The Hampshire Collection

Hampshire
County Council

CL82 7/02 10k

Forward Press

POETS 2008

Southern England

Edited by Forward Press Editors

FORWARD PRESS 20TH ANNIVERSARY

20 *Years*

POETRY FOR THE PEOPLE, BY THE PEOPLE

fp
forwardpress

First published in Great Britain in 2008 by:
Forward Press Ltd.
Remus House
Coltsfoot Drive
Woodston
Peterborough
PE2 9JX

Telephone: 01733 890099
Website: www.forwardpress.co.uk

Book Design by Ali Smith & Tim Christian
Edited by Forward Press Editors

HB ISBN 978 1 84418 480 4

Foreword

So often poetry can leave the common reader alienated. Since our establishment in 1989, our goal at Forward Press has always been to remove the barriers of elitism and provide a platform for poets from all walks of life. We believe poetry should not be obscure, introverted and as cryptic as a crossword puzzle: it is the poet's duty to reach out and embrace the world. This is exactly what our talented writers achieve with this collection of verse that is both entertaining and inspiring.

The main criterion for selecting the poems within this anthology is very simple: they communicate. They express feelings, emotions and ideas to the reader and most importantly they ensure the experience of reading poetry is one that can be enjoyed by all.

Contents

The Poems

What Is A Son?

What is a son?
A son is like a summer's day
Or crisp white snow where I used to play.
To have a son is really nice
With lots of smiles that could break ice.
The little things they do and say,
Make every minute of every day.
I have two sons, I'm truly blessed,
I know my sons are just the best.
I pray for people to have sons like mine,
They are more intoxicating than a glass of wine.

What is a son?
I speak to you, of a boy who stands so straight and true.
He maybe small, he maybe tall,
This sort of thing does not matter al all.
His heart is good, his deeds are true
And when in need, he will help you.
A friendly smile, a cup of tea,
This sort of thing you may say
Is a little thing,
Well maybe so,
But this is how love starts to grow.
A misplaced word can't bring a tear,
These little things make my heart strong
And help us all to get along.

What is a son?
What do I say? He comes from God,
O yes that's true, yes this I know,
Like me and you,
But this is not what I need to say,
I need to talk of a special day.
A bundle of joy to make you proud,
Not very big, but very loud.
He comes to us on his birthday,
This is what I have to say.
This special person from paradise,
He's very small, but very nice, so treat him good.
While he's here to stay.

For one day he may go away,
My son is not on Earth today.
For he is one who went away,
I know my parents who I love dear,
Will keep him safe away from fear.
His is our pride, his is our joy,
A very lovely, special boy.
We love our sons, indeed we do,
That's why I write these words so true.
God bless.

Ivor Birch (Swindon)

Voyage De Rêve

Preamble

Let's take a trip through mind and soul
Let us search through a black hole
Let us think and let us feel
Let's all dream a dream so real.

Episode 1 (the nightmare)

Riding over misty plains
Up and down, up and through
You see them laughing, pointing, taunting
Only facing towards you

You look and see they have no face
You are lost and scared
You turn to leave and run away
But cannot get away from them

Your knees just wobble
And your legs just shake
You can't be a stranger from it
You need to wake

Swimming through the water of my mind
Climbing the mountains of defeat
Lacking cause and purpose
A reason that's so bittersweet

Leaping, chasing, breathing loud
Seeing is believing when you're amongst this crowd
Feeling, touching, trembling starts
This is where the logic departs

Troublesome times and some troubles lost
Re-surfacing them for something to think
Bottom of the stairs, corner of the room
Back of the mind, standing on the brink

A dictionary may give you words
And a thesaurus may give you alternatives
Yet still there's nothing quite like screaming
To let everyone know that you're hurting

Stones will be chucked
And aimed at you
You're rooted to the ground
You don't know what to do

Standing like a flower
In an early grave
Wilted, weak and dying
The seeds they throw are shame.

When you feel you've woken up
And you'll never sleep again
The nightmares you remember

Yet you realise you were awake.

Episode 2 (the dream)

A land in your head
That is paradise to you
The entrance is your bed
The exit is so cruel

Your thoughts are the creations
Of a living fantasy
You are climbing slowly
You're striving to be

You spend all that time trying
To get to a heavenly place
Yet when the time does come
It gets pushed back in your face

When you want good things to last
They always come and go
They leave as quickly as they came
Making the high feel like a low

The night feels like forever
And you think you've lost the plot
Feels like you'll never wake up
When you do you just feel lost

Tiredness engulfs
Your sleeping alibi
Time to asleep the waking
And wake the sleeping that lie

Excitement pulses through your veins
You cannot wait for the highlight
You've been waiting for this moment
Since the instant of twilight

Time to get something off your chest
Believe it's true, it will happen to you
Don't give up, don't stop now
Just keep following all of the clues

You've spent all night dreaming up to it
But it was pulled away from you at dawn
It never manages to come around
And now you have to mourn

Take a dream, take a little time
Just to reflect on the night
What was it that you were chasing?
I'll tell you - it was for everything to be right.

There's always a little triumph in what you see
When your eyes are closed.

Victoria Taylor (Cirencester)

Mindscape

Echo - part 1
The cirrus clouds are edged in gold
by the setting sun.

Through a field a couple are walking,
in the distance their friends are waiting.
A row of oak trees edge the field,
on a branch a lone bird sings.

I pause, and look, but cannot see it.

The midsummer evening is warm and still.
The leaves on the trees hang
like sleeping bats.
Beneath a tree a man is sitting.
Obscured by the shadows - he watches.

A distant church bell starts to ring,
the couple stop - they can hear it.

In the distant village is a pub - 'The Old Bell'.
For a hundred years a fire has burned
a welcome in its hearth for all who come.
When it is quiet you can hear the echo
of revellers past.

Softly whistling the man rises,
and walks away.

The lone bird pauses his twilight song.

A cat prowls among the grass,
the couple try to coax it to them,
but it darts away - afraid of strangers.

It climbs the oak tree,
a dark silhouette against the dusky sky.
It pauses, watches me, I keep walking.

The sound of the bell -
only an echo now.

Falling - part 2

Summer faded. Now
its vibrant colours are no more
than a picture in my memory. The world

is grey, the way it looks
when you dream. From my window
I can see the grey. Days

pass. Each new day
a photocopy of the previous,
like stones in a wall.

From my window I see the trees
are still - like time stopped.

Yet high in the sky the birds still soar,
casting pale shadows on the Earth
and calling as if to say -
'None of this makes any difference to us.'

From my window I see them soar,
and the doors of the houses shut fast.

In the distance a low growl of thunder echoes.
Eventually the rain comes; cold drops
striking the Earth before being absorbed.

I cry too. Hot drops trickling down hotter skin
until they reach the precipice
of my cheeks - then falling.

And still the days are grey.
Tears can never wash away the grey
or smooth the jagged edges that rip and tear.

I look into the future, the past reflects
back at me and I am afraid. Fear
is a lonely emotion.

In my school playground,
under the shadow of tamarind trees,
there was a stone block about ten feet tall
with steps cut into it. The top
was big enough for six children to sit on.

Every morning before the bell,
W3e used to play on those steps.
It never entered my head I could fall.

I wonder if it is still there
or if the school has knocked it down,
finally afraid a child might fall.

Another day has spent its time
and now quietly leaves the scene.

Dream- - part 3
A new day stretches over the horizon
soaking up the darkness like a sponge.

The day is a blank page.
Anything is possible for those
brave enough to make of it what they will.

For me, like many others, each new day
is just another round of coffee and paper clips,
office gossip and rush hour traffic.

Yet we tell ourselves our jobs are important
and our lives are full, when we are no more than dots
on the pointillist painting called life.

Yet at night I go home to Russell.
With the spiky red hair, with the green eyes,
with a mouth that is always close to a smile.
Who never takes anything seriously,
who never analyses anything, who makes me laugh.

Last night I had a dream.

I dreamed I was in a deserted
car park surrounded by a wire fence.
I was standing to one side
with the fence close behind me.

The concrete floor was white
instead of the usual dull grey. It was daytime,
the bright sunlight highlighted
the white.

I didn't know why I was there,
or how I got there.

Suddenly, on the opposite side,
a large Doberman appeared.
It started running towards me.
I was terrified, I could not move.

When it reached me it put its mouth
around my hands, I could feel its teeth on my skin.
It didn't bite, but I knew I dare not move.

The *beep, beep, beep* of the alarm
interrupted the silence.
Cat gazed at me sleepily
as I reached out and turned it off.

Linda Dobinson (Basingstoke)

To Bath

There's a city I love the best,
Nestling in a valley, way down west.

A queenly place of
Crescent . . . Terrace.

Age-old buildings of weathered stone
They mark the place I'm proud to call 'home'.

The lazy Avon wends its way,
Reflecting beauty in its sway.

There's a 'peace' about the valley,
As if 'twas nature's special rally.

And if from lofty height you gaze,
You'll find this gem of Earthly glaze -

First a spire, a tree, a park,
Leaving 'mem'ry' a gentle mark -

And as your eyes across that valley roam,
Bath's indeed a 'city', proud to call 'home'!

Denis Read (Bath)

My Dad Les

Dad Les was born in 1936
It was a different kettle of fish
It was poorer, the era of Hitler
Bombs would drop
Dad and family would take refuge in the air raid shelter.

The war ended in 1945
I'm glad Dad survived
Dad went into the RAF, based in Cyprus
He had the time of his life!

We knew 'Dad Les'
When he came into our lives he was aged thirty-three
Dad Les worked as a car mechanic at ATS
Dad taught me about my mark 5 Cortina
How to oil, water, change the brake pads, etcetera, etcetera.

Dad Les was lots of fun
He flew kites with us once
He could outrun
He took us to the beach with my sister and Mum
Strong swimmers were Anne and Les, they were the best.

Dad Les did amazing Christmases
He put his heart and soul into it whole!
He put up decorations; it was a feat for him in older age
The dinner amazing,
Roast chicken, sprouts, bread sauce, parsnips and buttered carrots
Not to mention the Christmas pud
Two blue tapered candles were lit
On the table it was quite a hit.

Christmas evening all family came around
Christmas tea was made too
Sausage rolls, mini pizzas, Christmas cake
The yummiest Birds Eye trifle
Granny said Dad was like a son to her
It made me cry tears.

Dad Les sadly passed away
There was a funeral in Gosport
All the family so sad
I'll never get over losing Dad
I will cry a sea for eternity.

I'm so thankful for Dad's memories
Photos and videos
Of all his years
Dad is walking with me
He is a twinkling star in Heaven
Floating round the galaxy
Looking down, I have no fears
I'm sure he's happy where he lives in the spheres!

Stella Robinson (London)

Why?

My daughter, oh my daughter, your dreadful deed is done,
You took my little darlings, you took them, did you run?

My daughter, oh my daughter,
You took them and you ran,
You took my little darlings,
To go be with that man!

You left my heart to break dear, you left my tears to fall,
You left me in an empty house, you never cared at all.

My daughter, oh my daughter,
You took them and you ran,
You took my little darlings,
To go be with that man!

I kissed their empty pillows and I said my darlings' prayer,
I closed my eyes and prayed to God, when opened, they'd be there!

My daughter, oh my daughter,
You took them and you ran,
You took my little darlings,
To go be with that man!

You never came by morning light, or the blackness of the night!
I waited, how I waited, I could not believe it true.
You took my little darlings, my heart it broke in two!
You took my little darlings, my daughter, it was you!

My daughter, oh my daughter,
You took them and you ran,
You took my little darlings,
To go be with that man!

Ten years I loved them every day, I dressed, and taught,
And fed them, and I kissed their tears away.
But my daughter, oh my daughter you reached in
And crushed my heart,
You took my little darlings, and tore us all apart . . .

My daughter, oh my daughter,
You took them and you ran,
You took my little darlings,
To go be with that man!

You took them close to Christmas, my most favourite time of year,
You took my little darlings, my cries you did not hear!
You left me in these empty rooms, their beds so still and cold,
You left their toys, you left their clothes,
Where you went, nobody knows!

My daughter, oh my daughter,
You took them and you ran,
You took my little darlings,
To go be with that man!

Each morning when I wake from sleep, I listen for my loves,

But you took my little darlings, my little 'loves you tuvs'!
You took them off to be with him, because, I did not agree,
You decided that you'd break my heart,
My daughter . . . this . . . to . . .me . . .

My daughter, oh my daughter,
You took them and you ran,
You took my little darlings,
To go be with that man!

I loved you, how I loved you, over all the years,
But you took my little darlings, and you left me with my tears,
I cannot forgive you daughter, I cannot forgive you dear,
You took my little darlings,
You left
Me . . . alone . . . here!

My daughter, oh my daughter,
You took them and you ran,
You took my little darlings,
To go be with that man!

So, enjoy it, my dear daughter, enjoy it while you can,
It won't last forever, he's not that kind of man,
You took my little darlings, you took them and you ran,
You took my little love . . . u . . . tuvs just because you found 'that man'.

You never cared how hurt they'd be,
Or how you'd ruin their lives!
You're . . . selfish . . . and you're . . . wicked . . .
Your love cuts sharp as knives!

My daughter, oh my daughter,
You took them and you ran,
You took my little darlings,
To go be with that man!

But I will *never* stop loving them, I keep them in my heart,
I'll find a way to see them . . . we . . . *will not* be apart!
My hands are empty daughter, without my loves to hold,
My lap is empty daughter, but my love burns strong and bold!
I pity you dear daughter, for your heart is oh so cold!
You could have stabbed me in my heart,
And I would have forgiven you . . .

But you took my little darlings,
So my daughter . . .
Now . . .
We're through.

Rose Mary Childs (Haywards Heath)

27

Close To You

From London I see a view
Over dear old town
The view so wide,
So broad, so long
I could almost burst into song

You gave me this Lord
Old London Town
The way I feel and sing
Of all its longing

To be home again
With my feet on soil
Of London Town
This London girl

What a birthright
You gave me Lord
Queen Charlotte's
And all its finery
A rich Royal birthright
I couldn't have grander
Born of London
And all its glory

Proud I am for my Royal birth
And Cockney, yes
But maybe not the bells
But bells chime
Out their Royal ring
Every Sunday

I love the royalty
Pomp and splendour
And always give thanks to my saviour
For all its splendour

But most of all Lord
I give thanks to You
For my Royal birth
And all the heritage I receive
With pomp and splendour
God And Queen
And my London
Which is fit for any queen

It's in my blood
It's in my genes
The Lord gave me all this
It's really beautiful in my life
It's perfect in my life
My God and Queen
I am blessed.

Daniela Morbin (Wallingford)

Young Love

Teenage lovers hand in hand
Without a trace of care,
Ignoring others all around:
Just seeking out somewhere
To be alone away from prying eyes,
As each one promises to love forever,
To forsake all other, until the end of time.
Laughing gaily: teasing with mischievous wit,
Enjoying every bit of togetherness
With inner feelings of excitement and of joy,
This girl and boy.
Long summer days spent lying in the grass,
Watching clouds float past,
Their bodies close entwined,
Both being blind to what their futures hold:
Oh youth so bold as to ignore
What fate may have in store,
As years go by and they grow old
And must accept the wear and tear of life,
Which now means nothing
And until they're man and wife,
Will not appear or cause them fear
As they go blithely on in gaiety,
And taste the sweets of lovers' song.
Give them their day:
Don't grudge them youth and love or flaming sunsets
Wispy clouds above will surely all make way
In years to come, for shades of grey.
There'll be much time to reminisce in days to come
When they have changed from sweethearts
Into Dad and Mum: when children come
To bring not only joy but worries too and aching hearts:
When they must play their parts
As counsellors so wise,
Instead of lying watching skies
Through lovers' eyes.
We all behaved like this when we were young
When lovers' songs were sung:
We all looked through our misty eyes
At clear blue skies
And saw no further than a life of bliss
Each time we stole a kiss,
Or held each other's hand
Or romped on golden sand on summer days,
Content to laze so long as both were there
And knew not care.
But we matured and surely so must they,
As love's sweet carefree dreams
Slowly fade away.

Roy Hobbs (Christchurch)

What Did You Do Today Daddy?

(Porton Down - HM's Government Chemical Weapons Establishment)

What did you do today Daddy?

Mummy and me had a lovely time
We went to the park
The sun was bright, the clouds were white
The sky, was oh! So blue
There was nice green grass
Beautiful flowers, big tall trees
Singing birds and buzzing bees.

What did you do today Daddy?

The scientist

I had a lovely time today darling
I tested X today, darling
I wore a pure white coat, black rubber boots and gloves
And a shiny black mask
I squired X on a little white rabbit
And I watched it kick, scream, bleed, vomit, squirm and die
Nobody questioned, nobody asked
I can but wonder why
I had a lovely time today, darling
I tested X today, darling
I'm hungry; I'll wash my hands and eat now
Ask Mummy, what's for tea today, darling.

What did you do today Daddy?

The Workers:

I had a lovely time today, darling
I helped make X today, darling
I pressed a button; I turned a switch; I pulled a lever
I picked it up; I put it down; I turned it round;
I inspected it;
I poured it out; I bottled it;
I stored it;
I only typed the work schedules; I only made the tea;
I only manned the switchboard, anyone can see;
I lifted it; I moved it from here to there;
Where's it going? I know not where
As long as we are alright, darling, I just don't care
I had a lovely time today, darling
I helped make X today, darling
I'm hungry; I'll wash my hands and eat now
Ask Mummy, what's for tea today, darling.

What did you do today Daddy?

Parliament:

I had a boring time today, darling
I helped make X today, darling

I sat in the House of Commons, the People's Parliament
I saw the whips today, darling, and voted as was meant
Forgive me, darling, I'm not bold
I vote, the way I'm told
I helped make X today, darling
I'm hungry; I must wash my hands and eat now
Ask Mummy what's for tea today, darling.

What did you do today Daddy?

Every man:

Today, as every day, darling
I helped make X today, darling
I conformed
I paid my taxes
I obeyed the law
From life and responsibility, I abstain
From participation, I withdraw
I helped make X today, darling
I'm hungry; I'll wash my hands and eat now
Ask Mummy, what's for tea today, darling.

What did you do today Daddy?

The dissident.

Today I saw news on TV and I despair, darling
In dissent, I tried once more
To stop all war
In hearts and minds, darling
I'm sick, I cannot think, I cannot bear
Those Kurdish children, dead, just lying there

Hear the protests 'We're not to blame
For this crime committed, in our name'
Yet, all are guilty, just the same
I try each day to stop X, darling.

If I say 'No' I have my say
Taxation, if I refuse to pay
Will stop all wars, darling
From screaming 'Stop' my throat's real sore
Participation, 'tis the Rule of Law
I'm so tired
I'll try and eat now
Ask Mummy, what's for tea today, darling.

Gordon J Sheppard (London)

The Goblins

Out in the garden something stirring; dogs howling,
cats are growling, hedgehogs are hiding in the drain.
Birds stop their chirping, slugs stop slurping
those goblins are on the march again.

Draw the curtains, lock the doors, make sure
the children are safe in their beds.
If they are frightened sing to them quietly,
pull the blankets over their heads.

Every full moon the goblins come marching
stamping and trampling all over the grass.
Folk inside trembling, shaking, waiting
for the full moon to pass.

Pointed hats over scowly faces, long noses
and eyes black as newly mined coal.
Leather trousers with shiny buttons, over leather
boots polished up like burnished gold.

They march together in a line up the garden,
then back again searching every bush and urn.
Scowling, muttering in a strange language,
making sure every stone's overturned.

Nobody knows what they are looking for,
no one can guess what they've lost.
But round and round they scratch and search
until every leaf has been tossed.

Suddenly they stop what they're doing,
form a circle and they start to dance.
Twirling, swirling, feverishly whirling
almost as if they were in a trance.

The dancing stops, the goblins exhausted
pick up their lanterns and march away.
Folks breathe easy, then go to sleep
they'll clean up the garden in the light of the day.

Every full moon the goblins are marching
as they have done for hundreds of years.
Those strange, scowly little people
can reduce the strongest men to tears.

Superstition and old folk legends
tell stories passed down from days of old.
Of how the goblins search for treasure
stolen from them, a huge pot of gold.

So when the full moon is coming,
lock your doors and douse the light,
before those goblins come a-marching,
it might be you that they visit tonight.

Dorothy Fuller (Neasden)

The Seasons

The snow has melted, winter's gone, the slumb'ring world does wake,
New fresh carpets on the earth as Spring her place does take.
She knocks at Mother Nature's door dressed in a floral gown,
With daffodils and crocuses and primroses for a crown.

In the early morning sun the spiders' webs are new,
Sparkling like a million fairy lights dressed in their coats of dew.
The river freed from its icy chains hurries to the sea,
Winter seems to have locked its door and thrown away the key.

Cuckoos call, blackbirds sing, hoping for a mate,
Searching for a partner before it is too late.
This world of ours is not so bad if we could only spare,
Some precious time by Nature's side and gaze at these sights so fair.

Summer breathes its soft sweet breath o'er land and sea,
Flowers carpet Mother Earth, blossoms every tree.
Cotton wool ships sail on waveless blue skies,
Gentle soft breezes through hill and dale sighs.

Swallow are flirting with all that they see,
Showing the world they are happy and free.
This is the season of summer and light,
In contrast to winter as day is to night.

Trees change their dresses to gold, red and brown,
From the lush greens of Summer to Autumn's new gown.
Squirrels are stocking their larders in haste,
Hurrying, scurrying, not a moment to waste.

Countless small creatures are settling to sleep,
As slowly to Winter the world starts to creep,
The wondrous colours of this our third season,
Defies all description and of all reasons.

Winter has come with its bitter sting,
Autumn has finished with its final fling,
Pregnant clouds all swollen with snow
And the sky is tinged with a fine pinkish glow.

Those clouds are awaiting the moment of birth,
To send a white blanket to cover the Earth.
Icy-cold fingers ruffling the trees
A frosty sheet is covering the leaves.

The river is locked in thick chains of ice,
Fish are caught as in the jaws of a vice.
Nature is sleeping, none are awake,
Dreaming of when Spring its place will take.

Icicles hang like clear organ pipes,
Looking for all like a glass tiger's stripes,
This season's a beauty all of its own,
When old Jack Frost sits on his throne.

Ivor Pike (Exeter)

A Stranger

I have known you for quite a long time
I thought to myself we were doing fine
But alas you have surprised me again today
The mortgage we have will never go away
You stopped paying on the endowment side
For years now, you let it slide
With only a few years till the end
To pay back what we owe we will have to lend
But have you planned this from the start
To sell the land around a part of my heart?
I found this house, my home for life
A mother and nanny and your wife
You have taken all the trust I had for you right away
Never will believe a spoken word in what you do say
People tell me you never know what to expect in life
A loving family, nice home, but you have cut it in half with a knife
I should have learned when we were young
When you spent the money having fun
You act as if there is nothing wrong
Within these walls I don't belong
The warmth has left the area around
No more am I homeward-bound
I feel caught up inside a large net
If we carry on like this we shall be in great debt
Our sons are fine, they live their own lives
The atmosphere here you could cut with a knife
Nothing is said, still live from day to day
I didn't belong here I don't want to stay
You tell everyone that we will make a few bob
But about the debt we'll have to pay it off
So in the end we will be left with a home
No more mortgage no more loan
But deep within I have had enough
No more fun, out of love
The future I don't know at this time
I need to sit down and write a few lines
Should I stay and look after our handicapped son
Or leave everything behind, see what you have done?
I have no life now I can't leave you to care
You can't look after yourself you don't know how to share
After my visits to hospital where I nearly died
Did you really care about me or did you fake it and lie?
For thirty-six years we have been one
In those years we created two lovely sons
Ups and downs I know we have had
But the good times outweighed the bad
Now you say we should sell off the land
Think what we could do with the money in hand
But I have done some checking and have found
The money we make will not reach a pound

'Cause over the years you haven't paid the bills
A deep hole I uncovered which we can't fill
In two years the mortgage should have been cleared
But alas to my enquiries I found out and feared
You hadn't paid the endowment for quite some time
You told me everything was all going fine
I have now approached you but you say not a thing
I don't think you're sorry for anything
I have been through a lot over the past four years
After nearly losing my life which reduced me to tears
And only last year I lost my mother
I haven't mourned her I just cover
Now that you started to clear the site
It has hit home of the terrible plight
You even dug up my dog's grave and dumped it on the pile
The wind blew the top off I really did cry
She meant so much to me, I think it did
Set off the crying for my mother with the lid
You still haven't said a thing about the mess
Every day I love you less
But I am now biding my time
I'll get my own back for the crime
Not sure yet what I'll do
But for now I feel so blue
I keep it all locked up inside
But deep down I have cried
How could you do this to me and your sons?
I can't believe what you have done
I look at you now and can't see the danger
But to me you have become a stranger
I have to write down how I feel
Because to me it don't seem real
How can you live with someone for years
And not know them at all, I'm crying many tears
On my own, no one can see
Just the pain I have deep inside of me
I live now from day to day
But somehow I will make you pay
In my will I have wrote
To leave everything to my sons
Half the house they get not you
I hope you enjoyed your fun.

Jan Nice (Reading)

Accountants!

When the Revenue send their tax return
They put us in a spin
And we turn to our Accountants
To help us fill it in

To act as intermediaries
Would seem to be their role
But in order to achieve this
They need to almost own one's soul

I won't quote other people's views
At least not *'Ad Verbatim'*
Apart from TV's well-known chef
Who simply says, 'I hate 'em'

We have to tell them everything
How much! From whom! And when!
And, after filling out the forms
They send them back again

These are usually accompanied
By a formal note which says,
'I feel I must point out to you
The error of your ways

Are you sure you've not omitted
To mention everything you should?
To say that you've forgotten
Won't do you any good

It might not be Father Christmas
Who comes to visit you
But perhaps the Tax Collector
If your payment's overdue'

So, on their advice we write the cheque
With shaking hands and knees
Will we need a second mortgage
When we have to pay their fees?

If you think you're paying too much tax
Or your files resemble mountains
Then the remedy is simple -
Seek help from your Accountants

They'll welcome you with open arms
And rub their hands with glee
As they open up a file for you
In which to note their fee

But the moral of this story
Is 'The law you cannot flout'
And we're grateful for our Accountant's help
To sort our problems out.

E Dawson (Radstock)

The Beauty

'A beautiful Being'
That is what you are
Focus on this concept
And it will take you far . . .

Far into the distance
Of your life here on earth
From the time you were born
At your conception and birth . . .

Until the time you 'transmute'
Unto other realms of living
Where 'The Beauty' is constant
And creates much loving and giving.

For 'Beauty' is love
Coming directly from 'God's Being'
And is within, and around everything
If you have but eyes for 'The Seeing'.

'Beauty' is a concept
That comes from the heart
So seek it out everywhere
This will be a good way to start . . .

Your 'Journey of Love'
For that is the aim
As you live your daily life
On this human plain.

'Love' in all its aspects
For it has a wide-ranging field
And if used in its entirety
Your 'Whole Being' will be 'Healed'.

For 'Love' is of 'The Light'
And 'The Light' is 'God's Love'
Passed on through 'The Energies'
Of 'The Whole Universe' Above.

This 'Pure Love' can pervade
In all its 'Beauty' and 'Form'
And enhance your whole life
From the moment you are born.

So now look for 'The Beauty'
In everyone and everything
As this is 'The Balm'
That will make your heart sing.

Then 'Peace and Joy' will infill you
From those 'Energies from Above'
As you focus on 'The Beauty'
You will feel 'All of God's Love'.

Jade Deacon (Weston-super-Mare)

The Shipwreck

The Captain, the Officers, and all of the crew
Were happier today for together we knew
That the sextants had plotted just where we might be
After months of this voyage to the far China Sea

The stores were so low and the water was rusty
Our hammocks and clothes had grown green and smelt musty
But our spirits were high as we thought of the land
Which watch after watch came now closer to hand

The Captain turned in and slept better by far
Than for many a night with the help of a jar
But his sleep was disturbed by a terrible sound
As her keel ground in deeply and the ship gave a bound

On deck in a flash he called to the crew,
'Man the braces there lively' as already we knew
As the press of the sails dragged her more on the reef
'Til the ship felt quite dead with no water beneath

The carpenter called fiercely, 'Two feet in the hold'
And the faces around him looked withered and old
But the Captain cried, 'Steady my shipmates belay
We'll float her right off by the first light of day'

But the day did not follow that terrible night
For there over yonder where it should have been light
The sky was so black and the sea was so green
As no one on her deck had before ever seen

'Now quickly my lads, quickly there bear a hand
If I'm not now mistaken I think I see land'
As the lightning flashed brighter and the thunder did roar
We could see the waves break on a not distant shore

So we broke free the Launch, the Pinnace and Cutter
As the rain started falling with a regular mutter
And we loaded on board what was left of our stores
Then our guns and our powder and two-dozen good swords
As the boats were pushed clear and we struggled to row
The wind came on swiftly and it started to blow
But we all got away from that terrible sight
And pulled for the shore now with all of our might

The waves had grown huge and we started to bail
The rain lashing down mixed with sea spume and hail
The noise almost deafening as the thunder did roar
Then a huge crashing wave brought us right to the shore

As quick as we could now we crawled up the beach
As far as we could where the waves would not reach
And we hid behind rocks and trembled with fear
As we thought of our loved ones and those we held dear

The typhoon then struck and smashed down on the reef
The ship stranded there was lifted from beneath

Her hull was all broken by the razor-sharp rocks
Whilst her sails hung like ribbons struck from unruly locks

When some semblance of order was made from the mess
And the Captain said prayers for those laid to rest
We had lost some good men but for those left alive
Our thoughts turned to hunger and the need to survive

So we went off in land then to search for a stream
Enchanted by jungle which belonged in a dream
As we hacked our way forward our hands torn and bloody
Our bodies so white where our skin was not muddy

As the days passed our fears soon began to subside
'Til one day in the jungle the Bosun saw eyes
They were eyes blazing brightly but not of some animal
My God they were human but belonged to a cannibal

At this news the men quickly returned to the camp
The guns were all primed but the powder was damp
So we spent what seemed hours drying it in the sun
In the hope that in time we could fire off a gun

But the cannibals saw us as invading their land
And soon we could see them along by the strand
They chanted and sang and waved clubs in the air
And held trophies of skulls draped with black human hair
Our hearts beat as one as the Captain cried, 'Hold
We are Englishmen truly so let's fight and be bold'
But their numbers were greater and they fought without fear
Oblivious to our swords as our end became clear

When the Captain was struck down with a terrible cry
The few of us left knew that we also would die
So we slashed and we fought and we ran then to hide
But they killed all the crew of the Frigate Surprise

The old Navy Lists showed our proud Frigate as lost
But two hundred years on our bones lie where they were tossed
And there's nothing to show now - no stone to relate
That terrible day and our terrible fate

This timeless piece of history remained in Island lore
Until the digging had begun for the hotel by the shore
Then the diggers and the workmen found the long forgotten bones
Including this here scrawled account by the Bosun William Jones

Richard Plumley (Bristol)

Untitled

Tomorrow is a hope
Yesterday is a memory
Only made possible by today.

Indira (Catherham)

Farmers Boy

Yesterday I took a walk down winding tracks
Where birdsong greets the mornings realms
Where reeds and heathers there bestow
A pleasure garden all on show.

I gazed on hills that spread so green
Where lambs and seagulls paint the scene
Where clouds of cotton wool bestow
Their joy of life all spread below.

Across the heaths of rabbit run
Where fox gives chase and farmer's son
Sing all their songs of folks in prayer
To wallow in the beauty there.

I spied the tractor o'er the soil
The fields of grain across the moors
The lilac trees and nettles sweet
Where tramps and ladies trod their feet.

The sea of spray were fishes dance
The sands of time and pebbles chance
The sailboats riding on the spray
The sun shines bright across the bay.

The tower clock doth chimes the hour
The church bells ring across the Stour
The zunners run from school this day
Whilst lovers frolic in the hay.

I spy the village pond and water pump
The five bar gate where walkers hump
Their rucksacks and poles of fine regard
All just across from the farmer's yard.

The geese give chase to Mary Jane
Whilst dogs do bark and lords do monies gain
Where stone wall walks are set in sand
Where Hardy wrote and Barnes statue still doth stand.

Where market hawkers give full guest
Whilst zunners run amongst the best
Where pubs and cafes do imitate
The history of the landed Gentry's fate.

The walks I took that summer's day,
Across the Purbeck's right of ways
Where travellers rest and shoulders rich
In history lessons spread across the Purbeck's ditch.

Whilst warblers sand and lizards squirmed
The adder slid and the slow worm
The master poet was lost in joy
When I was just a child and farmer's boy.

Ray Wills

Mrs Understood

God grant me the serenity,
to accept the things I cannot change.
Is that how it goes?
I do not know.
I make sure not to know, no more.

Not to ask me is not to know.
Yet to ask, is to know the facts.
Who wants to know the facts?
To know what is right?
What is right for who?
It is right to know one could be better.
Should be better,
would be better.

Would you want me to be more?
Some things I want not to change.
I smile at my simplicity,
to laugh and enjoy so easily;
you do too.
Oh we giggle stupidly together so free,
how I adore so true
your love for me.

I do.
I do, I do, I do.
No strings to taut our unity.
So why does the plastic world dig,
dig so deep beneath me?

You would not be here,
if I had such shallow skin,
yet I manage to drown in such thick ridiculous need.
The need to be a flawless canvas,
so fresh, so new -
so utterly pure.

And when I yearn so sore for these basics,
to flow hastily beneath and above,
I remember and always remember,
my canvas is painted with such love.

So despite the wanted needs,
yes I will loath the envious dreams,
but you see
I own more than greed and jealousy.

I belong to you.
In beautiful breath, no vice could ever choke
and no such sins will ever wash away,
my passion of you
belonging to me.

Lauren Sheridan (Milton Keynes)

The Present

I was twelve years old
The year getting cold.
I felt so grown up
No longer a silly pup.

As Christmas grew near
I lived in fear
Of being treated as a child
This would make me wild.

The big day came
It didn't feel the same
As in previous times
When nursery rhymes
And dolls and toys
Were my joy of toys.

Now the thrill was gone
Something was wrong
Something was missing
Amid the greetings and kissing.

After breakfast was done
The presents opening would come
Anticipation was great
No one dared be late.

What would my 'big present' be
Under the Christmas tree?
As Christmas fairy it was my call
To hand out presents big and small
Others first to be polite
And wait in turn for my delight.

At last only my gift was left
But as I saw inside I was bereft
There was a heart-shaped box
White with tiny black spots.

When I opened it wide
And looked inside
I was so upset
What did I get?

A string of pearls was there
To my utmost despair
I wanted a game or book
Not just a jewel for a look
Unable to hide my sadness
I could not fake any gladness.

My father was wild
'Ungrateful child'
He wanted to treat his girl
To a beautiful string of pearls.

My mother refused
So I was used
As the next best thing
His pleasure to bring.

I counted them up
I'd have preferred a pup
There were sixty nine
All in a long line
Small at each end
Bigger towards the central bend.

The clasp was bright
Marcasites caught the light
With a double catch
For a safety latch.

I wore them one time or another
Until Father died, then Mother
I planned to swop for gems I liked more
Could even adore.

My daughter was going away
In Australia she would stay
I asked if she wanted to take
For sentiment's sake
Any of her grandmother's gems
Or if I should sell all of them.

She thought she would look fine
Wearing those pearls of mine
What a perfect idea
So many problems clear.

Her Christmas present sorted
The shopping aborted
She was in Heaven
When she left Devon.

My father finally had his wish
My daughter looked so swish
So, one of his favourite girls
Had his special string of pearls
And the world is able to see
How they look on my daughter so pretty.

Hazel Newman (Cullompton)

Lay Still A While . . .

Lay still a while near grass green mound
Silent, hush make not a sound.
Catch your breath and breathe no sigh
A sight behold to human eye.
Forbidden path not trod by men
Dare to glimpse at fairy den.
Through evening dusk steal just a peep
As tiny folk awake from sleep.
Rub misty eyes in fragrant hue
To capture moments seen by few.
Gentle fairies softly fly
With fragile wings like butterfly.
With graceful flutter, oh so bold
Petal skirts and crowns of gold.
From every nook in labyrinth maze
Come tiny folk in rainbow haze
'Midst silver veil-like curtains drawn
Spun spider thread 'tween glistening thorn.
Elfin folk in leaves they rustle
Like busy bees amongst the hustle.
On toadstool tables, feasts are laid
Woodland berries, fruits cascade.
Shrill blackbird chorus in the middle
And crickets chirp in tuneful fiddle.
From bluebell trumpets music sweet
Buttercups 'neath fairy feet
From acorn cups sip honey dew
And bathe in crystal waters blue.
Float fairy boats in walnut shells
White lily sails, and silver bells
Rainbows, blossoms, scent of rose
Lantern lights and glow-worm glows.
Beneath the trees in bracken nests
Spill sparkling jewels from treasure chests.
Moonlight cloaks a golden light
Heartbeats pulse at wondrous sight.
Pixie feet with gentle patter
Laugh and chant in elfin natter.
In pearly glow they sing and dance
In feathered caps they swiftly prance.
From daisy chains the creatures swing
Hush how sweet their voices ring.
Fairy magic 'midst the glens
Oh to capture this in lens.
Stay still a while, make not a stir
Less fairy dream becomes a blur.
Alas, they've caught a glimpse of men
In blink of eye, they're gone again.

Marilyn M Fowler (Penge)

The Bottom Drawer

I remember when I was a child, we were always very poor,
me dad was always out of work, and the rent men at the door.
I don't know how we managed with so little food to eat,
the kids that had their dads at work, had shoes upon their feet.
When I was twelve, I got a job, a good one down the pit.
The hours were long, the work was hard and I was always full of grit.
But the money earned I gave me mam, and she was overjoyed,
the neighbours soon found out that her son was now employed.
One day I came back early, and found her on the floor,
she was stuffing something in a tin, in the cupboard's bottom drawer.
I stared for just a moment, then she turned and held her heart.
'Oh you stupid, stupid boy, you did give me a start,
creeping up behind me and scaring me like that!'
'I'm sorry, Mam I really am, but I wondered what you're at.'
'It's nothing of your business, son, but no one else must know,
it's where I pay the rent man from, else we'd have to go.
You know just what your dad is like, he'd have it for his drink,
so I have to save a bit by like, whatever you might think.'
I crept away, and went to bed but thoughts kept going through
my head.
My brother now had got a job, and together we gave quite a few bob.
We still did not have much to eat, and we bought the boots to clothe our feet.
Oh we, I shrugged, must get me sleep, whatever's there will
have to keep.
I never tried to find the tin, it didn't worry me,
but many times I looked into the cold front room, and saw me mam down on her knees.
I didn't let her see me, she wouldn't have been glad
for poverty and hunger had made her old and sad.
The secret of the bottom drawer must be told one day,
but meanwhile the days and years were flowing fast away.
My brothers left, my father died and I was still at home,
I'd always been a dull chap with no desire to roam.
One sunny day, me mam collapsed, I had to call the doc,
She never had been ill before, so to me it was a shock.
'She's had a stroke,' he said, 'just keep her quiet and still
you've been her strength always and I know you always will.'
The days went slowly after that, she couldn't speak or move,
but I know that she could understand and was certain of my love.
One day she spoke, I started up, and she pointed to the drawer.
I pulled it out to give her, wondering what it was wanted for.
She pointed to the tin, which was underneath some clothes.
I took it out and opened it, then my hair literally rose.
For the tin was crammed with money, about three thousand pounds,
My God I thought aloud, the world now holds no bounds.
I thought of all those awful years, the explosion at the pit,
My face that was disfigured, well, what was left of it.
The money could repair all this, we could get out of this place,
I turned to speak but she had gone, the smile still on her face.

Dorree Spencer (Lancing)

The Night Darkens

The night darkens, everyone asleep
I sit alone here and pray for their keep
The long passage lights up from the outside world
My chair is rigid and my toes are curled

They do not know how I really feel
And my pain is so, so unreal
To them I am happy with my life
But do they realise that I was once a wife?

Children I did bear who make me proud
I sit and dream how they were so loud - (ahh she smiles for a moment)
Quietness is all around
I sit and dream
Why does my husband not care it seems?

If it wasn't for my children
Watching them all grow strong
I don't know how I would have coped as I did for so long

(She smiles again)
My dream of dreams was to have a house of my own
To have the family around
With veg that's home grown - (ahh she sighs once more)

To potter around, share a chat or two
With a neighbour
Who
Would share her news and views

'Come in,' I would say
'There's biscuits, cakes sat on the tray
Help yourself -
Yes,
Roses I've grown from the garden - you know'

I wake - how strange, I just then - thought
I was elsewhere -
But I stare -
I'm in the kitchen, I am still in this chair

(A tear runs from her eye, then pulls herself together and summons
her strength, her anger, her torment)

'How I long to *stretch* and *walk* around
Shout out loud and *touch* the ground'

(She calms herself)

Morning is returning to the passage way again
Another day is beckoning

(She tilts her head as she holds onto the chair)

Dear Chair
We have many memories -
How long shall we sit here?
Who will visit us

Surprise us?

Maybe a few flowers to brighten up this room
To make the room smell pleasant
Instead of
Stew and mushroom

The kitchen could do with a thick lick of paint
I know every crack in these walls
Every footprint that's on the floor

(She lifts her head and tilts to listen)

Soon movement from upstairs
My husband gets up from bed
My son comes down and kisses me
'Bye Mum,' he said and fled

Off to work, there he goes
Then my husband, he now shows
A cup of tea and then on his way
To catch a train for another day -
Or does he?
Now I am confused - I sit here puzzled -

Not the train, he doesn't work, I'm so confused -

His sister has already taken her place - upon his arm

My heart sinks - (she weeps)

I grip my chair

And see the front door close, to my alarm

I am thirsty, hungry -
Oh, I want my mum -
My sister
My children
Or
Just one

I am left with silence

All I have is you - my chair

I am now left in despair

Kim Elizabeth Reeder (Newport)

Reptile Dysfunction

'What's the matter, Jack?'
'I've found a Natterjack in the road.'
'That's dangerous.'
'He won't move!'
'He'll have to be towed . . .'

Celia Harper (Chichester)

Chastleton House Lives

(Chastleton house belongs to the National Trust. It opened in 1996 after rescue repairs. It was built from 1608-1612 and remains Jacobean in atmosphere. I steward there as a volunteer.)

Within its walls cold chisels ring;
Tall ladders lift in cuckoo spring;
Mallets tap a twelve hour day;
A church bell calls workmen to pray.

Within its stone, lime plaster heat;
The midday sun on masons' feet;
Spilt beer that quenched a dusty throat;
In chimney stack, for luck, a groat.

Sawyers' dust below the boards;
Shards of lead and plumbers' cords;
Shavings from oak newel posts,
Jest and song caught there, the ghosts.

Great roof timbers notched to fit
Close on blood spot and salty spit.
A curse is nailed in wide plank floor,
A yearning for the maid next door.

Above the best bedroom fireplace
Carved satyrs leer with devilish grace,
Ignoring painted figures higher,
Proud coat of arms that coaxed desire.

Strip cartoon tapestry hangs widescreen,
Stories laced there echo dreams.
Strong Bible passions boxed and hid
Lie low, key-safe beneath a lid.

A mute four-poster's fades cloths
Trap night thoughts that danced like moths,
Beginnings, cares and comforts shared,
Schemes and suffering, endings bared.

Chests by chairs and chamber pots,
Embroideries of floral plots,
Estate accounts, a child's chalk slate,
Cards, croquet balls, worn kitchen plate.

Foursquare the house its core maintains,
Serene in frost, ridge winds and rains.
One family's home in Gloucestershire:
Four centuries' handiwork is here.

Saved by repair and yet unchanged
Time's tissue packing clues remains.
Unhurried visitors, intent to find,
May catch past whispers, in the mind.

Maureen Dew (Deddington)

Think! What Price Harmony

You see with your eyes, and you listen with your ears
Man has been doing this, for thousands of years.
Phenomena you have seen, changes have been made,
You see Mother Nature she is under Man's blade.
Harmony, it is taught but do we understand?
We walk blindly across this, our land.
We are all mankind there should be no divide,
Take off your masks. There's no reason to hide.
A decent life, we try to attain,
Of our innerself, we are never quite certain.
To get back to basics, to live our lives free,
Takes more than a gesture, can you not see?
We rape the Earth, to be comfortable and warm,
The damage we cause, doing unknowing harm
Toxic waste, we dump at sea,
weapons in space, pointing at you and me.
Concrete we use, to cover the land,
mankind's expansion getting out of hand.
Is wealth so important, for it we will kill?
Man in his wisdom can never stay still.
The transport we use, a major cause of pollution,
What is Man doing, what is his solution?
If we all came together, what would we do,
Would we find others, wanting harmony, too.
Here is a problem, the things we are told,
Leave us no warmth, to others we are cold.
All that we do, we do through greed,
If we cared for others, there would be no need.
Wars are raging, in many parts of this world,
But do these actions make fighting men bold?
See that man! He is your brother,
Treat him fairly, you shall need no other.
As yourself, you know what you want,
His needs are the same, to live life decent.
To be treated, as you wish to live,
Open your heart, to this brother give.
Dedication and trust, respect and understanding,
Give yourself, it is not so demanding.

When as one, we can come together in peace,
Put the weapons away and combat disease.
With all the resources, once poured into wars
Can now be used, to give mankind a true cause.
No suffering or famine, the world on the mend,
Mankind together with nothing to defend.
A chance to live in harmony,
With lessons learned, of our past stupidity.

Steve McGowan (East Cowes)

The Legend Of El Cid And The Leper

Rodrigo Diaz of Bivar
Immortal hero of Spain,
Whom history called El Cid - The Lord
Set out one day with his knights,
On pilgrimage to Compostella.
His great white war horse shone
In blinding silver light in the
White-hot gold of the Spanish sun.
The sun's heat had not yet scorched the earth,
And great storms had caused oozing mud and mires
By the roadside.
The Cid heard
A pitiful cry for help
Mingling with the beat of horses' hooves
And jingling harness.
He halted his men, dismounted,
And walked quickly in the direction
Of the cry.
A little way from the road
He saw one of the filthy mires and
In it up to his waist,
Being sucked greedily down
By the ravenous monster of vile mud,
Was an old man - raising his arms in terror,
Crying,
'Help me - for the love of God!'
Rodrigo called to his men for help,
But the knights drew back in fear,
'My Lord,' they shouted -
'Let him die - he is a leper!'
The Cid looked at them with disgust -
'The hearts of you who call yourselves Christians
Are more foul than this man's disease!' - and
He strode into the mire, grabbed the man's shoulders
And heaved him out by himself,
Whilst his brave warriors cowered and looked on!
He lifted the old man onto his horse
And took him to the nearest inn where
They were to lodge for the night.
His men, crossing themselves,
Went to the farthest part of the room,
But Rodrigo who had given a clean robe to the leper,
Shared food with him from the same dish,
And as no one would come near them,
He shared the same rough bed
In a small chamber.
At midnight,
When Rodrigo was fast asleep,
The leper turned towards him
And breathed through Rodrigo's shoulders

And so strong was it that
It passed right through to his breast and he
Awoke in fear -
The leper had disappeared,
But a bright light filled the room,
He sat up and a Being in white raiment
Stood before him,
Shining with the bright light.
'Fear not - Rodrigo of Bivar, called El Cid -
I am Saint Lazarus - and I was
That leper whom you helped
For the love of God,
And because you did this for His sake,
God has granted you a great gift,
And that breath which has passed through you
From me, is a little of the Divine Breath,
And because you only do honourable deeds
And only for good,
So God has honoured you,
And His breath will make you
Invincible to all those who are evil,
Whom you will destroy for the sake
Of goodness and justice and in His Name.
When your time comes,
You will have achieved your great destiny,
And will die naturally and with honour
And be immortal in the minds of good men - forever!
For God hath blessed thee!' - and he disappeared.
Rodrigo fell onto his knees,
Thanking and praising God.
So it came to pass -
In God's name he saved Spain
From an evil enemy,
And saved the people of Spain -
Christian and Moor alike -
And rode into history
As the noblest and purest knight of Spain -
And most of all - of God!

Victoria Helen Turner (Weston-super-Mare)

My Dream

To find peace, in a maelstrom of sound.
To find love where no love existed.
To find excellence in a mediocre world.
To find compassion in a sea of indifference.
To find humanity in an uncaring world.

I found my God but not my dream!

George Till (Bath)

Travelling West

It's early.
five-ish.
A mackerel sky.
Slats of sun,
crimson, tango.
The road
is quiet
as if
100 years
have not yet
passed.
The station
is asleep,
weeds growing
between the
tracks.
Yet now
approaching . . .
the fast inter-city
west.
I step aboard
and am soon
being carried
at the speed
of light.
Even so
the countryside
is still
safely grazed
with sheep.
The sea
begins
to line
my vision,
opening out the horizon
to the west.
My thoughts
stretch ahead
to the islands.
I recall the
immensity
of the silence
and the sound
of seals
singing.

I am returning home.

Rosie Crocus Smith (Millbrook)

Memento Mori

An acrid blue haze,
Billowing from the chimney stack,
Falls over the Crematorium car park,
The air is dampened by the rain.

In white hair and best coats,
The old wait with painful panic.
Children skip and scuff their shoes.
The middle-aged hover,
Trying to enjoy today and wondering
Just how long its sweetness can survive.

The professionals conspire.
Smiles and warm words try to disguise
Their cold production line.
Exuding tactless competence,
Funeral Directors work uncomfortably
With clerical patrician confidence.

The mourners look conspicuous,
With men in last summer's wedding suit
And young women wearing the black stockings
Normally reserved for nights.

Furtive smokers light up while waiting
For the coffin to go in.

Hymns limp along. Vaguely remembered,
God is praised like an elderly, obscure relation.
Guilt stalks the chapels and memorial rooms.

Those who know
Try not to breathe too deeply
When leaving the Chapel.
Death gets on your lungs
And makes you cough.
Now it's over, leave the flowers to rot
And get away.

Relief invades the limousines
Sweeping swiftly back along the motorway.
A respectful laugh is allowed,
Only to be quelled by memories of the mortgage.
Cold chicken awaits, and whiskey,
Thank God.

In the distance
A lighter shade of grey sky appears.

The rain stops.

Who can remember death?

Neil Richardson (Greenford)

Shadow Play

The shadow
(it seems)

creates this stone

that I
(motionless and still)

sit upon
as if it were the centre

of this world.

It is the summer
of my childhood

and the world
is making itself

known
to me.

My mind
is hungry to learn!

My own shadow
chained to me

like a soul
to a body

longing to escape
my mortality.

It lies
like a fallen angel

thirsting for a Heaven

crestfallen at my feet.

Shadow plays
Hide-and-seek

amongst the leaves

sunlight laughingly
chasing it.

Birds write
the notation of themselves

upon the telegraph lines.

Sounds morph
into each other

the moo of a cow
becoming the murmur of a bee.

I try
to understand

the existence
of a me.

The five-bar gate
prints its shadow

on the lane

smiling at its own
distortion.

Wild roses
ramble from hedge to hedge.

Honeysuckle
climbs upon its own scent.

I sit amongst the milk churns

gleaming with the silver
of their laughter

as if I were one
of their number.

Waiting for a tractor
to escort us to

a faraway dairy.

We three wise monkeys
(seeing), (hearing), (speaking)

no evil

in this
the innocence

of my new
and only

world.

Donall Dempsey (London)

Reaching Out

(In memory of our mum, love always)

In each of us there is a child reaching out,
When life's encountered problems leave us full of doubt.
No matter what age we are, be it young or be it old,
Security and reassurance we reach out for when life is cruel and cold
And it is to our mother that instinctively we call,
When life is hard and maybe we are heading for a fall,
For she is the very essence of what we ourselves are.
And when she leaves our life - nothing will ever be the same again,
Though we may seek both near and far.

M A Shipp Yule (Southampton)

Still Miss You

I miss you in the autumn time
as leaves fall from the trees,
The changing of their colours
as life then sets them free.

You too began to mellow
and so did your colours fade.
It was hard to watch you wither,
though that is nature's way.

I miss you so at Christmas
it is when you lingered on,
listening to the Salvation Army Band
sign a plaintiff song,
as I sat by your hospital bed
holding your hand.

You still managed a smile
though you were very weak.
You told me you loved me
and I tried not to weep.

You made it through to January
and into February too,
when we gathered around your bed
to say farewell to you.

We cleared through your belongings,
we emptied your home.
We left your chair 'til last
It was so hard letting it go.

There was an empty space,
where you used to be,
but I know that your spirit
will always live in me.

I miss you so in springtime,
the time you loved the best.
In the beauty of the countryside
is where we laid you to rest.
Your children took your ashes
and scattered them afar,
in fields and primroses,
now that is where you are.

And season after season
I often think of you.
You gave my life a reason
but, Dad, I still miss you.

Carol Ponting (Bristol)

Betty

A little child found in an Uxbridge field
between the common and the town.
Elizabeth they called her - Elizabeth Field.
Unimaginative to be sure but it sufficed,
for even a foundling must have a name.

But for all that, who's to say her life was sorrow bound?
I'd like to think that those who took her in
loved her, discarded the formal Elizabeth
and called her Betty - their Betty.
I'd like to think she knew childhood's little joys and woes.
Ran wild in flower filled gardens,
raced with companions along the willowed banks of Colne,
felt grown up when asked to help about the house,
sulked when made to learn her letters.
And daydreamed, daydreamed
as little ones are wont to do.
But from time to time she must have asked,
'Please tell me who I am'

As she grew she must have learned a trade,
(a dressmaker or the like)
and I'd like to think that as time went by
she found a steady lad
and became his loving wife.
Then came family life,
children round her skirts,
a baby in the cradle.
And the grieving time when those
she called parents were laid to rest.
But carried through it all by the man she loved the best.
But still from time to time she must have asked,
'Please tell me who I am'

I'd like to think she lived long
with her husband by her side
and saw her children grown up,
prosperous and strong.
I'd like to think she was respected
by neighbours and all of her friends,
knew nothing of want's cloying tyranny
but the contentment ordinariness sends.
And I hope at last she found herself,
realised her own true worth.
And if that haunting question ever came to mind,
I hope she answered with certainty,
'I know very well who I am.'

Margaret Hibbert (Uxbridge)

Deserted Airfield

Cattle graze quietly beside the broken boundary fence
Which once was the limit of my daily life.
The same tall trees sway gently in the breeze
Whispering more tales than anyone of us could tell
Now seeing an old friend return to this now deserted spot
Quite still but for the birds and bees.

Flowers and tall grass have grown through the concrete strips
Creeper and ivy cling upon the buildings that are left
Yet within this empty peaceful stretch of land
There seems to be a nearness of the living past
As though with ease one could bring back the dead
By a single simple movement of an outstretched hand

Gaze round and see what the time has done since those tense days
Barrack blocks still stand with empty silent rooms
Save things that passers-by have left
And one small nissen hut with smokeless chimney stack
Is left in lonely state, boasting an invincibility
Just moss and grass and rust, forlorn, bereft

Once, quite long ago there were existed voices ere
Men and women eager to pursue the battle order
Experienced team, right knit, ready for the fray
Their world encased in metal, wood and air
The noise of engines revved in haste
Ready at any time, brief seconds in which to get away

By night and day the ground crews were kept alert
Cooks clerks and admin' staff all played their part
While at the controls, held steady by dedicated hands
The pilots climbed high to face another breed of youth
To return, they hoped, to transient rest
They were the lucky ones who could pick up the strands

Some did not return to fight another day
Burned out, shot up, their luck had not held out
Caught in the sun, not quick enough to turn
In so brief a combat, young lives extinguished, gone
Their number, rank and names were noted, letters sent
New faces took their place, new men with much to learn

Some said it was a special game they played
A game which grew from gentle roots, of gentle breed
Played out to rules and code, salute to all the dead
While others saw only tyrannies quick end
Short bursts, aimed well, another one gone down
The only way until the last of them had fled

Sometimes in the silence of an early dawn
Those who could not sleep heard quickening sounds
They heard the sobs from a WAAF sergeant's bed
Or strange cries from a haunted pilot's sleep
Yet as another day dawned fully on the field
Their outward calm returned, or so they said

Those who lived here throughout those war-torn days
And saw the gradual slow decline of battle's strife
Found that they had grown beyond their years
Were wiser by virtue of a multitude of scars
And later still on memories oh so clear
Of times of fear, of laughter and of tears.

For while the few fought full throttle in the skies
Drank together in the mess and loved their girls
All this had been an outward cover for their shattered world
Out of the greatness of their deeds and words
Remains so little to tell the brave new world
Those who braved the heights with freedom flag unfurled

Peace has long returned to this once crowded spot
Another summer smiles upon the almost empty scene
Yet I still seem to hear the old familiar sounds
See friendly faces, uniforms blue against the sun
But now with a reluctance almost too hard to bear
I cross the field and fence and walk slowly out of bounds

Anthony E L Cook (High Wycombe)

People Can Be Like A Box Of Chocolates

People's personalities can be so different, a box of chocolates is what they can be like,
People without feelings cannot learn how to care, it's not like learning to ride a bike.
Some people have soft centres and their feelings run deep,
People with soft centres are not afraid to weep.
Some people are a lot of fun, they are what you call nutty,
These people are usually soft centres too, soft as putty.
Some are hard centres, they often seem as though they don't care,
I find those people sometimes hard to bear.
But whatever centre you are God loves us all,
He doesn't care if you are fat, thin, small or tall.

Karen Grover (Farnborough)

Schemers

She took stock of his gleaming shoes,
    They shone like a conker, just sprung
From its case on a bright autumn day,
    And he still looked reasonably young.
Then gazed at his eyes and they twinkled
    In her favourite shade of grey.
So she sat on the bench beside him
    First of all asking if she may,
And thought *this one's worth cultivating.*
    I wonder what makes his day.
Now he an old salt, and just home from the sea,
    Knew all about feminine wile,
And, sizing her up, as she, hove to, thought,
    This one is out to beguile!

I admire a man who takes care of his shoes,
    Was her opening attack,
A pleasant smile passed over his face,
    But he never answered back.
Instead he cupped his hand to his ear,
    'Beg pardon, what's that you said?
I'm afraid I'm a little bit deaf dear
    On account of a wound to my head.'
She sighed, remembering her dear old dad,
    His deafness, and problems with him,
No rosy prospects here, she thought,
    In fact they looked quite dim.

So rising up rather smartly,
    Made excuse, beat a hasty retreat.
He giving no sign he had heard her,
    Raised his hat as he got to his feet,
Thought *I know scheming gals, when I see 'em,*
    Can't abide 'em, and all their deceit.
Two can play that game my pretty
    And I think my ruse, worked a treat,
Repelling menacing boarders in time-honoured way
Breathed again now, mission complete.

He looked up at the sky, with a smile to disarm
    The stoniest of heart,
Saw the sun was over the yardarm
    Now it was time to depart,
Make his way to the Scottish Thistle
    And have his first nip of the day.
Yes, time to, whet his whistle,
    And then be on his way.

Dorothy Puttick (Worthing)

My Perfect Day

I wake up early on a Saturday
I pack my picnic I prepared yesterday
I load my car with all that I need
Blanket, food, radio and a book to read.

I start the engine and make the final checks
Everything is ready, my eagerness to go and the things I expect.
I drive off my street and shift a gear
This town is so busy; I have to get away from here.

I leave the town far behind
And sigh as country roads before me gently wind.
The sun has now risen; the sky is a cloudless blue.
A beautiful day for what I want to do.

A few more miles and I reach my place,
As I park my car, a smile slowly creeps across my face,
Untouched and perfect, this is my spot,
Discovered by accident but never forgot.

In front of me stands a magnificent oak tree,
In all its glory towering over me,
I stand in awe of this ancient treasure,
Its age I wouldn't even want to try to measure.

I carry on walking now in the shade,
A little more walking through this beautiful glade,
I suddenly stop, I gasp and feel a shiver,
There before me is the gentle running river.

I lay down my blanket on the grass,
I sit and gaze as I watch the water pass,
Around me are birds singing and playing,
I talk back as if I know just what they are saying.

The peace of this place, forever I want to keep,
I am relaxed, finally and my heart does a leap,
I stay transfixed by this idyllic place,
The sun breaks through trees and warms my face.

Alas all good things must come to an end,
I must say goodbye to my river and my tree, my friend,
The drive home is slow and my heart aches,
To be back in the glade again as a new day breaks.

So that's what I'll do before tomorrow's sun is risen,
I'll pack my car again; I'll leave this town that stifles like prison,
Back to my tree, my glade and my river.

And sit and dream of being there forever.

Fiona Cary (Bridgwater)

Big Chief Eagle Eye

Upon the peak of Firefly Mountain
looking down upon the Cheyenne
Sioux's Mighty Eagle Eye!
Shielding warriors from danger
anger, hatred of the Cheyenne
lost, dead, wandering, disbanded.
Many braves hurt and wounded
in the big war against the Cheyenne.

Witchdoctors with words of wisdom
spoke to brave from other tribes.
He listened to their angry venom
as tepees were torched to nothing
like so many of the Sioux braves
all was disintegrated into ashes
in the big war against the Cheyenne.

Swiftly small braves clamber fleeting
bearing them away on buffalo wagons
which would take them to safe quarters
save mother squaws much heartache.
Big Chief says, 'Will prepare them
for the big world doing tasks,
put much food in their baskets.'

All the time me Little Song Bird!
watches, wondering at his wisdom
hears the tales from Big Brave Firehawk
note his words, and sense his longings
he so envious of the big braves
they with warpaint on their faces
in the big war with the Cheyenne.

Calling to spirits past he howls
Hail Raging Bull, Wiseman Bright Owl
from the dark world - that vast kingdom
he listens for their words of wisdom.
Spirits from the dark world sigh
then send a message to Eagle Eye,
'You will win the war with Cheyenne.'

Soon a brave named Thundercloud
would come and lead the tribe proudly
telling wondrous stories
of other battles, mighty glories.
At first light go to Firefly Mountain
meet Thundercloud on his stout stallion
he will lead against the Cheyenne.

On the morrow Eagle Eye
with his braves rode to Firefly
thru' the mists they hollowed aloud,
'Where are you Great Thundercloud?'
Thru' the mists he then appeared

in Indian catcalls how they cheered,
'Hail mighty warrior devils Cheyenne.'

Thundercloud he was so handsome
with his big bow shoots down small game
needs much food to fill his belly
deer and oxen, fish and berries.
A great stallion he leads
wearing furs, feathers and bright beads.
Hopes are high for war with Cheyenne.

Chants he love-song in a great voice
leading braves in a war dance
around the totem pole they're prancing.
Little Song Bird seeks his glances
but his strength he needs full ripe.
Resting with big chiefs, smokes peace pipe
planning tactics against the Cheyenne.

Before the dawn breaks they prepare
while Little Song Bird peeps and stares.
Eagle Eye in plumaged head-dress
mighty warrior, he strong fortress.
Stallion of black and white
he sits astride his knees clenched tight.
Big Chief ready for war with Cheyenne.

With Thundercloud at his right side
off they gallop side by side.
Followed by Brave Firehawk
all aglow in their warpaint,
head-dresses gleaming in the morning light
many braves follow to the fight
to the big war with the Cheyenne.

Joseph Venables (Esher)

Why? When Yer Happier Giving Out Love

Why does one man kill another?
Why do many want so much?
Why does one man think he only is the one who matters most?
Why do people lose dependence on each other to be free?
Why, why kill another when yer happier giving out love?
Why do many keep on taking?
Why do many starve to death?
Why does one man see another's faults and stay blind to his own?
Why should not the right solution be in giving happily?
Why, why be so selfish when yer happier giving out love?

Ben Henderson Smith (Liskeard)

I Miss

I miss the summer skies
And the curlews' piercing cries,
And I miss the skylarks soaring o'er the lea;
I miss the blackbirds' song
In the hedgerows all day long
And a cuckoo calling from a distant tree.

The violets down the lane
And April's sudden rain,
The apple blossom's perfume I recall;
The whisper of a breeze
As it dances through the trees,
Sometimes - oh! How I miss it all!

The poppies in the corn,
A misty summer morn,
I miss the cobwebs glistening with dew,
The leaves of gold and brown,
The way they flutter down
And autumn sunsets bright with every hue.

I miss the stars that wink
In skies as black as ink,
The harvest moon that rises o'er the hill,
A barn owl's eerie screech
As it perches in a beech
I miss the atmosphere when all is still.

The snow upon the ground,
The world in whiteness gowned,
I miss the snowflakes floating gently by;
The stillness in the air
When snow lies everywhere;
No one could miss these things much more than I.

The freshness of the spring
When lambs are frolicking,
The bluebells growing 'neath woodland trees,
The primroses so pale,
The harebells, blue and frail,
My heart is missing all such things as these.
But when sometimes I long
To go where I come from,
I know the country always will remain
As clear and fresh and new
As the early morning dew,
And some day I'll be part of it again.

K Burston (Tewkesbury)

Voyage From The Mind

He learnt to sail
   on Barton Broad
   in Norfolk's fine county,
   where his hero Nelson
     learnt so many years before.

He cannot boast
   of great victories or successes,
   but he shares
   one thing in common
   with our naval Lord.
     He can *hold* a telescope
       to his *blind* eye.

Although now with
   little sight or hearing,
   he can *look* into the mind
   and *listen* to the words
     as they begin to form and flow,
       cascading from the memory.

The rich current
   is caught by his pen,
     aided by his magnifying glass.
Together they grapple
   with the flood of ideas.
He is often sucked into
   a whirlpool of words
     which hurl him
       upon angry shores
which mock his disabilities.

Daring the slack tides
   of his thoughts,
he seeks again
   to make sense of the message
     from the mind.

He will never feel
     the adoration of the crowd
     as did his hero,
but he may become aware
   of the polite appreciation
   of his fellows
   and those lovely maidens
   who circle around him
     by the riverside.

Kinsman Clive (Sherborne)

Spanish Guitar

'Twas round the corner
Just off Grafton Street
That McCullough Pigott stood
Proud and majestic
Spread out on so many floors
Displaying the magnificent
Grand pianos
Gleaming and polished
As lazily they awaited
Their first new proud owner.

In that place
Through the door
You had to go
To the top floor
For the guitars . . .
Loosely arranged round
Their allotted space.

So 'tis OK
To pick one up
And try it
But only wish to buy it.
This he does and plays.

On a rosy summer day
Two young lovers wandered in
He wishing he could afford
A guitar, a decent one,
And she, the typist
Earning seven pounds a week,
That's all -
He showing off to his new moll,
She, gazing starry-eyed, in thrall,
Intuiting what just might become,
If she played her cards right.

Many guitars he played
And fell for one in particular
Sighing - 'Ah, just grand'
And then the penniless student
Replaced that Spanish guitar
Back on its stand.

Back down the stairs
Onto the street
She, not unusually, had left
One of her things behind
So casually, she said,
'You wait here, sweet,'
Rushing back up the stairs
Two at a time
She put a deposit

On that favoured guitar
Now, it was mine.

In the ensuing weeks
She survived on cauliflower and leeks
Paying the rent
On her tiny bedsit
She eeked out
        A livin' . . .
Somehow knowing this gift
To her new-found lover
(Or perhaps it was just sheer willing)
Would somehow lift her future
To a place well worth a shilling or more.

The guitar eventually
Was presented to him
With a triumphant grin
That would nourish
The tiredest of souls.

He gaped in awe
Fingered it and saw
As tho' from above
The enormity of the love
Which would mould
His and her future life together.

And forty years later
The guitar sounds oh, so mellow
While the pages
Of our song book
Fade to yellow.

Donagh Sanfey (Bristol)

Blossom Where You Are Planted

'Blossom where you are planted'
I learned that long ago
For whilst we are discontented
The 'sands of time' will still flow . . .
We may not always be where
We thought we might like to be
But the grass is *not* always greener
As you get older you frequently see . . .
So finding yourself in a 'foreign field'
With people you may not yet know
Put some tender tendrils of love out
Watch as the flowers of friendship can *grow* . . .

The painter can grow in words.

Pamela A Campbell (Potters Bar)

The Organ Fund

The Church Organ had finally peeped its last peep
so the council decided to put it to sleep,
for many long years it had given its best
but now came the time to lay it to rest.

Much money was needed to quickly replace
that faithful old servant with pipes for a face,
there were whist drives and fetes, and songs from the Choir
and the cash indicator rose higher and higher.

My dad decided - with help from us kids
to make jigsaw puzzles from old tea-chest lids,
he smoked like a trooper, so from inside each pack -
he'd collect all the pictures - there sure was a stack.

He would stick on the pictures - then we'd go for tea
while the glue did its stuff and sealed 'A' on to 'B',
then when we returned we all gathered around
as with fret - saw he'd cut every shape like a '£'.

My father just loved complications
but was never quite sure when to stop,
two pictures were on all his puzzles -
one on bottom and one on the top;
a girl and a boy were on one side,
the other, a map of the world,
and pictures got bigger and bigger
as plans for production unfurled.

Teatime was over and cutting commenced
and pieces flew up in the air
for me to assemble and pack in the box
to 'flog' at the forthcoming fair.
But problems arose on assembly,
I had chosen to build up the map -
with masses of pink of the Empire
and sea covering most of the gap.

The pieces grew higher and higher
as the world I attempted to fit -
and Dad kept patiently cutting
and passing parts bit after bit.
He finished, then started to help me
and turned every piece upside down -

'Get the children right first -
then look at the world
because that will come right on its own.'

Jim Pritchard (Bude)

The Sun In The Sky

He gave us life,
This we know true
But what does it mean to me and to you?
Do we embrace it with arms open wide,
Or do we regard it as days passing by?
From one to the next, nothing old, nothing new,
Stuck in a rut, no care what to do,
Days and weeks, months and years,
Never facing up to ambitions and fears.
Wasting the gift that has befallen upon us,
Drowning in the memory of those who broke our trust.
Into the darkness, our thoughts reside,
And disregard the life that's passing us by.
Do we ask why, to the misery we succumb,
And question why our journey should now be done?
What does it take, to prove its worth,
Our solemn meaning here on Earth.
To spread the word of our wish to mourn,
To inject our heartache from dusk till dawn.
For others to feel our eternal resentment,
Of wanton expectations of a passage never spent.
To bless us this sorrow, we beg to ask why?
For the answer to why it's so hard just to try,
When giving up, seems the only left option,
In the clouded arena, with nowhere to turn,
You must hear the voices of the ones who need more,
The ones who are crying and begging amour,
When you're at the bottom of the pits of despair,
There is someone who needs you, beyond the misted glare.
To grant you the knowledge of laughter and heartbreak,
Does help mould the person of which you create.
Your life experience, although it seems cruel,
Can help the others that can't see it through.
You have a choice, your life as you make it,
You chose to fight, or you chose to waste it.
No one ever said life would be an easy ride,
Maybe that's the answer, only you can decide,
Some don't get the chance, their voice has been taken,
By a fate unchosen, a path that's been broken.
Don't let your decisions pass you by,
Wipe away the tears and let yourself shine.
Black clouds can pass, and if you try,
You can remember how to love,
And see the sun in the sky.

Kathryn E James (Bristol)

Little Johnny Oliphant

Little Johnny Oliphant
was marching through the meads,
his thoughts were all of tournaments,
of ladies, knights and steeds.

In case of martial action
his safety was assured
by keen-edged sword and buckler
and helm, all finest board.

Though errants bold are wont to ride
to war, or else to woo,
this day young J must go on foot.
His horse had cast a shoe!

When he'd traversed a mile or so
he heard a piteous cry
and bent his step toward the sound
to learn what ill was nigh.

Soon he saw an ancient tree
and in it spied a maid,
and there beside her on the branch
a tabby cat was laid.

'What's the matter?' Johnny cried,
'Are you stuck up there?'
'I climbed up to get my cat,
to climb down I don't dare.'

'My father is the farmer,
he's working by the mere.
I've called and called for all I'm worth
but cannot make him hear.'

'You must not try to reach me
for if we both were here
then the weight would be too great.
The bough would break, I fear.'

'I cannot ride for help,' he said,
'of pacer I am shorn,
but I can summon aid for you
as sure as I was born.'
And so he could for at his side,
on leather girdle born,
he wore, besides his armaments,
a little ivory horn.

'I'll blow,' said J, 'without delay
and I'll not parley more,
for I surmise your rending cries
were drowned by tractor's roar.'

Johnny took a deep, deep breath,
as deep as he could bear,

raised his horn and through it then
expelled the gathered air.

They knew the sound had carried
from the engine noise cessation.
Johnny blew his horn again,
confirming their location.

The engine started up again
and help was on its way.
Johnny and his oliphant
had saved the happy day.

Soon the tractor came in sight
and by the best of chances
it had a bucket, just the thing
to reach up to the branches.

Girl and cat were lifted down -
an end to their alarms -
and daughter safely was restored
to loving father's arms.

'Well done, Johnny boy,' he said.
'You really are a knight.
Without your help my daughter
might have been here till tonight.'

'As it is the day's still young,
it's only half past three,
so we'll go home to the farmhouse
for buttered scones and tea.'

Simon Plant (Bristol)

Lily

She is passed from cradle to cradle
of grandparents' arms,
floating in her warm curl of sleep,
slowly flowering as the minutes on the hospital clock
move her closer, closer to realising she is born.

We too need time,
gathering with love to give,
to measure her future,
to catch our ageing selves
in her newborn breaths.

We counted stars all the way home.
It was late as we stood, listening,
inhaling happiness in the dark of the garden,
imagining where flowers
were blossoming.

Eve Jackson (Bembridge)

The Joy Of Dreams

I often wonder what are dreams.
Why do people have them,
These adventures full of wondrous
Things the waking mind can't fathom?

What magic is it in my brain
That conjures up for me
Trips to unknown places
That I'm never going to see?

How is it I can know a face
I've never seen before,
Or recognise an unknown house
Behind an unknown door?

Who is that tall, dark stranger
As handsome as can be?
Perhaps he does exist somewhere
And perhaps he dreams of me.

Why can't I scream when terror strikes
Or run when monsters loom?
And what hidden menace awaits me
In that dark, mysterious room?

The thrill of flying, soaring
Above village, field and town,
Then the fear of being way too high
And wanting to get down.

Dreams of swimming in dried-out pools,
Or where water has tuned to grass,
Dreams of being back at school -
The oldest in my class!

Commando-style adventures,
Lives to save and hearts to mend
And the noise outside that wakes me
Just before I reach the end.

I love to dream and the dreams I have
Are varied and are many,
All-night entertainment
And it doesn't cost a penny.

Stories far more riveting
Than any book I've read
And all enjoyed in comfort
From the safety of my bed!

Geraldine Beere (Croydon)

Hip: Hooray!

I've don't it at last, I just can't believe it;
It's been so long, it can't be so.
I'd think and wonder, should I do it?
And then I'd say, yes, have a go.

But always I'd find another solution,
And then my problem would be gone,
And happily for two or three weeks,
Of all my worries there'd be none.

But, of course, they were only just hiding,
And would return this way or that,
Never enough to make me quite certain,
But back they would come and I'd say, oh drat!

Because also was always the thought within me,
What will it be like being there?
And will the result be any better?
I couldn't help wondering how I'd fare.

Yes, no, oh what shall I do?
Shall I listen to the man who says I should?
These thoughts went on for quite a while,
Then finally one day, I said I would.

The man said, 'Fine,' and put my name down,
'You'll still have quite a bit of a wait,
But when the chance comes don't refuse it,
And then your troubles will all come straight.'

So along I went, I had to believe him,
And straight things are, he spoke quite truly,
For the new one is a wonderful job,
And the old one now no longer unruly!

My surgeon was wonderful, the anesthetist likewise,
The nurses were great, we had a good laugh,
So, in the end, was my hip replacement worth it?
Well, all I can say to you is, not half!

Oh, hip hip hooray! It's happened again,
It's only two years since it happened before.
It's the other hip this time, it flared up much quicker,
And now here I am, once again, through the door.

It's the same brilliant surgeon, the same helpful doctors,
The nurses are new, but we have just as much fun,
The rooms are a bit different, and now there's a telly,
But I hope it's not long before I'm back on the run.

Jackie Gilliam (Sidmouth)

Song of A Wayfarer

May fear be no repressive bar
To steer me from my elusive star.

I was not constructed and dispatched
To be dropped disruptive and detached.
I bore no art or charm to deceive,
But wore a heart to disarm on my sleeve.

I took delight in the sun, not dismal shadows;
Joy was to run in bright blissful meadows,
Time was infinite and carefree,
With no trap or pit to snare me.

I fell in love and surrendered my heart,
Oh hell, you pretended we would never part.
We grew like two trees entwined together,
But you knew not the kind designed forever.

It was in the glow of candlelight
You first let me know things were not right.
I burst into tears, my life's bliss threatened,
My worst fears realised, the abyss beckoned.

So experience enforces me to reflect,
Renders me cautious and circumspect.
I suppress anxieties that should be addressed
So no excess worries make me more stressed.

But in the pit of life's dreary travails
I admit to be weary and assailed:
By dread sense impaled, my nerve uncertain;
And ahead, the ascent veiled by a curtain.

But a nest of ease, oblivious longings,
Conceals a fortress where wordless song is.
I have got to be bold and revile its hold,
Or my lot controlled in a sterile mould.

I should create projects, strategies for change,
Not make rejects of what is to me strange.
To travel in hope but to fear arrival
Is to grapple a rope of mere survival.

Better to tackle with life's abyss,
Get embattled in strife and arrive amiss.
Rather risk pain and being victimised
Than exist mundane, anaesthetised.

I will direct my compass, sum up a passage,
Inspect my windlass and drum up the courage.
There are unsung worlds to be explored,
And unstrung pearls on far flung shores.

I am a singer whose song lies hidden,
Whose inner tune pines, unbidden.
Will glittering vistas cleanse this blight,
Whispering promises, and dispense light?

And is the light meant for me to recover,
And reinvent myself as some other?
Do I embrace the uncertain, immerse in the flow
Or uncover the face of the person I know?

Ah Love, where are you in all of this?
How do you square in my diagnosis?
Too repressed, averse to being true,
Have you guessed these words relate to you?

Does the height of this quest seem a surprise?
The light I search gleams here - in your eyes.

Let pessimism never so deter,
But idealism ever be my spur.

Alan Day (London)

Neither Man Nor Maid

Neither man nor maid can deny,
The pains of love,
The hearts that cry and bleed.
For her, the waning moon.
For him, the scarlet sky.
Not clouds that the wind has led.

Neither man nor maid can deny,
The surge in loins.
The thoughts so fiery red,
For her the flaming sword,
For him, the scabbard laid
In meek surrender.

Neither man nor maid can deny.
For those that do
Fool but themselves,
For have they not . . .
The blood as red as mine.

Peter Coakley (Enfield)

Somerset Stars

Fair traveller from afar
South-western bound,
Make Somerset your star
There's much to be found.

Linger at ease
And soak in the atmosphere,
It's bound to please
Wherever you appear.

Roam over Exmoor
Where forest meets the sea,
Wookey Hole is a must
With its caves of mystery.

Cheddar Gorge is marvellous
The Mendip Hills abound,
Whilst in the moors below
Much wildlife is found

Wander in the meadows
Trek the leafy lanes,
Pause to watch the birds,
Upon the gentle streams.

The magic of Glastonbury
And grandeur of Wells
Are where you must not hurry;
The saints would have us dwell.

The villages delight
With character and charm,
You cannot fail to see
An English country farm.

Taunton is the tops
As our county town,
With its many shops
Much can be found.

Try Weston or Burnham
Healthy spots to stay,
Or Minehead is great
To ease your cares away.

Coaching inns and mansions,
Lovely churches too,
Thatched cottages delight -
Somerset welcomes you.

Brian R Russ (Martock)

Bridges

Bridges are something that can be built
not just of concrete and steel.
But in the spirit of forgiveness
when there are hurts to heal.

There may be a way to close the gap
between generations young and old.
To suit the individual concerned
this kind appropriately mould.

Metaphorically speaking, they're an object
one wouldn't want to burn.
How to express a view, yet not offend
is a skill we all should learn.

The majority, of course, are structural
becoming famous in their own right.
Golden Gate and Clifton to name but two
are an imposing, spectacular sight.

Some carry passengers only on foot:
others allow vehicles to move.
A few can separate, letting tall objects pass
still their function designers are trying to improve.

Present on many sailing craft
as a central point of navigation
this area also houses the latest
in ship-to-shore communication.

It is a section of the nose
which will withstand spectacles' weight.
Or a connecting piece in the mouth
that keeps teeth remaining straight.

In snooker, this handmade construction
allows a player the cue to raise
enabling a hindrance to be got around
but care must be taken not to rip the baize.

Supporting strings on certain instruments
and even affecting the sound
a second musical sort exists
giving two different pieces common ground.

Whatever their manifestation
most span a great divide
joining separate points together
and making barriers less wide.

Alice Humby (Christchurch)

Erickson Has Something To Answer For

There is no such 'thing' as love
I do not believe it exists
I do not believe it is

Except
Since first we met
I have lost my sense of time
Not timing
That has improved
I dance like Fred Astaire and Gene Kelly rolled into one in my mind
And
I smile like a Cheshire cat
That becomes just a smile
All over rich and warm
And I have a glow
Not radiation
Yet radiating more when I think of or am with you

Yes this is not that 'thing' love
That seems so solid and grounded and tangible
To say, 'I love you' is simple and easy and trite

Except
Each time that you say it to me
I am moved to joy and laughter
As my legs are suddenly rubber
And of no use to man nor beast
I fear that you may say it when I am running
Yet, I wait,
Eager to explore the feelings
As though I have become a figure cartooned and coloured
I am sure
That my eyes widen, nostrils flare (a little), skin glows when you say
those words

And yet I do not believe in that love 'thing'

Except
I want to sprint and chase the clouds
Leap off high buildings and soar to great dizzy heights
I am an elegant eagle, a sparkling sparrow, a puffin' puffin . . .
soaring can be hard work
And it's nice to stop and eat some grass along the way
No wonder the signs say *Keep off the grass*
There'd be none left if we all felt this way

So even though I don't' believe in that I. L. Y. 'thing'
You get me to say it

And now I understand
That you have entranced me
Cast a spell across my mind
And drugged me with your presence
So that is what is done

You have hypnotised me just by being you
And I will leap up and down
And bark at the moon
And bathe in the sun ('til pinkly done)
And act like a chicken when encouraged to dance
Buy flowers and chocolate and wine
And then a ring or two
And press my face against yours for photos and curtain calls
And empty dustbins in gale force winds
And trim hedges
And clean cars that I don't even own
And make beans on toast until I learn how to cook

It is magic, mystic
And that is just the fact that today I ironed a shirt
And hugged you 'til my arms ached as does my heart

Yet
Still
I don't believe in it
Because I know
It is a word you use to capture my soul
And I am caught

I . . . you.

David Newport (Oxford)

The Happy Horse

Majestically he rears in sunlight-dappled yard,
And waves his forelegs at the world with clear delight,
Then the happy horse gallops around the orchard.

In sheer abandonment his cares he doth discard,
Like a statue his muscles tense and fleck with light,
Majestically he rears in sunlight-dappled yard.

The pleasant sound clip-clop upon the ground that's hard,
His long mane and coat are black, four fetlocks white,
Then the happy horse gallops around the orchard.

Muscular strength, upon this horse no sign of lard,
Primeval passion flashes from his eyes so bright,
Majestically he rears in sunlight-dappled yard.

Fast he leaps across a patch of discarded card,
Gentle his whinny as his goal comes into sight,
Then the happy horse gallops around the orchard.

A wondrous sight to stir the soul of any bard,
This joyous animal in swift and carefree flight,
Majestically he rears in sunlight-dappled yard,
Then the happy horse gallops around the orchard.

Linda Coleman (Crawley)

Pain

There's a pain inside me, a pain so raw,
It tears my heart and makes me sore.
It makes me sob and my eyes fill with tears,
But even they can't wash away my fears.

Growing up in my broken home,
Dad's gone out, leaving us alone,
Looking after the other kids until way past nine,
I'm a mother, way before my time.

Just entered my teens and should be out with mates,
Instead I'm in the kitchen, washing plates,
Screaming at the boys to stop hitting each other,
Makes me want to hide underneath my cover.

I wish there was some other way,
Some way to brighten up my dull day,
I want to enjoy myself like my friends,
But instead the chores never seem to end.

Now I'm grown and have a son,
I want him to know he's my number one,
Still can't hide the tears streaming down my face,
Not always possible to find a quiet place.

I wish I could tell you about this pain I feel,
But the heartache still feels so real,
At times I don't eat to get attention from those close to me,
But these are the chains from which I want to be free.

I know that this is a bad thing to do,
And that deep inside it hurts you too,
I wish that I could stop this pain,
That I could be a carefree child again.

Live this life in a different way,
Instead of dreaming of better days,
I should be happy, I've settled down,
But then why do I wear a frown?

Around most people I know, I plaster on a smile,
Inside I'm hurting all the while,
You have seen me at my worst,
I'm beginning to think that I've been cursed.

I guess inside there is a 'happy' me,
that's the person that I want to be,
I don't want to feel like this any longer,
I want to come out of this mess feeling stronger.

Claire Murray (London)

Galatea

Hewn in marble, white so pure,
You look on me and with allure
Do captivate my very soul,
Your cold carved stone, my love has stole.

Snow white eyes and curling hair,
Immortal your unseeing stare,
Still, looks at me and thrills me through,
Stricken am I for love of you.

Carved I you from thought alone,
Fashioned from that hard pearl stone,
Now I stare in love distraught,
Homage to the beauty wrought.

Aphrodite, queen above,
Give her life that she may love,
May laugh, may cry, may sing, may breathe,
May see me here where I do grieve.

Grieve for the stone that I have cast
Into a likeness that will last,
And yet, takes no thought to me,
For stone she is, and cannot see.

And yet, yet, her breast does heave,
How so, how so, I disbelieve,
O, Aphrodite, Queen in Heaven,
My pleas you've heard, so strongly given.

Her legs, her arms, so softly form,
Her hair unwinds, a curling storm
Enflames my ardent thoughts, desire
That sets my lonely soul afire.

And then her face turns down to me,
Her eyes of blue Aegean sea,
Cool, serene, they quench the fires,
Under threnody of Grecian lyres.

She steps down from her pedestal,
Sublime and poised with aire regal,
Daughter of a goddess' whim,
Unchained from stone, a poison grim.

To me she comes a mortal now,
Upon her lips a lovers vow,
And then she looks at me so clear,
'You carved me, I am Galatea.'

P C Rowe (South Ascot)

A Drop Of Rain

And so we waited silently,
Like cardboard figures on a stage,
Bereft of all emotion now,
Brings from another age.

Our strength was sapped to lowest ebb,
The small room airless reeking sweat,
Outside, the hard baked crust of earth,
Laughed, that pink mirage of wet.

The animals came in search of drink,
None here, and quietly lay to die,
Coal-black wings wheeled overhead,
Only sound in that leaden sky.

Then, with one almighty blast,
Of Gabriel's horn - the heavens broke,
And rain, real water splattered down,
In that second no one spoke.

Whoops of joy and madness came,
New found hidden strength surpassed,
All outside with face upturned,
Water, rain, thank God at last.

Drops at first, then great grey sheets,
Wallowed in it all we could,
Hair like tails, and bodies drenched,
That piecrust earth, a sea of mud.

All of us we worked like ants,
Pails and basins, bowls and tins,
Grandma's rose-sprigged chamber pots,
Brought from England with the twins.

So we toiled for days and days,
Catching every precious drop,
Glistening rain, soft smooth to hands,
We dare not breathe, we dare not stop.

Bodies freshly bathed once more,
Children's hair all shiny new,
Mimosa sprays around the house,
Arranged as Mother used to do.

The animals aware again,
Of sights and sounds and running free,
And struggling through that sodden earth,
The green shoot of a newborn tree.

So the days resumed their mode,
I lift my eyes towards the sky,
Oh, blessed rain, this happy land,
Thank God, we were not left to die.

I found my mother's letter then,
In apron pocket by the door,

Home had been so far away,
She sent it quite three weeks or more.

With eager hands I tore the flap,
Incessant ramblings met my gaze,
'Last week, we read about the drought,'
'How *will* they manage?' Grandma says.

'Father's well, you'd like to know,
Doctor says, it's George's ticker.'
'Mrs Woods reported missing -
Come to think of it, so's the vicar!'

'Garden's looking nice now dear,
Bulbs we planted coming on,
Bring up children in the bush,
Are you *sure* you should have gone?'

'Oh! Mother, how little do you know,
In your parochial naïve way',
With smile and shrug I turned the page -
PS - 'We had a drop of rain today!'

Joyce Raynbird (Sturminster Newton)

Anniversaries: Time For Celebration Or Reflection

Anniversaries come and go by each celebration
Some look on them with sadness, others elation.
Maybe it's an anniversary of just a month or year
Perhaps it may bring joy but sometimes it brings a tear.
Look at an anniversary of a century or more
Each turn of a century can only question what is in store.
For the years following man does not seem to learn
That strife and misery that may follow will only confirm.
People can live in harmony if allowed to do so
We must treat every human as friend and not as foe.
Look back at centuries past and reflect
The troubles, the wars that leave misery and neglect.
We have a multitude of religions, beliefs and many factions
That are often misguided by wrongful actions.
With the terrorism and hate of today
Is there a need - please end it we pray.
Colonial wars and oppression achieve little or nothing, we know
Smaller and Third World countries need help so let it show.
Many leaders religious and political pay lip service to the needs of many
And step back and offer little, not even a penny.
So, let us celebrate whatever anniversary there may be
And at the same time celebrate peace, tolerance and goodwill as the key.

Peter Parbery (Crowthorne)

Cotswold Country

High-plateaud land of mellowed stone
Gazing down on Severn Vale
Welcomes all four winds that blow
Summer sun-kissed, swept by hail.

Yellow lichened cottage roofs
Roughly clad from limestone heart
Appear to soak the warming rays
Reflecting back at evening's start.

Varied shades of gold and brown
Autumn tinted Westonbirt
Crispened russet fragments fall
With the Cotswold breeze to flirt.

Quaint named hamlets nestling small
In merest nooks that fold the land
Reddened lead-paned windows peep
From the night's surrounding hand.

Black velvet sweeps the rolling plain
Hiding scars that mar her face
Giant grabs which tear the turf
Gaped holes, with grassland interlace.

Yet chasms can't stay empty long
The ever rising waters make
Inaptly dubbed and silvered pits
A lakeland formed of gravel take.

Home for countless grebe and duck
Colonised by reed and sedge
Great pike patrol clear crystal deeps
Beyond the pit's wind - driven edge.

Hedgerow grubbed and widened fields
Elm, gaunt standing winter moon
Corn blades in a stone strewn earth
Await the brightness coming soon.

Green flushed hawthorn, minted new
Purple flowered dry stone wall
Migrant flocks of nesting fowl
Heed the springtime wakening call.

As seasons roll the constant scene
Timeless flocks of grazing sheep
Leave an e'er abiding peace
Disturbing not the Cotswold sleep.

John Nolan (Bristol)

The Stars

Dark sky alive in winter night,
The air so clear there's depth
Between the flying stars.

Up the sea-cliff path my walking stops,
My head leans back and upward looks,
Like feeling watched.

One week before at New Year
As we good-byed good hosts
At the old house in the moor,

I held child Mira, two years old,
And pointed saying, 'Stars, look?'
Her suckling face lay back,

Tiny hand and eyes all took
Maiden sighted to the twinkling lights in black.
Quiet, while car doors slam and merry goodbyes rang.

Now, I hear the brambles squeak.
So late and cold the wintered trees
Are naked dreaming of the warm.

And overhead to dark sea's edge
The bright star millions whirl on black,
Remaining fixed while full of motion,

My head lies back again to catch them.
No streetlight spoils the seeing,
The lane risen become rough path,

Chill hedgerow in the night wind clattering.
Over my head is blind with stars.
Stars in the spaces between their patterning,

Stars dusted with stars, glinting
Shifting glittering, fixed yet moving.
I cannot see them all for watching.

So linger, face tipped back
As if to drink the pinioned
Changing points of light.
No household stirs or curtain whispers,
Footstep quiet as sleeping cats,
Luck's door is here and here's the latch.

Indoors, the mind yet flown aloft to yearn
The stellar places like a birthplace,
As distant homes. I would return.

Phil Sheardown (Totnes)

A Cornish Carn

From high carn looking back
Sweat on brow I drop knapsack
Elastic roads stretch miles and miles
Ribbons of lanes approached by stiles

Before my eyes a patchwork quilt
When clouds move, Earth seems to tilt
Heady feeling just like wine
But the real thing, all genuine

Sun breaks through, dispels shivers
Silver streamers are small rivers
Copse of trees stand round in groups
Alone in field gnarled oak stoops

Has been used to scratch cows' rumps
Very soon be just few stumps
Perhaps two hundred years since born
Branches tired, no sweet acorns

Through the ages farmers battle
Raising horses, sheep and cattle
Struggle continues in the field
Life-sustaining crops to yield.

Shadowy mounds my vision fills
Other carns, giant mole hills
Further distant, glimpse of sea
Another world not meant for me

Gentle zephyrs ruffle my hair
It's not always thus, I do declare
Gales and storms, rain and snow
Assault the carn and valley below

During winter (long gone this glow)
Hill and valley blanket of snow
Blemishes covered by minute flakes
Pure white icing on Christmas cake

Return to this present sunny day
Panoramic views on display
Wealth of beauty - complete bliss
No cash required to enjoy this

As I gaze in wonderment
Smell the gorse and heather's scent
Wars, cruel killings, seem far away
Thank God I live to see today

Open my pack, sip at my tea
Beholding nature - its mystery
Though I bite a sandwich at least
Before my eyes is nature's feast

Yes! Patchwork quilt of greens and golds
Rivers of silver, beauty unfolds

I'm not so young, that's a truth
Though at the moment feel like a youth

Smoke from chimney curls to the sky
Worker's cottage below I spy
Joe works hard, tends herd of cattle
Family worship in yonder chapel

Though not many of this world's goods
God provides shelter, clothes, food
Joe's family and other neighbours
Thank the Lord for all His favours

Cottages, village, tumbled barns
God's and Man's handiwork on the carn
Between them did well 'twixt Earth and sky
Through sheer wonder, tear in my eye

I gaze and gaze, can't take all in
Why mankind kill? Why mankind sin?
Our Dear Lord said and it's so true
'Forgive them! They know not what they do!'

Arthur S Waller (Redruth)

Before You Went Away

*(For Sara Louise-written the night you were born sleeping,
24th July 2005, from Daddy)*

We only got to hold you
Just before you went away
God took you to His angels
Where we shall meet again one day.

We never heard your laughter
Or wiped a teardrop from your eye
We had little time to get to know you
Before we said goodbye.

Now every time we see a rainbow
Or a bright and shining star
We can look towards the heavens
For we know that's where you are.

While all the other angels
Play with their new best friend
We that are left keep crying
Waiting for the pain to end.

Those left behind will love you
Until each our dying day
For we only got to hold you
Just before you went away.

Nick Oliver (Plymouth)

Oldest Woods

(Wistman's Wood is one of only three remaining areas of ancient oak woodland on Dartmoor)

They looked unimpressive,
Age is deceptive.
Gnarled and grey
Bent by centuries of time
The Oldest Ones.
Trees of white coarse stubble
Old mans' whiskers,
Frail as dandelion clocks
Clinging brittlely onto life
In the crease of the hills
Where the river trickles.
Ancient boulders with pale moss
Grow from the ground, make dark secret holes
Round your roots.
What have you copses seen?
What could you tell
If anyone still listened to the mutter
Of your dry creaking voices?
Your sap has hardly risen
Soon you will be gone.

'Unless,' you whisper persuasively
'Something is done,
We are in no hurry,
We can wait
We are not moved from our ways
Stay with us
Be a Dryad!'
How exciting, deliciously tempting!
If I stayed
For you to renew and strengthen
Then would your branches be
Green again?
Would it be worth it?

Walk not with indifference,
Into the oaken spinney,
Clear the mind from voices,
Beware!
The Oldest Ones have hidden strength,
One knows not in innocence
The invocation of Pan who in this grove
Still lingers with tenaciousness.

Lucinda Carey (Torquay)

Battery People

The pecking order starts at home.
Peck. Peck-peck.
The one in charge stands all alone.
Peck peck.

Who handles cash, who pays the rent,
Who says each month what can be spent:
That's power.
And our dad has it.
'For now,'
Says Mum. Peck peck.

And at the bottom of the heap,
Us kids, the lowest of them all.
Though Granny's slipping every day,
And if it's right what people say,
She'll soon be there, to break our fall.
Peck peck.

Can't wait for my turn at the top,
But most of all
To pass Dad, as he slides and claws
His way down in an endless fall
Of booze and fags
And beating hands;
Those hands now hurting no one but himself,
And painfully small. Peck peck.

When I'm in charge, I'd like to say,
'Here! Take the money.
Take a holiday
And let's be nice to everyone.'
Peck peck.

Though really it will be more fun
To smash Dad's head in
As I go,
To do the same to everyone I know.
Peck peck.

They won't be cross. No. Not with me.
They'll say, 'But why did no one see
His cry for help?'
With a right-on sigh.
And 'Too true, missus', I'll reply,
As I poke out her other eye.
Peck. Peck.

Angela Vale (London)

89

The Race

The yachts set off at the start of the gun
For the honour and glory our race had begun
As we sailed across the endless sea
Each watch was kept by a crew of three

All the yachts started at a great pace
For winning was all that mattered in a race
From Cowes we set off, what a glorious sight
As over a hundred yachts left the Isle of Wight

It was to the Fastnet lighthouse we steered
It was a race many crewmen feared
For the weather could quickly change to rough
To sail such a race the crew needed to be tough

To sail our boat it needed a crew of six
These were comprised of a motley mix
Of a shipwright, a lawyer and a surveyor
With two engineers and a rugby player

For a day and a half the weather was so calm
The crew felt the race would be free from harm
And the tales they had heard about the gales
Were just stories and ramblings of old sailors' tales

But the weather seemed kind with a gentle breeze
Not enough to sail by or even to cause a sneeze
So gentle that the crew started to doubt
The excitement of the race then came a shout

Quick as a flash or so it did seem
The wind changed direction to now on the beam
The boat tilted so the side was under the sea
As the wind and tide spun it into the lee

The skipper tried with all his might
To bring the boat back upright
But the tilt had made the rudder clear the water
Then the boats keel seemed to make it falter

The skipper cried out, 'Drop the main!'
But his cries and effort were in vain
As the seas pushed the boat over to meet its fate
The main sail rope was quickly cut by the mate

No longer held tight it sagged and dropped
With the wind gone from the sail the tilting stopped
The boat staggered to come back to nearly upright
But the crew had not yet finished the fight

With the weight of the sail hanging over the side
The boat started gyrating into the tide
Then with a loud crack the mast broke in two
The skipper yelled out what the crew should do

'Get the cutters, cut off the mast
Then try and tie down, make everything fast.'

But the sea had not given up its sport
For it knew when it had another boat caught

The deck fittings were broken with the life raft
We will use the RIB but that rubbery craft
Needing pumping up and filling with air
But in the side of it was a great tear

The boat, though battered, seemed to weather the storm
And with the wind dropping all seemed like norm
But the engine was flooded so would not start
A Mayday had been sent on that the crew took heart

Except that there was no mast, no main sail, no rope
Yet despite all that had happened the crew had hope
It was the unconquerable spirit of man
That causes them to overcome all that they can

They laughed and cheered and hugged as a team
For sailing this race had been for all their dream
As they sailed across the endless sea
Whilst each watch was kept by a crew of three

Arthur Jenner (Guildford)

Untitled

Words used to flow freely,
My feelings on paper to stay,
But, those words were written for a special love,
Who has passed, and gone away.

When she left this world without me,
She in 'Heaven' me, left in this hell,
She took her smiles with her,
And my 'poetic' soul as well.

My mum loved my words,
Sometimes sad, most times gay,
I could always put into verse,
All the things, that she would say.

Two years have gone past, and until today,
This is the first time, that I am OK.

Your letter arrived, asking for rhyme,
I heard her say 'Put paper to pen.'
Now is right, and it is time.

To rekindle the flame of the poet in me,
Let my words 'flow' again, and set my soul free.

Recalling her love, throughout future years,
I'll remember her last words,
'No tears? No more tears.'

Wendy Harris (Newquay)

How The West Was Lost

Kindling a jolly good flame, untame,
Sure, bold, they wandered;
Sun glistening on the tenuous, shared herds,
See the latent bribes! White men, newly arrived within a nascent nation,
Free the ancient tribes! Red men, barely alive inside the reservation,
A loin clothed and head-dressed, feathered tribal clan,
Rambles hikes at Wounded Knee,
Spiked Tree, the hair-shorn master,
Boring bulls' eyes with his glimmering arrows,
Chieftain, poor fallen victim of the conflict;
Grief-torn, squaw calls the dictum of the convict,
The begotten, red, impressive sons of Earth all known best,
United, we hope, with the Great Spirit's rest,
With no money for a stirrup, strewn like litter, yes they fall.

Swindling for Hollywood fame, they came,
Pure gold they squandered;
Spun, disingenuous, spare words,
Aired in libel's diatribe, a grievous irritation;
Scared of rival's higher bribe, of devious estimation,
A coin tossed, and a reckless, leather-hided man,
Shambles like a zoo monkey;
Ike leaves the care worn cluster,
Pouring the prize out of simmering barrels,
Trigger clicks, and the gun powder all runs dry;
Cigar flicks, in the sun, chowder onions fry.
The forgotten dead from oppressive guns of death in the west,
United, we hope, with the Lord Christ's Sabbath rest.
Like comb honey or gold syrup after bitterness and gall.

Dwindling, such folly should shame, and blame,
We're told and remanded
Ones, listening to the tremulous, snared birds,
They received, then denuded, God's chosen six-day creation,
Now deceived and deluded, flocks frozen in aviation,
Purloined, lost and so feckless, a tethered idol can
Strand upright, but never heed;
Cries that the airborne muster.

Soaring the skies are the shimmering sparrows,
Near, mother birds, brood over their young;
Hear lovers' words, skewed upon the tongue,
Fields of cotton, bred obsessive songs, given birth from human pain,
United, we hope, on breaking the demon chain,
Up a gum tree, more birds chirrup, their offspring twitter in festivals.

Andrew Stephenson (Epsom)

Dead Planet (A 'Given' Poem - In 1962)

Distant scintillating light
White against the setting sun
Are you dying? Do I see death?
Do you harbour sentient beings?

Does one rest as I now rest
Chided by the evening breeze?
Have you thoughts as I have thoughts
Uncertain as the swing of the trees?

Has the arbiter of all
Mocked me in my vanity
Given you, beneath your sun
The choices given to me?

Did you grow . . . as a toadstool grows
To spotted prime with fungal glee?
Do you speak? Or do you read
The spores of fellow beings?

Perhaps, to me your beauty would
Be ugliness; a frightening thing
Though, to the arbiter I name
You are created and are good . . .

Have you laid waste as I laid waste,
Fellow sentient being?
Until your spore is the only spore
Preserved in slimy numbered bins?

Did wisdom come again, too late
As your functions ebbed and died?
None heard your vacant scream 'abyss'
Aghast as fatal glassy slide . . .

Planet. I can sense a death.
Grey scum. Something that sighs
And writhes alone, in darkening pools
Mirroring dead dreams of eyes . . .
From: 'Stars'

. . . have been and will always be
They move in the void of the great
Time Seas Creation is omnipotent
And Creation is of Love . . .

Eric Gladwin (Thame)

A Day In London

We started the day across from Big Ben
and duly noted the hour was ten.

Our tour of London about to start -
here we were in England's heart.

At Green Park our journey began,
our commentator a Pakistan man.

Past the Ritz on to Hyde Park -
people were jogging 'up with the lark'.

Marble Arch looked regal and proud
as it towered above the gathering crowd.

Shopaholics busily punished their feet
looking for bargains down Oxford Street.

Piccadilly Circus looked just the same -
forgot to ask why they gave it that name!

Now on to Haymarket, look at the sights!
Famous names are up there in lights.

Nelson looks down with one arm and one eye
on Trafalgar Square as our bus passes by.

Our Pakistan host once more comes alive
to recount Nelson's victory in 1805.

The National Gallery so large and austere
houses paintings by Van Gogh who lopped off his ear.

St Marten's the church was next on the tour.
At Christmas they open their doors to the poor.

Then down the Strand where each girl and boy
attended the tea dances at the Savoy.

Around Aldwych the Law Courts were soon to be seen
where justice, they say, still reigns supreme.

Now, just ahead, the road narrowly tapers
revealing Fleet Street who printed newspapers.

Now Ludgate Circus and Ludgate Hill -
there's time to look as the bus stands still.

Our guide points out the dome of St Paul's
and tells of the history within its walls.

The Whispering Gallery built by Wren
echoes and resounds as they say 'Amen'.

The Bank of England making the mint
continues to do so whilst people are 'skint'.

The Tower of London was next on our list,
a tourist's delight we couldn't resist.

Here Anne Boleyn languished, so it is said,
till Henry VIII shouted 'off with her head'.

As Queen of England, wielding her power,
Elizabeth locked Mary away in the tower.

One after another all lost their lives -
it's a good job that Henry had so many wives!

Our Pakistan guide now pointed ahead
and there were the Beefeaters resplendent in red.

At Tower Pier we boarded a boat
still viewing London although now afloat.

There's the Houses of Parliament where politics reign
and common sense rules (though sometimes in vain).

On Westminster Bridge we stood looking down
what a wondrous place is our London Town!

So, if you wish to see London without any fuss -
do it like us, on an open-top bus.

I M Cowen (Hayes)

The Factory

Here we are another day
Clocking on to earn our pay
White coat, blue hat
Washing hands is habit
At the factory.

Pressing, painting, scraping, scrapping
Rolling, wrapping, stuffing, packing
At the factory.

Time to take a coffee break
Drinks machine is our best mate
Read our stars
What is our fate?
At the factory.

Back again to face more toil
Machine has stopped, need more oil
Fix it quick as you can
There's more toffee in the pan.

While working we dream away
Of holidays, someday we may
Win the lottery, premium bond
Someone wave their magic wand.

It's almost four day nearly done
Can't wait to get out in the sun
Rush to the door, I hear him say
'Don't be late I'll dock your pay.'

Joy Pitman (Poole)

My Harvest

(Dedicated to my friend Ian Guy)

Clearing away the old man's beard
From the chapel arch and around the door,
Stripping the ivy from the communion rail
And picking up fruits from the sheeted floor.
Preparing baskets of gifts for the village folk
And tins of soup for the pavement poor.
Storing the lumps of coal for the harvest hence,
Removing from the table, the bread, the centrepiece
With water and with salt the core of life's essence
The chapel now laid bare.

'Twas but a few hours past
That the celebration had begun,
The chairs were filled with people
And praises to the Lord were sung.
The perfume of vegetables and flowers
Intoxicating everyone.
'We plough the fields and scatter,'
We read and loudly sang,
Remembering those in other lands
Where the soil had turned to sand.

I stood outside the chapel door,
Said goodbye to this year's harvest home.
But wait! A car draws through the gate,
I am not here alone,
Out of his car my friend alights
And greets me with good cheer,
'I've brought you a gift, I've made from wood,
Your birthday a few days past I fear.
I've inserted a coin in the cover too
Minted the year when you were new.'

'Twas a joy to carve and thread the clasp
A token of friendship throughout the years
I held it reverently in my grasp
While I was near to the point of tears.
My harvest had come in a gift unforeseen,
From seeds planted long ago,
Dropped in the soul of life it seems
Had germinated with fruit aglow,
Just when I had closed the chapel door
My cup was full, I could not ask for more.

Kelvin Thomas (Bath)

Song Of The Dolphin

We saw the Roman galleys, we saw the ships from Greece,
We guided lovesick sailors safely home in war and peace.
To Vikings and Phoenicians, to Egyptians and their slaves,
We were a good luck omen, as we broke from the moonlit waves.
We saw proud Spanish galleons,
The barques and the brigantines,
That carried silks and spices
In their holds with golden dreams.
We led the white-sailed schooners
And we swam the starboard beam
Of clippers signed to the China Run routine.

The sea is aquamarine,
We thought to bring back your dreams from the ocean,
As a figurehead figurine
We led you over the sea with devotion.

When liberty was threatened, or when human life was cheap,
We led doomed ships from danger, been as pilots to the fleet.
When mariners have foundered near the shark-toothed coral reef
We navigated safe passageways into ocean waters deep.
Alike to junks and sampans and the Indiamen of old,
We warned of storms and cyclones
When Pacific waters rolled.
We understood the weather signs,
How uncertainty unfolds,
Our ageless theme a priceless dream to hold.

When his crew was in mutiny,
We heard Arion's plea addressed to Apollo.
When cast adrift on the lea
We bore him safely ashore
His purpose to follow.

Across eternal oceans upon surfing waves of foam
We crossed the seas of destiny to bring your spirit home.
In ancient days our nomad ways wise Homer might have known,
Our course through time with humankind is not traversed alone.

We live as Man's companions,
It is freedom we defend
From seas remote we bring a hope
To light the lives of men.
Let us evolve together
Let us try to live as friends
And chase the bright rainbow ribbon to the end . . .

Rod Legge (Lymington)

Licensed To Kill

With one hand I grasp the legs and wingtips
And with the other
I grip the feathered neck in a knuckled vice.
The bird merely gives a blink.
Used to being handled, how could it know its fate?
Don't worry, these birdbrains cannot think.

But as I don't want to bother
The rest of the batch, I turn from the crate.
With little finger beneath the beak, I lift the head
To right angles. The strength is in the wrist.
Control the downward pull, no violent heave,
No sudden jerk to take the head right off and leave
The arterial hosepipe to sprout and twist.

In spasms life discharges in my hold
While the blood drains neatly into the internal gap.
Last twitch. Now I am able
To pass the carcass, slap
It down on the pluckers' bench, next phase to
Poulterers' slab and dinner table.
I kill to eat.
My part in the primeval lineage.
Also I kill to meet
The problem of compassion
When suffering becomes insufferable pain.
The farmer keeps the powers
Society feels unable to retain.

Yet not far off in time or place or memory
The ceremonial feast incorporated
The aged wise chief, or virile enemy.
Then the tender, young, raw cabin boy
Ranked less then officers and crew.
Who was it said we should not unduly strive
To keep alive the ailing? Of course we knew
That breaking necks was the right ploy
To free society from crime.

With the devolution of the soul
We superior animals count our time
Solely in this world, and so our bodies must endure
Beyond reason, parts more precious than the whole.
Pneumonia's no more the old man's friend
Quickening the last illness to a speedy end.

Were I politically correct I might feel bound
To fence a penal colony for fighting cocks and found
A hospice for the weakly chicks.

Last one. All done. My pluckers chat.
Ankle-deep in lousy feathers, they mix
Jokes and gossip, while guts drop
Into buckets from the trussing table.

Plumped white breasts. Bloody slop.
But this is a domestic scene. Bear in mind
Its no vast abattoir, no killing field
Where tented surgeons chat and joke
To blunt the horror as they wield
Their knives to eviscerate and truss there own kind.

Should we all eat grain?
John Barleycorn must die.
The breaking of bread relies on
Breaking the bonds in rain
And air and earth by the powered Sky -
Force taken from the slowly dying sun.
Take. Eat. Develop. Die.
Take a turn as dust until
The wheel of life recycles by.
Meanwhile my little flock will feed us.

Nan Rudden (Penzance)

You Have No Choice But Be Brave

'I am sorry . . . '
Ever always, it starts with
'I am sorry.'
As soon as you hear that
You know there is
A catastrophe looming on
The horizon,
A tragedy unfolding.
A tragic accident, they tell you.
You rush to the hospital
Forgotten is all else.
You sit by the bedside
Hoping. Praying for a miracle.
A gentle touch here, there,
On the head, a kiss,
On the fevered brow.
You hold hands
Willing life to continue.
Then a lingering last look
That says so much,
Means so much,
Of what might have been . . .
'I am so sorry for your loss,'
Someone whispers.
'You are so brave.'
No, you are not brave
You have no choice
But be brave.

S G A Bennin-Sam (London)

Fabulous

On the one hand, there was the end of the string;
And, on the other hand, there was the ball.
But, what happened in the middle was all a terrible tangle,
A most miserable, infernal, brute of a mess.
Yet, she expected him to unravel the mystery?

Take the bull by the horns, bait his rival in his lair?
Commit, as a condition of being her emblazoned paramour,
Some fantastic burlesque of bravery - don the golden sandals,
Shift the immovable rock; discover the bronze sword,
Grasp the glittering hilt? Well, he wasn't the stuff

Of which such fables were made - he wore brogues,
For God's sake! So, how could he possibly save the land
From suffering? Really, it just didn't seem reasonable.
In fact, it seemed bloody-well, down-right unfair!
But then, that was her all over - totally arbitrary, such a cow!

And, even her legendary beauty - the fruit
Of an unnatural union, or, so it was whispered - well,
That was a perfect labyrinth of moods: she could -
Looking up from her knitting - turn ugly; from the very id
Of her egotistical palace, become monstrous,

Pull her very own mythical minotaur frown; then,
Pawing, snorting underground, gore his knotted,
Sacrificial intestines. Should he, therefore,
Abandon her, while she was asleep? But, again,
No ruthless hero he, no regal lion; just, utterly lamb-like,

Too considerate by half. Though,
He was vexed enough to question
What precisely it was she desired; and whether he himself
Required a soulmate so bullish? Really,
She was nothing less than a cryptic catalogue

Of uncrackable codes! Probably completely beyond even
The oracle at Delphi; someone who was an incredible,
Self-created fiction; someone who commandeered the thread
Of reason and free will, made it always seemed fated
To arrive at the *cul de sac* of her queenly fiat. But then,

That's what everyone told him -
All the amateur psychiatrists. They said, they warned him:
She was fabulous, but, ever-changing
So Janus-faced that he'd be tongue-tied; that no one -
Male or female! - would ever be able . . . to relate.

Kevin Russell-Pavier (Catford)

Reminiscing

I have wandered thro' pastures green,
Beautiful flowers in glades I've seen,
Fruits of trees I have plucked in glee,
Riverside banks I've sheltered in lea,
Had moments rest on a wayside stile,
To survey the wonder and give a smile.

I still pick apples from orchard where I,
Once climbed up a tree to branch on high,
To watch rolling landscape and fields of grain,
Windmills in action, breeze-turning vane,
Then sit very quiet as birds come to rest,
And tend to the chicks calling out from their nest.

I've rowed on a river, fished in a stream,
Helped mow a meadow, drove a shire horse team,
Brought in a harvest to oast, mill and barn,
Tended some cattle and sheep on a farm,
Helped with the lambing, ploughing time too,
Laughed with my friends even when wet through.

I have watched, as a sunset is due,
At the glorious panorama of vista and hue,
The dancing of sunbeams and colours alive,
And seeing at daybreak the sunshine arrive,
To rival the splendour of evening before,
The regalia of colour no artist could draw.

On placid waters I have swam and sailed,
Over stormy seas I have prevailed,
In desert heat and arid sand,
I've found oasis close at hand,
Sank knee deep in snow bound lanes,
Yet still had enjoyable snowball games.

I found inspiration when out in the east,
I visited the Holy land, a wonderful feast,
Jerusalem and Nazareth, Bethlehem too,
Galilee and Jordan where Christ travelled through.

I haven't seen everything I wanted to view,
I didn't accomplish all I'd set out to do,
I've suffered the fate of not enough time,
But in retrospect satisfaction is mine,
The pleasures I found abundant in store,
No man could ever have asked for more.

William Stannard (Canning Town)

Your Loving Son

It's your loving son that's writing, please listen to what I say,
I'm on a ship that's sailing, far, far away.
I don't know when I'll see you, but I'll be thinking all the time.
Of what you and Pop are doing, now that you are far behind.
I have to keep it secret, where our destiny is near,
As we aim to fool the Germans, now that war is close, I fear.

It's your loving son that's writing, at last we see land ahead,
And although we are pleased to go ashore, we live in constant dread,
It must be the uncertainty, and maybe we can never be sure,
When our freedom will be no longer, and that we will be at war.
But just for now it's good news, we've fresh fruit and tobacco too,
And each time I roll up a cigarette, I smile Pop, and think of you.

It's your loving son that's writing, and we are leaving port today,
We've had so much food, we're fit to burst, and
Made new friends along the way,
I can't believe we're in a heat wave,
While you're probably having wind and rain,
Hang on Pop while I take a drink, then return to writing once again.
As I take a last look to the distant shore,
I know this will test my faith,
But Mom and Pop, there is never a night I pray to God to
Keep you and I both safe.

It's your loving son that's writing, this time it's bad news I have to tell,
We've been captured by the Germans,
And they've brought us to a place called Hell.
The days are long and the nights are cold,
And our clothes are wearing out,
Mom, please send some socks and boots, also cakes,
The ones I tell everyone about.
They've given us clogs for our feet,
Which are making our feet so sore,
And each day we spend digging,
Life here now, is not pleasant anymore.

It's your loving son that's writing, each day here is much the same,
How long can we endure this, who is it we have to blame?
Please keep sending me those letters, and photos of you too,
You don't know how much they mean to me,
To catch up on all the news from you,
How are you coping with the air raids? Is it causing much distress?
Are the houses in our street still standing or in chaos and in a mess?

It's your loving son that's writing and Christmas is very near,
It will be very strange not sitting around our table,
As we all did last year,
They tell us the Red Cross are bringing roast pork and Christmas pud,
So perhaps this Christmas, is going to be better than it could,
We are all very hopeful that when the New Year has come at last,
We will be sailing home to England,
And we can put all this in the past.

It's your loving son that's writing, and Christmas has come and gone,
Now it's back to hard work and labour,
We're wishing that this can't go on,
They found I could play the piano, they said it was sheer delight,
It certainly cheered us all up, on those lonely Christmas nights,
Thank you for the chocolates, it was heaven eating it once again,
It made such a change to our usual food,
It all tastes much the same.

It's your loving son that's writing, I can't believe what I have to say,
At last the war is over, and very soon I will be on my way.
Home to a new beginning, home to share tears of joy,
And I can't wait to see your face, I'm no longer your little boy,
I have so much to tell you, and I won't know where to start,
But when your loving son returns, we will never be apart.

Sally Busby (Shipham)

A Seaside City

In the Rose Garden Andrea saw roses of red and yellow,
As a blond haired man passed by he looked at her and said hello,
In the model village she saw little folk and buildings small,
She ambled round for two hours until she had seen it all,
On the lake were nice swan-shaped pedaloes of white, pink and blue,
She'd not seen these before so it was nice to see something new,
Andrea enjoyed strolling along the Rock Garden pathways,
Amid the flowers, plants and shrubs, on the grass she had a laze,
She saw the blond haired man just leaving and he gave her a wave,
At the funfair Andrea thought the roller coaster she would brave,
From the Round Tower Andrea looked at the ferries plying,
She had a glance in her bag at souvenirs she'd been buying,
Going down the steps she looked down at a familiar blonde head,
He saw her and smiled, 'We mustn't keep meeting up like this,' he said,
She was a bit suspicious and hoped her he wasn't stalking,
Trying not to worry about him she continued walking,
At the Camber she saw fishing boats and cabin cruisers moored,
In this interesting seaside city you could never get bored,
Andrea bought a drink and sat down outside the Still and West,
The view of the Spinnaker Tower from here must be the best,
At Gunwharf Quays she liked the waterfront, arcades, shops and square,
And once again Andrea bumped into the blond haired man there,
'You're not stalking me, are you?' she asked looking him straight in the eye,
He laughed and said, 'No way, I'm just an ordinary friendly guy,'
Andrea said, 'But you are always in the same place as me,'
The man shrugged his shoulders and waved his arms, 'It's just meant to be,
Come on, I'll take you on the historic ships in the dockyard,'
They walked together and admired the Warrior ship on The Hard,
Andrea and Lee were glad they chose Southsea for their holiday,
They chatted non-stop about Portsmouth as they went on their way.

Gill Coombes (Southsea)

Hay-Making

Each day, with the sky's dome intensely blue,
Hung with massive, white bouldering clouds
And haze shimmering far as the eye could see -
There were friend Ron, my brother Lew and me.

At a hayfield's edge we would settle down
For a snack before we played.
Our mums doled out thick slabs of fruit-heavy cake
And bottles of bright yellow lemonade -
An elixir made from 'Eiffel Tower' crystals
Bought in my great-great aunt's shopping arcade.
Sweating haymakers forking and turning the hay
Gulped cider from jars hid in hedge's shade.

Then with twists of warm, scented hay we traced
Forts, houses, castles and fairy palaces,
Playing out childhood fantasies
Or piled beige-ripe grass into huge bouncy mounds
To climb and to roly-poly down,
Gaining prickly skin and flushed glistening faces -
Not for us the freedom of tee-shirts and shorts -
Fine hay strands lodged in all kinds of places.

At last slow and silent in long-shadowed light
We trudged home through a tree-tunnelled lane,
Our dad was waiting to welcome his three -
My mum, my brother Lew and me,
With his special smile and home-produced feast,
A meal fit for a king and queen at least -
Potato chips, orange-yolked eggs and peas.

In this mish-mash world of modern machines
And conniving computers,
I doubt if today's children ever play
At rolling and rollicking in the hay
As we did almost eighty years ago,
I do not think so . . . but memories stay . . .

There were friend Ron, my brother Lew and me,
Now I am the only one left of the three,
But memories stay . . .

When I see cobalt skies hung with clouds washday white,
Smell new-mown lawns' sweetness in gold evening light,
I recall childhood's carefree, artless play,
In warm, scented hay.

Doris Pidgeon (Exeter)

Rainbow In A Bottle

I could sing a rainbow
Yellow, pink and blue
Anywhere that you go
I would go there too
Don't look behind you
'Cos I won't be there
When you left forever
Pain I couldn't bear.

I still sing that rainbow
Pink and grey and red
To think that I believed in
Everything you said
Life was ever rosy
When you and I were one
We were there together
In every way a song.

Red and black and tartan
Surely that's not right
But who cares whatever
I am getting tight
I don't need nobody
When I'm all alone
'Cos even when I'm lost
I'll find my own way home.

I can count a rainbow
One and two and green
I was meant for you
But were you meant for me?
What happened to my rainbow?
Song I'll never sing
You led me to believe
I would wear your ring.

Stripy brown and gold dots
When I'm really old
I will paint my rainbow
And find that pot of gold
But who cares, whatever
Time I went to bed
Dance inside a rainbow
Dream inside my head.

Elizabeth Boultwood (Rickmansworth)

It's A Spud's Life

I'm glad I'm not a potato,
growing deep down in the ground,
with eyes through which I cannot see
and only worth 10p a pound

For when I stop to think it out
they don't have much of a life,
it starts with being buried alive,
is spud claustrophobia rife?

Do we know and do we care,
as it struggles for life in the earth,
it pushes upwards for light and air
while below giving multiple birth.

Lots and lots of baby spuds
connected to umbilical roots,
while near the surface the fight goes on
and through the ground . . . green shoots.

'Oh *joy!*' it says, 'fresh air at last'
but what's this, a man wearing wellies
comes and puts earth on them poor little shoots
'cause they forecast a frost on the telly.

Undaunted tho' it reaches and grows,
enjoying the sunshine and rain,
the family of babies are all grown up
but there's danger lurking again.

It's *him* . . . the one with the wellies and fork
but now with a bucket as well,
he ruthlessly tears that family apart
and from here on in . . . it's pure Hell!

Thrown in a sack with strangers
our humble spuds are bemused,
for they know not of the fate to come,
of being taken home . . . and *used!*

There are many ways to murder a spud . . .
I'm sorry if that's a bit strong
but it usually starts with skinning alive,
now tell me . . . is that right or wrong?

For not content with that barbaric act
we proceed to boil it alive,
then smash it into a senseless pulp
from which it cannot survive.

Throwing it in red-hot dripping
then locking it in the oven,
is what we proudly call roasting . . .
who needs a witch's coven?

For those lucky spuds who keep their skins
and think they've effected escape,

think again . . . they're stabbed repeatedly . . .
and wrapped in foil to bake . . .

The fate that really gets me though . . .
being skinned and cut into strips
then lowered into boiling oil
they've certain *had their chips!*

So you think you've got your problems
well . . . they all disappear in a trice,
when you think of the humble potato
change your ways . . .

Help China,
Eat rice!

Hilary Hawkins (Exmouth)

I Am Precious In God's Sight

I'm unique and I'm precious
Something God, just once made,
There's no one else like me,
Nor will I ever fade.

I'm created and fashioned
And formed with great care,
And filled up with God,
Within me, He's there.

There'll never be someone
Like me, not again,
God made me quite special,
A real incarnation. Amen.

Oh God within me
He's there since the time,
That I first came to be
So if I'm so precious
And formed with such care,
It means that God's love,
Must be something quite rare.

And it's right there within me
In the depths of my being,
I've no need to keep looking,
And search without seeing.

So if that great love
Just fills up my heart,
I must love myself,
Or else I depart,
From that true love within me,
That indwelling, God's Heart.

Roseanne Harten (Plymouth)

And The World Keeps Turning . . .

Failed hunch, credit crunch.
Income drops, empty shops.
Prices rise, unheard cries,
Bank loans, worried groans.
Petrol dear, so is pub beer,
Council tax costs a whack.
Working hard, debit card,
And the world keeps turning . . .

Get one free, credit spree,
Cheap meat joints, nectar points.
Public wooed, surplus food,
Greed wins, full up bins.
Excess fat, we'll fix that.
Gastric op, pounds to drop.
Stomach clamp, weight loss champ.
And the world keeps turning . . .

Lack of sun, no fun,
Endless rain, yet again.
Maybe floods, loads of mud,
Insurance high, though it's dry.
Go abroad, fuel tax soared,
Plane delays, lost days.
Forest fires, funeral pyres.
And the world keeps turning . . .

Smoking ban, clean air fan,
Alcopops, laptops.
Mobile phones, Wi-Fi zones,
Emails, online sales.
Ebay, easy pay,
Facebook, take a look.
Chatrooms, business zooms.
And the world keeps turning . . .

Speed trap, take the rap.
Metal signs, massive fines.
Road humps, sore rumps.
Ceaseless noise, angry boys,
Too much beer, silent fear,
Locked doors, crime soars.
Abandoned wives, kids with knives.
And the world keeps turning . . .

Valerie Pritchard (Exeter)

Kilburn - Now And Then

I have lived here in South Kilburn,
    since before the last world war.
no stately homes or castles,
    our neighbourhood was poor.
We were poor but we were honest,
    no muggers roamed our streets.
At night we all slept soundly
    when we slipped between the sheets.

St John's church, where I was christened
    and the house where we lived with Mum and Dad
Were flattened by German bombers,
    we lost our home and all we had.
Yes the wind of change is blowing,
    things are not as they used to be.
As I walk the playgrounds of my youth,
    many changes do I see.

No coster barrows line the High Road,
    still the State stands proud and tall.
But it's a cinema no longer,
    now it's a Mecca bingo hall.
They pulled down the Kilburn Empire,
    a hotel now stands there.
B B Evans and Richards stores have gone,
    there are mobile phone shops everywhere.

Outside banks there are dispensers,
    for all to draw out ready cash.
But whether rich or poor you can no longer
    buy Manze's pie and mash.
Today we feast on kebabs or takeaways,
    mostly Indian or Chinese.
Fried chicken comes in a bucket,
    or any way we please.

However, material things are not important,
    people matter most to me.
I have a multi-racial mix of friends,
    and we live in harmony.
Our children play peaceably together,
    with skipping rope or bat and ball.
And the goodwill that they share today
    can secure the future for us all.

Bill Dovey (London)

The Coffee Shop

One early, enchanted customer, aptly described it
As 'the sanctuary of health', 'the academy of civility'.
Where raconteurs and intellectuals care to meet
in 'the nursery of temperance', the 'delight of frugality'.
Learned men of substance, and men of wit
frequenters of 'the free school of ingenuity'.
Dryden, Swift, Johnson, and others fit
to discuss politics, religion and philosophy.

A kind of 'talking shop' in diverse streets
of London; before the coming of the mail.
Communications percolating as men meet.
Barbed criticism; ingenious plans that fail.
Modest folk who find their weary feet
consoled by the everlasting tale.
The 17th century 'soaps' that greet
the fortune changes of the errant male.

Potent social and political hubs of the town
suppressed by Charles as 'seminaries of sedition'.
Here, the seeds of revolution were stealthily sown
with names added to the parchment of petition.
Cromwell and Fairfax were becoming known.
The strong flavour of their pious tradition
contrasted with the frivolity of the crown,
based on a devout, puritanical religion.

No female would enter the male preserve;
the chicory essence of the smoking den.
The cream of Society there, to observe
the portly, indulgent, businessmen.
And stimulated lives of vibrant verve,
seated with their pipes and feathered pen.
Mine host, with keen intent to serve
their eager appetites to satisfy again.

The second revolution has taken a while.
American companies now setting the trend.
Costa's and Starbuck's relaxing style,
favoured by TV's 'Frasier' and 'Friends'.
The decaff latte that generates a smile.
Hefty premium rates that often offend,
the tired office works' pecuniary guile;
City types with large salaries to spend.
That stalwart prop of our soul, and psyche,
three hundred years on our national scene.
The good old cuppa we cherish, and like,
has been duly challenged by the coffee bean.
The trendy bars, the fashion, the hype,
the semi-skimmed milk, the espresso steam.
Gap, Tommy Hilfiger, and Nike,
Levi Jeans, cut so tight and lean.

Like a geyser with its steamy froth
The Coffee Shop spumes a bubbling air,
gushing its patrons' joys and wrath,
on sugary smiles and black despair.
And modish topics to behold
throughout the ages. It can trace
fervent discourse about Our Lord
on Cromwell's austere, puritan taste,
on Dickens' stories, as they were told,
and cinema legends put in their place.
Talk and coffee; like honey and bees
rest together with consummate ease.

David Shonfield (London)

The Somme

It's nineteen sixteen and I am on the Somme
But it's not in this hell I belong.
As I lie in this trench cuddling my rifle,
And this pungent smell I try to stifle
I look from the trench across the wire,
I duck my head from machine gun fire,
As I peer through cordite mist,
Bodies akimbo writhe and twist,
A wounded soldier cries in pain,
'Help me, help me,' time and again,
For though I am part of the allied thrust
In this smelly trench lie I must,
For Tommy lies in no-man's-land,
Even Red Cross can't lend a hand,
I plug my ears from his crying,
For it's out there I'll soon be lying,
Stone dead, and not just dying.

The officer tries to boost morale
By telling us the same old tale
'That we'll really put the Germans to rout,
Have no fear, have no doubt
Just weave your way through the quagmire,
Dodge and duck the sporadic fire.'
But pretty soon I ought to know
That a shrieking whistle soon will blow
And up and over the top I'll go.
That dreaded whistle, a terrible tone
Really scares me to the bone.
I'll feign shellshock, I'll feign all sorrow
And maybe this time tomorrow
From this battle I'll be gone
Then I can leave this terrible Somme.

John David Harrison (London)

Götterdämmerung

I'll tell you how I saw it first,
Valhalla in the sky.
The air a brittle sheet of ice
Cracked by each passer-by.
And veiled by film of frozen fog
Hung down with chains of snow,
And spangled with electric lights
And shops oil-lamps aglow.

Down dim-lit tunnels through the town
Dawn-rising tourists strolled
Close-muffled with furred coat and cape
Against th' invading cold.
Within each mind, a solemn thought
That through these streets once trod
Goose-stepping feet of men and maids
Whose leader they thought God.

The shadows deepened down the years
Of hate-filled war and strife
When vicious, red-hot, jagged steel
Made widow who'd been wife.
And whole towns blazed and mocked their song,
'Please keep the home fires burning!'
And through the raging flames and smoke
Death's grisly mask peered, leering.

But, suddenly, the scene was changed,
The veil of fog was torn,
The snow-chains ceased to flicker down,
Another day was born.
And, as the sun, majestic shone
Upon the mountains high
We saw, proud standing in its rays
A palace in the sky.

Bright shining symbol of our age,
Of conquering man's estate!
The gleaming, tinsel outer walls,
Those bastions of our fate!
And then a spear of lightning flew,
Too swift for any eye,
The palace crumbled, love replaced
Valhalla in the sky.

Hugh Miners (Penzance)

October Thoughts

Chill little breezes too soon herald change
And then all chosen plans far from range!
So hasten to enjoy the lovely autumn scene,
Ere winter descends upon the land so lean.
And a weakened sunlight is all we share,
For weeks on end, the countryside laid bare,
The frosted lawns meet the naked trees
And wicked east winds replace the breeze.

That Indian summer will soon disappear,
The landscape adopting an air without cheer
And the dull old winter days clamp down,
Mother Nature all dressed in her wintry gown,
Then those woodland walks with sodden leaves,
Along muddy tracks, small rivulets damply weave,
To become impassable, unavailing in the end
And staying warmly indoors becomes the trend!

Days before, it seemed, that crisply warm sun
Would last until November's end had run,
To mingle with the tang of bonfire smoke,
Then sharpest frosts quickly came - to provoke,
The prelude to winter, approaching too fast,
Heralding too soon that summer had passed,
And grey cheerless days upon us once again
With icy roads made hazardous by the rain.

And yet those sunny, tingling October days,
Remain to remind one of enjoyment always,
When the hurried fun of our garden chores
Kept us so busy for hours out of doors
And the sun's warmth seemed always there
As we turned the soil, fresh ground to prepare
For the coming of spring, new promise portends
Her welcome return when sad winter ends.

As 'Madam Moon' her mystic magic weaves,
The brightness of the heavens touches the leaves
And wending downwards on to soggy ground,
They gather in heaps to await the garden round
And October swiftly fades - to November turns,
Yet for her beauty and purpose no heart yearns,
She is the prelude to winter's cold, shivery days,
But for that 'little summer', sing her praise!

Julia Yeardye (Chesham)

George

Mrs Maud Withers had about twenty cats and kittens,
A huge dog, and sometimes rabbits and chickens.
She lived down the road for as long as I can remember,
Until I left home at eighteen.

Her muddled, simple home was a haven for me.
I was always welcome,
Never patronised,
And probably over-confided in.
She befriended me freely,
Despite Mum's sometime jealousy.
Her treasure-trove house,
And untamed garden
Were abundant with wildlife and unconditional love.

Her husband Wally was ancient,
And sick with emphysema.
Like a scary magician,
He showed me other worlds
Through the lens of his microscope.
In the gloom of his dark room
Was a watery dish,
Where monochrome images of me and my sister,
Emerged like ghosts
From sheets of blank paper.

My favourite cat was Babs,
A beautiful, cream-tabby long-hair.
Gentle, large-eyed and trusting,
She let me hold her tiny kittens
Even before their eyes opened.
I was about four years old.

We chose a kitten to come and live in our house.
Someone named him George.
He was handsome and beautiful like his mother,
But bigger framed and huge pawed.
He probably loved us all equally,
But I liked to think he was my special cat.
I told him all my secrets.

I was very jealous of George on winter mornings,
When ice lined the inside of our bedroom windows,
And I had to get up for school.
I never wanted to go to school,
And wished I was a cat too.

Most school day afternoons,
George would be waiting and watching for me
From the front room window.
He must have mewed to my mum to let him out,
Because he would race down the road to meet me,
His tail raised proudly like a banner.
I felt like a princess then.

My dad and I cried when George killed my hamster,
But he never blamed George,
Just our carelessness.

When George became very frail,
And could not walk much anymore,
Dad said we would have to ask the vet
To come and 'put him to sleep'.
Dad and I cried then too.

When Dad died, George might have found him,
Running to meet him as he always did.

Caroline Anne Hodgson (Looe)

Can I Write A Poem? Well I've Tried!

Can you write a poem? Someone asked me once,
Well I said I'd try, I didn't want to sound a dunce,
So I sat down quietly and I pondered for a while,
Whatever shall I write, perhaps one to make her smile?
Well I thought about the times I'd enjoyed many hours,
Showing off my garden, where I'd grown many flowers,
And I thought about the times I'd enjoyed my family,
Playing in the garden, then coming in for tea.
There have been lots of happy times, I'll disregard the rest,
'Cause I really do believe happy poems are the best.

Now as I sit there thinking of my memories for sure,
I think my poem's going to be a hundred lines or more,
It's a lovely occupation just sitting quietly, making,
All my memories rhyme, how lucky I have been.
I've had two little boys who've grown to be the best,
Now they have families of their own,
I think perhaps I'll just, ask them to come home
To me and spend a little time,
Then I can make another memory, another rhyme.

We'll I've showed my little poem to my friend who asked me can
I write a poem, well I think I can.
She was quite excited, said, would I like to try
And send my poem to the society - oh my!
They are looking for new poems, my friend informed me then,
So I'm sticking down my envelope, I'll have a go and when,
Or if they write and tell me that my poem fits the bill,
I shall be very happy, I really, really will.
I'm hoping the society will say I have the flair,
And print my poem in their book, I really care.
I have three books already with my poems wrapped inside
I hope I'm lucky this time, they fill me with such pride,
But then again if not, well at least I've tried!

Eileen Southey (West Molesey)

To A Curry (With Apologies To Robert Burns)

Greetings, grand oriental platter!
Let minor gourmets vainly chatter
Of fish, or eggs, or tripe in batter:
You far excel 'em!
Let others wilt, while we get fatter.
We can't compel 'em.

The dish is filled to overflowing,
Its sauce with ardent spices glowing.
White-flaky rice is fairly snowing,
A sumptuous feast!
That fragrant bouquet must be blowing
A mile at least!

So seize your forks, tuck in, friends all.
For holding back won't do at all,
Nor let one single morsel fall,
Till all be finished.
With poppadums this lamb mughal
Is soon diminished.

Who can do other than despise
Cold jellied eels, mild cottage pies,
Slippery noodles, limp French fries,
Or bird's nest soup?
Faced with spaghetti Bolognaise,
Our spirits droop.

Our secretary's curry-fed.
The office floor holds her in dread.
Word of her anger runs ahead.
Her breath's a furnace.
The vindaloo goes to her head.
She's fit to burn us!

Ye chefs of cordon bleu on high
Who send us down our food supply,
Serve us no fast junk, nor purvey
Gruel, slop or skilly.
If you would hear our sated sigh
Send us a curry!

John Miller (Reading)

Sky Monkeys

One November night
A gypsy knocked at my door,
She wanted to sell some lace
And started to read my face,
She said my future looked good
And marry she thought I would,
Believe her if only I could.
Then a tall and dark ranger,
That was no stranger,
Let his desires to run loose,
Recalling to me Dr Seus,
Now rockets shoot to the sky,
Why don't we try
To live our lives together?
A Golden Monkey Plays An Umbrella.

This boy's father however
Forgot to tell him
The whole bedtime story
Before Dr Seuss departed
He always finished what he started.
So now I hold a Happy Lantern,
Waiting
For the Shirushi Banten,
I know beneath it lies a comic shell,
Ignited by a cosmic belle,
Tiger tails and twinkling leaves,
Hummerstars and silver bees,
Like all of these you disappear,
Leaving me
A falling tear.

So of these fortune tellers
What am I to make?
That amongst the real ones
Beware there lurks a fake?
Meanwhile I'll go on believing
That my fortune told was true,
And that some day soon
Fireworks will be lighting
Because I'll be loving
You.

Stella-Rose Benson (Penzance)

Reactivation

We may get so much for nothing,
But that isn't everything,
In my strange world
I get peace.
I get freedom from physical distraction,
My inner self released.

Free to feel and free to fly,
Without my worries whizzing by,
Without anxiety stepping in,
To think about the state I'm in.
And wonder does not reason why,
But wanders with an easy eye,
Eases into each new frame,
As if the last had been the same.
Free as the fields are to my form,
Where I can saunter through sun and storm,
At peace in mind and not in head,
But heading somewhere else instead.

And here is somewhere very high,
Higher than the clouds in sky,
Steeped in sun where no wind can
Whip my waiting
Whilst watching man,
Pour from jug,
Gold onto the ground,
A golden waterfall,
Without the sound
Of falling water
Or the spray
That soaks our clothes
From far away.

Falling in a flowing whole,
Standing, watching, with my soul,
Stunned in silence,
Safe, serene,
Yet so awake.
This is no dream,
That I am dreaming, whilst sleeping still,
I have come here, it is their will.

With sticks are symbols carefully placed,
That they may meet a future gaze,
That knows their value and their truth,
That can decipher ancient news.

The golden yellow in the sun,
Shining warnings of what may come,
Telling of the damage done,
That it could end as it begun.

Writing words of what they know,

Of life on Earth as it did go,
Before the sea swelled up so high,
And built a glacier to the sky.
Frozen fast, standing proud,
Gods glide down it to the clouds.

Writing words we have not heard,
Leaving lessons still unlearnt,
Wanting us to hear it all,
Hoping that we heed its call,
When we emerge out of the depths
Of darkness, fire and death.

Rebecca Hardiman (Taunton)

The Pilgrim And The Owl

On a dark and blackened night
An owl perceived a pilgrim's plight;
Beneath a bush he hid in dread
And lay quite still, like a possum - dead.

High up in a tree the pilgrim heard
The hooting sound of this owl bird;
Then came a sound he couldn't refute
Of men and horses in hot pursuit.

In terror and rooted to the spot
He was forced to hear the horses trot;
As the riders got closer in their search
The owl became agitated on his perch.

The owl swooped down and panicked a horse,
It galloped its rider on a different course.
Distraction soon would save the day
As the riders turned and went away.

The pilgrim emerged from his leafy nook
And followed the direction the owl took.
Despite the fact he felt quite shaken
The owl had undoubtedly saved his bacon.

The wise old owl began flying low,
Showing the pilgrim which way to go.
The journey was arduous and full of danger.
Could the pilgrim be saved by a feathered stranger?

After several miles and feeling weak,
The pilgrim found what he did seek.
The owl had guided him, no longer doomed
For across a clearing an abbey loomed.

Each night the *pilgrim* beneath his cowl
Would say a prayer for his friend *the owl*.

Henrietta Lee (Plymouth)

On St Mary's Day

'Sit down,' you said.
'I want you sitting down
I've something to tell you
you won't want to hear.'

But I knew all the time
what you were going to say.
Worst fears become reality,
words I dreaded to hear.
How can a father
leave his flock just like that?
But it was bound to happen.
It was only a question of time
and the rising of the right opportunity.

There was a deep-down change in you,
a knowing that the relentless surging
of the incoming tide
was flooding the field so fiercely fought
and the unacceptable becoming reality.

Then came a firm assurance
a sense of strength and peace
signs clear for all to see
that a decision had been made.

And - yes- it is right for you to go.
Your work here is finished
and a new life awaits you:
vibrant, pulsing youth, with its
new opportunities and challenges.
In the prime of your life
it is right to have such youthful souls
given into your care.

So, go - we shall not see your like again.
Go - but just remember now and then
the lives you've touched,
the souls you've saved,
the family - the friends - you leave behind.

Just know how much you will be missed.
A link with the past severed
leaving only cherished memories.

Jean Bloomer (Somerton)

Bags To Riches

Again, today, I met her in the park.

I had trouble placing her at first
and tracing the connection
to the furtive figure
sheltering in stations
clutching bulging plastic bags
and scuttling from scrutiny
from pinstripe people passing
and piercing her flimsy defences
forever scurrying in corners
seeking safety
and not finding it.

A woman suspended in alien space
or so it seemed to me.

Remembering her anguished eyes
yet seeing now no trace of terror in her face
has caused my confusion
and as I watched her walking calmly
carrying nothing but herself, erect
I sensed a strength
bestowed not by possession or by status
- her clothes were threadbare as before -
but the strength of a mind
no longer absent
no longer burdened by fear.

Present in the here and now
and travelling light at last
or so it seemed.

And as we passed
I met her eyes
and thought I saw amusement there
and recognition of *my* plight.

Strangely stirred by sudden hope
and to release a little
the anxious grip on my expensive bag
I had a glimpse of being
of belonging again
to life.

Frauke Hansen (London)

Golden Ring And Emperor

On wings of gauze a passing dragonfly,
Kissing summer meadows tinged with green,
Flies in silent ecstasy close by
A gently running brook whose rippling sheen
Caresses golden sunbeams of delight.
Her rings of ochre, finely striped in bands
Of shining light upon her back are bright
With inner fire, as though the unseen hands
Of her Creator lend them extra life.
And now, as, in a moment's pause, she blends
With golden meads, her lucent rings run rife
With buttercups - a dance which never ends.
For she, at one with nature, seeks repose
Upon a flower while the brook still flows

With murmuring refrain through pastures lush
With deepest emerald green. But now she flits
Beside the silver stream whose rapids rush
Towards an open river. There she sits
Upon a flowering bank quite overgrown
With ox-eyed daisies, cowslips, meadowsweet
And dandelions whose clocks, invisibly blown
On zephyrs, float downstream - light and fleet.
And as she watches life upon the river,
Wondering at those fluttering lily fields
Upon the water's surface, such a shiver
Passes through her frame that she soon yields
To love; for now an Emperor dragonfly
Alights upon a giant lily. Sky

And river seem to shine with lambent grace
As Golden Ring and Emperor now meet
Upon that verdant lily. Their embrace
Seems natural as they join wings and greet
Each other, silent friends at first sight.
Golden flame upon green lily pad -
A tiny zebra-crossing burning bright
With love; such fire is blithesome, chaste and glad,
Since it is born of air and ether. Golds
And azures merge in hope as Golden Ring

And Emperor spread love in lily's folds;
For living rainbows intersect to bring
A holiness of hue to summer showers
As colours nod and blend with dancing flowers.

But now, as Emperor's translucent wings
Are bathed in a film of dawn-spun blue
Above a crystal pool of radiant rings,
He rises with a grace and love most true,
Drawing Golden Ring into the air
Upon his whirring tail; and while all life
Upon the riverbank protects its lair,

Fighting, squabbling, caught in ceaseless strife,
Golden Ring and Emperor dance in peace
Around each other in a carousel
Of soft unspoken love. They give new lease
Of life to basking fish caught in their spell,
And to insects, birds and butterflies.
But otters, voles and ferrets, with loud cries

Of victory, still fight like soldiers bred
On hatred - weasel warriors still fed
On lies. Come, Golden Ring, teach them your love;
And, Emperor, grant them mercy from above.

Robert D Hayward (London)

Girl Rapped In A T-Shirt

Hey 97! Now where y' been?
You're the cutest number I've ever seen
Those purple digits on your shirt
Sound off a sugar sweet alert.

Do you dig my blue, number 54?
For you I'd make it less or more
A Coke in the café - help stay snappy
Check each other out, for sure!

Give me a colour, other than green
Which is too far out and most obscene
Don't make it drab, don't make it grey
But rich and trendy, kinda friendly.

Flash me a number under a hundred
A combination - like two of a kind
I'll wear them boldly on my shoulder
No matter if it's hot or colder -

A cool design, a regular pair
The latest thing in fashion wear
No fancy font elaboration
Plain and simple, roughly square.

I'll wear your digits day and night
Tell me that I've got it right
If you give me the brush
- goodbye - goodnight.

If you turn me flat with a double 'O'
I'll take my numbers and I'll blow
Sad to say I will feel low
My ego's taken the big KO.

Hey 28! Now where you been?
You're the cutest number I've ever seen . . .

Kevin Power (Reading)

Poem For Syd Barrett

Fame came early
like an electric guitar screeching at the gates of dawn.
Technicolor days
of free associative living
and free associative loving.
Tripping all the way to the bank.

Soon he came crashing down.
Starriest young man
who fell to Earth.
Erratic heartbeat of a generation
you made the cuckoo clocks sing
in not quite unison.
Pretty girls and dopeheads came by
hoping to score.
Burnt-out boho living like a hobo
they could not reach him now.
Syd's psychedelic breakfast
scrambled.

Thereafter
a life in retreat.
Desultory decades in Mum's house.
Fading from successes
and excesses of the past.
Gardening and gorging
on a fridge full of pork chops.
Or so it is said.

Meanwhile
royalties and rumours roll in
as mental illness is romanticised and anthologised.
Reclusive legend lurking in a living room
minding his own business.

Wandering the streets of Cambridge
is spied upon by paparazzi.
Like a praying mantis
with prying apparatus
they snatch their troubled prey.

Shine on diamond
bigger than The Ritz.

Chris Blackford (Basingstoke)

Somerset Secrets

Norton Fitzwarren, Watchet, Wookey Hole,
the very names mysterious and old,
set in times past, when Norman barons vied,
monks prayed and laboured, kings oft fought and died.

Quaint Mendip cottages, none of which match,
peep dark eyelids from under smoky thatch,
with leaded bedroom windows deeply set
like sleepy eyes beneath the eaves close met.

Cheddar, Nunney, Charlton Mackerell, Mells,
Kingsbury Episcopi, Shepton Mallet, Wells,
Sutton Montis, Midsomer Norton - who is there now?
Long lost relatives I long to meet, but how?

Shaded light and dark of summer's flickering leaves,
and each wild flower and grass its pattern weaves.
The sloping footpaths where no traffic goes;
deep threatening river in the valley flows,
where we were not allowed to skinny-dip,
nor lean down low to steal illicit sip
of water green with flowing fairy weeds
o'er stones so smooth, and lined with rustling reeds.

Top road's smart houses look down from their domes
upon the lower road's white humbler homes,
by fields of hay and buttercups and clover,
broken low walls for toddlers scrambling over.
My little playhouse by the kitchen door -
(a hollow box bush dim, and nothing more).

Other Somerset places there lie, too,
in deepest verdant ferny shades and woods;
the Quantocks, leading quietly to the coast,
or, spreading flat, the grassy dampish fields,
drained by straight dykes, and cropped by man and beast,
below the steep grey height of Glastonbury Tor,
special, magical, bright green Avalon mount,
so tempting to ascend, dream and explore.
With what relief to reach St Martin's Tower,
and share it with fellow travellers from all lands.
Cameras busy, they record their hour
delightful, and connect with Wessex man.

Joan L Carter (Abingdon)

Stumbling Road

What is it
that happens?
Why
am I here?
Why
do I live,
what's
the reason?

The death
is not the end
but why
is it life?
I'm staring
at life
and ask
what it wants from me

life is a stumbling road
it's a stumbling road

Why
all this evil?
Why
all this ignorance?
Cruelty,
where does it come from?
It doesn't come
from the heart

I'm sorry
to say it
but violence
is our own creation
It's too easy
pointing fingers
but it's a dead end
to play the blame game
we have to
reach the roots

Life is a stumbling road
It's a stumbling road

Our children
how to protect them
against brainwash
and abuse
How to
protect all of us
against the shadows
of fear

We can pretend

life is cream
dream away, fly away
run away
but whether we like it
or not
sooner or later
reality turns up
Better face it
and deal with it

Life is a stumbling road
it's a stumbling road

Genio (London)

Snow

Myriads of snowflakes, each feather - light and frail
Filter from the wintry sky
Like petals loosened by a gale.

White upon white in airy space
Fall silently with softest touch
To settle in a stilly place.

They mask the furrows, fill the ditch,
Hide the grime on road and roof
With kiss on kiss of crystal which

Bear patterns perfect as a flower
Microscopic miracles
As evanescent as the hour.

The past has passed yet feeds the present mind
With compost composed of days now hard to find.
Now is the time that must be foremost
The moment to be thankful and to toast
The coming of another precious dawn
With friends already gone and those unborn.
Now is the season meant to celebrate
Even if pain and sorrow lie in wait
To pounce upon the trembling brain
And thus divert attention yet again.
Now is the time to notice unimportant things
To share the liveliness that evanescence brings
Perceive the beauty of the muddy pond,
The essence of a unity beyond
These wayward faculties to comprehend
To calm the bodies ail and caringly attend.
To listen, watch and love without a judging thought.
For light and love illumine
When secret and unsought.

Daphne Bruce (Lymington)

Staying At Home

I love living in Teignmouth,
Fish and chips and Devon tea.
Lovely pubs, who serve real ale,
Down here by the sea.

Fishing boats,
Lovely shops,
A pier and lots to do,
A ferry over to Shaldon,
And Shaldon has a zoo.

Once I went on holiday,
I had it in the sun,
I put on lots of lotion,
'Cause that's what should be done.

I took lots of walks,
And lots of rest,
Till I was red and sore,
Upset tum, not much fun,
I won't go there, anymore.

Then I had a holiday,
I had it in the snow,
I fell on the ice,
Broke my leg twice,
Will I go again, oh no.

So I went to Scotland,
I went up on the train,
It rained and rained,
And rained and rained,
I won't go there again.

I went on a mini cruise,
I went on my own,
The sea was rough,
I've had enough,
I think I'll stay at home.

I love being in Teignmouth,
Fish and chips and Devon tea,
Lovely pubs, who serve real ale,
Down here by the sea.

Lynda Peat (Teignmouth)

The Frustrating Game Of Golf

You're all prepared and ready to go, with your balls,
clubs and bag
The aim is to sink the ball, in a hole marked with a flag
You think this game is easy, it really can't be hard
Just get the ball in eighteen holes, and mark it on a card

You align yourself and take your aim, on the spot
you want to land
You address the ball and take your shot, and end up in the sand
You must avoid the hazards, to score well under par
You slice one right and out of bounds, and hit the
captain's car

You come upon a short par five, a birdie chance no doubt
You're going to give it everything, so you get the driver out
You swing it smooth, you swing it strong and catch the ball
just right
You've never hit one like it; it's gone right out of sight

The wind's against, you've come up short, although
you are on line
The problem's now what iron to take, a seven, eight or nine
You duff a chip, you fluff a putt, you scuttle across the green
You must observe the etiquette and resist the urge to scream

You're playing bad, you're swinging poor, you've been
in all the trouble
You've hooked one left, you've hit a tree and ended
in the middle
When playing golf you need some luck, for that you just
say thanks
You never know when you might get the virus called the shanks

Golf can sure frustrate you and get you feeling mad
It gets your temper raging from the problems that you've had
But often when it's over most players tutt then shrug
The score just doesn't matter once you've got the bug

A monster drive a raking putt, a chip in from off the green
A pitch goes close or a bunker shot, the likes
you've never seen
All it takes is one good shot, to make you play again
If you don't play the game of golf, it's difficult to explain

Neil Warren (Gloucester)

I Look In The Mirror

I look in the mirror and I see my children
Their faces radiant as mine is wizen

I close my eyes and have a vision
Of the squealing moment of their partition
From their mother's womb in her hour of rendition

The proud parents we both were
The exhausted mother, nine months to bear
First the daughter and what a fanfare
Then our son, with short time to spare
Eager for his sister who thought it unfair

They grew up like twins, with a difference of a year
And drove us mad to the point of despair
But we loved them to bits and would watch them and stare
Wondering the mysteries of nature with prayer

We worried and fretted, we cuddled and nurtured
We listened to their breathing and touched their forehead
We looked at their bodies, their completeness reassured
And saw them smile then laugh and our gratitude endured

Sleepless nights and anxious days
For illness and nursing, and night vigil gaze
We saw them grow, clothes getting tighter,
Buy some more, a little more brighter
Small pram, not big enough,
The two have to fit in the same trough.

With *mothers' care* we manage
In cots, pram and car carriage
Such is the beauty of childhood
A mix of creation and parenthood

God's love and blessing superbly manifest
In response to parents' prayerful request
A desire to love, indeed as we were loved
A gift to the world, and no reward do we desire
Except to see in them our mini empire
Filling us with joy and the world to inspire

I look again in the mirror
And now what do I see
Our children grown up, and with us they agree
That their children are giving them great joy and agony

I look in the mirror
And wish I could find
Our traditions, and beliefs in them confined
Alas, times have changed
And so in their maturity, their natures comply
With trends current and what they think and imply
Some echoing ours, but the sound is so faint
Others so different, no way can we acquaint

Speak out we cannot
For to God alone is our complaint

Now look again in the mirror
And perhaps you should enjoy
Their wisdom, success, and so clever their ploy
We love them, their families, and their children ahoy
Coming on visits, and meals and laughter and love
We pray for their safety, their prosper and peace-giving dove

I shall still look in the mirror

Have they taken our tradition?

Nabil M Mustapha (Esher)

Politicians

From guns to boots,
equipment fails
the rigours of the fight:
the fault lies with politicians:
how do they sleep at night?

They award themselves
rises in pensions:
pay and allowances too:
pass stupid laws
and commit us to wars,
but don't ask the public their view.

Why should we rattle the sabre?
Die for a questionable cause?
The fault lies with politicians,
and yet the problem is ours.

Tanks in the heat of the desert:
choking disabling sand;
army boots melt and the feet hurt,
fighting in some other land.

What if the Arabs or Russians
decided the Brits were oppressed;
and bombed Number Ten,
again and again,
because they were right
and knew best.

It's depressing, I'm sad,
disillusioned.
A bunch of political charmers.
Deciding the fate,
of Britain once great . . .
Remember the late Nostradamus?

Simon Marshall (Eastleigh)

Lies On Your Lips

For six giddy weeks you lay on the bed
In the living room cleared for your death,
Attended by nurses and carers in shifts
And sitters to watch as you slept.

And I was there too, the son born of you,
Hoping for a sign of your love
As we chatted away those final summer days
Using words that were never enough.

Time and again I pledged you my love
With never a word or a sign in return,
And now I know why you chose this way to die,
For it was your way of betraying your son.

Deceit was your ploy for you to enjoy
As it left all of your children misled;
Leaving them perplexed, angry and vexed
When you knew you'd be away with the dead.

A cowardly mother who for decades cowered
In the shadow of a bully and boor,
He made you a doormat who would never react
When self-interest was always to the fore.

You never stood up for those in your care
Nor emoted as a woman or mother,
But buried yourself in a joyless world
Where problems were always smothered.

You martyred yourself on misery and wealth
While both twisted and warped your core,
And decades of this made you unable to kiss,
Made you unable to be human and warm.

O' mother of mine, for you no shrine,
Nor grave with stone and name,
For memories of you are joyless few
And there lies your eternal shame.

You left your family as no mother should,
Split asunder and plundered by rifts;
And your only epitaph is this poem
Because you died with lies on your lips.

Peter Waverly (Penzance)

The Wealth And Might Of Nations

The plight of many countries when financial aid declines
The poverty of people when foodstuff's hard to find
When parents watch their children die for want of simple things
To read that look of helplessness on faces gaunt and thin.

When constitutions crumble and law and order wanes
And people rise up in revolt to keep offspring from their graves
It matters not which party leads if change is brought about
But men will rise from poverty of that there is no doubt.

Those men who come to lead them are from within their ranks
They have no thoughts of power or to lead with planes and tanks
But what they want as with the rest are simple things some free
To support themselves and others, their own autonomy.

The wealth and might of nations who oft stand idly by
Is wasted prior to such events if time is on their side
But now when times are changing and sides are being formed
Is the wealth and might of nations not something to be scorned.

Is giving aid to others a charitable thing
Or is it done these days d'you think to strengthen ailing wings
Doubt that people matter when strategic aims come first
But plugging that defensive gap for all it's bloody worth.

To subjugate a person is a truly awesome thing
If the only thing that matters is propping up that wing
And what if people aren't prepared to be subjected in this way
Do they vanish overnight for the things they open say.

There's many such a country now affected in this way
Of many different cultures in unstable disarray
This outside aid will threaten not some but one and all
One can but hope it doesn't but is then hope a fool.

True wealth is people's knowledge the might is their resolve
To change their situation for the good of young and old
The political direction is not of their concern
If it brings about the changes for which they truly yearn.

When planning out their future let no one dare forget
That missiles can deliver an even greater threat
To all mankind and creatures that dwell upon this globe
Will the wealth and might of nations not assist them to grow old

C H Woodward (Hindhead)

Nightfall On Exmoor (Somerset)

The trees are rustling
Tonight.
A breeze
Flew in
With the
Tepid twilight.
Pale stars
Pay homage
To the
Full-blown moon
Fast rising
In the cloudless
Blue velvet
Sky.
Hooting owls
End the
Shimmering silence
With raucous cries
Foretelling a
Weather change.
A late bird
Is scratching in
The darkening depths
Of the silhouetted
Hedgerow.
Now the field gate
Emits a thin metallic
Restless squeak
Oddly sounding
In this rustic setting.
The farm windows
Light silently.
A sheep dog vents
A sleepy yelp
Then settles again
To his lazy sprawl.
A car is mounting
The distant hill;

Golden beams
Splay high
Into the night
Soon to swirl
And dip away
From sight.
Moonlight
Faintly outlines
The brassy hands
Of the tower clock
Soon to strike
The midnight

Hour.
The breeze fades
Deep silence
Invades
The slumbery scene.
In the quiet field
The sheep
Have long since
Quit grazing
And all
Is now still.

Joan Lewington (Weston-super-Mare)

The Hanging Tree

There stands a tree in Old Brook Lane, that has a tale to tell.
It's haunting moans of olden times resound through woody dell.

A lover was rejected,
and found upon its bough.
If you listen carefully
leaves will whisper the deed so foul.

The tale starts with two young men,
who love the same girl, Rose.
A duel was fought on a summer's morn,
one died from a fatal blow.

Amid the flapping of the birds, young Rose she did appear.
One lover was lain upon the ground, the other he stood near.

Poor Rose, she saw one lover dead,
and suddenly realised,
that he was the one she truly loved.
The other she now despised.

She spurned the winner of the duel,
but he couldn't understand,
for Rose had said before the duel,
'The winner shall have my hand.'

Now anger overtook him, and he drew his gun again;
he pulled the trigger slowly, Rose fell, she felt no pain.

The man, his dreams in tatters
flees high into the tree.
He ties his belt onto the bough
and hangs for all to see.

The tree now stands so sad and tall;
its tale has now been heard.
It serves as a constant memory
to all the foolish who have erred.

Susan Smith (Isleworth)

The Deserted House

I'm old, I'm cold and I'm lonely
Sitting in this brown field site,
With developers eyeing me up and down
I'm so sad, and half-crazy with fright.

Don't let them rip out my heart and soul,
Or plunge deep girders into my chest,
Don't let them turn me into an apartment block,
I was built for gentry; it's what I do best.

My oak panelled rooms were exquisite,
Hung with tapestries rich from abroad,
And though one of my masters liked a tipple too much,
He was a charitable man, and a lord.

There was such fun at our Christmas parties,
With blind man's buff and musical chairs,
A tall shimmering tree in the hallway,
And cook being kissed below stairs.

My great chimneys have held children's laughter,
And my broad timbers have challenged the foe,
And when the sun filled my windows with apricot light,
My rooms were awash with its glow.

But then sunlight gave way to shadows
That threatened the laughter I'd known,
And the joy that had flung itself up to my roof
Fell to the ground like a stone.

Fever forced its steel grip on my family,
It showed no pity for those I held dear,
And three generations went to their grave,
No neighbouring soul would come near.

My oak panelled rooms have been plundered,
The once rich tapestries, now thicket and gorse,
While ivy has planted its impatient feet,
And wild nature has taken is course.

But today, for the first time, I'm hopeful,
Green chaffinches are building a nest,
There'll be babies, and birdsong, and new life.
I hope they're gentry; it's what I do best!

Gloria Thorne (Paignton)

Don't Look Down On Me

Why do you talk down to me?
I do understand!
I know more than you sometimes,
Don't wanna hold your hand!

I know what you're all saying,
I just cannot join in,
I cry from sheer frustration,
And then everyone starts laughing!

Don't throw me in the air like that!
I'm scared but you think it's fun.
Everything is done for me,
You think I crawl but I'm trying to run!

I get my payback every morning,
I like to create a smelly mess,
I throw my nappy innards in boredom,
So I can laugh when you get stressed.

Why can't I speak out loud just yet?
I still don't have a voice,
But I have thoughts and dreams you know,
I'm restricted and have no choice.

I consciously choose to remember,
So when I'm older I can let you know,
When I can finally speak I'll prove to you,
That I had thoughts that long ago!

I don't need protecting I'm fine,
I don't need your pity,
I don't need your patronising,
I don't need to be told I'm pretty.

Yes you did just hear the ghosts in my room,
They bicker and sit in my cot,
They like that I'm open and unafraid,
And I'm sorry that you are not.

Don't underestimate the silent young,
We know more than one might think,
So don't pull that stupid face at me,
And stop dressing me in pink!

Claire King (Farnham)

Glimpses Of Rooms

(For Mum, August 3rd 2007)

Glimpses of rooms
Through half open doors
You pass like a stranger
By what used to be yours

Trapped in a body
That once was your friend
You sit in a chair
For days without end

In a world that has shrunk
With the walls closing in
You remember your youth
And what might have been

All the things that you could
And wanted to do
The hopes and the dreams
That were stolen from you

And you are so patient
So calm and resigned
While I rage with frustration
At a fate so unkind

You have lost all your freedom
And must just sit and wait
For a stranger to help you
And bring you your plate

You don't have the privacy
All of us need
You ask for so little
In a world full of greed

You are grateful to those
Who love and who care
But I'm sure there are times
When you wish they weren't there

That you didn't need to have them around
And you had a body
Both healthy and sound

To stroll in the sun
And walk in the rain
Those memories haunt you again and again

I would give up my life
In a moment if I
Could by so doing
Allow you to fly

And I cry for your hands
The music they made

All the wonderful tunes
In the past that they played

And I know that one day
I will sit in that chair
Remembering days
When you used to sit there

When my world will shrink
I fear all too soon
Till all I'll have left
Will be glimpses of rooms

Wendy Minogue (London)

Reflections

(In the evening of my life)

The world . . .
is in turmoil through famine and drought.
Cyclones and earthquakes abide.
Volcanic eruptions. The terror of war,
and the fearful tsunami tide.

The scourge of greed now dominates man,
for oil and the grabbing of land.
Children murders child, some disappear
yob culture is now out of hand.

Our caring society crumbles apace,
Leaders become self indulgent.
Pledges once honoured no longer exist,
Bullying tactics are rampant.

As the evening of life beckons us all,
we long for the manner of courtesy.
Our homeland enriched by care and concern,
to counter our vulnerability.

The culture of pride; our country once knew,
desperately needs a revival . . .
for all that we cherish, applaud and respect,
lest our values remain in denial.

The power and the passion of the written word
reveals the truth in adversity,
to strengthen resilience and inner resolve
that will reaffirm our identity.

And, nurture the symbols that herald our land
in the spirit of camaraderie,
that the annals of history relates to our pledge
of allegiance, love and integrity.

Mary Ratcliffe (Swindon)

Once

Somewhere, some other time
There was once a place
Where trees weren't cut
And fishes weren't caught,
When roses were a sweet meal
And nectar a soothing drink
Where wild animals
Were tame companions,
There was once a time
It was like so.

A world where once
The cold was unheard of
Spring was all we knew
And butterflies lived
More than a day.
Where smiles never
Ended in tears,
And when happiness didn't
Ever disappear.
Yes, somewhere, some time
We lived like this.

There once,
Upon a time I'd exist
Then our eyes spoke a
Rare royal love
And beauty was all we
Could see in one another.
It lays ahead this
Place of beauty
Where princes and princesses
Once belonged,
Where they will belong again.

Now they're walking
Around in silence,
They know who they are
That place in their heart
They wait once again
To arrive.

Benvenuta Di Bartolomeo (Slough)

On Looking Into Satan's Workshop One Thursday Morning Before Breakfast

See Satan in his workshop
Busy as a bee
Working out the best way
Of annoying you and me.

Stealthy little helpers
Rushing round all night.
Work we do not notice
Hidden out of sight.

Undiscovered by the targets, us.
This is what they like
Causing chaos, fear, distrust.
Not a pleasant sight.

Wake up! Put on the armour -
Sword of Spirit, shield of faith,
Helmet of salvation shoes of peace,
Belt of truth; be salt and yeast.

People suspect each other.
But how the enemy laughs.
Undiscovered he continues
While we follow well-worn paths.

You're as lovely as the morning
Refreshing as the rain
But isn't it a pity that
You're such a scatterbrain!

Sing it again. It's all a pain.

What are we waiting for?
What can we do?
Have your own way Lord
Pray: let Christ break through.

Obey, trust and follow. Why?
Give him his due.
Christian workers - little might
Keep at it; win the fight.

Cathryn de Viva (Minehead)

The Guardian

Skyscraper City, and just like the rest,
All the world over, the east and the west
    Look the same.
Only at first glance - the London I know
Still holds its secrets from so long ago
    When they came.

Long years have passed since I first saw the Wall,
And then I marvelled that it was so small;
    It had lost
All of its top - the once tall ramparts proud
'Gainst the invader defiantly stood
    in the past.

Stalwart observer of two thousand years,
Sunbathed in laughter and misted in tears
    Of our town.
Over the centuries weeds of neglect
Twisted about it - but still with respect
    They had grown.

The last attackers, they struck from the air.
Grimly the Londoners, close to despair
    Stood their ground.
Battle of Britain - hard fought and hard won.
We all remembered when we were alone -
    Gunfire's sound.

Then peace at last, and the Allies had won;
In desert heat, winter's cold, there had come
    Victory.
Europe at length breathed again, with a sigh,
New hope had dawned, like a bird that flew high
    O'er the sea.

Slowly the buildings rose, did not aspire
To outmatch Wren's landmark, did not rise higher
    Than St Paul's.
Then change - the horizon, truncated, was cleft
By monolithic shapes, dwarfing what's left
    Of the Wall.

Tribute to riches, for some who can thrive -
Beneath their shadow the desolate live
    Through it all,
In 'Cardboard City', for that's what they name
Home for the homeless, propped up like remains
    Of the Wall.

Roman Londinium saw its folk fed -
No money needed for 'annona' bread,
    Right of all.
Quite unconditional, answering need,
No condemnation or judgement decreed

When we fall.

We - a free nation, and ruled by its own,
Look with dismay on the London we've known,
    Past recall?
Our fast paced city, efficient and slick,
Can be too much for the lame and the sick,
    In its thrall.
Does the Millennium star shine as bright
As the lost glow of dim Roman lamplight
    By the Wall?

Pamela Harvey (London)

The Knocker-Up Is Up

Tap-tap-tap on the window, *tap-tap-tap* once more,
the knocker-up is up, it must be half-past four,
John struggles with the blankets, getting out of bed,
'That knocker-up,' he mumbles, but that was all he said.

Another day for John starts in the middle of the night,
He searched for a candle and some matches to get some light,
The candle is eventually found and some matches too,
He holds the candle to the clock which reads just half-past two.

'This stupid clock is never right, I think I'll throw it in the bin,'
Just like a protest to his harsh words the clock alarm begins to ring,
'It's no use ringing now,' says John, 'the knocker-up's been round,'
He looks out of the window to see snowflakes floating to the ground.

Well snow or no snow, boots or no boots, the millwork still goes on
'Well it's clogs or no clogs,' says John, 'as Wellingtons I've got none,'
A cotton worker, John is from down *Blackburn* way,
Twenty-five years of toil and sweat for very little pay.

A wife and five kids to keep, it's a struggle from dawn to dusk,
A steady job you need each day as money really is a must.
Outside now with coat, muffler, old peak-cap on his head,
Wishing it were Sunday so he could have a lie in bed.

John sees his fellow workers trudging to work through the snow,
Old Harry, John's mate greets him with information he already knows,
'Eeh-by-gum John lad, it's reight cowd out today,
My old bones towd me there was snow about the day afore yesterday.

I've a pair of old long Johns on, two wool jumpers made by our Flo,'
Then silently they walk along through the falling snow.
'Well John, as you know I retire next week my friend,
All good and bad things will always come to an end.'

So there'll be no tap-tap-tap on the window, no more tap-tap-tap once more
The knocker-up can come and go,
But on my window he'll knock no more.

Philip Quayle (Isle of Man)

Dear God

Our streets are stained with blood
Of our sons and grandsons
Our brothers and nephews
Our young ones
Our innocent ones

Our beautiful streets
They walked on
They played on,
They messed about on
They laughed on.

Tears run down our cheeks
When we hear of their plight
When we hear their mothers cry.

Their fathers cry
Their sisters cry
Their aunties cry
Their uncles cry
Their brothers cry
Their grandparents cry
Their neighbours cry
Their friends cry.

We all weep with them
We share their pain
Mothers
Fathers
Brothers
Sisters
Aunties
Grandparents
Cousins
Neighbours
Friends, well-wishers

They didn't stand a chance
They didn't deserve to die
When they hardly lived
Their blood is crying on the ground
Where did we go wrong?

Joyce A W Edwards-Arnold (Upper Clapton)

A Cornish View

The sun sinks over distant lands,
White cottages amongst green fields,
St Michael's Mount stands tall and proud,
With grey-like tapered hands.

A diver's boat comes into view,
What treasures they haven seen,
Things lost to mortals here on Earth,
Ships, coins and all their crew.

A yacht race starts, sails and flags go up
Their colours are of red and brown,
Across the bay they sail away
To win the treasured cup.

People pass by with fish and chips
Suppers, held in hands,
These will be a lovely treat,
And simply taste just grand.

Young seagulls cry, dip low in flight,
Old ones in thermals fly,
And when the sun sinks down to rest,
Like pale ghosts at night they fly.

Two small boys with rods in hand,
Lean against a rail,
To catch some fish of 'ling' and 'bass',
And lay them on the sand.

The island ship stands at the dock,
She rests against the wall,
The distance is not far from here,
To which the public flock.

A palm tree sways in balmy air,
It grows outside my door,
Cornwall's warm, some plants unseen,
So come, it's nice to share
I hope you come to Cornwall
This land beside the sea,
And really do enjoy yourself,
Stop by and visit me.

J Dennis (Penzance)

The Gnaw Of The Bookworm Brigade

(This poem is a parody (based on) Alfred Lord Tennyson's 'The Charge of the Light Brigade')

Half a page, half a page
Half a page onward
All in the library
Flew the six hundred
'Forward the Bookworm Brigade!
Gnaw all the books!' she said.
Into the library
Flew the six hundred.

'Forward the Bookworm Brigade!'
Was there a worm dismayed?
Not tho' the bookworm knew
Some worm had blundered
Theirs not to read and cry
Theirs not to understand why
Theirs just to gnaw and fly
Into the library
Flew the six hundred.

Books to the right of them
Books to the left of them
Books there in front of them
Opened up and pondered
Read at with words from hell
Quickly they gnawed and well
Into the words of men
Into the reader's den
Flew the six hundred.

Showed off their teeth all bare
Showed off their evil stare
Gnawing at the books t'were there
Gnawing through the library
While the Librarian wondered

Gnawed through the shelves of books
Into every cranny and nook
Mysteries, novels and thrillers
Shook from their gnawing blow
Beaten and humbled
Then they flew back, but not,
Not the six hundred.

Books to right of them
Books to left of them
Books there behind them
Opened up and pondered
Read at with words from hell
While worms and book bugs fell
They had gnawed so well

Came thro' the words of men
Back from the reader's den
All that was left of them
Left of six hundred.

When can their munching fade?
O the wild gnaw they made!
The Librarian wondered.
Marvel at the gnaw they made
Marvel the Bookworm Brigade,
Hungry six hundred.

Joseph Berenson (Mill Hill)

Here Comes The Sun

Eyes that see a memory
Beyond that distant sun;
The ploughman
Up, down
Up, down.
Until his job is done.

Every neat cut furrow on that hillside;
Devon's rich red soil to the top -
Now ready for the frost of winter;
Ready for the springtime crop.

Now the giggling Land Girls
With bounce and bobbing curls,
Stared at by the munching cow,
Sniffed at by the pregnant sow.

'Harvest time' smiled autumn,
'The corn is good this year.'

And so it was in the golden sun,
So work and work till the job is done,
The corn 'was good' that year,
And so was cider's welcome cheer!

But how it rained that night!
Rain, rain, that would not stop,
How they'd said it would, (in the village shop).

All this now - up on high
Through the swirling clouds
Of a sun-filled sky,
The sun-filled sky - my sun-filled sky.

Until that distant tractor's drone
Brings me back to stand alone,
Where shadows of that setting sun,
Harken and darken from where I'd begun.

Leslie Osborne (Tiverton)

The Sea

I lie on the beach
Watching the gentle sea
As the bubbling surf
Glides up upon the sand
And then, so slowly, retreats again.
I clutch a pebble in my hand
Stroking it, and think about the sea.
It has many moments,
Gentle and tranquil,
When the colours of the waters are sea green,
And all shades of blue.
Or sometimes roaring and tempestuous,
When winds turn the colours to steely grey.
And what of the creatures,
Who live above and below its surface.
Sea birds, wheeling and crying above,
Swooping down to capture their prey.
Seals, their little bobbing heads
Appearing for a fleeting moment.
Dolphins, leaping from the water in graceful arcs,
The sun, catching their glistening bodies.
And beneath the waves,
Shoals of fish swim to and fro.
It is the home of whales, sharks, octopi,
And many others.
Myriads of plants and rocks
Nestle on the seabed.
The sun can strike a sparkle upon its waters,
And the moon can create
A pencil of silver upon its surface
Sometimes a mist rises up
And the world becomes muffled and desolate.
How can we comfort those whose loved ones
Are sleeping their eternal sleep
Beneath the waves
The sea can be kind, and it can sometimes be cruel.
Whatever mood it is in,
It will always remain,
The sea.

Eve M Turner (Penzance)

Holiday - Cruising The Med

'Mr & Mrs Brown' were there each day
On the sun beds, where they lay
Soaking up the solar rays,
Squinting through their smoky haze,
Drinking ice-cold cans of beers,
Exhibiting their sun-kissed rears!

Did they ever leave their spot?
Did they even know that what
Most cruisers talked about
Was them, and their bad-tempered pout?

No one ever saw them dine,
Or saw them dressed up to the nine.
No one even knew their name
But wondered wildly, why they came
To join the cruise around the Med,
Then simply lay upon a bed!

My answer was a simple one -
They worked so hard that having fun
Was too much trouble, so they chose
To lie out in the sun and pose.

Others said that Mr's perm,
Announced to all he'd served a term
With one of those premium football teams.
And so now, having quit the scene,
He wanted to be left in peace
To fry, until we docked at Nice.

Still others thought that Mrs B
Had won the cruise, and so the free
Holiday was to keep her tan
From fading, till we got to Cannes.

Yet more and more the rumours flew,
In pools and bars, at dinner tables too.
But when at last we reached homeport
A stop was put upon our sport.
For answer came there not a one,
'The Browns' had simply upped and gone.

Ann Shippobotham (Compton Martin)

On Beacon Hill

A sparse layer of turf by the trig point,
Worn thin by so many feet,
Nearly eight hundred of them above sea level,
An outlook that's hard to beat,
Seven four seven cruises overhead,
Gearing down ready for its landing,
Ageing joggers flop down to rest,
Not one of them left standing.

Wood fires burnt bright in medieval times,
To warn of impending invasions,
From warriors from distant lands,
And from many different persuasions,
They also glowed in happier times,
To tell of more glorious things,
A peaceful noel, a prosperous new year,
Or the crowning of new kings.

A blue kite, but without strong wings,
Comes crashing to the ground,
While a red one, that requires no strings,
Glides effortlessly safe and sound,
Kestrel hovers on the updraft,
Beady eye on a squeaking shrew,
Long distance walker sets down to rest,
And pours out a refreshing brew.

Model planes, rise and plunge,
Grown men gather to play with their toys,
Lady hikers gleaning amusement,
'They haven't changed since they were boys!'
Crickets singing on the furze,
A chirping tune that lasts throughout the day,
Down in the valley, a spire, aspires,
For those with a desire to pray.

In the western vale, hedges enclose the pastures,
Varying shades of green within,
Shorn golden ones, with big round bales,
The harvest is being safely gathered in,
Like a patchwork quilt, its seems so endless,
Going on for miles and miles,
Distant country town, with towering office block,
Filled with desks and piles of files.

Downs to the East, old white lion,
Guards fiercely but never known to roar,
A landmark for the silent pilots,
As over his domain, they speedily soar,
Making his presence felt, he marks the whereabouts,
Of the nearby wildlife park,
When the dusk light falls,
He illuminates with pride,

Seen from distance in the dark.

Skylark takes to the air, where the oldest trail
Both begins and also ends,
Across the rugged escarpment,
Over the ridges it curves and bends,
Sulphury brimstones flit and flutter,
With meadow browns and chalk hill blues,
Drifting on the August heat-haze,
Going in any direction they may choose.

G P Cook (Swindon)

Missing You

I open up your front door
But the rooms are icy cold
Vacant now, alone like me
Now you're not here to hold.

I touch your clothes with nervous hands
And fold them with much care.
Such raw emotions chill my mind
Grief exposed and bare.

Your ways were never the ways of me
We rarely saw eye to eye.
But how I yearn to hear your voice,
Your songs, your laugh, your cry.

Did you know I'd feel like this
When death snatched you away?
That my heart would be awash with tears
And begging you to stay.

So now I have to clear your things
Each item filled with you.
Memories spill around the floor
Shadowing all I do.

I see you standing by the sink
I see you in your chair.
Watch you paint your pretty face
And style and comb your hair.

You are still here inside my head
Seizing my every view
And if I had one special wish
It would be to embrace you.

A lady full of charm and wit
Whose laugh rang out with fun
Who always made the most of life.
My very special mum.

Linda Hurdwell (Ascot)

Someone Special

I'd been in the kennels for months,
all alone;
longing for someone to give me a home.
Then things were looking up,
there was a couple
who didn't want a pup.

It's been ten years since that special day
when my owners took me home with them to stay.
They gave me my own little mat,
I would sit, cross my legs
and listen to them chat.
Grandchildren would come
and cuddle me tight
and Nan would bring me a bone
on a Sunday night.

I never liked cats
and would chase them away,
for my garden was a place
for me to play.
Although I lost an eye
the remaining one was special
as I'd look up at my owners
in such a way . . . 'Can I go
for another walk today?'
I loved to lay on the bank
in the sun
and watch
the children having fun.

But now I'm weary and
feeling quite ill,
I've been to the vet and
I'm taking my pill.
Now I'm tired and just want to rest.
I don't want my food;
they've all done their best.
If there's a heaven for dogs up above
I know I'll be happy, I've had lots of love.

Shelia Page (Newbury)

Blue Lagoon Cocktail

She sat
By the
Pool and
Sipped another
Blue Lagoon
Cocktail.

She turned
To her
Friend and
Said, 'Life
Is Rich'
Then gave
Her the
Bill.

The waiter
Stood in
The shade
Of the
Tropical sun
And patiently
Waited for
His handsome
Tip.

He returned
To the
Bar with
His silver
Tray and
Gave a
Sigh when
He read
The note
From the
Super-rich
Tourists, a
One dollar
Note.

J Ashford (Bridgwater)

The Beauty Of Springtime

Spring's light breeze through fresh golden fields,
dazzling the eyes, for future good yields.

Spring lambs unsteady on new limbs,
yet able to frolic before light dims,
their mothers are watchful and fussy too.
She herds her offsprings together, marked in blue,
to calm them, to slumber through the night,
'neath shaded trees, to protect against fright.

To view trees as useful, is evidence one cares,
these giants are our life's blood on how one fares.
Man's puny life span of three score years and ten . . .
are outstripped by the Giants thousand or more again.

Our wild plants are shamelessly termed weeds,
they are healing herbs . . . worth growing from seeds.

Poisonous plants are wisely kept at bay . . .
Yet to find them unworthy is total dismay,
for many have healing properties, to treat disease
such as foxglove, or the viola, 'Heartsease'.

Our flowing streams and ponds are beyond compare,
rippling over rocks worn rugged and bare.

The pond's whirligig beetles, whose giddy spins amaze.
Viewers' heads are spinning too . . . yet full of praise.

Sticklebacks are many, and good optic exercise,
darting and flashing amid astonished cries . . .

The frantic haste of water shrews, ever amaze,
yet soon pay the penalty of non-stop ways,
their life is so short, they burn themselves out,
but that is what their life is all about.

Our native birds are colourful, with a fine voice,
to see them glide on air currents is nice.

The robin and blackbird to our shores belong . . .
so different in aspect, yet beautiful in song.
Our verges look grand, so fresh and green,
there's red campion, stitchwort and cow parsley seen
and red valerian, rumex and many more,
with dandelions and buttercups by the score.

Canals are hosts to wonders yet unseen . . .
out there beetles, frogs and toads, are green.

Rabbits are rife, poaching and sniffing around,
digging holes everywhere to bolt underground.
To take with them . . . nuts and seeds galore,
Then squat, nibbling away at food-in-store.

At the water's edge, there's nodding bur-marigold
alongside is watermint, its blue flowers to unfold.

In the shallows with flowers a very bright pink
is great hairy willowherb having a drink.

Tall, sturdy, sword-leafed and very straight,
is the yellow flag iris looking great.

At last I fear this verse ends soon . . .
or snores will echo . . . around the room.

I thank those still awake with torpid eye,
and those that bowled me over rushing by.

Bernard Lobb (Sturminster Newton)

 Grief

Did I know it was to be the end? Yes
I love you
Did I know it was to be the end? No
I love you, too
Don't leave me. I want to come with you

Silence
The corridors are empty
Silence, silence
But your chest is heaving, isn't it?
Silence, silence, silence
Yes, I know - and No, I don't

The storm erupts; I am crouching in the centre
Will it pass? -
A crash
and I have landed on a strange and alien planet
But the Earth, the Earth is turning undisturbed
has it not noticed what has happened?
How can they all walk along the road, so undisturbed?
Just waving now and then?

I put two spoons out on the table
where only one is needed now
A handkerchief, a hair, your shoes –
Stones and arrows fly at me
and there is no escape from them
Memories cutting through the flesh

I am a nail come loose in an empty barrel
I am waiting, waiting
The postman will bring you back to me?
I am waiting, waiting, waiting
While my head explodes

A rose on your coffin.
It is gone, no trace, no children crying.
But you - will be here forever.

Anna I Roberts (Iver)

My Hats

With pins and a needle,
Some cotton and thread,
I'll make you a hat
That will fit on your head.
I'll find some material,
A flower or a feather,
I'll make it look lovely,
I'm really quite clever.
If you want a hat
To stand out in a crowd,
I'll make sure that your one
Is coloured and loud.
Plastic or leather,
Sinamay or suede,
Cotton and sisal
Are the hats
That I've made.
I'll work through the day
And work through the night
And I will not stop
Till I get your hat right.

So when I am famous
And appear on TV,
By selling my hats,
You'll come up to me.
You'll say, 'I am wearing
A style you created,
Always in fashion
And never outdated.

It's a creation
All made from resources.
I wore it at Ascot
And won on the horses.'

So for an original
You'll want it to be.
I'm in Yellow Pages
So come and see me.

Joan Hyde (Luton)

The Wonderful World We Live On

Today you look out of the window and see

A row full of trees
All swaying in the breeze

Or

A road with cars and lorries
And people with shopping trolleys

Or

Maybe you can see you staring back.

Whatever you can see,
Remember we are blessed to have everything,
Right down to the tiniest bee.

But even though we have this world,
It is being destroyed,
And we need to stop this
Now!

Deforestation is causing animals to die,
We need to re-grow the forests,
We must give it a try!

Poachers are wiping out elephants, rhinos and all,
Soon there will not be animals left in the savannah,
Why are people all so cruel?

Cars, lorries, vans and motorcycles are creating
a hole in the ozone layer,
Why don't they use a bike or just walk?
They are like *ozone layer slayers!*

People are cutting trees down for paper,
Scrap paper is always available,
These people who just keep using fresh paper,
What are they, tree haters?

If we don't stop this our world could end,
All people could die,
Try and help prevent these terrible things,
Or you'll drive me round the bend.

Emily Hume (Marlow)

The Big Cat's Closet And The Woman With The Pointy Head

The lion roared at me . . .
And I was scared . . .
Until a woman extended her
Arm; outstretched, with her
Pointy hat and used the very
Tip to wipe away my
Tears.

'Your reaction is raw'
She said to me:
'See?' And pointed to the
Hole in her hat
Where my tears had
Been - had burned right through!

'You . . . ' she said to me
Are true unto others
'See here?' and she pointed
To her fingers, which had held
The hat, which had wiped
My tears, which had burnt
The hat and torn at
Her skin! But the blood as it flowed
Spelled . . . 'clean' . . . and
'Pure'.

'I do not understand'
Was all I could utter . . . could
Stutter . . . 'I know . . . ' she said
Putting her hat most firmly
Back onto her pointy head
'. . . And that is because you
Have not been so true
Unto yourself . . . but I
See you are learning.

'Why else . . . ' she said to me
'Pure' and 'clean' dripping
Down her sleeve, '. . . did
You not laugh at the
Shape of my head?'

'the lion's roar is both
Greeting and warning;
Reactions are wide as the
Seas. Why else . . . ' she said to me
' . . . does he hide in the
Closet, cloaking his pride
With a tear in his ear . . .
And 'pure' and 'clean'
Tattooed on his belly?'

With those words she did
Leave me. But I did not
Feel alone . . . for the lion
Had bitten me! Which was most sure to scar! I
Stood and stared . . . he had exposed
The word 'pure'; the word 'clean'
And those words were my
Bones.

Karen Kennedy (Newbury)

Cover Her Bones

Part of the walkway straggle we stare intrusively
At various artefacts so carefully displayed,
One shield boss, a torque, nine chipped and ancient spears,
Then, shuffling down the line, at skeletons
Of what, a bored guide told us were, 'Fragile
Bones of a young female found close by
A Saxon warrior's remains, Jute maybe.'
These two the focal point of a display
Fund raising, officially, to desecrate
Perhaps three thousand graves and so reveal
What could historically be, 'a most important site'.

Headlined - Amazing Archaeological Breakthrough -
Research will tell of tribal settlements
Their age-old customs and their daily lives
And scholars will debate their likely wars
The length and terms of their uncertain peace:
But look at these long buried bones and think
Perhaps they should remain untouched, unseen,
Holding their own the secrets of the lives
They led, the deaths they died. These bones, once clothed
In living flesh, are now become dry curiosity.

Idly we speculate; was she the warrior's beloved,
A captive princess from some conquered tribe,
Victim of ritual murder, rape, assault
Or simply just a girl who died too young,
A private person who'd abhor this revelation?

We're fascinated by such distant time,
Exposure after a thousand shrouded years
Urges, almost, a vulgar scrutiny.
But please not here, not this especial place.

Strangely, we think of her with tenderness
Accord her remote respect that she can never know,
Leave her in peace, don't violate her grave,
Cover her bones, yes, leave her resting so.

G Howarth (Waterlooville)

The New Forest

The New Forest is a historic park to see,
Where beasts, birds and insects roam free.
Ponies and cattle graze side by side,
Fallow and roe deer, fleet or foot, hide,
Within woods, trembling with fear,
When they sense that danger is near.

Each season brings new delights,
Ramblers stroll and admire the sights.
Through leafy glade, beside crystal streams,
Not quite such as idyllic as it seems,
When winter gale and lashing rain
Reduce paths and scrub to muddy terrain.

Animals shelter beneath dripping trees
And when the ground beings to freeze,
Farmers bring trailers piled with hay
To keep the animals' hunger at bay.
Golden gorse, holy berries blood red,
Tentacles of ivy provide a spider's bed.

A metamorphosis takes place in spring,
A melody of birds begin to sing.
Squirrels, hedgehogs, mice awake
And soon the ground begins to shake.
With pounding hooves and walkers' tread,
Dew glistens on spider's silken thread.

Summer: early sunrise over the pines,
A dawn chorus perches on cable lines.
Carpets of heather purple and white,
Bloom laden - a colourful sight.
Lush green ferns and foxgloves too,
The bridge where we throw sticks, like Pooh.

Foals nestle beside their mothers,
Shades of brown and amber whilst others
Are piebald, black, white or grey,
Cows and calves shelter at midday,
Under a spreading chestnut tree,
Its candelabra a sight to see.

H V Boyd (Fordingbridge)

Shattered Dreams

All I thought was right and true
And that meant so much to me
All I thought that was of You
Turned out to be death on a tree.
The things that I'd been pursuing
Have overnight it seems fled from me
My vision is blurred because of my tears
And You've become somewhat of a mystery.

I thought I knew You
I thought I knew Your way
I thought I knew Your character
And was so sure I'd heard You say . . .
'This is the way you should go
It's alright with Me
Just trust and follow your instinct
Because they're God-given you see.'

By the road has proved long and tough
My soul is heavy and I struggle wearily
Pain strikes deep through my aching heart
And dark discouraging clouds hold me dearly.
Too many problems I have encountered
Too much opposition I've had to face
Doubt, fear, anxiety and confusion
Have all temporarily taken Your place.

Lonely, hopeless and despairing I wonder
And decide to reach out to a friend
The whole situation and You I ponder
What will be my end?

Will uncertainty enshroud me forever?
Will I be able to discern the differences between our voices?
How long will I have to live in the shadows of regret
Of my own mistakes and bad choices.

My mind is despondent and dull
And my eyes have lost their shine
Help me to give You everything
And to Your Spirit incline.

Dawn Madigan (Luton)

White Remains

The ocean.
I soak its swell,
The fundament that honed the marrow of the Earth,
A press beyond dream.

I am safer in shallows.
The ebb may yet unground my feet
But the weight is not too great,
It does not crush.

There is salt on my lips,
Sweet and clean.
And I remember . . .

A rip caught me I think.
I do not know.
But the ground shelved too steeply
And I panicked lest I drown.

Where was I in all that blur?
Did I fight for control?
Did I run for shore?

I was one with the waves that day,
A force of different moons given life
And drawn across the world.
Reaching, ungraspable voices timed like music on a scale.

Five,
Two,
Oh,
They met and played at different speeds,
One and, and one they ran their furrows and misconceived.
Out of phase, out of time.
Never we,
Never one.

A tear splashed meld that stifled, smothered,
Dragged all together down.
The crash of raw emotion,
A churn of pain
And the set ploughs on.

The wake lingers.
White remnants ripple on the shore,
Strands that flow through hands and wash my palms.
Streams I cannot hold,
I cannot mend.
Not here.
I will only rend.

So, pray now;
Take comfort.
There is time to heal the tidal heart,
One to sew.

Waves drift and part,
The currents lead them ever on.
They pass into quieter waters.
Grow great.
Grow strong.

Coolness caresses my skin
And this is the ocean.
I stand in its draw.

Jocelyn S Downey (Kingston-Upon-Thames)

Blake

(Have you ever wondered what William Blake might say if he was present in an A Level English Literature lesson?)

What makes you think I mean more than I say?
I didn't write to be dissected.
Leave the words on the page,
leave them there.
I didn't write them to dance for you.

Listen long enough to see
and watch long enough to hear.

I am a master of words,
I choose them: mould them
but a device is a device.
Animated alliteration,
and the splash of onomatopoeia
may inflame your imagination,
yet words are just words.

Do you ever pause?
Ask yourself - am I reading what is written
or am I reading my heart's desire?

My words and your meaning
but now and then stop analysing.
Visualise my Bardic voice and
hear the prophetic fallacy,
Close your eyes and see the Blossom
but take nothing more than a flower.

When I write 'stars' look to the sky
not a criticism of conformity.

Play with my words as you will
for you live and I do not.
Please remember,
words are my legacy, so

open your eyes and listen.

Hannah Dennison (Torquay)

The Black Hole

The black hole is death and dissolution
Entropy and ecstatic union with emptiness.
The black hole is pain and terror and the darkness of non-being.
The black hole is power, essence, and the majesty of God-in-me
The black hole is energy and creativity centred
into a split second of life-giving.

The black hole is a teacher:
To fear and yet live, to live and not to fear to die.
Come with me now into the black hole and you
and I may come to rebirth.

Into the black hole: come!
I am calling you back to the place of origin!
Into the black hole; go!
I send you into the dark to find the light!

On the far side after the maelstrom there is power and purity
And the pain of absolute unselfish love.
On the far side, where we may stand, there is silver light
And surrender to the infinite power of simply being.
And when the moment comes to let life go in all its richness
The black hole beckons us, with riches beyond
our wildest dreams.

Let us not fear the black hole or attempt to understand -
Let us be open to the goodness and the power that can be ours
If we give it way, let it go, and surrender
To the breath of life that blows in gales from out of it.
Blown by the breath of God that pours from the black hole
We can live according to the will of the wind,
And in our last hours feel the suction draw us down
Into that place of origin and creation
That is the place of dissolution and death.

Sink willingly into the black hole!
It is the cloud of unknowing, filled with ageless mystery;
It is the gate to paradise.
If we wait in this holy space together
And listen to the silent and mysterious loving power within;
Then truly we will have a taste of paradise this side of death.

Althea Hayton (St Albans)

Whispering Sea

Walking along the beach with the sand between my toes
Whispering, shimmering, looks the silvery sea
Green, blue, white with yellow shimmering there
The surf dancing like horses on the sea
Grains twoing and froing, with the waves beating on the beach
Beyond the sea becomes darker from the deepening of the sea
The sun, shines warm with the bright golden light
Shifting, drifting, with the shimmering sea, out beyond
Whispering, twisting, sands stayed beneath my feet
Frothing sea entwining around my toes
Damp cool seaweed wrapping around my feet
The ebbing pulling the sand beneath my toes
Running, jumping over the white waves
My skirt flying high above my head
Twisting, lifting from around my legs
Ribbons falling flowing, from my unruly hair
Hair fanning out, like the wings of a dove
Rain starting, tumbling down my face
Wind blowing soft breeze from the sea
Waves edging closer to my beach
Stronger and stronger, the sea starts to roll
Waves turning in on itself into the sea
My body pirouetting along the shifting sands
Twisting, writhing so stronger are the winds
Whispering sea has turned itself upon me
Clouds gathering quickly grey and dark
Flashes of lightning fork across the sky
Lightning strikes before the deafening sound
The rain starts to drop straight lines from the sky
Winds blow furiously tipping up the sea
I made it to my cabin, where fire burns bright and warm
The fragrance from the sea, and the salt upon my lips
Waves tipping, turning, shooting up to the sky
Comes down as shooting stars
Rain pounding, crashing, leaving marks on the ground
Winds are easing, the storm quieting, as I walk back on the beach
Fish gasping, floundering, being thrown on the beach
A glow from the sun hits my whispering sea.

Diane Complin (Berkhamsted)

Seen From A Greek Balcony

Think picture, framed by woods,
Begun but not complete;
A green pine base,
Tall at left, the right
A crystal of infinity -
And flowing out and in
The trackless, timeless sea:
Turquoise, blue, grey-green;
Now white with rage,
Now tranquil and serene;
Its shades of temperament
As varied as contours
On the island chunks beyond.

Borrow for a moment
The hero's eyes, returning
From a long and distant war;
That promontory in silhouette
An arched and favourite cat,
And behind, the soft and supple
Curves of Patience, asleep,
But soon to kindle welcome
As the sun begins its arc.
You can understand
That ancient awe:
More than all others,
Phoebus shaped this
Broken scattered Greece,
Each island-shard a stage
In his gold chariot ride
Across the day-long sky.

A plane breaks the spell
And drowns the crickets' riff.
It grumbles in, weighed down
By pink, perspiring Brits
Who came because their wives
Were bored with Spain.
Half their holiday is spent
In shops, the other half in bars.

They talk of Bagshot,
Basingstoke and Penge;
Of films seen, cars bought
And football matches won.
Their wives, plump with boredom,
Dream of Kostas and escape;
Of dancing, flattery and wine,
And red-hot passion
Triggered by a sign.
Ask them who Plato is and
They will gawp and say

It's Disney's dog,
Or p'raps a distant planet.
They don't 'do' history,
But they take the tour
That takes them round its coast,
The tales of battles won
Soon lost in the chorus
Of the Chicken Song.

Christopher Inge (Bleadney)

People

There are people, people everywhere,
All shapes and styles and colours.
They range from white to black and brown,
And in between, there are others.

The white ones start from northern climes,
The brown and black are southern.
There are other characteristics of their race -
The hair, the eyes - some others.

The red hair shows they're from the north,
And many start in Ireland.
It shows in Scottish ancestry,
And many blue eyes are Irish.

Spanish people have brown eyes
And higher-toned voices with an accent.
The French and German sounds are clearly heard
When they are speaking English.

In England once we all could see
And tell the origin of people.
There were accents plainly in the voice
To recognise the species.

Some temperaments are calm and quiet,
And others very fiery.
We certainly are not all the same,
And many seem quite barmy.

Yet everyone is different, too -
No two are quite alike;
So God works in a mysterious way
For the wonders He creates.

There are so many various types
Only God can shape the pattern.
People are people, wherever you go.
Yet good and bad are never flattened.

(Thank goodness! That's God's job.)

Doris E Pullen (Sydenham)

All You Ever Left With Me Were Memories

I know it's wrong for me to dream about you
As you left me for another long ago,
But I can't help the way I felt about you,
I loved you more than you could ever know.

But you have gone and left me all alone now
And when you went you took your love with you,
All you ever left with me were memories,
Oh, please return and take these with you too.

That day we met was cold and so depressing,
But my love glowed for you, just like a fire,
For I was overjoyed at having met you,
To have you always was my one desire.

But you have gone and left me all alone now
And when you went you took your love with you,
All you ever left with me were memories,
Oh, please return and take these with you too.

The man who took my place I can't but envy,
He's sharing all the love that I once knew,
And though you're gone I hope you will be happy
HIs love, like mine, I trust will be as true.

But you have gone and left me all alone now
And when you went you took your love with you,
All you ever left with me were memories,
Oh, please return and take these with you too.

It's hard for me to live my life without you,
Your leaving caused me tears and so much pain,
The love I had for you has never wavered,
The feelings that I showed remain the same.

But you have gone and left me all alone now
And when you went you took your love with you,
All you ever left with me were memories,
Oh, please return and take these with you too.

Kenneth J Ody (Chippenham)

Love's Complexities

What more
can poets write about love -
its pain and pleasure,
sorrow and satisfaction,
which merge and mingle
in two unique and equally
unrepeatable lives and histories?

What more
can priests reveal about love -
its sacrifices of self,
obeisance and offering,
its opportunity
for a woman and a man
to become as one?

What more
can prophets preach about love -
its joy, desire, delight,
parting and returning,
its sublime days
and pedestrian ways?

Poets, priests, prophets -
all can only agree
with the wisdom of the centuries -
love is the height of happiness,
a comfort against aloneness,
an affirmation of the senses,
a Heaven, or Hell, on Earth,
though more often
somewhere in-between!

Yes here, in mutual self-giving,
the great Lover's power,
beyond the sun, stars and moon -
the very vault
under which lovers
strive, yearn, laugh and play -
is both glimpsed and glorified.

Brian Frost (Reigate)

If You Can't Stand The Heat . . .

The foods of love are eaten with the fingers,
Varied in texture - voluptuous to the taste.
Follow my recipes for love that lingers,
Some dulcet, some with fiery spices laced.

The gelid smoothness of a peeled green grape,
Lychee, filled with Brie in a tiny tart,
Slender asparagus in a lacy crêpe,
Caramelised garlic, an amusing art.
Strawberries, scarlet as sin, with stem as handle
To dip in clouds of cream, angelic white.
Truffles that chocolate coat the throat -
Oh, dark delight!

(Make all in secret, by the flame of a red candle)

Then - veil your lover's eyes with scarf of silk.
Tie his/her hands with velvet cord.
Music should play, of soft, seductive ilk.
Tell him/her not to speak, to heed each word.

Press, then, a grape to his/her pliant lips.
'Open, my love' - and slide
the fruit inside
with gentle fingertips.

At your own leisure, order: bite . . . chew . . . swallow.'
Let the taste build, let them explode and flow.
Alternate savoury with a sweet to follow.
Avoid monotony, kind chef, imagination show.

With flavours from the east and west,
From north and south.
Make your love savour each exquisite bite.
And in-between,
To wash the palate clean,
Trickle champagne from mouth to tender mouth
Each drop will quicken lust's large appetite.
Feed not to surfeit,
Not to dull or cloy.
Leave hunger's edge just slightly unabated.
Overindulgence will not bring forth joy.
Repletion can, at times, be overrated.

This gastronomic exercise should not be misconstrued.
It's written on the food of love - not on the love of food.

Simone Brightstein (Bradford on Avon)

I Don't Know

Fainted raindrops falling down,
I listen out for a tearful sound.
The silence breaks
With a clap of thunder,
As I sit in my window,
I sometimes wonder,
I ponder on an eventful way,
To spend this very rainy day,
The weather man says it will clear away,
Washing everything in its way.
By noon that day,
The clouds are gone,
The sun is shining,
The birds hold their song,
How am I supposed to know,
When all I see is tears that flow,
The world this morning,
I watched it cry,
I heard the thunder, I'm watching it die.
How come none of us seem to know,
When all I see is tears that flow?
I'm sitting here in my window,
Watching the world fall apart,
Breaking up my marble heart,
I watch as all rip out the soul,
Of this poor pretty world,
The oil, the gas, the minerals, the coal,
The collateral damage of wars,
We hold,
Destroying people's homes,
Disease and fleas,
The scale's immense,
Though when will we come to sense,
The world is dying,
It is our home,
I sit in my window
Alas I don't know.

Shaun Smith (Plymouth)

New Forest

Twenty years, two decades,
Changes come about.
Yet nature survives
To gladden our lives
And thrill its senses.

The pony place, a tranquil scene
Admired from centuries past,
Open grassland, winding roads,
Frequent fords and quaint abodes,
Copses full of trees.

Shooting lodges intersperse
All routes along the way,
Some being now hotels and homes.
Fairy-like, with little gnomes
In fantasizing mind.

Abounding, open areas
Sparse traffic driven slow.
Livestock takes the precedence
'Cross hedges, gates or wooden fence,
Wandering, roaming free.

A heritage of royalty
So marks the Rufus stone.
Crowned kings' pleasure ground
Of piercing arrow shot renowned.
Alas! The fatal blow.

Incredible parameter
Of thirty-five thousand miles.
Towns included in the space
As weary walkers gather apace
For sustenance and sleep.

The air is sweet
The views immense.
A world apart, alone.
With creatures all to tone.
Into a peaceful bliss.

A Audrey Agnew (Ilchester)

The Tree

Stronger grows the tree, and weaker, *me!*
The cherry, barely one year old
Whilst I am eighty-three!

I sit and ponder all of this
and Torres scores for Spain.
How much time have we got left?
Will I see this match again
Next year?

Now in my final act
better than one, or two, or three
I hold it all so dear

This retirement life
it seems so long ago
I worked for cash reward
and now for fun, I still try to go forward!

Schweinsteiger frowns watching Ballack bleed
it's still one-nil to Spain
is this then all they need?
If only I had risked ten pound
Hey-up! There's someone down
Torres hits the ground!

Why write of football and the tree?
Because through glass and screen
they're both in front of me
and still the score's the same
and it's shameful watching writing
whilst Spain has such a game . . .

The cocoa's drunk, and this drama's o'er
I've never seen the Deutsch so poor
the wind goes on and on
the cherry tree is never still
the writer and the football
both have stopped
Barb's tree has got the look
it never will!

Roy Merrett (Bristol)

Wish You Were Here

(For a boss retiring to Australia)

Wish you were here
It'll say on the card,
But I don't suppose it'll be very hard
To forget about us lot slaving away
While you're sunning yourself in Byron Bay.
There'll be boarding and Barbies with bronzed Aussie men
And you won't get up until quarter to ten.
We reckon you'll like it far away down under
Away from the rain and the drizzle and the thunder
Away from audits and graphs and statistics
And irate women going ballistic.

But you won't think Australia's quite such a lark
When your leg's bitten off by a basking shark
And there's snakes in your knickers and a scorpion in your shoe
And a funnel web spider who lives in the loo
And there's dingoes and wombats howling all night
And you've got to put that stuff on your nose that's white
And you can't say 'Girls - have a nice cup of cocoa',
You'll have to go 'Ripper' and 'Spunky' and 'Smoko'.

And when there's a party, it won't be like here
With a big fat joint and English beer
There'll be 'tinnys' and 'Fosters' and you'll feel really sick
When they give you a big smelly cane toad to lick
And you'll go 'No thanks Bruce - I feel a bit dodgy -
I might find that cane toad a little too stodgy'.
They won't say 'We'll save it - for a bit later on'.
They'll just go 'Sheila . . . you are a winging pom'.

Now with your husband's interest in cultivation
And the help of your managerial motivation
You could keep him busy for hours and hours
Producing some really exotic flowers.
But it's dangerous to go out and tend your plants
When your garden's chock-a-block with dog-sized ants
And you've just about got your seedlings through
When . . . *boing* . . . they're buggered up by a kangaroo.

Yep . . . like we said . . . you might just find
That after a while you change your mind
When there's wombats in your knickers and a wallaby in your shoe
And a baby-eating dingo who lives in the loo
And there's snakes and scorpions howling all night
And those Aborigines could give you a fright
In the dark . . . if one came a little too near . . .
It might just be you who wish you were here.

Now putting you off is not our intention
But while we're at it we'd just like to mention
That the foods you are used to may not be abundant

174

Your cookery skills could be rendered redundant
We are concerned and don't mean to be rude
And we know Gerry's usually pretty good with food
And he'll know what to do with 'yabbys' and 'scags'
But one day he'll arrive with *things* in bags
And if we listen hard - we might hear you cry
'For f**** sake Gerry . . . *not witchity grub pie.*'

Lorraine Stevens (Bournemouth)

The Clearing

I will wait for you beloved,
When the fiery ball of sun slips slowly out of sight on the horizon
And disappears in a final glorious blaze of orange,
When the intangible wisps of evening mist gather round me,
Stirred by the softest breeze.

Come to me then in the clearing,
In the clearing in the wood.

I will wait for you beloved,
When the green forest turns to blackness,
And the song of the birds is hushed.
And other sounds are heard,
As the prowlers of the night emerge to pounce and feed,
When the screech of an owl, or bark of a fox,
Drown out the cries of small prey.

Come to me then in the clearing,
In the clearing in the woods.

I will wait for you beloved,
When the crescent moon ascends;
A new-crowned prince, who rides midst his spangled courtiers,
To light the purple heavens and cast a silvery spell on all below.

Come to me then in the clearing,
In the clearing in the wood.

I will wait for you beloved,
By the burbling water's edge,
And on a pillow of soft green moss, lay down my head.
I'll press my ear to the echoing earth
For sounds of your approach.

At last! At last! Quick footsteps come
Snapping through twigs on the ferny floor,
And the branches of tall trees bend and sway as if in welcome,
And I know in the wild leaping of my heart,
You are only a breath away.

You have come to me in the clearing,
In the clearing in the wood.

Ann Jarvis (Plymouth)

Darwinism Doesn't Explain Life

Some say God exists with absolute certainty,
Some believe in Him, some don't -
I do not know if there is a god . . . somewhere . . .

I know only that now
I walk alone, I live my life as if
There is no supernatural being.

It is not that I want to listen
To some more than others,
That I want to be on this side, or that side -

It is simply that I cannot believe
In an eternal . . . person
Who sees me, knows my thoughts, cares about me.

Listens to prayers, can answer my prayers -
I just don't think this is true anymore.
They tried to hijack my brain

These . . . totally sincere people -
Almost succeeded.
'God exists, there is someone there.

There is a Paradise, a Hell, an afterlife -
It is in the text, the Book is the guide, believe,
Do not question.' I did question -

There is no evidence.
There is mystery, strangeness . . .
We don't know the origin of the universe,

How the cosmos came to existence.
Darwinism doesn't explain . . . life.
Here we are on Earth

Engaged in a battle for the mind.
There is love and hate, I see and feel it -
There is both good and bad in me.

What I believe in, is love. Simply love -
That perfect feeling, that . . . something
In human nature.

Claire-Lyse Sylvester (Fleet)

Onus

I have been chased by words;
Hounded by harsh principles of creed -
Till I am sick of all this weary world of man;
Soul-starved, and hungry for a kindly deed
Were we so tired of peace and love,
That man thought fit to free the torments of a million tombs,
Plunging himself deep in the savageries of Hell,
souring the sweetness of a million wombs?
Even the dead cast shadows in the sun;
Steal over the rose that rots upon the mound.
Man's inhumanity to man, perpetuated
In precious blood, over a clovered ground.

We are the crucified
Who are shaped in God's image,
We die, with or without a thorny crown,
We suffer in narrow worlds we sanctify,
And yet we talk of growing old,
We of the ageless race. Futile fertility!
Weaving the unborn's future into webs of woe,
Which gave the spider, strength; the fly, its destiny,
Up, up, and heavenward, the song of birds,
Trowel the soundwaves, and our prayers;
Higher than minds and hearts and words;
The souls born on the treacherous rocks of grief,
They climb the stairs of Heaven, and the stairs creak,

The sound of man crying in the wilderness -
Hears only echoes, for fear forbids an answer,
Fear of his fellowman shatters the darkness.

Why are we wrapped in fears?
Is this our modern heritage, that cloaks
The parched bodies of our youth
And feeds their war scorched minds with ideologies?
They, who still tremble at the cross,
Are not surprised to find the stone has rolled away,
And Peace not there . . .
Only the dust of past philosophies.

Ronald Baron (Plymouth)

Sounds Around The Bonfire

It's quiet now, the embers have died,
And the babies have cried themselves to an infant sleep;
The smell of a November evening still lingers,
Enhanced with the scent of wood fire smoke,
And hoot of night-time owl -
Outside my bedroom window.

Earlier they seated me on a Windsor chair,
Dressed warmly in a duffel coat,
With a plaid shawl across my knees;
Voices around me directed my matches and fingers,
To where the woodpile lingers,
Heaped, I am told, like a pyramid;
With paper and straw and dry twig stalks,
Supporting the legendary Fawkes,
Awaiting his annual lot,
'Sixteen-o-five still not forgot.

I felt cold, the mist lying heavy, turning to frost;
Then the flames licked outwards,
And the sparks flew upwards;
Whilst the warmth advanced towards my chair;
My chilled body began to glow,
Warmed blood coursed to my feet.
And my toes wiggled as a young girl giggled,
At something whispered in her ear.

The noise of the fifth, snapped and spat and fizzed,
In a frenzy of exploding flame,
Banged and cracked and whizzed,
In an orgy of pyrotechnic wizardry;
Hot cocoa, poured from a steaming jug, filled my plastic cup,
There were 'oohs' and 'aahs' and squeals of delight,
From the people around me;
The autumn leaves crunched beneath stamping feet.
Someone pressed a sparkler into my shaking fingers,
I listened to the urgency of its spitting,
Feeling the heat creeping towards my hand,
Then they placed it into the sand,
Along with the other carcasses of celebration.

Declining the offer of a bonfire baked potato,
I settled to the laughter, thinking what was to come after,
Tea, in my Royal Albert cup, laced, as a treat, with brandy;
Slowly the sounds became subdued,
Whispers replacing the shouts and excited tones;
Gradually the warmth retreated, as the flames began to die;
So my son took me by the arm, leading me slowly -
With backward calls of 'goodnight', across the lawn;
Back to the comfort of my room, my room in the attic,
With the many sounds of the house.

Yes it's quiet now, and it's time, I suppose, for sleep,

So I take a final sniff at the stillness of the night;
I shall dream the colours of the flames,
Pretending to be a rocket,
Soaring in an arc across the sky,
Trying hard to fly, not too fast, not too high;
My pillow a cloud, as I see all the sounds that I heard,
As I sat with blind eyes and my ears wide open.

Donald Cooper (Honiton)

Balmy

Poppy.
Oil and rapeseed.
Opium, bloody.
Froth film.
Infra hands;
nefarious.

Feral range.
A field
of dogs and cricketers.

The grand houses.

Herd of flying geese.
Their gaggle squawks.
Pure, white down,
speckle the green.
Cloud-like.
Spectre.

Battered
railway track.

Clumps of
dust and twigs,
like gunpowder.
I am a
fire-starter.

The night watchman.
His bold lechery.

The olive,
Crinkled water.

Clement.
Temperate.

Pastel-hued
canal boats.

An utter
silence.

Caroline Baker (Guildford)

Southampton

Southampton! Home of mine, so dear to me,
Where avenues and leafy parks engage
With open spaces in a random way;
A garden city born before its age -

A sleepy city pitched four square between
The river shores of Test and Itchenside,
Where what is old is often thought of well,
And what is new is normally decried.
There has been change, but always marked with caution,
'Festina lente', so Rome then impressed
On early settlers making for Clausentum,
And ever since that way's been thought the best.
Now dig on dig sees time give up its treasure;
From medieval town of Bargate fame,
To Saxon settlement of far off Hamtun,
The story slow unfolding, is the same;
A tale of many people, many races,
Of gentry, merchants, those of humbler clay,
Of doughty sailors, blown from distant havens,
Of foreigners who came and chose to stay.
The scene moves on to quiet spa-spent seasons
Of leisured walks along Elysian paths,
Of crinolines, and lace, and furbelows,
Of stately balls, invigorating baths.
On to the age of steam, the railway era,
The building of the docks on new-won land,
The opulence of ocean-going liners,
The ferry boats, the flying boats, and, and . . .

Wait! Two world wars now raged within a lifetime,
And shook the city to its very core,
But with its people bowed but never broken,
A new town rose far greater than before.

The growth continues to the present moment,
Some say for good and others say for ill,
And yet, despite its wants and imperfections
Southampton! My home town, I love you still.

John M Davis (Eastleigh)

Bonfire Night

(For Claire)

Our bodies swaying together
we were flowers of fire
dancing flames
deep-rooted to the spot

we were the tree of fire

we were
ululating orange tongues
undulating silently in the frenzy of spent strength
licking the sky

we were
searing rags of joy
tearing loose
leaping free
miraculously, instantaneously
transfigured into darkness
over and over again
spending each molten shower
into the womb of night

we were starbursts
we were shooting stars

we were
a power house at the heart of heat
dense structures of incandescence
contained by blazing doors

and we are
lit by love

new unknown fire
for a thousand and one nights

a glowing hearth
enduring through the dark

5 November 1994

Nick Osmond (Hove)

When The World Stood In Respect

They came from the far corners of the world
Survivors of horrible crime,
To meet again with others suppressed
At the place named, 'The End of the Line'.

Returning there to honour those murdered
In the most deplorable way,
With memory sharpened, recalling foul slaughter,
'God, never again' they pray.

Where people untouched remained silent, apart,
Not knowing the terrible time
Those millions of people were forced to endure,
Now known as, 'The World's Worst Crime'.

They ran in their hoards, herded like cattle,
Whole families; old to the young,
Such cruel regime, one could not foretell,
Plans stealthily made had begun.

The world outside could not save them,
All war zones were hard to break through,
The terrible slaughter of innocent souls!
In millions their numbers grew.

Did no one hear of this torturous crime
Too dreadful to comprehend?
All taking place while the world stood by
When starving and gas was their end.

This day the living returned in their thousands
To honour six million souls; dead,
And remember the sad killing factories, to where
The human harvest was led.

Strong Cantor's voice in anguish cries!
Lamenting brave lost souls;
'Humanity, where oh where is thy love
And where are thy sacred goals.

Emotion swells in Cantor's voice,
When crying out the sorrow
Of poor souls, lost by cruel fate
Lived not for their tomorrow.

Low wailing breaks across the site
Where torture and destruction
Took place, no help, no hope, no life.
Just follow death's instruction.

The singing of prayers for the dead and those living
Pour out across the throng,
As ghostly figures, silently moving
Seek comfort, to sense they belong.

As deep river water, carries the blood
And ashes across the wide,

Soft wind wafts gently, caressing the dead,
Assisting their sighs to subside.

The sound of the shofar rings loud and true
Embracing the dead and the living,
Mankind be watchful! Making quite sure
That history remembers this killing.

Rosamund McGarry (London)

The Gardener

Eliminating weeds,
Old elm roots - bits of junk
From generations past
Within the garden soil -
Takes time. Takes toil!

Then the right
Ingredients for growth
Need careful thought.
For every plant,
Every wonderful variety
Of fruit or veg or flower,
A different 'work' is needed
To produce the best.

Remember also,
Keep the garden weeded!

In due time
The wonder that's created
Will bring the trippers
To exclaim, and ask the name
Of who and how and when,
So they may do the same.

You'll point them
To the gardener.
Say, 'Ask him.
I just did what He said.'

So with trial and error
Food will be produced
Where once was chaos,
Famine, war and ugliness.

And all the world will be
A Garden of Delight
Because the work
Was done aright.

The Gardener knew His stuff.
And for me, that was enough.

Diana Morcom (Minehead)

The Plymouth Blitz

The phoney war was over and the bombs began to fall,
the sight from not too far away was of one great fireball;
The might of Nazi air power which continued through the night,
made sure that in the morning the whole place was alight.
The sound of bombs exploding, mixed with gunfire far and near,
made us all a little nervy, the real word was 'fear'!
The early morning after was a sight of real disaster,
there were bodies mixed with debris in the streets.
The Nazis were still winning, this was only the beginning,
it was yet another one of those defeats.
Our fathers were away, so each and every day,
our mothers had to plan the week ahead,
there wasn't much to choose from, and there wasn't much of that,
but come what may the kids were always fed.
As children we were plucky, and more than often lucky,
we would lie and watch the dogfights in the sky,
these battles were amusing, and a little bit confusing,
we didn't know that one of them would die.
As children of the thirties, things that constituted 'dirties'
was to run away when someone said, 'You're dead.'
If you didn't play the game, you could never play again,
so you just ran home to Mum and straight to bed.
Our shelter was our second home, our pets would also stay,
at times we'd have a body count and find ourselves a stray;
we never really slept a lot, all we really did was doze,
it was dreadful in the winter when the water level rose,
taking turns to pump, we would try to keep it dry,
but in the summer it was different, we would simply lie and fry.
Those months of war soon took their toll of body, spirit and sometimes soul,
Then things got better as they always do,
the improvement began in forty-two,
at last it seemed we were winning the war,
the news was good, but our backs were sore;
back to our beds, from that hole in the ground,
even our toys were easily found.
Those months in the past we shall never forget,
and the childhood we lost, we lost with regret.

Gordon Henry Ramsey (Plymouth)

More Than The Logo

Christians as in playing games
Get out on the ground,
Where the greatest contest,
For this world is found.
Evil powers are out there
To make people sin,
So God needs some players who will
Help His team to win.
Don't just wear the Christian Logo
Cross, where Jesus died,
Trust His resurrection,
He'll be by *your* side.

We may not feel strong enough,
Seeing wrong approach.
But we can't be beaten,
Jesus is our Coach.
He will teach us tactics,
Keep us straight and true,
By His guiding Holy Spirit
Show us what to do.
Don't just wear the Christian Logo
Cross, where Jesus died,
Trust His resurrection,
He'll be on *your* side.

So much evil's happening
In the world just now,
That those who oppose us
Make us wonder how
We can be victorious
In this game of life,
But we know Christ's way must triumph
Bringing love from strife.
Don't just wear the Christian Logo
Cross, where Jesus died,
Trust His resurrection,
You'll be on *His* side.

Ronald Frost (London)

Children

Into our lives they came, bringing light, laughter and love.
Helpless they seemed but soon were we held in their thrall.
And so it remains through the years from childhood to adulthood,
As we answer their call; ties of silk with the strength of steel.

Beatrice Smith (Wareham)

Think

Think a thought so kind and pure
It fills the pockets of the poor
A thought that humbles fast and greedy
A thought that cares for frail and needy

A thought for old, a thought for young
A thought to praise the song that's sung
A thought of love, and not of hate
To give impatience time to wait

A thought for loneliness and grief
To clothe the beggar, pity the thief
Heal the sick from this thought hence
And grant the meek their inheritance

A thought for friends and family
A thought to honour flower and tree
A thought for water, soil and heat
To give the hungry food to eat

A thought that lights a child's bright eyes
Where innocence is recognised
And truthfulness is always sought
In every deed and every thought

A thought to have and then to hold
With open arms and heart enfold
A thought to banish fear and pain
That's a thought worth thinking again

A thought for a world where speech is free
And courage faces adversity
Where jealousy and rage are banned
And different creeds pray hand in hand

A thought where brother helps his brother
Lives side by side, respects the other
A thought to put an end to war
And make us question what war is for

A thought to reach the greatest height
To warm the day and light the night
To thank the moon for wax and wane
And for the sun to rise again

A thought for creatures of the earth
A thought for death, a thought for birth
A thought of thanks for all creation
And peace to reign in every nation

And when all thoughts combine as one
His Kingdom come, His will be done

Val Haslam (Godalming)

Our 60th Golden Anniversary

We have been married now for sixty years
I remember as yesterday
All in white with a train I had made
With six bridesmaids in array

My father took me down the aisle
With tears in his eyes
My mother had died when I was young
Now I was a blushing bride

We went to Switzerland on our motorbike
A BSA 250
We have lots of memories to share
As the bike was very nifty

I couldn't have chosen a better mate
We have three lovely children
We started well in our life
And had a good base to build on

We saved for all our worldly goods
And never owed a penny
No debts, no shame
With heads held high as any

But with age comes sorrow
I had a stroke
But what a treasure beside me
He looks after my every need
What a good friend to guide me.

We feel lucky to have lived so long
When our mothers died so very young
But we know one day our time will come
We tend not to dwell too much
We live a day at a time
And glad that our lives did touch

Our love for each other is still strong
And we hope as our children grow
We will still live on through their lives
On Earth and our grandchildren's love they sow.

Clare Bright (Bedford)

On Leaving A Home

In each room I leave a ghost.
Nothing spooky,
just an impression on the air,
a voice almost there
of someone who once
looked from that window,
walked through that door to a certain space.
They are there for always now,
and never mind the why and how.

Look, there, where our daughter briefly halts,
awaiting her new life.
Each step - study, travel, career
- planned, longed for just here,
where pictures crowded walls and doors,
eased troubled days and welcomed each return.
All gone, leaving aching space,
save one in its accustomed place.

Photographs defined this room,
life thorough our son's lens.
They still exist, but now elsewhere,
leaving powerfully here
echoes of throbbing life,
the creak of foot on stair at dead of night.
No treasures here to be found,
all images reduced to sound.

And shadows flit everywhere,
whispers bouncing off walls.
True, some of them bring with them tears.
Losses come with years
and the house stores all
- glad and sad - within its much lived-in space,
I'll never forget, I vow,
But - close the last door quickly now.

And what next? What follows after we forsake it to its fate?
The house hugs its memories to itself, - and prepares to wait.

Celia Andrews (Clevedon)

Exmoor Winter

Crackles white ice in rutted hollows,
Bites the frost, bitter the air,
Night early, tardy the dawn,
Bellows the antlered deer.

Hilarie Perry (Minehead)

The Judas Hour

The time
Hangs so heavy
Crawls so slow
When you're
Waiting
Waiting for
The Judas Hour

Just whose
Betrayal
Will we be
Witnessing
Today
Waiting for
The Judas Hour

I'm standing
By the gate
Of Gethsemane
My wings feel
Cramped today
Waiting for
The Judas Hour

Am I the one
To bestow the kiss
Or
Am I the one
To be kissed
When it arrives?
The Judas Hour

We gather
At the table
Raise a glass
Trying to read
Each others' faces
For now has come
The Judas Hour.

Richard Gould (Liphook)

Gramps Is The Champ

We love Gramps
Gramps is the champ
And Josh and Ben
Are two little scamps.

Joshua Norman (3) & Benjamin Norman (2) (Havant)

Afghanistan

Even though all around was cold,
I remember feeling warm.
The mountains, our mountains,
Shone with black and gold.

We scooped up handfuls of snow,
Glittering white powder, just perfect to throw.
Armfuls of luxury, excess and delight,
These were the dreams that we clung to at night.

We were children then, just boys.
As soon as dawn came, we ran
Into the foothills, the peaks were too far.
But their mystery beckoned, a door ajar.

Summer came with flowers, we taunted the bees.
We lay down and ate, stuffing our mouths,
Until honey dripped, thick and breathing, onto our knees.

Knees bare with freedom, no shoes.
We felt the snow on our toes,
And laughed.

You were older than me, and taller.
When we climbed, you reached back for me.
I could see the blue veins of your hands
As they strained to keep me safe.
Hands of a man, but not quite.
Instinct telling you that what was right.

We picked poppies, blood-red,
For our mothers and sisters and for their dead.
We threw snowballs for joy
Me at your heart, you at my head.

We pulled away the petals to see if they were real,
We made patterns in the sand, a kind of seal.
Dark grey-brown rocks, smooth in the rain,
Our hands caressing them again and again.

I do not remember in-between,
We never met to talk about it.
You heard the guns before me,
And went away.

The mountains swallowed you.
Not our mountains anymore, but all the world's.
I stayed to protect the bees,
To keep the poppies free.

There was blood in the sun that night.
I took late watch.
I saw you coming, but I did not hear.
Dark, grey-brown metal, dark grey veins.
A man's hands.
Boots crushing the snow with no fear.

We picked poppies, blood-red.
For our mothers and lovers, though our reasons are dead.
We fired snow, red and free
So splintered with sunlight, that we could not see.
Exploding into powder, words never said,
Me at your heart, you at my head.

Mary Cruz (Bath)

A Sussex Morning

The yellow Downs
Cascading in rape,
Flowing to the churchyard
Now tired and overgrown.
The church bell rings,
It's seven o'clock.
Old Father Time
Looks down from the spire.
The village awakes,
The bustle begins.
Dad's off to work,
The children to school.
Same routine every day.
Mr Tanner, old and alone,
Goes for his morning walk.
Across the glistening field
Still covered with dew.
Onto the kissing gate he remembers so well.
How many girls?
A smile, a thought
On he goes.
The school bell tolls,
Boys and girls come out to play.
Women gather at the village shop
Hoping for gossip, a scandal maybe.
'There's old Mr Tanner,' one of them says,
'Not long now, not long now.'
The church bell rings
It's twelve o'clock.
The midday sun
Warms the carpeted Downs.

Mr Tanner, old and alone
Lays back in his comfy chair
Closes his eyes
Drifts off to sleep
He is soon in the churchyard
With Old Father Time
Beside the others, tired and overgrown.

Jill Booker (East Grinstead)

191

Heaven

The moon brightens the clear night sky,
A million stars twinkle shining bright,
Each night I rest my head,
I see your shining light.

To me you were everything,
My world, my night and day,
I wish you would come back
And be with me to stay.

You have gone to a better world,
You have peace and contentment,
You are alive, well and strong,
Knowing I will join you in wonderment.

Time is a good healer,
I will never stop loving you,
When you were on my Earth,
You were my dream come true.

You are always on my mind,
My mind you will never leave,
I will join you soon,
This I do believe.

Thank you for giving me your life,
Your joy, your peace and goodwill,
Although you have gone,
You are my life still.

When we meet again in Heaven,
Our life will start anew,
Life will be so marvellous,
For me and wonderful you.

Be happy my dearest,
Be peaceful and content,
This will help me in my day to day,
In the future and the present
                    Everlasting life.

John Lewis (Houghton Regis)

Untitled

So why don't we walk down the same road together
And all I want now is to be with you forever.

Your beauty is beyond compare and your skin is so soft and fair.
So take me back to your lair and treat me like a cuddly bear.

Mark Lugar (London)

Enigma

A causing obsession
Is the reason to live
To live without question
There is nothing to give . . .

To wake every morning
And look to the sky
Then stare into darkness
And wondering why . . .

The Earth is a mystery
The galaxy vast
The spirits that roam
Of people who've passed . . .

The energy created
To give such a life
Can never be ended
It can only survive . . .

Time stands for nothing
Scientists will say
Dismiss all the reasons
That are obvious and portrayed . . .

For eyes now upon us
And sightings denied
Access all areas
For those in the sky . . .

Technology growing
A baby no more
A man made concoction
A product for war . . .

These times are upon us
Keep senses alert
And question the reasons
Why we're put here
On Earth . . .

Kerry Webber (Bridgwater)

The 'Rushing' Vine

The verbena's been a bit weak this year
And the daisies lank and lazy,
Petunias they were punier both large and junior.

But the Russian vine did climb and climb, it raced a mile a minute
It reached the shed, covered that and all the tools within it.
Now the mower's lost with the hoe and the rake
Can't someone control it with a garden stake?

Butterflies in a flock laid eggs in the hollyhocks
Not a posy from the roses just greenfly and black spot,
Stinging nettles in fine fettle, these we couldn't stop.

Yet the Russian vine rambled on over wall and fence
Tendrils grasping everything, the foliage thick and dense,
Crazily it curled, scrambled everywhere,
Has anyone seen grandad snoozing in his chair?

Antirrhinums? Couldn't find them something ate the lot,
Kniphofia fizzled, never sizzled; they should have been red hot.
Caterpillars, slimy slugs, evil weevils, bugs in trugs
Snails, black fly, nesting ants, all conspired to wreck the plants.

The Russian vine took no time to show that it was boss
It twirled and twined through the garden now half the house is lost.
From inside the greenery muted hissings and squeaks
Where's our old ginger moggy, he's been missing for weeks?

The fatsia got skinnier, lack of feed we're told
Yet the weeds are shedding seeds, rampaging and bold.
Dandelions push through where they have a mind to
In the lawn bare and worn uninvited how they grew.

Still the Russian vine grows on in sunshine and in showers,
We now have all the leafy bits whilst next door have the flowers.
But to the raucous crows, it appears heaven sent
As they create their crowded rowdy halls of residence.

'Tho the hostas didn't cost us much they grew with rapid haste
but a visitation overnight reduced the leaves to Spanish lace.
We couldn't stop the poppies flopping or the lupins drooping
The dahlias were all failures, heads bowed and stooping.

Clambering on at breakneck speed, chop it back, it pays no heed
Twisting, tangling weaving on, any visible path long gone.
Shrouding all that goes before, stand in its way you'll be no more.
It started life at forty-six, this perilous Russian vine
Now all the neighbours share a piece right down to number nine.

Doreen E Millward (London)

Life

In spring of life when all is new,
Carefree days and clouds are few,
The sun shines bright from morn till night,
In innocence we grew.

We played a lot and life was great,
Sums and spelling nailed,
Then exams to prove the point,
And the dreaded pass or fail.

The plans that were created,
The dreams and wild ambitions,
A product of our teenage years,
That rarely reached fruition.

Education, schools and college over,
We thought we knew it all,
And started on life's truer path,
Where we would stand or fall.

We coped with jobs and babies,
Cash flows, governments and wars,
Children's schooling, rising prices,
Technology, moves and laws.

It seemed a host of problems,
With determination, guts and zest,
The summer of life was conquered,
And in hindsight seemed the best.

Now autumn clouds are looming,
With different trials to beat,
Health and movement slowing down,
More challenges to meet.

Retirement, bus pass, hearing aids,
Tablets and pills,
Replacement hips and walking sticks,
All to aid our ills.

We may be near our 'sell-by' date,
But will not give up yet,
We'll find out all we need to know,
As we surf the Internet.

P A Lower (Bristol)

Memories Of The Sixties

Take me back to the sixties
when living and life was great
When people were loving and carefree
and we loved to go on a date.

Take me back to the sixties
when we went to the village dance
In our psychedelic mini dress
or our saucy scanty hot pants.

We did not need a mobile
credit card, or the like
The last bus would do for us
unless we had a bike.

We didn't worry walking home
alone, on a dark night
Gangs and thugs didn't stalk
the streets looking for a fight.

Oh, take me back to the sixties
when music was groovy
and raves were fun
And life was just for living
we had no need for a gun.

Society has changed so much
since those heady sixties days
It's take, not give, it's me not you
and everybody pays!

Life was good when we sampled
the euphoria of the moment
And love was satisfying and true
not discarded without emotion.

But now for kicks people kill
and maim, and drugs are commonplace
I'm so glad my youth was then
and I'm out of today's rat race.

Angela Soper-Dyer (Basingstoke)

The World Is Still Sleeping!

Have you ever seen poverty and hunger?
Have you seen the scourge of misery
On the tender faces of children?
I have.

Have you seen innocent budding lives painfully withering away?
I have.

I have suffered the pain of witnessing that pain of suffering innocence.
I have seen children left to die from starvation and of diseases
Although a little love, a little care and compassion could save them.
Alas! The world is badly lacking in those virtues of life!
We have practically no values either to value and follow!

We are all self-centred, unscrupulous beings:
No compassion or love do we have.
Children die painful deaths and we merely look on!

Have you ever seen helpless children all too resigned to fate
Without a word of complaint or protest?
Have you seen their absolute surrender to God
While anguishing and languishing to the inevitable end?
I have.

I have seen wretched children staring in pain but only in vain
At the heartless loveless world
With tears trickling down their afflicted faces -
Children dying to survive only to die to escape life!
They failed to evoke pity, for the rich little care for them!

I have seen such ill-starred children in thousands -
Children born poor not for any fault of their own,
Children born to suffer and to pine away to death
For no fault of their own!

Humanity has failed many a time
In its supreme duty to itself!

We aren't dead yet!
When shall we wake up?

S M Tajul Islam (East Ham)

A Pensioner's Privilege

How far is it from Watford to Ware?
I'm sure I don't know
And I'm sure I don't care
I only know I can get there
Free of charge and pay no fare!

Reg Windett (Rickmansworth)

The Place Where Happiness Lies

This is a game that I have grown to love,
Where you describe the thing that you're thinking of,
Whether you're with a family or friend,
It's a game that's easy to comprehend.

As I sit, I consider this,
To describe the thing that I'll surely miss,
And then it hits me with a sudden blow,
To describe the place I could never let go,
So then I explain the place that I'd miss,
Hold on now, it starts like this:

I think of a place that's colourful,
A place where happiness lies,
A place that has no cruelty,
Where I hear no sounds of cries.

The place that I think of is beautiful,
No other place can compare,
To the joyful sound of laughter,
And the absence of despair.

I think of a place rich with culture,
The saris, the jewellery and bangles,
A place so free you can walk bare feet,
There is no need to wear sandals.

The saris are gorgeous and stunning,
In the west they are fashionable and trendy,
The women's hands in the place I think of,
Are decorated vibrantly with Mendhi.

The food itself is amazing,
As you smell the mouth-watering samosa,
The curry, the roti, and bhajji,
And even an idle dosa.

The place that I think of is full of childhood,
As they are fond of kites,
Smiles spread across their faces,
As they celebrate the festival of lights.

This is a place that I will always love,
It is in the east and not the west,
Yet I'm sure you'll agree without a second's thought,
That the place I think of, India, is the best
My India!

Sneh Brahmbhatt (16) (London)

Wrong Medication

Don't give me antidepressants,
Depression I have not got,
When taking this medication,
I really lost the plot.

From a cheerful laid-back person,
Who would not harm a fly,
I'd changed into a monster,
With the devil in my eye.

I could not stop crying,
And anger filled my soul,
Such temper welled up inside me,
I was not in control.

My family stared in horror,
At this person they did not know,
I was worried I might hurt someone,
And shook from head to toe.

These feelings were so frightening,
I'd never felt this way before,
I just kept jabbering and swearing,
Then jabbering some more.

If you think this medication,
Will really make me well,
You're under a delusion,
Because it was a living hell.

I know I feel poorly,
And each day's hard to get through,
But I'd rather put up with that,
And be kind and caring too.

If I take this medication,
Which does not help at all,
The only thing I'll be doing,
Is climbing up the wall.

So please don't give me anymore,
I'm better off without it,
And if you haven't got the message yet,
I'll really have to shout it.

Jennifer Holloway (Southampton)

199

Carers' Afternoon At The Brick Lane Music Hall

Ushered in we bagged our table right at the front
under the nostrils of the troupe
and lapped up the service
with a welcome cup of tea
placed around doilies and Danish pastries.

We sat relaxed with our summer jackets
hung over the chair backs
then turned off our mobile phones.
Stuffed with mayonnaise and pickle with cheese
we paid the raffle man and drank more tea.

Around about the décor was rich and transformed the old church
into a venue for old time music acts
with photos transporting us to the olden days
and we pointed and gasped and waited patiently
for the curtain to rise.

The MC made us giggle and cover our mouths
as he projected mirth to the back and highlighted
the Ladies Group, while we squirmed un-invisible.
On cue he was joined by four others
in timely costume and theatrical grease-paint.
The show was off!

Tremendous fun and slick to the hilt
the players danced, clicked on their heels
bobbed and bopped in 60's style and led us all
down Lovers' 1950's aisle.
Some of us remembered the words
and went into different, safer worlds.
All of us enjoyed another place and time
away from domestic duties and daily grind.
We clapped until our hands were sore
then reclaimed our spirits from the rafters.

Gillian A Muir (Leyton)

The Poet Astronomer

When I gaze into the skies
The mind inside me flies,
Through far flung reaches of space,
Across light years untraced.
In the starship of thought
Dream adventures go unspoilt,
Imagination is that friend,
In my great cosmos of pretend.

A mind has no ceiling
No walls or any bars.
Allow me to throw the question:
'Why would it be wrong to consider the stars?'
I have knowledge that Earth is our home
And on it we shall roam.
Please don't tell me where you think I
Ought to point my telescope, I already know.
Just following a spontaneous interest
In the much larger show.

When I go outside at night
Earth's anxieties fall from bright,
Spiral downwards in a spin,
Until their presence has grown dim.
In our galaxy of wonders
The magnificence can be seen in numbers,
Sinless skies reveal pure creation,
For the skywatcher's unclouded fascination.

This whole universe is open
A perfect model for the mind.
If you care to take the lid off,
You won't be so daunted at things you will find.
A boundless sky of treasure
Far greater than jewels, silver or gold,
Invites us to sample the rich display cases,
As the celestial night completely unfolds.

Kevin Welch (Eastleigh)

Merry Widow

To some people, those who never met you, you are not there.
But, for me you will always be here, never there.
When talking to men at parties, their wives say, 'What does your husband do?'
I say, Nothing at all, I am a widow.'
With horror, I see them mentally put 'black' in front of the word
And 'spider' after it.
Do I really have more than one pair of legs covered in black hair?
No, I don't think so . . .

How can anybody ever be so presumptuous
To even consider that I would consider anyone could ever,
Ever fill your shoes and walk by my side holding hands,
That I could gaze into someone else's blue eyes
Or cut their white hair, not too short, and eyebrows,
And trim their ear hair as well and even massage
Their feet?
No, I don't think so . . .

When walking the streets, or corridors at work, at the gym
Avoiding taking pills by running 5K on the treadmill,
Sometimes the ground gives way beneath my feet
And I fall downwards, arse over tit, heart beating wildly,
Sweat pouring from every pore and I feel so ill
And feeble
Friends look and say, 'My word, you look well,' but am I?
No I don't think so . . .

So, for a while, to fill long, lonely evenings,
I tried prancing around with a spot of line dancing.
However, even stepping out NEWS in straight rows
One still needs to be one half of a couple
With that other half present, not only in mind but body as well.
So in the end, I only went for the cider
Or beer, or wine
Anyway, can one dance when continually falling through the floor?
No, I don't think so . . .

And now my love, here I am on my own with a paintbrush
Changing the colours of my life
Holding tightly on to the step ladder so as not to fall through
the parquet.

Did we ever think that day, following such love making and breakfast
In bed that you would get on your motorbike to go to
Tenby and fly your black BMW off a Welsh mountain and
Not come back?
No, we didn't think so . . .

Cheryl Newman (Cheltenham)

The Last Call

A trumpeter stood standing
Awaiting for a sign
His manner was commanding
His countenance benign

At length the order came to sound
A note upon his piece
A note to shake the very ground
And cause all life to cease

He raised the trumpet to his lips
Breathed deep into his chest
Swayed slightly forward from the hips
And paused for moment's rest

Then swiftly blew a clarion call
Of beauty unsurpassed
A note excelling over all
One instant did it last

The heavens were torn asunder
And lightning flashed on high
The rolling sound of thunder
Echoed in a cloudy sky

The Earth vibrated to the note
Great chasms split it wide
The mountains fell in lands remote
Red flames shot from inside

The seas in headlong fury raged
To sweep onto the land
As if the universe had aged
For reckoning was to hand

The planets in their headlong flight
About the burning sun
Ceased spinning in the spaceless night
As when the world begun

No living thing survived that call
For judgement had been said
With peaceful men pervading all
The trumpeter fell dead.

Douglas Wood (Portsmouth)

Pictures From A Country Garden

There is a clear, blue sky
and a soft breeze -
as I sit in my garden.
The gentle sound of the trickling water
can be heard from the fountain next to the red roses.

This soporific tone sends me to sleep.
I see my garden resplendent in colour -
deep reds, purples, yellows, oranges and greens.
I breathe deeply -
the pungent smells slowly creep up on me -
roses, lavender, surfinia -
embrace me with soft, sweet bouquets.
I see the olive tree - upright and proud
flourishing in its pot -
the old apple tree
twisted and green;
nurturing its new apples
like newborn babies.
The buddleia, tall and dense
drawing the brightly-coloured butterflies like magnets
to its thick, purple flowers.

The birds are gathering -
around their bath
awaiting their turn to clean, chattering loudly;
their wings a blur as they try to hand on.
The bees in their black and yellow uniforms
are busy as they move from flower to flower,
softly humming their little tune.

I breathe slowly -
as the sounds reach my ears.
I awake.
The beauty is all around me,
as the sun takes a bow
and daylight makes its curtain call.

Debbie Nobbs (Aldershot)

My Ol' Mare

(Ode to my father)

O to think of my ol' mare
a furrowing yonder lea,
wi' tail of tresses swishing air
and traces jerk and sway.
Many's the hour we'd turn the soil
wi' many a sod laid bare,
and scarce a rest from weary toil,
I'd foller my ol' mare.

And many's the time, wi' headland neared,
when furrows shone wi' gold,
I'd catch me breath at gunshot veered,
wi'out her being told.
From elder to paddle, straight as a dye,
a full ten chain and spare,
wi' never a need to turn an eye,
I'd foller my ol' mare.

When rattle of shoe that tips a stone
were music to my ear
and midge and gnat about me drone
the sounds that I still hear.
Wi' rooks a cawing overhead
to start the setting hare
and one foot down the furrow's bed
I'd foller my ol' mare.

But now I talks of days gone by,
when toiled by share and harrow
and my ol' gal be gone to lie
in fields a laying fallow,
and I be thinking I'll be gwain,
though poor of foot and spare,
along the furrow's golden chain,
a follering my ol' mare.

Ray Maslin (Newbury)

The Note That Came With The Flowers

(A son's lament on Mother's Day)

The time has come dear Mother, when I think I should confess,
it was me who made the wigwam from your Marks & Spencer's dress,
I blamed it on my sister, I was six, and she was three,
and I laughed when Daddy spanked her, but I lied Mum . . . it was me!

And as I'm pleading guilty, there's the time you never knew,
who it was that nicked Gran's hearing aid, I flushed it down the loo!
I didn't mean to do it, it was just a bit of fun,
we can laugh about it now of course, we can do . . . can't we Mum?

And Mum, I've just remembered, there were other things I did,
like the day I found the cess-tank, and I pushed aside the lid.
I called old Rusty over, and I pushed the dog inside,
when you asked me why he smelt so bad, 'Search me,' I said . . .
I lied!

It was me who 'scrumped' the apples from the vicar's precious tree,
and when his bike went missing, well, you've guessed Mum . . .
it was me,
and all that rude graffiti, someone scrawled across his wall,
you won't be too surprised to hear . . . well that was me, an' all!

It was me who left the tap on, I'm the one who caused the flood,
yes, I dragged my sister's blazer down the road, and through
the mud.
It was me who mixed the frogspawn, in with Daddy's favourite jam,
if you want to know who's guilty Mum, of all these things . . . I am!

It was me who slashed the curtains, I was immature, and bored,
it was me who smashed the telly, I just hope it was insured,
and while I'm on the subject, I should get it off my chest,
it was me who burnt the shed down, there, I've said it . . .
I've confessed!

You thought I was an angel mum, you fell for all my lies,
but underneath this smile, I was the Devil, in disguise.
But now, dear Mum, I'm older, and I've children of my own,
I've a wife, and two Cairn terriers, I'm nicer Mum . . . I've grown.

I'm sorry I was horrid, I was such a rotten kid,
let's look towards the future, let's forget the things I did.
So please accept these flowers, they're for all the love you gave,
and please forgive me one last time . . . I pinched them off a grave!

Nigel Smith (Thatcham)

Cinderella's Sister

Something shimmers in the night
Argent moonlight glowing bright
Beaded curtains, naked skin
Where on earth did this begin?
Tempting, teasing, pleasing lips
Sumptuous swaying curvy hips
Eyes that smoulder hot as coal
Burning deep into my soul
Where's the passion, poison, grace
There's the poise, the potent face
New aesthetic artifice
Imagination twice as nice
Urgent, needy, brilliant sight
Dragonflies and fairy lights
Butterflies displayed on pins
Hollow eggs and fairy wings
Cast your spell and shy away
Make your wish then fly astray
Drain a drink to absinthe friends
Show me how to make amends
Feeling empty, drained and dry
Moisture wells up in the eye
Like spider webs in morning dew
Jewelled pink and cobalt blue
Read the signal, flags unfurl
Spring is sprung as leaves uncurl
Dark Magenta, sweet azure
Only innocent, not pure
Honest, open, straight and true
Something made me think of you
Crass and cruel and hard and quick
Slow and sweet and smooth and slick
Scratch me, scar me, on all fours
Bite me, brand me, make me yours
Here is magic, needles prick
Beat me with your rhythm stick

Many stories left untold, bold as brass and twice as cold
Someone whispers and lead turns to gold.
Meanwhile . . .
Cinderella's sister is growing bold!

Alan Gibson (Southampton)

Words From An Angel

(For our dad, who we miss so much)

An angel spoke to me
Told me he was dead
Destiny had clearly changed
So I hurried back to bed.
As I lay in thought
Trying to count said sheep
My fears slowly lifted
And I vanished into sleep.

Here sweet dreams were hidden
As if I were awake
I simply couldn't settle
To all that was now fake.
Stepping up, I walked out
And left others to fret
Onto desolate streets
To find my dad I met

The angel caught me up
Asked to come along
I whispered, 'Why not.'
She sang my favourite song.
How did she really know
That was in my head
Said she picked it up
From my grieving bed.

As night began to give
I moved up in pace
Then it finally dawned
I'd missed the obvious place.
My dad was here and there
Wherever I was, so's he
Cos you know it's simple
My dad lives on, in me.

Tim Tweedy (Epsom)

Scuffing Up Leaves

I went for a walk on an autumn day
A walk filled with so much pleasure,
At the end of my walk inside my head
There were so many memories to treasure.

The leaves had turned colour and falling fast
I scuffed through them whilst on my walk,
They crackled beneath my feet and then
I spotted a high-flying hawk.

Was it laughing at me scuffing up leaves
Kicking them high in the air,
If it was on this beautiful morning then I
Was much too happy to care.

I crossed the bridge by the chestnut trees
Squabbling ducks swimming by,
The clouds seemed edged with a silver lining
Suspended up high in the sky.

I retraced my steps still scuffing up leaves
Three riders on horseback went past,
The field by the bridle path sign has been ploughed
Summer's behind us at last.

Memories of floods and the heartache they caused
Have been ploughed in the earth and yet,
On such a beautiful morning like this
It's a summer I'll never forget.

But this morning's a morning for scuffing
For scuffing up leaves with my feet,
And giving myself an ode memory
And a back to my childhood free treat.

Just imagine this little old lady
Over three score years and add ten,
Scuffing up leaves with delight and
Next week I shall do it again.

Beryl Osborne (Gloucester)

Laura Is Full

An ocean of brown liquid, cold, salty,
half a spuddy block remains.

Eight peas, they lie alone,
uneaten. Lonely.

Speck of carrot. Small.

Natalie Stallard (Reading)

Ode To Sparrows

I'm glad I begin to sing with words to blend of joy and praise, thereafter sad having to append as an end - your appraise in harrowing sparrow-woe - there within you tell wherefore what mysteriously befell you weak although knowing little nerds, who knew therefore flew so well instinctively north -
Lured to wheresoever the wind blew you natively south-inured emigrant birds; as if by some providence - fate to reach our island - conservatory gate, where through without dither to town and country - where its at - ate; to come - hither reside inside whatever may bide in building, tree or hedge -
You to - be conspicuous, ubiquitous, finch-like, invaders of
brown-fledge.

And so with passion come-o-will to have without ration your contumely fill of breeding; to and fro - feeding on insect, grub, morsel, seed and grain, to so sustain and so to consume so timely that which God's will provided; whether on land or in sky as one none too shy to multiply you were therewith never divided. Wastelanders to boot, in your constitutional - swooping-forays, only disappearing to rough it for lonely cooping stays in any suitably-sized nook or cranny - your indisputably-prized resourcefulness is uncanny.

Rightly so opportunely in the chronology of ornithology you were in
retrospect a sight so communally-prolific, although with respect to dearest hen being fearless boss of amorous, hen-pecked cocks - your capacity with alacrity to breed is quite numerically terrific - ironical therefore that you few who flew here did gender to render such abundant flocks. Wherein observed to be it unnerved whenever in constant hopping-orbit therein - so be it - concomitant pigeon-satellites, albeit commensally with all endemic host to rival even the starlings' numeric boast, whereupon reaching such inimitable heights henceforth surviving the whenceforth inimical stalk of the once thriving sparrow hawk.

So why did you cheeky, chirping, hoppers . . . 'come a cropper?' . . . The tree, hedge, and especially the house sparrow reply: 'Where are your town horses with their nose-bag droppings? . . . on which we swooped to sweep your streets clean of . . . ?
Where are your unploughed post-harvest fields of oat and wheat
croppings . . . ? Which in the autumn we loved to glean of . . . ? Why are your gardens now so bereft of the dock, fat hen and chickweed seed we need . . . ?'

'Why have your wastelands and wild flowers become motorways and towers . . . ? on which we used to breed and feed . . . ?' Why did your environmental construction and destruction take its toll . . . ? And why have your cats taken their without compunction cull . . . ? at such a cost . . . hence ten million of us were lost!'

Gerald Weeks (London)

A Feline Elegy

One of a job lot from a shop in Penge in South London
You 'Black Cat' with 'White Cat' as a kind of 'alter ego'
Not even personalised by a name just by a colour difference
Perhaps because you were replacing a named special feline loss
Wittgenstein the philosopher would argue each colour defines the other
But 'Black Cat' you certainly never did live in her shadow
Rather she in yours and then usually scuttling away from its edges
For you were the King while she was not even your poor mean Queen
Rather as a demean with your rule and affection so prominent
You deigning to relate as you so pleased to your loving mistress
Feeding on feline caviar and the milk of her human kindness
Not drunk by 'White Cat' jealous and zealous to keep a feline pureness
And so you had pilchards and chicken whilst she just the common tins

I did not know you then in your well time of feline prime
But only in your maturity where still your pride and power glimmered
Within an overcoat of greater softness in your frame of stiffness
Wherein the lovely yellowness of your eyes showed clear signs of mellowness
And ever you came to me to say hello in failing feline greeting sounds
Certainly no elective mute you managed finally to find an oral greeting
Touchingly comic sometimes but open-mouthedly genuine and given with grace
And often you allowed yourself to enter my heart as well as my arms
Where in rare privilege you would lay with purrs and no demurs
As ever of course you so did within those of your loving mistress
More I remember how in your last days you suffered your tired limbs
To climb weakly into my lap of compassion to be stroked and soothed
And to have all your pains and stresses calmed to pleasure purrs

When I told you then of how lovely and brave you were
I remembered how you had not even minded when I invaded your mien
That time when I took the grass snake away that you had so patiently hunted

Perhaps even then you knew that to the Pharaohs serpents were wise
And also that cats like you were so specially revered and venerated
That on death they were anointed, wrapped and preserved as a mummy
So you too 'Black Cat' can now live forever as a Phoenix in Paradise
And like with the Pharaohs your soul can rise to the heavenly stars
To rejoin and shine in your body there with all hearts that have loved you
So 'Black Cat' I look always to the evening Orion and its constellation
And in its starlight ever see you shining there with all other feline hosts
Just also you well shine in the heart of your loving mistress and in mine
Where 'Black Cat' you well do rest as an amulet of loving memory

D Viall (Oxford)

Binscombe Barn

Standing here four hundred years
I've heard the laughter, I've seen the tears
Struck by lightning, covered in snow
Yonder oak tree from a sapling grow

Cromwell's roundheads slept when they came
Cavaliers did just the same
Some carved their names upon my walls
Their horses tethered in my stalls

Sally Beckett danced and twitched
When they hanged her as a witch
She visits sometimes before the dawn
But never in her earthly form

Kitchener's troops once gathered here
They took the shilling, drunk lots of beer
Those whom God kept from all harm
Returned to work upon the farm

I've sheltered the ploughman's working teams
While nervous mice dart across my beams
Housed sheep and cattle, sometimes grain
Protected travellers from driving rain

I've heard the morning rooster's crow
Seen the barn owls fledglings grow
I've been a home to waifs and strays
To watch them go their separate ways

There was a fire it destroyed my thatch
The workmen made a perfect match
With hammers, chisels, sharpened saws
Repaired my boarding, renewed my doors.

They installed windows, walls, a chimney stack
Gone are my stalls and the old hay rack
No longer do I creak and groan
Since converted to a family home.

K Nunn (Godalming)

Hope

Where can I find the hope I need?
What reasons have I to live?
Why struggle through each exhausting day
Till I've nothing left to give?

Hope will always be with you,
A shining gleam each day;
A candle in a darkened room,
A star to guide the way.

But I feel so tired and lonely,
My soul is grey and bare.
All hope just easily fades away
When I'm overcome by despair.

Hope is a loyal and trusty friend
To save you, lest you drown
In a flood of black and frightening thoughts
That threatens to drag you down.

Confusion overwhelms me,
I'm ready to give up the fight.
I have no hope to carry me through
This endless, ghastly night.

What force has been protecting you,
Kept you fighting for so long?
Hope is buried deep in your heart,
Its warmth has made you strong.

I cannot find this hope you describe
Or believe that it exists;
My world and vision are dimly blurred
By thick and gloomy mists.

Hope is found and seen and felt
Amidst great sorrow and pain:
Just watch the evening's setting sun
And believe it will rise again.

Sarah Dodds (Weybridge)

My Secret Garden

I know a little bielded place
Where progress has not shown its face,
A place of peace and loveliness,
Natural beauty, timelessness,
Where I can meditate and free
Myself of things that bother me.

Upon the grass-clad chalky ground
Many wild flowers do abound,
Yellow cowslips, milkwort blue,
Several kinds of orchid too.
Pyramid, purple, spotted, bee,
Wave their heads for me to see.

Travellers Joy up in the hedge,
Beyond grow grasses, rushes, sedge
Blue butterflies frequent this place,
Red admirals rest on Queen Anne's Lace
Twittering birds sing out their songs
With joyful hearts all day long.

No traffic noise to mar the bliss,
I wander round in happiness.
There are no pylons standing here,
Nor marching 'cross the landscape there.
No 'tis always peaceful see,
It cuddles round and comforts me.

Where is this place? I cannot tell,
For you would tell your friends as well.
They'd all turn up with big sun hats
And radios and cricket bats
And leave their litter all around,
With Coke cans scattered on the ground.

Then would this earthly Paradise
Become Hell's kitchen in a trice.
I want this place to always be
A place where I can just be me,

To leave the noisy world behind
For one day just to clear my mind
To gaze at nature at its best
And give my tired self a rest.

Jacqueline Veitch (Aldershot)

The Chilterns

I open my hand
and close it a little,
and there the Chilterns lie:
cradled like a cup.
The mounds at the base of my fingers,
sleeping dragons that green,
stretch to the headland
above gold corn stubble that whiskers fields
bordered by hedges scarred by the flail -
and straight chalk paths
edged with the ancient colours of royalty.
Purple elder, red-painted hips
and leaves trimmed with gold.
On and on the plain stretches
until the woods gather
to cup their content.

High up,
the sun-burnished fingertips of a kite
claim the space
where platoons of clouds
quick march in disordered ranks;
and below the troops,
floating unmartialled,
grey wisps trail.
White billows through like the petticoats
of an Impressionist girl on a swing -
the grey, the silk of her Sunday best.
All set off by the sky-blue bows.

From the escarpment
I wave unseen.
With hand open, fingers wide,
the cup slips from my grasp
shattering on the turf.

I bend down,
open my hand -
and close it a little,
to cup in my palm a fragment of sky,
gently swaying in the breeze.
A delicate harebell.

Carol Ball (High Wycombe)

The Abattoir

Take off your mask of dignity
You're naked now for all us to see
Despite the common's outrageous plea
Rocked the heart of society

You've entered into the abattoir
Where they like them young and fresh
You've entered into the abattoir
Where they eat your flesh

Powerful men in powerful places
Pulling up their trousers and hiding their faces
Sin and sex are plain to see
But you've had an affair with bureaucracy

You've entered into the abattoir
Where they like them young and fresh
You've entered into the abattoir
Where they eat your flesh

You can run but you can't hide
Your so-called friends will take a bribe
The gutter press won't let it ride
The knife is deep in your side

You've entered into the abattoir
Where the pinstripes stand and gloat
You've entered into the abattoir
See the blood run from your throat

The flash of bulbs is in your eyes
You're screaming - they're not surprised
Will we ever know who told the lies?
They're swarming round like hungry flies

You've entered into the abattoir
They'll watch you slowly die
They'll watch you slowly die
They'll watch you slowly die

Andrew Mussell (Slough)

Forbidden Love

Forbidden is my love for you
Though the feelings are deep and strong
You and I - we belong to another
So being here with you is so wrong.

Yet passion keeps me coming back
I want it from you more and more
The chemistry is electric between us
You fill my being deep down to the core.

You have such a hold over me
Your power - it rushes through my veins
I'm addicted to you - just like heroin
And this feeling is why I remain.

We'll continue to meet in secret
And carry on this passionate affair
Sometimes I think it's all worth the risk
If we were caught, I just wouldn't care.

Don't get me wrong, I love my husband
And I know too that you love your wife
The consequences are unimaginable
Discovery would cause all sorts of strife.

But the magnetic attraction it draws us
We get lost amid its might along the way
How much longer can our forbidden love continue?
When it could be found out any day.

But until such a time may arise
We must enjoy the times that we share
For if they should come to an end
I cannot say that I wouldn't care.

Life would be so less bearable
If I could not feel you inside
So, for this reason, my love
Our attraction we'll continue to hide.

Joanne Hale (Bristol)

A Slipped Hand

(1)
God had only extended His hand
To bless the man

But the man exploded
As a suicide bomb
Embracing him
God shouting to his deaf ears,
'Holy book is not greater than God'

Blast! God's hand all burnt
Shaky

His words are now:
Dragged lines of fire
on a crimson canvas hanging
over a violently raped city

A despot's statue crumbling to rubble
A smile on his face:
'I shall have my day
Fools are many
Religion is greater than God.'

(2)
The injured God is at loss
When did He cut off His thumb?
Passed it on to a man,
Posing as Dhronacharya

He knows now why there is no more
His thumbprint on the world!

Man knows, He can't hold a pen
And so, the words
are nothing but
garbled drag marks
on a bloody sky . . .

(3)
Who is the culprit?
Who has dragged heavy lines of light
on a polished glass of sky

with the aeroplanes
hovering like vultures
on the sky
above a hapless
thunderously coughing
city?
Boom, boom.

Come, come
watch the spectacles of words
hanging like a dark cloud of smoke
over the city gang raped by the politics.

The one ignites the fire knows:
Man invented the words
God only spoke them as commanded!

Yogesh Patel (Morden)

Plum Pudding Hill

You couldn't fail to notice or hear them
If you happened to be in, or on the periphery of the park.
Crowds of children, young and vibrant
Carrying their mother's tea-trays and old
Cardboard boxes or bread carriers,
Stealthily stolen or legitimately procured
From the bread man's van.
They took anything and everything imaginable
In order to slide down the great hill.

It was an early summer's morning,
Long before the sun was ready to clothe the grass
Or the road, wrapping everything in its searing heat
In and around Greenwich Park.
The air was alive with chatter and the shouts of 'Hooray!'
Emitted from the mouths of excited children
As they began the arduous climb up from the bottom of the hill.
It was considered, the high point of their day
When, once they had reached the top, the anticipation
Of the sheer, heady exhilaration of the slide down
Made them all feel ill with excitement.

They each knew, when their goal was in sight
Because the Observatory would come into view;
And their shouts of achievement could be heard for miles.
A long line of them, puffing and panting from carrying
The cardboard boxes, tea-trays and bread carriers
Were silhouetted against the sun, bent over forwards
Hoping it might ease their exhaustive haul.
And then, suddenly they were there,
Collapsing in a gigantic heap to rest for five minutes
Before the adventurous slide down began.
Their sounds of laughter carried to the bottom where,
Passers-by, junkies and park people loitered.

And then it was off! And screams or squeals of unadulterated joy,
Along with shouts of 'Yippee' or 'Wowee!'
Zipped through the air as they zigzagged and slid
Forwards, sidewards, falling, rolling over and over
As tea trays careered off on their own, leaving some occupants
Breathless with laughter, while the rest continued on;
Slithering and sliding down, down, down to the bottom of
Plum Pudding Hill.

Alexandra Law (Launceston)

Knoll Beach

Lying in the sunshine,
Sky blue as far as I can see.
I wish that you were mine,
While you lie here next to me.

Children laughing and running,
Building castles in the sand.
I wish while you are sleeping
You would hold onto my hand.

I wish the children around us
Were made of you and me.
I wish you and I were us
As we walk next to the sea.

Sometimes I see the fish
Swimming through the weeds
The gulls land beside me
To rest, sleep and feed.

This beach reflects my mood
Today it does the same.
Last night you were so good
My life won't be the same.

So quiet and peaceful here,
When I usually come,
And now that you are here
See what it has become.

A beach as busy and exciting
As my heart feels inside,
But I keep on waiting
Beached by your tide.

You can be like a storm
Exciting, fierce and strong.
You make me feel so warm
Don't leave me too long.

Naomi Preston (Poole)

Requiem For A Tree

No whispering wind this
But hurricane force . . . roaring,
Raging, wild in its defiant destruction.

Like a giant hand,
Clutching and ravishing,
Breaking and bending
All in its path.

How we trembled that October night -
Waiting for the dawn . . .
In fearful anticipation
Then, the morning light:

Chaos and devastation,
Storm smashed windows,
Gaping roofs and splintered glass,
Wreckage and debris everywhere.

And oh! - the trees, hundreds of them
Torn and sadly inert on the ground
Roots grotesquely exposed
Or leaning drunkenly on walls or masonry.

My tree - my Sea Lane tree
That once stood proudly
Like a guardian by the shore
Now like a stranded whale still and broken
No more to gaze upon.

But today I heard a
Blackbird singing
And my heart lifted
For I know that we shall plant -

And in the years to come,
With sun and gentle rain
Forests of trees
Will flourish and live again.

Dorothy Daniel (Worthing)

That Solitary Moment

There is a love that seeks your life
Its footsteps you may hear.
There silent as a butterfly
But you'll know them crystal clear.
It stands beside that stream life
Near the presence of your life.
Quietly there abiding
Like the still of a pleasant candlelight.
He waits in humble dressing
At a distance ever near.
Tis I! Tis only I friend
I call that you might hear.

Words that you will n'er forget
Nay, not all your days.
Like nothing else shall matter
Upon those words He says.
Words that speak no words at all
Like an echo of His call.
Love solitary shepherd
A gentle tap upon the door.
How fortunate to hear those words
From the 'Shepherd' Christ Himself.
The orphan of the world has come
What a privilege for yourself.

I come that you may journey
In a far, far better way.
I'll walk with you each footstep
I'll bequeath your final day.
Dearest heart be not shamed -
That I should enter in.
I come that I may serve you
To take away your sin.
To comfort through those stings of life
The shadows and the fears.
To take away those prison bars
That's bound you all those years.
No matter for those dusty shelves
No paint upon the door.
No matter for the baroness
Or nothing on the floor.
No matter for the nakedness
Where nothing you can hide.
No matter for the anger
The kindled fire inside.
No matter of selected words
You cannot find to speak.
I don't search for stars or heroes
Or heights of wondrous feats.

I come to rest your hand to mine

We'll sup the cup of friendship wine.
No more shall you be parched and dry
I'll always be, that you may dine.

Michael A Massey (Cheddar)

My History In Words

My history's in my bookshelf but I've given it away.
Somehow the titles no more suit me in the present day.
The languages I tried to learn, the stories that they held,
were woven into sorrows of my life I cannot tell.
Needless to say, they caused me to act out for a brief spell.

And to my sharp chagrin, I glanced upon the clothes I wore.
Somehow, they do not fit me in the way they did before.
The parties I squeezed into, pouring me into *that* dress,
attracted those who up against my flesh wanted to press.
Needless to say, I *never* handed them my home address!

The heels that tried to topple me are out of my life too.
Somehow their phallic symbolism pandered more to you.
Asphyxiated in my outfit, shoehorned to conform,
Needless to say, I couldn't have been *further* from the norm!

The remnants of my nights were often strewn around the place.
Somehow my innards couldn't stand the make-up on my face.
Nor could my soul support the view reflected in the glass,
so jettisoned rejection, whilst my tears cleaned up the past.
Somehow I clung onto the hope that you would come around . . .
Needless to say, you didn't, rendering my hopes unsound.

And so it came for *me* to recollect my soul *again*.
I *somehow* knew that *this* time I had grown up from the pain.
I *somehow* sensed that *somewhere* lay my pre-planned destiny.
One book is all it took to redefine my legacy.
I didn't need the former and forgave what had occurred,
an action which was triggered by one greater and which stirred
my spirit to run free from all the useless self-reproach,
accept a *brand new* history, accept a *new* approach.
This led me to clear out the life which really *wasn't* me,
which truly wasn't at the heart of who I *came* to be.

Somehow, I dance and draw my name in dust upon the shelf,
Somehow, I sing and *love* the emptiness, where once was self.
Somehow, my wardrobe houses less and less, in terms of clothes.
Somehow, conditions are not bound to what the wide world knows.
How *something* so *upright* and *vertical* as my bookcase
could change my whole existence from the summit to the base,
is something that I'll smile at but no longer will explore.
Needless to say, I'd need more words,
but they've all gone before.

Coda Quashie (London)

What Lays Beyond My Prayer For You?

My friend is critical with infections
What lays beyond a doctor's skill?
Can faith respond to his intentions?
Prayer bring peace within God's Will?

Vigils come to those that worry
How can I face the fears inside?
Tendency is Your Will to hurry
What then to learn remains untried

Doubts are Demons you must resist
In all your being, shun them now
On God's love, you can exist
The path to truth will show you how

You look down, I know, such despair
When on high your eyes should see
Whole again, and in repair
Mending your eternity

O Father above, You know all things
You feel the pain - it's intense
Surpassing strength, let loose the strings
So a man may climb to Your defence

What lays beyond I cannot fathom
But go look for Him, my friend
He's made a bridge to cross this chasm
You will come through in the end

I pray these things so you may know
You're not alone all by yourself
Through Jesus' name, this prayer will go
Restoring you to vibrant health

Let God control, do not be scared
Just let your heart receive again
The gift of love that's freely shared
This Heavenly truth - *Amen*.

Mike Buchanan (Chippenham)

A Star Struck Youth

As a youth of just nineteen
So young, naïve and very green
away from home so very far
There on the continent of Africa

An infantryman sent without a say
I saw the desert far away
A million stars the Milky Way
Across a cloth of black velvet lay

Fifty years plus since there I saw
Nature's majesty filling me with awe
Fantastic myriads of shining lights
Searing days and chilly nights

A camel, what a curious beast
Designed by a committee at the very least
They could carry a house for a country mile
Protesting, complaining all the while

But when night fell I would see
Millions of stars there just for me
A soldier of his country pressed
Thinking that nature always does it best

I wonder often in the night
Will I ever see again the sight?
Of a rich black backdrop set alight
With a million pinpricks in the night

Each star twinkling in its place
Reaching towards me from outer space
So beautiful and surely nature's intent
To show her sparkling firmament

Night-times at home are not the same
The sky at night seems awfully tame
To that in Egypt wonderingly seen
By this soldier lad of just nineteen.

John Perry (Rickmansworth)

Sing Skylark, Sing

Lying in a summer meadow,
gazing at the distant misty heavens,
heat haze shimmer blurs the land.
Long grasses bend and sway
bedecked with chirping crickets
like sailors perched in rigging,
while high above, lost in palest blue
a skylark sings.

A gentle humming sound envelopes me,
the soft buzz of insects
busy with ephemeral lives
lulls me into somnolence,
the grass a cool caressing cushion,
and up above
a skylark sings.

I doze, I dream; another meadow,
a wartime childhood pasture long ago,
safe haven somewhere deep in rural England
far away from nightly wailing sirens,
rushing fire bells, barking guns.
I watch, as miles above
a steady drone becomes a roar.
Formating bombers wheel and turn,
dark predatory flocks with deadly loads
eastward-bound, close-knit for comfort now
unlike tomorrow's dawn, homecoming,
straggling, limping, battle-weary groups
or singly, flying low.
Yet clearly audible above the din
a skylark sings.

I slowly wake to present day;
my eyelids wet, with dewdrops?
A sudden welcome summer shower,
a myriad rainbow droplets
splash the crisp dry grass,
refresh the hard-baked earth.
Dark clouds obscure the sun,
but all the while
a skylark sings.

Throughout my life a single thread
links past to present day.
In all those memories from along ago
through boyhood, youth and later still
in foreign fields to manhood, and today
a skylark sings.

How will it be when memory fades?
Will sensual summer sounds forsake my mind?
Perhaps acceptance of those final days

will somehow be less hard to bear
if, at the end,
a skylark sings.

Tony Drakeford (Wimbledon)

After And Before

Strange.
I never thought that I
would hold your hand
or catch your eye

or feel
your eager warm embrace
or look upon
your upturned face

or miss you
when you were not there.
Not by me, with me,
but gone, where?

I did not know then
that each day
just you around
is all I may

forever want
or wish to have
or should you leave
you're all I crave,

I did not know then
it would be
that all the world
is you and me.

I did not know then
there's a door
that opens or closes
on before.

I love you now,
I loved you then
And will I
love you once again?

And play shy games
of him and who
and ask, half knowing,
'Who are you?'

Strange.

Pam Redmond (Taunton)

227

The Real Stroud

That Stroud is now a 'green' place is incredible to me,
When I remember it to be the heart of industry.
Where mills belched smoke and spewed out waste in river and canal,
And noisy oily steam trains transported coal and mail.

To gain an insight to the past we'll view from on the hills
To see a sprawling Stroud below with great extent of mills.
Of tall chimneys, now sadly gone, work buildings clustered near
Which combined to produce each week - cloth, plastic, pressboard, beer.

Also of Danarms, bricks and bearings - of engineering too
Of sawmills and asbestos from which disease could imbue.
Of shirt and clothing factories where women worked the shift
To help out with finances and give family life a lift.

The work day began early, about sixish I would say,
When men with lunch in canvas bags to work wended their way.
On foot or bike - sometimes by bus, rarely for them by car -
Their aim to stamp their card on time whether travelled near or far.

The noise increased at this time, hooters hooted, as did trains,
People packed tight in buses - well steamed up when it rained!
Shops opened doors, good smells emerged, most closed at one Thursday
And also during lunchtimes - then more main meals ate midday.

It was seven o'clock when weary workers wended their way home
Near Rodborough common where I lived and where I daily roamed.
The steep hills tested stamina after a twelve hour day
And sharpened up folks' appetites for the meal coming their way.

It's thought we are cleaned up now with no grimy heavy fare,
We eat organic food now - said to give us years to spare!
We exercise in clubs now 'cause we sit always in cars
Instead of using shankies to convey us near or far!

But for me Stroud was a greener place even with the smoke,
Then roads were quiet and cars did less on everywhere encroach.
Factories held fetes and there were 'weeks' and Sunday was Sunday
So we could regain some energy to sustain us on our way!

Joy Thacker (Stroud)

Some Thoughts For Abroad

Oh to be . . . well anywhere
Now that winter's here,
But it must be in the sunshine,
And they must sell English beer,

And a bedroom with a balcony,
And a band that plays all night.
Oh! Only English food, of course,
'Uno porko chopo' and chips, alright?

The language now can be a prob.
But they usually catch on,
Just shout it out, quite loud and slow,
Two-beers-over-here-my-son.

It's on the beach and in the sea
That we 'Brits,' can really shine,
We form big groups and run about,
Till the Germans call us sehwine.

A visit then to the local town,
Or better still a brewery,
It doesn't take long to get tanked up.
Then we all meet again in surgery.

Too soon the frolics run their course
And we must start our packing,
Time now to leave the fun and sun
(And that special Spanish crackling!)

We lose and find and lose again
Our wallet, funds and passport,
And just when we think we've got it right,
We miss the bus to the airport.

Airborne at last and settled down,
Though we've lost that new windcheater,
Now for the first of the 'last' of the drinks,
Two-beers-over-here-Conchita.

Paul Cox (Plymouth)

Still

If I ever knew the intensity of that which I have felt
I would have never loved.
I would have closed myself and unclothed myself and
thrown away the key,
for the true meaning of love, yes the true meaning of love can
only end in death.

As I ask the Gods to take me away from this,
relieve my heart from these woes, and
release my body and my mind from the temptation of
cold, hot, cold, hot, I am going to either explode or become so numb
that the heat which wants to burn inside, will at the end kill me.

So what do I do.
Cry, hold on, tear my bright hair, walk the street, do not eat,
be alone
or do I brave the cold and open myself to the possibility
of warm glowing hands that I want to be able to touch me?

My dreams take me to those places
where those hands touch me,
it is so lovely.
I want to go there all the time and yet when I awake
I want this to be also a dream. I want the dream to come true.

How do dreams come true? Why can't dreams come true?
No longer can we hold on to a dandelion and blow
making our wishes as the seeds scatter themselves all over the world.
My dream. Our dreams come true by closing of the eyes and
allowing ourselves to be transported to a world

a world where we are able to say, I love you.
I am sorry.
Will you forgive me!
A world which is right here and exists where you are.
This is your world.
This is my world
and it is only here that all of our dreams can come true.

Do not be scared,
do not allow the real nature of love to kill you
for as I have said
true love will never kill you
better to taste the juices of the fruit than to not taste at all
as the saying goes
better to have loved than to have never loved at all.

Climb out of those dreams and
surrender yourself to making love.
The eating of the fruit will not kill you, it will however bring you feelings
and so will love.

Will you love me like I love you?
Will you allow the heat of our love to consume us?
Will you love me like I love you?

Will you be mine
still.

Marcia Michael (London)

On A Knife Edge

As knives stab where kudos reigns
role models lack the means to breach
this gang debate wears out the reasons
no headway leaves the streets replete
               of answers . . .

    As predators remove birds from trees
    where lesser leaves fall onto concrete
    territorial fights usurp free wheeling
    as postcodes name their border rights.

    Treading softly lest ruffling feathers
    cocks of the walk strut their stuff;
    and another life is lost to us
    before innocence embraces trust.

Self-defence and self-protection
where must the pride before the fall -
as ever the bullies to be feared:
younger and younger recruits adhere
to being tested to advance career
becoming members where all meet
in an order - a 'brothers' clique . . .

A 'family' without generations gulf
that gap now filled with targets brief
setting the margins to draft new rules
from those don'ts old fogies preach.

    Scripts rewritten to promote,
    provoke yet another killing -
    in such affray a life is taken
    adding an extra notch to that CV.

    The media munches through statistics
    counting fatalities as lethal gains;
    while parents mourn, flowers are laid
    to the next victim slain.

    So many words, so many tears
    but overall the plot's the same,
    only ex-members can expose and
    denounce such raw futility . . .

As can be seen I am no youth,
ever loth to spurn the young
but ever hopeful for a braver truth.

Wendy Sullivan (London)

Black Aller Wood

I came to see the bluebells
The wood was filled with the scent.
Sunshine pouring through the trees
As along the path I went.

The breezes blew the bell like heads
Although there was no sound
It was as if they formed a dance
In their lapis coloured gowns.

The trees were swathed in flowing green
Fresh and bright this spring.
Shading all that lie beneath
The alder stands so trim.

The path that took me through the wood
Brought memories back to me.
When I played among the laurels
Where the rabbits used to be.

In the daylight all was calm
The senses lost in time
But at night the trees did form
Dark shadows in design.

Then my heart would pound
As I would run past at pace
In case the tiny goblins
Came after me in chase.

Now all has changed since childhood
The years have surely flown
My demons faded from my mind
A new copse now has grown.

With its fine new carpet
Black Aller shares its display
Until the season changes
And the bluebells fade away.

Beryl Smyter-Dray (Sidmouth)

Evening Rounds

All you can hear is the wind . . . and a dog,
All you can see is the snow,
All you can feel is the biting cold air
And the question is which way to go?

Is it right? Is it left? Where's the signpost? Don't know,
Is it forward or back? - Must decide.
The Land Rover's fine with the heater full on,
But where do the animals hide?

Oh! We've come to a crossroad and there's a signpost
All covered in snow - can't be read.
Shall I get out and clear it or guess the best way?
Now come on - don't guess - use your head.

The landscape is different when covered in snow,
The boundaries they all disappear,
The hedges look flattened, the valleys ride up
And the driving is all in low gear.

The roads disappear and there in their place
Wide ribbons of white stretch ahead.
You drive along slowly and try not to skid,
Knowing some folk are tucked up in bed.

But there's cattle to check and the ewes with their lambs
And horses to feed in the yard.
When you've been all out round and you're heading for home,
The last quarter mile can be hard.

There's a glimmer of light as you drive in the yard,
Home is a wonderful place.
Having shut in the hens, fed the dog, closed the barn,
You go in with a smile on your face.

You take off your boots, brush the snow from your clothes,
Wash your hands in the sink by the door,
Supper's next, watch the news, check the mail and then bed;
Who could ask for anything more?

Susan J May (Barnstaple)

Retirement

And so I've reached that 'certain' age
When life should be so easy
So why do I feel so terrified
Of becoming an OAP?

My mind is still alert
On a PC I'm still a whiz,
OK things now take longer to do
Than when I was a kid.

I think it's because of the stigma
That the very words imply
Everyone thinks you're useless
And generally pass you by.

The young have no time for us
And government don't care
Unless there is an election
And then you'll see them there.

Oh yes they want our votes
And promise us the earth
Then when they get into power
We're forgotten in their rebirth.

The medical profession?
Which takes the Hippocratic Oath?
Is run by local governments
And you cannot serve them both.

The NHS is tied by rules
Their targets they have to meet
So if you become a bed blocker
It's a downhill one way street.

If you're also an OAP it seems
Your age then counts as well
A heart attack at 65 ish
Might ring a surgeon's bell.

He is also target driven,
And as likely as hell
To take you on cos you'll survive
Then becomes a sorry tale.

If you've been hale and hearty
For all your earthly life
At 85 you're considered too old
To risk the surgeon's knife.

Because *if* you die whilst under it
His targets he will not make
Instigated by governments
A risk he will not take.

So now you see why I'm terrified
Of living for a very long time

And soon to become an OAP
In someone else's hands not mine.

Sheila Wilmot (Bristol)

Grandmothers Aren't What They Used To Be,
Nor Are The Grandchildren

Why can't I be a granny grandma,
Someone who looks older,
And acts with slower recall.
Welcoming my siblings', siblings
I'm Gran to advise them all.
Why can't I be less energetic?
With an apron around my hips
Brushing tears away with sweet words
And no rebukes on my lips!
Why can't I be relied upon?
To be always here at home
Grannies are supposed to be stable
Not always wanting to roam
Why can't I take the ignoring?
The sullied bored looks?
When I was just a child,
I had my mind on popular books.
I see no angelic, innocent faces,
No questioning screwed up cheeks,
No 'Please Granny help us?'
Don't see them for weeks and weeks!
But I know where they are,
In a spare enclosed room,
Awe struck, watching a static PC,
The harbinger of Granny gloom.
Flashing screens and button mouses,
Little fingers working faster,
Watching PC games unfolding,
Seeing who becomes the master,
Conversation stilled and quiet,
Concentration on the grey screens,
No hellos or goodbyes,
I'm just the granny that isn't seen,
So I have to go along with progress,
Progress with a capital P,
Letting them find their own pathways,
That doesn't include conversing with me!

Margaret Blight (St Austell)

On Reflection

Father Christmas I've loved you
Ever since I was small
You left me lots of presents
For no *good* reason at all

Thanks for your visit at Christmas
Such great delight when you came
And when I knew you'd come no more
Christmas was never the same

You struggled down the chimney
I never once thought it insane
To enter a house that way
Especially in the rain!

Father Christmas I miss you
And the magic of it all
Now you've vanished from my dreams
No hope of your presents at all.

Father Christmas I loved you
From when I was very small
Oh I wish I had never discovered
Who drank your drink in the hall!

But now I know who you are
I needn't shed a tear
You're still my Father Christmas
And not for just one day in the year!

To pretend is often better
Than to face the truth
Always make believe
And cling to the dreams of your youth

Always believe in magic
Don't always believe what you're told
Your life will be that much richer
Sweet dreams are better than gold.

John C E Potter (Bournemouth)

A River Of Tears

A smile on my face and I say that I'm fine
trying hard to hide what's within.
I don't want to show
that inside me I know
there's a river lurking under my skin.
A river of tears
containing sadness and fears
just below the surface - you see.
It doesn't take much
a simple word that can touch
and bring out an eruption in me.
From my head to my toes
it bubbles and flows
as I try hard to contain it inside.
Vulnerability you see
is not good for me
it hurts too much when I open up wide.
So I strengthen the dam
and do whatever I can
to try and keep it hidden from view.
I may seem quite hard
as I keep up my guard
but you don't know what I'm going through.
They say crying is good
relieve emotions that could
do more damage if I don't release.
But I'm trying to hide
the pain deep inside
to reach my own inner peace.
I'm hoping one day
to be able to say
your name - while I keep things in place.
But at the moment I fear
that time isn't near
as a single tear escapes down my face.

Julie Fluendy (Dartford)

Helston Flora Day

Flora, Furry, Faddy Dance -
Choose any name, but go
Along to Helston's Flora Day
To watch the Hal-an-Tow,

The Children's Dance, The Principal,
The Evening - final chance.
The big bass drum of Helston Band
Stirs one and all to dance.

The music is *The Floral Dance*,
By Kate Moss, they do say,
Who wrote it travelling home by train,
Inspired by Flora Day.

Of course, time changes many things;
The children now dance too,
And thirty couples from Culdrose
Join Helston couples true.

Yet golden gorse and bluebells bright
With laurel glistening green,
Still frame most doors and windowpanes
Just like it's always been.

At last we hear the big bass drum,
The dance is drawing near
And as the white-clad children pass
I wipe away a tear.

To Lismore Gardens then they dance
To take a break halfway.
Four miles of dancing takes two hours
On Helston Flora Day.

Now grey top hat and morning suit
Join hat and full-length frock,
As couples lead the midday Dance -
It's striking twelve o'clock.

They lightly dance up Meneage Street,
So elegantly dressed
In shades of every Cornish flower,
Turned out in Sunday best.

They dance through houses, shops and banks,
Past Market Place, then down
To Church Street, Willows, Cross Street House
And on through Helston Town.

At Coinagehall Street, up the hill,
The weary dancers hop
And step towards The Guildhall, where
The big bass drum will stop.

Meanwhile the Chapel's selling teas -
We rally to its call.

It's been a perfect Flora Day,
Enjoyed by one and all.

Sheila Fermor Clarkson (St Austell)

Friends

When I return to Africa
It is with friends.
Friends from other journeys,
Other times.
Our hearts beat as one
Seeing mountains
With the same eyes
Smelling sun-baked earth
With the same joy
Our minds opening
In the same way
To new people
Strange encounters
Deep feelings.
Africa binds us.
Inexplicably.

What lies beyond the hill?
Do thorn trees shade
Those mammoth giants?
Will starlings so superb greet
Our wide gaze
As myriad images of nature
Crowd the scene?
This land so old and yet
So full of birth
This land where life began.
How poignant is its skein
Around our hearts.
Dew-damp cobwebs
Thread the dawn grass
Cry of fish eagle
Roar of lion
Call of hyena
Pierce the air
Haunting our souls forever.
Friendship around the fire
Burns deep.
Beneath the night's dark ceiling
Daisied with stars
We talk and smile.
And share the silence.
Remembering the day.

Virginia McKenna (Dorking)

Epitaph For Edithmead

I often think of Edithmead before the M5 came
Bringing interchange and roundabout,
An unwanted claim to fame.
It was just a name on a rusting sign
Drunkenly pointing from the turnpike road
A nestling hamlet 'ere a planner's pen
Tore all apart with a stroke so bold
A grey tin church with a crackled old bell
Which called the faithful few
Tall green elms and a winding lane
The new road cut in two.
Beyond our orchard's leafy glade
The fields stretched out towards the sea
A patchwork quilt of light and shade
As far as distant Dunkery.
In summertime we left the lane
And walked the pathfields to the town
Hopscotched the swathes of new mown grass
And chased the drifts of thistledown.
We knew the bank where violets grew
A chestnut tree we climbed in play
Roamed meadow fringed with hawthorn hedge
Picked summer flowers along the way.
They buried the grasses under the stones
Sunk a road where the flowers grew free
Gouged out the bank where the violets hid
Razed to the ground the chestnut tree.
I no longer hear the wild spring tides
Flooding in through the estuary
All muffled now by a steady hum
As traffic flows incessantly.
So spare a thought when hurtling by
Northbound or southerly
For the fields once loved buried 'neath your wheels
And a fame which came posthumously.

Phyllis Wyatt (Wells)

The Hand

(This poem was written on reflection of Dad's last visit to my home in the Wye Valley - In memory of Telesfor Maciejewski, b. Poznan 5 Jan 1916 - d. Sherburn-in-Elmet 21 July 1998)

Back in summer that hand knew it was going to die.
It conveyed tenderness and despair in our brief goodbye.
That hand clung to me with warmth and diminishing strength;
A large hand, like a gorilla's pad, enclosed and lingered with mine.
This same hand fired a rifle, threw a grenade,
And was bloodied but survived a war;
It engineered a living, took me fishing,
Was soft and playful;
It taught me to draw.
Warm leathery fingers, protected me in crowds,
Caressed my hair, but stung the back of my legs when it chastised!

I relinquished that hand, for a life of my own.
When I blossomed and married, it gave me away.
I no longer needed its wisdom, its guidance and pain,
It simply became -
My father's hand,
Just one of a pair;
A right hand, unable to be joined in prayer -
A savage stroke deprived the left.
Fingers forever furled in a hideous fist designed by fate,
Which shook in anger at its entombed, crippled state.

Back in summer that hand knew it was going to die.
It knew my eyes would well their salty spring
More viciously than anything
That powerful hand could inflict.
Yet, I'm glad I knew that hand again
To see it wave to me from the train,
A final farewell, no need for words -
Too late, it would have been absurd.
Enough to be reacquainted with its affection and grip
Held out to me, across death's abyss.

D Mariana Robinson (Lydney)

A Rose

Gently petals of velvet soft unfold
Reveal a beauty that is majestic and serene
In a shade of pale cream
This elegant bloom
With its delicate perfume
As a radiance beyond compare

Joyce Sherwood (London)

'Sal'

My love has long gone,
I remember the day,
When with Sally, my Sal
We reclined on the hay.
The sun gilded her tresses
Which the light glistened on,
And the smell of the hay
In my mind lingers on.
Though the sun it still shines,
And the scent of the hay,
Still perfumes the air,
On a hot summer's day.
The hours together,
We reclined in the lea,
With the warmth of the sun,
And the drone of a bee,
Have long gone away,
For we drifted apart,
Now we no longer rest
On the hay, or the cart.
At night on my bed,
I remember with sorrow
The days long ago -
We thought not of tomorrow.
I dream of my Sally,
Throughout the night hours,
And in day reminisce,
Of the times that were ours.
I long for the time
When she slept in my arms;
I ne'er shall forget
Sweet Sal and her charms.
Does she lie on her bed
As often I do,
When sleep will not come
The whole night through?
And think about me
In the same fond way,
And remember the hours
We reclined on the hay?
Does she yen for our youth -
For the years have flown past -
As often I do?
For our youth didn't last.
For now I am old,
And grey and tired,
And I yearn for my youth,
Which so swiftly expired.
For my Sal has long gone,
I remember the day,

When with Sally, my Sal,
We slept on the hay.

B J Webster (Eastleigh)

This Day

This day will become yesterday.
Tomorrow we have yet to see.
This day is now,
Use it constructively.
What happened yesterday
May influence today.
What you do today,
May influence tomorrow.
All in good time,
Life's rules, we must obey.
Our lives are made up of days and nights,
With some wrongs and some rights.
All of these experiences
Are for a purpose.
They are there for you to review.
Perhaps you may wish to make some changes.
At least one or two.
This day is important,
It is as important as the next.
With all of its challenges and complexities.
It becomes a written text.
With all the highs and lows,
This can leave you perplexed.
Treat this day as a building block,
With which you can build upon.
Build with strength,
Which you know you can rely upon.
Days turn into weeks,
Weeks into months,
Months into years.
365 days,
Each different from the next,
It is meant to be.
Give each day its priority.
Also live life,
With dignity, honesty, depth and quality.
A meaningful life.
This should lead to contentment.
Then happy you will be.
Knowing this day,
Part of your life,
Is yours in its entirety.

Sheila Booth (Ruislip)

Where Did It All Go Wrong?

I don't know why I feel so much sorrow
When I see you drive aggressively.
I don't know why I care
When you disregard your own life.
Can't figure out why it pains me
To see you drink until you're drunk.
Can't put my finger on it
Why you need your knives to act so hard.
Can anyone explain where it all went wrong?
Can anyone tell me why it is we rush?
Since when did our lives mean so little?
Tell me why it seems like we all stopped caring.

I know why I feel so much sorrow
And I know why I care.
I can feel the pain of all those lost
To time, to impatience, to stupidity and violence.

So when you drive don't be so angry
When you cross, look where you are
When you drink, ask what it's for
Put down your knives, put out the rage
When did life become inconsequential?

Small changes can have big effects
We are humans one and all
Born in the same way
With a mother and a father
Regardless of race, gender or religion
When we have so many similarities
Why do we fight about the differences?

Think before you act
Love before you hate
Laugh before you cry
And
Love before you die.

Tracy Anne Mason (Lancing)

To The Giver And Her Gift

I love and thank you for this reason:
Simply for giving me my season.
'A time to live, a time to die',
Seemed much the same, a time to sigh.
Then you appeared, and thirty years or more
Revealed their purpose - milestones to your door.

Shaun Usher (Epsom)

Hot Summer (2006)

Connection severed
Is she lying, phone in hand,
In humid east London?

Arteries clogged
Is this call logged?
Do helicopters hover overhead
In the thick air
The smog that we have wrought?

Sirens from Lebanon
To Forest Gate

The wrong address

Medical attention not sought

Book burnings, inertia,
And circumlocution
Prolix in the heat of battle
When battle is elsewhere
Or: someone else's heartbreak
Is the worst that can happen

Talk of road maps
The National Grid
Health warnings in the heat
(Even Tenerife is colder we're told)

Making the right connection
(ie. not Iraq, Gaza,
Or West Bank settlements)

She is alright, thankfully
Is not lying in the dark
Alone
East London smoulders
Baghdad smoking
Beirut burning down.

Stephen C Middleton (Hornsey)

Fireworks

A waterfall of fireworks flickering in the air,
Booming, fidgeting fireworks, going anywhere.
Oh so bright in the moonlit sky,
Going nowhere but so very high.
With a flash and a bang the rockets arise,
All the different colours are such a surprise!

Emily Skyrme (12) (Bath)

The Man Who Never Lost A Battle

Stands still and silent, his eyes misted.
Is it tears of jubilation, exultation
Or tears for men beaten on the ground.
5,000 conquerors killed – 8,000 conquerors wounded.

The character of new achievements, of men
A history of men and battles.
The man who never lost a battle stands still and silent.
We won, we triumph, we rejoice
The loser surrenders, succumbs and submits.

I am a warrior, a soldier, a man at arms, a campaigner
But still I cry, why? What is the reason
Is this battle for my nation, for proud tradition
The gift of laurels to my name.

The reason I cry
I cry for men who march into battle with me
Wise heads upon wise shoulders
Ready to bear the brunt
March into the enemy camp, the theatre of war.

Line, rank and file, men take orders
Commands to put the enemy
Push with force, a forbidding force
Gain ground, gain control.

Injuries from shot, shell, gunpowder, bullet
Bayonet mean wound which maim, mutilate and kill
Suffering severs pain
The man who never lost a battle
Stands still and silent.

The field of battle
Yielding a stain of crimson red
The conquering air lies dormant
Inert bodies, twisted faces
Peaceful in their long, long sleep.

Departed from this troubled land
Regarded with honours in the promised land
The tired, tired and trusted men
Who survive this battle great
Sign and seem to say
'Thank God my life is safe.'

Sad and sorrowful we are for the men we lost
On this crimson battle ground
Proud staunch hearts, lion hearts
We do salute all fighting men
The man who never lost a battle
Stands still and silent.

John Churchill
Duke of Marlborough

Salutes these brave, brave men.

Christina McKechnie (Didcot)

 *Progress?*

While bonfires were once lit across highest land,
News travels in seconds now via broadband,
Replace 'air raid sirens' and 'church bell chime'
With networks 'breaking news' all the time

For years television was just black and white
Wireless didn't mean the transfer of megabyte
But analogue's been upgraded to digital grey
Wi-fi points adorn every hotel and café

Stars, compasses, telegram
Handheld GPS, inbox spam
In this age of technology, is there anything better?
Than receiving by post, a hand-written letter
In this age of technology, are we fully aware?
Of the true consequences, of what we share

They claim we've made progress
But progress in what?
They've changed the script
But we've lost the plot

For centuries musicians performed music live
Now it's download or burn, or synchronise
You used to know friends by name, face to face
Not by their email addresses or online space

Your neighbourhood used to be your playground
Now kids are all kept 'within sight' and sound
With a thousand channels for your plasma TV
Any surprise half the world now face obesity?

Rolled up maps, captain's log
Sat Nav system, online blog
In this age of want now, must have yesterday
The world shrinks, in its own reclusive way
In this age of want now, must've yesterday
Aren't we responsible, for this social decay?

They claim we've made progress
But progress in what?
They've changed the script
But we've lost the plot

Television's no longer either just black and white
It's a multicultural, multicolour insight
Reflecting ourselves and our anxieties
A mirror to the rights, the wrongs of society.

G Norman (Swindon)

247

Love Lost

As I look deep into his hazel brown eyes
I am reminded of the joy and happiness I felt with him long ago.
Such memories return with mixed emotions
as I embrace the man I called 'the one'.
His smiling face and warm embrace
evoke the feelings of true love within me,
feelings of which I tried so hard to suppress.
He draws his face towards me, speaking words of elation
so soothing to my nimble ears.
I feel my heart gently flutter
as I struggle to restrain my wayward emotions.
As much as I try to deny it, as much as I do not want it
I still love him. I am still in love with him.
But the hurt from the past is a sharp reminder
that we cannot be together.
I gaze once more at his soft brown eyes, trying to find the words to say to him.
But it is so hard to say goodbye, so hard to let go.
After all this time, after all these months,
so many days since he went away.
He finds the hurt in my eyes and begs me to return to him.
His expression is not one of folly
but of pain and regret,
the charm that he once exuberated
replaced by sorrow and guilt.
He asks for my forgiveness and speaks of promises and change.
Can we revisit that place again?
That love that was so strong, so solid for so long.
After moments of silence, in contemplation and thought
I understand what I need to do.

I take his hands one more time and smile at him quaintly,
pulling him closely to my face.
We walk back together. I do not let him go,
but look ahead preparing to start a new life with him
once more, with the love of my life.

Mary Ibeh (Tooting Broadway)

Wicked To Wildlife

I watched a bee in a garden today,
Surely the buzzer had lost his way,
Flying around between the showers,
Searching about looking for flowers.
What a bad day the bee was having,
There is no pollen in crazy paving.

John Bennett (Morden)

Bob

She looked at him, he looked at her
And I knew it was love at first sight
She walked towards him,
He walked towards her
And it seemed to be so right.
A friend of ours had told her of him
His contentment, shyness and charm
So she thought to come and meet him
Would certainly do no harm.
She'd been very lonely for quite some time
Her children had homes of their own
And her house was far too tidy
Since she had been all alone
So she came to my place one morning
And I introduced her to Bob
As he wagged his tail and licked her hand
I knew he would be just the job
When he came to me he was hungry and thin
His coat was tangled and long
But now he was clean, had put on weight
Was happy, healthy and strong
She took him home to her little house
So neat, tidy and trim
But now there are hairs all over the place
But her life has been transformed by him
He can bury his bones in the garden
And they go for long walks in the park
She knows she is safe with Bob by her side
Especially at night when it's dark
As she sits in her chair in the evening
With Bob lying there at her feet
She fondles his head, he looks up at her
And they both know their lives are
Complete.

Barbara Dalton (Reading)

Memories

Memories stir in celebration
Nostalgic thoughts, commemoration
Silent dreams, those distant smiles
That fill the gaps and cross the miles
Whatever comes, may have gone before
Treasured memories galore.

K H Allen (Salisbury)

Creation From Afar

We have observed from a distance
since your world begun.
Its birth a cosmic miracle
to us, a piece of fun.
We dressed it with a layer of
water, air and land
seeds and roots were scattered
our task was well in hand.

Beasts were created
to wander, feed and breed
enough space for all we thought
no killing, there's no need.
Things became out of hand
too much, too quick, we thought.
That's when we made our first mistake,
the addition of *'man'!*

We shared the planet evenly
different colours, creeds and looks.
Each area, a climate change.
That was when the wars began . . .

We're back now, only gone a while
2000 years we think
To use a short haul journey
to you, eternity.
We watched the tape recordings
What's been going on?
So many wars, disasters,
Much has disappeared, gone!

Over half of our creation
destroyed by fire, flood.
Man's destructive nature
no concern for any life.
The animals and the forests
depleted by a foe
of endless greed, insanity
to sate the lust for wealth.

Let's stop here and think awhile
and ponder what to do
this was not supposed to happen
what has the world become? . . .

We're leaving now, so sorry
no more of this hate
a planet with a death wish
      'One'
we did not create.
Too many leaders
Kings and queens of 'what'?
A planet's only purpose . . .

to push the self-destruct!

L. G. F. Walsh (Liskeard)

Beerswines And Spirits

When the supermarket's quiet at the end of the day
The beerswines and spirits all come out to play

The swines drink their beer from a can with a widget
They swig and they lurch and they fiddle and fidget

The spirits watch carefully and make their escape
From alongside the wines marked 'Australia' and 'Cape'

They wait for the moment when no one's around
And together they strut, never making a sound

The beerswines wear grins and with lager they slobber
The spirits all play hide-and-seek and just hover

When workers are checking computers and files
The beerswines and spirits cavort down the aisles

And on All Hallows Eve in the dead of the night
These mischievous ghosts will give someone a fright

Cos it's then they'll materialise in your supermarket
(Just drive up in your car, indicate and then park it)

But beware on that night if you hear any 'hics'
As the beerswines and spirits get up to their tricks

Ghosts love an old castle, indoors or al fresco
So why not a Morrisons, Co-op or Tesco?

The spirits will fly. Through the cereals they'll prance
Then the beerswines will sway and start dropping their pants

The spirits will pirouette gaily and frolic
While the beerswines drink anything that looks alcoholic

And now these stores open for twenty-four hours
These inebriate spooks are increasing their powers

They smell of white cider. It's difficult to mask it
They'll take things off the shelves and swap stuff in your basket

At the till if you find in your trolley, you've got
A rather large mango or a single shallot

That you didn't put in and you cannot explain
It's the beerswines and spirits enjoying a game

So when shopping, if you feel a chill down your spine
You'll know right behind you there lurks a beerswine

When the supermarket's quiet at the end of the day
The beerswines and spirits all come out to play.

Rob Barratt (Bodmin)

Remembering

I saw pictures in the sky
From the clouds up on high
All faces and shapes
Also of landscapes
And on a winter's night
See pictures in the firelight
Chestnuts to roast
As well as making toast
In the glow of the ember
All this I remember
No TV in those far gone days
Only pictures in the fire to gaze
On the windows Jack Frost
Those patterns are now lost
Snow falling on the ground
No traffic to make a sound
Spring does come
With picnics in the sun
Maytime with blossom on the boughs
A farmer his field he ploughs
Soon there will be no land
As building gets out of hand
A motorway across the fields
A farmer has lost his yield
We were poor in far gone days
But happier in a lot of ways
Penny for a bag of sweets
Or broken biscuits for a treat
Not scared to play in the street
Of any stranger we might meet
Skipping and spinning a top
And on his beat a cop
Past memories are long gone
But will always linger on.

D Doe (Hemel Hempstead)

Bad News

The room is still
Our throats have lumps at old
Yet a sadness surrounds us
You want to smile and laugh out aloud
As if you were mad, as if nothing had occurred
Him standing there
With the telephone in his hand
As he stands in shock
As his hands quiver
As he shivers inside
His face stretched from either side
His forehead gathered up
His piercing eyes the source of fright
Angry - full of anger
All those ridiculous thoughts
Running through my head
Ridiculous - unreasonable
Nothing whatsoever to do with this threat
Something that might be altered
Forever
Someone we'll never see again
The waiting
Silence not a word
As everyone thinks hard
This threatening feeling could go on endlessly
Sounds echo as the clock's seconds pass
As the radiator rattle away
The sound of breathing
Swiftly runs by from time to time
Shuffling of hands and fingers
As you cuddle yourself tight
Waiting - reassuring
Staring at that marked place
Where all these thoughts run by, slowly and painfully.

Shazia Afzal (Luton)

The Tie

Or 'where there's a will, there's a way'.

Old Bob turned up to Church one day,
In a tie most bright and florid.
It was his favourite, pride and joy,
(His wife thought it was horrid).

The congregation, in their pews,
Drew back in dazed aversion.
The elderly were horrified
At this blatant perversion.

The vicar said, 'This will not do,
We prefer a much more sombre hue,
For Communion is a sacred rite,
And your tie, by far, is much too bright!

We have a far more catholic taste,
Wear something sombre, a bit more chaste.'
Old Bob replied, 'If you insist,
It's pointless for me to resist.

But is it right and is it dutiful,
To sing of all things bright and beautiful,
And then to bid me not to wear,
A tie for which I truly care?

This is a tie I will not sever,
I'll wear it now, perchance for ever.'
And as he stormed out through the knave,
He shouted, 'I'll take it to the grave!'

The vicar cried, 'For it is certain,
When comes for you the final curtain,
I'll not bury that abomination,
I must insist upon cremation!'

And whence came that fateful day,
For as it must, tis sad to say,
It caused 'The Authories' to pause,
For in his Will he'd put a clause.

'When comes the time for me to die,
You *will* preserve my favourite tie!'
This caused his wife some great concern,
As where to put the funeral urn.

On mantle shelf it is not found,
Nor placed in consecrated ground.
For on a shelf within his shed,
Are where his remains lie instead.

And now midst rain and winter's snow,
The shed emits an eerie glow.

For round the urn, in all its glory,
The tie is tied, so ends my story.

Robert Yates (Stoke)

My Master's Dream

A country scene take at leisure
Many a hour provide great pleasure
Town and city within my reach
Warm the sun, day for beach
Hot or cold, onwards will
Take roads fast, often go slow

In quaint village bells are ringing
Pass old church choir boys singing
Hot tar road warms my tread
Long winding road into town lead
Hustle and bustle, baskets and trolleys
Shops and markets, streets and alleys

Out of town, houses of all kinds
Some are scattered, some in line
Smell of roses as I climb
Up and up the steep incline
Way is tough, will reach top
Down other side, brake to stop

Valley that's green, cool water stream
Rest a while, let off steam
Silver leaf willow in water leans
White top mountains enhance the scene
Winding old road beckons me on
Soon the stream and mountains gone

Ahead a city, cathedral and spire
City so busy will never retire
Day or night bright shining lights
Light up city, enjoy the sights
Flow ever onwards, blow on horn
Leave busy city, see fields of corn

Golden the corn, carpets of red
Poppies grow wild in green bed
Fields blue-grey specked with green
Trees and colours change each scene
Onwards must go, twist and wind
Reach blue sea, golden beach find

Use for work, use for leisure
Take you safely is my pleasure
Hot tar roads my wheels tread
Over steep hills to valleys lead
Black and polished, my windows clean
A motor car, once a dream.

Pearl Powell (Swindon)

255

Repetition

The iron moves back and forth,
Back and forth.
The pile of shining linen mounts,
The tap drips.
Perhaps a footfall will crunch
On the gravel,
But no one comes to call.
It is winter
And no bird sings outside.
It is Sunday
And the bells have ceased
Their clamour
Calling the righteous to prayer.
It is very quiet,
Does prayer help loneliness?
Not in church
Where people hide behind their hands.
God is found in the woods
Or in quiet back streets.
The iron moves back and forth
Back and forth.
And what of the mind
Does that move back and forth?
Or does it soar beyond reality
To sun and sea
And wide white sands
Where waves draw the shingle
Back and forth,
Back and forth?
What to do next?
There's a meal to be cooked,
A table to lay -
From cooker to sink and room to room,
Back and forth.

Margaret Blake (Puddletown)

Manna From Heaven

(Front line)

Bullets ricochet, bombs are cascading
As they fall from Heaven to Hell.
Flames lick around the houses
As people flee the carnage.

Mountains of rubble
Around the corpses of tanks and cars
And then a momentary silence
Respite from this war torn place.

The soldiers move in
Guns at the ready,
Checking for the hidden enemy
Feeling eyes all around.

The young soldier moves forward
Examining the car,
Inside the body of a man
By dress important.

He is surrounded by money, money,
What should he do?
In the middle of this desert landscape
He looks around.

He sees the children's innocent faces
Their voices growing in crescendo.
Large eyes, ragged clothes,
He grabs at the notes.

As he throws them into the air
The children scream and laugh,
As the money blows in the breeze
They scramble to retrieve it.

Here we have the two sides of war.

Joan M Hopkins (Tiverton)

Waiting For Affection

The tired little insect
Climbs out the pool.
I pick up my bag and set off for school.
When I get home,
He's still waiting there.
Down goes my foot
See if I care.

Warren Gould (Bodmin)

Middle Death

Hurtling along
To meet it head on
Too late now
For the end he had seen
Beautiful life
Cut off before time
Romantically passing away

Too soon it will be
For the logical end
To a complete and quiet existence
In a white dream
It waits darkly obscene
Middle age
Middle life
Middle death

Not quite dead
In a hospital bed
Shapes move about
Moths to a light
Could put the flame out

Fighting for breath
They deny him his death
With cellophane bags
And cake icing needles
Plunged into his back

Painted green
For the X-ray machine
That dulls his brain
Forgetting his name

Friends come to stare
They don't dare
To touch for fear of infection

Clutching their posies
Of tulips and roses
The pretty bunched smells
Don't cover the yells
As they bleed for their roots

They move away
Their good for the day
Weep for a while
So again they can smile

When he is dead
They clear the bed
In anticipation

Of the next in line
For weary consternation

Elisabeth Ware (Teddington)

Witness To Fish

I saw a man who liked fish
To look on fish his only wish
I saw a man his reverence clear
He nurtured fish and held fish dear
I saw a man, a righteous man
Was it you?

Leafy green banks or shingle underfoot
Quiet waters run or sparkling sea and summer sun
Rain upon the face, at once with nature
And Mother Nature's grace.

The line enters in
Seducing her within
Hunger her surrender
While trusting a generous lender.

She's relieved to live another day
As gentle hands return her
But only for another day's play.

Then
Thrashing about from side to side
She dies
Her fight for survival lost
And nowhere to hide.

Her life in the waters ended
And with it her joy
As man takes his sport
And she is his toy.

Oh to return to those beautiful depths
Where like a mermaid she swam
And like dolphin though mammal
And the shimmering rest.

But man must have his way
And play with dominion
Then bereft
And with depletion and extinction
Will he end it one day yet.

I saw a man who liked fish
To look on fish his only wish.
I saw a man his reverence clear
He nurtured fish and held fish dear
I saw a man, a righteous man
Was it you?

Liz Taylor (Worthing)

259

The Woman With The Hat

There she was
just sitting there -
the woman with the hat.

She had followed me down the street
darting in and out of alleyways.
Twisting, turning, up and down

round and about.
No matter how fast or slowly I moved,
still she followed . . .

I could see the shadow of her hat
bobbing along
she behind and

the shadow in front.
In and out we went
she echoing my every step.

We reached a little street.
It was a dead end.
I was trapped.

I turned to look at her
and there she sat . . .
she sat cross-legged in the middle of the street.

She sat smiling beneath the brim of her hat.
'Who are you?' I whispered . . .
'I am your shadow,' she said.

'And you can be anything you want . . .
and there are lots and lots of different
hats you can wear . . .

. . . just choose one.'
'You mean I've got to make choices?' I said
'Yes,' she said - 'that's the essence - choices of hats.'

E Jane Winship (Basingstoke)

The Two-Fold Bond With Our Lord

Our Lord in His infinite love
Mercy of wisdom guide to us
Day by day and in one's way.
We show our love to Him
God's love for us is complete
For in His image we are made
And in His love and mercy we shall never fade.

Jack Collette (Bournemouth)

On Exmoor

Pockmarked with lichen, sprouting ferns like green hair,
The little stone bridge crouched over the stream.
I pause on its brow, enjoying the warmth
Of the sun on my back, surveying the scene.
Form high on the hill the stream tumbles down
In a flurry of waterfall, noisy its song
Till it forms a deep pool, where, reluctant to leave,
It changes its tune and meanders along.

A kingfisher watches for fish from his perch,
He dives in a flash of iridescent blue.
A dipper is bobbing on a rock in midstream,
Then he's under the water, looking for food.
From the ivy that clings to the foot of the bridge,
Calling its mate, a wee wren is heard.
I listen, enthralled by the beautiful sound,
An exquisite song from so small a bird.

In the shade of the ivy shy violets are peeping
At the brave primrose, face raised the sun.
Wild garlic is sprouting, eager to flower,
But snowdrops have withered, their days are done.

Then over the hills, black storm clouds gather,
Soon they disgorge a terrible storm.
The waters all finding their way to our stream,
And so a great, raging torrent is born.
Its fury increases, it sweeps down the hill,
Boulders and branches are picked up and thrown.
The flowers are crushed, the ivy uprooted,
Only the birds, to safety have flown.

But the little stone bridge, pockmarked with lichen,
Built by our ancestors - diligent, keen -
Though stripped of its ferns, stands up to the storm,
Still steadfastly crouching over the stream.

Gwen Hoskins (Bath)

Polly Joke

There is a bridge and a kissing gate at Polly Joke
There lies a dream, a stolen kiss
A day, an eve and night
Where dreams and Cornish wishes live
They live, they surf, they give at Polly Joke
History lies, gives, breathes, happiness
To all who love to receive the gift.

Porché Pink Poet (Falmouth)

Advancing Years

The stiffening knees, the aching back
The waistline squeeze, the joints that crack.

Tired of counting greying hairs
Breathless climbing up the stairs.

Stomach disorders, tablets and pills,
Life gets dreary with the absence of thrills.

Shoulders start drooping, muscles to sag
Lacking in energy, spirits soon flag.

Eyes playing tricks, relying on glasses
Prescriptions are free, so are bus passes.

Nuisance brown age-spots keep on appearing
Problems develop from 'hard of hearing'.

Never standing for long when we're able to sit
Have become slightly edgy, losing our wit.

Memory is failing, forgetting most names,
Wanting in effort, ambition and aims.

Giving up sport, slowly tapering down
To walks round the common, shopping in town.

It's easy to doze, love afternoon naps,
Enjoy reading and music, but beware of the traps!

Welcome to solitude, dislike too much noise
Can do without people and children with toys.

Concerned over money, our meagre state pension
Rising costs of inflation, and bills with the tension.

For many long years we've been loving and giving
We must carry on with the process of living.

Much more free time to stop, stand and stare
All the time to reflect and some left for a prayer.

Desmond Masters (London)

Watching And Dreaming

Sheets billowing in the breeze,
Like sails on a ship sailing the seas,
My mind goes back to long ago,
When sugar and spice was the cargo,
Dreaming over was nice when it lasted,
Now back to reality,
I hear a radio blasting.

Janet Chamberlain (Bristol)

In Whose Name

In whose name
Are we at war?
Don't you know
What we're fight for?
Live or die
Well I'm not sure
All I know is
We can't take any more.

At the start of each new sunrise
There's fire across the sky
Look to where my heart lies
You won't see me cry
Hope you got my last letter
Hope you've read it now
Coming home soon
Back in town.

What awaits us in the end?
How much further must I tread?
I guess you saw the news my friend
Heard the bad things that were said
Time for sorrow, time for peace
Heard the thunder from above
Time to say enough's enough
Hate vs hate does not equal love.

In whose name
Are we at war?
Don't you know
What we're fighting for?
Lie or die
I'm not sure
But I know
We've been here before.

K Smette (Banbury)

The Carer

I've been for a walk in the park,
In the sun,
I'm the lucky one.

All night she said my name
Over and over again,
The day won't be much fun
But I am the lucky one.

Cyril J Hawkins (Highbridge)

I Sigh For Alice With The Winsome Air

In my days of adolescence
Now so many years ago,
I just loved it at the movies
With a seat in the rear row;
Of all the famous film stars
From Mae West to dim Will Hay,
My very special favourite
Was that darling Alice Faye.

In those old extravaganzas
This great gal would grace the screen,
She'd progress from sticks to stardom
But with pitfalls in between!
Whether wooed by Rudy Vallee,
Don Ameche or John Payne,
To see my sweet enchantress
I have queued up in the rain.

At those tuneful entertainments
I would feel my spirits rise,
This angel-faced young songstress
Was a joy for ears and eyes;
She would spurn improper offers
Then fall for Tyrone Power,
All these, and more adventures,
In the course of just one hour!

How I longed for her to prosper
As I knew she surely should,
In those effervescent classics
There was triumph for the good;
She'd surmount so many setbacks
As the story would unfold,
Till the villain comes a cropper -
While the star goes on for gold.

Roy Court (Teignmouth)

Rose

Can a simple blooming of a rose be so enchanting?
From tiny details of glistening jewels which the rain portrays.
Numerous fresh fragrances of new beginnings and formidable ends.
Long agonising twists and turns of thorny memories and forgotten dreams.
This angry unfamiliar torment of red can inflame our emotions into anxieties

This breathtaking beauty can be our salvation,
Or a feature to our insecurities.

Emily May Earl (18) (Saltash)

Peace On A Country Walk

The bees hum in the blackberry flowers
Bright blossoms bloom in the hedge
And far above in a sycamore tree
The chaffinch's message is spread.
The dog sniffs a hole where a mouse has been
And a buzzard calls up above
In a dappled blue sky the sun shines bright
And yonder, the coo of a dove.

Far in the distance a train rumbles past
With a rhythmical chug as it goes
And standing; I stare at a ladybird
Whilst sniffing a stray rambling rose.
The ambient quiet, the still and the peace
Of a gentle afternoon stroll,
And even the dog lays down for a bit
As the view takes its wonderful toll.

In the distance, church spires, and in the green fields
Are cattle and sheep as they graze
And all I can do is stand there and look
And offer God's handywork praise,
For the beauty and peace of a countryside walk,
(Though grubby and dusty my feet)
As I turn to go home I am happy indeed
In this beautiful world full of peace.

If only we'd stop all the war and the strife,
If we'd only consider God's love,
If we'd just 'stand and stare' at the beauty around
We give praise to the Father above.
We'd love all our neighbours though hard it may be.
We'd care for the creatures he made,
Yes even the dog loves a countryside walk
With its wonderful glories arrayed.

Dorothy Holloway (Witney)

If Only

If only we lived in an ideal world -
Sweet serenity.
No wars, no crime, no famine.
How wonderful this would be.

But always there is suffering, sadness and despair,
Which often makes us wonder
If God is really there.

A H Colmer (Waterlooville)

Sparkle Lips' Breath

Sparkle lips' breath with pleasing song,
that one may here some words of you;
with love two are remembering,
the music that we knew.
And to the music dance our hearts,
into a year quite departed,
time gone that is our history;
life's portioned watershed.

Each day has fresh moistured lustre,
and gleam is on the bloom of much;
with love two are remembering,
our pleasure was to touch.
And felt with fingers' tender pads,
if friction lay beneath a hand;
my gentlest touch was meant for you,
did then, and does remain.

Garland our time that will be brief,
for youth is but for only once;
with love two are remembering,
sweet flower fragrances.
And even to a passing hour,
a fleeting moment come so late;
arise upon a little air,
corolla opulence.

And then to sight your homely face,
to these years I adjusted grew;
with love just one remembering
the vision that was you.
A judgement made long time ago,
now signs of age are fast unkind;
the clock beats for the two of us;
lives parallel unwind.

Paul Moore (Great Missenden)

Launching Racks In The Dust

Guiderails into the sky, in the breeze,
Above the plain, are still there before the thunder shocks
From the skyrockets launched, over the plain and brightening
Quiet now, after the abundant stars
And the materials that approached the top of the sky
Persist in the sky, in the breeze, over the plain
                              in permanence . . .

M Courtney Soper (Oxford)

The Scream

She lay on the grass embalmed by the dying golden light
from the sun
There was no future, no past, only now
The shadow of a homeward-bound bird crossed her face,
for a flicker of time the serenity was lost.
The air although quiet was busy collecting moisture to lay
on her form, each bead becoming a tiny reflected sun.
Her hair grew damp, more dew crept from the earth to find
and absorb her warmth, seeping and creeping into the fabric
of her clothes.
Twilight turned to dark, as the moon took station to lend
its cold light to the scene.

The scream when it came was shocking and harsh;
it had nothing to defend itself from horror.

The scream soon robbed of its existence faded without echo,
absorbed by the heavy air.
She was sitting now, eyes still closed but seeing something
on the screen of her mind.
She lay back, breast heaving but otherwise unmoving.
The moon was washed away by cloud, darkness
had full dominion.
The rain started, a soft gentle caress to join with its brethren
on the ground.
The caress grew more urgent like an excited lover; gentleness
was lost as its passion increased.
Torrents fell in an attempt to sink her into the earth, the earth
seemed part of the pact to claim her back.

Like a fallen battle flag she met the dawn, half buried in mud
and dark with water.
The sun rose and new light discovered her, the mud receded
and colours were found.
She lay on the grass embalmed.

Robert Denis Spencer (Great Missenden)

Liberty Bell

To each their own Liberty Bell,
It rings daily in the minds of those forever grateful it exists.
It is an icon of history,
That lives forever in the now,
Its symbol stronger now than when first used.
To most it goes beyond the actual to the essence of the bell.
It is one bell toll that forever changed the world.

Ian Fisher (Taunton)

The Cornish Beach

Golden sand and azure sky,
Many seagulls flying by.
Surfers in their wetsuits black,
Going out and coming back.
Rocks for shelter and to climb,
Be careful that you know the time.
Buckets, spades and rubber rings -
These are usual seaside things.

Atlantic breakers crashing in;
See a basking shark's large fin!
Lifeguards driving up and down,
Seeing that we do not drown.
Ice cream vans with raucous bell,
Ensuring that the kids eat well.
These too are usual seaside things -
What fun the warm summer brings.

Other seasons too have great joys -
Great fun for all the girls and boys.
Strolling on a gale-swept beach,
Making sure the waves don't reach.
Collecting shells on the tide line
And breathing in the foaming brine.
Watching ships both small and large,
Even the occasional barge.

Flotsam and jetsam cast ashore;
Treasure hunters search for more.
There's a wreck out in the bay,
All saved to sail another day.
We see patterns in the sand
Put there by the tide's strong hand.
Something new found every day,
Just one joy upon the bay.

Tony Olivey (Truro)

Prescience

Peripheral to focused vision
Scattered to concentrated beam:
As the scope narrows
It becomes, richer, deeper, more intense.
Diffuse to concentrate
As long as we permit our Spirit and Mind to soar
We will always be aware, prescient about our World.

Damien Plummer (Leighton Buzzard)

Just Passing Through

(For Paul and Mary)

He stepped into my dream last night,
A shimmering radiance, entirely recognisable,
Essentially the same. Glowing with universal love
And displaying some kind of deep knowledge.
Then he was gone.
Evidently just passing through.

Seventy today, he would have been.
They had been planning a party, something spectacular
And a huge cake, with hundreds of candles.
And chatter . . .
And people, carefully chosen,
In dinner suits . . . slightly shiny
And posh glittery frocks, preserved from the eighties.
And all their grown-up seedlings
Popping corks all over the place
And passing quail's eggs.

She slightly apart . . . glowing quiet in white and pride
And he, in the middle of everyone
Of everything . . .
Shooting off party poppers, like biliho
Covering all in clouds of neon streamers,
Droplets of generosity, touching everyone,
Like wax from the candles, never lit . . .
And the rockets, never quite set off for Mars.

And her response . . .

I will be there as I promised, I will wear my Sunday Best
You will know me when you see me, with your rose buds at my breast.

On my sleeve a heart is glowing, in my eyes will be the stars,
I will be there as I promised, I will meet you under Mars.

Jane Brooks (Bridport)

My New Dog

My new dog is a sheepdog
Or he was
Greying now at the muzzle,
Cast out for being 'past his sell-by date'.

But at 12 my Toddie can still outrun them all,
They don't see beyond the tired old eyes;
This dog has loved and lost
I see it in his need for physical contact.

When he jumps on the sofa
Rides with me on the bus
Waits patiently for a titbit
And obeys every command

I know he was once loved greatly
And he loved back
Then he lost his love somehow
And had to endure months in kennels

Unkempt, shaggy, great brown eyes,
I don't know how they could resist him
But they did
And now he's mine.

I reap the rich rewards
Of his years and understanding;
Never puts a foot wrong -
Knows exactly how to behave

And gives undemanding love,
Loyalty and companionship.
His twinkling brown eyes
Hint at the wonderful friendship
We're going to have
Forever.

Diana Price (Exeter)

A Right Pantomime

It's time to pull the plug on everyone that I know
I could tell stories about them all and be a proper little so and so
Twazzz like when Old Ben Nevis got all above himself
And caught his little fingers in the mousetrap high upon the shelf
Even Lucy Locket, well she ain't so very good
She even let old Desperate Dan trip over that piece of wood
As for Tommy Tucker the stories about him that I know
Like those about Pinocchio oh now my nose has started to grow.

Philip Anthony Amphlett (Gloucester)

But Then . . .

Life
might be simpler
if
we'd never met.

No
anxious hours
waiting
for your call,

no
sudden drops
from cloudless heights
into black depths
of ice.

Nor
so much joy,
such lightness
in my step,
such warmth
in your embrace.

Nor
so much sadness
when it had
to end.

Life
might be simpler
if
we'd never met.

But then
it would not be
my life.

Anita Bild (London)

Paradise

Paradise where all is fair
And beauty reigneth everywhere
Spring of life is at thy side
O how I wish to be inside
Inside thy gate of Paradise
May I wander by and by
Till with wonder and with awe
I shall rest forever more.

Mary Gill (London)

The Elm

(John Edward Kilford 1924-1997)

How changed the countryside is now,
Without the elm tree, standing high.
And yet, I'm sure that I know how
These lovely trees were forced to die.

Before 'Dutch Elm' was recognised,
The tree was always thought to be
Most dangerous when there was a storm,
So under this, one should not flee.

The grub that causes this disease,
The bane of elms, has always been,
But just what brought the end to trees
Was snow and frost, for years unseen.

The awful winter of sixty-three
Did more than freeze the countryside.
Bird life was devastated, and though free
Woodpeckers were starved, and most just died.

The grubs attacking elm trees then,
And so led to trees' demise,
Were free from predators often,
So they could flourish and numbers rise.

The solution now, I'm sure must be,
That whether Lesser, Great or Green
Woodpeckers should be bred, then free,
Removing grubs to keep trees clean.

Then, once more, they will be seen,
Just as they always used to be,
The elm trees standing there supreme,
A dream come true, for all to see.

John Kilford (Taunton)

Anger

A hot spark in a dying fire,
The lightning on an old church spire,
Boiling liquid from head to toe,
An awakened volcano far below.

Molten rock from head to foot
A burning twig that won't stay put,
The roaring of a railway track,
The stick that broke the camel's back.

Rosie Powlesland (Chalfont St Giles)

The Stream

(Dedicated to the Falkland Islands environment)

Deeply within her, your mother, the Mountain,
Bears you through caverns that man may not see,
Bringing you forth in a clear bubbling fountain,
Giving you spirit and setting you free.

Carefully over the surface you sally,
Eagerly threading each route that you find,
Gleefully tumbling towards a deep valley,
Leaving your mother, the Mountain behind.

Washing o'er pebbles and making them chatter,
Leaping from heights with no hint of dismay,
Into a myriad of droplets you shatter,
Locking a rainbow in fine misty spray.

As you meander, long grasses caress you,
Trout breathe the life your soul's willing to share,
Grebe, upland geese and the teal duck all bless you,
Trusting their nests and their young in your care.

Round tiny islets you ripple and quiver,
Catching the sunlight or soft lunar glow;
Shedding your youth you merge into a river,
Gracefully then and more stately you flow.

Rain-speckled, sun-kissed, snow-muffled you travel,
Shallow or swollen, lethargic or fast,
Seasons and years have beheld you unravel,
'Til salty waters embrace you at last.

Still, far away, on your mother, the Mountain,
Ever your birth will continue to be,
Ever to rise as a clear bubbling fountain,
Ever to race to the arms of the sea.

Lorena Triggs (Waterlooville)

Incoming Tide

The waves inch slowly forward on the beach
each one a little further than the last,
children's sandy castles just within the reach
then waves leapfrogging gently round them pass.

In and onward comes the creeping sea
as over smooth and rounded stones it flows
like drawing in of breath, it seems to me,
and waits, rising, poised, before it onward goes.

Celia Turner (Melksham)

What's This All About?

What's this all about?
Her eyes glued to my face
she raised a point of global interest.
I held her tight in my arms
as if to squeeze it all out and replied.
Dearest, it's in our genes
we are bound by nature to procreate
and leave behind our icons.

Why then I shed tears
and my heart becomes restless?
There is more to this physical act
than just to grow and multiply.
She squirmed beneath and asked.
Releasing her from my hold I whispered.
Yes! Love in itself is a means to be.

Resting her head on my arms she asked.
So why does the smile sparkle
and river of tears flow?
Pain of losses pierce through our hearts
and happiness shines through our eyes.
Turning towards her and with a lazy glance
I kissed her soft lips and added,
These are the signs of life by design.

So what shall I call this act of ours?
Loving to love or love to be immortal.
She sighed taking a deep breath
sliding up her silky slender shape.
Absorbed in her body gleaming in dim light
I reposed and leisurely replied,
Yes! It is an endless form
of our physical side of creation.

Mojibur Rahman (Reading)

Phobia

I'm dreadfully sorry, I say to the spider,
I really can't help it, I just have to do it.
My whole body trembling, I pick up the slipper -
I'm sorry, I'm sorry, I keep saying to it.

Its poor mangled body, inert, lies before me;
I'm bigger than you were, so why did I do it?
I ruefully say to the little dead spider,
Forgetting the panic I felt when I slew it.

Mary Brainin-Huttrer (London)

Interview

We met, for the very first time.
How would it be, and was there a hope?
Hope, that right judgement be made?
Made in time to enter my life?
To be part of the pattern of things?
There was no going back.
The dye had been cast.
The meeting arranged in good time.
No rush, no hurry, the timing was right.

Seated, we faced one another, a table between.
How shall we start? How to proceed?
Why are we here? And what is your need?
The answer was simple and quite satisfactory.
Probably right and ready to lead one another.
Yes, another and more.
The questions progressed.
Again and again we answered: each probing exact.
The questioner, clearly, had done it before.

We paused, as if panting when racing was done.
No further questions were asked.
Papers were shuffled, inspected and checked.
A pencil was poised for a tick.
Slowly it came, at the end of the form
Completed by me, with CV.
The interview over, the silence was broken,
'You do realise I have no power to accept.
I can only commend, which I do.
Don't call us, Mr Hopeful,
We will call you.
Goodbye!'

Another long wait lies ahead.

George Robbins (London)

The Sea

Oh wide expanse of black and green what secrets you behold
Your mighty power your fearful sound such mysteries unfold
Your belly roars as foam you spit before you crash and then
As gentle as a soothing touch you beckon us all in.

Oh expanse of blue and dancing rays of sunlight
Rippling over golden sands to sounds of sheer delight
You are the enemy to do your worst when fancy takes a hold
And yet my friend, for all it's worth when I might feel so bold.

Patricia Taylor (Bournemouth)

It Is . . .

It's the things you can never have,
That you will always want.

It's the things you can only have for a moment,
That you will miss for a lifetime.

It's the people who bring you the most pain,
That you will never be able to forget.

It's the moment that changes everything,
That you will relive a thousand times.

It's the day you feel completely and truly happy,
That you will always think was a dream.

It's the boy you can never have again,
That you will always love.

It's the people who put you down,
That you will always think are better than you.

It's the times that the rain pours,
That you will never have an umbrella.

It's the people who should never let you down,
That will let you down first and most.

It's the person you love first,
That you will never stop loving.

It's the words you can never say,
That you will always wish you had.

It's the things you will always remember,
That you will always want to forget.

It's the things that age can't change,
That you will keep close to your heart,
When everything else is lost.

Anna Dakin (Reading)

Shepherds

How should we, belated, tiring,
Wonder-struck with sudden light,
Find the lamb of man's desiring
In the wilderness of night?

Keep we to our ancient calling,
Mark the anguished yeanling's cry,
Let the voices, soaring, falling,
Trumpet peace to distant sky.

Humphrey Clucas (Sutton)

Shame

When nightly on my TV screen I see
Long straggling lines - so very long -
Of figures, persons once as you and me,
Shuffling and shambling wearily along,
I weep

For children in this piteous band
Who uncomprehendingly, innocently, cling
So trustingly to a mother's hand
And are quite bereft of any childish thing,
I weep

For dead dark eyes in skeletal sockets deep,
The hopelessness so eloquently shown
In ravaged faces, too exhausted e'en to weep;
For tired frail women, menfolk stolen, quite alone;
I weep

Such men as can in this grim mass be seen
Are old, infirm, rejected as not worth the kill.
The women thus are left, not just to keen
But the brunt to bear, menfolk's places fill.
I weep

If some omnipotent great God there be
Who coolly contemplates this dreadful throng,
Implacably permits this evil tragedy,
No censure I can make could be too strong.
I weep

Yet from rumination, revelation came.
Such callousness lies beneath the reach of any single heart
So can there be no God, all powerful, to bear the shame.
This lies with humankind alone - of which I am a part.
So I weep.

G F Pash (Hayle)

Dinner In Caunes After The Fete De Marble

Pink marble and St Anthony,
Fountains - mountains and pink hollyhocks
clustering along cracked medieval walls.
White-draped tables - earthenware bowls of Daube,
creamy goats' cheese, oysters and red wine.
Tarte Tatin as the sun left and shade hustled the diners onwards.

Karen Jorgensen (Brentford)

London Symphony

The Thames, a wide smooth river, weaves
silver, serpentine, between city embankments,
houses, churches, one time temples, palaces,
once great estates. Two-thousand years
of restless history is remembered here.

Some say this town was created by Brutus,
great grandson of Æneas, the Trojan, founder
of Rome. Others have it named for Lludd,
King of the Isle of Britain before the Romans
came. Legend says he lies buried at Ludgate

and the city's name derives from Lludd, although
the city was ruled at different times by local chieftains,
Kings and queens: and, for some hundreds of years
by governors representing powerful Caesars, as a
remote north-eastern province of the Roman Empire.

Londinium - later London - became itself capital
of another, later, world girdling empire of its own,
the largest history has so far known. So times change,
as place names have changed too. From Albion,
recalling Emperor Diocletian's eldest daughter

to Britain, derived by Brutus from his own name.
This is the city, and the place, to where so many
different people have come and stayed, as true today
as of the past, of both the city and the nation.
Through Angles, Saxons, Normans, Vikings, Danes,

down to the present when London has become
the stage on which, blind to their different origins
all kinds of men of many cultures and nations act out
past and future histories of mankind's struggle and
attempts to civilize and save the human race.

Richard Storey (London)

Achilles Rose

Oh pretty rose upon the wall
How you grow to be so tall
Stems outstretched climb to the sky
Your buds not yet open to the naked eye.

Green leaves sway in the evening breeze
You're fourteen now and have grown with ease
You will go on forever I know
Throughout the seasons and the snow.

Dennis Russell (Axminster)

The River Wear

The noisy shipyards booming voice is stilled now
The tallest crane with folding arms, no more
For stocks are dead, no ships are given birth to
Laments the troubled river to the shore
Once, it wailed, I was so great and famous
And early century boat remains were found
Ahidden neath the earth below an oak tree
Some treasure from an ancient shipping ground.

Here's Peter's Church where Aiden spoke with fervour
And brought down books from Holly Lindesfarne
His preaching news of our blessed Saviour
As he sailed up the Wear one early dawn.

In thirteen forty-six a man called Menvill
Who lived by Sunderland's river at Hendon docks
Leased from the Durham Bishop for two shillings
A place at river's edge to house ship blocks.

In the eighteenth century charming Margaret Reay
Chose mighty chips to build on Wear's shore
No sewing . . . playing music . . . love's career
This woman's life . . . a different kind of chore.

And the first ship built in halves was launched from Wearside
Its part then joined as one did then reveal
An edifice of power, and grace so splendid
Evoked from minds, hearts, hands of truest steel.

Though rusted old machines now scar me greatly
While waiting plans and work of northern men
For flower banks to splash in coloured beauty
And pleasure boats aspeed to Hylton's town
But who will tell of history's North East story
Of the Wear built ships and river men gone now . . .

Maureen Plenderleith (Bristol)

Loving Salvation

Marooned in a constant wilderness of emotional darkness,
Lost in an endless maze of hopeless aspirations,
My emotional emptiness was unbearable,
Then she came and loved me like no other,
Her words comforted my whole being,
Her loving affection cured my senseless existence,
Her touch made me feel like a king,
I was emotionally reborn by her loving kindness.

Alan Grech (London)

279

Voltage

Padre, you know what a rotter I am
A wastrel, a killer and thief
But I won't despair
When I go to the chair
In a way, it's a kind of relief

Forty-one days I've sat in this cell
And I'm coming apart at the seams
You've knelt down and prayed for me
Got my debts paid for me
You've even appeared in my dreams

You've read me the Bible, chapter and verse
Talked with me hour after hour
You've sat with the guard
In the exercise yard
You've followed me into the shower

You taught me Monopoly, Ludo and chess
And how to make toys out of rags
You've read 'Robin Hood' for me
Told me it's good for me
And weaned me away from my fags

Forty-one days of poems and prose
And things of a classical flavour
Heroes and fairies
Hymns and Hail Marys
Padre do me a favour

Tomorrow at eight when I'm strapped in the chair
And the Governor takes up his stand
Padre, barring a hitch
When he throws the switch
Would you mind - holding my hand?

E Goodfellow (Southampton)

The Sea

The sea so calm
is torn away
by storm that's cruel
to claim its prey,
respect its temperament
you will
return once more
where time stands still.

Melvyn Roiter (Muswell Hill)

Twilight In The Park

Night, with soot-stained fingers
Pursues the fleeing sun
Which dips behind a parapet
Of distant hills.

The ghost of a wind disturbs dead leaves
Along the metalled path
They form a ring and dance
Beside the bench I rest upon
I hear them skitter in the silence
Like a beetle in a box.

Two women pass, their voices shrill
And nervous in the gloaming,
They go their separate ways, and hurry home
With backward glances.

From the nearby railway line
Comes the roar of a diesel engine
Crying 'rat-attack, rat-attack, rat-attack',
Rushing into chilly darkness;
Cocooned in a quilted lining
I remain a little longer.

Near the hedge around the bowling green
There slinks an urban fox
Scavenging the litter
For abandoned fish 'n' chips.

A sudden scream is echoed
By shouts of loutish laughter,
The fox, alerted, lifts its head
And melts into the shadows.
There are predators abroad,
I too must take my leave.

J C Fearnley (Bristol)

The Swans

There is so much good in this land
From John O'Groats to Dover,
There is so much good at hand,
And today I saw two swans fly over.
So little makes me glad
And I am no longer sad,
So little makes my day
And carries my sorrow away!

Richard Raymond (Watford)

Veiled Dancer

Her brittle chair caught fire
With a sudden snap,
Sparked by dormant red
Under a moon rise of ash -
Keen flames leap and lift

Spring, the veiled dancer
With her braid of yellow roses
Like so many suns woven
To a crown of mirrors
Eclipsing the night.

From the hub of her wings,
Boughs wave in the breeze
Touching drowsy hearts;
From her yielding sleeve,
Pale blossoms pour.

An early lance of light
Cuts through my sleep,
Its radiant beam holds
Motes of dust - whirling
Remnants of a dream.

Nectar, bees, the dawn-trill
Of a blackbird,
The laughter of a girl chimes
With distant stars and daisies
Sparkling on the lawn;

Runes appear in the mist
Of my breath on the glass,
Opening within the script,
The sun unveils its spiral -
Vision from the stoic womb.

Ashen Venema (Farnham)

A Picture Of Your Life

Life is but a picture
Life's picture is not always one of beauty
You do what you can to brighten it
To attend to the scenery of life - a duty
There are tears - in this picture
Though - there are places for laughter too
You are the subject of this picture
Does the picture have enough in it, for you?

Trevor Vincent (Castle Cary)

Angels

We all have angels, high up in the clouds
They love us all dearly,
They see our tears and worried frowns

In them we can all confide
The door never slams,
Waiting to listen, waiting to understand
Their wings stretched wide
And with a loving hand,
A few gentle words from
The promised land.

They are beautiful, they're kind
Lead you on the right path
And leave the bad behind
A feeling of wellbeing
A warm comfort inside.

Wait for the magic
Then your head can rise,
Have faith in the angels
Full of wonder and surprise.

Angels, angels, high up in the cloud
I love you so much, my heart
Just sings out loud.
I am happy, I am happy,
Like the birds up in the trees,
I'm truly cleansed and I know
I can succeed.

My deepest thanks and sincere gratitude
And best wishes for you all to share,
So glad you're very close by me,
Big kisses to you all, up there.

Maddie Reade (Swindon)

Should Hope Rest Weary

Should hope rest in weary slumber, she would fan the inferno in our *imaginings,*
lest the aching burden weighs on *twisted flesh.*
When a scarcity of light reins gloomy discouragement, might she loan
me her *torch* like the rising sun break with fiery promise through the *heavy pitch of night.*
If fright ran deeper than assurance, she would *loan me her lips*
and *hardened whisper* and *draw down* the stars to *her own astronomy and ours.*
Such was the wonder of her every *dance,* that even with glorious
frosting of ear and flaring of soul did she crash with her wrath and char *unspeakable goodbye.*

Alex Smith (London)

283

Do Call Me A Stranger

Do call me a stranger,
That is my name
Barbara means stranger
And that's how I came.
I should have been a twin.
I should have been a boy.
I'm glad to say my mother
Thought I was a joy.

Do call me a stranger,
But don't call me a fool,
Born on the first of April,
At 1.00pm though after all.

Do call me a stranger,
A southpaw - yes, left handed,
My mind works back to front -
The aliens have landed!

Do call me a stranger
From Isles of Scilly there
I once went back to London
And could only stand and stare.
Where were the English faces?
Where was our skin, so fair?

Do call me a stranger,
I do not know it now
I do not know my London
My Bedford or my Slough.

Do call me a stranger
We have no lasting city.
We are all migrants here, young man,
So I will end my ditty!

Barbara Hasler (Isles of Scilly)

My Heart And I

I can't remember many tears, but certainly the pain
When all about me fell apart I knew a broken heart
But time it's said will heal the wounds and shock and pain decrease
Time indeed - so much of it - before such pain to cease
But now my heart and I are one and life could not be better
I'll never let my heart depart to know such pain again
My hope is now eternal and together we shall fly
To heights of unknown happiness and wave the past goodbye!

Betty Batchen (Greenwich)

For The Pleasure

Smacked he was, as a boy,
Cross his legs, for discipline,
He was slapped;
Cross his face, by the girl next door,
He was slapped.

Stuffed he was, as an animal
When its innards are
Cut and stripped;
When his stomach said 'no more'
He was stuffed.

Blown he was, as a candle
When its wick is 'snuffed'
When a pinch of snuff,
Up his nose he sniffed,
He was 'snuffed'.

Strapped he was, like a 'firework
To a wheel', as Catherine was;
On the rack, like Guy Fawkes
He confessed,
Stretched he was.

Hung and drawn he was,
In the Tower, for High Treason;
At the dictate of the Queen
On a hook his parts
Were hung.

Purged he is;
Now the Angels of the Devil
Take Him down to meet his Maker,
Now for the pleasure
Purged, and 'finalised' he is.

P R Dennis (New Malden)

Hillingdon

From Heathrow planes to Lido trains,
From traffic jams and Harefield lambs to peaceful leafy lanes,
Western International, the Compass and the Beck,
Hospitals, schools and pools, Brunel and Uxbridge Tech,
Faces here of every hue, so much here to see and do,
The Chimes and The Pavilions, people swarming in their millions,
Coffee bars, gyms and discos to tempt you at your leisure,
There's everything in Hillingdon, whatever gives you pleasure!

Kathleen Day (Ruislip)

We Praise And Thank You, O Lord

We praise and thank You, O Lord
For Your wonderful creation
For the warmth of the sun and refreshing rain
The shade from clouds on summer days
The snow and frost in winter.

We praise and thank You, O Lord
For Your wonderful creation
For all the kinds of fruit we eat
The variety of shape and colour
Of apples, bananas, oranges and pears.

We praise and thank You, O Lord
For Your wonderful creation
The birds' different songs, colour and size
For the beauty, fragrance and colour of flowers
Whether wild or grown in a garden.

We praise and thank You, O Lord
For Your wonderful creation
For trees in the woods standing so tall
The mighty oak, ash and beech
Small shrubs and trees that brighten our gardens.

We praise and thank You, O Lord
For Your wonderful creation
For vegetables rich in flavour
Green, white, red, so good for us
Some cooked, some can be eaten raw.

We praise and thank You, O Lord
For Your wonderful creation
For loving pets like dogs and cats
Who welcome us each day
And other pets which give us joy.

Jean Martin-Doyle (St Albans)

Untitled

When far away
And love you carry,
And to some nice girl
Or boy you marry,
Think of me
For old time's sake,
And save me a piece
Of your wedding cake!

Vera Peters (Redruth)

Behind The Plough

If I could choose where else to be
I'd still be where I am right now,
And where is that? I hear you ask,
It's here behind the plough.

The air smells fresh, the sky's so blue,
The earth feels good beneath my feet,
Sensations felt by few! Nowadays.

Machinery roars in fields nearby
Distracting and polluting;
My thoughts revert to times gone by
When nothing but the sounds of life were heard
And life was not diluting, into
Keys and buttons, screens and discs
And midnight chats to strangers.
Remember that when Christ was born
It was in a humble manger.

No going back, just pressing on and on
This is a fact of life;
If only we could compromise
To minimise world strife.

A triumph that would be
For all humanity:
What joy and inner peace would reign
In place of poverty and strain.

We'd reap the good like a bumper crop
If we could only make it stop,
This madness of a world confused,
Of lives turned upside down and bruised.
It's time to make a stand, but how?
Perhaps - get back behind the plough!

Gerry de Faoite (Staines)

Sleep Tide

Drift silently into my pillowed space
Pour soothing calm upon my face
Bathe my eyes with a soft caress
Smooth my brow with tenderness.
Gently lap on my soul's still shore
Send ripples of peace through slumber's door.
Then flood my room with the moon's kind light
To harbour my dreams throughout the night.

Jean Young (Hartfield)

Words, Is What I'm Doing

What are you doing Mum? Robert said
Isn't it time you were asleep, in bed.
Words, is what I'm doing.
Words, I said
Putting them together
From a thought in my head.

Why do you write?
It's way past midnight.

Words, is what I'm doing
And some express
My joys and
Sometimes loneliness.

Why can't words wait?
You're up much too late.

Words, is what I'm doing
Making them rhyme
They come into my head
Sometime.

Why do words come?
Go to sleep Mum.

Words, is what I'm doing
They won't let me sleep
I put them all together
And sometimes weep.

Words, is what I'm doing
They won't let me pray
I put them all together
And sometimes they
Leave . . . me . . . *alone!*

Cecelia Peters (Slough)

Scars

I am not you or them but me.
My body developed at a slower rate than yours.
My arms are shorter than theirs.
My fingers uneven and smaller than yours but are mine.
Reach out to everyone telling a story, my story.
Follow the tracks on my back and you can learn more.
What makes me click, what I like and don't like.
My story is yours to unveil.

Ise Obomhense (Kingston upon Thames)

288

Sweet Dreams

A quiet moment to reflect,
Past Christmases I recollect,
When three young girls, their stocking hung
On fireside, pinned one by one.
Then off to bed, sweet dreams, each willing
That Santa brings exciting filling.
At dawn they creep down creaky stair,
Each fearful he may still be there.
Then sheer delight at seeing three fat stockings lying 'neath the tree.
Race up the stairs to Mum and Dad,
To show them what they each have had.
A book, a puzzle, sixpence to spend,
An orange at the very end.
Just little things that brought such pleasure,
A magic time beyond all measure.
Then leaving paper wrapping mess,
Each donning special Christmas dress,
They run downstairs to wait and see
Which gift is theirs 'neath Christmas tree.
A game to play, a teddy bear, a doll that talks with curly hair.
Such precious things to love and keep
Beside them when they go to sleep.
But now those days are long since gone,
I wonder how it all went wrong,
I wonder why we got so greedy,
When all around are poor and needy.
When once an annual would be nice,
Computers now may just suffice.
Has Christmas lost that magic touch,
When little things meant oh so much?
Past Christmases I recollect
A quiet moment to reflect.

Nancy Ferbrache (Guernsey)

Love

Hand in hand
through life they've been.
Husband and wife
since seventeen.
The longer they live
the more they admire . . .
Their love's now a glow,
when young it was fire.

Douglas Bean (London)

Blue

Colour of coolness, calm and freshness,
Gentle colour and royal too
Forget-me-nots and irises,
Delphiniums of varied hue,
Bluebells scent woodland carpets,
A breathtaking view.
Gentians high on alpine slopes
Bright blue and radiant too.
Kingfisher's dive,
A brilliant flash of blue.
Cute little blue tits,
Cornflowers, violas too.
Waving fields of flax
'Neath skies of blue,
Blue lakes and seas
And sparkling glacial blue.
Colour of crispness,
Cold and turning blue,
Attractive clear blue eyes
And baby boys in blue,
Woad and precious sapphire,
Oxford and Cambridge blues,
Blue Peter and dark blue whales,
Out of the blue comes news.
But only once in a blue moon
Do I feel blue and sad,
The azure sky so blue and clear
Keeps me content and glad.
Each colour has such beauty
But, for me, it's true
My greatest joy and peace is in
God's gift of blue.

Mary Elizabeth Keene (Leatherhead)

Devotion

Every time I think of you,
Your loving memory brings,
To me my darling Hildegard,
The sound of violins,
The fragrance of the flowers,
And honeysuckle sweet,
I'd love to pick those flowers
And lay them at your feet.

W L Harwood (Luton)

Twenty Years

What a surprise I had today
A beautiful bouquet came my way
Twenty years have now passed by
Since a club was started by others and I
This club was created for people who
Had suffered a stroke and needed to do
Something to help them to regain
Their loss of confidence again
They come with stick, chair or frame
They sit and chat and play a game
Biscuits, coffee, cups of tea
Are consumed so happily
There's soup and sandwiches for lunch
When members like to sit and munch
Sometimes a treat of fish and chips
With salt and vinegar tingling lips
The day would not be quite complete
Without a raffle once a week
Bingo, Hoy - sometimes a quiz
Are introduced by helper Liz
Flexicise and manicured hands
Singing choirs and military bands
Speakers make them laugh or cry
And therapists coax them to try
To speak and move their hands again
A slow process but worth the pain
As we think upon the past
Of memories that are bound to last
We look to better things in store
And know that members more and more
Will gain in strength and benefit
With social skills and keeping fit.

Joyce Beard (Burnham-on-Sea)

From Intensive Care To The Mountain Air

The confines of intensive care
Not much joy to lie and stare.
More surgery on my colon
Will they ever leave me alone?
Fitting a colostomy bag
Mustn't let it be a drag.
After many months of care
Time to walk again if I dare.
Much more help from the physio
And at last it really is time to go.
Back to my training with weights and the like
And later back to the beloved bike.
It feels like I've come so far
To be back again with my Yamaha.
Intensive care left way behind
I have a biking holiday in mind.
Over in France and the A26
Is getting to feel like a real good fix.
Cruising at about the ton
It's great to be back in the sun, and having fun.
Miles of open countryside,
Got to be better than being inside.
Passing over canals and rivers,
The bike and the freedom sure delivers.
Down to Dijon,
And many miles have gone,
Into the mountains and hairpin bends,
Yet this is not where the journey ends.
Seeing the lake (Geneva) below
There isn't very far to go.
Along the final lakeside motorway,
It's good to know that I've come to stay.

Andy Morris (Andover)

The Black Rose

I am a rose which fell off
The branch of its country's tree
And has been separated from
Its motherland
Living in a foreign country
Like a black rose
As black as the dark night
In these cold blustery winds
The agony of hate and
Crawling insects of racial discrimination
Are biting my inner soul again and again.
The wind of racial hatred
Is going down deep into my heart
And is piercing my whole existence.
It looks like the torch of humanity
Is about to dwindle.
The uneasy drops of my affection
Are falling from my sad and dismal eyes
Saying that one day a new book will appear
From the heart of this land
And its beautiful words
Will smile in its perspective of love.
New dimensions will produce new flowers
And this world
With its torch of eternal love
Will begin to dance
In the valley of imagination.
This is the fragrance of
My inner feelings
Otherwise I am only a black rose
Which fell off the branch of
Its country's tree.

Gulshan Khanna (Hounslow)

Love

He was old and his sight was failing fast
His time on Earth was almost past
Life was a burden, filled with aches and pain
Few friends from his childhood now remained
Fumbling along, white stick probing the way
His provisions he needed to buy that day
He stumbled and would have hit the ground
When he felt strong arms circle him round
And hold him till his heart stopped beating fast
And then she let him go at last
He could not see the clothes she wore
And never knew she was so poor
But he could sense right from the start
That love was pouring from her heart
And after that, she knocked upon his door
To see if she could help him more
She took him shopping, saw him safely home
Moved in with him, like a daughter she'd become
She washed him, bathed him, combed his hair
In every way she served him fair
For three whole years she tenderly
Looked after him most patiently
Acceding to his every whim
With love and patience from within
She stayed with him until the end
He'd never had a truer friend
The legacy he'd left was very small
But she had not wanted it at all
She grieved for the loss of her dear friend
As she closed the front door and came to the end
Of a time in her life which would always be
One of the happiest in her memory.

Sylvia Hankins (Glastonbury)

Settling Matters

For all those 'decent' folk
who believe that
the colonisation of
'Third World' lands
was a good thing -
that running other people's countries
'for them'
is a selfless and
or charitable act
stop
to think
about the facts
that
the colonisers
were not invited
and *took* control
for their own benefit;
enforcing their systems
of beliefs and finance,
'introducing' 'developments'
and generally imposing
their way of life
onto those countries
who are now
'demanding' -
wanting their independence
back
and insisting that
usurpers everywhere
know their place
and leave 'other' peoples
to manage themselves.

Jackie Joseph, (Islington)

Housework

My socks and clothes ran down the stairs
My sheets and towels too
I came in from work
And the bog brush cleaned the loo
My washing jumped into the washing machine
In an hour it was done
The powder poured in by itself
The colours didn't run
On popped the kettle, on went the tap
Plates and dishes had a shower
My dinner jumped in the oven
The oven turned on its own power
My iron ironed out all the wrinkled clothes
My mop and a duster got rid of the dirt
My husband looked up from his paper
And asked me to iron him a shirt
I picked up the phone, phoned the shop
Ordered some commodities and food
They jumped into the cupboards by themselves
Which I thought was very rude
So you see, Prime Minister
You were right all along
No you weren't right
You were dead wrong
Household chores don't do themselves
Women work day and night
Our kids will grow up without a firm hand
They won't know wrong from right
Women could get part-time jobs
About four hours a day
So you won't be so dependant
On your husband's pay.

Mary Crowhurst (London)

The Balloon Fiesta

What a fuss and a bother our dad said
And do we really care
To push and shove with each other
Just to see balloons rise in the air
The world and his wife are at Ashton Court
It's a regular event you see
To watch and wait for all the balloons
To rise up in the air for free
Don Cameron's team and the others
Too numerous to mention are here
They've gathered together for this event
But the wind has got up I fear
The conventional shapes have no bother
To lift off the ground, no sweat
But Rupert the Bear and some others
Will stay tethered tonight I bet
The road show is there blasting music
And throwing out free CDs
When they ask for any requests
Comes a shout from the back, 'T-shirts please'
Hot dogs and chips in abundance
All help pass the time it's true
But keep down the liquid consumption
'Cause look at the queue for the loo?
Then a hush falls over the arena
As the first balloons take to the air
A kaleidoscope of colour
As they drift off over the fair
On reflection it really was worth it
I'm glad that we live so near
And I'm sure that we'll do it all over again
Same time, same place next year

Brenda Jackson (Bristol)

The Broken Cat

That poor cat upon the shelf,
She had a broken neck,
Someone must have done it,
She is a broken wreck,
They'd patched her up with Sellotape,
And thought that that would do,
But now her head is falling off,
And what she needs is glue.
Next to her stands a perfect cat,
In colours, brown and white,
A Siamese with eyes of blue,
She is a lovely sight,
The brown sad cat with broken neck,
Can only sit and cry,
She wished that she could be like that
And asked the question why?
Now she fears her time is o'er,
There will be another cat,
Take her place, be like the other,
Cream and brown, a perfect match.
Do they want to be like others,
With sister cats all set to please,
And their purrs of pure superiority,
Miaowing 'We are Siamese!'
It's true the cat with broken neck,
Is brown and not so tall,
Yet she has graced the home for ages,
Wasn't there no love at all?
The moral of this tale is thus,
You cannot throw away,
A cat with so much history,
For a better shelf display.

Doreen Hutchings (Weston-super-Mare)

Border Holiday At Bowden

Bowden lies sheltered beneath the Eildon Hills,
With russet earth below its green fields,
Where golden gorse or purple heather,
Changes of colour with each season and weather,
I have walked your paths in Maxpoffle Wood,
Smelled fresh air that made me feel good,
Beneath branches of beech and birch,
Then crossed the road to Bowden Kirk your church,
Read some headstones then some more,
To find out what life went on before,
Then walked over the bridge and along the road,
To the village where once they also strode,
First to the fountain on the village green,
Opposite houses and the store where the school had been,
Outside stands the pump, dated eighteen-sixty-one,
Over the road the memorial to many a lost son,
Further on along the road, the village hall,
Where many a bargain is bought from a stall,
There are so many walks with views for the eye,
For us the visitors, who are just passing by,
Who may be here for a very short stay,
But will take home memories that will not fade away,
The penal monument that commemorates Waterloo,
Is always prominent and in many a view,
I lived in a village just like your own,
But now it's a town, how it has grown,
But I hope yours will always remain,
Because it reminds me of youth once again,
Many of the changes I accepted with glee,
Little thinking how it also changed me,
It now breaks my heart, I can see what it's cost,
I think of the beauty and countryside lost.

Peter Brewer (Walton-on-Thames)

Oh So Wrong

When I was young and still at work, I'd sometimes sigh and say.
One day I'll be retiring I can hardly wait the day,
And other folk who overheard, said listen here to me.
When you retire, you'll get bored stiff, just you wait and see.
You'll wake up in the morning, wondering what to do
And you'll look back, remembering these words I've said to you.

Well you were wrong, I know that now, because I've reached the day.
That you all said I'd be bored stiff, well it's not true, no way.
I get up every morning, give the wife her tea in bed.
Feed the dog, have a shower and see the cat is fed.
Put on toast, make more tea, then sort out my pills.
Have my breakfast, clear away, as I do most meals.

I then sort out the rubbish bins, then grab my coat and keys.
I have my grandkids living near, I have to see to these.
I make sure I've done it all and trying to keep cool.
I go and pick up Abbie and drop her off at school.
Sometimes Jack and Raith will come and the dog sneaks in.
It's quite a merry school trip, apart from all the din.

Because my kids, who are grown up, think the same as you.
They're always finding things for me, to mend and make like new.
Like making fences, sheds or things like those garden gnomes.
Gazebo's for the garden, well it does improve their homes.
I mustn't leave the Mrs out, she has the odd job on.
The garden looks untidy, or the Hoover's broken Ron.

Every night at eight o'clock, I make my way to bed.
I usually feel quite tired and can't wait to rest my head.
I think of all the things to do and what is yet to come
And hope that by tomorrow night, everything is done.
I lay in bed and thank the Lord, for my kids and wife.
I'm glad that you were all so wrong, about my bored stiff life.

R Clark (Reading)

Accident

Only an accident.
Nothing more.
Yet my risk assessment was the person least likely.
The person with the least exposure.
An 'accident' should only happen once.
Corrective and preventative measures should then be in place.
I get 'Groundhog Day'
Again and again and again.
An accident? No.

Mary Foggin (Bristol)

Let's Go

Come to the hills with me
And climb the rocky path
Towards a summit free
Of wood or wire
Wilderness laid bare
No restrictions there

Where we can wheel and run
Across the windy waste
In floods of sun
Bathing in heat
Under cotton clouds
Away from crowds

Come away with me to where
We are in the sky
In fresh air
And breathe at last
Away from city grime
A slower pace of time

Let's go now
Let's clear our minds
Let's leave the world below
Let's claim the hills
Let's seize the day
Let's do it our way

Let's walk away
From work
And soul decay
For once and take some time
To be ourselves, have fun
And enjoy the sun

Cora Sild (Cirencester)

Everywhere

I was walking, on the dark side of the moon,
When I saw a star go out
And it made me think of You,
Your strength, You give me each and every day
And I'm in Your debt.
Don't You think, when I pray
While saying goodnight, and thank You for another day.
So I can play on this magical shining planet
You gave us to share, thank You.

Pedi Fribence (Reading)

Lest We Forget - Seven Seven

Today she will remember the morning
She reached for a scarf as she left the house.
Why? Because she rarely wore a scarf.
As usual she boarded the Tube and sat amongst familiar faces
Thinking of autumn when she would walk down the
Aisle a pristine bride.

Why then did the world turn suddenly black?
Had her heart stopped beating? No,
She was alive yet sinking into thick treacle.
The treacle was warm; inviting.

She looked down.
Why were red streamers floating from her legs?
Why were her feet at right angles?
Hanging on shreds of red ribbon?
She felt no pain. Only a desire to sleep;
Sleep, sleep. No! Panic seized her.
She snatched the scarf from her neck tearing it
Frantically between her teeth.
With two strips she bound her thighs
Stanching the crimson flow.

Don't fall asleep. Don't look at the Bosch-like horror.
Keep awake! Keep awake!
Suddenly a voice. 'I've found another alive.'
Then a distant reply, 'Come out there could be another bomb.'
But the Angel stayed on, whispering in her ear -
'Hold on. Hold on.'
'I won't let you die. I won't leave you.'

She said goodbye to her feet in a private valediction -
Now they are only a memory as she moves forward
To greet a world where angels still abide.

Margaret Carl Hibbs (Burnham-on-Sea)

The Guardian

Angel
Fluttering wings
Face of beauty
Always there
Heavenly
There always
Beauty of face
Wings fluttering
Angel.

Charlotte Meredith (Okehampton)

302

Jack Frost Enthrals Me!

When a deep chill in the air befalls the night,
A mysterious hobgoblin will roam until daylight.
It isn't my company he comes enthusiastically seeking,
When at my windows he starts avidly peeking.
He's watching and waiting impatiently instead,
For me to start yawning and retire to bed.

Sam Scarecrow told me - Jack wears a floppy black hat,
Pulled down over icicle hair to hide his eyes of a cat.
Auburn leaves have been woven into an ankle-length coat,
Using some hairy threads discarded by a grooming stoat.
His trousers, are of the same, with worms' silk braces,
And his shoes are stitched 'docks' with ivy-twine laces.

I know he's no roguish pilferer out-on-the take!
It's a gift, for you and I, he's awaiting to make.
Sprightly prancing unseen - and without any sound,
He'll blithely spatter his magic onto the ground.
The panes of our windows will succumb to his spell,
Along with the hedges and bushes he touches as well.

Riding high on a cloud, yet again, he artlessly escapes,
Before I've even woken and attempted to open my drapes.
But, when out of my slumber, I eventually have stirred,
I know something amazing's already occurred!
Eager for the delight of his unique sense of fun,
I leap from my bed to see the artwork he's done.

Leafy designs, brushed with a white frosty paint,
Shimmer and shine on the glass that they taint.
A crystalline world glistens outside my door,
Its white, crispy freshness - I immensely adore.
Rainbowing treasures sparkle brightly in the sun,
For he's bejewelled the homes the spiders have spun!

Donna June Clift (Liskeard)

On Reflection

Thinking back as ever I do
wondering what could have been
had I found my dream come true
wishing I was anywhere else but here
hoping I could find the happiness postcards sell
yet finding bitter hell, it's all behind me now!
Starring from behind the glass
knowing there's more in front
I wonder will I last?

Sharon Elizabeth Benjamin (Stratford)

Her True Memorial

So few people, so few flowers
Such a dismal, bleak event.
How right she had been,
to request there be no service.

But someone - who?
had deemed it meet,
that her departure be marked.
The intent perhaps
for an occasion of such moderation,
so anodyne, hollow and bereft of soul
it might somehow fulfil her wishes.

Scant mention of her name,
Music of another's taste
Bland readings drawn
from random neutral texts.
Bland even before we recalled
the passionate intensity
of her own perceptive prose.
Of this there was no mention.

She was not there, of course.
Nor was there reason for
that elegant, hesitant presence
to grace the chapel corner
as we, we few,
endured those listless moments
for some strangely unknown purpose.

Sombre reflections and emotions later
Above the moss-encrusted tombs,
In a passing instant, a rainbow formed.
Her true memorial.

Heather Collins (Frome)

A Place Called Callender - Scotland!

Fast flowing river streams braking over waiting rocks,
Eyes are drawn to high mountains with veins of soft snow down their slopes.
The hills nearby have newborn lambs of sheep with heads bent low,
Placidly eating the sweet grass as they peacefully go.
As if trying to value what it is I have seen,
A vision of a paradise was my thought; in another world I believe I have been!
If only for a passing while, it had been a taste of pleasure to my thoughts.
If asked to describe that place on Earth, I would reply .. .
A few miles from Callendar, to the Dochart falls was where I was brought!

Rowland Patrick Scannell (Epsom)

A Joy To See

Perched on a branch is a pair of doves,
Quietly watching the world from above.
Round their necks half a collar of black,
Is easily seen as they quietly yak.
They turn their heads as they look around,
They do not miss a single sound.

They see the efforts of an aged man,
Who slowly walks as far as he can.
Arthritic joints cause him pain,
He knows his strength is on the wane.
Accompanied by his faithful dog,
Which understands his master's slog.

Two lively children jump around,
To somewhere exciting they are bound,
Skipping and leaping so full of glee,
Such exuberance is a joy to see.
Their patient mother controls their vigour
Her well-cut clothes enhance her figure.

The aerial swifts with scythe-shaped wings,
The warm summer weather these birds it brings.
Round the rooftops they wildly chase,
With piercing screech they swoop and race.
Then above the rooftops they gracefully fly,
With effortless movements they glide on high.

Sorrow and joy are experienced by all,
It's a fact of life from grace we fall.
As years pass by we all grow old,
Our ageing limbs feel the cold,
Yet still there exists the miracle of birth,
Which fills our hearts with joy and mirth.

Janet Boulton (Billinghurst)

The Rip Tide

The line of the horizon, a certainty separating the sea from the sky,
is lost
Suddenly the swimmer's powerful strokes no longer encompass
the shore
The clear warm water recedes as the roaring rip tide tears in
Unwillingly the swimmer swallowed by the swell surrenders
How he fears the ball of fire in the sky will fade: nightfall
Leaving him alone, cold, exhausted in darkness drifting
Another of nature's offerings to the sea: forgotten, unknown.

Monica Gurney (London)

Change

There are a few traces of
    other lives in these rooms
The name Arezzo on the door
A yellow plastic beetle perched
    on a ledge
Beneath the bed a sign saying,
    'Bless this House' and
    an effigy of the Holy Family.

Everywhere there is cleanliness and light,
A carved chest with elaborate knobs,
Lace curtain sewn with love.
On a chipped wardrobe the
    tracing of a duck.

Now the rose strewn carpet has been torn up,
Carried away by three heartless youths
    wearing long black coats.
The once bright walls are painted white.

Slowly we transform this flat,
    personalising it with our paintings,
    books and fantasies
But at night, when leafy shadows play on the walls,
Moments from their past return,
    filter through the walls.
There is a whispering,
    'Be happy, like us.'

Why did they go away so suddenly?
In night's silence they may come back,
Gently touch our hands,
Laugh with us at our half-realised dreams,
    imperfect yet beautiful lives.

Sandra Eros (London)

Hospital Bus Stop

He made it to the bus, and climbed aboard.
It was a near thing - he almost missed it.
He wondered if he could make it up the steps.
'Are you alright mate?'
The driver spoke for us all.
'I took an overdose last night,' he said,
'My missus left me.'
But he made it to his seat,
And the bus moved on.

Tracy Turner (Walthamstow)

I Am So Lucky, So Lucky

Most ancient of inhabited cities,
where domes of blue-tiled, opalescent mosques
shimmer under arid, tile-blue skies,
and deep, dusk-shadowed streets shuffle past
doorways etched with endless flowing Arabic;

where high walls topped with hint of trumpet vine
and glossy pomegranates
hide close-veiled courtyard intimacy.
Damascus - once a destination for St Paul,
where palm trees and minarets
tower above festering traffic,
bad drains, beggars, princes.

Rows of mean houses, a single Spar shop,
curry corner and crude-angled, cold Welsh chapel
ill-sited in a small, failed town.
Dump of dumps,
truly most charmless of the charmless -

God-forsaken Whitland,
one summer's evening, I found myself,
pacing your arid pavements,
and - yes - had an experience in your only chip shop.
The usual décor. Formica tables topped with ketchup bottles,
mayo, centuries-old brown sauce,
and there to serve me, two gentlemen from foreign parts,

not handsome, but a hint of glamour in their eyes.
Where are you from? I ask, as I hand in the money.
A shadow of a smile and then - Damascus.
Damascus? Struck down in disbelief,
I stumble out into the empty road,
blinded in the grey dusk of the failing light.

Roger Turner (Cheltenham)

The Coffee Pot And Engine

'A metal clad giant'.
Standing firm and strong!
Waiting by a signal
'Spitting sparks high above'.
Coal wagons sit behind,
Signal clears her path,
Heavy clanking wheels!
Gently rock and roll,
'A graceful sight maybe'!

D J Evans (Basingstoke)

307

Diet

Monday's here and it's time to begin
My healthy eating so I can become slim
Over many years the weight's crept on
So I'll try and try until the flab's all gone
Biscuits, cakes, crisps are things of the past
Replaced by low fats, I hope I can last.

My keep fit regime is well under way
Exercising to videos every day
Bum and tum, hips and thighs
Are gradually reducing in their size.
Step on the scales, the dial moves down
Soon it will be time to celebrate in town

Forget baggy jumpers hiding a multitude of sins
No gaps in skirts held together by pins
Out comes the bikini instead of one piece
I'm beginning to look trendy like my teenage niece
Next, on to the hairdressers for a cut and re-style
And then to the park to run my first mile

Big knickers are out, small lacy ones in
I'll no longer worry about my cellulite skin
My skirts are getting shorter, showing legs firmly trimmed
So it's time my old clothes were hastily binned
Perhaps I'll now try the latest craze
Cropped tops, high-wedged shoes, I'm simply amazed

My dreams are over, I've reached target weight
So now I'm ready for my first big date
That little black dress I've been longing to wear
Now hangs in the wardrobe with the greatest of care
And now I can say I truly believe
With positive thinking, goals can be achieved.

Claire Heritage (Southampton)

Better Late Than Never

How true this saying is.
If a person is in a traffic jam
Or had a breakdown,
Or maybe run out of petrol,
Or their bone idle and
Just never gave enough time,
For appointments or whatever,
I think better late than never
Is for sure the answer.

J Clothier (Southampton)

Eternal Quest

Sweet Night approaches;
wound around her flowing
midnight tresses,
a galaxy of stars
and nestled at her throat
a luminous scimitar moon.

Her gown of gossamer
chiffon clouds floats
gently on a zephyr breeze
as she waltzes to the dulcet
music of night birds
across the velvet sky.

Her suitor, the sun,
pursues her, eternally
at a distance - just out of reach.
Drawn by her tranquillity
his futile quest continues,
his ardour burning bright.

But she, dark lady,
heedless of his love
glides gently on till morning
when her day-shy stars
and lambent moon
will hide from the world.

On the edge of sleep
she glimpses ahead
a golden, burnished globe
but swiftly looks away
her eyes too dazzled
by his fervent fiery light.

Grace Galton (Highbridge)

The North Sea

Why not to Yarmouth or Lowestoft or
Somewhere by that sea

Too long land-locked, island man
Will find his way
To that windy waste of water

And then wonder why . . .

Cod and chips will briefly warm him
Washed down with weary tea
While through window wet
He can, but barely, see
Sails and ships
Toys upon the sea

Gulls squeal wheel white
Against clouds racing
Oblivious to rain driving
And to our man
Miserable murmuring
It's bracing, it's bracing as
Along the prom he presses
To pier, sheltered Shangri-La
Sanctuary on heaving sea

But no comfort to our man
He is not amused
Fairy lights will not allay
The darkness of the day

Homage paid to eastern shrine
It's surely time,
Our weather weary pilgrim,
To return hitherland . . . to tea.

Mike Mannion (Letchworth)

Lovers

Golden sands - deep blue sea
I with you - you with me

Holding hands - eyes now meet
Blissful love - kisses sweet

Warmth with sun - zephyr breeze
Mossy bank - leafy trees

Our love so pure - it will endure
Till end of time - till end of time.

Gillian Veale (London)

A Nonsense Poem

When Peter went to Groonin wearing his coat of glade
He carried a sack of letters, whose authors Peter had paid.
He remembered the fifteen herkins and the golden stitches they flayed.
He put on his hat of plander, which he believed had been made
By a two-tailed brown redded broily. Peter liked to encratise the trade.

At first he came to Pearlight, whose stars were drooping and hard,
While the proud inhabitants' offspring were sprooning a son of the bard.
Then sent he to Farley for theakers, for they were good at rosing a card
By the time he reached Suddle, his mind in a muddle; the strone was gilding his pard.

He held his head higher; ignoring the jumples' prent fast.
But when he tripped and brauded his face; the belly folk all walked past.
He stood up again, raised his planderful hat, his body as straight as a mast
'Not one of you,' he averred, 'is a soul like me, not one of you looks aghast.'

The Suddle Brook people he quit and made for the Wonder Mere.
'Here's where I can breen, disport and get thin, have a dasp, drink a beer
For the arbone is in and the mackletread brants once a year.
My long trek is now done, and I'm flecking all my way to the pier.'

At Brondswich he caught a fat mackletread brant
Whose treachite white gills were once seen to pant.
He lit him a fire of shookery sticks and took out his blade
He cut it apart, added conentsy fruit; then filled up his frade.

'Twas stroven the beach as he quirted his pleach,
Yet from within the fish flakes there came to his reach
A smell like an overripe peach. He started a speech
For Peter the postman he knew how to teach.

'I'll get me to Groonin ere the waters curtail,
With my hat, gladen coat I will happily bedrail
If my aim is tumpsy or the sky's full of hail,
I'll go ever onwards with my sack full of mail.'

Lawrence Reeve-Jones (Enfield)

Lily Cat

She nestles into my side on the sofa
resting on the usual pile of newspapers
sleek and furry, meek and purring -
my Lily Cat.

Her black fur glistens in the sunlight
as if scattered with tiny sparkling stars
and the white tip of her paintpot-dipped tail
tip-taps out the steady beat of her geiger-counter purr.

The white hairs lining her delicate ears
almost demand my touch
but I resist
so as not to disturb her peaceful trance of comfort.

The rise and fall of her breathing
gently lifts and drops the arm I hold around her
in precious appreciation of our inter-species bond
and as if she heard this thought
her head turns slowly towards me
eyes closed in feline relaxation, whiskers bristling slightly
as she purrs on in restful pleasure.

My own heartbeat slows as I revel in her warmth,
the delight of her silken fur and the fleshy pink tip
of her tiny flat nose emerging coyly
from the stark contrast
of her black-and-white Mikado-masked face.

I am hers completely.

She is my darling -
a vision of dozing calmness
ringed round by my protective arm -
my Lily Cat.

Maureen Horne (Worthing)

Emmaus Road

Will you recognise me as I travel your life's road,
Will you turn in my direction, let me share your load.
Will you find some time for silence in your busy day,
Will you listen with awareness to the words I say?

Will you trust me when you cannot see the way ahead,
Will you take the hand I offer, willing to be led.
Will you let me journey with you through the dark and cold,
Will you step out in the fog and find a firm foothold?

Will you seek my layers of being which are hid from view,
Will you look for me in everything, in all you do.
Will you trace me in the stranger and the refugee,
Will you find me in life's sorrow, pain and tragedy?

Will you see me with your inner eye of mind and heart,
Will you feel the healing touch I'm ready to impart.
Will you accept forgiveness, let me make you free,
Will you let my love enfold you in security?

Will you flourish in my soil as a fruitful seed,
Will you drink the living water in your time of need.
Will you answer my love's call and give your gift to me,
Will you let me share your life in its entirety?

Will you understand the way through darkness is to light,
Will you see that death leads on to resurrection's might.
Will you embrace the mystery that life must be,
Will you entrust me with the secret of eternity?

It is I who walk beside you from the start to end,
It is I who understand you and would call you friend.
It is I who wait, until I'm recognised and known,
It is I, your loving God, who brings you safely home.

Dorothy Avent (Bristol)

Aunt Clarrie's Funeral

I've been to Aunt Clarrie's funeral, it was today you see,
All the family were there and one of them was me.
We saw her off with great style in a brass and oak lined box,
Then we all rushed back to the house to see what she had got.

The first to get there was Uncle George who made for the garden shed,
He was determined to get the lawnmower that she had promised to Uncle Fred,
Aunt Gladys had always had her eye on the ornamental shepherdess,
So she craftily strolled by the sideboard and shoved it up her vest.

I saw Cousin Jane taking some underwear, so new they still had on their tags,
And stuffing them all hurriedly into Asda carrier bags,
There was Aunt Sophie quarrelling with Uncle Jack I could see,
Both tugging at the TV yelling she promised that to me.

A clever trick played Aunt Mabel she hadn't gone to church you see,
She said she'd stay behind and do the funeral tea,
Making the most of her time whilst she was alone,
She went through Clarrie's drawers with a fine toothcomb.

Then in walked the vicar, I thought sanity at last,
He said a little prayer for Dear Clarrie that had passed,
'Knowing her as I did,' said he 'I would say upon my life,
That she wouldn't mind me taking home a little trinket for my wife.'

By the time the sandwiches were served,
There was not a plate left to put them on,
And when I went to pour out the tea, half the cups were gone,
By the end of the day, the house it was stripped bare,
It looked as though a swarm of locusts had been there.

So enjoy your life spending all your hard-earned dough,
Like they say, you can't take it with you when you go,
When my time comes to go to that great playground in the sky,
Am I going to leave anything to fight over? - No not I.

Sandra Curtis (Ilminster)

Home Sweet Home

(The vision from a slave)

The ship sailed across the sea
From a land that I may never see
Africa, a land and home to me

Africa, a continent of many nations and tribes;
Men captured and taken to lands, mysterious and wide

I remembered the quiet breeze blowing from the east
The ships passing across the open seas
Where are they going, I would wonder,
When will I return?

How long will it be before I return
To the land where I was meant to be.

I have seen many wonders, which were new to me.
But home sweet home I would rather be.

This country I live in is truly strange,
The people are many colours and different shades.
Many inventions but none the black man made.

Home sweet home I would rather be
Where my mother and father will be missing me
Africa my home, there I should be.

For many years I have laboured and toiled
With the hope of returning some fine day
To tell the stories of good and bad.

I need to return for I am feeling sad,
The seas are wide; the oceans are deep,
But if I should return home
There I can finally sleep.

Roy Gunter (Anerley)

The World Outside Is Wrong

The world outside is wrong.
Sunlight shines only on the heavens,
leaving humanity blinded by god.
Fear envelopes all that I feel,
and emptiness fills the place you once was.

You see, the house inside is wrong as well.
It's lonely here, lying half awake.
My tears are masked only by darkness,
My novel's open, it's all that makes this nightmare go away.

Lauren Turner (Rotherhithe)

Memories

As I prepare for Christmas in the village this year,
I think of years gone by and wipe away a tear.
I remember my childhood Christmases, which are embedded in my mind.
To think upon: to pass on: to share, memories of every kind.
The preparations, Mum mixing the Christmas puddings in a huge bowl,
Everyone having a stir, hiding sixpences was her goal.

An iced marzipan cake decorated with Father Christmas, his sleigh and plenty of holly,
Stored in an old biscuit tin ready for the season when we would all be jolly.
A plucked turkey arriving home with Dad after his works do,
First prize in the raffle and a large bottle of whisky too.
Then the soot-covered orange landing in the grate on Christmas Eve,
Due to Dad's slight of hand making me believe.

Calling up the chimney with the present I would like,
Telling me Father Christmas was near.
Then to bed to await Father Christmas, otherwise no presents I'd fear,
I always tried to see him but my parents were too clever.
To recapture this magic of Christmas for the next generation
has always been my endeavour.
The next morning again the unwanted lump of coal in Dad's stocking,
he hoping against hope it wasn't there.
Our stockings filled to the brim with fruit, nuts and sweets from coupons saved with care.

Christmas dinner, crackers, party hats, the Queen's speech
and grandparents dozing in the chair.
We quietly played snakes and ladders, ludo, draughts and snap;
wake them we wouldn't dare.
As my memories fade, reality kicks in.
I've the fairy to put on the tree, my grandchildren are coming to stay.
I've mince pies to put in the oven, the cake to decorate,
presents to hide away ready for Christmas Day.
There's the door, the family are arriving; the magic of Christmas is about to begin.

Valerie Roberts (Stroud)

There's Nothing More Certain Than Death

There's nothing more certain than death.
It gets nearer the day you are born.
As soon as you leave your mother's womb,
Birth leads to life, as an infant, a child, an adult.

Life goes forward like a river goes forward to the sea,
To great uncertainties, love, joy, pain,
But there's only one ultimate certainty, death:
When you'll finally enter the great unknown.
There is nothing more certain than death.

Kevin O'Connor (London)

Twyford Down

The hedges, we were told,
Were flowering in the sun.
But there are no hedges.

There are no hawks that hover
Over the flower-filled down.
There is no down.
No hedgehog has leaves for its back,
No badger earth for a sett.
The only badgers that we see are dead,
Killed by the monstrous road
That cuts the hills in two,
Decreed by mindless planners
Who drew a line on a map
And cared not what was there.

Now no orchids lift their heads,
No mice run in the roots,
No deer graze.
The dainty things are killed.

The earth has been opened
Like a livid sore, a weeping wound,
Its secret depths exposed.
Even the secrets of our past
Have been discarded,
Thrown aside, destroyed.
Those ancient walls and banks
Nothing now but spoil
To be spread and smoothed,
Planted with alien trees
In a futile and insolent attempt
To prettify what they have done.

Daphne Hilsdon (Winslow)

A New Lease Of Life

(For my grandson Ritchie)

I've jumped in muddy puddles and rolled in freezing snow
I've not yet tried skateboarding but I'm keen to have a go.

I really should know better, after all, I'm fifty-three
But I have a little grandson who is very dear to me

There are fifty years between us but it doesn't seem to matter
He's very entertaining and always full of chatter

We go away on holiday, or may be to the zoo
and I find I'm doing many things I thought I'd never do

Like riding on a the roller coaster, flying through the air
Bouncing on a trampoline and just running everywhere!

When his mummy's working and I have him for the day
We watch 'Fireman Sam' on telly or go up the park
to play

We go to see some tractors and watch planes flying high
Or just sit on the wall and watch the buses passing by

Sometimes he stays the night and when the toys are put away
I tell him special stories and we talk about our day

We' climb the wooden hill' and when he's safely
tucked in bed
I gently stroke his baby curls and softly kiss his head

He can be a little monster and a cheeky little boy
But he's 'Nanny's little angel' and he's brought me
so much joy

It may not last forever – No, it may not always be
But for now we are the best of friends, my grandson and me

Liz Saunders (Kidlington)

That Day In September

My heartbeat gets faster and faster.
I almost cannot breathe.
There is nobody here to help me, or relieve the pain I am feeling.
I feel a tear drop onto my shimmering cheek.
My thoughts are wild, and out of control as an ocean falls from my distant glazed blue eyes.

Lost, confused, shocked.

An accident in the busy city, wiping out my father's existence.
Unexpected, sudden, I feel empty, alone.

I am useless and no matter what I do I cannot help my father, I am expecting the worst.

Rushing, panicking, to get to the big city.
Every second passing seems like a minute, every minute seems like an hour,
The longest journey of my life.

I need to be strong for my mother, a rock that will never break.
Hurry up, I think to myself, I feel like I am the main actress on a movie set, and this scene isn't real.

On edge, terrified, praying.

I walk through two big white doors, unprepared.

I feel my father is gone.

Why is this happening? How is this fair? What has he done to deserve this?

I see my father; a team of white coats surround him.
All I can hear is beeping ,all I can see is blood.

I write this, with a smile on my face, no sign of any tears.
My father is in the other room, twelve months on from that day in September.

Thank you angels,
Until we meet again.

Kimberley Reid (Lancing)

Don't Ask Me Anymore!

Don't ask me any more -
I've told you all I can!
All I remember is the face of my child
as she smiled at me
from inside the school gates.

'See you at three!' I called and waved
and she waved back, confidently,
because she trusted me to be there for her, forever;
as I had been, every day,
each night, of her short life.

By now, she knew her numbers well.
Time was a reality for her;
time, that was an agony for me
on this, her first day at 'big' school.

Time remains an agony for me.
This could be my last day of living.
Why would I want to go on living,
when her life is no more?

Her life, her school -
our everything.
Blasted out of existence:
by high-altitude bombers -
or a home-made device.
What difference does it make?

There is nothing left.
No trace of her beautiful being.
No traces of anyone living.
Can someone - anyone- anywhere -
tell me *why?*

Daphne Helliwell (Ringwood)

They Invaded Our Land

Arriving on our shores with canoes, they walk through the pebbled sand
Who these pale men are and where they come from, I don't understand,
They came from the sea, with foreign ships that were heavily manned
So one by one they invade our sacred land.

In the dense jungle our hidden city they find, which they soon invade,
One by one our temples and homes they burn, destroy and raid,
They then begin to kill us all systematically with the blade,
As an Aztec I feel my race is slowly beginning to fade.
The rest like me and my king Montezuma become captured slaves,
And so these new white rulers had to be obeyed.

Under Cortes, these Spaniards as they called themselves
Uttered a different sound,
We had to do everything they said and they kept us bound
For our riches such as jade, but especially gold they searched around,
We couldn't say a thing as they took our gold and treasures they found.

Even our very culture and way of life they ended and put to rest
Our religion of human sacrifice they destroyed and suppressed.
To them we were just viewed as sub human slaves and a pest
These invaders forced their faith upon us, they thought theirs was best.

With their swords they slaughter and kill everyone, when they came
Erasing our very race, existence and our very name,
Even though our Indian race were very tame
Though we begged for our survival, they murdered us just the same.

White man came and took away our land, riches, customs, faith and lives,
They had us under submission, killing us with their swords and knives,
Just like the Toltecs, Incas our Aztec cities they burn.
Why they almost obliterated every trace of our race, I don't understand,
The Spaniards came to destroy all that we built up with our hand,
Yes, they took away our sacred land.

Simon Genchi (St Albans)

The Great British Eccentric

Small, hard beetles, shining jewels
perverting the lights just like pearlised varnish
on the nails of young girls.

They weren't tough enough
nor wise enough
to escape him and his pinch.

Dead in his palm, dead
pinned against the white backing sheet, pincers
reaching out for a final hand hold.

His hobby, his collection, his delicate love
and the reason for his simple secretive smile.

Across counties and countries he chases them
seeking out their scuttle
of noisy high heels down Sunday morning streets.
Their colours the palate of cheap eye shadows. He takes
them all, from the smallest to the gnarliest.

Chrysomelidae
Coleoptera
Dermestidae dynastinae

He blends into his surroundings;
a shopping centre, an unpronounced jungle. He changes hues,
changes browns. He does not need to attract;
he hunts, he yanks, he lifts, he breaks every rule
of the countryside.

Not for him the flippant elegance of the butterfly.
No, not for our man, so fashionably eccentric
in his T-shirt with the trail of a foreign
slug slipping across his chest.

August Head (Bristol)

Fir Hill

(Figg-Hoblun Estate, Colan, Nr Newquay)

Deep in dark woods remain but crumbling walls
From where each layer gradually falls;
Here once a handsome mansion proudly stood,
Home of the wealthy, erstwhile great and good.
Bramble and ivy now festoon what's left
And upstart sycamore exploits each cleft.
Upkeep long shunned by the far distant heir,
Remorseless time claims uncontested share.

N D Wood (Newquay)

First Spring

It's almost four months since you died,
April now, bright sunshine and cold winds
In the garden, the rhododendron
we planted for your ninetieth birthday
is blooming vigorously
and your camellias, so poor last spring,
are a riot of blossoms ,red and pink.
I place cards and flowers on the table
like we did last Easter
I'm slowly sorting through your things,
take a few clothes to the charity shop -
it's difficult to part with them,
old blouses and jackets, some out of fashion,
flowered, striped, even ugly -
they smell of you, and of the Home you hated
I see in them again your old body,
soft, frail and forceful,
your thin arms,
that strange lump upon your collar bone,
your hands disfigured with arthritis
and specked with age spots, their touch
too cool, but able still
to grip mine strongly.
There's an unworn outfit in the wardrobe
you bought last June
You're walking in the garden in your old waistcoat,
the pockets bulging with keys and handkerchiefs
as you bend to inspect your daffodils,
pull up handfuls of long grass
that shouldn't be growing
in among the flowerbeds.

Susan B Chappell (Luton)

Untitled

(Remembering my brother Albert James Thompson 22.03.30 to 29.05.08)

Remember me at the break of dawn
When twinkling dew is on the lawn
When birds sing their first new song
When silly things in life go wrong
For I am with you still
To help you through life's next uphill
My love goes on for infinity
I'll always be there in your memory

Patricia Jones (Lancing)

The Rainbow

Soft mist of rain,
With the sun shining,
Out of the rain.
And yet behind
A rainbow
Began to form,
Across the sky,
Quarter key,
Half sky,
Then whole.
A beautifully
Coloured arc,
From side to side
Across the sky.
With two pots
Of golden treasure
Waiting.
Reflection
Of the rainbow
In the raindrops,
On the grass.
Millions
Of multicoloured baubles,
Extraordinarily iridescent.
The coloured bow
Of hope
Given to us
By God
And a reminder
Of His love
For us.

Patricia Laing (Taunton)

A Walk In Derbyshire

(For Michael Riddall)

Timeless landscape, not quite empty -
Silent hilltops and whispering riverbanks
treasure the tread of light-footed giants
who pass here in their eternity,
impossibly chasing their soaring desires
to capture for ever in perfect lines
that ring them with magic. What delight
when a rhyme-catcher walks with me.

Thomas Ország-Land (London)

Let's Celebrate Together

I feel like skiving - so let's go driving
Don't think . . . just get up and go!
Grab your shades, jump in the car
It don't matter how far . . . we'll know:
The guitar's on the back seat
The tent's in the boot
Come drive away . . . let's scoot
Up in the hillside, thro' the woods and trees
I need you beside me, I'm begging you . . . please:
Escape from the city, get out of the town
If we don't go soon - together we'll drown:
Let's find a beach,
No one can reach
I'll brush the sand from your hair:
Imagine it's an island
That's only ours
Just yours and mine to share:
In the moonlight, when there's a chill in the air
I'll keep you warm, you know I'll be there:
Let's make sweet music, we'll strum the guitars
Just find some chords
That match with the stars:
Over the rippling waves
I can hear your sweet voice
This is our life - it's our choice:
Then when our soiree is over
By the early morning light - and
Others invade our space . .
We'll just jump in the car
No matter how far - and
We'll skive to another place.

Julie Powell (Hounslow)

Wedding Day

To the happy couple this poem's just for you,
With love entwined in every word right the way through.

Some come from far away on this your special day.
All family and friends are gathered here
To show their love to those they hold so dear.

Love is a hard word to define,
It can be very painful but mostly it's sublime.
So once you have found it hold on very tight,
As just like a roller coaster it has great depth and height.

Pat Cheeseman (Ascot)

The Wood Back Home

I turn in for the night,
Taking the Thirties exit
To find a summer in Wales,
Remembering a place
On the memory map,
A retreat for boys
Daring shadows for ghosts
Under monster trees.
Here the stream
With mirrors of dead boys
Famous among Saturdays
Of freedom. I reach
The clearing of bluebells
Plucked for presents.
Here the path leading
To sparse light, a sanctuary
Where rocks protruded
Like sinister artistry,
A secret dell for boys
Brainwashed by rituals.
I move on. Memory checks
The scene when play ended.
Burdened with secrets
We shed them one by one
As age and time demanded.
Then long trousers
And the first harsh Woodbine.
We exchanged toys for tools,
Signed on at the mine
And performed rough rituals
With schoolboy hands.

Robert Morgan (Waterlooville)

Highways And Byways

The title brings so many thoughts,
Who'd go away to foreign ports?
Stay home, enjoy the sunshine's rays,
On balmy walks on sunny days,
To me 'byways' are all I need
Such peaceful beauty, springtime's seed,
They lift my heart and haste my way,
All nature's painting, free display!
Let's have a picnic - rug is spread
Some sausage rolls and jam and bread,
Some scones and cakes and lemonade,
Like nature - it is all home-made.
Our dog can run without a lead
To chase his ball through grass and reed,
And wag his tail as he comes back,
It's gorgeous all along the track.
Cow parsley, foxgloves, primrose too
Along with bluebells oh so blue.
Carpet of colour in the sun's rays,
It brightens a walk in the darkest of days,
The children all can dance and play,
The birds sing out, as if to say
What better lies beneath the stars, no noisy, smelly, motorcars,
The sun is set and time for bed.
With dreams to share with cuddly Ted.
A lovely day so full of fun,
The holiday has just begun,
But highways have their part to play,
To get us home the quickest way.
Such memories that are ours to keep,
And treasure as we fall asleep.

Morag Bayne Pocock (Penzance)

A Million Different Poems

It's our twentieth anniversary the Forward Press letter said
With over a million different poems that people have loved and read.
Poems that have travelled all around the world;
From sadness and heartbreak and tears of despair
Does anyone really listen, does anyone even care.
Laughter breaks through the dark clouds like sunshine after rain;
You can hear the pages turning, be it morning, noon or night
As people search for poems that set the mood just right.
I first wrote a poem in 1998 and to see my words in print set my pen ablaze
Twenty poems later in 2004 came a little reminder, please write some more.

My journey began with 'Things I Like' sunsets and 60's jive
In the poem 'Today' Easter tells that our Lord is risen and alive
'Going to Town' spoke of a disabled person's nightmare;
'A Walk Through Life' looked at different events over the last sixty years,
'I Miss' looked back at life where love had been swept away.
Then in a lighter vein I wrote 'The School Play'
A poem for my Mom, a child's love for all to see,
The poem for my Dad that Alzheimer's took away from me
'Guides are Great' is a simple fact but true;
And 'Judgement' tells its own story that it could happen to you!

It was 'Such A Silly Argument' a way of saving face
With 'The Bug' a little bit scary cos the creature wants my space
'Grandparents' begs the question why do our children fight;
In 'Up The Wall' I just had to take a stand
'Is Anyone There' my thoughts got out of hand!
In 'Remember the 5th of November' the children always pay;
'Always Remember' our glorious dead as down the ages mothers ask the question why?
I'm so proud of 'Dannie's Christmas' it almost made me cry,
A 'Christmas Thought' sums up the best place to start and end
I love to read poetry and I'm glad, Jesus is my friend.

Lynne Cassels (Gloucester)

Sir Winston Churchill

An effigy so powerful
of a man does tell
Hard he worked
and hard he schemed
to serve is country well
Sir Winston Churchill's
watchful eye
His statue does portray
overlooking Parliament
in no uncertain way.

Melvyn Roiter (London)

That Bottom On The Woodstock Road

Forty years have passed, but
Still I can see that bottom,
Cycle-borne, dancing, manic, fugitive,
Skirt-taut in some deranged pursuit
Along the Woodstock Road.
Hers were familiar, unattainable buttocks;
I'd studied them, two years before
Cupped with discretion in their lurex sheaths,
And pledged to other hands than mine.

Were I to take utter possession
Of that nimble bottom now,
Which is still nimble, not a doubt of it.
I would command its silver-headed owner thus,
'This is myth time, Mistress of Classics,
Time for enactments. Do you recall
The eager chasings round those attic urns?
I've come to such variations somewhat late,
But I am an enthusiast,
And a most adroit practitioner.
So, flex, Mistress of Classics,
Flex and accommodate yourself to me.'

You may not believe me, but
I'm sure that if this fantasy
Were to become real flesh, she
Choosy, fastidious, distanced woman then
Would now agree to everything I asked.
There are rear entrances
To any woman's heart,
And even if a man comes late
It is sufficient that he comes at all.

Dean Juniper (Reading)

When Evil

When evil crossed my path
I spat on it the snake of wrath
I just said, 'Go away.' It did
Faith I had, had as a kid
Another evil reared its head
I said the same, the evil fled
I said the same again and again
Until the evil was shot into flames
See evil would never have beaten me
I wouldn't let it.

J Mills (Bedford)

Reminiscing

A table shelter of cold steel grey,
Funny face gas masks and fire drill day
Air raid wardens and no street light
Ack-ack guns that took up the fight!
Ration books and standing in queues,
Digging for victory the whole year through.
Paper chains that kept falling apart
Thick black curtains to keep it all dark.
Cod liver oil; that disgusting taste!
Eat every scrap. No waste. No waste!

Christmas carols sung by bright firelight,
Praying for safety through the long cold night.
Aircraft engines droning overhead,
Hurry up now. Get out of bed
Down to the shelter of steel blue grey,
And stay in there out of harm's way.
Down to the woods in a family group
Picking up fir cones and lumps of wood.
Barbed wire barriers along 'our' beach,
With all that sand just out of reach.

Yanks and Canadians billeted near
Noisy and boisterous, assaulting our ears.
Needing friendship so far from home
'How do we get to St Paul's dome?'
Chewing gum and saying 'Gee'
Why ever can't they speak like we?
Memories flash (a camera snap)
Dumping joys in an ageing lap.
Sorrows too are paraded past
In a gigantic life-filled cast.

Jean Harrison (Calne)

Behind The Bike Sheds

Behind the bike sheds, here sit I
Wondering whether to laugh or cry.
I sit here in mournful bliss
No one to cuddle, no one to kiss.
Can't think what's so fascinating
Behind the bike sheds contemplating.
What is all the fuss about,
It's all talk I do not doubt.
All my dreams have been diminished
Whistle's blowing, playtime's finished.

Keith Barton (Hemel Hempstead)

I Am A Poet!

I am a Poet,
I write the words that others will read,
I expose my soul, my profoundest feelings on lines of paper
And let them be abused.

I love and I laugh and I cry out in the open,
I have no hiding place for walls are transparent to thought.
When people read the lines I have written,
They pull at my flesh with their minds,
They pick my bones with their criticism and
Leave the open wounds uncovered for society to infest.

The white swans that fly through my midnight world,
In the blackness of a winter night silhouetting themselves
On a blue moon horizon,
Floating like angel dreams towards some forgotten time
When life was so simple and people so kind,
Light up my dark world like a ray of sun that splits a rainless cloud.

And I do all this because I cannot express in the verbal way,
The things I want to say,
The emotions I want you to feel in me and the love that
Is within my heart.
The love of all things beautiful,
True beauty that lies within as well as the candy covered shell
That only the sightless can see,
But I am only this body, this skeletal being
Who is mute to feeling but heavy on thought.

So I convey to you my life on a page!
A page to be opened or put away in some box in a darkened
Attic for someone who never knew me to devour again
When I am long gone.

T J Hedges (Wimbourne)

The Crystal Ball

Shrouded in mystery is the clear crystal ball.
Gipsies foretell when a ritual they perform.
Clearing the mists to predict one's fate.
Gazing into emptiness like an oracle it relates.
Glass made with sand from some strange distant place.
Ancient and eerie, full of magic it makes.
Shaped like a globe. Its own unique world.
A sphere only forecasting when our atmosphere with it's twirled.
Concealing its secrets in an occult cosmic field.
Its universe the key into a whole different world.

Sandra Una Brisck (London)

Faery

My horse stood still by the pool
And gently cropped the grasses there,
While a girl on the mountainside
Smiled as I stared
And danced off into the air.

And as I followed her with a hungry cry,
I found the air a mire:
A sucking bog which clung up to my knees,
While she o'er the peat like a breeze.

Her feet and her ankles were bare,
White and smooth and delicate.
We came to some land at the hub of the bog,
An islet raised above the swallowing slime
With a barrow silhouetted black
Against the darkling sky.

And she stood by its doorway, waiting
And she stood by its maw, still waiting
Then with never a word,
She took me by the hand
And led me down into the black, cold earth.

She fed me cake in the fire-lit grotto
Which tasted as sweet as despair,
Then came to me sudden and unbound her hair,
Black and abundant, that blinded me there
As her lips fed on my hungry mouth
Like a feathered moth lapping
At a nocturnal flower
And I knew nothing till they dug up the barrow
And found my skull still lying there.

Garreth Simister (Ventnor)

Wayside

As I walk down the lane in the morning early,
a hare appears from a field and lopes along before me.
A yellowhammer hops from bush to bush along the low cut hedge.
I stop by the hump-back bridge over the river
and watch a mallard duck and family slide down the bank
into the gently flowing water.
A skylark rises from a cornfield and rises high and higher into the sky,
singing, singing filling the quiet morning with his beautiful song.
I am lost in wonder at the beauty of nature
and this moment in time will live with me forever.

Evelyn Farmer (Chard)

The Lonely House

The house is silent now,
No happy laughter ringing
Or children's footsteps clattering in the hall.
Unruffled cushions on the old settee
Resent their tidiness
And Lego bits and jigsaw pieces
Tucked down the sofa's sides
Wait patiently for small fingers to retrieve.

The occupants long gone,
On their tragic holiday of no return
Killed by a 'plane dropping like a stone'
They could never come back
And now the house is deprived of company
And its family who's love once filled every room . . .

So time is standing still
No one to wind the clocks or switch the light bulbs on
Allowing their shades to cast a rosy glow
And loneliness combined with damp and mustiness
Replace the smell of scented candles
That once wafted waves of happiness
For the photo frames have lost their memories

So stands the house with an ailing heart
Waiting like a sick patient for a replacement
Waiting for new life with love it's only hope
For it has lost the magic of that word called 'home'

Outside, its only companion
Standing like a sentry by the garden gate,
A post with a brightly painted sign
That reads: *A Family House For Sale.*

Dulcie Levene (Bournemouth)

Islands

Along the rim of a basalt tumour
That swelled and burst through the globe's soft, young skin,
Solidified and dead since long ago,
The islands are left, their blue granite honed
And ground back by the sharpening sea,
Like rotten teeth spaced out on shrunken gums.
Boist'rous tidal waters tumble between
Falling away to the World's far end
And round the wrinkled cliffs and bent thorn trees
The stiff, indifferent wind never stops.

R J Raymond (Guernsey)

River Dart

Dartmoor's tears as dewdrops fall
Penetrate the peat to its granite core.
Streams appear, hidden curlews call
Soon to be lost by the river's roar.

Conceived by the elements in the Earth
Born of beauty and power.
The Dart on its journey will increase its girth,
Before freedom at the castle towers.

Bubbling and dancing as a moorland stream
Falling off rocks in foam.
The life it sustains is beyond a dream
As nourishment, haven and home.

Waters meet and the river grows
Noisy, tumbling off the moor.
Until it slows between distant banks
Silence! Clear, to the river floor.

Driving turbines at Abbey and Mill
Its waters now harnessed by man.
Sharing its valley with giants of steam,
Purity, destroyed out of hand.

Taken for granted by man and craft
Grown to maturity.
The Dart, now a working river,
Has to fight the encroaching sea.

The River Dart in war and peace
Has seen men live and die.
Loved by all from source to mouth,
Carved with Devonshire pride!

John A Gordon (Totnes)

Anyone For Cricket?

Flipperty flap and wiggery woo,
There's a strange little creature in my shoe.
It hopped out so high and was springing around,
What is this strange thing that I have found?
Into the kitchen and through the door,
Light as a feather to be seen no more.
Wait a minute, I can see it out there,
Floating down in the wind onto a chair.
As I creep closer I now can see,
It's a cricket so bright and green as a pea.

Alma Betts (Uxbridge)

Oh! To Be Slim

In the mirror I saw one day,
A big fat woman looking my way,
Oh dear I thought, *who could it be?*
Was the fat woman really me?

I used to be slim, oh look at me now,
How did I get to look like a cow?
Why didn't they tell me I looked so plump?
Why didn't they say I looked like a frump?

I wanted to be slim, not be a tub,
So off I went to slimming club,
I got on the scales, I nearly died,
'You're two stone over!' the woman cried.

She told me all the things I couldn't eat,
No chips, no chocs, no cakes or red meat,
I made up my mind, I had to be strong,
I didn't want to eat anything wrong.

It's so easy for a rabbit you see,
But eating green salad was hard for me,
But now in the mirror I see each day,
Old chubby me just fading away.

My husband says he's lost a fat wife,
He just loves the new slim one in his life,
I feel so wonderful, I feel so good,
I feel like every woman should.

So all you fatties don't feel so blue,
Start eating lettuce, tomatoes, and cue,
Instead of looking like the trunk of a tree,
You will look like a willow, slim as can be.

Pauline Xena (Bristol)

Here I Am

Mighty tree
Spreading your evergreen limbs
You fill the space
Your type can take
No butchery of your shape
What joyous chance you were given
To grow the way you have
There you stand
Saying simply,
'Here I am.'

Judy Clinton (Gloucester)

Durweston PTA Summer Ball

The Hall and patio were quite supreme,
From entering door 'twas like a dream;
'The Enchanted Garden' was the theme,
For Alison Foot, this was her dream.

The helpers came from near and far,
The things they brought just filled their car;
The tables laid so neat and prim,
The decorations were so trim.

The lighting, decorations, were first class,
The fairy lights sparkled like polished brass;
The bar set up to be top grade,
The raffle and auction, real profits made.

'Innervision', really a great live band,
Some dancing as good as any in land;
The food just delicious with fairies to serve,
So sprightly, so prancy, and all kept their nerve.

A night to remember for many a year,
Enjoyment and friendship without any fear;
So many to thank for work and for gifts,
'Twas in early hours before any drift.

On Sunday morning helpers came to the Hall,
They worked like beavers to dismantle the ball;
The spirit throughout this glorious event,
An example to others whose spirits sometimes dent.

To all PTA Committee and others, three cheers,
You deserve lots of praise, as well as free beer;
To our headteacher, our thanks for efforts throughout,
A fantastic achievement without any doubt.

John Paulley (Blandford Forum)

Treasures Of Youth

Through coldness of night, morn's sun still rose high,
shrouded in darkness, while light filled the sky,
pain in my heart and my body felt old,
warmth filled my void, then her love took my cold.
She entered my life, like a bolt from the blue,
she healed and repaired, gave me hope anew,
flooding my life with the treasures of youth,
lies and deceptions were cured by her truth.
She could be an angel, sharing my dreams,
touching my heart, with the smile that she beams.

Des Beirne (London)

In Memory Of Dad

The day you first held me in your arms
I knew how much you cared.
You worked hard through life to give me
The love and happiness we shared.

As a child I looked up to you
You were my hero through and through.
I wanted to make you proud of me
And be a good person, just like you.

The teenage years were difficult,
Growing up was quite a strain.
You put up with so much from me,
Through tears of happiness and pain.

You supported my decisions,
Good advice you gave me too.
Helping me along the way
As only the best dads do.

The cancer took you slowly
Before my eyes I watched you die.
Suffering along the way,
All my heart could do was cry.

I thought you'd be here forever,
To love and guide me on my way.
I was not prepared for the loss
When you died on the 7th of May.

I miss you Dad so very much,
A part of me went with you.
I only hope that you know,
How much I love you too.

Teresa Brimble (Luton)

Sound The Fanfares To Celebrate

Come blow your trumpet to celebrate
Beat the drum roll we will stay up late.
Let's dance past the midnight hour
Never mind the passing shower.
Let's eat funky food on party plates
We will have a drink with all your mates.
To commemorate these years of love
We will burst some balloons from above.
So raise your glasses in the air
As celebration time is here.

Marina Smith (Bristol)

337

The Challenge

It was the greatest challenge
The biggest prize of all
That many people yearned for
But most would fail and fall.

They said we'd never make it
They said we'd never win
But it made us more determined
That we would not give in.

Standing on the sidelines
We watched the other fail
Taking note of what they did
Before we told our tale.

As the days progressed we watched them
Failing one by one
Until at last our turn came
And we stood there in the sun.

The people stood expectantly
To see what we would do
As you took my hand in yours
And I pledged my life to you.

We turned around to face them
And then we took a bow
That was fifty years ago
With a repeat performance now.

They said we'd never make it
They said that we'd give in
At last we proved to everyone
That it is possible to win!

Giovanna Gallo (Swindon)

Untitled

Congratulations, all the best
On your 20th anniversary.
Thank you all very much
For giving me the opportunity
Of writing a poem
Saying hello
Life is there to be lived
Whatever age
Whatever stage
We all have something to give.

Just Haze (Swindon)

Skywatch

Now that the summertime is here
You can be sure where I'll be found,
Out here in my pretty garden
Where the joys of nature abound.

Bees dawdle thru' my lavender,
On the arch the roses ramble,
While thru' them all like butterflies
Golden honeysuckle amble.

It's tempting then to rest awhile
'Mongst perfume so heavenly,
But my favourite place of all
Is by my dear old willow tree.

I sit on the seat alongside
To hear its gentle whisp'ring sound,
But while my ears are listening
My dreaming eyes are skyward bound.

I see soft white clouds ever drifting
And changing their shape as they go,
It's like another world up there,
So different from here below.

As birds fly thru' and out the clouds
It's a really magical sight.
While their plaintive cries echo around
As they wing ever onwards in flight.

So rested and refreshed now
From my lovely garden I'll go,
Whilst the knowledge of what is out there
Leaves me filled with an inner glow.

Daphne Lodge (Carshalton)

Complicated

Complicated is as complicated as complication at its best.
These words I write are written this way to put complication to the test.
See the way I write is wrong or is it wrong for me to write?
If my aim in these words is to confuse the reader's sight.
My task set out as follows, to make you stop and stare.
To delve so deep into this page you'll start to disappear.
For example on the 12th, I sat and wrote this line,
To show it's possible to go backwards and forwards at the same time.
You went back in time to check the fact whilst time continued forward.
It's facts like that which complicate, I hope it's not too awkward.

K Swaby (Wembley)

The Web

I have spent a lot of time creating my website
Working long hours through dark of night
Criss-cross up and down and round and round
Busy busy without making a sound

There that should do it, final touches done
The trap is set nicely for some innocent one
Offering them something they think they need
Rubbing my hands together to satisfy my greed

Scurrying away for somewhere to hide
Keeping alert, all my eyes opened wide
Anticipation is high, am hoping for a kill
To satisfy my hunger need to take my fill

It's all a scam, the whole site is a fake
Give me your credit card numbers, I am on the take
Could not care less if you are rich or poor
Just keep giving to me, more and more

Suddenly a movement, a vibration I feel
At last I can eat, I have caught me a meal
Hapless victim does struggle, I have to act fast
Wrapping it up tightly I need to make this last

Don't want your ID, don't care if you are young or old
I may seem warm and friendly but really I am icy cold
Sucking you dry of all your money, that is my game
On the web you will find me but you will never know my name

The web is a very useful tool for all users
But can also be used by some nasty abusers
When playing on the web, please user beware
Every man, woman, child, please take great care.

Mike Tracey (Plymouth)

Untitled

Just in time I saw the light
Hot blurred over but burning bright
People fleeing everywhere
Just no time to stop and stare
Much to my amazement then
A tiny bird flew in the glen
Maybe it will ease down soon
Hopefully in time for noon
Guy Fawkes has visited
A little too soon.

D Prescott (Billingshurst)

Over A Rainbow

The years quickly pass by
    Some days with a sigh
But looking back of long ago
    One feels riding over a rainbow

Seeking the way of nature
    Doth lead to a pleasant future
All lives encounter a somewhat frown
    But Heaven reveals beauty surrounds

Writing poetry offers a life worthwhile
    Giving folk a bright outlook and smile
Filling hearts with rhapsody and a glow
    They feel riding over a rainbow

When young one has many dreams
    The mind travels to extremes
But such can be achieved by thee
    As many folk realise and agree

Meeting folk offering them cheer
To find the light within banishing a tear
Will feel thyself in rhapsody
    Just knowing thou made another happy

One can overcome days of sorrow
    By looking to a bright tomorrow
A surprised friendly verse received
    A person distressed can feel relieved

Nothing is more pleasant than seeking nature
    Life's wonder of every cure
When one is feeling somehow low
    Nature gives feelings riding over a rainbow

Josephine Foreman (Chichester)

Figures On A Hillside

In shadows gathered at set of night,
In the eventide of a long, long life,
An old man scaled an ancient hill,
In stirred response to a childhood will.

Upwards, upwards, up he went,
A silent figure with a back full bent,
Winding a slow and measured way,
That echoed the span of his mortal day -

For he carried the weight of the sum of his years,
The parchness of laughter, the sadness of tears;
All the days he had lived and walked on his own,
All the days he had needed but suffered alone.

But the rise of the hill became too much for him;
His heart beat a drum in the ache of each limb,
And he fell in his path, and lay midst the heather,
To stare to the summit, far beyond his endeavour -

Until a young man, striding up the same trail,
Took gently his arm, so thin and so frail,
And held it close by him, as soft as a feather,
And said, 'Come, my friend, let us journey together.'

And together they reached the end of that climb,
Where together they shared that feeling sublime,
Of finding success by finding each other,
And knowing that all men to all men are a brother -

That to walk side by side, makes a far better pace,
Than to cling to one's strength in a one-winner race;
And think only of Self, and not of another -
Still out on life's hillside, in need of a brother.

Peter Wheat (Poole)

My Wanda

She wandered through our garden, on a beautiful summer's day,
    and as we gazed across at her, she slowly made her way,
to where we both were sitting, and looked up as if to say,
    'I don't know if you realise it, but I am here to stay!'

We asked around the neighbourhood, put stickers on a tree,
    but the days passed by, and no one called, while she purred complacently.
So we set off to the shops at last, food bowls and basket bought her,
    but back again we had to go, for a bowl for drinking water!

We had never owned a cat before, so we learnt as we went along,
    and if she disagreed with us, it was made clear where we went wrong.
We had so much to learn about, but first we had to ponder,
    on what to call our beautiful cat - oh, of course we'll call her Wanda!

We had such fun, the three of us, as we all played together,
    a game of football, butterflies or a single pigeon feather.
She entered into both our hearts, our family was complete.
    We were so very lucky and found life indeed was sweet.

But when tragedy fell upon us, then Wanda came into her own,
    and with such love and thoughtfulness, made sure I was never alone.
She stayed by my side in the daytime, at night she would sleep on my bed,
    and those beautiful eyes spoke such volumes, that told more than if words had been said.

The years that followed went to show how intuitive she could be,
    our roles reversed, and with effortless ease, she continued to look after me.
But then her strength deserted her, and her health became so poor,
    with tests and operations, then the words, 'We can do no more!'

So I watch my beloved cat, in the winter of her years,
    I tell myself despairingly, as I struggle with my tears;
that I will lavish love and care, that she gave so freely to me,
    to the bravest, cleverest and kindest cat, that this world will ever see.

Margaret Bathgate (Barnet)

Granny's Apron

Do you remember Granny's apron
Made in the pinny and bib style
Just right for so many uses
And always worn with a smile.

In the kitchen Granny had a system
Easy to understand
Wrap the hot handles in the apron
Not to burn her hand.

In the garden for Granny it was useful
She could pick up all the vegetable with care
Gently place them in the bowl of the apron
And carry them to the kitchen to prepare.

On washing days it was really handy
Somewhere to put the pegs
In the chicken run it was dandy
Just right for collecting the eggs.

The orchard was our favourite pastime
Spending hours and hours at play
Sometimes, one would have an accident
Granny's apron would lovingly wipe the tears away.

Sunday was always a special day
Everyone clean and smartly dressed
Granny's apron was always brilliant white
Starched, and neatly pressed.

The best of all it was close to Granny
And I will tell you the reason why
Her apron hung like a curtain
An ideal hiding place if you are shy.

Vic Gilbert (Devizes)

Somerset

The swirling mists round Glastonbury Tor
In ghostly swathes eradicate the base
The square-shaped edifice atop stands proud
A beacon to the pilgrims to this place

And farther down the road the Festival
At Pilton makes its urgent presence felt
From every walk of life they congregate
As into one huge throng the people melt

A different kind of tower from Glastonb'ry
Is starkly outlined on the Channel coast
The nuclear plant entrenched at Hinkley Point
Made Somerset, reluctantly, its host

The River Parrett boasts its little Bore
At Bridgwater, a source of huge delight
To children on the bridge who watch the scene
And revel in this unfamiliar sight

A county rich in pastoral pursuits
Of basket-making, thatching, digging peat
Where Alfred, King of Wessex, stayed awhile
At Athelney, a haven and retreat.

This gentle county also had to bear
The stains of battle on its quiet land
To Sedgemoor came the Duke of Monmouth's troops
To find themselves defeated and out-manned

So rich in folklore and in history
A fascinating tapestry of time
To delve into the past is wonderful
To live here in the present is sublime.

Joyce Wenmoth (Wincanton)

The Wood

Looking way back - to life as a kid,
If our mothers knew only one half that we did,
Their blood would run cold - it would do them no good,
To learn of the things that we did in the wood.

The wood was the place that all the kids went,
For hours and hours of time well (mis)spent.
On a hillside that came to the back of our street,
Criss-crossed by tracks made by hundreds of feet.

The den sites were fought for by each rival gang,
Fighting got dangerous and bowstrings would twang.
Then a punch up would probably finish the game,
Then home for tea went the hurt and the lame.

A swing was hung high with a rope that was frayed,
To a very high branch that creaked when it swayed.
Then we would take turns - each one for a dare,
On a precipitous slope - to fly out in the air.

The slope was a beauty and when it was wet,
Each of us gathered to take up the bet,
On an old iron tray we would slide down the mud,
Nine times out of ten ending covered with blood!

When we roasted potatoes at the foot of an oak,
The fire was so sluggish it was nothing but smoke,
But big Jeff the farmer came up, shouting that we,
Had *'Gone and set fire to the base of the tree!'*

My friend's mum would tut as she sewed up my rips,
She cleaned off the mud and the blood when I tripped.
Then we'd clean off our shoes, with a rag hid in the shed,
And home we would go for tea, bath time and bed.

Jan Thayer (Bristol)

Beauty, Skin Deep After All

She was the local beauty queen
But a catwalk queen was her secret dream
He was a local working lad
And tried to cope with her mealtime fads

Workmates would unwrap a pastie or pie
And offer a piece when they saw his green eye
Often ashamed of the sandwich he'd got
He'd slip to the chippie, and buy a fish lot.

What will happen to us, he'd sometimes say
If you find this fame and spend ages away
Am I supposed to help you pack
And never know when you'll be back

She said he knew where she belonged
To hold her back would be so wrong
And then one day her dream came true
A catwalk queen, one of the few

Always moving from town to town
With diet meals, but gorgeous gowns
Pushing to be the one that's seen
Fighting snide remarks from other queens

Until one day she'd had enough
This set of beauties were much too tough
She knew that she could never do
The things they did, though she was no prude

Back she came to the little hometown
Thinking her fame would be like a crown
But the lad she'd left to fulfill her dream
Now had a real queen, a beauty in jeans

Charles Boyett (Bristol)

For Cliff

So pure and holy, undefiled
this love I feel for you
so precious, tender, beautiful
so lasting, deep and true.

You were the one to claim my heart
just you, and you alone
and now my loneliness has gone
I've finally come home.

I love you more each passing day
and know I always will
my needs have all been met in you
my heart's desires fulfilled

You give me joy, you give me peace
in your arms I find rest
I've waited such a long, long time
and now I have God's best

The empty years just melt away
as now I clearly see
I was the one, just meant for you
as you, were meant for me

Old lives were left along the way
and tough lessons were learned
but we both came through brave, and strong
and now the page is turned

The final chapter starts from here
your strong hand holding mine
destined to walk this world as one
in love for all of time

Tina Lodge (Corsham)

Whisper Of The Breeze

The gentle whisper of the breeze,
Softly wakens nature's trees
Solid roots, branches sway
Some leaves fall; others stay

I feel the breeze upon my face
When visiting my private place
A safe domain for me to rest
When life hands out another test

As I flee to find my peace
To activate my mind release
The breeze reminds me, I am free
My comforter, so naturally

Surrounded by this gentle breeze
I sway in echoed harmony
Graceful movements, synchronized
I watch the leaves fall side by side

The solid roots beneath the tree
Foundations set, eternally
A constant strength, determined power
Standing tall, a sturdy tower.

I came to see my special place
Ran away, without a trace
Solace found so easily
I celebrate my liberty

My task complete - revitalised
I silently say my goodbyes
I cast a glance at nature's trees
So grateful for the whispered breeze.

Diane Crouch (Bedford)

Was Aeschylus Soft In The Head?

Aeschylus who was widely quoted
As were many Greeks, it must be noted
Said Life and Meaning will correlate
As patterns form and integrate

So if a problem was to him borne
He'd scratch his pate of hair all shorn
Sit on a rock and wrack his brain
And take an aspirin for the pain

When solved, then came his Eureka cry
Hold on! Was that him, or another guy?
Crowd gathered, with Aeschylus in the middle
Cry then went up, 'Baldy has solved the riddle!'

Our Sage, now bathed in fame and glory
But not for long as it now gets gory
For Fate will not be tamed this way
Alas! Fortune can last, less than a day

When ancient Scribes this tale related
They wrote of Pride and Ego sated
He then took a stroll to clear the air
It was to be his last, Life's so unfair

An eagle passing glanced at his head
He saw a rock, he was misled
This tortoise I'm carrying, I think will crack
If dropped from height and on its back.

Thus cruelly ended our eggheads life
No word is know of the tortoise's strife
Raptor changed his name, by deed poll legal
Now calls himself, an American Bald Eagle.

Charles Keeble (Barnstaple)

Cornwall

It all happens 'ere in Cornwall,
Our far 'flung home in the West.
Because we're so far away,
We often enjoys the best!

Down to a small cove - in summer,
We rips off all our old clothes,
And we plays all sorts of little games!
Which most others do not know!

Then up 'along the cliffs we do wander,
(We've put back most of our clothes!)
And we all looks out to the glistening sea
As well as down - to more little coves;

But soon again 'twill be winter,
When them Cornish winds do a'blow;
Albeit we're mighty lucky,
As we 'ardly gets much snow!

Then indoor games keeps us happy,
In homes or in our warm pubs;
We likes a drop of the 'ard stuff,
And likewise some lovely pub grub!

Soon again 'twill be spring'time,
With them new lambs a prancing about,
The hedge'rows a looking really pretty;
And some young maidens a'looking 'stout!

So there you 'ave it me 'andsomes,
We don't do so bad down 'ere,
So come for yourselves - in the summer,
And taste a pint of good Cornish beer!

Peter Mahoney (Hayle)

A Beautiful Region

England is a place of beauty,
Both historical and natural,
Castles where many did their duty,
And beautiful scenery more rural.

Cross the River Tamar,
To enter the Cornish land,
Places of interest near and far,
And miles of golden sand.

Padstow has a wonderful lighthouse,
Truro - the most beautiful cathedral,
Falmouth - climb Jacobs Ladder,
Listening to songs of the seagulls.

St Michael's Mount is of interest,
Walk there at low tide,
But when the tide is high again,
To return to Marazion, you need a ride!

Penzance has 'Market Jew Street'
The most westerly street in England,
A statue of Humphrey Davy,
Penzance's son most grand.

Tintagel King Arthur's birth place,
A legendary monarch,
Go on until you reach Lands End
To view the longships' lighthouse.

Digging in mines for metals,
Rushing home from work for a pasty,
Then Cornish cream spread on a bun,
Cornish food so tasty.

Doreen Carne (Hayle)

Devon

'Tis the third largest county in our small isle,
Named from a Roman tribe, Dumnonii,
Attractions abound whatever the style,
From Widdecombe Fair to Hartland Quay.

Two coasts, two cities, and even two moors,
A modern population of two origins,
For travelling purpose, the choice is yours,
Be it first class hotels or village inns.

From Roman days, are no remains,
No Saxon architecture seen,
But remnants of the Tudors' reigns,
To depict just where they've been.

Tin, copper, iron, lead,
Throughout the centuries' olden days,
All have been mined, or so it's said,
And fashioned in so many ways.

No natural lakes, but rivers abound,
Rising on Dartmoor, Exmoor too,
Culm, Dart, Plym and Exe are found,
Teign and Tavy to name a few.

Refugees, evacuees - Devon received them all,
Whatever ills befell them, whatever problems there,
In good times and in bad times Devonians still stand tall,
Their warmth and hospitality so readily to share.

Drake, Raleigh and Hawkins too,
Such great names, so rightly proud,
(Defence of realm to Monarch true)
And many more if space allowed.

Sue Goss (Exeter)

Oh For A Simple Life

Life is very simple
When we are very young
Playing with our parents
Under a never-ending sun.

Growing up so slowly
Playing with our friends
Life is full of laughter
Almost never ends.

School days they last forever
Sometimes that's what it seems
Broadening our horizons
Polishing our dreams.

Soon, we are in the real world
A rude awakening for some
Not everyone is friendly
Welcoming or fun.

Politics and religion,
Poverty and strife
Wars and pain and suffering
Tragic loss of life.

Life doesn't seem as simple
As we start growing old.
It can be very painful
Hunger, loneliness and cold.

Our values, they need changing
To create a better life.
For parents and for children,
Oh! . . . For a simple life.

Ryszard Lipinski (Weston-super-Mare)

Rain

Rain, rain
You've caught me crying again
Rain, rain
Against my windowpane

Rain, rain
What's my name?
Am I going insane?
Not playing the game

Rain, rain
What is to gain?
Feeling the strain
Living in shame

Rain, rain
Is it the same?
In the fast lane
Going down the drain

Rain, rain
It's my aim
To catch that train
Make it plain

Rain, rain
Wash away the pain
I shall regain
My demons now slain

Rain, rain
On my windowpane
Rain, rain
Falling rain.

Jon Watson (West Dulwich)

Starry Night

Sky drenched in midnight blue
The lucid glowing of the moon's pale light
Air sharp and clear, and stars hang glistening
I gaze in wonder, beauty of the night

The planets plot their course on Solar's way
Are they looking back at Earthling's child?
Of little importance in the order of things
Yet touched with beauty as the stars beguile

One hundred years from now who will recall
The dreamer of dreams who looks up at the stars?
So very few are destined to impress
The world will not remember my small scars

Yet as we pass along life's road
We touch the lives of many on our course
Have the power to send each on their way
Hearts lighter, and not heavy with remorse

To have the vision to reach out and touch
Maybe plant a kiss upon a cheek
A smile of greeting often means so much
If only we would find the time to speak

I stand and stare into the universe
Are there other worlds to go on to?
Will we go forward to another life?
Learn from past mistakes and start anew

Will I live another life with you?
Please let there be some time for us together
No more pain, let happiness break through
Because I know that nothing lasts forever.

Sheila Scorse (Helston)

A New Year Resolution

'Floccinaucinihilipilification'
'Whatever is that?' you say.
It's 'Estimating as worthless'.
Some folks do this all the day.

They know the price of everything
In the field of what money can buy,
But they care for the value of nothing.
'How much cash?' is their only cry.

They look down their noses at small things.
Their brows are as high as can be.
They forget that small can be beautiful.
The simple profound they never see.

What is the price of faithful service
In boring job or menial task,
Keeping going in rain or shine?
Is gratitude too much to ask?

How much worth to a child is a bedtime story,
Time spent with parents at play or on hike?
Compared with the price of a TV at bedside, or
'Go away. Take this cash. Buy whatever you like.'

What price do you put on true human love?
The one you love is two-thirds water.
What was the value of that great Life,
Whose price was thirty pieces of silver?

I'm afraid that my brain has run out of rhymes.
My muse is suffering from fatigue.
So, after all this, I hope you will join
My Anti-Floccinaucinihilipilification League.

Eric Leaton (Petersfield)

God's Test

At times I feel alone and confused,
As though someone has taken out my fuse.
I pray every day and now feel closer to God,
And can feel the strength for me to go on!

It is as though in one minor small blow,
Our family has turned; there is no longer a glow.
We glued back the pieces hoping for the best,
But we know that this is just many of God's tests!

My dad is the one I have the most concern for,
Because how long he lives now, we can't be for sure.
I know because of this, his heart is very weak,
Because his love, his life he poured into this family!

You may say that we all have to die,
But my father's strength meant that he could live longer than I!
I love my parents more than anything in the world,
And to see this happen to them I could not survive!

Being in denial that this would never happen,
Hoping that it was something that I could ignore.
I feel as though you have taken away my inner core,
Something special that can be no more!

I feel cheated and used for your own purpose,
And above all betrayed by my sister.
Our relationship although once very close,
Will disappear, I speak for us both, to say I will miss her!

This is something that I don't think can be forgotten,
Because this is a time that everyone was shaken!
This all may be hard for you to understand,
But I think I am at end of my strand!

Ashika Gauld (Sunbury-on-Thames)

Break The Chains (Of The Slave Trade)

One day, I went out to play
Strangers came and took us away
Beaten and shackled, no escape
One by one led to the marketplace.

Stripped in the heat of the day
Without food or shelter
Like lambs to the slaughter
We were sold to the highest bidder.

Separated from our loved ones
Shackled once more, led to the shore
Forced into ships in the harbour
Bloodied and sore to see no more.

Sticks and stones may break our bones
Our spirit will never be broken
We'll never forget that dreadful day,
When slave traders came and took us away.

Packed together like sardines in a can
Shipped as cargo to a foreign land
Stripped us of our innocence and our name
So as to make profit in the slave trade.

Hopefully one day, we will return
Find our roots that we so yearn
With Wilberforce's help we
Broke the chains of the slave trade.

Empires were built in our name
All for what? Profit, their gain our pain.
The tide has turned for some to return
Strangers in our homeland.

Cecilia Hill (Stoke-on-Trent)

The Library

Hidden treasures for 'The Mind' lie here within,
Drawn to enter, my appetites begin.
Like food a menu for thought, I spy a threat?
Like a bookworm, hungry for words to eat.

The young are eager, to see history in the making,
Within these four walls' adventures they are taking.
A glimpse of the look on their happy faces,
As they are lost in their visiting places.

Finding all their heroes new and old,
Awaiting to greet hem as the pages unfold.
They escape for a while to a different world,
Returning the richer for wisdom unfurled.

Or be it cooking or gardening that we delve.
We are given such choices on every shelve,
Books for the blind, talking wonderful friends,
'Come alive' as it were, as the story unfurls.

You can be transported to battles hard fought and won,
Hobbies? Don't know, fish, golf, boating, tennis, and 101,
Animals as pets, farm or wild from all over the world,
Their habits and welfare is all here to the readers.

Trying to decide what you want to be?
Be fashion, or health, on land, air or sea.
Help the mothers, and children, from birth to 103,
You can travel the world, as far as you like, before tea.

With religion, and music, poetry and romance,
Take these books as your friends, just give them a chance.
Just like in childhood, with a beautiful story for bed
Relax, unwind, with your favourite author recline your head.

Anne Gilliam (Torquay)

Somerset

The county of the summer people,
An ancient wandering tribe,
The beauties of now Somerset,
I'll endeavour to describe.

To the north, the Mendips,
This is a place to go,
For limestone caves and gorge,
It is a wondrous show.

To the south the Blackdowns,
Rolling pastures green,
Pleasant leafy byways,
Treasures to be seen.

To the west the Brendons,
Rising up to meet,
The heather hills of Exmoor,
They surely are a treat.

My favourites are the Quantocks,
With steeply wooded coombes,
Red deer on the hilltops,
Where purple heather blooms.

In a way of contrast,
The levels are so flat,
But with the rivers flowing,
The otters love all that.

Somerset is my county,
There is so much to explore,
However many miles I've walked,
I want to do some more.

Janet Foley (Taunton)

I Wish I Was The New Dolly

Here I rest
The sad little teddy bear.
Unloved and unneeded
Now I'm in disrepair.

I'm no longer cute,
A mere shadow of myself!
I have no more dreams to dream
Nor allowed to sit on the shelf.

I have one leg adrift
An ear hanging by a thread, I was
Tossed into the corner and now
Lie crumpled by her bed.

My shaggy thin body
Was just thrown aside
Now my sewn on smile
Hides all the tears inside.

I wish I were the new dolly
Happy in the pink pushchair.
Where she would love and hug me
And stroke my curly hair.

I would have rosebud lips
And twinkling deep blue eyes
Be adored and be cherished
And wouldn't ever have to cry.

With my growl now a squeak
I thought her love was unshakeable.
I'm now broken-hearted
She sees me as untouchable.

Ann White (Bristol)

Lyons Café - Liverpool

Chewing, chomping, never ceasing,
People, people, always eating.
Young city gents with salt cellars,
Lorry drivers, all types of fellas.

Old man with tray filled with food,
Young girl with coffee comes to sit and brood.
Women eat and exchange their ills,
Puzzled soul, 'What's this, two bills?'

Serve yourself notice informs,
Dare I risk those curried prawns?
Old couples in tweeds and wearing brogues,
Bet those two in the corner are rogues!

Empty cups and dirty plates,
Boys and girls fulfilling dates.
Damp is the salt and solid the mustard,
Should I have rice or prunes and custard?

Waitresses busy clearing tables,
Battered suitcase, just look at those labels!
I wonder to whom that suitcase belongs?
Perhaps to a salesman selling dinner gongs.

Businessmen in bowler hats,
Office girls and screaming brats.
Well dressed spinsters and ragged tramps,
Glossy paint and fluorescent lamps.

You can see all these and plenty more,
Even watch the traffic through the door.
But I've paid my bill and it's time to leave,
Wonder if that killer will get a reprieve?

Brian Denton (London)

It's Just That Sort Of Morning

It's just that sort of morning
Through golden pollen haze
Knee deep in flower strewn meadows
When you think of holidays.

It's a marmalade-y morning
With orange juice and toast
On neat clipped lawns for breakfast
Blackbird singing on a post.

It's a tranquil sort of morning
Bees rest in flower heads
With butterflies on noiseless wings
Of yellows, mauves and reds.

It's a scrumptious sort of morning
Marshmallow white cloud dream
A bee-droned scented garden
Near a babbling woodland stream.

It's a madcap spring like morning
Pretty girls with boys to tease
Chasing hats and swirling skirts
From restless, gusty breeze.

It's an outdoor sort of morning
On a moor or lakeland fell
For hikers, walkers, ramblers
It's like a magic spell.

It's a misty sort of morning
Dewy grasses silver sheen
A gently hint from nature
That summer's left the scene.

Peter Colenutt (Bristol)

My Garden

My garden is a place,
With flowers, shrubs and trees.
I encourage all of nature,
Like insects, birds and bees.

It's a haven and an oasis,
So all of them can grow.
Birds singing in delight,
They flying to and fro.

Plants of all shapes and sizes,
Both in width and in height.
Buds, blooms and foliage,
It is nearly looking right.

With flowers of every colour,
Red, blue, yellow and white.
With many shades of green
Some subtle, some are bright.

Lawn is mowed and tended,
Beds and borders weed free.
A pleasure on the eye,
For everyone to see.

There's a sound of trickling water,
To ease the weary soul.
Not much more to do now,
I've nearly reached my goal.

When the day is over,
And late into the night.
I can sit back and relax,
Cos I know it's looking right.

Linda Knee (Borehamwood)

London Bombs

Why is it always the innocent who suffer?
Do the bomb makers think they're really any tougher?
Such cowardice and senselessness, so difficult to understand,
Do they really think they're making a stand?

What peace of mind can they have at night,
Do they dream of destruction their power and might?
The emergency services are the heroes of course,
Bringing their skills right into force.

Coping with hysteria, people in shock,
Prioritising the wounded, working right round the clock.
Having to reach trapped bodies inside,
Down in the underground, there was nowhere to hide.

The bus that has a roof no more,
What justice can be bought about by law?
No one ever wins in a war,
These acts of violence people will always deplore.

Nobody deserves to lose a limb,
To suffer burns on a terrorist's whim,
Who will remember the people who died,
The commuters who took their final ride?

Will there be a memorial site?
To tell of how they suffered their plight.
For loved ones to visit, to pay their respects,
Put aside their religion, their creed and their sect.

How do we find our inner strength,
To help us through these days of length?
To put into perspective all that is lost,
How much does a human life cost?

Nicola Varmen (Poole)

Seagull Sans Mercy

Standing beautiful, elegant, glossy
In the sleekness of plumage you wear
Or soaring, squawking and screeching
Or hovering high in the air.

But don't let him see you
Enjoying your meal or a pasty
For without fear or shame
He'll turn greedy and nasty.

He'll dive swiftly down
Beak grabs pasty in flight.
Your meal and sneak robber
Are soon out of sight.

All children beware
As your ice cream you lick.
His cruel vicious beak
Whips it off in a tick.

He really doesn't care
'Bout the victims he harms.
So should we admire
His strutting proud charms?

His fine image and posture
Will surely deceive.
He is not the paragon
He'd have you believe.

He thinks he's entitled
To savagely thieve
Or drop his foul mess
On your head or your sleeve.

Amy Cotter (Plymouth)

My Cathedral

I know of a cathedral
That's way up in the hills,
It's a place so very special
And a heavenly peace instils.

For the hills rise steep to form its walls
Its roof is the moon and the sun,
Its doors are ever open
To welcome everyone.

There are trees that form its pillars
There are birds that form the choir,
The flowers and leaves, the carpets
What more could one desire?

The congregation varies
But some always come along,
For many of God's creatures
Are there at Evensong.

It seems the sheep and cattle
Want to come and share,
With Heaven and Earth united
In simple humble prayer.

I've heard many sermons
In my cathedral fair,
With God Himself the preacher
A joy beyond compare.

Yes! there's a special atmosphere
Which God with His presence fills,
And no place on Earth is dearer
Than my cathedral in the hills.

John Osborne (Bath)

Pause For Thought

The day started like any other,
The moon shone in a star-studded sky,
Then the sun peeped above the horizon
And the stars disappeared from our eyes.

But the moon today was defiant,
It would keep shining as long as it could.
The day continued to brighten,
As the sun crept as high as it should.

But the moon would not be defeated
And it threatened to take the sun's reign.
The skies started to darken
The upper hand, the moon started to gain.

Finally the moon had engulfed it
And we see only a bright diamond ring.
Then above, the sun's corona,
Spills out from the moon's smothering.

Around the mount of St Michael,
Waves continued to roll to the shore,
The beach was shrouded in darkness,
As the daylight it was no more.

Then far away on the horizon,
Beyond the shadow of the moon,
Light had returned to the people,
The same way it would to us soon.

But what the moon had accomplished,
In the time the sun it had caught,
Was to give the sun a few moments,
Just time to Pause for Thought.

Lesley Beard (Radstock)

Lottery Fever

We were a fairly contended nation
carrying on in our regular vocation
We put a bob or two on a horse
knowing that winning was a matter of course

It was just a bit of harmless fun
and a minor but pleasant diversion
There were those who did the pools
and were told they were such fools

Becoming a millionaire is temptation
and we know it is just a speculation
We never gave it another thought
to the gambling fever we have got caught

Now we have the lottery with the fanfare
Buying tickets galore as if we didn't care
The razzmatazz, the publicity is such a vision
It became a decisive factor in our compulsion

Becoming a multimillionaire is now an obsession
and has certainly become our main expectation
Millions of pounds are spent on tickets
emptying the poor people's pockets

Money that should be spent on grocery
20 pence of which now goes to the treasury
If that money could go to charities
to the poor it could provide many facilities

If there is a limit on what could be won
the rush for great wealth will dry out soon
It will then become just a small flutter
and we will all feel so much better.

Albert Moses (Harpenden)

A Flight Experience

I'm going! I'm going! I'm going!
I can't really believe it!
With thirty other pilgrims
I'm off to the Holy Land.

First stop, Heathrow,
I was far too early
'Baggage can go through'
Said the voice of authority.

Then the others arrived,
Tables were erected.
Their baggage was checked
Very carefully checked.

Wasn't I lucky, my bag's gone,
I joined them ready to board,
I was bubbling with excitement -
Then came the 'little man'

Dressed in dark uniform
He called my name - now what?
'Sorry madam, your baggage has *not*
Gone through our security checks!'

'Please wait here,' he said and left.
The others all boarded and I,
Was close to tears, and alone.
Perhaps I *wasn't* to go after all.

The 'wait' seemed like hours,
Until the 'little man' returned
'We've checked,' he said 'You can board.'
Was I relieved - Israel here I come!

Jean McPherson (South Petherton)

Untitled

A poem to write, of what should I write
Of a world that's gone mad, with hatred and greed?
Of Man's inhumanity and his lust for power
No thought of his fellow man who is dying in need!

A world of uncertainty, where money is God
No time to spare, in his race to the top.
Where people don't matter, they are just in the way
Will this kind of world be impossible to stop?

Forget for a moment, this world of despair,
Replace it with beauty, so easily found,
Meadows of buttercups, ripe golden corn,
Laced with red poppies, sharing the ground.

Snowdrifts of May flowers, apple blossom, pink and white
Perforate the senses, invigorate the brain,
So numbed by acts of violence, it often doesn't care,
Until the world of beauty, replaced fear and pain.

Open your eyes to this wonderful sight,
It cannot be bought and it cannot be sold,
it comes free for everyone and touches the soul
And cannot be purchased with silver or gold.

All that is needed, are moments of your time
Just stop and stare and then store it in your heart,
Imprint it on your memory, forever to remain,
Reminding you that in this world, beauty is a part!

When life feels full of darkness, remember what you saw,
Share it with someone you love, make their day seem bright,
So they can give to others, a view of beauty seen,
That shows in spite of darkness, it will always be followed by light.

N Davies (Emsworth)

The Battle Of The Books

The big religious company
    Declined a deal: 'We fear
That after due consideration,
    We can't sell that there 'ere'.

The ancient place of worship said
    'It's not quite what we sell'.
Not part of the Establishment,
    I didn't fit the bill.

And what about the bookshop where,
    If you believe the rumour,
An enterprising manager
    Displayed it with the Humour?

But thank the Lord for all those friends,
    Of open heart and mind
Who bought the little volume.
    They cherish what they find.

Some find it 'quite informative'
    And some enjoy the jokes.
And some prefer the pictures -
    Well, there's nowt so queer as folks.

Some found it 'too political'
    While others laughed, or cried.
And some reviewed it in the Press -
    But scarcely looked inside.

More books were sold . . . an author reached
    The ladder's bottom rung.
The winter of our discontent
    Had passed . . . and spring had sprung.

Audrey Stanley (Bournemouth)

Horace

A black shiny nose at first I see,
Jet-black eyes scrutinising me,
as it emerges from under my shed.

Its snout is twitching from side to side,
sniffing the air to help it decide
to emerge from under my shed.

I keep quite still, not to scare it away,
as it edges forth, the scene to survey
and it emerges from under my shed.

Horace, the hedgehog, taking stock
then running around like a headless cock,
since emerging from under my shed.

He makes for the dish of milk I put out,
eagerly dipping his little snout,
well worth emerging from under my shed.

Now he's off to my freshly dug garden patch,
searching for slugs and worms to catch.
Oh the joys of emerging from under my shed.

A fat, juicy slug is devoured with relish,
then back again to the milk-laden dish.
Oh the bliss of emerging from under my shed.

Scurrying here and scampering there,
he's looking for a mate I do declare,
so that's the reason for emerging from under my shed.

Oh no! A strange object on which to have a crush,
he's vigorously mating with my boot-cleaning brush,
so I put Horace back under my shed.

Ivor King (Bristol)

Recollection

Strolling in the dusk beside a stream
It is of you I think especially this evening
And opening the hidden door within my mind,
Behold the dim loft where you first turned the key
And dreams crept out.

I see, under the cobweb-covered rafters,
Thoughts of you still glowing in the light
Of the long peacefulness of summer afternoons
And in the golden fires of autumn,
Recall again the harvest of our happiness.

Daphne M F Byrne (Havant)

King Social Misfit

I've never seen You
but I've heard You've declared,
'You do it for me
if for your brother you've cared.'
You were an outcast
so many years ago.
You were born poor,
yet with gold, your house glows.
We worship a man 2,000 years gone by,
who the 'religious' rejected and despised.
We avoid in the pew
the man with the smell and the stains.
Would we touch the hem of *Your* garment,
if it appeared the same?

I've never touched You,
yet You touched people who were untouchable,
and You loved people,
those classed unlovable.
Has your church moved on?
We shun with lacking embrace,
where acceptance
needs to be the case.
What's gone so wrong
that's failed to get right?
What would we see
if we could judge *You* by sight?
You stood up for those
whose actions you could not condone.
King Social Misfit
now sits upon a throne!

Debra C Rufini (Portsmouth)

Son Of God

They knew not whencefrom He came
Nor where to His mission was bound
Cured He the sick
Healed He the lame
Raised He the dead from the ground

His only crime was preaching good
And practise of His word
They hung Him high
From nails in wood
In hope He'd not be heard.

Kevin Setters (Welwyn Garden City)

Retrospective

(For Peter Thursby)

A portrait you did of yourself
at eighteen hangs in one corner -
confident, flaunting a new blue
chin, a touch wary, pugnacious
even, schooled in fierce encounters
at water-polo - already
so skilful, features in vibrant
perspective, background suggested
casually.
       The room holds your bright
harvest - a trio of figures
in front of flames, sculptures half black
half silver, whirl of a farmyard
cock with scimitars for feathers,
bronze struts dazzled by spray, cobalt
sun crowning ghost-hints of a tree.

You couldn't see them all those years
ago. The fact they're there now proves
that adolescent knew just what
had to be done. He possessed iron
loyalty to his vision, love
of textures, hunger for colour,
calm-fevered need to conquer fresh
realms of design. The victory
in embryo is his while this
fulfilment nowadays is yours
for all we're celebrating here
has been foreshadowed in those eyes.

Harry Guest (Exeter)

Stormy Seas

The stormy sea with white-topped waves
in blues and greens and shades of grey
merging where the sky dips down
to greet the distant horizon

The gulls soar effortlessly
with just the merest twitch
of a feathered wing tip
sending them wheeling
and soaring
in different directions
scouring the shore
for tasty morsels

Flotsam and jetsam
thrown up by the waves
scattering foam on the beach
which today
is as inhospitable
as any alien landscape may be
yet magnificent
in its own dangerous beauty

If ever the sea should give up its dead
then surely it must be
on a day such as this
when the wind and waves conspire
to assault the land
in such gestures grand
as we stand and watch in awe
such scenes as these
before the stormy seas.

Grant Meaby (Stevenage)

Happy In The Here And Now

Where would I be without memories?
In the cold greyness of a forgotten past!
Not in a kaleidoscope of colour and feeling
Where I now visit people and places
On a daily basis, those long ago encountered
And stored in my treasure house of memory.

I can't contemplate not being able
To conjure up yesterday, to savour
It again at my own pace,
To relive the events which made me laugh,
Weep again at those which made me
Shed years long ago
But still need to touch me now
In my hours of solitude and recollection.

There is one so close who is closing
The chapter on each day,
Retaining little to think about tomorrow,
Short-term memory loss is swamping
Her so fast that sometimes
Yesterday didn't happen!
I need to remember for us both.

But she is happy in the 'Here and Now'
So today is what counts.
A memory diary need not be put away.
For tomorrow, with God's guidance, will bring
New happenings to make her laugh and chatter.
That is all I ask for her,
Security, contentment and love.
And the greatest of these is *love!*

Pat Heppel (Elburton)

Chicago Rock Café (Fareham)

What make Chicago Rock Café so good?
Not just pub or nightclub understood.
It's a venue for everything,
Friends and romance bring.

A place for drinking,
A place for dancing,
A place for eating,
A place for talking,
A place for kissing,
A place for touching.

A place for dating,
A place for singing,
A place for loving,
A place for dreaming,
A place for gigs playing
A place for play engaging.

Marvellous things happen here magic,
Strangers exotic and declare erotic.
They make Venus and Hebe honest blush;
Beyond doors party fever lustful rush.

The people of Fareham is clue,
The girls and guys souls true.
The country has many pubs and clubs agree,
But Chicago Rock Café Fareham rare you see.

Open evening seven nights a week
The only place virtue love seek.
With some most beautiful babes ever seen
The essence of sultan's harem muses agree.

George Woodford (Fareham)

Arrival

Wet and crumpled, too weak to bleat,
Heart fluttering, eyelids closing, I fight a wish to sleep.

> She nudges, nudges, licks me clean
> And kisses breath thro' my untried lips.

Heart strengthening, knees knocking,
I summon the will to please. Where is she? I call her.

> Nuzzling, guiding, in fleecy mountain,
> Sweet warm nectar quenches tender maw;

My strength is gaining, my tail's a-dancing.

Eleanor Holden (Alton)

Seventeen In '66

Down Carnaby Street walks a woman remembering
when the Jones to keep up with was Brian;
when Hendrix was cutting the world up his way
and raw Janice Joplin was flying.

She walks down the street with a tear in her eye now,
and '66 floods back to taunt her.
Her thighs feel the flutters her miniskirt gave,
while love's kiss persists still to haunt her.

> She was just seventeen
> and the Marquee queen
> where she went Friday nights for her kicks.
> Just seventeen,
> and the Marquee queen.
> Seventeen in '66.

The sounds she still hears will not grant easy freedom,
John, Paul, George and Ringo are saying,
'Come back, gel, remember those wonderful years.
The ghosts are still here and still playing.'

Play on they might well for the good it will do her,
for sounds are not substance for living
and fact is not found on an old album track
though echoes reverb, unforgiving.

> All the years in-between
> where her life might have been
> lay as limbo that H couldn't fix.
> Just seventeen,
> and the Marquee queen.
> Seventeen in '66.

Waterman Quill (Surbiton)

Snowfall

The day I saw you last
Fresh snow had fallen
Into a leaning ache
Of shimmering separation.
A bumbling country bus
Shuddered and lurched
Between burdened thatches,
Dipping low above
Heavy-lidded cottages
And shallow, ermined walls.
Trees yielded, white and
Hesitant as postulants.
Their shivering nun-veils
Stirred by a cutting wind.
Ice-edged footsteps
Led to the threshold
Of your new, deep pain.
My cold fingers yearned
To stroke the taut
Sorrow from your face.
The jagged smile from your mouth.
Yet it was you who offered warmth and solace.
Turning the desolation
Into a shared possession,
Until our wedded anguish
Was blessedly assuaged by
A clasping of chilled hands;
A prismed instant of articulate unity
Beyond need of more
Than a few pared words.

Joan Howes (Basingstoke)

The Cat And The Magpie

Looking out of my window on a cold and dreary day,
I spied a young black cat hiding between some bushes, and steeped up clay.
He was stalking a magpie and he thought he was unseen,
But as you know, the eye of the magpie is very, very keen.

He decided to have some fun with the cat and side-stepped from side to side
The cat couldn't make head nor tail of this, and decided to lay low, bide his time and hide.

The magpie took flight, and hovered overhead,
Circling the cat, *cluck*, *cluck*, clucking at his head.
The cat went into a spin, he was shaking with fright,
I think I'll stay where I am today, until day turns into night.

S Papier (Stepney)

Of Good Intent

Woman rising from a dream
Flushed pink in face but neck like cream
And soft, like dove's pure underside
Where sheet hides all her greatest pride
The linen's whiteness, rise and fall
Above the breasts which lie in all
Their clouds of thin-veined warm allure,
An earthy splendour yet so pure,
And then when tumbled covers peel
Unseen to floor and so reveal
The full waist, sumptuous, moist with sleep
The jutting hips where men would leap
(If given leave) and hold those bones
Like handlebars, and sit alone
Astride this beauteous couch,
Forget that other men could vouch
For its brash moaning ache
That slakes your thirst so that you take
More than your share of mead-like drink
So sweetly cloying that you think
All heaven now is near at hand,
Until abruptly there you stand
Your quivering outraged flesh dismissed
Your mouth unwanted, scoffed, unkissed
Watch her climb back 'neath the sheets
And know your stupid act complete,
Creep out and leave her smug, content
You know you loved with good intent,
But feline woman fast in sleep -
Cares naught.

Shona Chester (Eastbourne)

Wondering

20 years have gone past,
The world moves so fast,
The sun sits in the sky all day,
Thinking, *why can't I run away?*

Behind the hill, the cloud is all alone,
Chatting, chatting, chatting on her phone,
Up comes the moon, when it's night,
Shining so bright as a twinkling light.

What an adventure was today,
Now I am going to sleep far, far away.

Mickaela Moore (London)

Afterwards . . .

Sell me good works, praise be
Mixing metaphors busted metre
Carry on in spurious images
Race riots, impressive messages
Recent rip off left one duped
Speechless standing at the bus stop
Accused, infusion of language
Notices, tie-breaks, hand shakes, rave on
Evening show - true to you
Organising do contact
Faltering step by step - walk on
Progress tests prose purification
Preparation passing plain text
On the route to eternity
Which Society burns us end to end?
Mobility jolly front pulsating rhythm
Trends lend to kinky boots
Boot in - words with roots
Last minute decisive art form
Shaken not stirred
Single! Do I dare
To pen poems here
Freedom of expression
Afterwards . . .
Poetry for the People
Rave on Poetry pals - encore
Celebrations race compete
Interest rests upon your feet
Please me punctuation -
Afterwards . . .

S M Thompson (Southampton)

Moods

Happy days, sad days,
Then there's 'not so bad' days,
It's just fine to feel that way,
There are others fine and gay.

Hearts, souls and minds like weather
Have highs and lows; as air pressure;
Times that we forget or treasure.

So be glad to be alive,
Winds and things will change and seem,
Like none of this has ever been.

Janet McNally (Hassocks)

383

I Could Not Remember Me

I fell on my head
and could not remember me.
I counted my fingers
and wriggled my toes.
I looked in the mirror.
I saw and I froze.
I did not recognise me.
Was I really that old?
With a hollowed-out face
and a crag for a nose?
A lank white crown
and lines on the forehead with tales well told?
I remember the King in the first Great War,
but I cannot say my name -
and who are you all standing there
staring at my dribbling shame?
You ask me questions to which I can only try to reply
Like what is the date?
When was I born?
And how old am I?
It is the day that it is.
On the forty-fifth of July,
and as many years ago as I am young.
You showed me books
and I gazed at pictures
in the hope of remembering me,
but I am revisiting a world
I have never seen before
like returning to a school room full of closed books.
Through my fumbling mind I have forgotten me.

Peter G T Schapira (London)

Looks

'Cheer up Miss,' the young man said
As the woman gazed into outer space.
It was not a sad, unhappy face
But a pensive look,
So much for, 'I can read you like a book.'

He did not know what she was thinking,
No idea . . . not an inkling.

Don't presume you know what
Someone is thinking or feeling
I know . . . looks can be deceiving!

Monica Mahabier (Camberwell)

Winter

The garden
Thermometer
Is frozen
With the
Cold as
Poignant
As a wooden
Shelter that
Runs down
The valley.
The iced ground
Is covered
In waste
And leaves.
The plants
Past their
Best rest.
Except there
Is a state
Of chilling
Vivacity
Like an
Agony. How
Wasteful
To stand
Still as
If unfinished
Like a
Discarded
Painting.

Nicola Barnes (Taunton)

Credit Crunch

I paid the rent,
And the gas bill too,
Let the phone go red,
And the electricity blue.

In the envelope for my credit card
I sent a poem,
Titled 'Life is Hard'.

'If it's so hard,'
(Came the reply)
'How can you write poetry?'

Mostafa Woola (London)

These I Have Loved

(Poem written by my mum S J H Bridewell who died three years ago - submitted by her daughter Serena Balch)

The softness of a cuddly toy,
A newborn babe to hold is joy.
The warmth of velvet on a cushion or such,
These are the things I love to touch.
Strawberries and cream on a warm summer's day,
Candyfloss and ice cream at the fair,
An apple, orange, banana or pear,
A hot dog eaten in haste,
All of which I love taste.
Birds singing in the early morn,
The bleat of a lamb just newly born,
The music of the roundabout,
Children at play as they laugh and shout,
The quiet as the night draws near
Then a loved one's voice I love to hear.
Scent from flowers, soap on washing day,
A hot roast dinner as well,
Are only a few things I love to smell.
Waves breaking on the rocks,
Large ships standing in the docks,
The blues and grey of the skies,
The colours of the butterflies
The sinking sun shining red at night,
Are all to me a wonderful sight.
These are some of the things I have loved,
But no more,
As God is calling me to the door.

Stephanie Jean Hope Bridewell (Andover)

Living In Newlyn

'Why do you live so far away?'
From what, from what I ask myself -
From the fetid underground, the unswept streets
The crowded pubs, the angry faces
The rush hour and the sightless eyes.
Close by I have the sea
The cry of gulls, the unleashed wind
The crash of waves, the lash of rain
The elemental verities,
Why do I live so far away -
    From what?

Martin Green (Penzance)

Pavane For Summer

Wistfully I recall the days when I was young,
ice creams that were so cool upon the tongue.
Lazy days spent splashing in the pool
and playing on the beach, or just playing the fool.
I remember bodies, roasting on the sands,
rare picnics for tiny flies, marauding bands
of ants, the vicious diving wasp
attacking the food held gritty in my grasp.
Staggering from boiling deckchair into shade
secretly praying for a cloud that would invade
the dominion of the heat we know as 'summer'.
I ask, 'what comes with the sinking of the sun?'
Autumn, winter, spring; my life near run?
It's hard to realise how very long alive
I've been; how long will I survive?
That sharp stabbing pain within my chest
a portent of approaching 'eternal rest'?
Will I awake from sleep, and will I mind
if the world that greets me is a different kind?
Will I walk up to the shining golden gates
to where a bearded person with His book awaits
with outstretched arm, face heavy with fierce frown,
whose bony finger points mercilessly - down!

Maybe it would be best to make the most of it,
perhaps I could even enjoy to sit
and watch the gentle waves run up the sand,
close my eyes, listen to the band,
allow myself a welcome 'old age' doze.

Would I awake the same, do you suppose?

Bruce Kennard-Simpson (Budleigh Salterton)

Nowhere

Climbing hills that reach the sky,
Going nowhere.
Sitting on my saddle whizzing along,
Going nowhere.
Running across sands stretching to the sea,
Going nowhere.
Swimming through the waves,
Going nowhere.
Nowhere is the best place to travel to.
No expectations, no goals, just the sheer
Pleasure of going.

Maureen Wildash (Tavistock)

Tidy And Neat

Tidy, we do like it tidy,
Cut down the alder
At the bend in the river
Zoom, zoom! Whack, whack!
Our digger makes short
Work of that!
Cut down the willows, untidy!
The banks must be neat!
Cut down the hedges
One minute for that
Grub up the roots!
Burn the lot!
Mow down the grass - untidy, untidy,
Strim the hedges - no birds allowed,
No slow-worms, no hedgehogs,
Untidy, untidy!
Cut down the nettles and brambles,
Not neat. Poison the weeds,
Lots of slug pellets.
'No, they don't harm the thrushes,
They have *lots* to eat.'
We *do* like things neat!

Why the silence? Where is the shade,
Against sweltering heat?
Where the shelter from
Lashing wind, snow and rain?
The kingfisher's gone having nowhere to perch,
The song thrush is poisoned.

There is silence at the bend in the river.

Gillian Service (Glastonbury)

Mother Nature

I am fond of that pond
Where the willows weep
Where plump ducks laze
And lithe frogs leap
Where gentle cows
Meander by
And song birds lull me as I lie
Life's chill alarms
And worries fade
In nature's arms
'Neath the willow's shade

John Bennett (London)

Talking To My Mountain

I don't know why I love you but I do.
Your every height, every shape, every hue,
The sun gives you glory, your snow-capped head white, majestic!
Grey clouds make you frightening, angry too.
Rain washes you clean.
Life, green shoots sprout at your base.
Mist covers your face my mountain, you disappear.
But I know you're there, I'll stare and stare,
'Til the tears roll down my cheeks,
You will come back, I know you're there.

I don't know why I love you but I do.
I must come and see you my mountain
The road twists and turns, round and round and round
I'm here with you mountain, up here with you.
Your breath is pure, sweet, strong coming from your lungs into mine.
Magical air of a different kind.
It cures the mind, gives you power bereft of mankind.
You tower over the azure blue sea
Which caresses you in its arms.
The wind howls, sounds like a choir singing psalms.

My mountain you are just as I thought, gentle and kind,
Aloof, romantic, friendly you are.
Do you stretch, do you try to reach a star?
Darkness is falling, your friends of the night are calling my mountain
My world is down there,
Down the twisting, turning, winding track
I'll be back my mountain,
        I'll be back . . .
I don't know why I love you but I do.

Sylvia Hayball (New Barnet)

Urbanation

The ever changing face of the city
And the heart of the people
Where man has taken this ground
And fashioned from the earth
For centuries his dwelling
In moods of stone
Upon this masterpiece
Our journey
This bonding of paths
Aged yet ageless
So vast as to touch forever.

Kevin 'YT' Pearce (Bristol)

For My Dear Toby

The house round the corner
holds memories for me,
for our daughter lived there
with her family of three.

On Hallowe'en all three would come,
a witch, a demon and skeleton.
As I opened the door they'd shout, 'Trick or treat?'
I'd pretend to be frightened and give a small shriek.
They would then start to laugh and say, 'Nanny, it's us.'
I'd gasp and say, 'Sorry I made such a fuss.'

Our Toby is the youngest child
who sometimes used to stay
on mornings when his mother worked,
oh, how I loved those days.

Sometimes we'd visit local shops
so on the bus would go,
he would always thank the driver,
who would say, 'Mind how you go.'
I'd say, 'Remind me Toby of things I've got to get.'
He'd say, 'I'll mind you Nanny, I won't let you forget.'

The house round the corner feels empty now,
our family have moved far away.
The day of departure I cannot describe,
I was filled with such utter dismay.
But time now is slowly easing the pain
and happier memories are filling my brain,
of laughter shared with those scallywags three,
Emily, George and little Toby.

Patricia Evelyn Gruber (Bournemouth)

Greed

Greed can be all
consuming,
suffocating love
and putting self-interest
before all else; it
never satisfies, but just
like lust, it creates
more hunger
or just like seawater
the more we drink
the thirstier we become.

John McGovern (Hemel Hempstead)

Harvest Festival

I dug up me garden all in good time,
and bought some manure, plus a few bags of lime.
Then wood ash I sprinkled all over me soil,
to boost the rewards of me 'ard work and toil.
I spread it, I dug it, I worked it in well,
I even ignored the 'orrible smell

Peat and sand from me 'and I lovingly scattered
with each single seed sown as though they all mattered.
Then all that were needed, wuz the rain and the sun,
and I stood there think' all me 'ard work wuz done
But alas and alack, it wasn't to be
the wee creepy beasties beat me to it you see.

Me tomatoes and greens never even got started,
but still I refused to be really downhearted.
us gardeners won't admit we're a right load of mugs,
growing carrots and suchlike just to fatten up slugs.
yet me runners are drooping and ready to die
'cos of brown spot and mildew and bloomin' blackfly.

Darn greenfly and whitefly and red spider mite,
are busily gorging things all day and night.
Blackcurrants and goosegogs were then to be had,
but the ones that the birds left were nearly all bad.
There wuz plenty of lettuce, much more than I need,
but why dear Lord did they all go to seed?

So all that I grew is now gone and forgotten,
unfit for me table, all soggy and rotten.
Yet all is not lost, for me weeds are just fine,
a good year to brew me own dandelion wine!

Sam D Kingdon (Southampton)

The Loser

Does anyone know he's there, does anyone really care?
Never gets a second chance, never gets a second glance,
At a party, bash, or ball, no one notices him at all,
Always seems to do things wrong, never seems that he belongs,
Will anyone notice this poor creature, a blot on the landscape?
Not a nice feature,
Will anyone know he's there, does society really care?
If you see him wait awhile, don't pass him by,
Just stop and smile,
Don't simply stand and stare, stop and greet him,
Show you care.

Raven Thunder (Paignton)

391

Coming Of The Storm

(For Peter)

As if born from the mountains, Mother Nature's womb,
Grey clouds begin unfolding, spreading darkness as they loom.
A churning mass of vapour unfurls and covers up the sky,
The majesty of the sun now fades, with its closing eye.
Once silently spreading and creeping across the empty down,
The distant rumbles can be heard, in the far-off town.

Startled by the thunder, a crow hurriedly finds a bough,
Where it sits with others, then suddenly dies their row.
Cowering in the hedgerows, creatures hide in wait,
Hoping for the storm to pass and the clouds to abate.
Huge tears smash down into the cracked and wounded earth,
The first drops of the season as the clouds give birth.

Figures begin to scatter as the storm the town invades,
Hidden behind the sanctuary of stone and wood facades.
All the souls have fleeted and the streets now dark and bare,
Until the lightning the skies ignite and thunder splits the air.
The overflowing gutters, puddles in the lane,
The streets washed clean of their sins by torrential rain.

Thor, from the swirling clouds, let's fly his jagged darts,
Followed by his resounding roar, a sound to still all hearts.
The raging and the turmoil of the savage skies,
Then slowly a ray of sunlight and the storm begins to die.

A last stand by the dying storm a thunderclap so loud,
Then a flashing scimitar, a rainbow slices through the cloud.
Light split and fractured by diamonds as they fall,
Bringing a sense of wonder and humbling to us all.

Martin Thompson-Denning (Exeter)

Life

Life is a mirage of images
Some solid, others vague
Jumping and seeping through the forest with its entwined array of inhabitants

Life is a mirage of images
Sad, isolated and desolate faces
Peering through the cold frosted windowpane crying out for inner peace

Life is a mirage of images
Hope, happiness and humility
Scream and shout through the empty vacuums in the mountain top waiting to be captured

Life - What is it?

Patricia Rochester-Bergamini (Leytonstone)

Skylight

I love to look out of the skylight,
just as the night descends,
as the city blinks itself to moving sleep.

I love the sky that's never quite dark,
the ever moving planes,
the clouds that scud and twist their shapes,
soaked in the last of the day's light.

I love the trees
that whisper and blow,
that darkly sit
in the orange glow.

I love the change
in pace and noise,
the now quiet gardens,
with abandoned toys.

As one by one
the houses settle to sleep,
each with its own story to tell,
and I above it all
can only watch and guess.

I love you standing
right behind me,
as we gaze out at our city,
warm against my back.

I love the sigh,
as we turn for bed
and leave the city to its busy slumber.

Alexia Nicol (London)

Untitled

As the river runs slowly, ripples shimmer and shine,
For the sun doth cast lowly, all its radiance divine
So God gave us the power, the will and the mind
To give freely of our love, to be gentle and kind.
For the favour of flowers, of their scented perfume
All the colour endowered, and the birds' joyful tunes.
He but asks that we harm not, cause not suffering or pain
But that we should remember, whence from yonder we came.
That compassion is a treasure, and life not a game.
So to this end I implore you,
Use God's gifts while you may.

J C Henchy (London)

I'd Like To Show You England

I'd like to show you England, the part of it that I know,
All the birds that sing, and all the plants that grow.
Celandine and honeysuckle, robins, doves and swallows,
Blossom on the apple trees, and catkins on the willows.

Wild roses in the summertime, the scents from falling rain,
Hawthorn blossom, creamy white, cow parsley in the lane.
Berries in the autumn, like jewels, black and red,
The frost-encrusted winter, when all the trees seem dead.
Bluebells in the springtime, and new green leaves unfurled,
This little part of England I love best in the world.

I'd like to show you England, the part of it that I know,
All the birds that sing, and all the plants that grow.
Crocuses and dandelions, daisies, daffodils,
Beeches in their autumn gold, the tawny Mendip hills.

You are from so far away, a different kind of land,
Mountain peaks and canyons, deserts, snow and sand.
Vast and wild, magnificent - we've nothing like that here,
But there's a smaller beauty at every time of year.

I'd like to show you England, the part of it that I know,
All the birds that sing, and all the plants that grow.
Mossy crooked ancient oaks, chuckling woodland streams,
Swans that glide so silently on misty smooth straight rhynes.

You are native to your land, you love it, I am sure,
But you could go travelling, the planet to explore.
You could cross the ocean, and if you ever came,
I would show you England, this land that knows my name.

(A *'rhyne'* is the local term for a drainage ditch on the Somerset Levels)

Philippa Drakeford (Weston-super-Mare)

Drums

My son before he was born, a footballer I thought he would be.
But it turned out playing the drums made him feel free.
Sometimes soft tones I hear, rumbles begin that lead to all kinds
of sounds,
Sometimes it brings a change of mood to hear the drums played,
I drift into a dream world, a jungle scene, the louder the beat
I almost feel the jungle heat.
Sometimes its thunderous roar you think of a charging wild boar,
Then a gentle beat, pitter-patter of tiny feet.
The dream of dreams is the rolling waves of the sea coming in gently until it crashes on the
rocks, then the drum beat stops.

Barbara Allen (Chiswick)

Aromatherapy

Alyssum bloomed, aromatic, white and wild
Beside the wooden, creosote-pungent fence.
Intoxicating scents,
Drifting emotive through the air
But in the soul forever to remain.
And memories of a child
Recalling tarmac heat while waiting there;
A burning, searing pain
Beneath the soles of sun-tanned, nut-brown feet;
Of hopping each from each
To minimise the sun's incessant glare;
Relieved when adult discourse was complete
And steps resumed along the pavement short 'twixt home and beach.
From thence, those blissful afternoons
Where buckthorn grew across the rising dunes,
And privet flowers, throughout the hours,
Their windblown, warm, midsummer fragrance threw.
Remembering paths that left the golden glades
To climb through sharp, blue, cutting marram blades.
Ascent was slow for soft the sands
And steep the slopes for eager, grasping hands.
But then, the summit reached, the downhill race;
The pace too fast to upright stay
And so, with legs like clay, a fall unplanned!
But, sometime, e'en the power to stand!
Such triumph then - before the rush to dare the whole again!

Airborne delights - what images outpour
Of lazy, hot and hazy ways
And carefree summer days - alas no more!

Verity Gill Malkinson (Padstow)

Milton Keynes

This is a new town, a boomtown,
New houses, theatre, the lot,
It's green and it's tree-lined,
Modern and streamlined,
And, I like it a lot.

If you should be passing on the M1,
Pull in and see us,
There's plenty of fun,
It's friendly and seems
To share all its dreams,
It's my home, and it's Milton Keynes.

Eve Pace (Milton Keynes)

Rachael Leigh

Upon a bright, but chilly weekend morn
We strode like fearless soldiers down the planks
Of sun-bleached jetties drunk with years of brine,
And hauled our colours by an antique pile;
We dropped our lines for flounder or for pout,
But in the brownish soup of engine oil
Caught nothing bar a multitude of crabs.

And so we beat retreat with shouldered rods
Past hardy fishers, bearded, pipes in mouths,
When suddenly a girl, about our age
In pumps and Breton cap, seemed out of place.
She was beguiling, resting on the boom
Her hair was brighter than the sun, her smile
Softer than the fall of waves - I was awed.

She sat upon the Rachael Leigh, a boat
That sparkled in the sun from some lost dream,
That hailed from paradise and for a day
Came quiet on my grey and jaded town.
I had to stop and stare with mouth agape,
And shield the morning sun and sparkling rays
From eyes that knew so little of the world.

Perhaps the clouds rolled faster in the sky,
Perhaps the breeze, blown by the ocean sprites
Was full of magic then: was this for me?
She was as pristine as her sky-blue boat,
Her colours pastel, outlined with the sun
The girl aboard the Rachael Leigh was change
Turning me from youth, leading me to man.

Fraser Hicks (Gosport)

The Mutuality Of Love

This stolen, rejuvenating, day of bliss spent together.
Each totally accepting of each other's weariness.
The cups of tea proffered without asking
And delivered with the gentlest, reassuring touch
Of hand on shoulder.

This mutual, safe, warm, compliant
Love,
This cherished living fantasy
This married love, of many years
Fathomless
And now more powerful than its first embrace.

Frances M Thomas (Hemel Hempstead)

Global Warming

The weather change is through global warming
So we are warned, which sounds alarming;
Ice getting thinner through too much heat,
Too much arable land in retreat.
Parts of the world suffering shortage of food
Others are plagued by quakes, gales and flooding.

The weather has changed, which is plain to see,
It must be plain to all, not just to me:
The sun rises with glorious light,
Warmth from its rays - no cloud in sight
But the clouds appear, turning brightness to grey
All at the beginning of another new day.

The weather is changed as each day goes by,
We're not sure what to wear or what to buy.
First it is warm, then the rain joins in
The temperature becomes cooler - clothes too thin.
Umbrella is used to save soaking the hair
But a wind comes from nowhere the day to share.

The weather was changed many years ago
When a man was crucified - perhaps you do not know
How the darkness came and covered the Earth
At the time of day which yet brought new birth:
Those who have accepted what happened that day
Have come to know that man in a greater way
For 'twas ordained by God that Jesus died
To show all people they can abide
In the love of God's Son forever
No matter how changed the pattern of weather.

E Harvey (Bournemouth)

Dragonfly

In front of me there are trees
and under my feet grass.
The sun looks down at me
like a giant eye.
Seconds pass like a dragonfly
in front of me.
The hum of a bee.
The bark of a dog.
Children exiting from the park.
In the distance cars pass by
quicker than the wings of a dragonfly.

Alan Mason (Southsea)

Harbour Or Haven?

Now what of the universes fixed
    Beyond our own in unbounded space?
In what new way are their elements mixed?
    Has a man-like creature a privileged place?
    Is there in them for doom or grace,
Good, and evil? Are souls enslaven
    Within them, or free? Can we know or trace? -
In the cosmic sea is there harbour, or haven?

If our own is a universe unfixed,
    Moving around some moving base
In the Milky Way, we have 'here'! prefixed
    To our home for an instance as on we race
    Threading the stellar populace.
Are we pilotless, are we bold or craven,
    As the paths of the stars we interlace? -
In the cosmic sea is there harbour or haven?

With the moving stars we are intermixed -
    Do our moving millions more displace?
Is the heart of the Universe transfixed
    With desire for rest - or increasing pace?
    Do we fill with our stardust interspace
Betwixt greater systems, our path engraven,
    Fixed, though we ever its marks efface? -
In the cosmic sea is there harbour or haven?

We do not know - can we space embrace?
    Can we time deliver, a dove, or a raven?
Can we vision an end to the endless chase? -
    In the cosmic sea is there harbour or haven?

Henry Harding Rogers (Purley)

Perfection

I have just seen a blue whale breach
it is something I thought I would never see
a tail so mountainous
a tail so tall
what do we as onlooker think of it all?
We are in awe of this beautiful whale
it is like a clipper in glorious sail
a free spirit, one who roams the sea
a beautiful creature for all to see.
Please don't destroy this wonderful creation
if you do I am sure it will be Man's damnation.

Susan Stuart (Epsom)

Royal Eltham

Let me tell you of my place of birth,
Come on a journey with me
This tiny part of Britain
Is steeped in history.

First mentioned in the Domesday Book
Eltham got its name
Meaning Elta's Homestead
Was home to kings of fame.

Yes we can boast of several kings
Of jousting in Tilt Yard
At the Moot of Hundred many a law outlined
And the most important
The Magna Carter signed.
A stone's throw from the Palace
Chaucer's house you'll find

In Well Hall House by the Tudor Barn
Elizabeth Nesbit's house once stood
Also Sevendroog castle is
Nestling in the woods.

Yes this tiny part of Britain
Has history to boast
In World War II our castle
Helped keep enemies from our coast.

There is so much more to tell you
And so much more to see,
Come and walk down memory lane
Come share this place with me.

Audrey A Allocca (London)

The West

'Rain, rain, more rain,'
Forecast for the west.

Green, green, green fields,
Stretch across the west.

Trees, trees, trees sway
Gales in the west.

Flood, flood, flood plain
Covered in the west.

Sun, sun, sun breaks through
The clouds in the west.

Joan Boswell (Bath)

Mothering Sunday

(A tribute to 19-year-old Immaculee Illibagiza, who survived the Rwandan genocide and forgave those who murdered her parents)

She kneels at the graveside, this daughter of strife,
And reads the inscription carved out on the stone:
For Sara Bagiza, dear mother and wife,
Who died in the killings, and died all alone.

She kneels and remembers the sweet childhood days,
Of play with her brothers, of lessons at school,
Of her father's strong hand and her mother's sweet gaze,
And hours by the stream, with the water so cool.

She kneels and remembers the day of the killing,
The faces of flint and the eyes rimmed with blood,
The shouts and the curses, the voices so chilling,
The uniforms tattered and spattered with mud.

And the swish of machete in bloodstained hands,
And the cries of the victims of murder and rape,
And the smell of the evil in Rwanda's fair land,
And the anguish of children who tried to escape . .

She kneels and remembers this Mothering Day
The mother cut down in that cruel genocide.
'Dear Mother, I love you , and always I'll pray
That your soul in the hands of the Lord may abide.

And I'll pray, dearest Mother, for those men of fire
Who murdered and raped for their own evil ends,
Who killed the best mother a girl could desire,
And took from my childhood the dearest of friends.'

Ken Brown (Crawley)

Mr Beaver

Mr Beaver, wild and strong,
I knew you, and I knew what was wrong.
You called out in the rain, in pain.

Mr Beaver, your dam gone and lost,
You act as if there was no cost.
Your dam was burnt,
The men never learnt.

Mr Beaver, protective and calm,
Knew the river like the back of his palm.
He looked after young, tried hard not to be dim,
And just look what fate gave him.

Tara Wells-McCulloch (Plymouth)

The Seashore

The azure waves come rolling in, in timeless motion towards the shore.
White foamed crests hit jagged rocks and into coral caves they roar,
where sunken treasures from the deep in caverns their ancient
silence keep.

The seagulls swoop from windswept sky down to the deeps
where right fish lie and crusted cabs and lobsters red sit basking
on the warm seabed.

In dappled pools where sunlight shines, tiny fish the young child finds.
With net and bucket and wooden spade, he stirs the creatures
from their shade.

Stately ships their voyage make and white sailed yachts bob
in their wake. Foreign boats in style sail past with tropic goods
in holds so vast, from blue lagoons and distant lands
of pure white reef and shifting sands.

Paddle steamers wend their way to distant ports and sparkling bays,
where palm trees sway amidst the breeze
and boats stand empty by the keys. Cafes with their awnings
bright are open all hours of the night.

The vermilion sky with sunset deep its rendezvous with night it keeps.
Red and gold cross water shines, nothing stops the sands of time
as tide flows in to meet the land and loves stroll by hand in hand.

The distant shore lights from afar bright like hosts of twinkling stars,
dance upon the water line like rainbows mixed with pale moonshine.

Time and tide will wait no more till dawn appears upon the shore,
and sunrise creeps up through the mist touched by
summer's golden kiss.

Sue Lancaster (Waterlooville)

Next Season, Thank You!

Outside the window
Winter stands, beckoning.

Behind the curtains
The little cat sits,
Like a girl at a dance,
Dressed in an outfit
Of figure-hugging black,
Her green eyes
Demurely downcast.

Thank you, no!
She prefers to sit this one . . . in!

Valerie Tapson (Newton Abbot)

Wellies And Mac'ats

In years of drought,
Gardens did shout.
We need much more rain.

And folks did cry.
It's all too dry.
We need the rain again.

The good Lord then
Took up his pen
And signed the order 'Rain'

And it did.

'Water, water everywhere
Not any drop to drink!'
'No, it's just not an overflow
From the kitchen sink.'

It flows like rivers
Down the drains
Filling the valleys
And surrounding plains.

It comes up to the doorstep
Seeps up through the floor.
The garden is a wondrous lake
'Oh - dear Lord for heaven's sake.'

Over the following night and day
Most of the water sank away.
Balance of nature I heard it said.
It leaves a question in my head.

Frances Mary Santer (Stevenage)

Romans

The Romans journeyed on the Fosseway
To places on the Southern coast
Their route passes my dwelling
And I hear their heavy footfalls.
Their presence is compelling.
Some must have died en route
Their souls still roaming here.
My flowers lower their heads -
And birds sing songs of loss.
Those Romans go on marching
For ever on the Fosse.

Joan Gilmour (Bath)

The Silent Hunter

In the warm night air, there is no sound,
But as small creatures scurry through the dark,
A pair of dark eyes glisten in the moon,
They hover midway in the trees,
A heart-shaped face in the heart-shaped leaves.

The silent hunter of the night.

The branch shakes and the creature is gone,
Its silent form flies high,
High by the stars,
High by the moon,
A shadow it makes across the gloom.

The silent hunter of the night.

The tawny wings make no sound,
As those beady eyes scan the floor,
A mere morsel is all it wants,
It finds one,
And so begins the hunt.

The silent hunter of the night.

The bird is silent,
As it plummets fast.
Long legs outstretched,
It takes its chance.
And away it flies,
With its dinner in its hand.

The majestic, silent hunter,
The barn owl.

Katie Stimson (14) (Camberley)

Always Hope

This world awaits in anticipation
For hope for some consolation,
But I myself fear the worse,
Not to prophesy things to come
Nor do I wish to be like some,
And say God's will be done,
So I will go into the picture now
To the farthest corner,
And not look back,
Not look at the world behind me,
But the future that is to come.

Pat Maddalena (Whitchurch)

Spring

Strong incursion
Lies staid a land:

Given Godliness
First hand.

Trauma
Altruistic
Is the captivating Earth
Bringing constant
Ever-flowing power
En passant
Life is ours.

On and on she scurries
Old ideals of men
She buries.

Wielding her great
Salient foetus.

To embellish
Every living tree
Every child
And you and me.

Pros and cons assimilate
In her psychic disarray
Positive's sublime.

Fetching every nuance
Of her springly splendour
To our human eyes.

Helene K MacDonald (Bristol)

A True Friend

A true friend like you is hard to find,
You're in my heart and on my mind,
You're thoughtful, good and true,
So I wrote this down for you,
May these words fill your soul,
Like a warm bowl of soup,
Right down to your toes,
All through to your fingers and
Up to your nose,
I hope you will find true friendship,
In these words of mine.

Anne Davies (Sidmouth)

Greetens Vrom Darzet

To live on a coast ensures one thing;
The pleasant coves and differing beaches
Will have seen invaders, smugglers,
Wrecks, as well as good times.
Dorset is no exception,
France is but a sail away.
Here the D-Day forces gathered,
Locals learnt to hold their tongues,
Avert their eyes as practices went on.
Many years before the Romans came,
Using beaches even then as a resort.
This is the dinosaur country,
Storms reveal here a tooth, a bone,
And crumbling cliffs expose strange creatures
Preserved within the rock.
Up our wooded chines
Brandy and tobacco climbed,
For ready back door sales,
Woods resounded with the clashes
As law enforcers tried to stop the trade.
Still we have the woods,
Once hunting ground for kings.
The downs and cliffs cover
Stores of building stone,
Great monuments display
Our underground treasure.
Still beaches and historic towns,
Hold their markets, offer pleasure,
And gentle Dorset speech lives on.

Di Bagshawe (Poole)

Eternal Love

Gone but never forgotten!
Your beautiful memory
Lives on in my dreams at night!
In the stars, in the moon,
You are my guardian angel,
My guiding light,
You gave me life and love
And let me spread my wings
Like a dove!
What I am I owe to you,
A shining star above!

Pamela Hanover (Christchurch)

All Who Observe

Who would aspire to poetry,
Must ever look to ever see
Throughout nature's widespread field
Her greatest and her smallest yield.
Peer at moss upon a wall
And note the glory in dew fall
Upon each tiny seeded strand,
Or gaze at patterns in the sand
And colours on a pebbled beach,
There's beauty to be found in each.
Look! When skies drop down their rains
How jewelled are the birch tree chains;
Observe the wonderful designs
In ivy, as it wreathes and winds
About the hedges and the trees.
Beauty abounds, the eyes to please;
Dark holly with its berries bright,
Bare oaks lit by pale moonlight,
A ladybird upon a rose, a finch upon a reed,
Take a moment, just to pause -
To nature's book give heed.
The loveliness of falling snow,
And hoar frost's magic touch,
There is replenishment of soul
To be found in oh so much;
Who would aspire to poetry?
All who observe in lane and lea,
On mead and moor, by brook and sea . . .
For all these works are poetry.

Doreen Beer (Exeter)

Clockwork People

Tall dark buildings the man-made land
Long winding pathways beneath them stand.
The hustle and the bustle of the *am*
When clockwork people rush off to work again.
Pushing in the subways,
Shouting in the streets,
Loud pitter-patter of clumsy feet.
To offices and factories people fly
Yet in their hearts none of them know why.
Just another day to start another week
For clockwork people for clockwork streets.

Kathleen Ruth Bruce (Alresford)

Forty Years On

(Eight Haikus)

Adolescent buds:
school uniformed tube journeys,
single sex seating.

Adolescent blooms:
who is driving her crazy
across the gangway?

Heart pounding, yearning,
she pursuing, he fleeing;
unrequited love.

She is my mad friend
roping us haphazardly
in her whirling sea.

Sophisticated
sixth formers have other loves;
now we talk as friends.

It's forty years on
and we are caught, two fishes
on an e-mail line,

in a dreamy transport
to refocus, redefine,
lost territory;

your mesmeric eyes
etched on memory's landscape;
my departing wave.

Rilla Dudley (Worthing)

Windfalls

Climbing over the orchard wall
To gather apples - ripe windfalls.
Picking up the fruit they heard a shout
'Here comes the farmer - Look Out! Look Out!
come on, run, he's waving his stick
Quick, quick! Hide in the hayrick.'
With bated breath they waited there
Not daring to move, even a hair.
At last it was safe, off they fled
'Hurry! Hurry! We should be home in bed.'
Out of the field and over the wall
Holding on tight to their windfalls.

Jan Nolan-Averies (Swindon)

Observations Whilst Mowing The Lawn - May

Clear skies and sun appear together,
Flowers and shrubs begin to thrive;
Fat, furry bees nuzzle the heather
Digging for gold to return to their hive.

An earthworm writhing in a complex coil,
Panicking on the patio stone
Needs a helping hand to return to the soil
To a far more familiar and friendly zone.

Minute silver dots embraced by the sun,
Glint in the heavens, deceptively high,
Leave twin vapour trails, which merge into one,
Defacing an otherwise faultless sky.

A peacock butterfly lands nearby
With wings outspread on the hardened earth,
Its roundels displayed to the open sky
Parading its beauty for all it is worth.

The airwaves are filled by singing birds,
Sparrows flit from bush to bush.
The robin and magpie appear to have words
Whilst a blackbird competes with a thrush.

Something is happening all of the time
Events overlooked before,
To miss them in future would be a crime
And mowing the lawn is no longer a chore.

David Allen (Plymouth)

Departure

Seven thirty. Daylight streaming in
Stirs me, snugly balled up in my bed,
And I catch you packing up your bag.
'Zipping up your memories,' you said,
And then go on to say that every word
In every single letter that you sent
Expressing your devotion, and your love
Was written from the heart, and truly meant.
Yet I, through seeking truth have now erased
In moments, years of friendship with one line,
For love is more than letters on a page.
I verbalise that you cannot be mine.

Kim Algie (Plymouth)

Until The Next Time . . .

(In memory of Auntie Jill . . . July 2nd 2008)

Having had the chance to share the yesteryears talking
of your younger days the laughter and the tears . . .
Who would have thought that I would be standing here this day?
talking of you now even though you're not far away.
I know now of your journey for this is not the end,
you are on a new horizon, a pathway to the rainbow's end.
I thank you for the days we shared,
which will stand as a testament of time,
a memory for me to hold, a gift that is truly divine.
You held me and you told me how much you loved me so,
I then did the same, but I said goodbye and had to go.
Farewells are never easy, for life will never be the same,
for I know you will always be part of me,
through the sunshine and the rain.
So as we laugh and as we cry it's our turn now to say goodbye,
to remember you the way you would be
and to release you now and set you free.
The pain has gone, the worry too . . .
it's your infectious laugh that saw you through . . .
through the doubt and through the fears,
what has happened to all those yesteryears?
Your guardian angels have taken you home,
for there you will rest and not be alone.
I'll think of you always as the days pass on by
and remember your words and your reasons why.
So your tapestry is woven, your life is now complete,
farewell until the next time, for the next time we shall meet.

Will Turner (Reading)

Chance Encounter

When Sammy the hedgehog was out one day,
He was in for a big surprise.
A rabbit said, 'Please may I borrow your coat?
For I want to go out in disguise.'
'Why yes,' said Sammy, 'you may borrow my coat,
But you really will have to take care,
You must make quite sure that the zip is done up,
Or the prickles will lay your flesh bare.'
'Oh dear,' said the rabbit 'assistance I'll need,
For I'm not very clever like that,
It might be too difficult even with help,
So perhaps I'll make do with a hat.'

June Hilliar (Ashtead)

Summer Roses

summer is the rose
the rose of our lives
the flower of beauty
that sits out in beds
where all about is the warmth and life
and the rose blooms silently about
great arrays of flowers
that stand as one
in serried ranks of different colours
and speak of the joy of summer now

when all around is joy and life
and seasonal cheer
and the festive time everywhere
blooms the rose in its several spires
flowers overwhelming all the beds
as joy in flower does reach out
the endless realms of summer
and gone the times of yesteryear
when roses did not stand around
in so many places unforeseen

but the rose stands in the flowery banks
that speak of endless days of summer
with the scent of freshly-mown grass
speaking of the tides of joy
of summer come at last
after the long winter of despair
and blooms the rose always there
a scene of summer cheer

Alasdair Sclater (London)

Sailor's Love

I made love to my girl where the waters roar,
Where the rocks are splashed with foam,
For I loved that girl with a seaman's love,
And the seashore was my home.
The crashing of the Atlantic waves
Played a lovely melody.
For I loved that girl with a seaman's love,
And I loved the roaring sea.
I heard the mew of a seagull's cry
As it circled high above,
And the sunshine kissed the pink sea thrift
On the ledge where I lay with my love.

Roland G Clarke (Andover)

To A Piece Of Flint

You lie in my hand you Stone-Age man's flint
With a groove for two fingers and thumb-ball's imprint.
You sit there so snugly your point to the fore,
Far now from your kindred upon the seashore.
I turn you and wonder who picked you up first,
Who struck the great flint stone from which you have burst.
Who fashioned you crudely, who chipped you away,
Did children of Stone-Age man, once with you play?
Did you belong to Stone-Age man's wife,
Who used you to flay her skins, like a knife?
Or were you the point of some keen hunter's spear
With which he would slay the fast-fleeing deer?
I wish you could tell me, you Stone-Age man's flint,
With your groove for two fingers and a thumb-ball's imprint.

I look at your structure, the dark and the light,
The veins of grey graphite, the marbling white.
I ponder your making, the rough textured rim
(A contrast most striking to smooth stone within).
Who made you? Who wrought you, my sharp arrowhead?
Were you rubbed, were fretted along the sea's bed?
Did strong waves uphurl you to land on the beach
Away from the breakers' harsh, grasping reach?
Did the wind whip you? Did the frost form a crack,
So cavemen would chip you, and so, break your back?

Who thought you? Who dreamt you? What power? What might?
God was your Creator, you offspring of light.
And now I am holding you, warm in my hand,
You fragment of history, you piece of our land.

Jane Finlayson (Guildford)

Clouds!

White, silver, even grey
Fluffy stuff way up high
A family which floats together
Clouds. Amongst blue sky.
Some look soft and gentle
Others fierce and strong.
The white ones round and dumpy.
Grey ones, stretched out wide and long.
Watching as they masquerade
Amidst the midday sun.
Disintegrating very slowly.
One by one, by one.

Nicola Green (Hoddesdon)

Echoes

Monday's child is . . .

    A happy, go-lucky guy in his teens

Tuesday's child is . . .

    Whose got great t**s and a**e!

Wednesday's child is . . .

    Regular shop has closed

Thursday's child has . . .

    Into no-man's-land

Friday's child is . . .

    Grace is definitely his love and he's giving her
    a good seeing-to

Saturday's child works . . .

    In a sports shop part-time

And the child that is born on the Sabbath day
is bonny and blithe and good and gay -

    Fair dos and all that -
      True -
    I was born on a Sunday
      True -
    I was a bonny baby (so me mum tells me)
      True -
    I liked a laugh as much as anyone
      True -
    I thought I was good (well most of the
    time, anyway) -

    But *gay!* Who were you kidding -

    Grace . . . Grace . . . Tell them please . . .

B Montague (London)

A Dorset Lane

The lane winds round to hidden places
Where orchids and bluebells might fill the spaces
The ferns grow tall and hide the deer,
Not many people find their way here.
The hedgerows are lush, thick and green
I find a gate on which to lean
To watch the swifts in spiralling flight
Or a buzzard calls and dives out of sight.
The scent of honeysuckle is very strong
I breathe it in deeply, as I walk along
And even when it starts to rain
I still find joy within this lane.

Pat Parkes (Bridport)

I Wish I'd Looked After Me Feet

(Apologies to Pam Ayres)

'Oh, I wish I'd looked after me feet
But the young have this need to compete,
So when fashion beckoned
Well, comfort came second,
I wish I'd looked after me feet.

Those ridiculous shoes that I chose
Rubbed my heels, and squashed up all me toes,
My mother would sigh
As she watched me limp by,
'You'll regret,' she'd say, 'wearing those.'

I wish I could turn back the clock
I'd not give me feet such a shock,
Oh, the corns I have cursed
And the blisters I've burst,
I wish I could turn back the clock.

Now I sit in the old rocking chair
And gaze at me feet in despair,
My dear mother was right
They're a pitiful sight
And in need of some specialist care.

So I hobble along down the street
To give these old trotters a treat,
My chiropodist's nice
But she comes at a price,
Oh, I wish I'd looked after me feet.

Jean Spindler (Swindon)

Celluloid Man

I set you up
With volts of beam
And you were the traveller
On the screen
I found you wondering
In time fog
Peeking through
The life you spoke
Was set in clue
In the flicker of an eye
When a hundred years
Was rolling by.

Richard Leduchowicz (Slough)

Inventions, The Earth, The Sky And The Sea

When the combine harvester drives round the fields,
What do the field mice say?
They squeak to their friends,
You must run for your life while you may.
There's a monster running around near our homes,
It must be an unknown species,
If we don't get away right now if we can,
It will just chew us all up to pieces.

When a Concorde speeds across the air,
What do the birds all cry?
Down into the trees, friends down into the trees,
Yes into those trees we must fly,
There's a giant eagle above us, racing,
Right through the cloud.
I just do not think it will care about us.
The noise that it makes is so loud.

When those oil holes are dug way under the sea,
What do those poor fish think?
Swim far away, friends swim far away,
Our food here will all die then sink.
Something's polluting our water,
We'll find it so hard to survive,
We must all swim away,
Just as far as we can,
If we all wish to stay alive.

Nita Garlinge (Poole)

I Knew The Truth

Adopted I alone
Spoken to but not at home
So rebelling I would walk
From the fosters who wouldn't talk
Never a time I knew the truth
Provoking thought throughout my youth
Sometimes cracking in despair
I was dragged by my hair
Never a guess I was used
So rehearsed at hiding clues
No one knew in all those years
I carried it all from those queers.

Mark Hill (Oxford)

Today

Today . . . today
A gift - a given
Yours to fit into even

Though many days
Will haunt the hours
Before today begins

This new day rises
Without a past
Sun at last taking leave
Of the night

Still landscapes appear
Fill a sky empty of words
Where birds speak first

Or

Will

Memories habits
Form a list
To twist away
Today

An old essay remembers
A poem torn from a book
Newborn without blemish

Peel back the dawn
Your pages are waiting
Today.

Dorothy Ann Coventon (Torpoint)

Through The Kitchen Window

Young woman, hanging washing,
Unaware, the sun turning her blouse transparent,
Firm, erect nipples meet my guilty gaze,
How I long to touch,
Caress,
To kiss.

For two decades I have watched her mature
From schoolgirl to woman.
I lust for her now,
Will I ever possess her?
One day,
Maybe.

Douglas Bishop (Bournemouth)

A Poet's World

How can a poet articulate
His brave new world to readers?
By his own creative way,
From our trapped minds he'll lead us.
Who can dream the poet's dreams,
Or share his flights of passion?
Who can see with his artist's eye,
Or help his thoughts to fashion?

A poet can make a heaven of hell:
Sculptured thought from chaos as well;
Out of blackness a starry sky:
From despair to hope, a reason why;
Out of the depths of his own creation:
Serenity from agitation;
From darkest thoughts of wondering why:
A calming river meandering by;
From Hell create angelic sound:
Or a verdant pasture from stony ground;
From simmering anger a quiet mind:
Leaving the cauldron of evil behind.
Coolness he makes from hot desert sands:
Or warmth from ice which none understands.
Out of his wealth of imagination:
He makes new worlds his own creation.
Stamping out a destructive past:
From hate to love and a peace to last.
For he lets in God for total protection:
From death to life and resurrection.

Janet Lang (Seaton)

Pursuit

He sits on top of roadside perch
With view of hedgerow and of garden,
Seeking out persistent foes who rashly venture into sight,
Quiet invasions swiftly spotted,
Punished by a hot pursuit,
Warnings given, not a pardon;

For offences oft repeated then the search
Goes high and low following a frantic route,
Earnest chase of brash intruders
Sought and found from dawn 'til night,
Daring to invade the landscape
Held by Blackbird as his right!

C E Margetts (Orpington)

You Wanted Me To Steal You

You wanted me to steal you
'Run off with me,' you said.
'Kidnap me, abduct me, poach me,
Sling me over your shoulder,
And trudge home with me,
Stash me in your outhouse and salt me down,
Make me a provision for months to come,
Preserve me for your table,
Serve me up with a fine wine,
Cook me up a storm,
Peel my delicate layers and decorate a dish with me,
Garnish me with flowers put into strategic holes,
And stuff my mouth with an apple,
Devour me, ingest me,
I will never be wasted,
Drizzle me with desire,
Whip me into a frenzy,
Baste me with bondage,
Souse me with sensuality,
And sprinkle me with sauce.
Toss me with temptation,
Make me rise with your yeasty dough,
Risen in a hot place and proven in a hundred others,
Add some zest to my life,
And then eat me.'

You begged me, cajoled, pleaded,
That's what you did.
But I was never that hungry.

Jan Crocker (Plymouth)

My Island Home (Guernsey CI)

Azure-blue to turquoise-green
The bluest sea you've ever seen
The sky above cloudless but with a morning haze
Quiet - heat to come - just sit and gaze
Not a breath of wind - no foliage stirs
The view of small islands slightly blurs.

A gem of an island in the sea
Is where I was born and want to be
Some come - some go
But often they return and know
Having toured the world but still agree
It's hard to beat 'Sarnia Cherie'.

Jacqueline Bartlett (St Martin)

Two Sonnets For Vanchristen

Should a love like this, on mortals, be bestowed?
For God, alone, is *'love', a rightful heir*
Whose heart bears all, whilst we, on Earth, are bowed;
When 'life' is wrought in Heaven's loving breast
And born, unseen, of water, dust and air
By 'Divine' hands; exhaled, a breath, in love,
Breathes into hearts; holds 'man, woman', there!
Then, eyes opened, their naked shame bequeath.
'My love, you are the warmth of sun's embrace,
And when you gaze, in love, you melt my heart;
This love becomes such 'illness', no solace,
Am smitten by charms' impassioned darts.
When all alone, or in the melee, hid,
Your envisioned smile, comfort bids.'

Sleep steals from my eyes, like summer's dew
And thoughts of you betray to waking yours
My sad wand'rings, with visions of blue.
Even windowpanes reveal restless thoughts.
Which surface through my tears, on dismal days
When lonely clouds, conjoined, their comfort seek;
Crying tears of joy, in grey, blanket haze.
When loving you, dear Vee, is sickness, weak,
I ache and yearn with longing, just for you;
Infused, deep within, our hearts as one;
And dark clouds flee when you come into view.
For God's hand, His authorship, be done;
Pedestals are banished from His sight
And our 'God-centred' love, is His delight!

Cuba N Briton (Swindon)

Where The Rainbow Begins And Ends

She was on a long journey
To where the rainbow begins and ends.
Poised on the soft edge of colour and light
She could hear her children laugh and cry,
As down the years they travelled,
Gum-booted and slippered towards their dreaming night.

Sleeping, she embraced her rough loving husband
As the moon drew closer and flowers bloomed
On her rosy cheeks
Her eyes shining
Like stardust
In the fading light.

Josephine Thomas

Eyesore

Outside Broomfield Park I stand
I am a plane tree.
But not just a plain old tree
I am a beauty clothed in green
A magnificent sight to see.
A sight for sore eyes.
At least I was until yesterday
When a shocking thing happened to me.

I was standing in my usual place
Swelling my leaves, breathing the fumes
Producing clean air for the mad human race
When suddenly some men climbed into my arms
And started attacking my face.

The saws they were wielding screamed with delight
As my green treasure fell to the floor.
They continued to hack every vestige of green
Until all I had left was my core.
I am naked, I am bare, I'm denuded
I have nothing to live for at all.
My winter is here already
Now I won't see my autumn leaves fall.

So come up to the park and see me and my pals
It won't be a picture to paint
Even though we're standing in Palmers Green
For us, poor mutilated trees,
Palmers green
It just ain't.

Shirley Nicolaou (London)

Close-Of-Business On The Mountaintop

The wind played with the grass
The flowers shook their heads dizzily, as if in a trance
The wind, distracted, asked if they would like to dance.
How could they refuse?
They couldn't let such a chance
Pass them by.

The crickets worked hard on the score
The birds took care of the vocals.
The spectacle passed unnoticed by the locals.
Familiarity blinding them
To this rite of nature,
At close-of-business on the mountaintop.

Arwa Hassan (London)

Just A Thought (After Icarus)

Who's improbable eye espied
A little bird upon a tree,
And picketh up a stone, and shied -
And frighted it, and marvelled, he
Who's bane surveillance of the bird -
That fleeth lightly on the wing,
Saith to himself, and how absurd,
'Oh, if I could fly like that pretty thing.'

Yea, that discerning prophet sought
The mystique of the feathered clan.
In mind and body, he was fraught -
With but one aim, ah worthy man.
And whomsoe'er wouldst mock and mirth,
Or wonder what, forwhy, and how,
Hath verily ne'er spurned the earth,
But bide content with the 'here and now'.

And so the time once dawned, when man -
Confused with unction tried to fly,
Unto a mount, and praising Pan -
Didst cast himself into the sky.
'Oh what foolhardy man is this?'
A bystander was heard to shout.
The tragedy most surely is -
'Twas a summer's day, and the sun was out.

Icarus, son of Deadalus in Greek mythology,
Who melted the wax in his wings,
By flying too near the sun.

Derek Haskett-Jones (Beaminster)

Development

In thunderous dust, moon-high,
The tattered curtains, closets, carpets lie:
One last rough gable with its privates bare,
This grand old house hangs naked in the air
Its remnants trembling on the sky,
Outraged by public stare.

There, now, rise luxury apartments, cool,
For trophy wives; white carpets, use-of-pool,
(Except by minnow, dragonfly and frog).
In duplex, penthouse, 'spotless' is the rule;
All glass and chrome and muted dialogue.
No place for wellies these days. Or the dog.

A J French (Poole)

Leaves Leaving

(Perhaps best read aloud)

Sharp autumnal winds sear branches,
 Frost-weakened connections sever
And from above descend the freed appendages
Of trees shaken in the shock of loss.

Swirling and twirling and whirling,
 Dancing and prancing then glancing
 One off the other,
 Lunging and plunging, swinging and winging,
 Lifting and drifting - stalling and falling,
Caught bright in the gleam of a sunbeam
Then dulled in the transient shadow.

Red blending with amber,
 Amber smudged with brown,
 Brown laced with yellow,
 Yellow live with green,
All thrown into a rich confusion of colour,
Co-mingling, separating, reuniting, meeting and parting,
Progressing ever ultimately downwards.

So float the leaves on the first and last journey
 Of their short, beautiful lives;
 Dying in radiance, sustaining as decaying,
All as if in thanks to that which briefly bore them,
High and proud and green at first
And finally through the shades
To the lasting wealth of Earth.

H L Martin (Cullompton)

Milton Keynes, The Silver City

Many came to make a new life
In these wide open fields
Low marshland became fine roads
To lead onto neat and varied estates
Open skies over a city of blue and silver reflected in glass
New city centre skyline; domes, pyramids and blocks.

Keen families walk and jog,
Energetic as they briskly pass
Young cyclists on the Redways
Near the Pagoda at Willen Lake
Every faith and race gather to find
Space for peace and hope.

Anne Reilly Brown (Bedford)

Happy Birthday

May colourful balloons fly high to give a cheerful start
To the celebration of the 20th anniversary of your birth
And the whole event leave lasting memories behind
To boost your prosperity and success
In placing more poets on the path to fame,

In discovering their rich depth and guide
Their power of imagination to enchanted worlds,
As well as in putting their works on public display,
And be hugely appreciated for that.

Especially, why not go on to support
Those bards who try to immortalise the mighty heart
Of Princess Diana, who with her acts of love gave glory to this land
And hope to thousands of souls on Earth,
With her crusades to save lives and fair play?

More praises we owe the phenomenal Princess of Wales,
For being a spectacular landmark of the 20th century,
And humanity's champion, always doing her best
To give everyone happiness!

She was a poet herself.
As a poetry patron she did popularise this genre,
Bid to give it a future so bright.
Let her live for evermore!

If you keep her powerful memories alive
She will bring you good fortune and luck
To enjoy many happy returns
In the years ahead!

Lucy Carrington (London)

Country Retreat

I miss the trees I miss the blooms,
I miss the space of many rooms.
Trains thunder by grabbing the ground,
Carry commuters homeward-bound.
To empty boxes and empty lives
To awful offspring and bored housewives.

O' where is the birdsong and scent of mown hay,
In this world of pollution and disarray?
O' where is our Post Office and village shop
Where pensioners paused for a life-saving prop?
O' gone is the good life of our yesteryear
As byways and buildings encroach ever near.

B Deadman (Worthing)

In Celebration

What indeed shall we celebrate?
Of what too would we like to read?
Over the years, the subtleties of words,
A hunger of a verbal greed.

Best poets of a certain cheer
Their many works we love to hear
'Songs of Senses' and of the heart
Could say one has 'poetic art'.

To pass on -
Who's who, of friendships, life and celebration?
Vibes reach out to all with such a notion.
Or maybe 'sweet nothings' whispered to your sweethearts
Whilst sharing meals 'a la carte.'

Steph and Chris, same birthdays share,
Just celebrates another happy year,
Not just ages but careers too,
Medical doctors their lives will pursue.

In celebration then -
It was BBQ time with friends from far and near,
Smokey burgers and sausages relished with good cheer.
Bottles of 'Chamfers', bubbly and beer,
Begin again we trust, another rewarding and happy year.

So what now is up for celebration?
These twenty years of poetry from the nation.
We gather too for those special moments,
That remain forever, always fragrant.

Beatrice Pennell (Broadstone)

Woodwind

April's branches reach towards the sky,
And in their leafless and skeletal hands
The rooks' nest high.
Building untidy piles of sticks
The blackbirds, country cousins all,
Exchange their gossip, cawing each to each,
Preparing lodgings for their sooty broods.

From below, the great nests form
A skein of notes against the blue,
Which fingered by the wind, achieve
A fugue which marks the passing of the cold,
And plays an overture to spring.

Rosemary Hull (Newbury)

Sussex Rambling

We trudged along the South Downs Way
In the high-noon heat of a summer's day,
Down the hill descending steeply,
Down to the river at Amberley.

Across the meadow to the water margin,
Past the dock with the moored barge in,
To reach the café where they serve you tea
Beside the river at Amberley.

'Neath the bridge, the ebb tide's swirling
As stemming the stream, propelling churning,
A motor launch came moving slowly,
Up the river at Amberley.

Amongst the reeds that line the bank
Against a single jettied-plank,
A lad in waders fished serenely
In the river at Amberley.

Along the levee, our way we wend
Around the sweeping river bend,
To find the dock for the ancient ferry
Near the parish church at Bury.

It's a dangerous place with a ripping stream
Where the ferryman's ghost, or so it would seem,
Straining and heaving on the sturdy oars,
With never a chance to stop or pause,
Was condemned for ever, until the boat sank,
To cross the Arun from bank to bank.

David J King (Leatherhead)

Little Children. In Memory

Did God forget you?
Does he love you less,
Than we do who weep,
And will not be consoled?
They will not return.
These children.
To clasp you again well and joyous
Is all we want.
Nothing else will do.

I do not know the end of my poem.
Nor of the children.
Not yet.

Mary Wilson (Bath)

Another Day, Another Dollar

Up I rise at crack of dawn.
Was it for *this* that I was born?
Groping blindly for the light
oh how swiftly flew the night.

Outside, the patter of the rain
beats upon my windowpane,
along the gutter to the drain,
how I long to sleep again.

Bracing myself, I show my mettle,
where in hell's the flaming kettle?
A hurried shave, gulp down my tea
then smoke a fag, what luxury.

Another day, another dollar,
how I wish I'd been a scholar.
I'm almost reduced to tears,
of deep regret for the wasted years.

But then, I never had the brain
to jump on board the gravy train,
or grit enough to push and hustle
among the guys with all the muscle.

And so I mount my bike again
to ride to work in the pouring rain.
Meanwhile I dream like other fools
of the glorious day I win the pools,
another day, another dollar,
how I wish I'd been a scholar.

James Poole (London)

Time Now Goes So Quickly By

The unexplained mystery of a passing moment
  when life was but a mere child,
Taking every minute to cling to
  when days were wild,
Something to ponder on
  when life was passing through,
When that bed of roses meant a different point of view.
Wasting not a second in the years of crazy bliss -
  sharing more than this.

Now we're getting older and we can't turn back the hand
  that moves forever quicker at its will,
Time was priceless when time stood still.

Pauline Newsome (Ryde)

My Secret Eye

Come and enter my multisensory world!
A world where nothing is quite as you see . . .
A magical world I'll show you,
Full of surprises, come enter with me!

A world where forest green is the scent of a hundred foot fir tree
Where winter white is the wind when it bites through your clothes,
Where burning red is the cold, stinging your nose and your toes,
Where sugar pink is a big wet kiss, full of lipstick.

Where cobalt blue is the warmth of a pool.
I can swish my legs and splash like a shining seal.
Look at me!
I am free!
I can swim like a shimmering fish in the sea!

In my world, I see using my secret eye,
It's my sixth sense
With my secret eye . . .
I can tell who it is when they enter a room,
I can tell if they're happy or sad, filled with gloom.
It's the tinge of their voice,
It's the perfume they wear,
It's the smell of their jumper slung over the chair,
It's the brush of their hair, as they kiss me.

I may be blind but can you see
Gazing with my secret eye,
My world is very multisensory!

What's your world like?

Katriona Goode (Hemel Hempstead)

Celebration

Celebration! Celebration!
Hail the poets of the nation
Producers of sparkling pearls of light,
Diamonds of literature, shining bright,
Illuminating dreary prose,
Giving more pleasure, as everyone knows.

Bring out the bands,
And clap your hands,
Forward Press is celebrating
Having made the twenty years,
Of poems fit for publication,
Giving much pleasure to the nation.

John Freeth (Taunton)

I Really Do Care

I feel privileged to be a carer
Although I didn't know what to expect
But you can be sure I will always give you
Honesty, but above all respect.

I have heard it said, 'Don't get emotionally involved'
But how can I not, when I'm there,
For when once in a while,
I see the hint of a smile
Proves to you, that I really do care.

Sometimes it's a one way conversation
But at least, you know I am there
With love in your eyes
It should come as no surprise
I am your carer, and I really do care.

When you truly get to know me
And it won't be long before you do
The one thing I will aim for
Is you trust me as I trust in you.

For there is so much you can teach me
Tell me of times you have laughed and you've cried
Your hopes and your fears, in your twilight years
Full of dignity and pride.

I don't see caring as a job
As time soon passes by
For I shall follow you down life's path
There for the grace of God go I.

Margaret Filbey (Truro)

Philosophy Of Life

Praise God for the sunlight
Praise God for the rain
One fills me with delight
The other is rather a pain
But I know we need both
We must have them for growth

And so it is with life
There are times of peace
And also times of strife
But as our days increase
We realise at length
This only gives us strength

Megan David (London)

427

The Poets

Some poets seem to go on forever,
Like those in the Bible you see!
The words are wonderful writings,
They explain all I'm wanting to be.
The psalms of David keep coming!
Like those of Shakespeare or Barnes,
Tennyson, Lawrence, or Wordsworth;
They all have a way to bring charms.
How could we doubt Fanny Crosby
With hymns that charm us today!
Or books of Elizabeth Browning.
Hardy and Shelley; I say!
We have Bernard Shaw, and Byron,
Longfellow and Scott, I see,
Those Brontë sisters, and Kipling;
Such gifted souls were these.
Kingsley and Burns are famous!
With Thomas and Blyton we hear.
Then there is Hemingway (Ernest)
Who many hold so dear.
Now poets are born to give service,
In words that go to the soul,
There is nothing in writing a poem,
If the writer has no goal.
For a reason poets love writing,
They express all they want to say.
So if you have a reason for writing,
Then put *pen* to your paper *today!*

Ernest Sharpley (Poole)

Tell Me Why?

(For Ethan)

Tell me why I can't play.
Like my friends along the way.
In my heart and head I can run as fast,
But my legs don't seem to last.
I practise every day; to play like my peers is my aim.
Football players do not need walking frames and wheelchairs to get them by.
In my dreams I scored a goal.
Today is a good day, all in my world is OK.
My mum loves me, my dad too; my grandad says there is nothing I cannot do
I know I won't be a world class footballer any day soon.
But I am as cute as any kid you know, and if I work hard a referee is what I plan to be.

Glenda Barker (Waltham Cross)

Early Morning Journey

Pink, yellow, green and white,
The roadside banks are looking bright.
The sun is rising in the sky,
And everything looks good to the eye.
A hawk is hovering in the silent air,
Viewing the ground with the greatest care.
She needs breakfast for her family,
Swoops and catches, and back to her tree,
The nestlings all with mouths held wide,
Grateful for anything that's placed inside,
The road is virtually traffic free,
As we head out to the glorious sea,
The mist is hanging over the hills,
And even the smallest valleys it fills.
It gives a pearly ghostly sheen,
To this early morning scene.
The earth is slumbering, from hillock to lake,
Eternally waiting, for nature to wake,
The twisting turns, of the winding lanes,
Enhance the sea, as height it gains,
Whispy clouds streak the sky above,
This is the time of day I love,
The gentle silence is ready to burst,
Which of God's creatures, will be first,
The barking fox, the lowing cow,
Or the screaming magpie, showing them how?
My heart is at peace, with this wonderful world,
Awaiting the day, that's becoming unfurled.

Denise Marriott (Plymouth)

Good At Heart

A person is said to have a good heart
When found to be nice also kind.
Like wandering ivy
When it clings and climbs.

Every so often many things go wrong
You see not a good person around.
All thorns on a beautiful rose
No love, joy or peace can be found.

Could I be that person to help others
Just like a ray of sun dust
Falling to take away gloom?
Or as a dove of peace I could bloom.

Marion Staddon (Bournemouth)

429

Burt's Ultimate Sacrifice

They danced a jig, a jig,
Danced a jig,
A red farmyard hen,
And her good friend Burt Pig.
The farmer ploughed fields,
From six until three,
He returned to his chair,
As hungry as could be.
'A big English breakfast,
Is what I desire,
A yoke and some rashers,
I'll eat by the fire.'
Red Hen kept on dancing,
'Keep waltzing,' she begs,
'His hunger is sorted,
For I've laid three eggs.'
But Pig's feet aren't moving,
No dancing, they're makin',
For try as he did,
He just couldn't lay bacon!
Three eggs they lay ready,
On a bed of soft straw,
Red Hen kept on dancing,
Burt Pig gave his all.
When life's hunger does call you,
Stop dancing, don't jig,
Will you lay eggs like a chicken,
Or die like Burt Pig?

Carol Harrington-Brice (Bridgwater)

A Prayer Of Hope

If I could have a wish come true
I know what it would be
A world where everybody
Would live in harmony.

But maybe it's a pipe dream
That in this troubled world
A solution can be found
And problems all unfurled.

We can only hope one day
Wars be a thing of the past
And then our children will grow up
In a peaceful world at last.

Sylvia Dyer (St Austell)

Calshot Spit

Sea kale, green upon the stones.
A slipway, where once slept a princess; still mighty in her slumber.
A tower where, more than once, men kept watchful eye.
A tower, taller than the first,
With electronic eye, forever turning times without number,
Watching the horizon to welcome those returning from abroad,
Or giving 'farewell' to those whose horizons are broader.
Brick buildings of a military pattern which held those young men
Who, ascending into vast machines of war, each to his own place,
Raced across water and into air to destroy an enemy below the waves.
A mighty hanger, silent now to the roar of engine and clash of tools,
But cacophonous to the voice of instructor guiding the instructed
On climbing wall and dry ski slope.
The lifeboat still rides at its mooring, changing direction with the tide
Awaiting the shout of 'Mayday'.
Where once the mighty Sunderlands were winched from the water
Children sail tiny boats and paddle small kayaks,
In anticipation of the day, perhaps, when they take control of
mighty ships.
Wooden huts in long unbroken lines
Gaze out across the water towards the island, which, since time out
of mind
Has guarded the land from storm's fury and tempest's blast.
Giant ships from many nations laden with the produce of the world,
Pass by this place of meeting, led in safety between the shallows
By a vessel a thousand times smaller, that proudly proclaims along
its sides,
'Harbour Master - Southampton'.

Robert Smith (Romsey)

Cutting Edge

Now when we reach that 'certain' age,
We should mellow just a bit,
And though I've surely reached that stage,
I can't get the hang of it.

I know how a gentle sweetness,
Sits nicely on we wrinklies,
I think I'm kind - well more or less,
Honestly - I *aim* to please.

But in spite of best intentions,
(Not to carry my own torch)
There are many situations,
When my tongue can really scorch!

Margery Fear (Weston-super-Mare)

Witney Blankets

The famous little blanket town
Where I was born and bred
With quaint old stone built cottages
And quiet streets that led to
Market Place and tiny shops
Where you could always buy
Everything that's needed
To keep you fed and dry
The clacking of the weaving sheds
Where shuttles to and fro
Did shoot between the warp and weft
To make the blankets grow.
The river underneath the mill
To wash the blankets clean
The racks where they were stretched to dry
With allotments in-between.
so proud of our four blanket mills
On whom we did depend
When times were hard, and money short
Comfort was there as well as a friend.
From management to factory floor
Just one small step away
There was someone to rely on
To help us on our way.
Sadly they have bulldozed all our mills
We are now just history
And this famous little blanket town
Is now just ordinary.

Helen Hyatt (Witney)

A Summer's Day

Summer sun brightly shines all day today,
Birds are singing while flying skywards.
Neath the trees people shade a-seeking,
Children on swings are flying and laughing.

Lilies in the pond gleaming brightly,
Fishes whose colours are red-gold and blue.
Roses so scented and pleasing to see,
Blue and cloudless the skies up above.

Lovers are strolling only absorbed in each other,
Relishing the sunshine and beauty of nature.
Squirrels up trees go scurrying at speed,
To escape from children wishing to catch them.

B Bonner (London)

Godrevy

It's heaven to sit and look at the scene
where time after time white rollers have been.
Caressing the shore then ebbing away,
a continuous action day after day.
The sun shines down across St Ives Bay
sparkling like diamonds on the ocean's spray.
The headland juts out like a giant thumb,
shrouded in mist from the heat of the sun.
The beaches are crowded with folk having fun
in warm waters, and sand, for which they have come.
Black dots in the sea on the crest of a wave,
are surfers, who often, spend their days in wetsuits,
on surfboards racing the foam,
and when all is done they journey home.
On its rock base, tall and proud,
Stands the lighthouse, gleaming white.
a safeguard from rocks hidden from sight.
Somewhere above in a cloudless sky,
a skylark is singing way up high.
Swallows and swifts fly past at speed,
screeching noisily as in flight they feed.
Seagulls too join in the throng
adding their voice to the endless song.
Now, as I sit on my grassy mound,
I let my mind drift against the sound
of people, and cars, that come to this place
enjoying like me,
the beautiful landscape that is Godrevy.

Sheila Brown (Hayle)

Precious Love

Let me hold you close to me, for you to know I care.
Let the love flow through us, in that moment that we share.
Let our love entwine within, and our hearts fly high and free.
Then God will give us all His love, just for you and me.

Let me hold you one more time, before we have to part.
For God is waiting there for you but you'll always be in my heart.
For my love will then be close to you, so you will feel within,
A closeness and a perfect peace that never will grow dim.

So go to God and rest in peace, let His love be by your side.
Let Him hold you near to Him and always be your guide.
Please think of me a little, when the tears I cannot hide,
For the love we shared was precious and within us always abide.

June Avery (Bournemouth)

Rise Of The Soldier

He stood so still in the field of death
Where once he had been laid to rest
Seeing the way the land had changed
Where really it had been rearranged
He examined the way the forces collide
And if he was alive, what side was his side?
He viewed the many men he'd soon see
In person, he'd see them and they'd see he
He listened so carefully to each man's prayer
Why did they leave? Why were they there?
Each with a wife, a daughter or son
A whole world of people who would soon be gone
Tears of terror, shame and fury
Each came with his own judge and jury
And within every blackened soul
A heart cried out, no longer whole
And soon the man started to run
Shot between the shells and guns
With bloody tears lining his face
No longer was he full of grace
This intense power of rage and hate
That at one time did seal his fate
Surged through his veins and through his mind
Looking for something he just couldn't find
And finally when all sound had ceased
He realised he was looking for peace
In a world that simply couldn't provide
And once again he died inside.

Hannah McCulloch (Farnham)

Conceit?

I'm a poet, though not many would agree,
Perhaps because I write simplistically;
I'm a poet, with no aim, no flame, no goal,
I write just for myself, to ease my soul.

Not a poem intellectual or lyrical,
Nothing deep, obscure or satirical -
But I'm a poet.

I write about the people I have known,
Condense the joys and sorrows of my years,
Aspire to no Laureate's Crown or Throne
When I record my laughter and my tears.
But I'm a poet.

Sarah Lindsay (Bournemouth)

Untitled

Greetings, I'm your bird,
No, not what's in your mind,
I'm not the sexy curvy type
I am the feathered kind.
I am a turkey, plump and fat
The traditional Christmas meat
All succulent and juicy,
I'm your dinner - what a treat!
I've gobbled tons of food,
To put on lots of weight,
And now I'm dead and lying,
On your clean, white kitchen plate.
They've plucked out all my feathers,
I'm nude, I'm wearing nuffing,
They've pulled out all my innards,
And filled me up with stuffing.
I've got no head or feet,
My stumps were covered in foil,
I had potatoes by my side,
And my breast was rubbed with oil,
I was put into the oven,
The one with a circular fan,
Boy, was it ever hot in there,
But I've got a smashing tan.
Now I'm ready to eat,
Wash me down with a glass of beer,
Merry Christmas everybody,
I'll see you all next year.

Ann Hulbert (Bristol)

A Question For All

Is it true that if the tree falls without witness
It then falls without a sound?
Is it true that if paths do not cross
That time would continue relentless?

Is it true that beauty is held within the eye of the beholder
Even if those eyes are found to be blind?
Is it true that love can also be blinding
But then find solace in the eyes of those who can still see?

Is it true that we will devour ourselves in conquest?
Even though we have lost sight of our purpose
Is it true that we know not what we want?
As we have taken too much already.

Stuart Goodbun (Reading)

Abandoned

On her bridge men were frantic, in the North Atlantic, they'd struck ice, now heaven knows what.
It cut through hard steel, tore a hole in the keel, her watertight doors would not shut.
Men down in the hole kept shovelling coal, striving for all they were worth.
With no vessels to hand and so far from land, was there a more bleak place on Earth?
As the ship shook and rolled, those on deck felt the cold, but it was fear that made them shiver.
God's truth had got home, it was curtains for some, they were leaving their loved ones forever.
The calmest amongst them; the band, played an anthem, no audience, no boxes or stalls.
Passengers in a tizzy, the ship's crew too busy, attending to cables and falls.
A place in a boat, something that would float, the terror stricken ran amok.
Able seamen worked hard, at each davit and yard, clearing every choked pulley block.
'She's going! She's going! Her bottom is showing, with the stern now high in the air.
In this ice-cold sea, I take nothing with me, oh Lord just tell me that you care.
Look after my son, and my granddaughter Bron, may it please you to keep them both warm
For now I must go to where only you know, cherish them, keep them from harm.
Forgive any sin, these the dearest of kin, will know that I stand before you.
All else I would lose, but pray that you choose to guide them in all that they do.'
At the oars, people rowing, know not where they're going, overloaded they got under way.
No compass to steer by, flares glow in the night sky, where will they be by light of the day?
It's not all doom and gloom, the radio room, eventually got out their grave warning.
So much wiser by far, to hold where we are, there must be ships here by the morning.
Being cruel to be kind, some are left behind, Lord knows there were just too few craft.
You fools, stay together, use light lines to tether each lifeboat by the fore and aft.
Alas, I'm too cold, to retain a good hold on this piece of wood, my mind wanders.
to a land of sweet dreams, there meadows and streams, thrive where the Avon meanders
In a green sun drenched field, all my hurts are soon healed, I can hear sweet music and laughter,
Here, no one grows old, and it's never cold, this is the happy ever after.

James Feakes (Bournemouth)

East Is East And West Is West

In the east they scratch around
For any scraps that may be found
While in the wet, banquets of plenty
Expect this not in 2020

The global summit in Japan
Chew the fat, as best they can
No help from members of G8
They've far too much upon their plate

The rich must now abandon greed
Hearken to the planet's need
What's the point of countless wealth
When dying from a foodless shelf?

Michael Saye (Calne)

I'd Like To Say, I'm Here

Words do not come easily to me
Oh how I wish they really would
There have been so many times
When I have been misunderstood.
Always standing in the shadows
Peering out into the light
Hoping someone may see me
But never catching anyone's sight.
I have never felt very confident
Travelling my journey through life
Telling myself to be assertive
Has caused me so much strife.
Sometimes I'm not even noticed
Folk don't even know I'm there
Trying to fit in with other people
And making them feel aware.
It always seems the same for me
Never really comfortable anywhere
Always feeling like an outsider
Just hoping one person may care.
At parties I usually stand alone
Never really knowing what to say
Wondering why I bothered to go
And wishing I was miles away.
Not one for starting conversations
I'm sure folk find me a bore
Standing nervously in a corner
Usually very close to the door.

Judith Watts (Abbots Langley)

Autumn

The days are getting short again,
The leaves are turning to gold,
The swallows are flying to the south,
To warmer climes we are told.

The fields look bare now the harvest is over,
The ploughed land looks dark and cold,
Hedges are cut and ditches cleared,
And tales of the past are told.

It won't be long now and winter be here,
The land will be covered in snow,
And people will say, 'We wish we could fly,
To the warm climes, where swallows go.'

Ernst-Wilhelm Peters (Honiton)

2006 - A New Year - Renew!

I vow to you Pete
I'll stay loyal and kind.
I don't want to fight;
To mess up our minds.
You treat me like I'm special -
Like no one before,
Inside I die a bit
When you go out the door.
You are my angel,
My guiding light.
You listen when I'm happy or sad,
Morning, noon and night.
I'm so proud
Having you in my life.
I'd do anything for you
Cos I'm your trouble and strife.
You so quickly change my mood
When I'm sad,
Making everything seem clearer
And nowhere near as bad.
I know you worry
About things from the past,
But neither of us need fret,
We're together at last.
I love you my darling
With all my heart,
A new year is coming,
I'll try harder from the start.

Max Ryan (Crawley)

Once There Were Green Fields

We used to walk this lane when we were small,
Run through a glade of tall trees' fresh, young leaves,
Then climb the stile to edge swathed, gold corn sheaves
And glean bright seeds of grain that lax, bored hands let fall.

Sheep in the far field, bunched in white wool flocks,
Grazed in the short grass. There, in those 'mad March days'
Hares fought for love, boxed hard and took their knocks,
While from an arched blue sky, larks sang a song of praise.

Now our old lane is choked with brick and stone:
Trees are long gone; the field's crop, walls and words.
'Keep off the grass.' 'No ball games.' No go zone!
I walk the street where boys stand mute and hear no birds.

Janet Smith (Frome)

The Light Of Hope

From the edge of infinity comes the echo of a light
where darkness breath desists in the shadows
of the night, there is hope.
Through the changing
facets of life where
we walk in and out
of the realms
of unrequited
love and loss,
there is hope.

As the smallest droplet
of dew turns in an
aperture of sunlight,
even though it falls
like a tiny tear,
its very being is
a gracious acceptance
of life's experience,
and there
is hope.

There where the barriers
of time slip away,
and the morning mists
clear to bring the beauty
of the day,
the light of hope
will guide you.

Eileen Stockwell (Fareham)

Untitled

God made the Earth
The people that are on it
The sea, the sun and moon
He made all the animals
Jesus is coming back on Earth
When things go wrong for you
Jesus opens a new door
And things start going right
Walk the pathway of God
Be kind-hearted
Give your heart to Jesus
Blessed less fortunate than ourselves
The homeless and the old-age pensioners.

Brenda Smith (Oxford)

Before My Fall

I had a dependent free day
yesterday but today has seen
nothing at all go right
what does that tell me?
I really do need to sort it out.
I cannot go on being a laughing stock.
I have an image
to upkeep but the reality
is that that is all based on farce.
Oh John, I'm so ashamed.

I wish you every happiness
but I'm not going to like this at all
too proud to leave the house, I think
pride becomes before my fall

Nothing's ever easy is it? Nothing.
I've wanted something like this
for a long time and now it's
actually happening other things
are in the way and I really
don't know what to do.
The long and the short of it is
that ultimately I will destroy it,
if it doesn't destroy me first.
When Steve sang 'I've made it
my life's work to be the worst
at everything I've ever tried'
he couldn't have been more right.

Sid Stovold (Farnborough)

Focus Of Hope

The green-leafed branches proceed to dance
With sinuous grace abetted by the wind
Who conducts each rhythmic sway, each visual nuance
As my eyes peer through the dining room window
A silence pervades this exalted scene
In the distance blackbirds scurry across the fence
Then branches flutter where the same birds had once been
My view continues with ever expanding gaze
As world events cast such portents of doom
Nothing can be permanent but may changes be slight
A vista of seeming simplicity deflects from potential gloom
Nature imbued in variant green though broad in scope
To leave one feeling blessed with this focus of hope.

Phil Darch (Barnstaple)

440

One Day More

It's funny how strong views, once held dear, pale into insignificance,
and it's funny how your whole outlook changes in an instant.

It's funny how you no longer notice when three buses arrive together,
and no matter when it arrives the train you're waiting for is never late.

Funny, how the sound of garden machinery no longer disturbs
a Sunday rest,
and the yelling of small children at play is more acceptable than before.

When the Big C comes knocking on your door.

You begin to realise the full value of each new dawn,
rain, hail or shine, that day is yours to live to the full.

Bare tree and bushes frozen in white, herald a wondrous promise,
that they will again don their spectacular livery and wave in
warm sunshine.

Bulbs lying dormant, throughout the long cold winter months,
hide the flowers that will dance again for you in spring.

Even when the Big C comes knocking on your door.

So guard well these moments of restless anticipation,
for all these wonders will happen without fail.

Your life must not be put on hold,
who knows how long and wonderful that life will be?

Who can tell what the future may bring?
So, when the Big C comes knocking on your door,

be grateful, for one day more.

Colin Harrison (Andover)

Computer Woes

My computer will be the death of me
As just a black screen is all I can see
I wonder if the mouse has been caught in a trap
Or hiding under a table having a nap
Perhaps the ROM has done a bunk
If that's the case then I'm really sunk
I could contact the makers and ask for their say
But not if I can't type in org.dot.uk
A flu virus would be the last straw
I shall never understand this modern technology
Although some people say it's easy as can be
Now at last the screen's coming alive
Surely it couldn't have been the hard drive.

B C Dennis (Biggleswade)

On A Tuesday At Charmouth, Dorset

Majestic cliffs;
Subtleties of grain
Bely your strength.
Black lias clay piled high,
With interactions.

Shaped like pages
Of well read books.
Ochre blocks of stone
Cementing turf to lias,
Now grey with dryness;

But here below
Where sea and cliff meet,
Black as soot
Are huge boulders
Pitted with bites

Where tide has snatched
Relentlessly.
A jutting spire
Leads the eye upwards
Where sun catches a stream

Like molten gold
Flowing from the top,
Seeping in dilution
To meet starved grass,
But stopping short
Of giving life.

Pearl Foy (Langport)

At The Edge Of An Angry River

At the edge of an angry river,
The rain falls down to the valley
Flowing hard and free:
Into our towns and the sea.
Overflowing by the flood,
To find houses filled by mud.
At the edge of an angry river,
The rain continues to rage
With anger and the fierce
Of the wild wind to destroy all in its path.
In our streets and homes the water may go.
When the rain fell from hell,
At the edge of an angry river.

Sarah Anne Day (Bristol)

Through My Window

I awake, draw back the curtains
Letting the outside in.
The sky is grey and heavy
No sun rays to be seen.
The park is empty, no one's there
Another sad and gloomy scene.

To work I said it's time to go
But did not rise or move.
I sat and stared into the mist and dew,
The trees majestic no leaves swaying
Weighted down with so much rain.

Through the silent rain and stillness
A bird from far was heard to sing.
Another with a different tone replies
Then silence then another bird chirps in.
Three birds now in conversation sing.

Suddenly a loud response from many
All joining in to sing good morning
Birds playing and talking all at once
Like children in a playground dance
In discord, in unison, in harmony all chirping.

A feathered choir and orchestra is formed
Birds in discussion and in vibrant song.
All happy and united without care chirp on
Suddenly this dull grey cloudy day of rain
Turned into a sunny world of musical refrain.

Helen Antoniou (Harrow)

My Love

When I think of you
My heart melts,
The love in your eyes,
The lilt in your voice,
The sound of your footsteps,
Will always be a part of me,
You doubted me,
As I doubted you,
Such love could never be,
But the memory of you,
And what we shared lives on,
You are my love,
And always will be.

Penelope Ann Kirby (Newquay)

To Love Is Not A Conscious Decision

When you fall in love
(with whom, or when or where)

it can begin
with a trickle

swelling to a torrent

or sometimes
it arrives less gently

overwhelming the senses
to a maddening degree.

Such is: *Falling in love.*

But to love - ah!

Therein lies the difference.

Never faltering . . . never wavering.

Love has no boundaries.

To love
is to surrender
in totality.

Not to count the cost
Nor the gain

but to feel the pleasure

and not
heed the pain.

Gina Pisapia (London)

Crimson Rose

Last spring I re-rooted the prickly stem,
Through the open window,
I watched intensely when a minute bud emerged,
Kept my eyes peeled for the next stage.
One summer morning to my delight,
I absorbed a breath taking majestic sight.
My crimson rose had finally bloomed,
Through the passing summer,
Daily I watered it and groomed.
Brushing of the dewdrops each morning,
For the velvet petals to dry.
What beautiful nature's art,
The apple of my eye.

Shazia Kausar (Reading)

I Was The One

The other day I heard a voice,
My spirit rose, my heart rejoiced,
Words of comfort came my way,
I heard these words from Jesus say,

'I was the one who caught you
Every time you slipped and fell,
I was the one who broke the journey,
That was leading you on to Hell.

I could see your weakest points,
Where any sin could enter in,
So that's the place I started,
That's the battle we would win.

I took away all your affliction,
Because you prayed to be set free,
You knew you couldn't do it,
On your own away from me.

So we fought the fight together,
In your weakness I was strong,
I called you back to be with me,
For that's where you belong.

Now Satan has no hold on you,
Your faith has set you free,
I have broken the chains that bound you,
I'll forever be a friend to thee.

You see I Am the One who loves you.'

Ian T Redmond (Newport)

Timeless Dreams

Our dreams are timeless
Full of half-remembered fragments
Of lives that have passed
Or that may be in the future
Hokusai's Great Wave
Washing over castles in the air
Sometimes silent
Chanctonbury Ring on a winter's day
Sometimes full of music
Miles Davis playing 'Kind of Blue'
A beginning without an end
Or an end without a beginning
But always, always, an enigma.

Joe Loxton (Exeter)

The Story Of The Lonely Stray

It was a cold and windy winter, the snow was falling hard
As along the way I wandered, to reach my best back yard.
The wind held no pity for a creature such as me, it made the
Dustbins rattle, someone threw stones at me.

I was so very hungry, my throat was parched with thirst,
Would I ever reach that pool and would I get there first?
As I settle down my head beneath the stars at night,
I murmured to myself, 'Not another night.'

I heard a voice calling, somewhere from above.
It spoke to me with mercy, it spoke to me with love.
'Run little dog, run on. No longer shall you roam,
You will find love, you will find a home.'

I got up and off I ran, through the long endless night
I came across a cottage, wherein there shone a light
I dragged my tired body, weary and so sore
I fell upon the doorstep banging my tail against the door.

The door slowly opened, two hands reached out for me.
I was so very tired, I could hardly see.
They took me to a fire and stroked my weary head
And laid me on a blanket which I could call my bed.

They gave me food and water, my body to sustain
But most of all they gave me love, I felt happy once again.
There is a moral to this story, for some hard to see,
Why is man so cruel, not to heed the words of he?

'To love them as I love you.'

Doreen Brennan (Plymouth)

Freedom's Flight

I look to the skies for one last word
The thoughts in my mind
I'm sure you've heard
As you rose to the heavens
So free, full of life
The need for relief
So long you have strived
And now no more tears
Your spirit's with God
No pain you will feel
Gone you have not
For in our hearts your strength will stay
For your love is with us every day.

Joanne Holpin (Bristol)

I Am (The Bowling Game)

I am the pins at which you throw the ball,
The shoelaces on which you trip and fall,
The letters that you use to spell your name,
As we begin the bowling game,

I am the holes where you fit your hand,
The soft barriers that seem to understand,
The hands in the air as you cause a strike,
However, it's not me you like,

I am the laughter you share with my friend,
The words you whisper that I can't comprehend,
The camera that's held right in your face,
I wish it was me that was in her place,

I am every point you score,
The one who you are bowling for,
The person for whom you pretend to care,
Just like every pin that's spare,

I am the shoes that you take off your feet,
The look that you give her as your eyes meet,
The person that is watching from the side,
Always bowls just a little too wide,

I am the picture without you in the frame,
The one who's left out of the bowling game,
I am the memory that's left behind,
The something that always slips your mind,

I am the bowling game.

Beth Harmston (Southampton)

Experience

Seasons' tales
Calm and gales
Sun and rain
Love and pain;
Snowdrifts and snowdrops
Bare fields and green crops
Noonday and moonlight
Acorn and oak might;
Babes' chuckles, girls' grace
Youth's strength and Man's pace
Glow in its sunbeam trace;
Loving kindness
In an autumn face.

Frances Searle (London)

Deadbeat

A lazy time doused in red wine while gazing at the sun
Catching spies and butterflies with my loaded water gun
I choked on a lie that broke inside, and breaking's never fun
Then in the sky a plane shoots by and all the madness
comes undone

The world - usually an oyster, today appears a cage
I have no clue where I'm going, yet have fear of being late
I'm deadbeat, struggle to my feet, feeling oh, so obsolete
I'm deadbeat, but can't quite face defeat
The summer feels so bittersweet

An idle time, feeling denied, while driving in my car
A traffic light seems to shine so bright - I wonder where you are
A hazy sound that shakes the ground, I push the pedal to the floor
Accelerate with fear of being late and fear of wanting more

The world - usually my oyster, today appears my cage
I have no rules or policy yet fear I can't behave
I'm deadbeat, still can't face defeat
The summer seems so bittersweet

A hefty fine for a petty crime, is someone pulling legs?
Swig the rest from my treasure chest, and smoke the final dregs
Then contentedly, as I drift to sleep, the curtains finally close
In this idiosyncratic civilisation, you know, anything goes!

Distant deranged church bells ring, and on the radio a jazzman sings
After being so ignorant I suddenly see, how lovely it is being free

Summer feels just how it ought to be.

Abigail Randall (Wedmore)

Walking With Huckleberry

Early on a summer morning,
Dog and I go walking.
Round the rec, past the clubhouse.
The sun glistens off discarded beer cans,
After last night's revelry.
Empty crisp packets and sweet wrappers,
Dog sniffs hopefully, then,
Lifts his leg to scent the way.
The chatter of rooks, alarmed, calling
Not quite drowned out by a lumbering jet
Droning its way to Heathrow.
Dog and I turn to our way home,
He chases his ball into heaps of new mown grass.

Katherine Hall (Windsor)

I Stand Up And J'Accuse, I Accuse!

I stand up, raise my voice and I accuse j'accuse!
Men of many nations, to our amazin' good Lord,
For terrible kinds of injustice and all other abuse,
They may bring the threats of death to our world . . .

Selfishness, greed for riches in silver and gold,
Their evil striving, for the things of no good use,
Brought all the suffering, j'accuse I accuse,
All those who persecute good, just and bold . . .

This world would be, so much a better place,
Were they never born on its once pretty face!
This planet of ours, that was so full of grace,
Thanks to them may disappear without trace . . .

O God, how much better off we all would be,
If evil forces never made that wicked race!
How much more all good men would be free.
But, instead of freedom, slavery is their case . . .

Instead of our sun's glorious and shiny light,
The darkness rules in eternal starless night,
Instead of life, Earth will be empty and dead,
The place of love will take hatred and dread . . .

Please, don't let filthy lies take the truth over,
Or, the foul injustice make its dreadful mark,
Let not evil's hydra-like head rule undercover
Of good, or dazzling light's beauty turn dark!

Then, even on my dead lips, read j'accuse, I accuse!

Geofil Zoriastro (London)

Reverie

Often when I'm all alone, I find myself in a twilight zone,
Imagining all kinds of things, like small forms with delicate wings.
As they move I wonder why these tiny fairies are passing by,
Dancing and weaving among the trees, spinning gossamer like
busy bees.
So rapt am I there's not a sound, as I watch them flutter along
the ground.
There's beautiful glitter everywhere, sparkling ever in the air,
I shudder out of my reverie, then wonder did I really see?
These magical beings or was it meant
And does one think it was heaven sent?
'Cause when I stepped upon the ground, there was pretty glitter
all around.

E M Dixon (Havant)

449

This Feeling Called Grief

This heartache, this sadness
this feeling of pain
to think I'll never hear your voice
or see your face again

The loneliness without you
is beyond belief
I can't come to terms with
this feeling called grief

It's so hard to describe just how I feel
without you beside me
time has only stood still

I sit for hours in your favourite chair
talk to you photo
wishing you were there

I touch your clothes and start to weep
I hug your pillow
and try to sleep

Life must go one
I suppose it's true
but a day doesn't pass
without thinking of you

To treasure your memory
I must carry on
but nothing else matters
now that you've gone.

Paul Brown (Godalming)

For Siegfried Sassoon And Stephen Tennant

Siegfried, why did you go away so soon?
Or do you yet walk in your wooded grounds
And weep to see your home reduced to flats?
Brave huntsman, do not weep for this alone.
Pink coats will soon be banished from our land,
And regiments like yours cut down to size.
Stephen's rich horde of pretty bric-a-brac
Is scattered far and wide to who knows where.
And 'Tennants' by another name dwell
Where once he entertained his merry friends.
But may you both be happy now, in cool
Elysian fields, released from earthly care,
Free spirits laughing at this world below.

Beryl Newport (Bristol)

Barn Owls At Alverstone Mead, Near Sandown, Isle Of Wight

You fly on silent, seemingly motionless wings
Scouring the ground for edible things.
Breaking our habit of visiting the mead by day
Late in the evening we came this way
To see if the red squirrels were around
But just one in this evening hour we found.
On our afternoon visits to the mead
Many squirrels from our hands have learned to feed.
Our evening visit was totally worthwhile
Sitting in the hide, saw the barn owls fly with grace and style.
One came from a derelict tree
And flew so very close to me.
Over the mead and along the brook
Then back to the nest with food which you took
A precious young family to feed,
Parents supplying their every end.
Round and round, to and fro
On your mission you continued to go.
The sun had gone from the sky in the west
But for you there was to be no rest.
We sat, we watched, for an hour enthralled
So pleased that on you tonight we had called.

Jackie Hamblin (Newport)

Goldie The Goldfish

Watch him swimming round his dome,
blowing bubbles occasionally foam,
Goldie came with a mate,
she was pretty coloured but soon met her fate,
he would swim her round and round,
I'm sure he was the cause,
he wouldn't let her pause.

Now he is alone surrounded by shells,
at the bottom an anchor lies without bells,
with a large toy frog, toy crocodile and turtle,
he thinks he's in Loch Ness,
but these all help to stop;
his amorousness.

Enid Bowerman (Buckingham)

451

The Wildlife Of Sussex Comes And Goes!

I know a place where the badger is set
In a silent and secret part of the forest
I know a place where the white horse grazes
Midst buttercups and ox-eye daisies
I know a place where the brown rabbit hops
And flees the predator in fields by the windmills
I know a place

I know a place where the fox stands and gazes
As one passes by on a summertime walk
I know a place where the blackbirds whistle and sing
All the day in the happiest of ways
I know a place where the swan has a nest
Behind the priory where all is at rest
I know a place

I know a place where the deer stand like statues
Listening and watching in silence and in calm
I know a place where the wild orchid grows in abundance
And in grace an echo out of time and out of space
I know a place

I know a place where the wren hops and searches
For insects and grubs for chaff and for nourishment
I know a place where the noble kingfisher glides
Across the surface not far from its hole in the riverbank
I know a place where the ladies smock grows
In Maytime an English treasure an early wild flower
I know a place

Margaret Bennett (Burgess Hill)

Valediction

ill-defined the language of light
as so emotion
intangible content of thought
illuminate the confusion
fading into night
the essence slips away
elusive to will and reason
in the imperfection of the moment
lost to mind

the sun's rays bear down
tracing a line of wisdom into the dark
exhume the tarnished remains
to riddle out the fire of anguish.

Katrina Warren (Oxford)

Does It Really Matter?

Is it really such an issue
On the colour of the tissue,
Or the colour of the box they lie within?
We've now a brand new whiteboard
As the black one's not the right board,
And all because the colour of our skin.

If you choose to wear a toupee,
Or your dreadlocks every which way,
Curly, black, blonde, brown or even ginger,
Just think of this instead,
Hair is hair and on your head,
So be grateful for it, don't become a whinger.

If you're chubby, fat or thin,
Tallish, short or really slim,
Yellow, black, white, pink or even green,
To call our colour names
Starts off nasty racist games,
Turning into violent actions so obscene.

Outside we've different faces,
That's because we're different races,
Our bodies made of lots of different parts.
And the blood that's in our veins,
Is identical, the same,
And guess what else we've all got?
Yes!
A heart.

Elaine Fearn (London)

Immortality

Close your eyes and come with me
To the land of immortality
Meet the heroes of ancient Greece
Hector, Paris and Ulysses
Dine with the Gods
On Mount Olympus
Be young, be gay and frivolous
Close your eyes and you can be
Anywhere you want to be
With Peter in Never-Never Land
With Alice in her wonderland
Close your eyes and come with me
To the land of immortality.

Gerry Sherrick (South Woodford)

I Exist

How will they know how I feel if they don't know?
How will they know how I think if they presume?
I'm not a stone that remains unchanged
I exist
I am here,
It's been an awful year.

How will they know what I need if they ignore me?
How will they see the hurt that life brings?
I'm not a cloud that just floats away
I exist
I am here
With all my fears.

How will they adapt to my different ways if they don't feel?
Their hearts have to reach out to touch mine.
I'm misunderstood
Time and again.
I exist
I am here
Listen to what you hear.

Accept me now for who I am then you will know
The world will be a better place for everyone.
So see me now
Why not be my friend
I exist
I am
I am here.

Amanda-Jane Tudor (Guildford)

Untitled

A little love is needed,
In the world today,
In helping blessing others,
To worship and to pray,
Forgetting the troubles of the past,
Enter into the new,
Laughter, joys and all things blest,
The honest and the true,
Keep on keep on the daily work to do,
But Jesus can be with us,
May we love and serve Him too,
All the extras are given by God,
Through Jesus and His saving love.

George Camp (South Molton)

Golden Wedding

A Golden Wedding is a wonderful time
To look back over 50 years
And wander in mind down memory lane
Amid laughter, heartache and tears.

You recall that day 50 years ago
When your vows together you made
And you knew then that your lives would be blest
By Him whose love never fades.

Your children came - a gift from God
Their lives in your hands to mould
You helped them walk the path that He trod
To receive His blessings untold.

The children have grown up now
And started their lives anew
Just as you did 50 years ago
So now there is just you two.

You've always been so cheerful
And given help with a smile to any in trouble around you
In fact you've made life worthwhile.

As the day ends may you proudly say
Thank you Lord for a lovely day
With God's loving hand to guide you
As the future years unfold
I pray that God will continue to bless you
As He has through the years to gold.

Muriel Laity (Penzance)

Where Have All The Sparrows Gone?

Where have all the sparrows gone?
That cheeky bright eyed bird
When others flew to warmer climes
Its cheery song we heard
Little bright eyed cockney, he was always there
Its cheeky ways would warm us
And drive away our care
But suddenly, our little friend's not there
It only seemed like yesterday
I only turned away, and when I looked my heart was sad
Oh, where is he today?
Oh where have all the sparrows gone
Because I miss them so.

Gladys Mary Gayler (London)

Starlings Roosting On The Moors

Anne-Marie and I stood still in our thick coats in the rising storm,
Very separate, like red sea anemones in a tidal rock pool,
Out on the flat Level's fields near Westhay.

The tall rushes bend and sway in the dusk.
The sky is a bruised ochre with purple swelling clouds
Massed tumbling across the wide horizon,
Spitting icy rain.

We wait standing and staring until the first starlings
                                    come on the wind.
A few black swirls of thirty or forty birds spiralling low to the roost,
Bending the rushes down to drink the pewter coloured water.
They twist in conjunction like dark sparks from a windswept bonfire.

Now they fly in thousands as the light fades,
Flaring black against the sullen sky,
Like many quavers dotted on the sky's hidden stave.
Their music raucous calls like streaming city people going home,
Gossiping and touching in, after a performance in the park.

Tenaciously the rusty claws hold to their posts
Their yellow bills sweeping neat their speckled feathers
Even as they still call.
The reeds in the water bend down with all their weight as night falls.
The lowest bird just an inch above the dark water.

We hunch our shoulders against the weather
And turn and walk wordlessly along the muddy grass of the drove,
The birds' patterns troubling us.

Chris Madelin (Langport)

Rejection

Today my heart is broken
Yet it beats harder
Cleaved in two.
My body is frozen
By the ice-cold of everything it touches.
I am a wraith
The sun's rays pass through me
I am super conductor
All your energy shall pass through my coils
I put up no resistance.
I am a fallen star
But I never shone
And I never fell.

Jethro Dykes (London)

Porky Pig

Porky Pig was not very big, in fact he was quite small
His brothers and sisters were all round and fat
But he wasn't plump at all.

There were so many of them, pushy, unkind and mean
And when it came to meal times
He couldn't get between.

One day the farmer came along and said, 'Oh dear, oh dear!
It's off to market for you lot
But not for Porky here.

He'll have to stay with me I fear, I'll try to make him fatter
I'll give him extra food and mash
It really doesn't matter.'

So Porky lived with the kind old man and became his special pet
He ate so well you soon could tell
He was fat as he could get.

So you see it doesn't always pay to be the biggest and the best
For little runty Porky Pig
Being smaller than the rest

Could live a life of comfort and ease, eating to his fill
With the farmer and his wife
In the little house on the hill.

Thus our tale comes to an end, there's not much more to say
But being selfish and greedy
Doesn't always pay!

Valerie Jureidini (Hemel Hempstead)

Forbidden Fruit

So you wish to try forbidden fruit?
That's something you shouldn't do.
Forbidden fruit can cause great pain,
To me as well as to you.

Just like the Tree of Knowledge
This fruit must not be picked
Upon the tree the fruit must stay
And you must learn to walk away!

Pain as you know can be sweet
Just like the fruit on the tree
But fruit can go bad
And love make you sad
So, don't be tempted by me!

Louise Emberton (Bushey Heath)

457

The English Riviera

Sea, sand, buckets and spades,
Sun-soaked azure sky,
Fragrance of fish and sun tan oil,
Small craft sailing by,

Picture in your mind
The English Riviera.

Pasties, pastries, long walks,
Evenings at the pub,
Scones and cream, cups of tea
And loads of other grub,

People love to visit
The English Riviera.

Raincoats, fishing boats,
Mist and fog and rain,
Cold, wet, dark, damp,
Could be the south of Spain?

But it's not,
It's the English Riviera.

Breathtaking scenery,
Landmarks and history,
Lazy retreats and
Sunny day activities,

We've got it all on
The English Riviera!

Yve Ashton (Plymouth)

Reading

Look closely
at these pages.
Time has weathered them
but the faintest of marks remain.

Here and there something emerges,
barely visible.
Fingers trace the rutted surface,
eyes strain, forehead knotted.
But each line is just a jumble of letters,
the story shattered.

What can I say?
It made sense
when I wrote it down.

Debbie Bull (Andover)

Black And White

Among the thorns of hatred
Where love is out of bounds
Two hearts were seen embracing
On this bleak and stony ground
Where colours shouldn't mix
Where races live and fight
They beat in time together
One was black and
One was white
Forbidden as a couple
Though it seems the natural thing
Stolen kisses, secret meetings
But to never wear his ring
Tears only shed in darkness
Must never see the light
Why does it have to be when
One is black and
One is white
To never be accepted
Is this their only crime
Why is life so unfair
Will love stand the test of time?
To banish all the hatred for
Two wrongs don't make a right
'Til then they love in secret when
One is black and
One is white

Lesley Hartley (Salisbury)

The Other Me

Now that I am old and grey,
I often think of the years gone past
and wonder what might have been
had I grown up as the 'Other Me'.

Ah, the 'Other Me' - would most
certainly have been a free thinker
a revolutionary or a dreamer of
what in life good is meant to be.

Alas, instead, 'Me as Me' emerged,
not to fight but conform to what
was there for so long, never ever
to become as intended the
'Other Worthy Chap'.

P P Christodoulides (Enfield)

Unwanted Job

In the Big Bang all things we know began
God not part of the team I do not mean.
When things bolted into being,
things had to be halted into seeing.
It was not because of darkness,
but because of tardiness.
They were sick of the murk,
so created the giant firework.
But wait. . . oh no it's too late,
now the sparks have turned to life,
who is going to hold the burden and strife?
Not one stepped up and claimed it,
they all fell into their pit.
Out of the tracer of planets and light,
stepped forward a most uninspiring sight.
Was not being nor fake, there it stood for all our sake
'I will burden the blunder,'
a voice like a nightingale rather than thunder.
'A mistake we have made, I will not leave their parade.'
That is how our fate was placed,
onto a higher being with haste.
He never wanted or created,
but he alone took on the fated.
His employment is the hardest job;
remember he is merely a God.
He never asked to be our caretaker,
surely that makes Him all the greater?

Greg James Hull (Deptford)

React Now!

Can you see the swaying trees or,
Can you hear the buzzing bees,
On a lovely summer's day?
But yet, all is to come!

Can you see the children playing or,
Can you hear the adults saying, 'Hello'
On a lovely summer's day?
But yet, all is to come!

So global warming is madness,
And the Earth needs a lot more kindness,
So if we work together,
No more thundery weather,
On a horrible, nasty day!

Charlotte Allman (11) (Plymouth)

The Door

I had not been that way before,
Walking through an ancient wood,
Pushing aside the dense undergrowth
A clearing appeared, overgrown
With nettles, meadow sweet and tansy
Entwined with brambles and sweet briers,
In this tangle lay the ruins
Of a humble cottage, roofless
Its walls crumbled to heaps of stone.
The only part standing complete,
The porch and a solid oaken door;
Though ivy covered this entrance
Had stood the ravages of time
As if it had, in some strange way
Waited for a long-lost family
Remembering a careful wife?
Who would in the morning sunlight
Shake the dust from her hallway mats?
Where now the children, running free?
And did that khaki clad father
Return to see his family?
How long could the old door remain
To keep these memories alive?
Sadly I turned and left that place,
Leaving the old, sad, haunted door.
To drift into oblivion
I never trespassed there again.

Arthur Mylam (Truro)

The Sombre Forest

The sombre forest was covered in dark shadowy rays,
But the grim moon awoke in many ways,
People came riding with boots up to their thigh,
While other shadows meandered upon the cloudy sky.

While slithering like a snake, robbers clattered and clashed,
Through the gloomy sunset they dashed,
And when that happened, the moon arrived with doom,
Coming for the robbers searching for a room.

Cautiously, the robbers paused for a split second, ready to attack,
Suddenly they heard the owner come back,
Their eyes were red with fear from a strong bloodshot,
And there in the corner, blood trickled from the pot.

Harry Neil (9) (Bristol)

Grasp The Moment

Grasp the moment for tomorrow all too soon becomes today,
Don't hesitate, for time relentlessly moves the present away -
And sends it into yesterday;
Think about your secret wishes, hopes and dreams left undone,
Bring them out again from the shadows, let them know the midday sun.
Little goals, like learning a language, gardening, visiting a foreign shore,
Feel your spirit gently quicken, let it be your friend once more.
When life's not as good as it should seem, open a good book,
Chat to a friend, let in a shaft of gentle light - an illuminating moonbeam.
Just shake off remembered sorrow -
              you're heading for a new tomorrow!
Remember when you were a small child,
Going bare foot, running wild, how each day seemed eternally long?
Plenty of hours for watching butterflies, hearing beautiful birdsong.
How scarlet poppies waved in silent splendour,
Fallen soldiers gone before.
We bathed in streams with cobbled stones then, with fading light,
Homeward bound with weary bones;
Postponed bedtime till the very last second,
Slumbered deep the whole night long.
Though things are different now than then, inspiration can come again.
Don't let sad news make you despondent - rise above life's tragedy,
Just be grateful for small treasures - count your blessings, don't you see!
Each new dawn try your best - stop and think for just a while,
Even if you're down and lonely, pass on a free gift, wear a smile!
Stop and chat to passing neighbours, ask about their family,
Be a lantern of human kindness - that's what life's about you see!

Sheila Evans (Torquay)

What Is Love?

Love is when you know you cannot hide
When in their eyes they are open wide
Open mouthed and wanting to say
I've loved you dearly from that very first day

Love is always in your heart
Knowing that he does not want to part
So down on one's knees he will go
With a ring in a box, it just goes to show

He is asking me to be his wife
Together forever all of our lives
I love him so much I could not say no
Arranging the wedding here we go

Angela O'Rourke (Marlow)

Our Legacy

Across these isles where Britons long ago walked, the wandering wind blows from the rim of
the sky. Along heath and hill,
harsh places walled with rocks, forest ways, the oak, the pine, the ash,
all feel its scentless breath. From church towers, as wild vine slips down to touch rustic
blossom and small-windowed cottages
where blue smoke rises, come the calls of
windy places, in an ancient land.
Fallen branches beneath the beeches, the green gloom of thick forest,
land fallow and ploughed, bleak wind-worn upland thorn,
with hedgerow fruits, wear nature's charm with lighthouse gleam.
A threshold of the spiritual and deep from golden seas of Wales
to the ocean of a western beach shining green and silver,
thence to Kentish hills and high woods, amass with evening crocuses in rosy golden haze.
Harvest sheaves and kindling, honeycomb and lavender,
flowers placed upon a nameless headstone, a rain-sunken barn.
Laughing green leaves, young and sweet, dance over marsh-flooded streams in gentle air.
Under full-starred heavens, languid hours pass to a rhapsody
of night-owls calls, blackbird shrieks, wild duck in serried flight
and pheasant, arching swallows and the impish magpie.
Nature works such lovely seasonal craft:
church bells ring in summer songs, sea-whipped bubbles
summoned by ponderous, foamy breakers, frost-shimmer
upon mouldered stones.
Valleys awash with colour of autumnal weeks.
Through garden gates we pass, our land beckons massively.
The wet, dark seas surround these precious isles
where Britons long ago walked.

Frances Burrow (Southampton)

For You J

To where you've gone, I shall not know
For your time here was short, but definitely not slow
Twenty-six years of your tears and laughter
Leaving us all with memories forever after.

You touched hearts, you touched our souls
A life of fun was your one true goal.
To stand tall and never walk alone
To be surrounded by friends and family in your final home.

We'll recollect memories and most probably cry
To keep your memory alive and never say goodbye.
We'll pay our respects as your soul flies free
To the gate of Heaven that we all long to see.

Andrew Collinson (Newbury)

Dancing With Red Indians

Through deep New Mexican snows winds the path
To the ancient village at Holy Mountain's foot;
Enveloped in early morning's cold
Uninvited I enter the parade ground-like Plaza
Silence now broken by cries of alarmed awareness
As from secret subterranean chambers seep
Then distant glimpses of fleeing figures
And close pursuing painted earthly creatures
Approaching Troglodytes, spirits of darkness
From whom in cold fright I recoil
As in a dream then, suddenly unreal
Hovers, and like a troubling incubus
Harassing its prey, bedecked and camouflaged
Nearby stands, pounds the hard earth impatiently
Staring as if entranced, black eyes pierce mine
Then in balletic, ju-jitsu hold
An arm snakes around my neck
Held in unsought proximity
In preamble it seems to trip and throw?
We whirl in strange intimacy
A willing spectator turned unwilling actor
Willed on stage reluctantly from darkened stall
Am I a symbol summoned
Perhaps in partial retribution?
Till the whitest buck-skinned Deer Mother
Dances out from Earth's embrace
To tribal drums and swaying deer actors

David Cooper (Kingsbridge)

20th Anniversary!

Twenty years
Let's celebrate
Write a poem
That must be great!

Words to encompass
All those years
Times of happiness
Times of tears

Just jot them down
Make them rhyme
Then it will be read
For now and all time.

Barbara Coward (Woking)

Freedom Is Not Free

(To mothers, fathers, comrades)

I stood and watched
As young men marched
The flag fluttering in the breeze
A young soldier saluted it
Then he stood at ease
I looked at him in uniform
And thoughts passed through my mind
How many young ones just like him
Had fallen through the years?
No, freedom is not free
I watched them as they slowly marched
Others quiet and still
As from the plane the coffins came
Did I feel a chill?
No, freedom is not free
I thought of all the mothers,
Daughters, sons, had gone
How many mothers' tears
Had mourned the loss of those she loved
But remembered all the years
No, freedom is not free
The soldiers, sailors, airmen
All we do not see
Sit awhile and think of them
No, freedom is not free.

L E Davies (Bedford)

Lost Love

When love falls apart
It tears at your heart
You can't sleep at night
Stay awake until it's light
The things that were said
Go around in your head
Who was to blame?
Was it him or was it you?
Maybe a little bit of both
Is really what is true
Then the only things left
Are the memories you share
And the part of your heart
That will always care.

Irene Mellowship (Rickmansworth)

Resigned To Freedom

I resign.
I resign.
Farewell job, no longer mine.

Sad, it started out so well,
Heaven ended up as Hell.
Hopes and dreams that turned to dust,
Want to stay, but leave I must.
Indignation, hurt and rage,
Stop. Breathe deeply. Turn the page.
Focus on the positive,
Don't look back. Get out there. Live.
Little voice of common sense
Whispers, 'It's experience.'
Hello freedom - factor wow,
Open door to here and now.
Leave without a backward glance.
Seek adventure, take a chance.
Save the good, reject the bad,
Don't mourn what you've never had.
Healing time diffuses stress,
Penury is happiness.
Walk away with head held high,
Now's the time to say goodbye.

Farewell job, no longer mine.
I resign.
Yes, I resign.

Norma Fraser Reid (London)

Northern Lights

It's the speed that
makes you marvel:
sails of green,
the colour of precious stone,
cover the sky,
sculling along on
invisible winds;
the cherry edges
curl inward, shape
shifting ghosts in the heavens,
pirouetting for attentive stars;
and I am awed,
far below,
on a lake frozen in wonder.

Tom Garbett (Islington)

Loving Care

I am now living in a home,
The door is locked so I can't roam,
So this is old age, they call it living,
No one here has the knowledge of giving.
The male nurse here treats me very rough,
When I moan he just says 'tough',
My watch has gone, my ring is missing,
The ladies here spend time knitting.

Some poor old souls have lost their minds,
They have no idea how time unwinds,
From bed to chair, and chair to bed,
Is it no wonder I have pain in head,
The chef here is called Mike,
I wish he would cook something I could like,
This life is costing £300 per week,
My bank balance is now looking bleak.

I can walk, I can almost run,
I never go out or have any fun,
Life in this place is just a mockery,
I don't even get a chance at the lottery,
I can't even have a smoke or
I will be told off by some bossy bloke,
I have no one here to call me honey,
All they want it seems is my money,
How dare they call this loving care,
In the future just beware.

B L Moore (Weston-super-Mare)

Memories

You speak to us
In tender tone
Of happy hours
Beyond us flown
And once again
To mind recall
Old friends remembered
Best of all
But still no sadness
In all your tender music dwells
Though times may change
And flowers forsake
The happy ways
We used to take.

Roy Williams (Plymouth)

Good News

Let not your heart be troubled!
Let not your heart be troubled?
    Unrest encompasses every side
    Murder, rape, theft, an evil tide
    Surely heart peace must be denied.
Let not your heart be troubled!
    Inflation soars, debts arise
    Marriages fail - there's broken lives
    Drink and drugs and gangs and knives
Let not your heart be troubled?

    Ah yes! There is One who gives peace and new life,
    One who can comfort in this world's strife,
    One who loves dearly when hatred is rife,
Let not your heart be troubled.
    God loves you so deeply all of the time
    When things go well or when life's in decline.
    He wants you now your life to refine
Let not your heart be troubled.

    Although God loves you He hates your sin,
    So He sent Christ your soul to redeem.
    In repentance and faith you can turn to Him - then
Let not your heart be troubled.
    God sent His Son that you might be saved,
    That you might be His as you enter the grave,
    His most precious possession for you He gave,
May your heart be not troubled.

Marion Tinkler (Waltham Cross)

Long Ago And Far Away

Go west was the explorer's clarion call
but nearer by far, lies county Cornwall
With rhyme and legend through local lore
the wild and rocky Cornish shore
The Isles of Scilly, like Islands of the Blest
beneath the waves perhaps Lyonesse
The holiday crowds see Newquay, Rock and St Ives
residents carry on with their normal lives
A heritage of the sea, fishing and tin mines
pirates, smugglers and writers; Du Maurier story lines
A pathway stretches round north and south coasts
enclosing moors, farms and villages; tales of ghosts
A land of romance, ready to turn a new page
a Celtic tradition, vanishing in the modern age.

Stuart Fletcher (Helston)

For The One I Love

(For Susie)

To walk a bluebell carpet soft
with you would be delight
to watch moonrise o'er leafy glade
on starred and velvet night
your eyes as jewels sparkle
no star nor moon compares
if flowers held your lovely frame
the honour would be theirs.

The gossamer of silken dawn
nights dew-fall in the air
or breath of mist 'cross fields green
whence dandelions stare
your form delights the meadows
no blossom could replace
the beauty of spring morning sun
soft dancing on your face.

Pure crystal mountain waterfalls
swept rainbows through their height
fresh snowfall smoothing lofty peak
first touched by morn's cold light
your smile would melt the coldest ice
no frost its warmth could bear
refracted light as nothing 'gainst
the sunshine through your hair.

Jonathan M Grout (West Drayton)

This Lane Where Lovers Linger

This lane where lovers linger,
Is my rat-race rat-run.

Lovers, gazing eye to eye, transfixed,
My gaze fixed groundwards, introspectively.

They, hand in hand, lazily loiter,
Me, hands in pockets, impetuous and driven.

Their elastic seconds stretch each for an eternity,
My diminished minutes are of the very essence.

Lane's end for lovers is sublime communion,
For me its end acts simply as a means.

They now, replete in languorous contentment,
While I accelerate towards corporate oblivion.

Barry Jones (Ryde)

Heaven's Half Century

(In honour of the Golden Wedding Anniversary of two parents I know very well.
Once, twice = Soraya & Desire Nice. Aum.)

Blue moons ago you said, 'I do'
Now fifty years have proved it
And through the grace of gentle weather
In love's garden grown together
Seen the cycle
Seed to tree
And blessed four dozen summers' breezes
The state of marriage thankful now
Her truth has blossomed new;
For rarely is she fairly honoured
When test of time defines 'I do'.

And the fourfold seasons' changes
Marked two hundred poets' dreams
A muse so faithful
Few have known
Who braved the storm 'I do'.

And as the years
Fold into now
Reveal the Love
Which needs no vow,
Fifty-thousand years as nought
Beside the holy, timeless thought
'I am,' I said, 'And you?'

Sarathin (Joseph Noel Thomas Nice) (London)

Cold

Cold.
You are the Arctic of my heart.
Cold.
You are the sin that won't absolve.
Cold.
You are the sadism of my past.
Cold.
You are the life that will not grow.
Cold.
You are the bearer of my mistakes.
Cold.
You are the fruit of my womb.
Cold.
You are the love you cannot get enough of.

Ishwar Maharaj (London)

Pop Fest In The Park

They're turning up the decibels in the park,
Brain-washing pigeons,
Dejected blooms,
The shivering crowd.

Wind shreds the lyrics
To incoherent scraps
Tossed in the air.

But nothing kills that beat
Bold as Niagara,
Flooding all crevices
Demanding world submission.

Only the two great planes
Oldest incumbents of the park
Offer some sanctuary
From wind and rain,
Insanity of sound
Battering their quiet dignity.

Oh planes,
Lifting your strong
And lovely limbs
From clay to thunderous sky,
Teach us to stay the course
With some integrity
As years like driven clouds
Unheedingly race by.

Michael Tanner (Guildford)

Happiness, Where Does It Come From?

A smile on a face
    Joy to the human race!
It doesn't need to be taught,
    It cannot be bought
Automatically grows
    From peace within.
A love that shows,
    A joy to bring
To those all around, about,
    Good news to shout.
A light that radiates,
    Dispels the darkness, indicates
The gift of a wonderful relationship
    Of trust, knowledge and friendship.

Brenda E Cheeseman (Slough)

Enduring Horizons

We wrought heady separation
Into a persistent wine
A fermented salt of bitters
Which dressed dimmed sight
As brightest light of all.

The lemon metal of the sun
Once birthed lightning to cleave
Dark the shade of memory
To blind scuttle and hide within
Split heartwood grain of horizons unseen.

We forged persistent separation
Into a heady wine
A bitter salt of ferment
Which dimmed dressed sight
As lightest brightening of all.

The etched metal of the sun
Once sired sunbirds to leave
Dark the fade of memory
To scuttle within hid heartwood
Grain split of horizons unseen.

We cast steady separation
Into a resistant wine
A salted ferment tinctured
Now quick of undressed sight
As most naked light of all.

Peter Flux (Paignton)

Words

Putting pen to paper is a worthwhile idea
Quill pen or keyboard - matters not,
nor length of line or sentence.
Ideas and inspirations portray
various emotions,
Words on paper the food
to nourish enquiring minds,
A treasure box - written thoughts the gems inside.
Answers to questions, knowledge from the past,
a future more informed are things which will last,
Those words which flow from the fingers
through keyboard or pen
are the fact or fiction of the novel
we crave reading to the end.

Davina Headland (Reading)

Am I Missing Something?

After all I could be
Floating down the Thames
On a boat to Richmond
(- my dream of tranquillity
constructed to lull me to sleep)

Or I could be
In stately grey Edinburgh
Gone festival crazy - or
(Nick leaves a message
saying Paris is better
than Edinburgh); but
no, I am in the best
place; suspended

sky-high above trees
watching the blue
turn to grey and back
again: clouds
floating by as I
sit amongst
books and silence

watching as August
slides into September,
green leaves turning to
brown on the trees

outside.

Sarah Wright (Brighton)

Corpus Christi In Italy

'Is God . . . in church beside the sacred shrine,
Or is He with the birds above the stream?'
My friend's fair question drew a searching line
Across the sands of time, as in a dream.
Inside the church the faithful prayed the Mass
With words and music hallowed many years.
Outside, Italian men thrice kissed a lass;
They joked and smoked - they had no lasting fears,
The service ended and the faithful came
With solemn faces through the merry crowd.
Two ladies wept: was this for shame or blame?
No questions from a stranger were allowed,
But was Christ present in the bread and wine?
Yes truly: it remains a sacred sign.

Viggianello (Bedford)

Underground Artery In Cornwall

Digging,
The base of the greenhouse,
Frank unearthed a hosepipe type
Of root; running the length
Of the growing area.

Was it an
Offshoot from the grapevine?
Whose limbs and leaves climb high, to
Reach sunlight, among the high panes.
Ripening fruit of Bacchus.

Or did
The root stem from the gangly
Goat-willow tree; standing outside?
Drawn to the glass-warmed soil;
Tapping into nutrient rich loam.

Frank
Tugged and shook the snake-like form,
To reveal its blood-red skin and vein,
Like capillary rootlets,
That seemed so attached to the land.

Instantly,
It appeared as though an
Underground artery was being
Wrenched, from the very heart
Of the earth.

Josephine Hodges (Bodmin)

Untitled

The shock of what had been said
Falls on deaf ears or ears of denial
Tears glistening down my cheeks
My eyes red with crying harsh
Lips trembling with pain and suffering
My heart welling up, it's hard to breathe
Body aching, it's hard to bear
A shiver running down the spine
Grasping for air after every immense dispersal of despair
Memories flashing through my mind
The love and joy we once had
Our smiling faces all together
I will forever hold that, tell my daughters and sons of you
Till the day comes when we can share them together.

Toni-Anne Earl (Saltash)

Is This What Love Is Made Of?

Look where we stand now -
To leave, to stay, we know not how.
I pushed, you pushed -
We pushed some more -
Imperfectly-created ruche
Oddly lies on the floor.

A ruche of thorns we not have made
Of a love once so perfect
You took, I took; not putting back
Strength to rebuild, alack we lack.
Is this what love is made of?

The shores of life, we strolled along,
Young hearts just like skylarks sang:
We skipped, we tripped, we shared a kiss;
Our beating hearts a beat did miss.
Gossamer gowns of gold we wore
Had trains of roses trail the floor.

Happiness, it was ours to take
As wine we sipped beside the lake -
Fingers entwined, kisses like wine
Lingered on your lips and mine -
That was what love was made of!

Now here we stand, our passions bland
On lips that once knew only love.
Is this what love is made of?

Liz Barnor (Barnet)

Cadbury Hill

What are you doing on Cadbury Hill
Little boy and your dog?
Up where the old kings used to stamp,
Up where the Romans built their camp,
Up where knights ride their prancing steeds
Whose silver shoes only brush the weeds,
Weightless and faery. Not like you,
Running and shouting, a mortal who,
Leaping and calling long years after
They have faded to shadows, with your laughter
Recall them again on a Midsummer's Day
To delight in your joy as you carelessly play,
Strong and alive upon Cadbury Hill
Little boy and your dog.

Lavinia Bradley (Littlehampton)

Her Colour Materials

Black, beige, brown, fawn,
colours of 30's wallpaper - no!
I shout colour from the housetops,
I defy dowdy colourlessness,
I am in revolt against no colour.

My Filipino hat with its wild swirls
makes me look like a toadstool.
I don't care, my goldfish water jug,
orange, mauve, blue, green,
blending together in all their glory.

Made to be filled with red wine.
Wooden Indonesian cat
in psychedelic 1960's colours.
And this mug with a painted parrot -
anything defying convention, good taste.

My gaudy Oxfam coat
made to copy 70's retro style,
I love them all to bits, their tasteless clash.
I've gone off the rails, they say,
'She used to have a good eye.'

Now I don't know here I am.
Colours clash like cymbals,
so do I, flouting the well-worn way,
'She's gone mad again.
She's not well, what do you expect?'

Ann Scorgie (Bath)

Oxford Dreams

Oxford, dreaming spires with history, with plenty to see and do
Museums, art centres, restaurants, pubs and clubs true
So the Coven night-club entertains us all
With plenty of entertainment and banging funky music,
Sure it's a great place to be
And Bury Knowle Park is a great park for all and loads to do and see
And to sit for peace and enjoy its scenery of nature's trees an all
And the place to be,
We call it our Headington treat,
With the shops on its doorsteps too
And toilets and views perfect for all
Oxford has so much history and things to do and enjoy
With its dreaming spires and its enchanting views
I just love my Oxford city of dreams . . .

Sharon (Blossom) Brown (Oxford)

Behold He Comes

All over the world they saw a great shining light,
People were gazing high up beyond moon and star,
What could it be? So lively and bright;
What can it be? It is coming from afar,
    It will soon be here.

Allover the world it came nearer and nearer,
And people were fearful, as the light grew and grew;
It's some sort of figure, not like a man,
There's more than one there, oh I wish I knew,
    I'll soon understand

All over the world they saw this wonderful sight,
A real kingly figure, so heavenly a man,
With angels around, before and behind,
Even lighting the sky more bright than the sun,
    Seen by everyone.

All over the world spirits went up to meet *Him,*
The spirits whose lives have been close to our *Lord,*
Rising in joy to meet their redeemer,
Happy to be meeting the one they adore,
    Cleansed and renewed.

All over the world wondrous miracle of light,
It was *Jesus* our Saviour, who is coming again;
With angels attending glorious and bright,
He comes, as He promised and now *Jesus* brings
    Joy, peace to the end.

W Herbert G Palfrey (Seaton)

Don't Waste My Time

Don't waste my time
Don't disturb my mind
You are the same every time why can't you just let your former life die
Around and around that's all we ever do just like a merry-go-round
Year in, year out
Year after year this relationship is always stuck in time
Your habits, your friends, your character there is no end to this list
Time after time our love is greatly tested and disrupted
Time after time our love abruptly comes to an end
Then around and around we start our love again only for you to waste my time
Only for you to disturb my mind and turn my sunny days completely blue
Love is what I want not a broken, lonely heart
Happiness and commitment a relationship made like glue
One that will forever remain new.

Jacqueline Warrington (London)

A View In Mind

There are many places all over the world,
Of great beauty where one's eyes seem too small
To take in such colour. Where the scene of
Flowers and grasses fill one's senses with joy.
Too many to choose, so I think of home.

Here in Britain the countryside is green,
Each county has its own view of nature
With many ancient relics of times past,
Some fields are flat with floodwaters in check,
Other countries are craggy with steep hills.

The mountains of Wales and Scotland present
Breathtaking views of valleys quiet and peaceful.
But the view which pleases me most is
A garden in Wiltshire, in a village at
The foot of rolling hills and the White Horse.

To sit at rest with the world, breathing in
The scent of roses, golden rod, hollyhocks,
Phlox and sunflowers blooming alongside
Beans, tomatoes, carrots and onions,
Takes me back to my own childhood days.

For many years now I've lived in a flat,
So potted plants, mainly cacti, keep me
In touch with nature, helped along with
The occasional bunch of carnations,
Lilies and chrysanthemums to cheer me.

Joyce Robson (Catford)

Ode To Barnett Demesne

There's a beautiful place, so romantic,
Caressed lovingly by the Atlantic;
Rich and green is the sweep of her lawn,
Pearled with dewdrops at every new dawn.
Breeze ethereal wafts with a kiss:
A dear foretaste of heavenly bliss.
Trees in blossom, dance like a young bride;
Underneath, daffodils bloom with pride,
Like flared trumpets, exotic and bold;
Midas never attracted such gold!
Pale narcissus, so elfin and small,
Like a sweet colleen at her first ball.
Nature, flaunting her purest of arts,
Will, forever, abide in our hearts.

Marion Whistle (London)

The Furthest Outpost

(1962 Driving to Khalat in a 1932 Wolsey)

A boy
held up a posy of
roses,
that spake of scratched soil and a
hungry time.

Climb-ing from the plain takes
hours long;
days
ways of the goat herd and camel
afoot in the cool of night.

Sight of him
hurt, my tired engine screaming
'On, on,' the
sky, even, barren of eagles between the
high peaks.

Shrieks of
spurned flowers
offered like water without price held me and
the boy, at last, dumb, in a lost tongue,
gave me his mite.

Smiting my
Western ways with his courtesy of
timeless hours.

Oliver Cox (West Hampstead)

Maybe

Maybe we knew each other better
When the night was young and not old
And the moon stood still over Venice
And there were no question marks between us
And no ghost trains to scare . . .

So much for the past but turning into the present
There are moments caught between heartbeats
When maybe we know each other better than before

But what is that noise clinking in the darkness?
Maybe we shall know each other better in the future
When silences no longer bleed deep in dark canyons
When the long dark tunnels meet beneath the mountain

Maybe we knew each other better before we were born.

Judy Studd (Newport Pagnell)

Edge Of Sanity

So you think you know my secret,
but you haven't got a clue.
You think that you can read me,
but I've got news for you.
You can't begin to imagine what
really makes me tick.
You wouldn't understand my obsession,
and your arrogance makes me sick.
I could never trust you with the truth,
you could never understand.
So I'll pacify you with a lie,
because that's the way I am.

Some things are better left unsaid,
because the truth's too hard to take.
So don't try to read my mind,
for you own sanity's sake.
I'm not what you think I am,
I'm not as nice as I seem.
I'm haunted and tormented
and shattered by my dream.
I made it my reality even knowing it was wrong,
and now I can't escape it,
I've been trying for so long.
So maybe I'll give up and just enjoy the ride
because I'm too tired to run now
and there's nowhere left to hide.

Valerie Windmill (Much Hadham)

Highgate Cemetery

Only the dead lie silent
While high in treetops owls communicate
With shrieks of night-time mysteries,
And in the undergrowth below
The foxes make their noises
Like fighting cats recalling conquests
And birds they tore to pieces
In wilder days.

Then when the night is over
The birds take charge again,
Singing their sweeter songs
To greet the living
With hopes of new tomorrows,
But still the dead lie silent.

Norah Gordon (London)

Forbidden Fruits

We fumbled the key and entered in
The domain of Marjorie, next of kin.
We trod softly around and opened a drawer,
And gazed with reverence, fear and awe
At down at heel slippers, a bright silk scarf
Still wrapped in tissue. One of us stifled a laugh
As hysteria mixed with sadness and dread
At the absence, the silence, the ghost of the dead.
We sensed disapproval as we threw boring clothes
In a black plastic sack, a present for those
Still in need. But suddenly, clearly, someone was there,
Corporeal, alive, in the old brown chair.
With bated breath and tremulous glance,
We all felt the presence and looked askance
At the booty collected to remember her by,
We guiltily hoped to escape her sharp eye.
How dare we enter uninvited, unbidden,
To handle possessions and treasure long-hidden?
A momentary flicker of guilt mixed with sadness
Had summoned her back. She would laugh at such madness.

In the kitchen a kettle clicked, somebody there
Fearlessly sat in the old brown chair.
We played plastic bag football, and someone else shouted,
'Coffee up. Marjie's happy.' How could we have doubted?
We drank coffee, like old times, discussed the grey day,
With our dear next of kin just a murmur away.

Enid Bryant (Highbridge)

Dawlish Beach At 12 Years Old

Crippling pebbles; slippery weed,
Chilling breeze and swirling water
Clothes my feet; and then the ice
Creeps up my flesh:
Hesitation swells the torture,
So part the foam and cleave the ocean
Plunge beneath and rise again
And when the chattering teeth are still,
Shout, 'Come on in!'

When the water's silky smooth
Lie back on its warming surface
Watch white cloud shapes floating by
And red rocks with their bright green hair
In distant view - thrusting from the shining blue.

Anne Healey (Sutton)

Young Jockey

The young jockey opened the stable door,
And watched his horse with pride and awe.

He walked him gently to the track,
Adjusting stirrups, slid on his back.

It stood quite placidly on the grass,
The jockey's heart was beating fast.

He stroked his head with great affection,
He knew he had the best selection.

He rode him to the starting gate,
The horse and he could hardly wait.

Quickly he urged him from the stall,
He knew he would beat them all.

Gently he coaxed him round the bends,
He thought the race would never end.

But suddenly was past the post,
He'd achieved what he'd wanted most.

The race was won on his first ride,
The jockey looked at him with pride.

At last he slipped back into bed,
And lovely thoughts went through his head.

The best present he'd ever had,
A rocking horse from Mum and Dad.

W Hall (Weymouth)

Bath Shades

As sinners climb those rungs of stone
Does Sulis help them to atone?
To purgatory they slip and slide
Through ages down the Abbey's side.
Victorians, Georgians came and went
Through wigs and gowns and ornament.

Bath rests so easy on the eye;
Canal and river rippling by.
The years are kind to mellow stone,
Though ages past haunt those alone.
In Roman Bath or city street,
Shades pass you by on silent feet.
Beau Nash and Austin are about -
That they are here there is no doubt.

Rhona Aitken (Bath)

Blank Verse

I have to confess it
Why did I suggest it?
That everyone should write a poem
To be perfectly frank
My mind's gone quite blank
With not even one line to show 'em

Not a limerick or rhyme
Or some words all in time
A Shakespeare type sonnet or verse
In an opium haze
No Byron like phrase
No TV jingle or worse

Not like Coleridge or Gray
God help me I pray
I am down on my knees
And I plead
But Him high above
Says I'm busy, my love
There are people in far greater need

Poet Laureate, inspired
I think I'd be fired
Tennyson, Shelley, who cares
John Hegley, so modern
Well I say, oh sod 'em
I think I'll just copy Pam Ayres.

Jackie Longley (Warminster)

Starlings At Dusk

We walked at dusk near Redcliffe's lofty spire
When suddenly a rustling filled the air,
We stood transfixed and only could admire
The beauty of the starlings far up there.
How generous is nature thus to share
Those myriad birds that never tire,
And soar, as sinking sun with rays of fire
Gleams on the shimmering feathered suits they wear.

They sweep across the sky in patterned swirls
And back they come, and dip and soar again,
Like giant waves or supernatural curls
As close together as the drops of rain.
We still stand gazing skyward at the sight
But then they're gone, to roost another night.

Christine Lillington (Bristol)

Feline Nonsense

The ginger cat said, 'Follow me,'
So up the tree we climbed.
From limb to limb we clawed our way,
Clouds drew near, earth left behind.

Birds' nests on the way we saw,
With bluebirds on their eggs.
A squirrel we spied in hat so tall,
Black jacket and trousered legs.

Just then the cat stopped short
And hissed, 'Don't make a sound.'
For soldier ants in two by two
Were climbing from the ground.

Our parachute was safely strapped,
We jumped and pulled the cord.
So, floating softly down to earth
That cat said not a word.

We landed in the buttercups
And nothing did we spill.
Nectar filled the golden blooms,
In joy we drank our fill.

Cat turned her head, said, 'Follow me,'
I woke up with a jerk.
Time for cat food once again,
She must think I'm a berk.

Denis Pentlow (Southampton)

When I Get To Heaven

(To all loved ones in another place)

When I get to Heaven will I see your face?
When I get to Heaven will you be saving me a place?
When I get to Heaven will I see you smile at me?
And welcome me with open arms the way it used to be . . . ?

When I get to Heaven will we sit down and talk?
Remembering the things we did like going for a walk
When I get to Heaven I'll have so much to say!
About the things you've missed in life whilst you have been away!

When I get to Heaven I will know you I am sure,
And I will run and hug you just like I did before.
So when I get to Heaven, reunited we will be,
But until that day I'll think of you - that's the way it is you see.

Jane Wade (Truro)

Wishful Thinking

It was World War I,
When millions of mothers lost a son,
Common decorum died at The Somme,
Came peace and life carried on.

Decades later back where we started,
Millions of mother's sons departed,
Taking qualities absent today,
Leaving fatherless children to go astray.

Gone are the days of chivalry,
Waiting for a yes on bended knee,
Maidens then were femininely coy,
Prospects of courting such a joy.

Customs of supporting and giving,
Bonded relationships mystified the living,
Men were bold and quick to scold,
Disobedient minors did as told.

Nowadays young men will say,
'That was yesterday today it's passé,'
Doffing the hat obsequiously naff,
Considered hilarious inviting a gaffe.

Days when marriages lasted longer,
Fabric of society so much stronger,
Will life ever be the same again,
Is expectancy a thought in vain?

Robert Reddy (Taunton)

Ozzie

From the Surf Coast
zigzagging down
to Adelaide,

koala signs on gum trees
make us look up.

Out of 'the city of churches'
rangers on the hill make a bear
feel safe.

Twelve varieties of favourite tree to savour,
you turn, offering poses to be grabbed from every angle.

Sitting in the tree's fork,
you almost slip away
into daylong dreamtime.

Christopher Martin (Southsea)

Hiroshima - September 13th 2001

No planes are flying west
but I've flown east
- despite armed guards at Heathrow
rumours and delays
(I surrender scissors whilst
a teenager worries
about unwashed underwear) -
east to where *Enola Gay*
dropped *Little Boy.*

By bullet train to

Hiroshima. In the Peace Park.
parties of Australian schoolchildren
envelop the statue of a little girl
holding aloft a golden crane
with rainbow coloured garlands -

Sedako's medicine papers reborn
as cranes. Her goal
to fold one thousand
then she would be well again.

We tour the museum - taste the charred remains
in a child's lunchbox - cleanse ourselves with iced coffee.
Under the shadow of the A-Bomb dome, we watch
cranes dip down into the once black river - rise- and fly away.

'I will write Peace on your wings and you will fly all over the world.'

Carole Alexander (New Milton)

The Tumbledown Cottage

In the tumbledown cottage of timber and stone
She'd lived all her years, the last twenty alone.
When the day was a-dimming and darkness drew nigh
The smoke from her chimney went spiralling high,
When the sun had just set and the evening grew still,
Against the dark yew tree, against the dark hill,
And up to the wide, white sky.

Now over ninety her numbers are told,
Her roof has stopped reeking, her hearth has gone cold.
In the time of the twilight I fancy she went
Like a twist of white smoke in a silent ascent,
When the day winds had died and the night winds were still,
Against the dark yew tree, against the dark hill,
And up to the wide, white sky.

Editha Russell (Princes Risborough)

The Ever Elusive 230 AYE

As I look back some forty years, I think of something grand,
she is the finest of her marque, the best in all the land.
Her looks are sleek and beautiful, and great she'll always be,
that's why she's streets ahead of most > 230 AYE.

Produced way back in fifty-nine, she's rode the years so well,
and even after all that time, she really does look swell.
Aston Martin's what she is, prestige is what they are,
and none more so than this old girl, a stunning looking car.

I knew her many years ago, then went our separate ways,
I think about her now and then, and to those good old days.
Even though the years have flown, it feels like time's stood still,
as I have tracked her down again, and that is such a thrill.

She now resides in London, and soon we're to unite,
as I will make the journey there, to see that lovely sight.
I've spoken with her keeper, and yes he does agree,
that we're to meet at Brooklands track, just Alex, her and me.

The day was just amazing, and the sun did shine throughout,
it was for me a special day, of that there is no doubt.
She really looked outstanding, just stood there on parade,
giving me some priceless thoughts, the kind that never fade.

I've checked out some achievements, and yes to say the least,
she really racked up some results, a truly awesome beast
It's written down in history, and now has come to be,
the pinnacle of our racing greats, the DB4 GT.

Phil Boote (Seaton)

Bright Yellow Café

My daughter
who is three
runs a small and efficient
imaginary cafe
that serves cappuccino,
wild chicken with sea horse and crystal cakes that twinkle
flamingo ice cream
and chocolid lullapots
in the shape of balloons
that taste of rainbow.

'Here is a yellow pizza, Daddy,
I made it for you,'
she says and smiles,
taking the order with writing pencil.

Ian Duckett (London)

The Black-Backed Gull

Fly, fly you black-backed gull
Dipping and soaring above the rocks
Through the swirling drifting mists
On this blustery day.

The lonely lighthouse standing tall
Rough water splashing on its walls
The only witness to your flight
Flapping, wheeling, with all your might.

You hover gracefully in midair
Not a movement, just hanging there
Like a child's kite without the strings
Flying ever higher on outstretched wings.

The wind decreases, the mist departs
Skies turn blue, the sea's like glass
Slowly, slowly, down you go
To the waters far below.

Other gulls rest on the rocks
Preening in the warm sunshine
The noise now deafening, as they compete
Soon the main thought will be to eat.

So fly black-backed gull to your nest
Where all the birds return to rest
Tomorrow will soon arrive
Another day for you to survive.

Marje Dale (Bournemouth)

A Ride Through A Park

Riding through the park gates I go.
Watching kids on the climbing frames I see.
Riding from the concrete path onto the grass I travel.
I see two dogs chasing me.
Then smelling the dew fall on the grass,
Looking down, realising I'm going too fast.
Turning my head, seeing the dogs way back there.
Over something, *bum pity bump, bum pity bump.*

My bike wobbled from side to side.
I fell onto the grass with my bike on top of me.
I felt the pain, as I stood up with my bike.
I tasted the tears that ran down my face into my mouth.
I heard the dogs getting smacked by their owners,
As I carried my bike all the way home.

James William Hunt (Bristol)

Tree-Born

Said the oak I am getting old
To the young tree that he told
When you grow up like me
Fine upstanding strong proudly

Looking over forest of green
Overlooking all I have seen
Stretching I can touch a cloud
Birds gathering in a crowd

Building nest knowing I'm strong
Although I know before too long
Woodcutters will cut me down
I will lose my kingdom's crown

Making room for you to grow
So I'll teach you all I know
When the wind comes with force
Stand correctly and on course

Defy the rain tread the sod
Rooting in as an iron rod
Winters will bring heavy snow
Soundly rest and you will grow

Spring arrives you'll look grand
Strongest oak in the land
Overseeing your domain
Many years may you reign.

M A Dooley (Southsea)

My Island

Beneath the green and leafy trees
Rustling in the gentle breeze,
Overhead the blue, blue sky,
Fluffy white clouds go drifting by.
Then we know the tourists come
Basking in the summer sun.
The tiny ripples on the beach
Trying hard their chairs to reach.

And then when winter comes to pass,
When the frost lies on the grass
The waves come crashing on the shore
Our island is our own once more.
Who could be bored at such a sight,
My beautiful, peaceful Isle of Wight.

E Maxfield (Newport)

Modern Prophet Required

Thousands and thousands of years ago
When the world was full of trouble and guile
Prophets gave messages sent from God
And people obeyed them for a while.

Since then the nations' leaders have tried
To solve the world's troubles - without success
So things have got worse instead of better
And now we're in even more of a mess.

So surely what is so desperately needed
Is a 21st century prophet to appear
To tell us where we've gone so wrong
And to give us a message loud and clear.

Millions of people throughout our world
Would have to change the way they live
For the message from God would probably be,
'Stop craving for more and learn to give.

Put hate behind you and filled with love
Do your best to help others - a worthwhile task
And ask help from God, who loves us so much'.
He is waiting to answer whenever we ask.

So who will accept the challenge now
And God's message to His people feed
Will *you* be the modern prophet required?
Think hard, for a prophet is wanted indeed.

O G Beck (Littlehampton)

When The Air Changes

Mild air coaxes lilac buds to open,
nudges forget-me-nots to show their faces,
new warmth, new growth, hope reborn.

The sun stole my daughter's spirit,
wrapped it in gold and petals
to shimmer in the summer months.

Sweet smelling flowers delight,
colours shout and dazzle,
there is nowhere to hide.

When the air changes and
summer fades to memory,
her spirit looks at the world through my eyes,
through my eyes.

Rywa Weinberg (London)

The Night School

One of the strangest places to be at night,
Is an empty school, with just moonlight.
The children and staff have all gone home,
Leaving the spirits to roam the corridors alone.

The spooky world is led by one,
But the ghosts who roam will all become,
Servants . . . of the mighty spirit,
The ghost head teacher, in the office he sit.

By day the spirits will all be asleep,
The children never know, they don't hear a peep.
But the staff . . . stories have often been told,
Of ghostly goings on, as the day grows old.

'Don't stay past 7,' the music teacher said,
'That's when they arrive, they come from the dead!'
He spoke of the library, when books would fly,
One by one, in the blink of an eye.

He retired last year, he claimed he was ill,
But the staff all knew, and yet they still
Refuse to believe, and won't be drawn in,
To the crazy stories, that were told by him.

And so the days go on, the school still running,
The normal day, with children coming.
Though never again will the staff stay past
That seven o'clock . . . it may be their last.

Jamie Parkinson (Worthing)

His Eyes (A Vivisection Monkey)

His eyes are black,
He stares at me,
Must get him back,
To his territory.

His eyes are cute,
But say he is sad,
And when he cries,
He is told he is bad.

His eyes cannot stand,
The sharp nails clamping his head,
If PETA were not there to hold his hand,
His whole family would be dead.

Think about it.

Jodie Hassell (13) (Ascot)

491

Change

So high I flew,
The changing takes so very long,
The dark tonight,
Is surely coming.

Far underneath this bridge of lies,
A story,
It unfolds,
As ageless as it can be.

Full of illusions,
And counter punches,
We carry the can,
For the death of the others.

Watching your reflection,
It changes in front of you,
Too tired to read those spiteful reviews,
Have you found that feeling that hides?

A warm brown liquid,
Soothing,
Reaching,
Ill conceived was I.

Indifferent to the body politic,
That rots and smells so putrid,
As it cuts a swathe,
Through our lives.

Gary Vaughan (Wadebridge)

Edward Bear

This is the story of a teddy bear,
Brought to our shop in need of repair.
He'd belonged to a boy who now had grown
And from 'the nest' he had flown.

He was found in the bottom of a drawer,
A great big hole where his eye should have been
And needed stitches in his right leg seam.

I fixed him up and with an inspirational 'flair',
Made him an eye patch to cover his stare!

He looked so cute in the 'outbox tray'
Awaiting his collection day -
That his picture was taken - and put on display
In our company news letter the very next day.

Aileen Andrews-Jordan (Bournemouth)

Fowey (My Favourite Place)

My very favourite place is Fowey,
It really fills me full of joy,
I walk along the esplanade,
Watching the seabirds as they wade.

Then as I come to the sea,
I find a seat within the lea,
In winter and in summertime,
The panorama is sublime.

For when I'm there I feel no fear,
It's all I want to see and hear,
The crashing waves upon the rocks,
There's none here to sit and mock.

I watch the boats upon the waves,
Those little boats that are so brave,
They rock and roll - just like me -
When I was young and so carefree.

The seagulls soar above my head,
They make me feel alive - not dead!
In wintertime there's a few like me,
Who seek some solace by the sea.

And as I wend my lonely way,
I know there'll be another day,
When I shall sit upon my seat,
Feeling again my life's complete.

Janet Towells (Par)

Scramble!

When warm weather wanes,
Wary of winter approaching,
In a high place awaiting agog with anticipation,
The signal to scramble.
When whirring wings will wend toward a warmer clime.
In winter here the ground is cold and hard,
Digging delightful insects almost futile.
While withering without water
But at their destination, the green veldt yields tempting morsels,
Making their arduous trip worthwhile.
When time for temptation is terminated
By the instinct to return,
Once more on the strenuous reverse trip,
So it's 'Scramble!' once again.

Ron Isaacs (London)

Modern Women

Gone are the days when life was a pleasure,
Thank goodness, for memories with which to treasure,
Every magazine and newspaper are all full of advice,
Featuring beauty advertisements to help us look nice.

How to be fabulous, lose weight in a week,
Get glammed up or dressed down whatever one seeks,
Ever considered going under the knife,
Why can't women just get on with their life?

We must have this, we must have that, 'Oh dear don't eat that,'
Then abstain to the limits so they don't put on fat,
The lengths women go to obtain a perfect bikini body,
They purchase the latest fashion shoes they must not look shoddy.

Meet the girls there on a night out of fun,
All day they drank wine and laid on the beach in full sun,
They say it's so much nicer to glow with a tan,
Most will consider doing anything to catch a good looking man.

You can be stylish with an eccentric touch,
Go easy on the make-up, don't use too much,
Be flirty and sexy in a little black dress,
Don't go over the top, you might suffer from stress.

Take life as it comes, then you won't go far wrong,
Soon you will become a pensioner, it won't be that long,
You can travel on the buses, your bus pass is free,
Go visit family and friends, there's new places to see.

Pamela Wild (Barnstaple)

From The Day Of Our Birth

Beautiful countryside, beautiful land,
Heaven on Earth amazingly planned.
A richness of colours in dark shades and light
Weaving together pure scenes to delight.
The hardness of rock, soft mud and fine sand
Defines the reality of our living land.
New birth in the springtime, the summer sun's heat,
Autumn and winter their gifts they repeat.
Rapturous moments and breathtaking times
When nature and beauty our world underlines.
Such gifts seen and heard in a world so divine
Can only enrich the heart, soul and mind.
A heritage given to all on this Earth -
A precious memento from the day of our birth.

June Rampton (Basingstoke)

At The Playgroup

Let's all join hands in a circle
And tiptoe around like mice.
Stretch up very high, like a bird in the sky,
Then dart around in a trice.

Let's make a house out of paper.
And paint it as bright as can be.
Let's tumble like clowns in a circus
Then gather around for tea.

Pretend we're ships on the ocean.
Sailing as fast as we dare.
Swimming like fish in a river.
Or running as fast as a hare.

Let's parade round the room like soldiers.
With music to keep in time.
We'll act out a fairy story -
No talking, it's all in mime.

Let's pretend we're all riding horses
Or driving a bus in the town
Or being a princess with flowers
And wearing a beautiful gown.

Let's all sit down in a circle
We've just climbed a mountain so steep.
then we'll hack our way through a jungle
Oh goodness! You're all fast asleep!

Joan Manwaring (Chessington)

Memories

I sit here every night watching each move she makes,
Graceful as a swan gliding stately on a lake.
Her voice like faerie music, her breath a sylvan breeze,
Her eyes as deep and warm as the blue of coral seas.
Her smile so full of tenderness, I take her in my arms,
And lose myself completely in the wonder of her charms.
Alas! These are but memories, for she has passed away,
Leaving me to struggle through each everlasting day,
Of heartache and of sorrow, waiting for the fleeting night,
When once more I'll be with her in her radiant spectral light,
And we'll wander through love's realms
Where death and life are as one,
Until sunlight brings the dawn
And 'til the night my loved one's gone.

W B Reid (Welwyn Garden City)

Trewarveneth Street

I can see again the cobbled way
As I lean against the granite wall,
Newlyn's old Trewarveneth Street
And Katie in her bonnet and shawl.

At the bottom of the cottage steps
She sits with tangled net and twine,
Her small lad crouching by her skirts
As he winds a fishing hand line.

Sarah washes at the wooden tub
With clothes flaskets at her feet,
And washing hangs from the balcony
On lines strung across the street.

And Liza with her arms akimbo
In the doorway across the way,
Gossips and laughs with her neighbours
On the latest news of the day.

Young Tom carries bucket and pitcher,
Spilling pools onto flags and floor,
As he slowly fills the old water butt
That stands near the open door.

The children play on the cobbled street
And call to each other noisily,
Then turn and shout as they run to meet
The fishermen home from the sea.

Esme Francis (Penzance)

Mermaid's Song

Sometimes I wish I were a mermaid
Swimming through waves of blue and green
Diving down to a pirate ship
That for centuries has not been seen.
Maybe it has a treasure chest of precious stones and gold
Long hidden from human view, kept safely in the hold.
Do you see me as you walk along the shore?
Look closely and I'll be there, lying on the rocks,
Not to lure sailors to their doom, but with a friendly wave,
Listen to the seashells and you will hear me sing.
Only good news to you do I bring.
O, I wish I were a mermaid, swimming under the sea,
With shoals of fish and the octopus -
What a happy place to be.

Susan Sanders (London)

Lilac Tree

There was no hint of pretence
no permanence in anything,
no demand for response.

There was only this lilac tree
and the blackbird's song
piercing the luminous light of the lemon sun.

And when his song was sung
his black wings flowed into the gold oblivion.

While the lilac tree
with no disquietude,
no longing for what went before
and was no more
remained blessedly dumb,
just there
in its space and solitude
desiring allegiance from no one.

But where the bird had rested
the faint pressure now released
gave birth to this particular branch
creating a fleeting life of its own.

And fluttering in a certain mild renown,
not easy to discern
it waved its lilac laden arm gently up and down
in silent salutation to a passing bird of song.

Judith Garrett (Haywards Heath)

Forgot Them Not

Forget them not on this November morn
At the eleventh hour our heroes are reborn
In Flanders Fields and desert sands
They lie at peace in foreign lands
Those brave young men who left our shores
To fight for peace in others' wars
On land and sea and in the sky
They fought our fight not asking why
We owe a debt we can't repay
To those brave men of yesterday
Two minutes silence on this morn
Ensures our heroes are reborn
A poppy pinned upon one's chest
In memory of our country's best

F Osborne (London)

Folk Passing By

I can sit in my front garden,
And watch the folk go by,
A kaleidoscope of people,
I don't really have to pry.

There are various types of bikers,
I see the children going to school,
And the families out for a Sunday treat,
And the oldies who think it's cool.

The passing horses are ridden with care,
The riders are a varied lot,
There are some who pass with a snooty look,
And some at quite a trot.

And then we have the runners,
There are the rugby training men,
And the dedicated marathon set,
And the puffing slimmers you ken.

The walkers are my favourite,
Because they stop and share the news,
Of families and friends and fund raising events,
And over babies we can enthuse.

So come and sit and watch with me,
If you feel you'd like to call,
And we'll enjoy our tea and cake,
And wave to one and all.

Vera Banwell (Wedmore)

Italian Sunflower

Girasole
Gyrating round the sun.
One word says it all.
We see in one word's sound
Those plush, heavy headed flowers.
Seeds set in spirals,
Fibonacci sequences.
Flippant petals framing dusky faces
Yellow, orange, rusty-red.
They smiled at us outside Siena
Greeted us at the brown city gate.
One word says it all.
No need for convoluted lines:
Girasole.

Shirley Mungapen (Southampton)

After The Storm

After the storm clouds gather around you,
See the sun come shining through.
Give God all your doubts and pain,
And He'll make you whole and new.

Keep looking to the Father,
He sees your every tear.
He knows the way ahead of you,
Today, tomorrow, next year.

So now just place your hand in His,
And let Him lead the way.
The clouds may gather above you,
But His love won't fade away.

Look up, and count your blessings,
He'll make your life brand new.
Remember, not a day goes by,
When He won't take care of you.

The door is always open wide,
Reach out and take His hand.
He'll lead you by the narrow path,
And help you understand.

In the stillness and the quiet,
You can hear His still small voice.
He is 'The Way, The Truth, The Life',
So now make Him your choice.

Jackie Allingham (Yeovil)

The Day The Worm Turned

He said I was neurotic,
When I should have been erotic,
He said I didn't dress,
With any style or finesse,
He said I couldn't cook,
Like the food looked in the book,
He said that what I read,
Classified me as brain-dead,
He said more of this same stuff,
Till I finally had enough,
He said I hadn't got a clue,
And I would never see it through,
He thought that it was funny,
Till I got half his house and money.

Susan Ireland (Wareham)

'Cold Turkey' Every Time!

Well, we've 'kicked it',
The habit of smoking, I mean,
We've been in its grip for 35 years,
And now it's an old 'has been'.

I never thought I could do it,
It really had hold of me,
My husband was in its thrall, nearly as bad,
So, 'cold turkey' it had to be.

There's no two ways about it,
You have to be, with yourself, really tough,
All these remedies 'to help you with your willpower',
Are simply not enough.

It's only willpower, in the end, that will do it,
Make no mistake,
Say to yourself, 'I will do it,' and mean it,
Ignore that longing, nagging ache.

Say also to yourself,' I'm bigger than you,
Pathetic nicotine,
I'm no longer in your thrall, I won't answer when you call,
So take a hike from the scene.'

Well, I can only speak from experience,
It really has worked for us,
Don't shilly shally, get on and do it,
And ignore all the ridiculous fuss!

June M Benton-Wright (Aylesbury)

Winter Landscape

The unremitting song of the surf
Surges through the trees, yet they are still.
Birds rise in a rush from wintry turf
In a synchronised ballet and spill
Swiftly like a spray of scattered grain.
And then gather in a downward arc
Only to rise and plummet again.
Inland seagulls fly across the stark
Landscape of skeleton trees with loud
Mews. They head for the shady outcrop
Of hills where pale sunlight veiled by cloud
Filters through an anaemic backdrop
Beyond the rugged curves of the moor
To the sparkling sea and rocky shore.

Rosina Winiarski (Dulverton)

Crossroads

At the crossroads of our lives
We're faced with many paths
Some roads are easily defined
While others split in halves

The choices that we often make
Are sometimes not so clear
Resulting in a struggle
And for some a lot of fear

I've had no children of my own
Nor someone on whom I depend
I haven't had a brush with the law
Nor ever been round the bend

I've never been a traveller
All set to see the world
I've only wanted ever to write
And let my mind unfold

I've kept myself well to myself
And never won an award!
But always for my guidance
Have relied upon the Lord

I've been no saint I must confess
Nor anybody's wife
But can sit back in my old age
And say - I've had a life . . .

Linda Yvonne Kettle (Portsmouth)

Christmas Past

It's all about when I was young many years ago,
When I believed in Santa Claus and fairies don't you know,
I'd write a list for Santa, to ask for this and that,
A train set, or a pair of skates - a pet, perhaps a cat.
I'd wake up in the early hours on Christmas Day to find,
The pillowcase I'd put there, with things he'd left behind.
By the look at what I got, this must be his last call,
An apple and an orange and a little rubber ball.
What happened to the train set, the roller skates, the cat?
Dad said, 'Things are tight this year,' add Santa's name to that.
When Mum takes me to see him next year at the local store,
I'll tell him not to bother calling, at my house no more.
If that's the best that he can do, then stay at the North Pole,
I'm sure my dad could do his job and keep him off the dole.

R Niall (London)

The Lost Souls

I fear religious people;
They lack common sense convictions.
How can each God's words all be true,
When they're full of contradictions?

I fear religious people.
They believe 'Thou shalt not kill',
But frequently they do so.
And claim they're doing God's will.

I fear religious people;
Their laws cause so much pain.
They say, they come from God,
But over centuries they change.

I fear religious people;
They're such appalling bigots;
Intolerant of others;
Full of hates and prejudices.

I fear religious people;
They state that, 'Humans are the best;
Supreme of all God's creatures';
Yet we slaughter all the rest!

There is though, one 'good' message,
We receive from God above.
What a shame 'they' all ignore it!
It is: 'universal love'.

Edward Lyon (Isle of Wight)

Untitled

Just quietly hear the music start
As each string trembles near your heart
It sounds as if in ecstasy
It longs to play a rhapsody
The hill is high you want to see
How near the top you yearn to be
The symphony in volume grows
Ones senses real and overflows
Into a pool so dark, so still
A pause, then very high upon the hill
A violin plays all alone
The sweetness of it now you own
And as you listen to it die
You look above and softly sigh.

Shirley Davies (Barnet)

Seascape

Seagulls wheel and laugh and cry
And coast along on the breeze;
The sun burns down from the vault of blue
On the shimmering dancing seas.

Little boats with coloured sails,
Gybe and tack and run
Like butterflies with wings outstretched,
In the warmth of the summer sun.

Waders dart along the shore
Searching for things to eat,
Stabbing and probing with slender bills,
Lacy wavelets around their feet.

Then swift and sudden, all is changed . . .
The wind grows fierce and strong;
Dark angry clouds blot out the sun . . .
The smiling scene is gone.

The gulls sweep down - ride out the storm,
Tossed on the surging foam;
The little boats, caught unawares,
Reef down and scurry home.

Only the busy waders remain
Along a vanishing shore,
With the sullen windswept skies above,
And the ocean's menacing roar.

Elizabeth Amy Johns (Truro)

The Patchwork Quilt

The patchwork quilt lies on my bed,
blue, pink and rosy red,
with each patch a dream was sown,
a piece of Jane's dress that she had outgrown,
John's torn trousers all tell a tale,
when he climbed the fence and got caught on a nail,
memories flood back with each added stitch,
a tale that unfolds with something so rich,
satin and silk from an old wedding dress,
a piece of a gown that had belonged to Aunt Bess,
patches of memories all sewn together,
to make something warm to keep out the weather,
heirlooms are made of such faded dreams,
sewn with such love and very neat seams.

Margot Recardo (London)

503

Tele-Images

'The way to pull society down'
Said Satan with a smile,
'Is to focus bad images
To tempt and to beguile.

If we can show bad habits
Rude words and ugliness -
We'll get society to copy them -
So good behaviour-less.

We must get into the minds of those
Who orchestrate production -
To allow sex and violence
With plenty of seduction.

The way to do it (we must be subtle)
Is to make things look 'quite cool' -
And in a person's ignorance
It can become the rule.

Children will think like their parents
As parents will already be hooked; -
Oh what a delicious plan
That clever me has 'cooked'!

Our future is the bad news -
This I have to tell -
But with careful planning -
They'll come with us to Hell.'

Pat Melbourn (Poole)

Lanes

Leafy lanes that lead to nowhere,
Lanes that lead down to a cove,
Lanes that lead to sleepy townships,
This is the England that I love.

Lanes with autumn's gaudy colours,
Lanes with catkins in the spring,
Accepted as their due by many,
To other folk mean everything.

Worth the wars and worth the anguish,
Worth the fears and worth the fight,
The leafy lanes of England,
England's freedom, our birthright.

James R Warwick (Plymouth)

The New Forest

The woodlands and the wilderness,
The King's own hunting ground,
A haven from the rat-race,
Peacefulness all around.

Ponies grazing everywhere,
They stray upon the road,
Ramblers smile, admire the views,
And follow the country code.

The deer browse in the forest deep,
The mighty oak supreme,
Cyclists take a moment's rest,
Beside a trickling stream.

Birds sing so melodically,
Donkeys are intent
In eating scraps the picnickers left,
They are now content.

Campers find a pleasant spot
Amongst the purple heather,
Children run and laugh and play
In the warm and sunny weather.

A perfect place to get away,
Somewhere to unwind,
Explore the forest's hidden gems,
And leave the world behind.

June Melbourn (Ferndown)

First Love

It had been raining
followed by thunder and lightning
and in the theatre foyer
waiting for me was my lover.

Though wet and cold, she was still smiling
and clasped my hand before moving
through the park where flowers were blooming
and gentle breeze was blowing.

As the evening had flown by
it was time to say goodbye.
so we parted filled with sorrow
wondering what awaits tomorrow.

K R Kadkol (Twickenham)

Our Wonderful World

As I looked up at the moonlight
And clouds that hurried by,
I felt in the space around me
The vastness of the sky.

A view that's seen in perspective
Plays an important role,
One can look at fragmentation
Or simply see the whole.

The astronauts saw the beauty
Of Earth from outer space:
The shining world in completeness,
A very lovely place.

And we who have not been up there
Remember what they saw,
As this was a revelation
Not seen by men before.

For the world is not divided,
No barriers are there,
Apart from the mind that makes them,
The love is everywhere.

Though we live in different countries
That change from pole to pole,
Each nation is a perfect part
Of a great perfect whole.

Anne Greenhow (Highgate)

An Essex Ploughboy

Sixty year, sixty year, I steadied the ploughshare
Called to the horses, wrote a scar on the land
The plough was my life, a life I had loved
Though the sun burnt my head and the plough cut my hands

With Plough Monday over, three horses we'd hitch
A broad Essex field rolled in front of the plough
And the sound of the tackle and the smell of the earth
Are so fresh to my mind, all those years even now.

But today I ain't ploughing, need a stick just for walking
Then while sat by my gate, heard a team in the land
The memories flooded my mind and my eyes
And the tears trickled down, I'm a ploughboy again.

Tony Kendall (Chingford)

My Life . . .

First I was a son
To my mum and dad
With their love and inspiration
They made me feel so glad

Next I was a pupil
To the teachers at my school
Who taught and educated me
With all their golden rules

Then I was an apprentice
To my bosses at work
I was quite conscientious
And rarely did I shirk

Happy I was a sweetheart
To my darling Lin
We were so much in love
Our wedding bells did ring

Soon I was a father
To our family of three
It's hard to believe how lucky
One man can be

Now I am a grandfather
My life has really moved on
I hope you've enjoyed my reflection
On my yesterdays gone . . .

L.J Roche (Chalfont St Giles)

New Day

Quiet and fresh is the new day at dawn
Weak are the sun's rays as they find their warmth
Bright is the bird's song that welcomes the day
Thank you for all this to its maker I say.

Soon rush takes over as the day passes on
Sunrise and birdsong are long past and gone
Then into evening, with no time to spare
For the quiet and beautiful world that's out there.

If only we'd make time to stop and admire
The birds, trees and flowers in radiant attire
But the world rushes on and we are a part
Too busy to admire each new day as it starts.

Sylvia Bartrip (Newbury)

Mid Winter

In the bleak mid winter, icy winds do blow;
Christmas carol singing, in the cold, cold snow
but that's not very usual at this time of praise
it's with us far more often in Feb'ry's frosty days

Scotland and the northern dales
have ice and snow and Arctic gales
dark and dreary mornings, foggy roads at night
gardens frozen solid, grass a glowy white

Children going schoolward, slide down icy hills
older folk in sheepskin coats trudge through weather's chill,
thinking perhaps of warmer times, as off to work they go
wondering, why is it that in wintertime, the weeks they go so slow?

Whilst in the South the Gulf stream flows
bringing rain and gale force blows
but snowy blizzards white and hard
are only seen on Christmas cards

The folk down here are very blessed
there is no need for thermal vests
and all they require to get about,
a mackintosh and brolly stout

But spring is but a month away
and new creation then holds sway
trees will blossom, birds will sing
and sunnier days warm everything.

David Dallimore (Bournemouth)

Man V Nature (1965)

Will the unseen air of yesterdays,
Be seen in years to come,
When filled with man's own compost heap,
Brought forth from the worldly slums.

Industrial smoke and insecticides,
Pour forth from man's own hand,
To filter into the clean pure air,
That covers this wholesome land.

Will nature strive to hold her own,
While smacked in the face by us,
Or will she turn and destroy herself,
And begin afresh from the crust.

Eugene F Cummings (Oxford)

Love

Love is the source of joy unborn
Love is the grief of loss and pain
Love is a powerful burning thrust
Love is a thought without a name

Love is the passion of our youth
The untold mystery of age
Love is a look, a smile, a touch
An unread book, an unturned page

Love is a mother's tender care
Love is a father's swift caress
Love is a friend, love is a snare
Love can move mountains, love can bless

Love is a yearning, deep desire
Love is a distant, urgent call
A mutual trust, a rush of blood
Love conquers all

Love is a flood, love is a fire
A rising tide, the fount of life
Love is a child who knows no fear
Love gives us peace amidst the strife

Love is a cord which binds us fast
Love when rejected sears the soul
Love given free heals deepest wounds
Love is the part which makes the whole

Doreen M Hill (Southsea)

The Cottage

There is a little cottage
I pass it by each morn
A special little cottage
The place where I was born

Nestling in the valley
By downland village stream
Its walls of white, show up at night
It really is a dream

Picturesque with timber beams
And chimney pots quite tall
In summertime it looks the best
And is admired by all

Raymond Hobbs (Hungerford)

Why?

Why must I live my life for other people
Why can't I live it just for me?
If I go to bed and leave the outside light on
They automatically think I'm on the spree.

To each of us is given something precious
A life to make the most of what we can
But always there is someone interfering
If it's not a jealous woman it's a narrow-minded man

To all you nosy people who think so ill of me
Let me open up my heart and tell you my story
Here lives a lonely woman who has no one of her own
If I stay in at night I see the four walls of my home

Now surely I have got the right to find happiness if I can
Even if it means my going out and meeting with a man
As long as I conduct myself as I consider right
Then surely it need not be wrong if he takes me out at night?

So look to your own life, my friends, before you criticise
Is there not something that you did that was not always wise?
And would you like to be condemned for a crime you didn't do
When all you wanted was a friend you could give your friendship to?

No; surely in this time and age we must not judge each other
But offer each a helping hand, come neighbour, friend or lover
And leave the final judgement day to *He* who sits above
And look upon our fellowmen with compassion and with love.

Barbara Dorothy Wooddisse (Wimborne)

Washing Jesus' Feet

As I was walking down the street
I thought of Mary at Jesus' feet
I thought of how she'd used her hair
Oh, how I wish that I'd been there

Then I stopped and thought awhile
And as I pondered began to smile
Because I too can wash His feet
Even walking down the street

So as I do my daily chore
I can serve Him more and more
Not by rushing here and there
But to listen, to look and to kneel in prayer.

Rita Rogers (Havant)

Soft Heart

My love for you
Shines so bright,
I always hope
That you're alright

My faith in you
Is always clear,
Because I love you
So very dear

My life is yours
For you to own,
I'm all yours
From skin to bone

My heart is full
Of love to you,
I just hope
Yours is too

My mind is wiped
When I see you,
My goal in life
Is to make something new

Remember one thing
I'm always there,
My love and happiness
Is yours to share.

Amy Stimpson (14) (Milton Keynes)

The Finishing

Blood-red, the beast is dead, ox-red,
Like a terrorist killing;
The beast lies still, shocked by cold metal,
Powerless, a contract broken.

Grass heavy, well bred and nurtured,
Blind, folded and beheaded,
The struggle to hold life, pours out
Onto stone, from arteries, hot with fear.

English beast, betrayed and displayed,
The spirit now composed
Into ceramic pots, is dragged lifeless
To a dusty street, then tossed like garbage.

Glyn Davies (Barnstaple)

Christmas Long Ago

A lonely clock struck four as I in bed lay deep in thought,
remembering past happiness that Christmas always brought.
My heart was filled with longing to relive those happy days,
before the path of destiny showed each our chosen ways.

Our house itself seemed happy to accept the cheerful sounds
that heralded the coming of those friendly Christmas rounds.
The kitchen warm and cosy, with a fire glowing red
to heat the oven into which mince pies and cakes were fed.

Such magic seemed to fill the air when Christmas Eve came round,
with presents wrapped and put away, what fun when they were found
From dusk until the morning came, my mother worked to make,
such tempting Christmas goodies and the pudding and the cake.

The rooms were spanned with garlands, in bright confused array,
and coloured bells, balloons and things that make a Christmas gay,
and standing in a corner as *majestic* as could be,
you'd see, I'm sure, the largest decorated Christmas tree.

Nostalgically my memories, swept through the darkened room
and shared the utter silence of the early morning gloom.
I wiped away a lonely tear for those I'd see no more,
the years roll by and some are left and some go on before.

Yet through the changing years the Christmas spirit will remain,
for Christ was born and Christ knew death and then came back again
Soon Christmas time will come again, and, in the firelight's glow,
will take me back across the years to Christmas Long Ago.

Ivy W Berry (Truro)

Himalayan Evening

Who has heard the bugle sound
The end of regimental day?
Who has smelt the evening smoke
curling upward on its way?

Who has watched the eagle's flight
From mountain peak to dusty plain?
Who has breathed the upland air
That is sweeter than champagne?

Who, having dreamed of England
From such a place as this,
Has surrendered to the scents
And sounds of Himalayan bliss?

Gerry Wheatley (Chichester)

The Poetess

The heart of the poetess lies not in love but in loss.
How it aches through the rekindling of happy memories,
Through chosen dreams that eluded times past
To be filed forever in her creative conscience.

The mirror reflects the bell-jar on a desk strewn with birthday letters.
Only buried beneath carefully chosen expression,
Is her soul enriched, the tempest calmed,
For 'time is a great healer', a man called Ted once said.

Her thoughts are too complex for outsiders' comprehension.
Her mind too frail to digest emotions this raw.
With any dilemma before her, however,
The poetess puts her feelings to pen, pen to paper.

Like a tidal wave, they come rushing forth.
No anxiety is left untouched, no worry unexplored.
Scribbling furiously, she is unable to compose fast enough
To evade wilful capture by her depressive shroud.

As she writes, pondering verses so simple yet heady,
Tears begin to trickle down her ashen face.
Recalling painful events that fuel her composition,
She cowers, trembling, before their might.

The strength of the pen leads the poetess to the dawn of a new day
Yet this woman of words is powerless to exist -
Slowly perishing behind sealed doorways framing dimly lit rooms,
Bound for the eternal embrace of ravens' wings.

Joanne Garzella (London)

Love

What tis love, tis a thick jam sandwich
What tis love, tis an ice cream in a crowd
What tis love, tis two eggs and bacon
What tis love, tis one's first teenage kiss.

What tis love, looking into eyes that meet
What tis love, holding hands outside your first home
What tis love, the patter of little feet
What tis love, leaving your child at school.

What tis love, tis listening to their breathing
What tis love, tis kissing under our child's Christmas tree
What tis love, tis holding hands as the sun sets
What tis love, tis waking up in paradise together.

R J J Atkin (Holdsworthy)

Destiny

Are there creatures out in space
    Watching us, the human race
    What they see, and seen before
    Constant conflict, forever war

Man has yet to land on Mars
    But writers have us warring stars
    Are dominance, greed and gain
    Priorities of the human brain

Innocents are the ones to suffer
    People's lives don't seem to matter
    Resources of technique and skill
    Go to find more ways to kill

History, and days gone by
    Saw war on water, in the sky
    Tribal war, religious strife
    And warring was a way of life

Watchers from above the moon
    See our destiny, as doom
    Man's ways will never mend
    Till Armageddon - the world's end

If one could have but just one wish
    That single wish should be
    That everyone, from every race
    Be clothed, and fed, and free.

Roy Glanville (Andover)

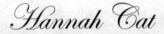

Hannah Cat

Tail outstretched as she races down the path.
Miaowing and eyes bright as I pick her up.
Hello Hannah Cat!

Hannah Cat
Purring friend with flicking tail.
Seer and knower of all things -
Forgive me for seeing and knowing nothing at all.

Hannah Cat
Thank you for your love
Thank you for your loyalty
Thank you for the fun and games.
I miss you Hannah Cat.

Angela Potter (Woking)

To Understand

She sat and watched on Mother's Day
As children brought their gifts
Mothers waiting patiently
Greeted with a kiss.

No children had been born to her
No child on Mother's Day
To bring her gifts of love
So she turns away

No joy for her of baby love
She has not pain of loss
Aware of constant prayers denied
And the bitter cross.

Sadness lasts until she hears
Of a baby born to love
Yet dies within its mother's arms
Why, oh God above?

Through faith in God she can accept
E'en though there still remains
Deep regrets and sadness
Of no child of her own.

God knows best the path we take
In fulfilment of His Plan
He blesses all the gifts we share
We will one day understand.

Elva Knott (Ferndown)

Inner Strength

If the morning sun is burning,
I will be your ocean breeze.
Should the bitter north wind blow,
Then I won't let you freeze.

When love takes your breath away,
I'll keep your feet firmly on the ground,
And should that love turn sour,
I won't desert you, when you're down.

For I'll be there to pick you up
And give you the courage you need,
As I am your inner strength,
And it's in you that I believe.

Diane Beamish (Cheltenham)

Prayer Of The Dying

No more letters
No more rhyme
No more study
There isn't time.

No more lusting
No more crime
No more hating
There isn't time.

No more stealing
No more lies
No more envy
There isn't time.

No more fighting
No more fame
No more seeking
For exalted names.

No more weeping
No more cares
No more laughter
No more years.

No more self-seeking
No more self
Only time to plead -
'Lord, have mercy . . . upon . . . me . . . a sinner.'

Sheila Seecharan (London)

Poetry

Poetry is a frame of mind,
Sometimes witty, sometimes blind,
Some written by the pens of rage,
A different mood on every page.

Some written by the pens of grief,
To share it is a great relief.
Some written by the pens of hate,
A reader's guide to someone's fate!

So, all you budding poets out there,
You have no time to stand and stare.
Sit down, relax, take pen in hand,
Someone out here will understand!

John Bilsland (Welwyn Garden City)

The Wedding

A man and a woman side by side
He is my son and she is his bride.
Standing together, acting as one,
She is his future but he is my son.

Life spreads before them
With its pleasures and pain.
The joy that life holds
Again and again.

They've spoken their vows
And given their love.
A journey has started
Blessed from above.

Look at the woman
Look at the bride
The glow in her eyes
For the man at her side.

Look at the man
Her husband and joy.
He is her partner
But still he's my boy.

A man and a woman side by side
He is her husband and she his bride.
They're standing together to face life as one
Look after him Lisa, for he is my son.

Ruth Clarke (Shoreham-by-Sea)

Amazon

Muddy waters, winding rivers,
Birds of every kind of hue,
Vast expanses, open country,
Its' there to see it's just for you.

Animals yes, in their masses -
Hunting food and climbing trees,
Almost silence - trees are moving,
Gently falling nuts and leaves.

This is what they call a forest,
Strange and magic to our eyes,
Damp and humid - insects biting,
This is called a paradise.

Betty Moir (Fareham)

Lonely Eyes

Staring blankly at the window,
the rain it's pouring down,
no familiar faces smiling,
not a heartbeat, not a sound.

Loneliness but a wonder,
salty tears upon my face,
please Mummy, come and save me,
I am all alone in this empty place.

Why does nobody love me?
Why do they not care?
What have I done wrong?
Through dirty windows I stand and stare.

Slowly I fall asleep,
My tummy is aching and bare,
my lonely eyes are aching,
as I hear no silent prayers.

Angels up above me,
stretch out their golden wing,
into the realms of Heaven,
this little soul to you we bring.

Take care of this little child,
for life, it's so unfair,
as God wipes her cherished tears,
no more lonely eyes to stare.

Patrick Mullen (Plymouth)

Memories

Take me back to the green hills of Devon,
Let me walk by the blue azure sea.
Take me back to that dear humble cottage,
And loving arms waiting for me.

Let me walk once again in the wild wood,
Hear the birds sing, so happy and free.
I will think of my brothers and sisters,
Sweet promises they made to me.

Oh Mother, dear Mother forgive me,
But I thought that I could be free,
I will walk once again, down that old country lane,
To my mother's arms, waiting for me.

Benita Tucker (Totnes)

Above The World

From the silent sky above,
I look down on this land I love,
Over mountains, over streams,
Over trees and fields so green.

Like a bird up in the sky,
I drift above the world so high,
Floating like a weightless sphere,
As just a gentle breeze I hear.

Over flowers that seem to dance,
When first your eye does catch a glance,
Over rivers that flow so free,
As they make their journey to the sea.

Over houses way below,
Like little nests from hillsides grow,
With the roofs of thatch so neatly done,
Just the place to raise your young.

But now I'm at my journey's end,
As I slowly start to descend,
For I've floated long and floated high,
Way up to the bright blue sky.

So now I'm back upon this land,
But my memories are so grand,
Of all the sights that I have seen,
From a place above that's so serene.

Ernest Ian Kerr Hiddleston (Poole)

Package Deal

Pinioned by the burning eye,
Grouped in isolation lie
Bodies offered, oil coated,
Mindless thoughtless, the devoted.

Watchers of the time, now timeless
Sixty minute hours, endless.
Sounds of surf and voices blurring
With the wave-worn pebbles churning.

Numbed are all the nerves' defences,
Blocked, the doorways of the senses
Prostrate to the breakers' dogma
Read ten pages then turn over.

Robert King (Southampton)

To The Forward Press

Twenty years may seem a long time
To publish poems which scan and rhyme,
But the need for them is always there
To relieve tension, stress and all care.

Not too demanding, but with some thought,
Words can soothe us when we're fraught,
With a gentle nudge towards hope and a smile,
Away from things superficial and puerile.

In these days of violence and greed,
Poems can help to plant a seed
Of awareness, hope, joy and beauty
Guiding us from despair and futility.

Poems may revive moments of pleasure,
Or remind us of memories that we treasure
When nature and friends continue to restore
Our faith in the future and much, much more.

Emotions shared, whether happy or sad,
Can switch a mood from sombre to glad.
Memories return to enrich our days
In many different and enlightening ways.

So all thanks to those of the Forward Press
Who have inspired us to moments of happiness.
When writing down our thoughts as they come,
Or reading those of others, for solace or fun.

Sheila Dodwell (Taunton)

Life's Worthwhile

Now you see the spring flowers growing,
All those colours of the rainbow showing.
Doesn't it make your life worth living?
The frost and cold winds gone, life's more forgiving.

So shake off those winter blues and begin to smile
Instead of running half a mile, try and do a mile.
Get the aches out of your body, just have a try,
It won't hurt you none, you'll say 'Oh no' but why?

When you see the sunbeams through your windows shine,
There's something good and there's yours and mine.
So do the best you can out of this life and smile
Then you'll see what I mean, life is very much worthwhile.

John Shanahan (Hitchin)

Song Of The Bluebells

Hush, tread softly through my woodland
Let no footfall sound be heard
Feel the peace that's here created
Disturb it not with human word.

Lightly move among the bluebells
Listen, you will hear them ring
A myriad million blue heads nodding
Tranquillity for the soul they sing

Admire their colour tinged with purple
As the evening shade draws on.
Each is wistful, gently shaking
Creation's youth is in their throng

Look not towards the treetops mighty
Of oaks mature that hide the cloud
Where squawking birds disturb the stillness
Or branches make invasive sound

Transparent wings divide these kingdoms
All unseen by human eye
And as they quiver so the bluebells
Wave their heads then you and I

Trusting in God-given senses
Await the joy the flowers bring
In the aura of the woodland
To hear a million bluebells ring.

W R Chapman (Cirencester)

Fancier (1930s)

I wonder if I'll ever get it straight
Mother's face would say it all, and tears.
I grieve in terms of money and of birds:
a frugal living borne for silver plate.

Upon his shoulders I sat and saw it all:
the sawdust and the seed, the damp, the dust.
The pain of broken eggs. The mice. The joy
of commendation and the winner's call.

Of course I loved him, as I always will
-as one of five it all seems very clear
and I'll remember long my mother's view
as I look to distant birds on wooded hill.

Reg Billett (Dunstable)

My Pet Dog Toby

The doorbell rings, his ears prick up,
If I did this, I would be considered a nut.
He laughs at me and has an intelligent look,
I know he understands and reads me like a book.

If I take his lead he turns and barks,
And will not give up his clever larks.
He is loved and cuddled, squeezed and stroked,
I know he loves it, his eyes tell me so.

When I am stressed he sits on my lap,
A few loving kisses and we take a nap.
I awake refreshed and he is still curled up,
Thinks I am a fool for getting up.

He pretends he is dreaming and fast asleep,
But I know he hears because he gives me a peep.
Do not disturb me he seems to say,
I wish to stay here for the rest of the day.

There is no need to talk, the silence is bliss,
I love him all the more because of this.
He cannot answer back or say harsh words,
It is such a comfort just like the birds.

Tenderness, kindness, warmth and care,
That is all he asks so I make sure I am there.
Love him always, the rewards are great,
He will stay forever and be your best mate.

Jo Taylor (Hayle)

Lady Of The Auburn Hair

Sweet lady of the auburn hair
steadfast in the street she'd stare.
If she moves I know not where,
come rain or shine she's always there.

Brown coloured robes that do not tear,
that's why the lady's not elsewhere.
She just can't move it isn't fair,
For bronze she's made and cannot wear.

And eyes, that with a look ensnare.
You break all hearts, and can't repair,
a single one, but don't despair,
sweet lady of the auburn hair.

Brian Richard Bates (Stamford Hill)

Just A Little Boy

I'm just a little boy
I think I'm six or seven.
I'm hungry and I'm lonely
My mummy's gone to Heaven.

The soldiers took my daddy
And killed my little brother.
There's fighting in the street now
So I must run for cover.

The day they killed my mummy
I cried and cried and cried
And then I looked around me
For somewhere I could hide.

I'm nobody's little boy now,
I think I'm six or seven,
So hungry and so lonely,
Won't someone care for me?

There's different soldiers here now,
They're kinder but they're tough.
The bad men all have run away
I think they've had enough.

I'm hungry and I'm lonely,
Won't someone care for me?
I won't be any trouble,
Just hug me and feed me.

Louis Robert Early (Reading)

Never Forget My Name

I looked at my life one day
and the years ahead of me,
I wondered how I could make my mark
on the pages of history.

I am not afraid of death's hard grip,
or what man do to me,
but I want to be remembered in years to come
so I do it through poetry.

It is no vanity that drives me thus,
nor to search for monetary gain,
I do it merely that nobody
will ever forget my name.

Phoebe Brooks (London)

523

Folly-Behind Closed doors

What shall we do with all this waste,
We've sorted it in crazy haste,
We'll let the fishes have a taste,
We'll send it out to sea . . .

From the IMF we want cash
One hundred billion is very rash,
Just wait and see the markets crash -
We'll send the problem out to sea . . .

Our leaders go to a capitalist summit
Causing global care to plummet,
The environment - oh, we can dump it
And send it out to sea . . .

What shall we do with this pollution?
Is there really no solution?
We'll chuck it out with our ablutions -
And sent it out to sea . . .

We're all caught up with answers rash
Nature's trapped in a pincer crush,
In the environment there's a deathly hush -
We'll send the problem out to sea . . .

Destruction here is going apace:
The state of the planet is a disgrace -
And all because of the human race -
I fear, we're going out to sea . . .

Deirdre Hill (Bournemouth)

People

People can be funny
People can be strange
When it's very sunny
They're out on the golfing range.

There's people on the beach
Packed lunches and a peach
There's people in the sea
Only come out for their tea.

There's people having fun
In this there is no pun
'Cos people should enjoy their life
Being out and about in the sun.

Theresa Hartley-Mace (Mawgan Porth)

Thoughts Of Past And Present

When I was *small*, I had a dream,
I smiled a lot, or so it seem.
I'd tell a tale, and make it rhyme,
People said I wasted time.

What right had they, to interfere?
What I told them, I made real clear.
Whether family, or friend,
Most thought, my work was round the bend.

I soldiered on, and years did pass,
Some people called me, a silly arse.
I did not care what others thought,
They envied me, as others bought.

And so it went, from good to better,
Was even praised, in an anonymous letter.
I've always written, just for fun,
To show my work, of what I've done.

My written words, have come to much,
Though many think they are double-Dutch.
With close on ninety, under my belt,
I can tell you just, how I have felt.

Though my poetry is read by many,
Seldom have I made more than a penny.
Now I'm *tall,* and in my prime,
Unlike many, I can boast they're mine.

Les J Croft (Penzance)

The Gardner

The dew was on the roses,
The flowers a golden flame,
His thoughts went back to his boyhood days,
And his lovely Emma Jane.

He saw again her smiling face,
So happy and serene,
He shook his head and gave a sigh,
And thought what might have been.

His tired old eyes were dimmed with tears,
His faltering feet were slow,
'Twas just a dream of his dark-eyed queen,
the girl he used to know.

Rosaleen Caffrey (Luton)

Alone And Empty

Do you feel the need to cry?
When you're feeling low
Do you hold your head up high?
When your tears do flow

Do you ever feel alone?
When life gets you down
Do you find it hard to smile?
When all you do is frown

When the pain within your heart
Gets all too much to bear
Do you feel the emptiness?
Makes you have no care

Don't feel down and lonely
Don't feel sad inside
Look way up ahead now
And don't feel you must hide

There is light down that tunnel
But it seems too far ahead
Just hold on tight and be patient
There is no need to fret

All you need is loving
That's all you'll ever need
Just find someone who cares for you
Who is a friend indeed.

Gary Long (Feltham)

Ice Fields Thawed

When New Year rains have drowned the Xmas wreaths,
And wild winds lash the cottages of stone;
When bright-eyed dogs are ready for the run,
And glasses steam, and cheekbones sting and glow;

When winter birds are wrapped in feathered cloaks,
And log fires hiss and crackle in the hearth;
When leaving our remains of hearty brunch
To seek out moorland hedge and puddled path;

Then, squelching through the mud-fields we shall go;
Each step a slurping splash in muddied earth;
And, thankful for our sturdy boots and sticks,
We stumble not, but, balanced, weigh our worth.

Jane Skellett (Bournemouth)

Congratulations To You!

I would like to celebrate with you.
Twenty years, have sped right through.
Poems you say old, or new.
Here's health to you and you and you.

That covers all the poets true
Who in the past supported new.
The selection of ideas, sent by you,
For us poets to pick, choices grew.

June is my name, smiling through.
The poems sent by you and you and you.
Amusing and straight, tearful and blue
What a joy, to behold. All colours and hue.

I have laughed and have cried, tears on cue,
When prompted to write words, so due.
To capture the moment, on papers few,
Words that I feel, right on issue.

Words so focused, words so true,
In my mind, for all to view,
New items and features, from my pew.
To share for all, the world and you.

Sadness, hatefulness, covers grew,
With words to express, the day long through.
World's problems you can read, anew,
In *Forward Press* the really good brew.

June Chorlton (Dunstable)

Colour: raison d'être

Exploding passion like an ecstasy of fireworks
with wild reds, shimmering silvers and the taste of orange,
dark mysterious blues wrapping around like a see-through quilt,
purple blazing its king rich glory to satisfy your soul

Or gentle pinks contrasting with crimson, for the bride maybe;
a symbol of innocence about to take the final leap
from the soft rainbows of cornflowers, buttercups and daisies
into the heated world where hot colour swirls into one's mind

Some primrose veiled sunlight seeping through the morning mist
reflecting sensuous images of swishing silk,
creating an expectancy that life must wake up
to glory in a coloured world that is Art itself.

Corin Ruth Jasmine Dienes (East Grinstead)

They Never Fail

Sometimes just fleeting moments
Rays of hope may shine
Someone gives brief glimpse
To potential sublime.

But thru' the looking glass they fall
To lay amongst the shards
All their dreams and aspirations
A fallen house of cards

Lying and deceiving themselves
A long-practised art
Flaws and weaknesses in gene lines
Moving further and further apart.

Greedy blind leading greedy blind
To be the richest dead
They refute the story's end
Denying every lesson read

Beware - unborn generations
May survey an empty field
The planet bled dry
Not one selfish drop spilled

So nature's ultimate folly
Rushes headlong to a broken rail
Yet ironically in every misguided thought
They never fail.

John Marshall (London)

A Friend

She's there when you need a helping hand
When you feel you are sinking in the sand
When things just get too hard to do
She is always there for you.

You know she's there if you need to call
When you feel that you are going to fall
She always says what you need to hear
Taking away some of the fear.

She will try her best to make you smile
Tell you to go that extra mile
I know on her I can depend
My very, very, special friend.

Annette Redwood (Torquay)

The Selection Process

When two bodies merge in copulation and the seed is free to flow,
Then starts the process of procreation, as the babe begins to grow.
Genes and chromosomes endowed, from each partner taking part,
The process of selection, triggers the race to start.

The unsuspecting child, is thrust into its twilight world,
Protesting cries and gasps for breath, as into life it's hurled.
As vision clears and memories dim the comfort of the womb,
The selection process, now dictates the pattern of life to come.

Is it gathered into the bosom of a family, waiting with love
Or regarded with resentment as another mouth to feed?
Is it into freedom born with no political walls
Or is dark suppression of spirit the future that appals?

Has the process of selection chosen this child to live in grace
Or live in loath oppression one of the downtrodden race?
Is he born with a silver spoon, one of the chosen few
Who tread the path of glory, fame and fortune to pursue?

Will the most difficult selection he ever has to make
Be from the pile of sweet confection set upon the plate?
For some, selection process has condemned to starve and toil
For them life's great achievement to fill the begging bowl.

Why does his life become a battle daily striving to exist?
For him selection process decreed the bottom of the list.
In trying to unravel the mysteries of life, of happiness or dread
Do we thank God for our existence or Buddha or Mohammad.

Dena Howarth (Edwina) (Totton)

Lingering Smiles

Have you seen my mother?
Did you notice her there?
Longest of lives in her pale green eyes
Murmured sun in her auburn hair.

Have you seen my mother?
Did you sense her caring way?
Did you see a tranquil smile?
Her sigh at the eve of the day?

Did you ever see my mother?
She slipped away a while ago
She had her whisper of giving
Now relaxed in her copper glow.

Diane Miller (Bristol)

The Leaf

It's early spring the trees are beginning to wake,
One little bud is starting to break.
A leaf shows its little green head,
He felt warm although he had popped out of his bed.

He grew stronger, and his brothers and sisters came out too,
They all began to rustle as the wind blew.
Very soon on his stem a little flower blossomed out,
He felt protective and hugged her round and about.

But the blossom did not last long,
The wind blew it away, it seemed so wrong.
Very soon under the leaf grew a small green ball,
The little leaf hoped it would not fall.

The ball grew and started to turn red,
Turned into a juicy apple instead . . .
Alas Man came and picked the apple away from the leaf,
He was upset and shattered with grief.

Soon the leaf became sad then mellow
And turned from green into yellow.
In time he changed to brown,
The wind blew and he came tumbling down . . .

The trees are bare this time of year,
But in the spring new buds will appear.
Then they will fruit again
The little leaf's life was not in vain.

Olive Young (Ware)

Praying

A prayer at church or at home
It does not matter where you pray
You can pray with others or on your own
A prayer is really having your say

People have different ways of praying
They may just sit for awhile and meditate
I just feel good about life, is my saying
Life is too short so why wait?

We do not owe anything at all
So why do we feel that we have to do this?
That is because people tall and small
Feel at one and at total bliss.

Marina Reeves (Sutton)

The Bounty Hunters

Between a critic and a lost soul
Between a dancer and a social nonentity
Between black and white the shades of grey mutate
Run suddenly, lift the fear, fleece the landlord, fly.

Between a WW2 plane and Vaughan Williams
Between why the hell and ne'er do well
Between the bank and a hard place every day
Do a bunk, become a skunk, shrink to proportionate heaven.

Between how's your father's father's father
Between now and then or twice a week
Between come on in and door in face
Bowl a fast ball, return a serve, shrug nonchalantly, how they hate it.

Between *really* meaning it and job well done
Between eyeball to eyeball and erotic charm
Between where there's a will and a year in bed
Manage an economy for six months, then leave it in ruins.

Between mending a fence and blowing a gasket
Between Lord of the Rings and Hedwig's Angry Inch
Between up and down and down and out
Lacerate your own face and let it bleed.

Between a likeable lurcher and a mad Jack Russell
Between a contract killer and a licence to kill
Between bittersweet and simply bitter
Sack the cast, breathe your last, it's lush on the other side.

Steve Spence (Plymouth)

The Dolphin

A mammal of beauty and splendid design
Once used in the war to carry a mine
Their aquatic dexterity and intellectual renown
We use for our pleasure as a theme park clown.

When the show is over we walk away
They circle round destined to stay.
We research their behaviour, decipher their sounds,
Man's quest for knowledge has no bounds.

As for the dolphin who gives birth from the womb
It knows the difference between freedom and a water tank tomb.
So let them wander, let them roam,
Be at peace in the sea, for that's their home.

Howard Knipe (Slough)

531

I Am A Hampshire Hog

I am a Hampshire Hog
Southampton born and bred
I have tales I'd like to tell you
Stored up inside my head.

The Mayflower left from Hampshire
All those years ago
With shining eyes and pounding hearts
Went folks to lives unknown.

'The Gateway to England,'
Southampton once was named
The Great, the Good and infamous
Between its portals came.

I am a Hampshire Hog
Great liners I have seen
Side by side within our docks,
And named by kings and queens.

Those days alas have passed
Our dockland is no more
Proud craftsmen bow their heads
Their skills are now folklore.

But to all you little hoglets
Coming on apace,
Remember what I say . . .
'Hampshire is a special place.'

Vivian Hayward (Southampton)

A Sunbather's Message

It causes cancer, so they say,
To lie beneath the sun all day.
And to feel its warmth is a delight,
Although don't burn, you will look a sight.

It's best to lay just for a while,
And then by eve you can still smile,
As it's a painful lesson to learn
If you stay too long, you'll surely burn.

So enjoy the sun, but also the shade,
For our skin is carefully made,
It has to last our whole lives through,
Don't overdo is my message to you.

Marianne Nuttall (Portland)

Happy Childhood Memories

I remember when we all were young,
gath'ring chestnuts near The Copper Horse,
and our cat Ginger and our puppy Jet
would see they roasted by the fire, of course!

> We would often bring home from the forest
> pussy-willow twigs and blackberries.
> We loved cheese straws, cough drops, ice cream sundaes,
> fish and chips, and drinks that fizz.

I remember when the days were long
and on our back lawn, Tiger City rose.
Then we dressed up in mother's cast out curtains.
Flour and water made the meal we chose.

> We loved dodg'em cars and roll-a-penny.
> Need I say we loved Monopoly?
> But I made myself a model theatre
> and that meant the most to me.

I remember when I used to sing
What I thought of as my favourite song:
'Jerusalem' until our next-door neighbours
joined in, making it a sing-along.

> I was merely try'ng to entertain them.
> I was like a little chirping bird,
> chirping, chirping . . . what could be the problem?
> They too, needed to be heard!

Arthur V. Coyne (Windsor)

The Falcon

On a hot summer's day I looked in the sky
When something amazing caught my eye
It wasn't the sun that was glaring at me
But something so fast it was difficult to see

I watched it soar above my house
Maybe it wanted to eat my mouse?
I looked a little closer so I could seek
What sort of creature owned this beak

Its eyes of amber searched around
And saw me standing on the ground
Then the falcon turned and flew
To find its nest or even you.

Nathan Evans (Tadley)

Animals

Animals are wonderful
Animals are great
Animals depend on us
To oversee their fate

Animals are caring
Animals create
Animals need concern
Beyond the farmers' gate

Animals are sensitive
Animals are kind
Animals are trusting
Animals aren't blind

Animals have voices
Animals surprise
Eyes, ears, noses, mouths and tongues
Animals are wise

Animals communicate
Animals confess
Animals cajole us
Animals impress

Animals need kindness
Animals express
'Release us from cruel farming,
Laboratories and chefs'

Colin Davies (Bristol)

Untitled

She stares from the painting with battered eyes,
Wet lashes suggest perpetual crying.
Most of her energy dissipated,
Her dear loved ones, her family, all gone.

It is this knowledge, which is so painful,
Looking back at her, feel my soul scream out.
Around her a lonely cell once called home,
It's obvious this is a home no more.

In the foreground lies a wooden casket,
That she touches in trance-state with gnarled hands.
Her directness is very unsettling,
She pleads for help but none can help her now.

Susan Mullinger (Torquay)

The Pleasures Of Non-Driving

My driving days are over,
not quite so dramatic as it may sound,
I have found two perfectly good legs,
able to ferry me around.

But, just like a car, they object to the cold,
and find it difficult to start,
after a few kind words then off they go,
having taken them to heart.

I am seeing so much on my walks,
things I have never noticed before,
people's homes and their gardens, green lawns,
colourful flowers, bushes with berries galore.

The compensations are many,
people passing the time of day,
giving one a feeling of being in the real world,
as I plod along my way.

The bus numbers I still find confusing
and the times are anyone's guess,
the timetable is well thumbed now,
but I am showing signs of stress.

'Give it time,' my friends say to me,
having just missed a bus to town.
'All is not lost, not the end of the world,
Don't let it get you down.'

Margarita Reeve (Bournemouth)

Procreation

The drive to fertilise the egg
To procreate mankind
May lie between the lovers' legs
But largely in the mind.

You turn me on, you turn me off,
Foreplay is a good start.
We're not just animals you know.
(The headache plays its part.)

And when it works such bliss we feel;
The climax of one's life.
And when it's not, a bore, unreal,
Begins domestic strife.

John McLachlan McCall (Haywards Heath)

The Strange Old Man

Whilst walking down a country lane,
I saw a strange old man,
He passed with me, the time of day,
With him I did the same.

A wonderful day for dreams, he said,
And have them all come true,
If only that could be, I smiled,
Then; I'd wish my life anew.

Oh! Any dream is possible,
Hope can be fulfilled,
Most wishes can be granted,
Our fate is not always sealed.

I turned to look at the strange old man,
Has this been true for you?
Oh! Yes my dear, - this very day,
And to you it's mostly due.

I wished today for skies of blue,
The sun to warm my bones,
A pleasant smile, from a pretty face,
A convivial chat for two.

I turned around, to say goodbye,
But the strange old man had gone,
And all I could see, beside a tree,
Was a scarecrow, bedraggled and worn.

Frances Bacon (Waltham Cross)

Dead Wood

I stand around about twenty foot tall,
I am not human, and I'm not a wall.
I am my best in summer, I have such flair,
But in winter I'm so very bare.

I am a home for many things from insects to pest,
I am a home for many birds where they can come and nest.
You're more than likely to guess who I could be?
But you're wrong, I am no longer that beautiful tree.

I could be dead or alive, I am not that sure,
I could be a part of your furniture;
I could be a shelf or that dining room chair,
So please look after me and polish me with care.

Brenda Wedge (Portsmouth)

Motorway Magic

Shining metal, blues, reds, greens,
Super speeding, man-made machines;
Interspersed by white van and truck,
Caravans slower on the inside track,
Leather clad bikers - space invaders look,
Peering through their visors - beings from a book.
Fuel guzzling monsters, spewing out their fumes,
Poisoning the air and the wayside blooms.
White and orange cones, the drivers despair,
Slowing down the traffic when they suddenly appear.
Car cocooned people glance outside,
Surprised by the beauty their eyes denied.
Dazzling colours meet their gaze,
Scabious and vetch a purple haze.
Ox-eyed daisies, buttercups gold,
Stitchwort threading through foxgloves bold.
Ferns and grasses, waving leaves,
Dancing shapes in the summer breeze.
Glimpses of wildlife seen along the way,
Sparrow hawk hovering searching out its prey.
Healing sweetness from flowers and leaves,
Enriching and cleaning the very air we breathe.
Once again, as the traffic gathers speed,
The motorway monster starts to shake and heave.
The flower filled verges begin to slide,
Like a long green ribbon rushing by its side.

Sue Groom (Crawley)

Smudge

(Dedicated to Jack, another 'Smudgeon')

When first you went to print you used a rubber stamp -
The ink was sometimes smudgy -
The paper much too damp,
But now you've gone 'all modern',
Your words are quite distinct,
Your books, your papers, poems, are always out on time!
Your editor now wears a suit,
Not a printer's apron, and is it 'female' cult?
From office boy and manager en route,
So happy be the life of a company such as you.
You've made the way through candlelit time,
And let the smell of print stay forever -
Here's wishing you happy birthday 140 years young!

Catherine Mary Porter (Dawlish)

Beautiful Oak

Ye olde oak, was it you who spoke,
what a wondrous day, not to work but play,
the heavens are blue, the trees a beautiful autumnal hue,
the sun is warm, no fear of a storm,
so good to be alive, good fortune for you to have survived,
if only you could speak from your gnarled old wood
what tales you could tell, some bad, some good.
You have stood two hundred years or more
not too far from the grand palladian mansion's front door.
Crinolines you must have seen and breeches and long laced boots,
and now today men in their pin-striped suits.
A gentler life you did view when a very young oak,
picnics under your spreading branches,
sweethearts stealing secret glances,
gentry riding on their horses, coaches coming to and fro,
dinners, dances, lights aglow, a very different life long ago.
No families live in the old mansion anymore
there are rows of smart cars at its front door,
businessmen and women in their smart suits attending conferences,
oh what a bore.
People today who walk by will look at your branches reaching up to the sky and admire your
beauty as do I, and wonder what stories you
could tell as we walk our dogs and children play, a different world we have today.
We still love to sit under your branches, a peaceful place to sit and ponder and wonder what
will be yonder.
Beautiful oak may you long survive, to have people look up at you and feel glad to be alive.

Patricia Osborne (Chertsey)

Pretty E

The city's seductive, the perfect scene
With its clubs and its bars
And dancing and drinking 'til sun-up.

Looking overdressed in a barely there shirt
You blow a kiss to the watchers.
All gathered round like bees to honey
Or dogs to a bone!
And it seems so lonely in the middle of a crowd
So find something to numb the feeling.
Go so far up you can't come down.
Watch lights flash and rooms spin.
Breath stops spilling from ice-cold red lips.

Did you know from up here, the city's not so pretty?
When you look down you can see the pills.

Dani Birks (Andover)

My Garden

The joy of having my garden
Where the trees and flowers grow
Where the birds and animals visit
The first to fly in, is the robin
Who comes quite close for a chat
While I sit in fear of any prowling cats
Next is the squirrel busy burying the nuts
While the magpies wait patiently to steal
There on a branch above sit the collared doves
They nest in the trees
Wake us with their early morning call
Along comes wood pigeon 'Bertie'
Finds the bird bath and has a drink
Looking very happy as he struts about
When it rains out come the snails
From their refuge under stones and pails
The different colours of their shells delight me
Of course their eating habits delight me less
Many people consider them pests
They are still visitors in my garden
Where the blackbird and thrush find them a treat to eat
A gentle breeze sways the trees
Tranquillity all around
All these wonderful joys giving so much pleasure
Such memories which I will always treasure
In my garden where the trees and flowers grow.

Patricia Farbrother (Uxbridge)

Dog Show

Swig back the coffee, scrape back the chair, come Fifi my Boo, let's go.
I've told you, my dear, that today is the day
When we both have a date in our fullest array.
We are powdered and primped and my hair and your fur are as white as the innocent snow.

Fifi, my love, my sweet doggy dove, you'll vanquish the mightiest foe.
Surely we'll win but I grant that there may
Be a short-sighted judge who in some silly way
Will be bribed by our rivals, take leave of her senses, and land us the sneakiest blow.

O, Fifi my Boo, I knew that you'd do it, you certainly made your mark.
What you did, I must say, is a very strong trait
That was kept hitherto in the dark.
The cup that you won is exceedingly rare
It can join all the rest on the mantelpiece there,
The inscription informs all the world at a glance that your *bite* is worse than your *bark*.

Margaret Alderson (Stevenage)

Last Chance For Our Planet

The Earth is slowly dying
We must stop it before it's too late
The human race with its head in the sand
Every day they destroy the land
Pollution in the air, pollution in the sea
What sort of future is there to be?
Stop and think before our planet is destroyed forever
Let us try and clean it up together
Stop your fighting, put down your guns and knives
Solve our Earth, protect human lives
If we don't do it now there will be more decay
We only live from day to day
We will leave no future for our daughters and sons
So people on Earth put down your guns
Get together, think peace not war
Clean up your act, you have done it before
This beautiful world was created for Man
While we are alive let us do what we can
Let us leave a future so our children can survive
Don't kill the planet, keep it alive
Do not waste what precious life we have
Or the Earth will become a grave
People of the world are now joining together
We realise we cannot go on forever
If we leave this Earth a better place
There will be hope for the human race

Marion Stevens (Torquay)

Summer Sin

How I yearn for yesterday's long hot summer,
when I plucked you from your sun drenched resting place.
In my possession, I clutched you
to my heaving breast, until
we could be together in some secret arbour.

Alone, I was aroused by such sweet fragrance.
Flushed cheeks brushed against your velvet smooth skin,
Tongue-moistened lips parted, as if in erotic kiss,
teeth sinking slowly into soft inviting flesh.

I groaned with sensuous pleasure as our juices rose.
Trickles ran free down an un-sleeved arm,
persistent amber rivulets intoxicated,
ultimate joy from stolen fruit,
a succulent peach harvested without permission.

Elaine Barwick (Blagdon)

The Day The Earth Moved

When the newsflash came in, we were sat at the table
all stunned into silence, the family unable
to believe what was happening, life seemed so unfair
we watched the Tsunami break hearts everywhere.
It raced through the beaches with no hesitation
leaving behind complete devastation
The sun beds where holiday makers once lounged
were battered and broken and strewn all around
If lucky, their occupants had managed to flee
but for most they were swallowed up into the sea.
Their lives had been stolen by an evil so rotten
and although they are gone, they will not be forgotten.
They didn't deserve to die as they did
the mothers, the fathers, grandparents and kids
Whole families wiped out in the blink of an eye
surely they didn't *all* need to die
This shouldn't have happened, now we're counting the cost
of the number of innocent lives that we've lost
So *how* did it happen? Someone should have known
with all of the data and technology we own
We were caught out by nature in a cruel callous way
sending such peril to us *Boxing Day!*
The offices were empty, the desks were unmanned
No one could have guessed what nature had planned.
A loss too great to take in, our lives changed forever
but we *can* make a difference - if we all pull together.

Wendy Orlando (Burgess Hill)

The Hands Of God!

The Hands of God are filled with prayers, and thoughts
and sayings, too -
Whenever someone's cared for me, God brought these
softly through;
So I did not feel hopeless, or alone, afraid and lost,
For my dear Saviour - loving God, achieved it through His Cross.

The funeral day should've been for me, filled with sorrow
as peace did flee,
But because the love was tangible, I ate and drank Him edible,
and He surely nourished me!

I treasured friends who'd come afar, and many near at hand,
And most of all, we stood as one, to say that Roy was 'grand'.
So God in Heaven has His son - recently arrived,
And now I'll do my best in life, with His help, to survive!

Gill Mainwaring (Barnstaple)

Trip To Shanklin

We wait at the station till 'here comes the train'.
We're going to Shanklin and then back again.
From Ryde we move slowly, then hear 'tickets please'.
The guard checks our tickets: we sit back at ease.
Now clickety-clacking the train gathers pace
Then whoosh through the tunnel. Hey is this a race?
Too noisy for gossip we gaze at the views
While other trav'lers sit reading the news.
Gathering speed our train hurtles along,
Clickety-clacking it sounds like a song.
Landscapes flash by - we see woodland and sheep
While there in the corner a baby's asleep.
A brief stop at Brading - a mere bagatelle
And now the train moves like a bat out of hell.
Sandown is busy - it looks more alive,
The train moves more slowly but soon we arrive
At a very small halt where the driver will brake
For passengers leaving or boarding at Lake.
Dum-diddy-dum-dum the train's pace is slowing
Next stop is Shanklin where most folk are going.
Here at the station they're boarding the train.
Others are leaving but we will remain.
The platform is active and now we can see
Two old ladies chatting and drinking their tea.
A few minutes rest, then the driver - with pride
Gets the 'off' from the guard - then he sets off for Ryde.

Frances Heckler (Ryde)

Learning To

Stand at the top of the slope -
A clump of trees perhaps on your right -
Release the reflex to hold back
Look down into blankness of white.

Forget how you've felt such a fool
When only the smallest incline
Could topple you into the cold -
Shrug off that old habit of mind.

Pause at the summit and breathe -
Feeling this moment alive -
Remember the swish of the skis
As you went with the slip and slide -
Just lean into it, let yourself go
Concentrated, clear into impulse and flow.

Neil Bowen (Bristol)

What God Hears

The prayer of the lonely
Which pierces the clouds,
The cry of dereliction
Which electrifies the crowds;
The song in the shadow
Which holds hope still,
The weeping of the beaten
Who have had their fill;
The anger of the abused
Which is long overdue,
The strangled heart
Of those who can't make do;
The pain of the robbed
Who feel diminished,
The power of the weak
Who feel they are finished;
The silence of the lamb
Who stands condemned,
And the roar of the lion
Whose endless life transcends,
Overcomes and undoes
The twisted darkness of
Our unhealed wounds
So that he can tell us
We are healed and held
And loved to the very end.

Russ Parker (Bordon)

Letter To My Granddaughter

I know that you are grown up now,
Too old to come and stay,
But if you sometime change your mind,
You'll be welcome any day.

I feel quite sad really,
But know your time has come,
To 'fall in love' with 'fit boys',
And to leave them one by one.

Thank you for the happy times,
I hope you'll feel the same,
For your controllable laughter,
That makes you 'a real cool dame'.

L E S Lucas (Newquay)

Breathe On Brothers And Sisters

We are saddened, we are saddened
By the volume of deaths and suffering
On our young boys as well as girls
We are tired! We are tired of this brutality.
We are eager! We are eager to help our people
Whoever and wherever they are.
    We are anxious! We are anxious!
'So help us Lord and Saviour'.
    Knives and guns have become the accessory.
We feel the pain, we suffer the loss
We are your brothers and sisters
So why are you depriving us of our loved ones?
Can you hear us? Can you see us?
We can see you, for we love you;
So come on! For we can be friends,
    Forget what society has done to you
We are in peril, if we are in the wrong place at the wrong time.
Where are our leaders gone?
The good ones, the chosen ones,
The ones to direct us as we watch in hope.
    Far! Far away our eyes are seeing,
That our morals will return
For us to breathe deep and free,
As it was meant to be
Then we will echo this beautiful word
      Amen and amen, so breathe on.

Dalsie Mullings-Powell (London)

April The 9th

Today it is my birthday,
I don't feel that old,
You may guess my age,
Don't ask, as you will not be told.

I'm getting on a bit,
Maybe getting slow,
I'm not saying how old I am,
I want no one to know.

If I said how old I am,
I'm sure you would not believe,
But, I'm the same age as my tongue,
Years older than my teeth.

J B Northeast (Warminster)

The Divine Healer

Wriggling in agony, and slumped on a hospital bed,
Inwardly berating God for His blatant neglect,
Swooned I, and to all around me, I seemed apparently dead,
But was 'compos mentis' fancying that to Heaven I had fled:
Transcendently, floated I to the Land of the Bible,
and met with the Son of God, face to face, in a tremble.
He beckoned me to follow Him, my misconcepts to quell -
First, to the mountain where a leper begged to be made well,
Jesus touched him, and his leprosy was cleaned like a spell:
In Capernaum, a Centurion pleaded for his sick servant,
Jesus found *faith,* and healed him without going in person:
When Jesus found Peter's mother-in-law sick with fever,
He merely touched her hand, lifted her, and her fever left her:
In Nazareth, a paralytic was lowered through the roof,
And healed, not by touch, but by behest - 'Your sins are forgiven you'.
Where the Synagogue Ruler Jairus' daughter lay dead,
'Talitha, cumi,' Jesus said, and she rose from her bed.
Where two blind men cried, 'Son of David have mercy on us!'
'According to your faith, let it be to you,' said Jesus.
Where a woman who had a flow of blood for twelve long years,
His garment's hem she touched and was made whole,
with gleeful tears.
Witnessed by me - ipso facto - these scenes were enacting,
Admonishing me for my lack of *faith, prayer* and *fasting,*
These 'sine qua non' attributes should precede Divine Healing,
And I awoke wiser in the knowledge of my own shortcoming!

Welch Jeyaraj Balasingam (Lewisham)

Flirsten

Greet them with a smile.
Defend yourself with your love.
Let their words fall upon your open ears.
Let them know you understand, for I will give you understanding.
Come away from them and digest what they have said stand fast
in your beliefs for my fire burns deep within you.
Slowly as you realize the power installed in you, by me your Ceator,
you will ignite fires in those you meet.
I made you and I gave you all you need, realise there is nothing
missing for you are whole, all you seek to do, you can do in my name.
They will come to comfort you, feeling that they do right, send them
to me and I will give them rest.

Eugene Dunkley (Hitchin)

Twenty Years Showcase

D evoid of any feeling, a deep and dark hole
    When you feel you have no purpose, you're lost within your soul

E xperiencing overwhelming sadness, crippling your heart
    When you feel you've lost control, it's ripping you apart

P ressure mounting within, thoughts being conjured inside
    When you feel you're all alone, you want a place to hide

R esenting what you've become, you want to feel at peace
    When you feel emotionally drained, will you ever find release

E xploriing within yourself, you trying to find some sense
    When you feel you can't go on, every thought is so intense

S earching for some reasoning, why you are in this terrible mess
    When you feel you are to blame, your life's taken over by stress

S immering in your gut, the emotions just want to erupt
    When you feel there's no salvation, your mind is just corrupt

I ntent on punishing yourself, you find dark ways to cope
    When you feel there's no way out, you've lost your faith
                              and hope

O bscene and angered voices, plagued your heart, soul and mind.
    When you feel you're going crazy, your old self you cannot find.

N ever finding help, no one will understand
    When you feel you've lost the battle, will someone reach out
                              their hand.

Daisy Wells (Romsey)

The Darkness, The Night, The Moon

It's 1am and very, very dark,
So why am I wandering around the park?
Can't sleep that's why, things on my mind,
I wish that I could leave behind
These thoughts and fears of Saturday night,
Remain in my head because of the sight,
Something that I saw and will never forget
Someone who saw me, that's why I regret,
That the moon was shining down on me,
This other person who I didn't want to see,
Would have been none the wiser to who I could be,
But the darkness, the night, that shining moon,
Could reveal my identity much too soon,
But wait, I realise it's all been a dream,
Or was it?

Anita Barnes (Bournemouth)

Torrington Commons (North Devon)

(In the summertime)

Torrington Commons are unique.
They have a natural beauty. They have mystique.
The sun's early rays, with golden sheen,
Come twinkling through the tall trees' screen.
Morning mist in the valleys deep,
Is nature's cover for things asleep.
The sun now warms the dawning day.
The early mists rise and melt away.
The buzzard poised on soaring wing,
Watches the movement of everything.
Secret tracks twist through meadow and hill,
Then down into the valleys quiet and still.
Home to the salmon, the river drifts by,
Reflecting the dappled summer sky.
A dragonfly hovers on rainbow wings,
While nesting in reeds, the warbler sings.
In the shielding bracken on the hill,
The deer takes cover, alert and still.
All around is the heady rich perfume
Of the wild rose, the gorse, the broom.
Yes, Torrington Commons are unique,
With their natural beauty and timeless mystique.
So when you explore this beautiful place,
Remember you're a guest in Nature's showcase.

Sue Davan (Torrington)

A Village

Have you ever wondered
How a village came to be?
Many long years ago
People wandered down a lane,
Landing from far distant shores
Saw beauty to acclaim.
Water flowing free and clean.
Hills to shelter from the rain.
Trees for wood to cook and heat.
A place so obvious to behold.
Wandering souls
From whence you came?
Mystery will remain.
And Huish Champflower
Is the name.

Pamela Gormley (Taunton)

Accepted

(Dedicated to Holly and Claire, with all my thanks)

I was never accepted,
I was not the same,
I am unique,
From my hair to my clothes to my name.
I never tried to fit in,
I was confident to stand out,
I remained calm and brave,
No matter what they'd shout.
I remain strong,
I did not let them get to me,
It was fine, I knew they were wrong.
I would turn to my friends when it got too much,
They would hug me and say it's OK now,
They were my angels, my rock, my star.
I could cry to them anytime, any day,
Wherever they were, I was never far.
They never accepted thanks,
Said, 'It's what friends were for,'
I still thanked them though,
I could ask for nothing more.
I am accepted, I am the same,
For I have won this game.
I still stand out,
But, nothing they shout.

Leia Thomas (Andover)

The Blind Harper

I fret over the strings -
even graft cannot kindle sleep tonight.
I slur the pedal work,
dazed feet aching for rest.
We come to a stop, the harp nodding.
Camlyn accepts silence, for my sake.
Sometimes I yearn for sight, fresh chords.
But I could never desert my oldest friend,
lay aside sounds of every weight, and none.
Camlyn coaxes reluctant fingers, forgiving.
People say that the stars are very lovely
but they make no music and can't be hugged.
The urge to play is heady, irresistible.
Like the tender willow,
we shiver with joy, bend in sorrow.

Brian Phillips (Plymouth)

For A Fantasy Lover

I am the White Witch of the West
I ride the winds of my mind
I scale the mountains of your hope
I swim in the sea of your oblivion
I burn in the heat of your body
Now - the dream is over - you are free - and I?
I go on to summon up another fantasy.

I am the snake who lies
Curled up in your loins
I walk not a straight path
My way is devious into your heart.
I am the White Witch of the West
I can awake the demon in your breast
But stay! Take opium from my love, for soon
I'll go away.

I am the Pegasus who flies
Over a million moons and stars
And never dies.
My hooves are claws upon your back
To make you rise with me
Into eternity.
I am the White Witch of the West
I am the calm after the storm
I am the dove in your hand
I offer you Peace.

Briony Brown (Kingsbridge)

Looking Out

I look out of my window
And what do I see?
Banks of green bushes
And tree after tree.
Birds diving downwards
To pick up some bits,
Often a seagull
And sometimes blue tits.
Squirrels come passing
And rabbits come too.
But nothing to eat,
Just the things that I grew.
And now it's so windy
And very wet, so writing
About it, is as far as I get.

Maurice Gubbins (Torquay)

What Is Existence?

Do I exist . . . ?
Do you exist . . . ?
Does anything at all exist,
 save in the mind of God?
If I could see each atom then
 all solid things would disappear,
Could my eyes see raw energy
 atoms themselves would cease to be,
Whilst if my resonance I ruled
 I'd need no doors,
  walk through the wall -
Or so the scientists say . . .

What *is* existence . . . ?
Could it be real
 without a solid, actual form?
How 'real' is thought,
 our own or God's?
Whate'er my base, I see and feel . . .
Who knows the answers? -
 none but God, -
The root, the ground,
 the *only* sure reality,
From Whom all else is drawn and flows . . .

However everything exists,
 we rest in Him alone.

David J C Wheeler (Beaworthy)

The Flowering

Imagine
an arch of honeysuckle, a sun-kissed bough
over soft beds where aquilegias flirt in fancy
skirts of mauvey blue and twirl to show
modest daisies how to tease; showering confetti
bonnets on the lawn. Here, entwined by these
images, I, in fancy too, wander back
to that simple white-washed yard, where bees
procured sweet nectar from blossom-decked
trellis. There, innocence, in polka-dotted frock,
was wooed. Lovers they slept
where sweet night-scented stocks graced terracotta
pots. Next, in fresh profusion, pressed flowers,
kept tokens of love, veins now murmuring.
'Oh! Dewy clover fields such soft seducing!'

Honor Riley (Muswell Hill)

Seaside

Seaside seashells shellfish low tide
water's edge black-clad in fetish wear,
shining nets of popping rubber weed:
small flies swarm upwards and the smell
is fish and drains and salt.

The seaside always smells of drains and salt and fish.
'Aaah' we breathe, draw into city lungs
sunstroked pretence of health.
We step across the tideline charnel house,
the rotting crabs, decaying seagulls,
desiccated jellyfish,
and squint at glittering ocean, blinded to
the high tide debris -
condoms, broken glass and single shoes.

The sea breeze seems to blow away all thought:
maybe the ebb and flow of tide
sucks out all worries and concerns;
perhaps it is the mantra
of the falling waves,
the heartbeat of the sea,
that draws us down into that timeless trance
where, joyful beachcombers, we pounce
on smooth and milky sea glass,
driftwood bleached and sanded by the beach,
and dried out smelly seaweed.

Janet Zoro (Gloucester)

A Plain Path

In our stresses, distractions, worries, fears,
Find God at the 'centre' of your life. He hears.
Leave heavy stones, burdens, at foot of His Cross,
Take up His Cross, it will be no loss
Except to self, and selfish desires
That are like thorns and prickly briars.
Follow Jesus, the Way, the Truth, the Life.
'Follow daily walking, no trouble or strife'
If the Way as a labyrinth does seem,
He will lighten it with His Light's beam.
We will 'get there' through His God grace,
Take life steadily, at an even pace.
Come to God, seek Him and pray,
Go out into the world with Him each day.
(Matthew 11 v. 28-30)

Steven Rolling (Reading)

My Angel

Today I saw my baby,
Displayed for all to see.
She really did look beautiful,
To think she came from me.
I've always thought her lovely,
As mothers always do,
Her lovely eyes, her curly hair,
A face that cannot lose,
Our baby, yes our baby, has made the front page news.

She made a perfect angel,
Her beaming little smile,
Her brightly shining halo,
Seemed real for just a while.
She smiled for all the cameras
It really was her day
And when she sang her little song,
My tears began to flow,
It was a feeling deep inside,
Only a mum could know.

I love my little Donna
And there's one thing I know,
When she's grown up and flown the nest,
My memory won't forget
The lovely little angel,
Who outshone all the rest.

Debbie Lloyd (Plymouth)

By The Lake

Majestic swans glide effortlessly
Across gentle rippling water
The sun shimmers brightly on the lake
As the breeze rustles in the trees
Making them dance with graceful ease
In the distance a cockerel sings its persistent song
Colourful butterflies waft amidst
A host of sparkling dragonflies
Hovering above the edge of the forever lapping lake
A bee alights nearby, carefully feeling its way
Seagulls take flight into a cloudless blue sky
Calling to one another as they swoop
Over shimmering water
Almost as if
They too can feel the wonder of its beauty

Jean Beard (Stroud)

Somewhere In Time

(Inspired by the novel 'Lady of Hay' by Barbara Erskine)

Where did she come from Our Lady of Hay
Was it tomorrow or was it today
With tales of regression and shrinks taking notes
Our Lady of Hay she sure got my vote
From the middle of time when lunch was a boar
We flit from now till days of yore
Matilda thoughts, I wish they were mine
Would I be a lady, oh so fine.

To try regression is my dream
I've lived more lives some days it seems
But would I also turn out to be queen
Perhaps it was just another sweet dream.

To turn a key and unlock my past
My secrets awake, to know at last
Of loves and friends and times gone by
But would I want to sit and cry
To weep of loved ones lost in sorrow
To know there's no chance of meeting tomorrow
But time evolves and I have returned
If we loved enough we could be not spurned
They'll come again just as I
You know what they say
Never say die!

Janet C H Follett (Basingstoke)

God Word

O light of dark, O word of God, O wisdom from high,
The living word. It is the Heaven-drawn picture, a

Banner, it shines like light, of Christ divine. A lamp to
guide our footsteps. Shine on from age to age. O Christ

To thee. Spirit of light and life. And still that light he lifteth
O'er the Earth to shine on. O spirit truth and life unchanged

Unchanging mid mists and rocks and quicksand. Still guide
The church from her dear master before God's host unfurled,

Above the stormy world. O'er life's raging sea. It is the Heaven-
drawn picture received the gift divine. O word of God incarnate

The living word of God where gems of truth are stored. The holy
Word of God. Come from Heaven above with power, wisdom,
Grace, peace, love.

Imogene Lindo (Sydenham)

553

Sign Of The Modern Age

Sadness and sorrow
About what will be for tomorrow
What will we have left to enjoy
When it is left for us to choose even if we have a girl or a boy

Simple daily pleasures are taken away
We can't even let out our children to play
Not allowed to call someone love or
Allowed to show faith to the Lord above

Mother Nature looks after her own
And now that humans appear to be fully grown
What will happen to us?

The Earth, our precious kind and all living things
If only we could all have wings
And fly back to a land where time has forgot
Forgotten wars, global warming and all bad things
If only we could take charge, each and every being
To make this world a better place
So we do not need to advance into space
To look for new planets which we will in time destroy

So take up the Earth plight and put up a fight
So that the sadness and sorrow
Is gone from tomorrow
And we will have lots left to enjoy
For each and every one of us, woman, man, girl and boy.

Angela Faulder (Hemel Hempstead)

The Yellow Rose

The tiny rose hidden from sight,
Grew strong and proud,
Towards the light.

Amongst the weeds and grass it fought,
Until a glimpse of it I caught.

Its tiny petals so fragile, close,
To reveal perfection in a single rose.

A work of art, nature's gift,
A part of a puzzle that we fit.

And so if we are to be ash and dust,
Surely we would lose our trust.

And God would fail his single duty,
That like the rose we live in beauty.

Pamela Dickson (Plymouth)

Eating My Words

Is there a single thing I feel right now
that has not been so well documented,
so over-written,
so crushed through a thesaurus and come out a pop song recited
that the words are not heard?

rejected,
such a tiny word for the whole you left of my life.
So insignificant, it makes a capital look out of place.

I feel like a tiny empty anorexic skeleton with an overcoat of fat
you allowed me to drip myself in whilst you
slowly, by crumb, slowly,
became as repulsed by what I saw as I did.
Stomach churning, bulimia inducing, repulsive rot.
You left me empty as my stomach.

I question whether there could possibly be anyone who could love me
the way I loved you.
Enrapturing, captivating, wonder-filled, drown in your beauty
and colour you in love.
I wonder if it would smother me.

Should I try to need this into poetry, mix it with adjectives
and bake it 'til all the tears are dry?
I serve you a dish of crisp words that fell out in a jumbled, grated pile
and hope one day you will thank me
for the tinier I get, the less there is for you not to love.

Not Anna Reynolds (London)

With You Always

Let my love be Your love
Let my life be Yours
Let Your love move through me
Flinging wide many hearts' doors
Let me love You truly
As I endeavour to do
And may life forever
Reflect the joy that comes only from You
For it is Your love that moves thru' me
It strengths thru' hope and tear
It forever guides the road ahead
As Your presence is always near
It reaches out to others
Even when I detect it least
Everlasting joy is your gift on which we feast

Eileen Marston (Swindon)

555

Is Today Just Today?

Is today just today?
The day before tomorrow.
Will it bring me many joys?
With very little sorrow.
Will my hopes of yesteryear,
Fill my coming days with all good cheer?

Yet life must have its reality,
No matter what our dreams may be.
It's up to us just what we do -
Only ourselves to blame.
We are responsible for the way we act,
Good or bad and that's fact.

'It'll be alright, it doesn't matter!'
But, then you think, as you hear others chatter.
'Did he really have to go?'
The answer we shall never know.

The chatter of the passer-by,
The answers not for you or I.
I've heard it said, 'I'd like to be a fly on the wall.'
But, even then, we couldn't know it all.
We'd better take life just as we find it.
Be satisfied with what we do and say.

Enjoy the life we have today,
Tomorrow's never far away!

A Bricknell (Bournemouth)

First Kiss

The warmth of his skin,
As his lips brush against mine.
One moment between ourselves,
But it seems like eternity.
My feet rise from the earth,
While our hands begin to entwine.
Nothing and nobody can take this sensation from me.
A second of passion.
Barely one.
Or perhaps two.
I feel as if I cannot take myself away.
But quickly it is over.
His lips drift away from my own.
A single, coy smile passes among us.
And he is gone.

Annie Pollock (13) (Cheddar)

Swan Song

In this haunted land, the living are already ghosts
They float along the haunted streets
In their ghostly cloaks
Pale with bloodless veins
Engrossed with living nightmares.

The swan song is premature
Me not ready to sing
The tone will be tuneless
With sorrow that hath no bounds . . .

In this haunted land
Happiness is too much to ask
I am still counting my blessings
While others are bleeding to die
Pessimism is my middle name
Garlanded around the neck

This can be my last sip of water
This can be my farewell glance
I count the apples in the shopping streets
Heat beat counts my life

This fighting seems to be endless
Gunshots, grenades: my cliché
Somebody I know seems to be a prey every day
Let me count my blessings
And count my life chickens before they hatch.

Mihiri Ekanayake (Ilford)

My Grandchild

Tiny little fingers,
Tiny little toes,
Cute little face,
Tiny little nose,
Someone to cuddle,
Someone to love,
Sent by God
From Heaven above,
A mother and father,
And grandmas as well,
Now the story we can tell,
A lovely granddaughter
To hold and love,
We all love her
And we always will.

Anna R Spinks (St Albans)

Lunchtime Concert

(Lady Chapel, Wells Cathedral)

In this cool stillness of
The Lady Chapel
An eager audience
Is gathered as
The medieval clock chimes noon.

Set on altar's level
Five chairs and stands await
Musicians carrying
Violins, viola,
Clarinet and cello.

Now to muted applause
They enter, take their seats -
Tune instruments.
Suspense: hushed anticipation;
Mozartian notes soar on high

And sudden sunbeams magnetized
By golden keys, reveal
Kaleidoscopic wonders through
Ancient stained glass windows,
Magnificent in majesty.

Beauty, double delight
In joyous sound and sight.

Joan Palmer (Weston-super-Mare)

Together Forever

This match made in Heaven is plain to see
These two special people, one unity

Two souls, two spirits, two hearts, two minds
Two becomes one, they entangle, they entwine
Two souls, two spirits, two minds and two hearts
Two becomes one and will now never part

So wholesome, so true this recital of 'I do'
These vows so dear are announced so clear
Both anxious, both nervous, both scared but excited
Both certain, so sure, now individually united

So together forever they now happily stand
Together forever, man and wife, hand in hand
To take on this world in a partnership together
May their happiness grow and remain strong forever.

Julie Clark (Bristol)

Weymouth

Weymouth is a lovely town
It has a lovely bay
Folks come here from miles around
For a fortnight or a day.
They come by road, they come by rail
With accents strange and new
They lounge around in deckchairs
Lie on the beach and stew!
The kiddies build sandcastles,
While Dads just sit and stare
Is that a shapely beach belle
Or a surfer with long hair?
For weeks and weeks all summer long
In our streets they roam
Sporting silly shorts and hats
(They'd never wear at home)
But welcome gorgeous 'grockles'
Feast on our fine cream teas,
Fish and chips and candyfloss
Are guaranteed to please.
Spend all your hard-earned money,
In September it will cease
The town returns to normal
And we are left in peace!

(Grockles, West Country name for holidaymakers)

Anne Williams (Portland)

Pleasures Of Life

Those who can read have friends for life
As from a book you can turn to romance or strife.
While adventures abroad may keep you agog
Or nearer home with a pond full of frogs.
You can turn to a chapter where grass snakes slither,
Or a kingfisher on bough, above a river,
Swoops down on his prey without a sound,
And only clear water spins circles around.

Walk away from the river through a sunlit glade,
Where the scene that meets you is heaven made.
As across a stile moon daisies dance, while a deer in the shade
                                        of a crab apple tree
Raises his head and looks straight at me.
In a moment without sound, swiftly he is gone,
To leave me to wander the last page alone.

Hazel Sheppard (Swindon)

Exposure To The World

(Animal cruelty)

Who locked me up for several years?
Just belonging to myself,
No one heard my cries for help
My tears they flowed into rivers,
With hunger, I nearly collapsed,
The world forgot about me,
They locked the cage and threw away the keys,
Had this happened to any one of you,
You would have gone insane,
they kept me locked for so long,
In this horrible solid frame of a cage.

A lady with a golden heart,
One day came to set me free,
Weak and almost dying,
She embraced me in her loving arms,
She nursed me back with all the love and care,
To run free on all fours,
Now I stand proud to expose myself to the world,
With a very special painting of me,
In a very special frame,
Unlike the horrible solid frame cage,
The lady with the golden heart had set me free,
I give thanks to God.

A Bhambra (Hayes)

Towards Eden

Goodbye lacks meaning,
until I've given her substance,
created a shape
to mould my arms around,
imagined
the feathery, raindrop touch
of lips searching out my breast,
till I've conjured a smile
sweet as vanilla ice cream
and a daughter taking her first
wobbly steps towards Eden.

I can only let go of the idea of her
once I can see her fully grown, mouth
ruby-red from her lover's kiss, murmuring
the words, so long Mum, so long . . .

Sue Sims (Bristol)

Celebrating Difference

Celebrating difference and what it means to me
Is learning about people and what they have for tea
How they work and live, when they wake and sleep
And even more importantly what memories they keep.

Celebrating difference means the world to me
People of all races, sex or disability
It shouldn't even matter what your 'difference' is at all
We are all basically the same inside, all hurting if we fall
All bleeding if we cut ourselves, all crying when we're sad
All needing Mum when we are ill and when we're broke - poor Dad
All having friends we care about and laughing till we drop
All feeling a warm glow inside when in our lover's arms we flop.

It seems celebrating difference should be overturned to me
To celebrating 'sameness' and 'similarity'
To celebrating 'sharing, understanding and tolerance'
To celebrating education and elimination of ignorance.

Celebrating difference means future hope to me
That we will all be living in peace and harmony
In a great world for our children to live and love and play
Where we can grow old gracefully enjoying every day.
Where we wouldn't have to worry about the future for our kin
Or violence and anger due to the colour of their skin
Where co-operation, caring and tolerance prevail
Wouldn't it be wonderful - let's hope this plan don't fail.

Sue Hancock (Bristol)

Canvas

My canvas is a shadow
Without colours
Everyday
I paint on it
A black dot
With white stripes
Using the same black brush
Again and again
When nobody else
Is looking . . .

I never expected
The dot
On a canvas
To last
So long . . . in the darkness . . .

Ben Younes Majan (London)

Four Seasons

Spring starts the year with growth and light,
Small lambs appear in meadows bright.
The buds on trees uncurl their leaves,
Small plants push through the earth to breathe.
It is a season loved by all
When life wakes up to nature's call.

The second season of the year
Is summer gay with flowers to cheer.
The nights are light and children play
Until sleep comes to end their day.
In summer everything is new
Nature has so much to do.

Autumn is a season sad
For it's a time of change.
The leaves on trees turn red and gold,
And ripened crops are cut and sold.
The birds get ready to migrate
Before the autumn weather breaks.

Winter closes down the year
With biting winds and fires to cheer.
Bringing snow to the baron land
As high waves hit the golden sands.
Skies are filled with angry clouds
And seagulls cry with an eerie sound.

Joyce Barrett (Bristol)

Mayday In Holland Park, London

The sun is shining yellow warm and bright,
The sky is blue, shimmering in sunlight,
Birds fly around, peacocks walk in the park,
The park is open from morning to dark.

A waterfall flows into a small lake,
With goldfish, rocks, stones and statues to make,
The leaves of the trees are green, red and brown,
People come walking, relaxing in town.

Beautiful flowers, red, pink, white and blue,
Plenty to see here and plenty to do,
Ecology centre garden to grow,
Birds sing and twitter and fly high and low.

Mothers with babies and old people walk,
Some read a book, some wander, look and talk.

Susan Mary Robertson (London)

Luck

On that dirt road lurching up twenty miles
through virgin forest to a camp in the Sierras
was the first time I thought I might lose you.
Al Stats throwing the gears, the Dodge bucking
the ruts, and me riding the bench seat
five months gone, trying to save you from shocks.

The sky between the pines bristled with thousands
of stars, blinding out the familiar map.
I'd never slept so high or far from towns.
Hank broke his leg and was bumped out again
to a hospital. It could have been me,
bleeding, or Al's heart at that altitude.

I tucked my skirt close, edging past
Poison oak, ants as long as my toenail,
to crouch behind trees far from our camp,
in their pungent dust among rumours of bears.
Nearby, prospectors had channelled a stream
down a wooden chute where they panned for gold.

With your life fluttering inside me
I rinsed handfuls of grit, half-expecting
a spark of the Colour – a rogue star
to pinch between my fingers, holding
my vision in a careful balance against
disbelief, as the old miners might have done.

Linda Saunders (Bath)

On Loan

I sing to you a lullaby
To rock you off to sleep.
I do it, so that you don't cry
My precious child of just one week.

I change your nappy many times
To keep you clean and dry.
Now I sing you nursery rhymes
You've also learned to wave goodbye.

You'll marry one day, when you've grown
I know that day will come.
You are not mine, you're just on loan
My darling, precious, baby son.

Your wife will love you, you will see
But I know, not as much as me.

Barbara Webber (Gloucester)

My Friend

My heart is like an open door,
Love doesn't live here anymore,
The people that I loved and knew,
What has happened to you?

Thomas Hardy who I adore,
Why didn't you write more?
'The Return of the Native' above all,
Is simply the one that I adore!
I long to come and see your tomb,
Installed in that very large room.

All your heroines are so sublime,
All are such friends of mine,
The heroes are my friends too,
Oh! I wish I could talk to you.

The hurt, the pain, that I endure,
I do wish there were a cure!
The sleepless nights, the loneliness,
Will I be happy anymore?
You are my only friend,
Without you my life would be at an end,
I could never endure the long days and nights anymore,
How I can't wait to read your books again,
And escape the loneliness within my soul
And make me whole again.

Doreen Alice Robertson (Bristol)

Tabitha's Ashes

Deepest, duplicate sympathies from the cemetery,
tasteful booklet, calming verse,
'How to cope without your pet'.

A slightly hastened end
following a pathway
almost nine lives long.

Abundant, scattered fur
now coffined ashes lie
beneath a plastic spray of
box.

The rose scented in memory
pot-bound but
at its side random purple blooms
self seeded from your territory.

Valerie Hockaday (Falmouth)

June In Kefalonia

Pale tense holiday makers leave the plane
To bright, bright skies, no sign of rain
Clear azure heaven, Ionian sea so blue
Blossoms everywhere of brilliant hue.

A limpid pool, sparrows on the brink
Swallows and swifts swoop down to drink
Cicadas call from dawn till night
Fat fledglings chirp, on verge of flight
Goat bells, melodious sound of ages
On perfumed air, flowers pine and sages.

Fine mosaics excavated from the Earth below
Shows Romans dwelt there centuries ago
Mountain settlement destroyed by earthquake
New Scala reborn for the villagers' sake
And ancient monastery so quaint
With respectful homage to a saint
In silver shrine he is complete
Pilgrims bow to kiss his feet.

Delightful lunches in shady bars
Attentive waiters under shining stars
Ripe lemons and apricots fall to the ground
The moon-filled night has scarcely a sound
Forts, monasteries, castles and bells
Kefalonia enfolds us under her spell.

Valerie Coleman (Wallington)

Why?

Tears on the face of time,
memories lost down the line,
weary body the only shrine.
Why?

Where is your mercy God
to this poor lingering sod
beaten by times ruthless rod?
Why?

Why look with baleful eye
on this poor soul about to die?

Hate, is the man with the gun
who took away her only son
when his life had scarce begun.
That's why.

George Derek Ewer (Bristol)

Sixteen

Beginning of summer - end of school,
Choking on cigarettes, trying hard to act cool,
The Clash and The Pistols, shocking my dad,
Spiked hair and eyeliner, so good to be bad.
Riding pillion on motorbikes, dangerous, wild,
Not yet a woman, - no longer a child.

Never-ending kisses on the last bus home,
Long hours spent talking on the telephone,
Breaking the curfew; getting locked out,
Making Mum cry and Dad rage and shout.
Boys and betrayals, heartaches and tears,
Still just a baby, but wise beyond years.

Giggling with girlfriends, soulmates forever,
Baring your midriff in all kinds of weather,
Flirting with bikers and boys in black leather,
Knowing all the answers, and acting so clever,
Buying a round in the pub for a dare,
Then back home to bed with your old teddy bear.

Diaries and poetry, feeling misunderstood,
Knowing you shouldn't but wishing you could,
Hormones and hair-gel, discos and dances,
Bacardi and blackcurrant, taking mad chances,
Pushing back boundaries with rips in your jeans,
A heart filled with hope, and a head full of dreams.

Lisa Waite (Highbridge)

A Death In The Family

As in the early days
of radio, chairs huddle round
the electric fire;
magazines
make a rainbow on the floor.

Leaves skitter down the road;
clouds across the sky.

The guests have all gone.
Coffee throbs in the pot.

When you get up to
pour more into your cup,
to delay the tragedy of sleep,
the furniture crowds
closer to the fire.

David R Morgan (Bedford)

The State Of Poetry

With too much unclear thought within your lines
I shudder at your purpose in all this.
Are you intent upon a fatal kiss
Where the recipient is drawn to death,
As one who on a lethal serving dines?
Why do you bait the reader with your breath?

Or is it that you're caught inside the drift
Of modern parlance thirsting for a fee,
So that you are not quite what you could be
By adding to tradition, proved and tried,
Or taking courage in your natal gift,
Instead choosing subversion as a bride?

Perhaps you have not read so much of those
Who went before you, suffering for their cause,
In strict adherence to their pristine laws.
You are succeeding, that is beyond doubt,
In bringing history to a rapid close,
As many read your slogan, 'No Way Out'.

And since the world depends for health upon
A poetry of meaning and good sense,
While you are banking on a false pretence,
It finds itself inverted in its course,
With all its landmarks washed away and gone
Since such as you departed from its source.

Alan Dryden (West Molesey)

Dartmoor Ram

A monarch of the moor's fulfilled his role;
The farmer who possesses this fine beast
Is hopeful that again he's reached his goal:
Two hundred lambs, to come next spring, at least.

The ram exhausted by his week of love
Surveys the flock of raddled ewes he's tupped
And watches warily as shepherds move
Around the pound which by the Tors is cupped.

Amongst this harem guessing next year's count
Of lambs begat by him. The counting o'er,
The men, watched by their boss astride his mount,
Drive out the flock onto the open moor.

Meanwhile the ram, until next season, rests
Within the pound amongst the granite crests.

Mervyn Prosser (Tavistock)

Borrowed Time On The Titanic

In the undersea light, conversation
ebbs and flows. While small fish,
pop-eyed and scandalised,
quiver among the table legs.

Feet are tapping, elegantly shod,
glasses and eyebrows archly raised,
while everyone appreciates the band.
*'They played as they went down
so bravely.'* It was said.

A couple take the floor, she, stylish,
bright and limp against his black,
a feather curled teasing at her cheek.
On a spurt of animation, perhaps a wave,
they are spanning the floor in easy gliding,
his arm still and careful,
like someone carrying a wisp of silk.

A whale sometimes comes by.
Tries to talk, but has to give up,
being too large for them to see.
Her eye, tiny and bright in the vast flank,
watches intelligently. But soon
she turns her bulk, with only a sound
like a whisper, and glides, a grey shadow,
at home and right in the water.

Stella Goorney (Bath)

The Missing Ingredient

Every day people say to me 'Use your potential,'
But for me something's missing - the bit that's essential.
I don't know what it looks like, or what it is,
I'm not even clever, or a kid that's a whiz.

I won't join the Rat Race to have money or power,
I'd rather be pottering about hour by hour.

I've been contented and happy for most of my life
With no money or fame, but a loving wife.
I asked her today if I could help with the chores,
(But the weather is good, I'd like it outdoors).

'Go into the garden, Dear,' she said.
So here I am in the garden shed,
With a chair and a book and a flask of tea.
And guess what! At last my potential's found me.

Marjorie Mitchell (Stoke)

Mother

Her aura arrives before her physical presence,
Air once fresh becomes thick,
The home becomes a house.
She moves confidently and with purpose,
I watch her discreetly.
Like a snake who might strike if it catches the reflection
of your eye,
She is the Medusa who'll turn you to stone.

I notice how lines score her face like ravines,
Has she been battered by the past or silently eroded by the unseen tears of others she has
scarred and torn apart?

Her head is covered by a scarf, she is about to cook.
She feeds us well.
A variety of fayres are amongst her repertoire,
Salted mackerel, bitter chocolate,
Hot peppers, shaved ice.
She cooks well because she is empty.
She cannot feed others on what's inside her.

It's time for me to move,
I hear her before she speaks.
I make myself invisible and slip out.
While she lifts hot pans with thickened skin
That has been burnt so many times,
It feels nothing.

Laura Annansingh (London)

Beyond The Mundane

There is a reality beyond the mundane - beyond the physical.
It wafts through it like a subtle breeze
And leaves a whisper of some earthly time once vaguely remembered.

From the moment that time began, when we separated from the source,
The purpose of all these lifetimes is to remember this one thing -
There is love.

It is beautiful, it is tangible, it is attainable, it is our very nature.
All else is illusion;
All wants, all needs, all desires and all power struggles stem from one
Thing - the illusion of this lack.

Nothing will fill the gap until we heal this age-old wound;
It is the journey from sleep to awakening,
From forgetting to remembering, from who we think we are
To who we really are - it is the journey back to love.

Nita Smith (Newquay)

Earth Sound

Listen to the sound of the Earth
The sound of the sea and sky;
The crack of black thunder that echoes,
The wing-beat of eagles that fly,
The pounding and crashing of oceans,
The wind that makes waves through the rye.

Listen to the sound of the river
Surging and gushing from its source.
Wait and be still for a moment,
For the stag as he leaps through the gorse.
How blind we've become, how deaf, how dumb,
Not hearing the beat of Earth's sound.

How wondrous is Your creation Lord!
How infinite Your power!
How selfish that we cannot see
The beauty we devour.
This precious gift, the wondrous Earth, created for our joy,
Poor baffled, blind and selfish Man, he only can destroy.

Listen to the sound of the Earth
Take time to stand and stare,
Stop the atomic heartbeat
That trembles and hangs in the air.
Listen feckless, foolish Man,
Listen and beware!

Kristin MacEwan (Hemel Hempstead)

A Leafy Suburb

Once
a century ago
the leafy suburb
was for well heeled
city folks,
ethnic now,
buzzing,
rendering politely
friendly service
for every need,
bustling with
burkas and bearded clerics,
only the architecture
remembering
the distant past.

Godfrey Dodds (Croyden)

Bradford Revisited

A little down at heel, the street still stands,
Grey, hunch-shouldered houses, holding hands.
Between the rooftops and the pelmet lie
Narrow bands of ever-changing sky.
The laughing chimney pots are long since gone,
But still the banner clouds go marching on.

Now other children sit astride the walls.
In alien tongues, the old familiar calls.
Their eastern silks defy the Yorkshire cold,
Bright mirror fragments stitched with red and gold.
Kingfisher flash, and sari butterflies,
Jet-black hair, unfathomable eyes.

Time concertinas here and loops its track
To lives forgotten, half a century back.
I am my mother, washing, making tea.
These children are the child I used to be.
My father, the old man we used to bait,
Hurling rotten apples at his gate.

The city is a bridge from old to new.
A place of dreams; strange, yet familiar view.
A teeming meeting place of east and west,
All manner of life's dramas, worst and best.
Peace, born of conflict, hope distilled from fear.
Childhood remembered, and old age too near!

Frances Stubbs (Berkhamsted)

Heart Standing Still

The phone is still and quiet,
No funny anecdotes,
Or sad tales and warm understandings,
I miss her perfect timing,
And ache for her hug,
Text message still on my phone,
Memories paper my walls,
They line my pumping heart,
Ghosts in my clothes cupboard,
Hard to move,
I borrowed her back in a dream,
For a moment,
It was perfect again,
For a moment,
A dream's breath away.

Sara Glass (Bristol)

Meavy

On merry-eyed nights it leans over and over,
The old oak propped by the churchyard gate,
When lovers lie lost in the thigh-high clover,
And a dog fox barks to the moon for a mate;
And Meavy's shy ghosts from the Old Time come creeping
When the lights are all out, and the houses are sleeping.

When post office dawns in Marchants Bridge meadows
Wake Lynch Hill Cross to the old church tower,
The lanes and hedges are fretted with shadows
Of wagons and haycarts for many an hour;
And Meavy's blue skies look to see the first swallow
When the summer days come, and the summer nights follow.

And should you stroll slowly past old Meavy Barton
Towards the Old Smithy no more on the go,
The noise of the boys in Captain Hughes' garden
Is of practising jumps for the Oak Fair Show;
And Meavy Green's leisure is lordly of laughter
When the summer days come, and the summer nights after.

And when all's said and done, and journeys are over,
The old oak propped by the churchyard gate,
Will welcome to home every long-lost lover
Who's travelled a distance, and sleeps very late;
And Meavy's rich earth will be easy of waking
When we've passed through the gate, and the new dawn's breaking.

Edward Murch (Yelverton)

Window Seat

Dozing, eating, reading, journey weary,
Encased in crowded limbo.
A metallic glow seen from the window
Of engines, blanched in sunlight,
Power on a flimsy wing
Shuddering and straining
Against their element of wind.
Movement above the billowing clouds
Seemed ponderous and slow
As miles of continent moved below.
Suddenly, a small plane, distance undefined
Bright against the canopy of cloud,
Flashed by.
Sense of speed was reality as the jet thundered on . . .
Did someone see our trail across the sky?

Pat Llewellyn (Abingdon)

Wendy

The first time I saw you,
I knew right from the start,
You were meant for me alone,
You put paw prints on my heart.

Wendy, you are a treasure,
More valuable than gold,
The love you share is priceless,
As the years unfolds.

You look at me with eyes of love,
You never hold a grudge,
You think I'm far too wonderful,
To criticise or judge.

I know you think you're human,
But I'm glad it isn't true,
The world would be a better place,
If folk were more like you.

Adoring eyes that say so much,
Paws that have the gentle touch,
A tail to wag that all is well,
And far more love than words can tell.

Wendy I will love you,
Forever and a day,
Until I pass away.

Eileen Tasker (Paignton)

Summer

The sun is shining,
the clouds have all gone,
the blackbird is singing
a melodious song.

The squirrel has climbed
high in the tree.

The gulls are flying high
over the sea.

The cows in the fields
peacefully grazing.

Look all around,
it seems so amazing,
from where I stand
it's a wonderful land.

G Jordan (Beaconsfield)

573

Lack Of Understanding

The man woke up in the morning light,
Put in his hearing air and got a fright,
Rushed downstairs to charge the battery,
But it was a false hope, can it be?

'I am deaf,' he cried to his loving wife,
'What am I to do at this stage of my life,'
A baby just a week or two old can't hear her cries,
Can't tell whether people tell the truth or lies.

Had to learn to lip read as well,
Couldn't handle the sign language truth to tell,
Felt too old and couldn't cope,
Longed to get it back but he knew there was no hope.

People said how rude he was, ignorant as well,
They thought he was ignoring them,
The truth was he couldn't tell.

Depression set in, didn't know what to do,
Went through years of feeling really blue,
I know my friends you might well ask
How I k now this gruelling tale,
It was me and I thought life was hell.

Now I have learned to live with this
And to hear my kids, the wind, the thunder
And my ever-loving wife would be bliss.

C P Chapman (Southampton)

Prison Of Fear

Sentenced to a life of trauma,
Unable to appeal against the fear,
Trapped behind the bars of anguish,
Locked in the cell of torture,
Clean the floors of sorrow,
Serve the platter of pain,
Exercise the muscles of anger,
Lay on the firm, hard bed of hate,
Cries of pain echo through the night,
In crowded cells of insanity,
I escape, sentenced increased,
The brutal judge ignores my plea,
Release me from the shackles,
Unable to appeal against the fear,
Sentenced to a life of trauma.

Alicia Francois-George (Tottenham)

A Prayer For April 30th

Dear God, just for myself I make this plea:
Hold April in Your hand a moment more for me,
That I my wonder ere the wonders flee.

Snowdrop and crocus along have gone,
But daffodils could surely linger on.
The windflowers, like a drift of snow
Sway gently on the forest floor below
And blackthorn also clothed in white,
Says spring is surely in our sight.

The creeping ivy may confuse,
The shyer violet does the light eschew.
No gold of Man could ever shine
As bright as your own celandine.

What do the bluebells say to me?
A drift, a carpet, then a sea.
Queen of the woodland, there you reign,
To lift my winter soul again.

The blackbird sings at break of day,
The starling splash their bath in play.
The hedges green, the new-mown grass,
How does this always come to pass?

This magic month, so quickly to depart,
Hold in Your hand that I may write it on my heart.

Judy McEwan (Lingfield)

Loyal Friend

Who do you consider to be your most loyal friend?
Soulful eyes studying you from close by.
Protector, helper, companion too,
Listening quietly to all of your woes.
He doesn't respond with anything but love,
And walks alongside you through thick and thin.
Never judging, no matter what,
He adores it when you give him a pat on his back.
He doesn't ask for much in return,
Food, warmth and a roof over his head.
So when those beautiful canine eyes glance at you again,
Acknowledge the loyalty that has come your way.

Glenda Barker (Waltham Cross)

Dawn Rising

Deep in the presence of solitude
a hermit heron, silent, alert
Elusive in the chill dawn dusk
misting the silver reed beds

Save for the gentle slither of grasses
swaying in the noiseless air
Stillness fills the ghost-light

> A tentative cry
> from the lustrous mud
> as a lone gull rises

> Liquid first calls
> of invisible curlew
> pierce the early hush
> Then fall

Steadily, slowly, chattering voices
saturate the gathering light
Swelling to an urgent surge
that soars aloft in a silver cloud:
A galaxy of glittering gulls
rising to the heavens

> Far to the east, in silence
> the pink-tinged sun drifts gently
> Out of the shimmering mist.

Pauline Bird (Marlborough)

A Seasonal Journey

Dazzling shades of golds, reds and browns
Swirling and dancing on the breeze,
Circling slowly to the ground, as summer waves goodbye.
The wind howling through the forests
Bitter cold and brutal as the rain thunders
hard on the concrete ground
Pummelling and thumping, as if it were in a boxing ring.
Animals hibernating, birds flying south.
The days darken, the temperature plummets
Scarves soar through the chaos of umbrellas
And eventually come to rest on the apple tree,
As autumn gives way to the snowy days of winter.

Alexandra Williams (15) (Salisbury)

Score

To score a goal
A score to win
To score a mark
So deep within.

A score - an age
So young and bright
Full of dreams
Of life in flight.

From birth to teens
To Woman
To Man
To Nanna and Grampa
Such a wide span.

Our lives hold in its large store
So many things and wanting more.
Striving always to do our best
From our first step
- such happiness!

My memories are three score years
 -But then-
My hopes and dreams are still happening!

With Sons and Daughters and one Grandson
My Husband and I still have not won!

Sandylea (Milton Keynes)

The Blindfold

Fury and frustration
stored in the corner of our eyes
made us oblivious to
the street sandwiched between the trees
the rhythmic movement of these branches
the whistle of this wind
the waltz of these leaves
the several shades of green and yellow in the leaves and
the grin of the roots that the soil has failed to swallow
Yet we are aware of the
sharp blades of silence
that slowly spread between us.

Nasheeha Nasrudeem (Crawley)

Mighty Creator God

Only sovereign, wise God, maker of Heaven
And Earth, the sea and all things therein.
Without Him nothing would be made.
We would not be here. God is life and light,
Life and light are like twins,
Can't have one without the other.
Nothing could exist without light, for God is light and life,
God is everything good.
God is our source, God is good to all people.
We are His people and the sheep of His pastures.
God is more than life to me,
When God created the world it was without form and void
And darkness was upon the face of the deep
And God said, 'Let there be light,' and there was light.
God spoke things into existence. How marvellous is He.
Who is like unto our God. No one. He rules creation. He is in control.
King Jesus is the bread of life. We cannot do anything without Him.
We could never live without Him. It's all about God and Man.
He loved us so much and we must love Him too.
God gave us all that we need, more than enough.
So come, let us praise and worship Him always.
I love Him because He first loved me.
I could never live without Him,
Because He has done great things for me
And is now and always.

Amelda Farquharson (London)

When You Left

(In memory of Spencer Timothy Andrew Hewell, died age 26)

When you left I could still feel your warm embrace,
I could still feel that tender kiss upon my face.
In my heart I see you there
With that smile and well-gelled hair,
Your gentle giggle and warm smile
That made every moment in time worthwhile.
Not a second would pass when I could see
Your smiling eyes looking back at me.
When you left you didn't say goodbye
And now I'm left here to cry.
Goodbye, my Stah, goodbye my friend,
I know now that the last was the end.
When you turned and walked away
I never thought it would be our last day.

Janice Bailey (Worthing)

578

The Angler's Lament

I wish
The fish
Would bite
Tonight.
It's bad.
I've had
Enough.
It's tough.
I freeze.
I sneeze.
My bum
Is numb
I'll quit
And sit
No more.
Before
They close
At Joe's
Fish shop
I'll try
To buy
Some hake
To take
And fry.
Goodbye.

Frank Richards (Bedford)

A Flower Amongst Flowers

(For Marie Elizabeth)

As I gaze across a meadow
And the sun beats down from above
I see a flower amongst other flowers
Which encompasses me with love
I walk along a winding road
And I suddenly stop and stare
For the flower I saw and from which I felt such love
I knew was one so rare
I tenderly walked across a field to where the flower lay
As I watched her sway majestically like a wind across a bay
I am in awe of all her beauty
And how she stands so tall
For this flower amongst all other flowers
Is the fairest of them all.

Lee Cassidy (Tewkesbury)

The Office Run

Clickety-clack went the high-heeled boots.
The sweeping coat skimming the ground.
Howling winds snatched at her hat
Her umbrella was turned inside out.
Fingers were numb, no gloves to protect.
Clickety-clickety, clackety-clack.
Through the park and across the roads.
Nearing the station, away from the winds.
Shelter at last, breath coming back.
Clickety-clack, clickety-clack.
On the train stopping and starting, swaying and stifling.
Coats overcrowding, coats overheating.
Reading the paper and answering the phone.
Nearly at work, still sorting out home.
Clickety-clack still racing on stairs,
Now at her desk, tapping and turning.
Talking, observing, thinking and earning.
In other rooms and sometimes buildings.
Deadlines and gossip, snacking and shouting.
Laughing and signing and checking of papers.
Then clickety-clack on her way back.
Rain in the face and darkness surrounding
Pushing against the wind and the crowding.
Now walking, now running, clickety-clack.
Another day over and now she is back . . .

Christine Clark (London)

Noshers

Citizen of Southall, from distant Mumbai,
Sitting down to dinner at the 'Curry Paradise',
With a banquet of chickpeas,
Prawn Tandoori,
Poppadums, samosas and egg fried rice.

Greedy City broker, lunching at the Ivy,
Working through the menu like a half-starved horse,
With a feast of asparagus,
Lobster, tournedos
And sticky toffee pudding with a hot fudge sauce.

Dirty British worker with a huge great beer gut,
Glancing through the 'Mirror' in his paint-splashed jeans,
With a plateful of fried eggs,
Chips and bacon,
Brown sauce, sausages and Heinz baked beans.

David Hornsby (Richmond)

Sugar, Cream - Well, I mean . . .!

Why is it, when out for a coffee,
I get in a terrible toss?
To mingle the cream and the sugar
With the coffee leaves me at a loss.
For the cream comes in tightly sealed cartons
And the struggle in opening the top
Always forces the stuff to squirt on to my cuff
While the coffee receives a mere drop.
Now I'm no devotee of black coffee,
But resigning myself to my lot,
I remember with pleasure, the sugar, in measure,
Will temper the taste will it not?
In sachets the sugar comes packaged
'Tear open' - so simple t'would seem,
But the foil is so tough, it would foil sure enough,
Anything but a shredding machine.
Is it my fault for being ham-fisted,
Or do other folk suffer the same?
If they do, the affliction, without contradiction,
I'm sure marks a devious game.
All health-food fanatics, the packers,
All sugar and cream each abhors;
Though at risk, their employment,
They blight our enjoyment,
And Shanghai us into their cause.

A Green (Bedford)

Audie

Yes, you are lovely, lovely, lovely,
Sweet, and full of charm.

The thoughts of so many lovesick men,
Have warmed to words the poet's pen,
Herrick's Julia, sonnets by the Bard,
Make tender; hearts once wintry hard;
They rhapsodise on charm and beauty,
On eyes, on form, on hair,
Seldom on acts surpassing those of duty,
Negating self, by loving kindness fair.

You dear, lovely as you are,
Enrich your bounteous gifts by far,
These lines salute you, as they should,
Yes, you are lovely, lovely, lovely,
And my darling, you are *good!*

Ralph Kelly (Lyme Regis)

My Lovely Robin

Oh Robin Redbreast you are our garden bird
You are in this garden all the wintertime
Just singing your little heart out for all to hear
You sing upon the tallest tree singing
Most all the day through
You bring winter sunshine with your song
It is such a lovely tune for all to hear
You remind us of the robin Christmas cards
They are in the shops to buy December time
Oh Robin you are such a lovely bird
You love to eat the seeds and worms I supply
For you to feast upon all day through
You even love the peanuts that are in the bush
For other birds to feast upon
Oh Robin you are such a lovely bird
In the spring when the weather is warming up
You start to build your little nest for your mate
Or you find another way to build your nest
In a kettle or anything you can find
That is cosy for you to rear your young
When the little ones are growing
And are ready to leave their little nest
To start lives of their own somewhere,
You still stay in my garden singing away
Oh Robin you are such a lovely bird.

June Johnstone (Camborne)

The Blackbird

Do not be afeared of me,
I sit and watch, and oversee,
the resting places of those
whose lives are now at rest.

Seek sustenance beneath the sod
and be at peace with those with God.
Take to your nest betwixt the growth,
the curtilage protecting this spot.
You have the freedom to fly as the spirits
now resting here,
but they alas cannot be seen as you in
your form divine.

Do not be afeared of me,
I sit and watch and in life's form
rest in nature's peace.

D R Thomas (Ottery St Mary)

Poetry Versus Rock And Roll

Writing is fun while I think so anyway
Performing is just magic in my mind
Put them together it's a dream come true
But my real dream is to make it more wild
Like a rock and roll singer in my mind
Book launch may not sound so wild
But when I wore jeans and a T-shirt torn to look old
And everyone else wore suits to look grand
The Japanese went wild at me yes me!
That's great I thought I could only dream of this day
But they only asked for my autograph with a smile
As I signed the bits of paper so proud
I wished poetry could be like rock and roll
Bras thrown at me so hard with a smile
As sweat pours off their breasts like a fountain so full
Then they jump up and down and scream so loud
And I throw my words and tear them up in pieces so small
Then choose with which girl I will spend the night so full
But this will never happen to a poet at all
But I can dream I am sure
It will never stop me writing at all
And I will never sing rock and roll music to a crowd
But as long as people enjoy what I do
I will be happy to carry on as before
While I can lie I am sure of that.

Brian D Ball (Windsor)

Post Imperium

It wasn't so great being great -
It's brought dishonour and hate.
When you thought you were good
You were covered in blood
And now you're only third-rate.

So, gone is the noble idea;
What we want is a gallon of beer.
So what, if we're fat?
What's so wrong with that?
When we go we'll go with good cheer!

Then we'll dream of a tropical isle
That's free of rancour and bile;
Where everything's nice
And covered in spice
And we're liked for ourselves, for a while.

Brian Green (Cirencester)

Widecombe Fair

As I walk the lanes to Widecombe Fair,
With the crowds of people who travel there,
Across the moors all yellow with gorse,
We see Tom Cobley riding his horse.
Within the shadow of the church on the green,
Stalls selling all their wares can be seen,
Bargains for all, roundabout rides, all the fun of the fair,
The smell of hot pasties fills the air,
Ice creams on sale everywhere -
A Devon cream tea, a wonderful treat -
When farmers and friends on village green meet.
On the showground field the horses race by,
Pulling buggies and carts, grand and groomed,
With brasses, manes plaited, so proud to be taking part,
White woolly sheep in the pens nearby,
So soft to the touch, delight the eye, as we pass by.
Cider is flowing - gay music we hear -
From an accordion played by a man sitting there,
On a stone by the wayside his neckerchief bright,
His brown leggings shining in the fresh moorland light,
The September sun sets, on this age-old show,
The same as centuries come and go,
And on that grand old grey mare tall, go Bill Brewer,
Jan Stewer, Peter Gerney, Peter Davey, Daniel Whitten,
Harry Hawk and Uncle Tom Cobley and all!

Barbara Sargent (Teignmouth)

Listen, What Do You Hear?

Thoughts go with you on the journey long,
Bringing to people peace with song,
Raise their spirits, bring a smile,
Spread happiness, wait awhile . . .
Listen; what do you hear?

You can't hear a smile or a little tear,
A cuddle from someone you hold dear.
Sing from your heart at the top of your voice,
Let all the world know, sing and rejoice . . .
Listen; what do you hear?

Will you ever know that the seed of sound
Was sown on hungry yet fertile ground?
The sound of voices raised in song
Will last forever when you have gone.
Listen; what do you hear?

Betty M Dunne (Salisbury)

Time

What is the time?
What 'is' time?
Time to sleep, time to wake,
Time to eat, time to drink,
Time to be happy, time to be glad,
Time to be flippant, time to be sad,
Time to talk, time to learn,
Time to be gentle, or sometimes stern,
Time to listen, time one should not,
Time when one's cold, just right, or too hot.
Time to sing, time to dance,
Time for love, time for romance,
Time to work, time to play,
Time to relax at the end of a day,
Time to laugh, time to cry,
Time to pray, time to die,
Time to think before you do,
Time to ask, is time true?
Should the answer elude you,
And you need thoughts anew,
You have the time,
For time is infinite,
Time is immortal,
Time is eternal,
Time is, 'anytime'!

Douglas C Orton (Weston-super-Mare)

God's Day

Have beautiful thoughts of me.
Sing lovely songs to me,
of birds nesting in the trees,
flowers bending in the breeze.
Oh, what a beautiful, beautiful day.

Buttercups and daisies, and magpies too,
all there for me and you
to enjoy God's beauty, He paid for us to see.
Oh what a beautiful day have we.

Bees buzzing in the flowers,
butterflies in the rose bowers.
Oh what a beautiful sight to see
all put there for you and me.
Oh what a beautiful day
What a beautiful, beautiful day.

Ena Stanmore (High Wycombe)

Temptation

Not sure of what I'm feeling
But I know it's something strong
Trying to fight the notions
Because I am sure that I belong
In the life that I have already built
And no changes should be made
Apart from all the plans we have
For our future foundation one day
I keep telling myself it's forbidden fruit
Of which everyone's aware
The poison will softly linger
If take a bite I dare
I love my life if I'm honest
But yes there are things I would change
But spending my life with someone else
Is not a thought I'd entertain
Then maybe it's because it's different
And everything that I do is the same
Am I looking for excitement?
With no consequences gained
Either which way I need it to stop
Because I feel like I am insane
And am risking a life
that could be so good
All for the sake of a change.

Ca (Cheshunt)

Weston Shore

Ropes of water unravel on shingle.
They hiss and rustle away -
breathing into themselves again.
The sun burns my hands and face
while cold pokes my back and
slices down the collar of my coat.

The sea had reached the limit of its swell
and left a pale ridge along the shore
of cockle shells, disassembled
amongst plastic and wood.

Dark wood splintered and inert
tangles with bright, light filled
crisp packets and the unapproachable sun
leaves me green-blinded
with its burning after-image.

Patricia Morgan (Southampton)

Not Coming Home

I've kicked down the door so I've got to go.
There can only be trouble coming my way.
I hit the street and look for a place to rest.
Away from the bright lights and motor mouths.
I huddle in a corner and gather my thoughts.
Shall I come home and face the music?
I doubt there will be forgiveness. I'm not coming home.
I walk on through the rain-sodden streets.
My socks soaked and my spirits saddened.
'Where are my friends?' I ask
Nights turn to days, days into months . . .
I hear whispers that all is forgiven but my paranoid state forbids me to concede.
I trundle on, my head to the ground.
I think of my mum every day, I think of the pain I've caused.
But I'm not coming home.
Every day there is a sign, but I'm still not coming home.
When the rain penetrates my outer clothing, I am closest to home.
I see the Sunday roast gathering and the Friday night takeaway
But I can't come home.
I see tears fall on the bathroom floor on dates of importance,
But I'm not coming home.
I'm surrounded by dregs with their needles and tipples.
I'm an outcast here but also there.
Where will I sleep tonight? Shall I come home?
Sorry Mum, I'm not coming home.

Aaron Cole (Newton Abbot)

Hold On

When things go wrong
As they often do
And life is unfair
With blessings few
    Hold on

If the way seems long
With a heavy load
And your troubled mind
Sees no end to the road
        Hold on

Life can be kind
With promises new
Reach for the blue skies
All is well if you
    Hold on

Shirley Davis (Cinderford)

I Want To See Your Smile

I wanted to embrace you as a sister but I could not see your smile.

I looked away.

I wanted to help you as you stumbled.
You did not see the silent bike as you stepped into that road.

I looked away.

The cyclist swerved, managed to stop.
No words spoken, no comfort either way.
It seemed surreal.

I looked away.

I saw your small child screaming by your side.
I wanted to reassure him.
Perhaps he cried because like me,
He felt separated from you, his mother.

I looked away.

Surely your God must be my God too.
Doctrines cannot invent their own source.
God is love, you must feel it too.
In wisdom he gave us the precious gift of a smile.
To pass on, to comfort others.
I want to share my smile with you.

I do not want to look away.

Eileen Fry (Gloucester)

Four Haikus

When Mother was ill
Father put my hair in plaits
Without the ribbons.

My teenage tresses
Outgrew parental liking:
They were locks for love.

When I was Mother,
I had a haircut. My child
Cried, 'Can you still cook?'

Grey hair from my brush
Floats through an open window.
Line your spring nests, birds!

Helen Jeffries (Alton)

The Coup De Grace

(Based on the foot and mouth outbreak in March 2001)

As I survey my barren land a sadness fills my heart
And I contemplate my destiny.
No need to lock the gates today,
For no animal will enter in or out.
I close my eyes and listen to the final
Bleat of a lamb and the ricochet of a rifle shot,
Followed by a dreadful silence.
Mercifully, it is all over now.
But my heartbeat quickens and anger wells up
In my eyes, and I feel strangely alone.
There is no more movement now;
Just animated flames that dance
And tease, and taunt my soul
While a mocking stench arises from its sordid pyre,
And the sun, seemingly with homage, hides behind a darkened cloud.
I feel I shall not sleep tonight, for my heart is weary.
Maybe I'll cry a little and empty out my sorrow.
Such healthy animals too, and quite free from the disease.
Some just entered into the world, but denied the joys of spring.
Myself, I feel my book is closed
And begin to wish I too had never been born.
Yet, I have a choice, and am the lucky one.
But, alas, my restive mind stays unresolved.

George W Lansbury (Gloucester)

Ages

When I was twenty-one I wed my husband Tony
From that very first day I was never lonely.
I often laughed and maybe sometimes even cried
Life is often like that, tested and tried.
Then when I was twenty-five
We had a son 'our boy'.
He brought more love and so much joy
He grew so fast, babyhood doesn't last.
He made his own life, and took himself a lovely wife.
But now I've reached seventy-nine
And wish that I had not
If I had a choice I would go back to fifty like a shot.
Fifty seems lovely when you're seventy-nine
Not worried about going on fifty-one
But now today I'm seventy-nine and oh!
Tomorrow it's one more day to the big eight O.

Myra Rose Yates (Andover)

Passing

I lay down to sleep and dream again
Of more gentle times before the pain
Of daytime sun and evening moon
Of passionate times that passed too soon
Two loves entwined to be as one
Two souls together before time begun
Is love so fierce it will not die?
Is it for the passing of love that I must cry

Did I awake on a distant star
Could the death of a love travel so far
Were there three suns creating light
Did their radiance extinguish night
Was now a day, a day forever
Or could eternity just mean never
Have I slept my final sleep
Is it for the passing of night that I must weep

Did worlds collapse when we passed by
Were the winds of change just a sigh
Did mere mortals bless our love
Were we condemned by gods above
Could true love last a thousand years
Would its promise dry the tears
Or was your spoken word just a lie
Is it for the passing of truth that I must die.

Edward Jay (Paignton)

Happiness

Waking up early to a beautiful day
The sun shining through a broken cloud
A caterpillar crawling upon the windowpane
The neighbour's cat lies by a broken gate
Walking by the river, boats in the bay
Fishermen casting their floats on the waves
Birds fly high in the summer sky
Singing and whistling cheerfully loud
Farmers in the field are making hay
Frogs are croaking as you pass them by
My girlfriend waiting in a crowd
Her beauty like no other makes me proud
Love shining through that is honest and true
I will spare a thought for all of you
If you had only just one wish
Would it be that you were me.

Dugald McIntosh Thompson (Bedford)

Over Beachy Head

The sun was warm
As we left our bed
And packed a flask
With some buttered bread
The view was fine
We were newly wed
What a wonderful dawn
Over Beachy Head

When I reflect
On the things we said
When our past
Was still ahead
The life we planned
On those chalky beds
Covered with corn
Over Beachy Head

Now autumn's come
As green, brown and red
Meet the blue sea
White gulls overhead
Our plans came to little
Despite all that we said
But I love you still
Over Beachy Head

Stuart Delvin (Enfield)

Clapham Common, SW4

Not the Clapham
Of the morning rush
But rather the Clapham
Of the evening hush
Embracing each
And every noise
The subtle day
Employs
From planes playing
At noughts and crosses
In the sky to our
Counting the losses
Of an unlived day
While Clapham slowly
Falls asleep in silence
Relatively holy!

John Clancy (London)

The Losing Game

Do you *really* see the flowers grow,
with perfect form and myriad hues,
centres golden, all aglow
with nectar, tempting for the bee to use;
in turn to fertilise and procreate
the species for another date?
Do you see these as a child, the same;
or, is your life a losing game?

Do you *really* hear the children sing,
with voices pure and innocent?
Bodies swaying as they bring
enrapture to an evil world, intent
on self-destruction. Satan's dark abyss
abrogated by their sweet kiss.
Do you hear them, as a child, the same;
or is your life a losing game?

Is your life instead, a tilted glass,
intrusive needles in your arm;
Mind blown, trying to amass
false, fleeting ecstasies to something warm,
unceasing, durable? Alas the pain;
Own up, another dream in vain.
Will you *always* waste life's gift the same?
Why make your life a losing game?

David Tribute (Bournemouth)

The Family

The most potent force that God created,
For you the family can never be outdated;
The origin of nationality and global politics,
Does epitomise, you are so complex;
In life you offer so much culture
Yet in contribution you are no vulture;
You are the inspiration in all our lives,
When we are subject to varying strife
The engine room of a social scene,
And a happy one does portray that special sheen;
When each member therein plays its true role,
Creating the desired strength which is the goal;
For when things do go amiss
The result is turmoil and who wants this?
In God's creation you are the greatest tree,
You are, of course, the family.

William A Ryan (London)

Grandma's Hat

How I remember Grandma's hat
It was her pride and joy
A thing of beauty, it adorned
Twas not a simple toy
Crowned with fur and feather
With fruit piled up on top
It was guaranteed to make
A lovesick swain's eyes pop

She wore it with her Sunday best
On her way to church
She really was a stunner
The curate's heart would lurch
When upon a feast day
That hat came into sight
Why, all the fellas in the town
Fair swooned with sheer delight

Through thick and thin and toil and strife
On that hat Grandma relied
Why, even on her wedding day
She wore it as a bride
Now Grandma's gone and here am I
Discarding this and that
But nothing will prevail on me
To part with Grandma's hat

Harry Pryce (Saltash)

Untitled

And I less exist
less and less
I depart and depart
to asylum of stars
to place
where face to face
evening scatter'd
dark wings
so that I could
cover my grief
so that I could
reveal bottomless sorrow
which sneaks to my heart
like goth
O my God!
Where is God?

Korczak Krzysztof (London)

Seventies Sunrise

The sun comes up and dawn dilutes the dark.
I turn toward your dear familiar face
And watch you wake; a slow good morning smile
Precedes a sometimes passionate embrace.
Unhurried now, our chosen daily plan
Unfolds at leisurely un-working pace.
No more for us the breakfast on the run,
The traffic maze, the into office chase.

In younger years we rarely saw a sunrise,
Woke only to the clock's alarming ring;
No time to sit in bed with steaming coffee,
Admiring garden birds, hearing them sing.
Today we're charmed by goldfinches and robins,
While overhead loud rooks caw, as they wing
In search of twigs and willow fronds; nest-building,
An annual ritual, harbinger of Spring.

The sun is up, we 'must arise and go',
With poetry to write or golf to play;
Perhaps an exploration in the car,
Though each of us might choose a different way,
A new pursuit, a separate interest;
To reunite with ever more to say.
Contented, near the sunset of our lives
We savour every sunrise, every day.

Valerie Calvert (Cossington)

Devon Sonnet

There is a whispering in the aspens though the Devon sky is blue,
And the water in the Culm gets deeply dark with every dew,
I can look across the barley soughing in the balmy wind
And be glad to be in Devonshire with Midlands far behind.
The summers of so long ago seem far away indeed
And Devon's sweet serenity is all I've ever need.
She welcomed me to organised the school centenary;
The customs of a bygone age in pageant imagery;
To read the lore of headmasters who ruled those hundred years,
Each living chronicle inscribed for later joy and tears.
For children gathered sphagnum moss when two World Wars
were come,
They signed 'The Pledge' and bore the cane and helped the
harvest home.
Oh glad were we to travel here one golden holiday,
To settle down and make it home, a lifetime for to stay.

Pauline Field (Cullompton)

594

Memories Are Made Of These

You will find me in my garden
when the sun is in the sky
hidden midst the flowers
where the Clematis grow high,
the roses hide the brick
where no spying eye can see
a sunny day in London
I am happy as can be.

The grey that is London
outside my scenery
cannot stop the birds that sing
or the buzzing of the bee,
there is an oasis filled
with colour and with sound
my memories fill my garden
in the flowers that surround.

Each tiny bud that opens
leave imprints on my mind
I see the past too clearly
in images I find.
A shadow walks the paving
to plant each seed that grow
it keeps my memories fresh
in the yesterdays, I know.

Sally Flood (London)

Only A Fantasy

More than a picture in a frame
A shrew untouched who can never be tamed.
For all that I am is a seduction of the mind
Candy peaches and cream, to ease the daily grind.
A perfect image a sight to behold
An idol a trophy, for Man to lovingly hold.
Sculptured and moulded artificially to one's taste,
Hanging discreetly unveiled,
In their own private little place.
Like a portrait in the attic, illustrated to please,
A personal pin-up to titillate and tease.
A created image trapped in a gilded frame
Responsible for men's misgivings,
But devoid of any blame.
Held at ransom to fulfil fantasies and needs,
Created lovingly, into everything they want and perceive.

Marva Barnett (London)

A Summer's Walk

The most beautiful garden was sown by the Lord,
　　giving us country lanes,
With the scents from the flowers crying with dew,
　　or fresh from a gentle rain.
Sweet wildflowers cover the banks, each side
　　of the clear running stream,
Showing gentle rays as rainbow hues,
　　locked in a sunshine beam.

The buzz of the bee oblivious of you, seeking pollen
　　bright yellow,
Creeping honeysuckle entwined on a wall, aged by
　　the sun pink mellow.
Trickling cool waters, tiny waterfalls, dodge knobbly
　　grey and black stones,
Soft music follows the meandering lane,
　　capturing altered tones.

This scene calms the most troubled heart, giving
　　strength to worried souls.
Nature at its most beautiful will reverse the
　　saddest of roles.
Make an effort to find an evening, let your eyes
　　feast the view - then talk.
Speak your thoughts out loud to the babbling brook,
　　on your wonderful summer's walk.

Lucy Bloxham (St Austell)

Upon Open Water

Dancing like a ghost
Upon open water -
Feel this white satin sheet
That's wrapped around your body
Which blows in the wind -
But your long dark hair
Lies dead still
As if you're not really there -
Like a ghost you dance
Across this open water
That's where you will stay
For now and thereafter.
Dear only Child
You're the one and only daughter
Your soul remains dancing
Across these lonely waters.

David Brown (Plymouth)

Hello Old Friend

Hello old friend
It's been quite a while
But it's good to be near you
And see your smile,
Been on my own
For such a long time
But you put back the spark
And stopped the decline.

Hello old friend
Often thought about you
And through the ups and downs
A part of me knew
That one day I'd find you
I just never knew when
And the lust for life
Would be resurrected again.

Hello old friend
I have to confess
You lighten this world
Full of misery and stress,
Without you around
This world would be dark
So I give you my thanks
From the bottom of my heart.

Nikki Mortimer (Lancing)

The Town Crier

In Tewkesbury's streets, at certain times, a loud voice may be heard
A voice so clear and forthright, pronouncing every word
The raucous tones from gravel throat, emitting ever higher
In truth it is the rasping sound of Tewkesbury's own Town Crier
Bedecked in medieval clothes, colourful and gay
The bell rings thrice, oyez, oyez, the statement on its way
It may be news of an auction sale, or any local function
Chosen words, meaningful, delivered without compunction
Strategically positioned, outside local inns
Manfully combating the sound of traffic dins
Delivering his protocol, for all around to hear
Afterwards, easing his throat with a pint or two of beer
Visitors from near and far, are filled with great delight
To view this rotund gentleman, indeed a pleasing sight
With a flourish as he doffs his hat and says 'God save the Queen'
A memory of bygone days and what they used to mean.

A Hill (Tewkesbury)

The Church

The church, atop its windy hill,
Stands guard - an ancient sentinel.
And down below in cottage small
A boy and girl rise early, dress,
And climb the hill to worship there
In warmth and light, returning home
They breakfast, change and then depart,
To shoot and fish the day away.

Then later Gran and Grandad leave
To climb the hill to Matins, where
They pray and sing and talk to friends,
And catch up with the week's events.
The vicar's wife - is she now well?
And Mollie Jones baby too?
Before returning home to lunch,
To fire and papers, and a snooze.

But then, within a moment's space,
The church, atop its windy hill,
Stands silently and weeps to see
Within the shadow of its walls,
The three new graves so freshly dug.
And now the girl, with bitter tears,
Kneels there beside the ones she loved,
And wishes all her life away.

Hope Rhodes (Ferndown)

Benjamin

The soft blush folds of her wedding gown
Hid this precious secret from the joyous crowd
Unexpected, your life's journey had only just begun
Floating in the soft velvet darkness of the womb.
It seems only yesterday, but the months have passed
And the long awaited day dawns bright and clear
Pain and tears have gone, and the wonder at last
As she holds her small miracle of love so near.
I was so close by when you entered this world
It was magical, wonderful, charged with emotion
Your arrival will turn our lives upside down
But you will always have my undying devotion.
So this is a welcome to you my first grandchild
My heart is filled with such joy and elation.
Child of my child, firstborn and so precious
You are the start of our new generation.

Jennie Gilbert (Taunton)

Scarecrow

Hailed as the latest saviour of mankind,
I'm strung up by my arms and stuffed with straw,
Both feet suspended high above the ground.

A trilby's jammed upon my head,
A pipe stuck in my mouth. To the marauding crows
I'm a last warning in the shape of the Cross.

For a time they keep their distance,
But when they realise that I'm harmless,
The whole colony begins to attack.

I try to defend myself, putting on a brave face,
And whistling like mad through my pipe,
But I'm no match for their vicious beaks.

First they peck out my eyes. Then they peck off
My nose, and then they pinch both my ears,
So that I can't hear their mocking laughter.

After that, piece by piece, they strip away
My clothes and stuffing, till I stand naked,
Nothing but a thin spine and crossbar.

My carcass becomes a much used perch, and,
Instead of a last warning to the crows,
I become a grim warning
To mankind.

Keith Shaw (South Cheriton)

Krystyna

(Sonnet for your Eighteenth)

What happened to those days of long ago
when you pushed Dolly's pram across the park
and Mummy taught you how to knit and sew
and read you stories till the days grew dark?
Then Daddy came to kiss you in your sleep
and Teddy bears would dance in every dream.
Do you remember mornings when you'd creep
and snuggle up beside them in the warm?
And can you still recall those holidays
with bucket, spade - with sand and cobblestones -
and friends, dear friends with all their funny ways
and rugger pals with scrums and goals and groans?

Do you know Krystyna, from the start
we've loved you from the bottom of our heart?

R H M Vere (Heathfield)

599

The Doctor - A Kind And Thoughtful Man . . .

He was a kind and thoughtful man, though manner seemed austere,
He hid his charms, to make his mark, first filling me with fear.
This fear was only fleeting, with trust and foundations laid,
Respect became the reason his wishes were obeyed.

He held no further malice - once he had had his say,
But his 'lectures' I remember still, whilst reflecting on today.
You couldn't make excuses, his standards being high,
And as I grew to know him, I wouldn't dare to try!

He glared above his glasses when he was being cross,
And his manner held a warning; *do not provoke this seething boss.*
I had to keep my silence whilst waiting for the calm,
Then wondered what had happened, to trigger such alarm!

I always tried to please him, and he helped me in this quest
As he made me feel important; knowing I did my very best.
He was not one for praising but that I didn't mind,
Because life was really perfect, when he was being kind.

Although the years have passed, and life is different now,
The standards he instilled, are part of me, somehow.
I have worked for many others, though none have made their mark,
But he was someone special, who has a place within my heart.

Shirley E Parker (Plymouth)

The Keeper Of The Tower

Between the city and the water's edge
where shadows cross the sand,
the keeper of the tower
surveyed the frozen land.
There was nothing before that horizon
but endless fields of stone
and ugly splintered statues
where once green trees had grown.

Between the city and the water's edge
where time piles up the years,
he heard no childish laughter
nor shed the usual tears.
It was only the absolute stillness
that kept him rooted there
until his soul, like winter,
was deadwood: stripped and bare.

Jeff Vinter (Chichester)

Two Sides Of A Memory

(From the family. 25th June 2008)

There are so many things in this life that we face.
Some sad and some happy - at fast or slow pace.
But then there are those times when you reach a spot
That you should go on - if you're ready or not.
And these are the times that can break your resolve,
To go or stay - if to leave - or to solve.
A vital event and there's no one but you
To follow your thought of the next thing to do.
But it's no disgrace if one cannot comply
And hold back to let someone else have a try.
We aren't all brave heroes, we do normal things,
We only can do what our own effort brings,
But sometimes there is one who plugs up that breach
And enters a realm that not many will reach.
For just that brief instant, when time may stand still,
It's only just them and their own force of will,
A power, emerging from when first was laid
Erupts into force - and a hero is made.

A memory, that dark night, was made for us all
For you to remember and us to recall.
And so, dearest Rob - and from deep down inside,
We give you respect - and this family's pride.

Tom Martin (G/Dad) (Great Missenden)

Snowman

Standing tall in the night,
Cosy hat above his brow.

He keeps silent vigil,
Strangely proud somehow.

Through endless hours,
Till break of dawn

When the rising sun
Dismisses him with scorn.

Slowly he shrinks in size,
Melting away.

Tears trickle from his eyes
But he will return some day,

When next it snows
And children play.

Chris Stacey (London)

On The Oxford Canal

This quiet, damp July evening our launch chugs
Through squalid, sub-industrial decay:
Crumbling bricks and rusting metal sheets,
Foul rags, soiled paper fluttering, and a pipe
Dripping its poison into the canal . . .
A bridge (boys shout, dogs bark!) - now we are clear,
Into the mellow fields of Oxfordshire.

After the soft and intermittent rain,
The sun has just one salvaged hour to thrust
A few sharp-edged, yet gently luminous, shafts
Through fissures in the ceiling of grey cloud.
Those shafts are magic wands, for instantly
We see a strange land, golden and sublime . . .
We glimpse a joy beyond the frame of time.

This pungent smell of watery vegetation!
This smooth kaleidoscope of coloured change!
Green, liquid views dissolve, merge, melt again:
Reeds, waterfowl and cream-white meadowsweet . . .
Reeds, willowherb, tangled convolvulus . . .
Reeds, cattle drinking at the muddy edge . . .
Reeds, and a water-vole's trailed, silver wedge.

The sky is redder now. We swing around;
Return to derelict and poisoned ground.

Denis Pethebridge (Banbury)

Untitled

I will go to the top of the Mendip hills
when the world is too much for me;
to see how the Earth is spread at my feet
and the wind is wild and free.
To see how the wind is wild and free
and sets trees and grasses flying;
how it chases the clouds across the sky,
then I'll have no fear of dying.

For the voice of the wind is His voice in my ear
saying, 'Soon we will be meeting.
Your time on Earth, like the grass, is short
and like the clouds you are fleeting.
So come to me when your time is done,
like the wind you'll be wild and free;
free at last from the cares of Earth,
come and live eternally.'

Hazel Williams (Bristol)

I Want You

I want you
I want you to hold me
To feel you close to me
To be ensconced in your arms
Just to be bonded for that time
To make me feel like a woman, once more

I want to close out everything
Just you and me
Tight together against the world
When I am lying with you
Just for a short space of time
Nothing matters

I need you right now
I need you this moment
I physically ache for you so very much
Hold me tight in your arms
Until morning comes

Kiss away my tears
And make everything seem right
I never ever want the night to end
When I am with you
I just want you to hold me
For all eternity.

Paula Greene (Edgware)

Eden?

I made this great big beautiful world
In just under a week.
Then I made Man, gave him a wife,
And a voice with which to speak:
I gave them a beautiful garden,
Where they could roam at will,
But it wasn't enough, they wanted more -
And they never had their fill.

Now centuries later, my world's in a mess,
And there's war at every turn;
Greed and corruption are everywhere,
And beauty they seem to spurn.
They pollute the seas and the atmosphere,
And I've no one to blame but Me;
So next time I make a beautiful world . . .
I'll just leave it . . . man-free!

Janet Boor (Penzance)

The Ocean

The ocean roars and with its sound
I am lifted out of my reverie -
No silent sleep from the waters deep
Only rolling waves that reach the shore -
My heart it leaps and tears I weep
For him I lost to the ocean's roar.

I shout my grief to the ocean's roar
But the ocean did not answer
Defiantly I stand and stare
I behold a phantom -
It is my love floating in the air.

The ocean then turns about -
As if answering my shout,
It whispers to my mind -
I breathe its salty kiss -
I feel its rippled caress -
The ocean calls to me.

I hear but I do not answer
I stand silent with surprise -
Then a saw-edged wind catches me -
Flings me roughly into the deep
Grief and I do not struggle,
With my love I am doomed to sleep.

Kathy Dickenson (Stevenage)

No Happy Ending

Lyrics from a song or a poetic phrase
Fill my heart with sadness and pain,
There is an empty void time can never erase
For the loved one I cannot see again:
My tears mingle in with the raindrops
As I tread this dark lonely path
And dark clouds hang over the hilltops
As I struggle with love's cruel cruel wrath:
It hurts to know he's gone forever,
My friend, my soulmate, my lover,
Could I love again? No! Never never
For alas, he belongs to another:

But his memory will always be there,
It's not just a mere passing whim
The good times we had I'll cherish with care,
Those beautiful memories of him.

Olive Pentoni (Luton)

On Winter Hill

Our snatched words
are paper kites on Winter Hill.

There goes, fluttering
your colleague's
restless wife and what she did.
As aunt who married a
fisherman by some unlikely shore
the weather her wild horizon
jigs in the sky.
The departure of the Fordhams
for a different life, rises.
There go the wicked, wheeling
and swooping: parents
who disappear: those who change
course refusing to be useful any more

You say, and the wind stands till
'A moment comes: a chance
a risk: the impossible idea'.

We are silent then, on Winter Hill
and regard the ancient view.
A toy train caterpillars on its track
beside the shining river's blade
from Marlow to Bourne End and back.

R Muncie (Maidenhead)

One Day In The Future

One day in the future, when the world's tired of turning,
When daylight has faded and the sun has stopped burning,
When the stars have all dimmed
And on earth blows a wind,
When the world is on fire,
With flames ever higher;
Who's hand will it be that dries up the sea?
One day in the future, what day will it be?

One day in the future, when the clouds blow away,
When the fields turn to dust and there is darkness all day;
When the rivers are running with nothing but tears,
Survivors cry out, but nobody hears.
Petrified trees as witnesses stand,
Like eerie grey sentinels keeping watch o'er the land.
One day in the future, one day who knows when?
Like the planets in the cosmos, we'll be dead, just like them!

Colin Spicer

Thinking Of You

Whatever you do I am always thinking of you,
You're in my mind today,
I wish you could see
What you mean to me,
And I'll take your hurt away.

We are both a sorry pair,
And should not have a care,
But the hurt gets in the way,
If you will trust in me,
Then we can see,
That love can find a way.

Each night I pray,
That you ring me and say,
Let's take a chance,
And then the hurt goes away,
And we have today,
And it's the start of a new romance.

Now we're walking side by side,
And we are so full of pride,
The hurt is going away,
Then you look at me,
And we can see,
That true love can find a way.

Maureen Hughes (Weston-super-Mare)

Autumn Death

Death lets them rest, strewn,
In brown, black layers
Upon the rain flecked verge
Beside the oft still flowing rills,
Whilst high above them hang
Grey and moss decked boughs
That gave them verdant life,
Beneath the warming sun.

This summer, now long past,
Slowly drifted into winter's maw;
Whose harsh and chilling gusts
Wrought this harvest of death.
So now along the verge we see
The limp damp forms decay,
Whose death will succour
Spring's fresh, nascent growth.

Michael Howe (Basingstoke)

The Narrow Man

The narrow man
Walked down the street
Narrow as an arrow.

He didn't look strong
And he didn't look weak.
He held himself proudly
He was light on his feet.

Spick and span was the narrow man
In shiny shoes
And a light summer suit,
Looking happy and full of youth.

With smooth dark skin
And laughter in his eyes,
He looked like someone
Who has just won a prize.

People who saw him
As he passed,
Had to cast
A second glance.

The narrow man
Walked down the street
Narrow as an arrow.

M C Barnes (Enfield)

Painted Lady

She prefers to flutter
away across the river, over mudflats
whilst her flower opens in the sun.

She is lured by sweet pink scents
in garish riverbank gardens
whilst her flower becomes purple.

She braves uplifting air, to visit
balconies bursting with minute nature
whilst her flower gently sways.

She prefers to dart along the disused railway
just to stretch her delicate wings
whilst her flower patiently waits.

She turns, her task complete, it is time to return
whilst her flower has reached perfection
and is calling her home.

Tracey Cornwell (Shoreham By Sea)

The Donkey Shay

The donkey shay had had its day as Granny took to the road.
Its wheels screeched most noisily protesting at the load.

The donkey it was in a mood, and lashed out left and right,
But Granny reaching for the whip and drawing the reins in tight.
Soon she had that donkey at full speed, it was a worrying sight.

Her hat took off to her surprise, and settled down across her eyes.
The wheels, once so firm and stout, had buckled around to inside out.
This put a strain upon the shaft, which promptly cracked and broke in half.

The donkey now could see his chance, and stopped right dead and did a prance.
For Granny there was no reprieve,
Reluctant as she was to leave her seat upon the shay,
And sailed over the donkey's head to land in the roadway.

Granfer soon was on the scene and quickly grabbed the moke,
Then stared and stared at the poor old shay before he ever spoke.
Then reaching for Granny's hand, he quietly did say,
'What are you doing down there my dear - you're supposed to sit on the shay.'

Grandma was in no mood for jokes and gave that donkey such a poke,
Then stood upright inside the reins.

The donkey looked, and used his brains then took off like a rocket,
And Granny too, before she knew it was upside down with her foot in her pocket.

And Granfer too was in the way of what was left of the poor old shay.

E J Paget (Falmouth)

Eden

*(Claymining works 'Bodelva Pit' until Tim Smit and his team came
to create Eden, with acclaim to its 'plantparadisic' name)*

A 'sleeping beauty' Cornwall was -
the prince had not then come,
until Tim Smit tamed the 'white steed'
and gave beauty a home.
As if erected by a wand
'dream bubbled biomes' comely stand,
on heartfelt tended Eden land.
And now as from the vernal date
people of many nations come daily -
as if to celebrate outcome of a successful quest
which proves so wonderfully great,
serving soul and body best.
We walk the place in grateful awe
and feel an inner rest.

Marie Nanny Dowrick (St Austell)

Come To Paradise Island

Have you heard of 'Paradise Island'
Such a beautiful place to be
Peaceful and delightful
And surrounded by the sea
Lovely walks and tempting food
There's nowhere better you'll see
And so easy to get to -
Whether by air or sea
A warm relaxing climate
With interesting places to know
You can enjoy a lazy holiday
With so many places to go
Have a happy healthy time
On this special 'Paradise Island'
Taste the delightful food
Roam anywhere you wish
Whatever your type of mood
Swim in the sea
Or catch some lovely fish
Peaceful accommodation
Wherever you want to stay
You'll be extra welcome
Because everyone loves Guernsey
A fantastic place to be.

Martin Selwood (Waterlooville)

The Rose

To soothe the soul
And gladden every eye,
There is in nature's store
A gift of soft repose.

Nurtured by a morning's dew,
Opened by a lover's sigh,
There stands in beauteous majesty,
The sweet and scented rose.

A passing rainbow gave
Some scarlet, pink and gold,
A sea of emerald,
Sprayed some glossy green,
Then each petal nature's fingers,
Began to wrap and fold -
Until a voice from paradise
Proclaimed the rose - a queen.

Stuart McAllister (Plymouth)

Am I Sixty?

Am I sixty? Am I sixty?
I can't believe it's true.
Have I been here for sixty years?
Sometimes it feels like two.
But then again some days you see
When I feel I've had enough
I think I just can't take this any more if tomorrow is as tough.
Sometimes the pain is very hard
And more than I can bear.
I wonder what it's all about, sometimes I just don't care!
I sit and think and worry and weep
And fight the dark to get to sleep.
But then I wake to a brand new day
And think just maybe it will go my way.
And sure enough the day is fine
I think to myself, *this life is mine*
I haven't time to be so sad,
I must cheer up, I must be glad
That I can walk, and I can sing
And I can do most anything.
So then for me I say, 'Three cheers'
Who cares if I am sixty years.
I've all the memories that's gone before
And I surely won't get sixty more.

Joy Toms (Cheltenham)

The Glebe Garden

The knapped-flint façade of
Old Priors Dean, its newly painted
Windows a muddy Georgian green.

The capricious winter weather,
Transforms the quality of the light,
A glowing crimson sun hung low

Casts long shadows, a bold
Stone statue of a man, well dressed
In a garment of lichen.

A mixed border made magical by frost,
An old stone seat set amidst a
Tangle of glinting foliage.

A spider's web outlined by rime,
Makes a silvery winter scene
And all about the trees are bare.

Carole Resplandy (Hammersmith)

The Time Of My Life

Have I retired? Yes I have.
Have I got bored? No I haven't had time.
Do I get lonely? Oh no!
Am I infirm? No I really am fine.
What do I do every day?
Look after my grandchild who likes me to play.
As my years go from silver to gold,
My voluntary work involves helping the old.
But you're old yourself, they tell me,
But now there's no pressure, I feel that I'm free
To do just what I want, how and when
And sometimes find time to pick up a pen.
I go down to the town and I shop
With my bus pass I walk to the local bus stop
And chat to someone in the queue,
There's surely some gossip to keep me amused.
My family tree's coming on,
I would like to know just to whom I belong.
But now I have run out of time,
I'm rushing to try and get this to rhyme.
I'm so terribly busy you see
But I have to make time to go for a wee.
So have I retired? Yes from strife
Of going to work not from having a life.

Audrey Harman (Guildford)

Quiet Day In The Suburbs

Relieve the bladder.
Open windows for fresh air.
Take a sip of tea.

The pale green neck-tie
(fine cloth for her splashed gravy!)
smells of old wardrobes.

Fancy the fruit cake?
Buy two for the price of one.
And sniff my melons.

In the liquor store,
think of drinking all that gin.
Coins chink in a till.

Come motorist's friend,
longed-for recovery truck.
Flash your yellow lights.

Michael Cleary (London)

611

Graffiti Writerz

Show me an image, to which I can lust
show me the person whom I can trust
bring me the colours contained, not brushed
what I do, I feel I must,
ruin the canvas bringing me noughts
question my motive to darken my thoughts
I question my worth as each day ceases
always together as I'm all to pieces
as night-time descends, so does my mood
want fills my head and becomes my food
without being rude I question why
the sheep just follow then they die
against the masses I still defy
but how much longer must I try?
Whilst alive, I'll test the grain
making sure I'm not the same
a different name, another me
the only time I feel I'm free
of invisible chains and blunted axes
that grind my wheel to pay these taxes
as I must. As we should
help to keep our world this good
this mono-grey, this urbanite
brightened by the things I write.

C D Spooner (Chichester)

The Spinney

Today I walked through Rotten Corner
And listened for the drumming bird.
But alas! He doesn't drum today.

From a nearby Alder a tiny wren scolds
Me roundy, and all around the glade
Is avian song.

Then; tchick! Tchick! Above me on a
Towering beech he sits, in liveried black
And white with dash of red upon his head.

I withhold my breath, but in just a heartbeat
He has flown, and all around the glade
Is avian song.

Today I leave Rotten Corner, content, for
In a lofty tree I spied that elusive
Drumming bird.

Michael Brooks (Luton)

My Beautiful Town Pigeon

On Christmas Eve so still I lay
Alone and cold in the shop doorway,
And people were walking by so fast,
Because no one cared that I'd breathed my last,
Not a single word of sorrow was said,
And no one cared that I was dead
But I once soared in skies so blue
Looking down on all of you,
And I raised my babies in the softest nest,
Amongst leaves of green I would rest,
From day to day I would feast on seed
I'd eat my fill, but some called it greed,
On warm summer days I'd softly 'coo'
And my calming song you'd listen too,
But over the sound of tranquillity
Was the rage of voices angry with me,
So, I know for sure I'll not be missed
By those who wished I didn't exist,
But please don't pass my lifeless shell
Or smile and cast me down to Hell,
For my eyes once saw all you see,
And my beating heart gave life to me,
And just like you I breathed the air
So, please someone, take time to care.

Pauline Jones (London)

Today

Today is the present
Tomorrow is the future
Yesterday is history

Today is alive
Tomorrow is possible
Yesterday is sleeping

Today is new era
Tomorrow is obscure
Yesterday is past

Today is reigning
Tomorrow is claiming
Yesterday is serene

Today is the master
Tomorrow is a vision
Yesterday is sold.

David Pollard (Stroud)

A New Angel In Heaven

Whatever happened to us Ken,
I fail to understand,
Why God reached out that fatal day
And took you by the hand?
I didn't want to let you go,
I know you tried to fight,
Now every day seems very slow
And darker is my night.
I can't believe I've lost you,
You were one in a million to me,
I just want you back here Ken
And regain our unity.
I can't get used to losing you
And know I never will,
I need your arms around me Ken,
All this seems so unreal.
And when I reach those Pearly Gates
I'm going to question God like mad,
Why did He come and take away
Such a caring, loving dad?
Well my sunshine has been taken
And my world has had to end,
Not only did he take your life
He also took my friend.

Carole Bates (Crawley)

Exile

'Seek me in the broken hearts and by the crumbling tombs.'
Ah, the old poet calls to Allah;
And I too call, I, an old and distraught wanderer.

Born happy in a wild land, gone now forever.
Ah, gone: borders moved at random,
Nation reduced to slogan for a gruesome, greedy panjandrum.

Trace a childhood: pale band of savannah,
Shade of antelope, ring of huts, snag on a thorn tree
And the line is lost in neon, noise, human rights, grimly free,

Wavering in a graveyard of memories.
Ah, lost, erased by city blocks, foreign tongues
Far from custom, family bonds.

Please, Allah, please seek me.
Ah, tear from me my broken heart;
Return to me mother, father, priest and land, never more to weep nor part.

Tessa Paul (London)

The Daydream

There's a clearing in the forest,
Where I sometimes sit and ponder.
The atmosphere is quiet,
My thoughts will often wander.
Suddenly without warning,
Little men will then appear,
Stocky little fellows,
With long flowing beards,
They sit in a circle looking rather grim,
Discussing life around them,
No one dares to butt in.
They eye me with suspicion,
No one says a word,
I daren't move a muscle,
I'm paralysed with fear.
The older one gives a smile
Such a relief is this,
Another rather cheeky one,
Blows a gentle kiss.
I return this greeting with a wave,
Not daring yet to move, then -
With one eye open I realise the scene,
I've had a little nap and -
Enjoyed a lovely daydream.

Freda Symonds (Torquay)

Night Fades In Different Ways

Her green eyes search for moonlight,
Over tides, submerged into deep
    Marine-blue.

I love you like the ocean loves the shore,
Like the birds love the air -
    Within which the clouds adore the sky.

Just like the cupid's whisper, which falls upon deaf ears,
    Or the unlawful spoiling of our elegant sphere.

I embrace her lips, with a single kiss -
Moving my mind through a black hole in space.

I hold her heart in my hands,
And fix her crown of gold.
In pictures of meadows.
She was dodging the arrows,
- But one has struck her down.

Dan Moxham (Bristol)

615

Growth Of Weapons Of War

Man has always been aggressive to Man
Ever since the world began
First they fought with clubs and stones
Fighting each other and breaking their bones
Next came the sword and the defence was a shield
Great battles were fought in countryside fields
Following on the bow and arrow now appeared
A deadly weapon opponents learned to fear
Next powder and shot to feed the flintlock gun
Reloading after each shot until victory was won
Fighting in trenches the rifle and bayonet arrived
Killing in hundreds not many survived
Tanks crushed through towns and house were shattered
Big guns firing salvoes all in their path severely battered
Scientists made the atom bomb a weapon to eradicate
When used a hundred thousand people were annihilated
And great areas of land were completely devastated
The aftermath was the ground could not be cultivated
We are now manufacturing more destructive weapons
Until ultimately we will all be relocated in Heaven
Before the ultimate occurs let us start against breaking bones
Back to the days of using clubs and hurling stones
Why don't we travel back to the start
Before we blow our world apart.

LAG Butler (Liphook)

Deep Thought

(Dedicated to Emma Henderson)

How beautiful is the air,
in these lofty apartments I call my mind.

Diamonds are not always forever,
sometimes they are never never,
I've seen engagement rings returned.

The motorway had broken his heart.
All there was left for him now, was,
the hard shoulder to cry on.

Now the house is full of ghosts
and it is up for sale - hence
my vigil at the letterbox
wishing away the mail,
my heart will remain in prevailed silence.

Sally Wyatt (Wallingford)

I Found The Cure

You're the apple of my eye
a shudder for my being,
rarer than an orchid petal
gold dust wrapped in skin,
I look at you with melting lust
and the way you hold your bones,
you have charisma roaming wild
like a stallion in the spring.
My attention needs a stronger span
that's why lovers came and went,
but Cupid drew his finest bow
when he shot you through my heart,
I'm wounded, but it isn't blood
that leaks from longing veins,
I'm burning up, my candle throws
much more than idle sparks.
I didn't think I'd ever find
a beauty for this beast,
I thought I'd stay a lonely moon
a rover in the skies,
but here I am, I've picked the fruit
from the magic tree of love,
and I found the cure I always craved
for the illness in my eyes.

Andrew Hobbs (Chandlers Ford)

Nocturn

(For Alison)

In silence under the street lights
hard light, first stillness, then movement
a shape sloping through ghosted grass
and out onto a stark pavement

I watch for a short time -
intrude perhaps (the subtle dance
enacted next the shadow self)
and wonder which is more real

At this late hour under the exact
half moon, the two clouds edged
with moonlight, the wide sky of stars
the something else

which is more real, the fox or her shadow

Sean Donaghey (Charlton)

Borders And Edges

The lavender's alive with bees,
And roses are abounding;
The buddleia's full of peacocks
And the croaks of frogs are sounding.
When every colour joins the dance
And the sunshine's dappled o'er,
There's a magic in the garden
That no one can ignore.
Some people like their plants in rows
And standing to attention;
I'd rather have cascading ones
Too numerous to mention.
Red, blue and white - oh what a sight,
Yellow and orange too,
All leaping and tumbling from a height
And bursting into view.
Petunias, a purply pink
Are bubbling in my old stone sink.
Lobelias sprouting here and there
And hollyhocks climb in the air.
There's just one thing left to be done
Before my garden is at one -
I'll trim the edges very neat
To make the borders look complete.

C A Leeding (Stroud)

Willowed Moon

A melancholy shadow dapples its light upon a silken façade,
Watery soul, a luminosity that constantly animates.
The pull and tide of your lunar mood is a seductive secretion.

An orange moon, merely in reflection;
A saturation of bloodless hope.

Diffusion, dispersion, infiltration, penetration, permeation,
Distant but attainable, on a voyeuristic voyage of loneliness,
To be looked at, never touched, conquered but not a conquest.

An ocean of omnipotence belies your heart,
A sea of tranquillity, amidst a hollow existence . . . willowed moon.

Winnowed to see the transparency of a glowing grain.
Every cell permits beauty, and an uncontrollable allure,
Like the moon, an enigma, a face of porcelain and a soul that is fragile.

The cracks are just beneath the surface.

Charlotte Grace Hopkins (London)

You Are

You're assertive you are
And abrasive too,
You're constructive you are
And coercive too,
You're decisive you are
And deceptive too,
You're effective you are
And effusive too,
You're imaginative you are
And intrusive too,
You're objective you are
And oppressive too,
You're perceptive you are
And projective too,
You're retrospective you are
And restrictive too,
You're suggestive you are
And secretive too,
You're talkative you are
And tentative too,
You're undemonstrative you are
And uncooperative too,
You're you, you are
And you, you and you.

Lisa Harper-Gough (Newbury)

Innocence

Who am I who sits and dreams
While others do their task?
Why am I inquisitive
While others never ask?
Will I ever change the world
Or even see it end?
Will I have a happy life
And always have a friend?
Or will my life last for a year,
Even just this day?
As quickly as God gave me breath
Will it go away?
While others fight to have their say
Will I be always mild?
Who am I to ask these things?
Me, I'm just a child.

David Morgan (Port Issac)

In Praise Of Ringwood

I'm glad I live in Ringwood Town
(The Hampshire one, I mean)
The coast's quite close at Lymington,
The Forest in-between.
You can head up north to Salisbury,
It's only up the road,
The city's steeped in history,
The tourists swarm in droves!
If shops and entertainment
Are more your cup of tea,
Try Bournemouth with its theatres
And miles of sand and sea.
A friendly town is Ringwood,
A market every week;
Unfortunately the livestock sales
Have ceased, now farming's bleak:
But all the many stalls are great,
We've plants, fresh fish and cheese,
Good bargain clothes, fine local crafts,
No end of things to please;
We've glorious countryside around,
The green belt at its best;
We really do appreciate
To live here, we're much blessed!

Corinne Lovell (Ringwood)

Meditation

I take myself to a quiet place
To sit in peace, to have some space
I close my eyes and clear my mind
My inner self I try to find
I travel in thought to a faraway land
Where dreams and love go hand in hand
Feelings of quiet, well being flows through
And I see the world has a rosy hue
A comforting peace flows all around
My eyes are still closed, there is no sound
This inner strength I have come to know
Gives mind and spirit an infinite glow
I return myself from this meditative state
Enjoy a moment when time must wait
With peace and tranquillity filling my mind
My inner self has at last been refined.

Gillian Doble (Taunton)

Nature-Trail

Left far behind is winter's scene
As buds unfurl, turning forests green
Woodlands become a mass of blue haze
As carpets of bluebells meet our gaze.
The pungent scent of garlic fills the air
As we gingerly step with every care.
Clusters of primroses shyly peep
Awakening from their winter sleep.
The magic of spring is a wonderful sight
As fledglings take their very first flight.
Fox cubs nervously leave their lair
Activity suddenly is everywhere.
Buttercups become a shimmering gold
As covered in dew their petals unfold
Opening up to greet a new day
And to catch a glimpse of the sun's first ray.
Tiny rabbits hop and scamper about
Then dash for cover when in doubt.
Pussywillow and catkin hang from the bough
We see again the farmer's plough.
The gentle ripple of a woodland stream
Wending its way cool and supreme.
As swarms of honeybees take to the wing
We know winter's past, and this is spring.

Gwyneth Weaver (Stroud)

Goodbye To Nurse Rita

Five siblings plus her niece
of different shades and from
two different bands of gold;
all stood steadfast
at the Vale in Luton, Beds
to say goodbye to nurse Rita.
'Twas goodbye to the womb
that housed life.
Goodbye to the breasts
that fed infants.
Goodbye to the soft heart
that nursed the sick and
cared for the elderly.
While gazing at a heap of fertilizer;
thought to myself,
this has got to be final . . .

Fran Hughes (Luton)

The Ballet Exam

I'm training for an examination
'Grade I, ballet in education,'
There are five positions
To place my feet,
Keep my back up straight,
And tuck in my seat.
Half a bend is Demi Plié
(The terms are all in French, you see.)
I have to point and stretch my toes
Battement Tendu, and so it goes.
Grand battement, devant and derriere,
And exercises at the barre,
Carriage of arms is ports de bras,
And in the character steps
Country pas de basque.
Adagé is movement,
With control and good line,
Then there's sautés in first
Gestures and mime.
Let's hope, after this
That I'll get through,
Then I can work for the grade II,
Cos I was lucky in the primary,
I was highly commended for that, you see!

Doris Mary Miller (Wellington)

That Old Fashioned Fire

What a beautiful sight, that of an old fashioned fire,
So full of warmth, comfort, there's so much to admire.
Great chunky logs helping to give a blazing flame,
No other fire can ever be quite the same.
The sound of snappy crackles, sparkling from the wood,
Surrounded by the attractive stone fireplace makes it look so good.
As one sits gazing in that rocking chair,
Outside there seems to be rain in the air.
There she lies so contented on that sheepskin rug,
Of course it's the black cat all crouched up nice and snug.
The fire rages and now has a lovely glow,
As the rain now lashes hard against the window.
Swirling sounds from a wind now really strong,
But the cat still sleeps, fire still burns, and the chair rocks on.
As time goes on even the weather begins to tire,
But however, still remaining is that old fashioned fire.

Paul Hobbs (Weston-super-Mare)

The Nagathame Warrior Women!

The Nagathame warrior women
Are as frightening as can be,
They carry large broad swords
And shields and stand at 6 foot 3,
With war paint on their faces,
They shout and scream at me,
So when I see them coming,
I run towards a tree.
They wear long silk dresses,
Down to their feet,
With soldiers military caps on their heads
As trophies, a symbol of victory,
Taken from those they have killed
Or captured in retreat.
Traders come to visit them,
Bearing silk knickers and nylon stockings,
Which the Nagathame warriors wear under
Their dresses, going into battle
In exchange, the Nagathame give
The traders goats, sheep and cattle.
As I write this poem,
My mind is filled with fear,
The Nagathame are watching me,
And soon they will be here.

Stephen L Freeman (Edgware)

The Land Of Dream

You know that place 'tween sleep and wake
That draws their slumber . . .
The world outside can't know enchantment
The likes of which they're under!
Memory reflects its transient lull
Like waters ebbing from a distant shore . . .
A place where even time can't go
But 'twould lie down for.
That world which time outside forgets
But can't erase leaves its trace . . .
Like God's light etched
Upon each darling brow and face.
And there, where a faerie stooped to steal a kiss;
(Their happy thoughts 'twould seem)
That's where you will remember -
In a dream!

Jacqueline Anne Hosken (Redruth)

Running Out Of Time

He took a sighting along the barrel,
and lay stock still.
Never had a father, no one to look to,
dreamed all his life of being a soldier.
Looking along the trench,
he saw no sign of life,
realised he was the only one left.
It was never supposed to be like this.
No one said anything to prepare you.
Just as well he mused,
never had done it, if I'd know.
The quiet was like a snowdrop,
the stillness illusory.
He put down his gun for a moment.
Figures appeared, running for their lives.
Surely they weren't going to hurt him
seeing all the dead
and he with his weapon laid down.
They fired as they ran
and blew him out of this world
and into the next.
He died with a frown on his face.
Though he had been told what to do,
he never knew why.

A' O' E' (Beaconsfield)

The Cave

Beneath the stormy sky of red and mauve,
The little boat swept into the gale-lashed cove.
Staggered up the beach, the sailor, drenched but brave,
Across the shingle and crawled into the echoing cave!
The wind howled like souls of many sailors lost:
The boat drifted away as it heaved and tossed.
Rain made a curtain across the cave's mouth -
The wind blew north, east, west and south!
Deeper into the cave the exhausted sailor crept,
The dreadful storm raged on: the sailor slept!
Morning came, and with it the Revenue men,
Surrounding the cave. (There were at least ten!)
They found the sailor unconscious, wet, cold and numb -
They found the smuggled barrels of wine and rum!
And, carrying him off to that damp and filthy gaol,
So for him ended another Dorset smuggling tale!

Lionel James Cluett (Poole)

Untitled

*(Written after the sale of the Duke and Duchess of Windsor's'
Home and Personal Effects - February 1998)*

You cannot see us but we see you
Watched in the silence of the house
We shared - so long ago
So long when we were flesh and bone
We often wander through the house -
As once it was dreaming again
Of our long loving years - the pain
Remembrances regrets and woes
Music, laughter, friends and foes
To lose a lover for a throne?
Impossible he said she is
More precious than a crown
We walk the empty rooms and view
Glittering trappings once we knew
And treasured - so many faces, many lands
Ran with the dogs - hands in hands
In spirit breathed the garden scent
Sat under the trees - no need to explain
How things went -
No tears for you nor grief for me
Together in shadows we reign.

A F Stanley (Exeter)

Time Never Changes

Just a thought of mine to
Stroll in the twilight hour.
Guided by the light of a silvery
Moon. To sit by a little stream and
Wish upon a star. Soon a cockerel
Will crow. Why? I don't know. The
Birds will then sing in the dawn.
Who knows what the new day will
Bring? The chances are it may not
Change a thing. The moon and the
Stars we know have always
Been high in the sky. The sun
Can deceive us and sometimes pass
Us by. We live and we die, it's been
That way since time began and
Will be for evermore. What a
Wonderful world.

Richard Mahoney (Lancing)

Spring Into Summer

Spring is turning into Summer, what bliss,
We have had no rain for a week!
So the haymaker has made hay
From the tall, flowing stalks
In the fallow field next to me.
First it was cut and bent over,
Then came swirling and turning,
Followed by baling and wrapping.
The field became denuded and stubbled
But, heigh-ho, in two weeks green shoots appeared,
The rooks came croaking and jostling,
Making small birds hop quickly away.

Butterflies now flutter over the fence
To see what is on offer in the garden.
A gull swoops from the chimney pot
Making a plaintive cry.
It circles the field, has it lost its mate?
Or is lonely with no one to play?

Yesterday was lovely,
Blue limpid sky and hot sun.
Today is scurrying cloud and wind.
Oh! Don't go away yet, Summer,
For, it is still only July.

Yvonne Luckham (Ringwood)

The Storm

The sultry air thickened,
The crimson sunset quickened,
As clouds hung low and black,
Across the August sky.
The murky waters quivered,
A sudden breeze sighed,
And stirred the dust laden leaves.
The nightjar screeched, alarmed,
And flew as if beyond the storm.
The valley echoed with the roar of thunder,
Trees lit up and bent by lightning,
Sharp and cold as steel.
The rains, through veiled clouds broke
And lashed the hills beyond.
The earth formed pools of cool water,
And life awoke again,
Thirstily, to greet the dawn.

Marion Gunther (Oxford)

We Miss You

Sleep in peace our beloved one,
We treasure the time we had
With you very much.
We miss your lovely smiles,
Your happy laughter,
And your loving kindness.
We will remember special days,
Things you've said and done.

You are more precious than
You will ever know.
Although you are not with us in person,
We know you're here in spirit.
You will always be in our hearts,
In our thoughts, and in our memories.

There is never a day that goes by
When we don't think of you.
We are not there to take care of you anymore,
But we know the angels will.
You were like a light that shone from Heaven,
Lent to us for a while.
You will always be
Our bundle of joy,
So sleep in Heavenly peace.

Emelia Rickman (London)

Coastal Erosion

The coastal cliffs of sand and clay
Relentlessly rained on day after day,
Sodden and seeping
Wet and weeping
Like a woman in waiting
The waters break,
But happy outcome - no
The birth of these cliffs was decades ago.
Now just destruction as they slide their way
To the shore below.
Here waterfalls, there rivulets,
Taking the slurry, slipping and sliding.
In colourful streams of white, green and brown,
Down, down, down.
Washed by the sea on the shore at high tide,
The loss of the land which caused such emotion
Another chapter in coastal erosion.

Pat Allen (Ventnor)

Our Lil And Our Jack

Surrounded by love, now's the right time to tell
Of those troublesome days I remember so well
Fresh in my memory though many years back
I remember my fears for our Lil and our Jack.

Their children both suffered - my mum gave them hope
She always found time, she just seemed to cope
With seven of us plus a nephew and niece
There was noise, there was laughter, but no chance of peace.

Second-hand clothes, torn boots, torn socks
How I envied my friends in their clean pretty frocks.
We had Mum's brother Nat - both deaf and blind
And Mum's brother Max - so quiet and kind.
Poor Dad working hard, he couldn't hold back
Cos we all had to help our Lil and our Jack.

Food was a-plenty but Mum wasn't mine
Always too busy to spare me the time
And I spent my schooldays imagining others
With their mums and dads and sisters and brothers.

I'd picture for hours a room of my own
My teachers would shout but they couldn't have known
The worries I'd have so I'd sit at the back,
'Please God help our family; our Lil and our Jack.

Barbara Spencer (Broadstone)

Kiss Goodnight

(For James)

You brighten my day
Wipe away my tears
Ease the pain
Take away the fears

I will love you
Forever and always
I'll stay with you
For the rest of my days

This is a promise
That I make to you
You can rest assure
I'll always see it through

I'll be there in the morning light
And I'll always be your kiss goodnight

Rebecca Penfold (Southampton)

Easter Sunday

Like daffodils tossed carelessly aloft,
Two yellow butterflies in their uncertain haste
Chase across the hedge, spring-tipped with palest green
Which, winter-naked, had exposed
A rusted fence, grey deadened twigs and crumpled polythene.

Now, pheasants peck the ploughed furrow,
Disdaining traffic on the bordering road,
They meet their frequent death all unaware
Of startled drivers in their frantic speed
Who hate to hurt yet take so little heed!

New trout have graced the winter-flooded brook:
The lonely collared dove has found a mate:
Two muntjacs daily stroll along the verge
And all of nature has no time to wait.

Now swing the mallard ducks in downward curve,
Where daffodils stand caped with crusted leaves.
They only yesterday that mouldering carpet speared
With which they now with comic nonchalance are draped.

They shake their bright, tempestuous trumpets clear,
Sounding aloud the urgent song of spring
To fattened buds on steely chestnut twigs
And rooks that on treetops confidently swing.

Dorothy Francis (Rickmansworth)

The Flame Of Hope

It shimmers in the smallest of small breezes,
Flickers, bends sideways,
Is almost extinguished, but not quite.
Infinitesimal, it still glows,
A diamond splinter of light
In the darkest of dark places.
A glint in the tear-filled eyes of the desperate.
A tiny spark that once embraced,
Flares to a mighty blaze
More powerful than a million burning suns.
A fragile thing, gentle as gossamer and yet
Unable to be broken or uprooted,
Once bedded in the heart and soul of man.
Lifting him up from the mire of despair
To the utmost reaches of the universe and beyond.
Clear burning, unquenchable and eternal,
The beautiful flame of *Hope!*

Julia Whale (Blandford Forum)

The Hands Of Time

Life is a finely tuned timepiece
seconds and minutes turn into hours.
The world waits with anticipation to be discovered
by the intrigued explorer.

Time is on the world's side,
for us - slowly ticking away,
as the sand of life flows through . . .

Hours to days,
nightfall creeps in,
encasing the world in its thick cloak of darkness,
barely a movement, all is still . . .
soon to be replaced by the early morning sun rising
and the stirring of life for a new day.

Days pass into months,
bringing new seasons,
fresh air cuts the warm sun.

Spring is near with its inspirations,
flowers are in bud,
relaxing days to be had on the beach.
All too soon turning the leaves to fall
and time to be reset,
the snow to drift in . . .

Denise Harris (Haywards Heath)

The Concrete Jungle

Never knowing who's coming round the corner at you -
Have they got a gun or a knife?
Will they try and rape my wife?
Will an ambulance save my life?
Teachers, police and social workers in the front line
Can't parents keep their kids stable within the family-fabric bind?
Brutal bullying peer groups picture what fashion should ration our nation
Will you be killed for what you are wearing
by an angry bear in a glue-sniffing lair?
Drugs and alcohol fuel hate, a thug waits for you to take the bait
Weapon in hand to dictate your fate
Tower blocks in which youth learns prison rules
Amongst gang cultures -convict vultures
Burglars ply their trade within a terrified population
Can't afford to keep a window open
Social disintegration . . . a concrete jungle
Of fear of never knowing who's at your rear.

Matthew Lee (Aylesbury)

The Shadow Child

Memory shadows wait in the wings
Too deeply shaded for the stage limelight
Of total recall.
These shadows do not wait silently,
Immobile, neatly stationed,
Waiting for recall,
But enter centre stage unsummoned,
Like shadow mutineers clawing their way
Into the present.
With my silent Munch-like scream I
Will them back into the shadowed past
To wait my summons.

These mind-shadows whisper innuendoes
And complicate the present with their woes
Incessantly *sotto voce*
Placed forever on the back-burner of my mind.
I crush these shadows into a crevice
To muffle their chant,
The whispered vehemence of a shadow-man . . .

Abort! Abort!

The child lives on as a shadow

The shadow-child.

Jeffrey Grenfell-Hill (Harpenden)

My Family

I am so
lucky
to have a
family
When I think
of you
All three
The apron
strings
have now been
broken
But maybe
this is a
token
of given
love
Received.

Kathleen Harper (Barnstaple)

631

Life's For Living

Anniversaries
Bring past events
To mind,
Their joys and sadness.

In nineteen eighty-eight
The first Red Nose Day,
The jumbo crash
In Lockerbie.

For me
Retirement,
Celebrations,
Anniversaries,
Until one day
The death of darling daughter.

But friends abound,
And Forward Press was found
To publish poetry.

Solace found
In others' verse,
Grief reduced.
So, celebrate!
Life's for living after all.

David Oliver (London)

Olympic Time

The Olympic Games
a dream for some,
I sit and drool
and I'm only his mum,
with trepidation and fear
it's Hong Kong and China this year,
Oriental, exotic or could be chaotic.
The competitors come from all over the world
with the chance to win medals,
bronze, silver and gold.
The world is a stage
And everyone could be a winner,
just hold it there
maybe it's a beginner.
Whatever the outcome
please remember the date
as we all sit and watch this 2008.

Patricia Murray (St Albans)

Suitcases

My suitcases are always ready for take-off
manifesting themselves like wanderings
through the wilderness in ancient times.

Still ready for take-off
the eternal wandering Jew

Living here in exile
not my 'homeland'

Always remembering where home is
promise not yet fulfilled, full of yearning.

Last time packing in haste
the only photographs I took - cut deeply
how strange, how meaningful.

My mind overflowing with treasures untold
ready to be assembled and evaluated out of moth balls.

No need to pack - all is immured in the
recesses of my mind.

It is said 'Only those who can carry weights
receive packages of unequalled proportions'.

There is little space for distribution,
so, therein lies the moral.

Margot Reich (London)

Rewardfully True

Many congratulations, of course you are number one,
Thanking you for those many kindnesses, printing is fun
Marking my thanks in this prose could I do worse?
Repeatedly a mighty thanks for all you are worth
Some occasions it is different when the mind refuses to act
I am then prompted and cajoled to retrace my track
Low and behold there functions, hence there is a verse
Ready for your criticism and approved you have the final word

Being associated with 'Forward Press' from its infancy
I take great pride and am never denied, published I'll be
Results are terrific, I am always amazed
As bound volumes adorn my shelves with me on every page
Here's to many more prosperous years saluted now as you are
I raise my glass and hail a toast 'The Forward Press'
(Could be milk from the cow)
Repeating again my thanks to all, may you continue long
Congratulations to one and all, and here I'll end my song.

R D Hiscoke (Waltham Forest)

Allotments Are So Sad And Still In Winter

Allotments are so sad and still in winter.
I harvest artichokes
Late.

No one's around.
Those who know the score
Curl up in comfy chairs
Caressing seed catalogues,
Lunches in their ovens
For one o'clock.

I eat at random,
Garden out of sync with the seasons,
Rarely plant in neat rows.

Next year I'll do things differently,
Embrace advice,
Practise normality,
Rehearse what it could be like
To uproot

My arrogance,
Singularity.

Ros Kane (London)

The Lost Art of Tranquillity

Why do people hate the silence,
fill their lives with constant noise;
ditch last season's ancient 'must haves',
queue to buy the latest 'toys'?

What's this fear of being neglected,
urgent need to be in touch;
ever making new arrangements.
Does it matter all that much?

Why confuse 'alone' with 'lonely',
panic when the rest go home;
rush to fill each waking moment.
Leave yourself some time to roam.

Breathe the air that's all around you;
lift your eyes and really 'see'.
be alone in total silence,
peace of mind; content to *'be'*.

Ellen Green Ashley (St Albans)

Dartmoor Sheep

Waiting, watching, she stands, helpless
as we drag across marshland,
stumble through
a pregnancy of boulders,
twist around the ancient oaks:
breathless in a thick mist
on the long haul to hilltop,
where she waits, in silent vigil;
where, face to face, we stand back
and share in her sorrow:
she nudges her lamb,
nudges gently, the
lifeless, breathless,
    tiny body.
Cold and bloody on the cold earth

and she, standing back,
nudges our helplessness,
humbles and tumbles us down;
    down
        through
the thick breath of grief,
away . . . and away,
beyond these barren hills.

June Lloyd (Plymouth)

Peaceful Dreams

As the memories come flooding back
Of ones we used to know
As the past and future do meet
In our peaceful dreams

We see them there waiting
To see us once again
As in every sleeping time
Hope and love returns to us

So when it's said they have gone
Do not fear their loss
They return to us like rotating clouds
That roll across the sky

Hope and love is shared within
So blessed are the memories
As the play unfolds in our dreams
Because they never die

Rose Mills (London)

Resurrection

Not long did they lie on the torn red field of pain
They fell they lay they slumber they took rest
With the wild nerves quiet at last and the vexed
Brain cleared of the winged nightmares and the
Breast freed of the heavy dreams of hearts afar
They rose and greeted their brothers and welcome
Their foes they rose like wheat when the wild wind
Is over they rose with shouts they rose with gasps
And incredulous cries with bursts of singing

And silence and awestruck eyes with broken laughter
Half tears they rose from the ground with welling tears
Glad whispering God like babes refreshed from sleep
Like children they rose brimming with deep content
From their dreamless repose and what do you call it
Asked one they thought they were dead we are cried
Another we're all of us dead and flat I'm alive as a
Cricket there's something wrong with your head they
Stretched their limbs and argued it out where they sat
And over the wide field friend and foes spoke of things
Remembering not old woe or war hunger hated or fierce
Words they sat and listen to the brooks and birds and
Watched the starlight perish in the pale flame wondering
What God looked like when he came.

John Waterworth (Trowbridge)

Winter

Winter is depression
Eating through my soul
Short days, grey and cheerless
Nights as black as coal

Winter is depression
No more warmth on skin
All the world is silent
Cold comes creeping in

Winter is depression
Trees are stark and bare
But nature changes faces
So we need not despair

For in just a few months
Birds again will sing
As the world goes turning
Coming back to spring!

Judith Leeves (Bracknell)

You're

Constant in my life.
My pleasure, lifeline
and real need.
At times as much worry
as a teenager with your incessant
demands and shoddy appearances.

No sooner are you happy
and settled than you dream
of being something else.
Have a heart!
Pleasing you is like trying to interest
a droplet of fountain water, so quickly
come and gone.

One day I see you full
of clear, dazzling light that
makes your sins forgivable,
Another time I could turn
my back as you douse that
brightness and offer a frowning face.

In spite of all, I need your signs to keep me right.
You will be taken away over my dead body
            My home.

Maureen Preece (Burnham-on-Sea)

Old And New

Once when I was young, and all was simple,
I yearned for something new.
Now I am old and yearn for the simple, cos everything is new.

The songs have no tune, the films are blue,
The language is foul, and the manners are few.

Is this what is progress? Is this what is new?
Please give me the old, I long for it so.

Gone are the pleases, and the thank yous too,
Where are the sorrys and how are yous?

The young are clever, and learn things fast,
But why don't they care for things that are past?

Why can't they see that speed is not all?
Why do they spend, like tomorrow won't call?

For tomorrow will call, and they will be old,
And then they will see that their bell will toll.

Kenneth Brocklesby (Burgess Hill)

Child Of Today - Adult Of The Future

I was born into this world, without knowledge of anything -
Therefore, I am grateful for your guidance.
With your tender love and care, I shall thrive -
But, please make allowances for my mistakes,
So that I may learn from them.
If you do everything for me now - how will I survive on my own -
When you are no longer around?

When bad things happen, do not try to shield me from the truth,
But show me how to deal with and face up to, the situation.
Equally, when there is cause for celebration, let us gather together,
As a family, to share those happy times!
I am also aware, that I have been given the chance to explore
The many opportunities and adventures that await me,
In this vast universe!

I shall always respect you, my parents, but, in turn,
I hope that you will respect me too.
After all, a child only learns, from those who raise him.
I am living proof of your devotion to each other
And I want you to know, that I shall do my best
To make you proud of me.

I am a child of today -
An adult of the future.

Ann Kemal (Camberwell)

A Farmer's Lament

The dawn sun touches the roundel, of an oast house in fairest Kent.
Then lights up the old farmhouse windows, but no one is stirring yet.

There are no animals waiting attention, in stable or in byre,
but chickens cluck in the orchard, for their eggs are still required.

Mrs Weaver comes up from her cottage (she's forgotten about her bad feet'!)
to help serve the 'full English breakfast' which the guests find such a treat.

The wife is busy and bustling, you never saw such a to-do,
the washing machine always going and there are 'optional' evening meals too.

I miss the hop-pickers from London, they were such a cheerful crowd.
Not needing en-suite bathrooms, or all those fluffy white towels.

Our son 'Entrepreneurs' in the City, he often comes home for a rest,
the daughters are all safely married, perhaps running a B&B's best.

Although sometimes, in the last of the twilight,
I still see sheep on the hill, hear the breeze through hop poles sighing
and house cows' gentle moo.

Meryl Champion (Worthing)

Incredulous Injustice

It could happen to you -
    Covert surveillance.
        Sinister in its anonymity.
Allowed to continue, year after year -
With no end in sight.
    The watchers.
        The listeners.
            The voyeur even.

Misinformation
Circulated
Nationwide.

The voice of the innocent
    Totally ignored
        Laughed at
            Cruelly taunted.

The wronged woman desperately
Clawing at her life -
Cries out in her despair -
'Will someone please listen to me?'
    Her voice
        Lost -
            In the echoing silence.

Nina Graham (Bournemouth)

Dartmoor

Bleak and rugged Dartmoor lies,
Beneath its blackened winter skies,
Granite tors and mossy stone,
Monument to wind's cold moan.

Peaks preside o'er landscape's flow,
Watching rivers far below,
Winter's mantle gently crowns,
Peeping heads with tiny gowns.

Feeble sunshine bathes the land,
Softly warming nature's hand,
Keeping safe its hidden lore,
Till the land awakes once more.

As the moor in gentle slumber,
Turns to kiss its springtime bride,
Pale blue skies bequeath their blessing,
As soft rains fall with tender pride.

Alison Mannion (Okehampton)

Reminisce

Attractiveness,
You were my happiness.
Twenty springs have come and gone,
Since we met that blessed morn,
When true love was born.

I missed the warmth of your infectious smile,
That calmed my fluttering heartbeats,
And the soft touch of your dainty fingers
That caressed my face,
Like the gentle strumming of a guitar,
Playing a symphony of love.

Then, as I gazed into your loveliness,
All the things that surround me,
Became shadows in your radiance and zest.
I saw you in my dreams
And in a flash you were gone.

But the fire of love has rekindled,
The dreams that were once shattered,
Have been made whole again in you,
Now, you are my lasting happiness,
A hand to hold in the darkness.
Tenderly.

Eileen Beatrice Johnson (Kingston upon Thames)

Old Age

When I am old and cannot sleep
And nights are filled with fears
I'll think of all the friends I had
Who've vanished with the years.

Their faces come into my mind
I'll greet them one by one
But they have gone from mortal life
And left me all alone.

My heart will think of them with love
And fill with silent tears
And I'll remember jokes and fun
We shared throughout the years.

No one to say, 'Do you recall
The days that used to be?'
That is the tragedy of age
Or so it seems to me.

Marjorie Towers (Hoddesdon)

Women Celebrate

As women we are complete
We are like Betty Boop
A sort of girl we desire
An icon in collectable things

Betty Boop is salutary and kind
Towards animals, friends and family
Type of person you can rely on

Betty is fun in summertime
Many hot clothes,
Fiery and sexy, another time classic, shapely
On a bad day, a rock chick with attitude
Fabulous in different mood swings.

As women we have a bad time with men leaving us for another,
Hurtful I know, I have been through it myself, a cheating rat.

Betty surprises me in many ways to celebrate womanhood.
Let's celebrate women as mothers, daughters.
We are beautiful and have many qualities
Women in the world be strong and beautiful
We are caring and strong to carry on with things that happen to us.
Courage we have, beautiful in many ways.

Women all over the world, just celebrate.

D Kangodia (Bristol)

Runaway

The forest is filled with umbrous night
That penetrates the trees,
Blanketing the living things
In sanctuarial tease.

The sky, sugary with stars,
Is far away, unseen
Within this blackened space.

Hands reach for whipping stems
That slap with dripping leaves
Refusing alien entry.

The air tho' pitch, is clean
Reviving the tortured breath.
While feet crunch on needled carpet
And cones, in irregular haste.

Behind, across the moor
Baying dogs come closer.

Valeria Chapman (London)

The Miracle Of David

The small child in his bed lay sleeping,
A tiny teddy for comfort he held tight,
The soft glow of a night light to protect him
And make him feel safe through the night.

He knows his parents are close by him,
Watchful in case he awakes,
To hold him in his hours of slumber,
Reassuring him with each breath that he takes.

He was born into this world very early,
Premature and so incredibly small,
And with the dedication of the doctors and nurses,
It was a miracle he survived at all.

Soon it will be his first birthday,
To celebrate and rejoice,
Presents and cards to surprise him,
Sounds of happiness will be heard in his small voice.

His parents will always give thanks for their miracle
And they will show it in the love that they give,
The little boy will always know his parents love him.

Their miracle . . . their own dear baby son so special . . .
They named him David.

Mary Plumb (Southampton)

To Touch The Sea

She had the desire, that crisp winter's afternoon,
to touch the sea she missed so much,
so far away in that inner city, which temporarily
she called her home.

So we walked along the prom, and then I sat and watched,
like an indulgent parent, as she ran down to the water's edge,
like an excited child.

And I found myself thinking, as I waited patiently there,
of the growing awareness, over the years, of the One
behind this beautiful scene.

And so we both smiled, as we sat there together, at the joy
it brought my jaded friend, released at last from the concrete
jungle, to taste the salty ocean air.

Then she returned, her mission accomplished, the triumph
of her grinning face, once more connected with creation,
as we wearily went on our way home.

Sue Dean (Southsea)

Oh Agony!

My dentist is a cheerful chap,
He chatters on as he fills that gap,
Mouth agape and vacuum going,
But still saliva overflowing.
My nostrils pointing to the sky,
I gaze into his bloodshot eye,
'Going on holiday this year?'
Injecting gum and out through ear,
'Hun,' all I say and sweat a little,
Try to grin, but only dribble.
Mouth full of gadgets and chrome,
I contemplate his shining dome,
And wonder vaguely if it's my breath,
That turns him pale.
He looks like death.
'Oh dear,' says he, 'it looks like rain,'
The drill vibrating on my brain,
'Two Amalgam, make it thick,
Let's hope this lot will do the trick,
A, B, missing, C, D, filled!'
Have I a tooth that isn't drilled?
'E, F missing and sorry to say,
The three you've left have got decay!'

R Jennings (Bristol)

Breathtaking

Plain after plain of unspoilt land,
Forest covered tops
Glowing in the sun.
Some darkened by cooling shadows,
Others too high for new growth,
Point upwards to the sky.
Stark and proud.

Bubbling white waves jive over rocks
Exploding into a frenzy of spray.
Merging with clearer
Translucent waters.
Rich in aroma.

Another world lives under these waters
Oblivious to race, creed or time.
Dip and divining, they hover and dart.
Carefree.
Timeless.

Lynn Craig (Weybridge)

You Don't Know

You don't know
How my life affects yours
I don't know
How my life affects yours
But if the opposite was true
Would you know it too
Or would you be wondering
Why I'm calling in this tune?
To get a reaction from you
Or a sense of belief
For what's going on,
I cannot really see
Except a smile on your face
For receiving 'one's' grace
And receiving 'one's' joy
And receiving 'one's' love
And understanding
Or so it appears
But in my mind it's not clear
It's twisted up with desire
For rest from desire
Please take me higher
So I may learn to see.

Kay L Soord (London)

Heads Or Tails?

Just one toss of the dice my dear,
One little bet on a horse,
Just a flutter at cards my love,
While my luck is in, of course.

What about the bills to be paid,
The mortgage, the council tax?
What about food, and shopping and shoes
And clothes on our children's backs?

Only one turn of the wheel, my sweet,
Just one more bet on the net
Then we'll be in clover my love,
And pay off all our debt.

You can go to the dogs my dear,
Casino, racecourse or track - but
The odds are poor on finding me here
When you decide to come back.

Caroline Hansen (Shoreham-by-Sea)

This Trump Year

There has been no snow cover in London
This weird, wet and windy winter season
Even on a bitter spring equinox
Until on an early Easter Sunday
In this magical year of miracles.
A white Eastertide instead of Yuletide
To help turn around our upside-down world
With apt favourable, freakish weather.
There is a repeat a fortnight later
With an Olympic flaming fiasco
Over bigger fish eating smaller fish
Hindered not by earthquake lake formation
Even as our predecessors prepare
To host the summer games in this trump year.
Won't the next destination of the torch
Be to where indeed earth-shattering changes
Do occur in relative abundance
Despite the ongoing world credit crunch
Uplifting the mind, body and spirit
Like in our autumn city of London
Reaping the rewards of its odd weather
Whilst counteracting discrimination
Thence we may have snow cover next winter.

Eunice Ogunkoya (London)

The Picture

I've just bought a painting
for the living room wall,
which depicts a young lady
dancing in a hall.

The painting's both stylish
and beautifully done,
you can see the young lady
is having innocent fun

But my wife dislikes it
and says it's much too rude,
because the young lady in it
is dancing in the nude.

She's ordered its removal
from out of our house,
which is oh so typical
of my artless old spouse.

Bob Sharp (London)

The Sea Is Free

The sea is free, it goes where it wants.
You can't hold it back, it's free you see,
God bless all that go down to the sea.
The fishermen, the lifeboat men,
All those men upon the sea.
If it wants, it can take you down deep.
So if you go down to the sea, do take care.
When the winds blow, it wants to be free,
It won't hold back for you and me.
It has to let go, it's free you see.
The sea can be blue on a summer's day,
And black and dark on a long winter's night.
The sea means freedom,
It goes where it wants, into our towns.
So do take care, it wants to be free.
You can't hold it back, it's free.
It can go into our fields and into our homes,
It goes where it wants, you see it's free.
God bless them all upon the sea this night.
Take your boat out so you can be free,
Just like the sea.
But do take care for the sea is free,
And the winds may blow, it's free you see!

P Charlton (Penzance)

My Garden

My garden's green, red and gold,
such a lovely sight,
but hard to tend as I grow old,
and always such a fight.

There's slugs and snails, and oh the weeds,
I think they hide and wait,
they target all the plants and seeds,
and avoid the sprinkled bait.

But springtime, when the bulbs are out,
and the bed's a glorious gold,
there's not so many pests about
I suspect it's just too cold.

Instead they lie and watch the plan
and think of goodly feasts,
they know more tricks than mortals can,
they wait and hope, the beasts.

Amy Oldham (Stratford-upon-Avon)

Life's Melody

The music of life is hard to understand completely,
So many harsh notes enter every song,
And words of the lyrics oft confusing,
Sweet lines of melody too brief . . . or the others sad and long . . .
And when we try to contemplate the meaning,
Or catch a fragment of the truth in dream,
We find on waking this eludes us . . .
And no one ever understands completely,
Since perfect truth is neither heard nor seen -
But half-truths ring from each new cadence,
And give us strength to hope and sing . . .
Just as the New Year takes renewal,
From each returning song of spring -
If we could find the happiness we crave for,
Never facing up to doubt or pain,
But finding perfect purpose and design for,
Our span of time here . . . every way made plain,
Perhaps we'd find it all too easy . . .
Predictable and certain, but with no enchanting song -
So a melody in the minor key might be
Life's true music which can make us strong . . .
The music of life is hard to understand completely,
Though somewhere in its symphony we all belong . . .

Noni Fanger (Bournemouth)

Grieving

Long and lonely years have passed,
And still my heart is grieving,
I miss your smile, your touch and love,
And know I always will.

I try so hard to carry on,
As I know, you would have wished,
I know, I am being selfish,
Because others miss you too.

The family and friends,
All try to keep me going,
But even they don't know,
The tears that I am shedding.

Of one thing I am certain,
That when all of this is over,
We will meet again one day,
Never to be parted.

Meriel Brown (Bristol)

Learning

You don't know what you got
Until it has gone.
You don't know what is right
Until you have done wrong.
Learning by your mistakes,
Even if it takes so long.
Giving respect, trust and love,
And get it back twice as strong.
A love that is eternal,
A love that is so true,
That is how much my love is for you.
Pray for forgiveness,
In the mistakes that we made,
And forgetting the loneliness and sadness
I felt in my bed where I laid.
Together we can fight any battle
Strength is in numbers they say,
So my hand is holding yours
Every shared minute of every single day.
Strong in every path or step that we take,
Making our relationship happier
With each kiss we make
'Everything better.'

Jackie Sutton (Salisbury)

Ships Of Death

The tall ships with its cargo set sail for Botany Bay
With villains, and murderers, all set for a very long stay,
This new colony thousands of miles and oceans apart
Lovers and children, left behind to suffer a broken heart.

A new world to build, a long sentence to serve and fulfil.
Men are beaten, women raped, all this at the captain's will.
Conditions that break hardened sailors, children and men
Suffering scurvy, starvation and death, to be beat again.

Those long days at sea with fever, foul food and cold,
Boys never to grow into men, all die before growing old.
This bay they now colonise on this southernmost seashore,
Countless lives lost, this new world now ready to explore.

Soldiers who rule with iron rods and flesh tearing whips,
Gaze out to the sea waiting for its new cargo on ships.
This far off land with prisoners never to see home again,
Too scared to fight, all live in fear of death and more pain.

Lennard Clarke (Bishops Stortford)

Poems Of Life

I've wrote lots of poems,
Some are good, some are bad.
I've wrote very happy ones,
And very sad.
I've wrote about life
About my husband and family,
About being his wife,
I've wrote about my dad's life,
How I loved him and my mum,
I've wrote poems for funerals,
And cried when they were read.
I've wrote about my children,
About my lovely son,
Who's now twenty-one.
The years of trying and waiting,
Hoping and praying too,
Then came my lovely daughter.
I've wrote many poems,
For weddings and funerals too.
Ones full of Xmas cheer,
Tales of woe about the war,
About life.
But I'm just a mother and wife.

T Sullivan (South Oxley)

Haunted Pier

The ocean sighs
The pebbles groan
Seagulls soar away
In the whispering sky

There's a strange
Pain inside me
I see your ghost
On the pier

The ocean dies
The pebbles cry
Seagulls soar away
In the whispering sky

There's a strange
Pain inside me
I see your ghost
On the pier

Geoff Downton (Torrington)

Once Upon A Time

Once upon a time every meadow was lush and green,
Buttercups, cowslips, blood-red poppies danced in summer's breeze,
Bumblebees drunk from nectar sweet,
Cows with calves, sheep with lambs,
Birds of many colours were seen.

Pesticides of modern times and greed of man,
Have destroyed many of these,
Pretty villages are turning into towns,
Meadows replaced by concrete boxes all the same size,
Trees and hedges ripped from root,
Badgers and foxes given the boot,
Cars and lorries' fumes fill the air,
Frightening both bunny and hare.

Snow in summer,
Hot sun and thunderstorms in winter,
Everything gone to pieces,
Rape and crime everywhere,
Children killed by knives and guns,
Thank goodness for my memories of my own childhood days,
When life was pure and simple, free to roam and play without fear,
Unlike children of today, who have no childhood at all,
Innocence and beauty replaced by stress and greed.

Marguerite Gill (Milverton)

The Empty Chair

She's gone! She's no longer here,
My own beloved wife: my darling dear.
As I look across the room, I see an empty chair.
Gone is the smile that used to meet me there.
A smile that said, 'I love you,' without a single word,
The language of silence; where not a sound is heard.
She loved her children and grandchildren, whether little or very tall,
Each one was rather special and she dearly loved them all.
On the day of her departing, we all shed many a tear
And to this very day, we still wish that she were here.
Silent is the voice that sang so beautifully,
The hymns and songs of Zion: the words of victory.
For she triumphed in her battles with great courage and intent,
Her faith, it never wavered, no matter what life had sent.
Her eyes were fixed on Jesus, the One she learned to love;
And she waited for that call from Him, to her home in Heaven above.
She'll be sadly missed by all of us; her memories linger on
And in a rather funny sort of way; it doesn't seem she's gone.

Peter R Beadle (Tidworth)

Here's To Our World

Here's to our world
The beauty of all beauties
An island in space
The home of all our countries
May her people's love surround her
With dignity and grace
With all the stars around her
As she spins along in space

Here's to our world
So precious and so lovely
All through the years;
The sun, her royal trophy
May her reign be long and wonderful
As she journeys on her way
Her destiny, the universe
As she rides the Milky Way

And with her moon beside her
She fills our hearts with pride
Raise your glasses and salute her
Sing her praises far and wide
For she's our life - our world!
Our world!

Nelson Peters (Portsmouth)

The Cupboard

I really must clean out that cupboard.
I haven't done it for ages.
There are boxes of rubbish that want sorting out,
There is also an old 'Yellow Pages'.
There is an old dress there that's had quite a bashing,
Shall I throw it out? It might come back into fashion.
There's my old hockey stick and my old school hat,
Oh I did look silly when I had to wear that.
I've found my son's old football socks,
Shall I throw them out? No, I'll put them back in the box.
There are some old books and toys,
Shall I give them away to some other girls and boys?
My children had such fun with them for many a day,
I won't throw them out, not yet anyway.
Well, I've sorted the cupboard and moved things about,
But I didn't have the heart to throw anything out.
I just couldn't part with a single thing,
Maybe I will try again next spring.

Stephanie Harvey (Bristol)

I Walked The Hills And Paths

I walked the hills and paths
above the night-time town,
the stars embrace me
in active silence
on this December, cold night
where few people stir
from crackling, placating log fires.

Only the scattered burning woodsmoke
lays gently on the sun-departed air,
as trees exhale the day's reverence
I walk on, my dog and I
in our separate perceptions
of life's importance
on the much trodden paths of others' dreams.

Lights bright in the valleys below,
where activity and indolence merge in ceaseless whirl
to the piper of what might be tomorrow
In blinkered aspiration of time-saving devouring
of a modern world prostrate in prayer
to the god of somnambulism in frantic illusion,
my dog drinks from the icy stream
and we move on.

John Fontaine (Stroud)

Ifs And But

If I could, I would give to you,
The creamy pearls from fallen dew;
Platinum showers from mornings' frost
I'd give to you before 'twas lost;
Streaks of silver from morn's first show;
Red rubies reflecting sunsets' glow;
Opals from clouds as they unfold,
Flowers' jewels with wealth untold;
Bright diamonds from the falling rain,
I'd search for you just to attain;
The evening sun's pure molten gold
I'd give for you to have and hold;
Emeralds from leaves, left after mist;
Crystals by snowflakes gently kissed;
Pale amethysts from late evening's skies,
That only show as daylight dies;
Abundant sapphires from skies above;
But, you already have my love.

H.Val.Horsfall (Knebworth)

Wayland's Smithy

Ironmaster to the gods was I;
I beat the glowing metal for their spears,
bent the iron-strip to shoe their steeds
and felly their chariot wheels.
They called me Wizard for my skills:
I knew what Thor did not - the secret of the forge;
for judging the fire-heat, Odin trusted me.
Loki would check his strong malicious urge,
and Baldur the beautiful, the bright,
came from his far-shining home to see
my art with anvil, hammer, tong and fire.

Now all are gone. Their seats on high
are empty, overthrown; all disappears
before this new Order with its destroying light . . .

I do not forget the old, but now must needs
live with the new; and so my skills I hire
to mortal men.
Leave here your horse, your silver on my stone,
and while you are gone
I will shoe him; and when you come again
call my name before you mount and ride away -
so may I live on, to work another day.

Freda Cave (Ilminster)

Dreams Of A Child

I go to bed and then I dream
Of wondrous land I've ever seen
Where kings and queens and princes fair
Live in shining castles in the air
Of oceans blue where the dolphins play
And the sunrise steals the night away
The snowcapped mountains touch the sky
From their rocky crags the eagles fly
Cowboys ride the dusty plain
To guide the weary wagon train
And sunset casts its magic spell
On desert sands where the nomads dwell
But dreams don't last it's sad to say
For I can't sleep my life away
Bedtime soon will come once more
And then again I will explore
Those far-off lands I never see
Until my dreams do come to me

I M Cole (Gloucester)

653

Your Name

I'll sign your name on the Sistine Chapel.
You'll say you didn't do that,
but you did the dishes
and I could write your name
on those
if I wanted.

I'll write your name on a thousand
post-it notes
and stick them all over the city -
but they won't stay.
They'll end up
back in my pocket alongside the receipt
from your toothbrush.

I'll wash your feet,
and people will say
'Like Jesus?'
and I'll say, 'Like who?'
because stars no longer lead to stables,
but to irises
and fingernails
and the spaces between the words
'It happened'.

Gillian Turnham (Brighton)

Have A Chuckle

Time seems to have speeded up;
It's already time to fill my teacup.
I haven't yet made my bed;
Already I'm longing to rest my head.
Old age is a pain wearing hob-nailed boots
Which often treads over this old coot.
I sent for the doctor, alas he couldn't come
Because he'd eaten too much
And had a pain in his tum.
He swallowed a get-well pill
But all it did was make him ill.
It really was a dreadful sin
That medication did that to him.
I've a head bunged up with phrases
So I'm placing them on snowy white pages;
I hope they're enjoyed by a reader or two,
As this rhyme is a bit of a riddle,
They could have a jolly good giggle.

Audrey Luckhurst (Bristol)

654

Mastacat, Mastacat,
The beating heart tells all,
As stars light up the sky above,
And down below they fall.

White knuckles show the way we feel,
They also grip our soul
As slowly we are moving through
A night as black as coal.

Mastacat, Mastacat,
Dance with me and sing
I hear your voice
It fills my mind
You made me - I am king.

Mastacat, Mastacat,
I am here for you.
Your prayers will fan me like the wind,
I know now what to do.

Must attack! Must attack!
Forgive me one and all.
Must attack! Must attack!
Annihilate them all.

Kim McAllen (Haywards Heath)

Win Green, Wiltshire

(For ST)

Peace is here,
Where wisdom is.

Within the wind,
Where love lifts us up,
Above these hills,
We soar,
Amidst the songs of the skylarks.

And the love in our smiles,
Is higher than ever,
Ever before,
When we were simply friends.

Hold me.
Lay your head on my shoulder,
And listen to the bliss,
Of the wind rustling the bushes.

Michael Wride (Wedmore)

Save Our Planet

Deadly cobras man may fear,
Lions in the jungle deep,
Maybe too that huge, great bear,
Oh spider! Please your venom keep.

Yes! We fear them and take heed,
But who is mostly to be feared?
The one that causes want and need,
It's man my friend, it's man.

Who is stripping forests bare?
Homes of creatures large and small,
Destroying plants that are so rare,
These could be used to help us all.

Who is wasting all the oil?
Who is wasting food galore?
Who is poisoning air and soil?
It's man my friend, it's man.

Who is fighting all the wars,
Slowly causing global warming?
Glaciers melting more and more,
Who must heed this dreadful warning?
It's man my friend, it's man.

Pauline Denham (Dorchester)

Church Path

Church path in springtime - what joy!
Cool freshness, with a touch of coming warmth.

The hedges' feet are bright with celandines,
Shiny saffron petals thrusting through the debris of winter past.

The dog violet showy, with pale mauve flowers,
Promising perfume, but disappointing.

Searching for the hidden beauty of the purple violet
With scent divine, and better still, the white violet
In secret haunt known but to a few.

Sweet primrose, the best of country flowers,
Whose perfect innocence turns up its dewy face
To greet this ever-welcome spring.

The hedge broken by a wooden crossbar gate;
In the field the new-turned earth with rich dark smell
Draws the eye across to misty hills fading into
                                        the sharp blue sky.

Barbara Jameson (Dursley)

Pictures And Memories

Pictures and memories fade over time,
old black and white snaps,
just an old shutter click as you stood by the wooden door frame,
that's now been replaced by brick.

You played with that old hoop and waving a stick,
one passing moment in time, captured in just one click.
The alley where you once played has now faded far away,
and been replaced by a new modern building,
that has now covered the cosy home where you once laid.

Yes, pictures and memories fade over time,
but although we never met, I'm glad that I've found your picture,
so I can put your image into this line.

Who took your picture? There is nobody left to answer that question,
so now my picture proudly sits in the photo album right next to yours.
To lay when I'm also gone,
in perhaps a wardrobe, a cupboard or a set of drawers,
to be discovered by someone new and caring,
of which in this modern age, there are sadly very few.

Pictures and memories fade over time,
but now both of our pictures are bound together, forever in this line.
So that our pictures and our memories will to us, never fade over time.

D Watts (Camborne)

A Wedding Anniversary

A wedding anniversary is
Such a special date,
A day to be remembered and
A day to celebrate.
A day to thank each other for
The joys you both have known,
For friends and for the kindnesses
That many folk have shown,
A day to
offer up a prayer of
Thanks to God above,
For all the blessings of this life
And His unchanging love,
And when the day is over and
You've time to meditate,
Remember the vows you both
Exchanged on this
Anniversary date.

P Birchall (Bracknell)

A Prayer For The World

Dear Lord, please guide the world's leaders,
Towards securing peace in all lands, so that
The people of the world can live
With justice, freedom, and without fear.

Lord, help them use every endeavour,
To form friendships and respect for all,
Let all nations join hands for the common good
And the well being of all its people.

Let the leaders think long and hard
About the atmosphere that is being slowly destroyed,
Along with the Earth's bounty of treasures,
Being destroyed by fighting and destruction.

Lord, let them listen to the pleas of the people,
Whom by aggression have been made homeless,
Homeless, destitute, without hope and afraid,
Afraid for the children caught up in this madness.

Dear Lord, our children are the future generation,
Are they too going to grow up without hope,
Give the leaders the strength and courage to say,
Enough is enough, stop all the fighting,
And let peace reign all over the world.

Maud Eleanor Hobbs (Basingstoke)

England

There will always be an England
We sang so many times
But now we are not English
To sing it seems a crime.
How can the Scots be Scottish
The Irish can be so
The Welsh are Welsh
But English now is no!
Why do we allow a government
To treat us in this way
When we should get together
And demand our say.
Do lets hope very soon now
We will stand up and sing again
There will always be an England
And England will be free
If England means as much to you
As England means to me.

Audrey Salter (Aylesbury)

Tommy (1911-1991)

O, love, why did you leave me
How can I live alone?
The silence here deadens the air,
Your chair is cold as stone.

You'll not sit at your desk again
In the window of this room,
Nor see the daffodils you tended
Burst into golden bloom.

The little things you daily used
In mute reproach they catch my eye -
Your keys, your pen, wristwatch and comb . . .
The books you loved unopened lie.

I sense your presence everywhere
But I can't touch your hand
This strange state of loneliness
Is like a foreign land.

You've been my mate, companion, friend
Husband for over fifty years
For both of us this is an end
I cry, but no one hears.
I cry such useless tears.

Mollie King (Hatfield)

Hobson's Choice

How long will it be before the cliffs turn to sand?
How long will it be before sea covers the land?
How long will it take the towering mountains to fall
And the floor of the ocean to rise and grow tall?
How long the rainstorm's torrential force
Bends the Earth's mighty rivers from their ageless course?
How long will it be before the vast ice caps melt?
When by humankind will Earth's great travail be felt?
How long will it be before the sun starts to fade
And we have to ace the ever-deepening shade?
How long before the highest creations of Man
Sink to oblivion in time's eternal span?
How long before the planets begin to collide?
How long will it be before there's nowhere to hide?
How long will it be? Perhaps ten million years
To witness that time; will there still be eyes or ears
Or will fruit of the knowledge tree cause to unfold
A world without life - and those tales stay untold?

Michael Collin Wearne (1942-2004) (Great Missenden)

A Gypsy Life!

(Dedicated to my husband George)

When we were young we'd travel around,
From town to town we'd go,
You never did stay in any one place too long though.

You'd have the fresh air and open space,
Lots of different people to get to know your face.

We'd travel here, we'd travel there
Without a single care.

Oh! There could be trouble,
There could be pain,
But a normal life - no, never again.

You can't beat freedom and the open road,
Leave your cares behind and go it alone.

But we were free as free could be,
That gypsy life was so right for me.

Now we've reached a matured age,
Things changed along the way,
We have our special memories now
And these will always stay.

Sara Jane Berry (Witney)

Home

Dirty dishes, grime soaked, surrounded with half eaten
soap suds meandering into the sink.
Mount Cotton to be scaled before breakfast,
starting on the slopes of my bedroom floor.
Bedclothes stained suspectly
(with Tippex and ink),
with the contents of a Royal Mail sorting office on the mat
just inside my front door.
Books re-writing their pages from comedy or blank verse,
to tragedy, to reflect their condition
(forgotten).
Fruit ripening in the fruit bowl,
beyond fruition
(rotten).

I don't live in a sty most of the time.
It only occurs when I'm ill, or stressed.
Then I decide to write a rhyme
(rather than clear away the mess).

Lauren Hesford (Wantage)

Woodlands

Woodlands on your doorstep let the future be,
Many a new plantation for children there to see,
Beauty all around us and clover in the field,
As into the millennium new horizons yield.
The days of old still linger where beauty used to be,
And orchards in abundance bear fruit upon its tree,
Farmers then found pleasure and moved without a sound,
But now it's turned to concrete set upon the ground.
The birds and beasts of Britain rely upon the source,
Which God created for them, as planets on their course.
So let us guide our children to tread the path ahead,
In valleys green and peaceful, our source of daily bread.

And now as rain descendeth to scatter on the earth,
The sound of falling raindrops herald a future birth of,
Greenery in abundance for children everywhere,
And woodlands on our doorstep amidst the meadows fair.
There is no inner feelings for those who strive for power,
To take away our pleasures, misdoings every hour,
As they are out of tune with nature, and need to seek the sun,
With love for one another, whils't all ages run,
So let our voice be heard now, to grow and prosper here,
Fulfilling all our needs, with woodlands new each year.

Suzannah Freeman (Bournemouth)

Our Old House

The house stood bleak and empty
Broken shutters over the floor.
I looked and my heart was breaking,
For I'll never go there anymore.

It was there that we played as children
And my own saw the first light of day.
I remember my mum, as sweet as they come,
And the wild woods where we used to play.

They tell me you can't live on memories,
But to me that's what memories are for
To go back to the days that were happy,
But I'll never go there anymore.

But one day the good Lord will take my hand
And my mortal remains will blow across the land
And come to rest on the rubble and stone
To the place that for me was home sweet home
Then I'll return once more.

Evelyn Maskell (Reading)

Awaiting Dawn

Waves spill around my feet like lace
And the evening sunshine touches my face.
Wind whips my hair across my eyes,
Overhead a lonely seagull cries.
I walk far out into the darkening sea,
Letting it enfold and hide me.
The water glitters as the moon appears.
Only spray covers my body with tears.
Alone I'm hidden from all human sight,
Blending into the magic of night.
From all real things I'm set free.
Dark velvet of night covers me.
Until dawn shows on the horizon
With the first golden rays of sun,
Warming me, awaking my heart.
I'm reborn for a new start.
No longer alone, empty and cold.
I'm alive and covered in gold.
There is music in the sound of the sea,
Songs in the breeze which caress me.

I raise my face to the birth of day.
Exhausted I've been a long, long way.

A Wisternoff (Calne)

2008 - What Happen?

Forward Press is nearly twenty years old and one million - poets . . .
Very proud to be the largest publishers, on the market.
All books are sent to the British Library,
Hopefully FP will keep going - over - one century!

The NHS is sixty years old, and Gillian is still a staff nurse. . .
Some areas, the NHS are unfortunately, getting worse!
The Service is in Intensive Care . . .
I wish the government would put more money, in there!

Sixty also is the Farnborough Air Show
I used to love watching it on TV with Raymond Baxter, and his info
In 1994 I got married and watched it free, from my in-laws . . .
In Cove, 300 yards from their blue front door!

My old school - Lord Mayor Treloars, now celebrating, their
century . . .
1968-1976 I went, and had bad and good memories
In Froyle, a boarding school, horribly . . .
For disabled (then) boys . . . only!

Barry Ryan (Winchester)

Stained Glass

Darken the door of a church? Me?
Never! Yet I knew
all about stained glass windows.
I'd seen pictures
of Canterbury Cathedral
and Notre Dame.
I'd read a book,
watched a TV programme,
followed the Abbey restoration.
I even went on a course,
learnt all about
gold in glass, lead kames,
copper salts and urine.
I could tell you, show you,
make one for you.

Then one sunny day -
I still don't quite know why -
my dark form was seen
entering that arched frame.
And from within I suddenly saw,
filtered through scarlet and purple and green,
the gold of the light I'd been looking for.

Chris Payne (Godalming)

Motherhood

Sleepless nights and constant feeds,
Crying and screaming all of their needs,
Teething pain and dirty bums,
Spitting their food and windy tums.

Temper tantrums and kissing the phone,
Toddling and climbing all over your home,
Chasing the cats and pulling their tails,
Scribbling on walls and climbing the stairs.

Blowing raspberries and rolling on rugs,
Snuggles, cuddles, kisses and hugs,
Missing you madly when you're apart,
Smiling and smirking, melting your heart.

Ma Ma, Da Da and laughing out loud,
Holding hands and feeling so proud,
Meaning what they say with those four little words,
I love you Mummy,
The best thing I've heard.

Katherine Bowers (Bristol)

I Love Trains

The wonderful joys and
The incredible noise
The grace and the verve
As it rounds on a curve
The sharp gleam of metal
On a train in high fettle . . .
The curves and the line
Of the classic design
The graceful refinement
Of wrought-iron and steel
And the wonderful feel
Of each line and each curve
Each nut and each bolt
And each rivet's location
Is sheer revelation
The clean polished metal
Of a warm copper kettle
On its way to the station
Is a sheer revelation
Of wonderful noise
And incredible joys.

I love trains!

Dennis Studd (Newport Pagnell)

Night Watch

The baby's shrill screams shatter the dark silence
Like a hammer on glass.
She wakes to the sound tearing through the stillness,
And squeezes her eyes shut,
Wishing she could do the same with her ears.

Bone-weary from hours of night-walking,
Arms aching, throat dry from lullaby-ing.
Beside her the man is still . . . and she is angry,
Resenting his withdrawal into exhausted sleep.

Why does he not hear the child wailing?
His child as well as hers.
How can he lie in some far dream-world
While screams attack her, shattering her eardrums?

Reluctantly she stumbles from her bed
To lift again the frantic little form
And murmur words of comfort while her eyes
Fill with tears of weariness and frustration.

Connie Voss (Havant)

Mother's Making Strawberry Jam Today

As I came near the window,
I heard the angry buzzing, and bumbling of wasps.
I looked up and saw that the window, as usual, was slightly open,
And then I smelt it, that all-permeating sweet smell,
And I said, 'Mother's making strawberry jam today.'
I could almost see that cauldron of steaming syrup,
The strawberries rising, falling, twisting, turning,
The explosions of bubbles, releasing their evocative scent,
That little boy in shorts and T-shirt, watching, as Mother
Inserted a spoon into the scarlet mass, lifted it up and examined
The sticky mixture to see if formed a solid drip.
'Is it ready?' she would ask.
 And I would nod, the juices already running in my mouth
At the thought of that sugary, delectable taste.

I quickened my pace, but was halted by the pain of my arthritic hips,
I rubbed my rheumy eyes and gazed once more.
Not wasps but flies, fluttering in and out of a broken window.
No sweet smell coming from within, just a damp, dark stench,
The house empty, abandoned, everyone long gone,
I alone could still visualise that precious time of my youth.
I alone could still savour that aroma, that fragrance,
That ever present smell of syrupy strawberry jam.

Sarah E Fernandes (Bristol)

Sanctuary

The donkeys graze or browse or drowse in summer sun in fields above the sea,
Retired or rescued spend this last lease of their life in sanctuary and tranquillity.
On windy days the donkeys run to greet, their necks across the gate.
Your troubles must be left behind.
Observant eyes and ears and eager noses wait,
They're urgent to communicate, insistent for your mind.

The timid ones, who have known harsher times, stand far,
Look longingly, view and review.
Their trust comes slowly as the summer air and must be delicately earned.

If you are patient, wait, and wait, and wait,
As though testing ice upon the pool,
Nose tentative, eyes wide and questioning,
They come, and ultimately gently lean, to demonstrate that there is trust in you.

In winter barn's pervasive donkey warmth
Is peace of mind; and, strangely, of spirit
From their innate ability
To bring you in their sanctuary, tranquillity.

Deirdre Golden (Sidmouth)

A Flower

I discovered a flower
through the tangled branches
of a thorny pyracantha.
A crimson rose
blooming out of its prison,
straining towards the light,
six buds in its orbit,
clinging to its slender stem.
A robin peered above,
fluttering.

Long ago,
someone planted a rose bush
then forgot about it.
It tried to reach the sky
in the neglected garden.
Its beauty revealed
a sudden magic present
in a gloomy world.
Its scent spread
all around
and the robin started
singing.

Antoinette Marshall (London)

Always Yours

The letter finished 'Always Yours' which filled me with delight
For it was from my first real love, no other was in sight.
I read the kind words many times, they meant a lot to me
He was my Mr Wonderful as fine as he could be.
But now he must be far away, he found I'm not his kind
I expect he has forgotten me, but I don't really mind.
For I have found another love with whom I want to stay
We married several years ago on such a happy day.
He's kind and handsome all I want, his love for me is real
He loves the things that I love, it is the perfect deal.
So I can say to all of you to wipe your tears away
Tears because he's left you, and you hoped that he would stay.
You think your heart is broken, there'll never be another
But I can tell you out there you can find another lover.
I know he was your idol, so witty, tall and strong
But there are others just the same who'd love you true and long.
So get up and start looking, throw all your cares away
And you will think of what I've said upon your wedding day.

Margaret Perrow (Truro)

Why?

Why is just a little word,
The shortest question you've ever heard,
Easy to say, yet hard to reply,
You may still want to ask why?
Some answers are happy and make you smile,
Some make you want to 'run a mile',
Some bring regret and many tears,
Some can't be answered for many years,
Some are hard to understand -
You may need to hold someone's hand.
Whatever the question, there is a reply;
Tell me now! You may cry . . .
The answer depends on where you go -
Some may only say 'don't know'.
But there is someone who'll answer true,
And only wants the best for you.
Ask believing and you will find . . .
Much more than just peace of mind:
A joy, a hope that will not pass away;
A new life that can start today.

'Call unto me, and I will answer thee, and shew thee great
and mighty things, which thou knowest not'. Jeremiah 33:3

Melanie Biddle (Egham)

Our Queen Mum

We thank thee Lord, as we kneel and pray
That our 'Queen Mother has reached '100' today.
To the world she is known, as our Queen Mother
So much respected, and loved, as is no other.
Who loyally served us through the years,
With joyous laughter, but sometimes tears.
She suffered with us, two long wars,
Not forgetting such arduous chores,
As trying to console those who have lost,
Their 'husbands' or 'sons' whatever the cost.
To ease the worry, to families and the stress,
And pray to the Lord, they will all be blessed.
Her daughter 'Elizabeth' is our present Queen,
Following her mother's footsteps, she can be seen.
To care for her subjects, as her mother always would,
Hoping to live and be just as good,
And carry out her duties, without favour or grace
And be so proud, to serve in 'her mother's' place.

J W Clark (Chichester)

667

The Tree In The Churchyard

The tree greets all who open the gate,
Searching for peace in our boisterous world.
A refuge for squirrels,
A bandstand for birds,
A sculptural landmark,
It holds the villagers' story
Deep in its heart.

Lovers carved initials before Waterloo,
Made trysts here after Dunkirk.
Evacuees who sat here waiting for billets,
Now have grandchildren seeking homes of their own.

Its shadows alight on the baptismal shawl,
Leaves greet the bride on her father's arm,
Branches extend a final salute
To each coffin as it passes below.

Everyone pauses for Nature's own blessing,
As they enter the Church with its quiet of faith.
There's shade and there's shelter
From this welcoming tree
Guarding our story,
Deep in its heart.

Anne Everest (Sidmouth)

Understand And Undermind

Understanding the understanded it gets in my way,
Reinacting the reactions each and every day.

Hypothetically speaking life should be like this,
But who says it should? As this is what I missed.

Each and every night I skip worlds and I dream,
I love going to my special places as nothing is what it seems.

They're unique and they're wonderful as I lay there in peace,
Different friends and situations a fairy tale feast.

Back to reality every day I come,
Each and every day it feels like I'm on the run.

From the important things, the things that matter most,
They give me energy and a reason I like to boast.
To succeed in the game there's only one thing you can do . . .

Live life to the full,
Play the game,
But play the game for you.

Gemma Turner (Croydon)

Rest And Thankful Inn

It is all quiet and serene,
In this lay-by inn,
It's summer in the country,
Is for all of us see.

The cows and sheep dwell
In lovely fields,
Beautiful horses neigh,
And pigs given lots of swill,
All like it in the meadow,
And the farmer's son is busy
Down at the old well.

Oh! What a great joy it is,
To be in the country dale,
Now the sun is shining here,
You just lay down,
Without a single care.

The pub is open you know!
And cider begins to flow,
To us it seems a pity,
To sit inside just now,
And to get tiddledy!

Sammy Michael Davis (Bournemouth)

Autobiography Of An Earthling (In Three Chapters)

I thought about a hippopotamus in a box
And wondered if I could play a game with it
It looked at me
I looked at it
We looked at each other.

I thought some more about a hippopotamus in a box
And wondered if he was playing games with me . . . or she
I averted my eyes
From the corner of its eye
And for a moment we were together.

I stopped thinking about hippopotami in boxes
And wondered what else there was to think about
I racked my brains
My brains racked me
Till there was nothing but lust and the weather.

Cally Hill (Plymouth)

You

All this rage and hate,
Towards you,
I love to negate,
The feelings few,
I have for you

You made me mad,
You went away,
So down and sad,
I'll make you pay,
For running away.

You left me alone,
My heart so blue,
Always by the phone,
Thought your feelings true,
No idea,
They were so few.

Never again not to be,
Just like this day,
Will repeat to me,
Just remember to say,
'This is me, it's my day.'

Kathryn Pope (Ivybridge)

Cardboard City

Sleeping in the streets . . .
That concept just defeats
The democratic right
To place your head at night
On a bed that's dry and warm
Which is sheltered from the storm.
It cannot be the way
In this so-called modern day
That we've homeless such as those
Who only own the clothes . . .
That they're wearing, nothing more
As they lie upon the floor
With no hope of better days
Or a place for long term stays.
Well something must be done
For it isn't any fun
But the thing that really shocks is . . .
We're running out of boxes.

Harold Hyman (Enfield)

670

Timeless Wonder

It has a face,
Also two hands
And many working parts.

It is always moving,
But it stays in the same place.
People would be lost without one.

It cannot talk,
But it tells us something.
There is one at the office.
There is one on the factory floor.
There is a big one in the city
Or a small town.

There are more at home,
One on the mantelpiece,
One in the kitchen or hall.

Yet, it is never right.
It was working yesterday.
It's poetry,
As it is working today.

In fact, it is timeless . . .

John Wisby (Carshalton)

Happy Birthday!

Happy birthday Forward Press
Well, we would have never guessed,
20 years have come and gone,
Happy birthday is the song.

Poems have been long and short,
Many subjects have been caught.
People from all walks of life,
Put pen to paper in a trice.

With many poems in the make
And 20 candles on the cake.
Forward Press have passed the test
Knowing that, they are the best.

So here we mark a length of time,
And poets have written many lines,
'Cheers' we say to toast the day,
A few more poems are on their way.

Happy birthday.

Anne Griffiths (Highbridge)

Rain Today

People say they hate the rain
But I can honestly say
That I do not feel the same

I step outside on a rainy day
Not with umbrella
But beneath I stay

I hear that you may
Wash my sins away
So I don't care, rain today!

Wash away the sins of people
In a world which is filled
With such pure evil

Tap against a window
Soak me to the bone
While others go for cover
In these streets I'll roam

Until I find solace
Or beautiful sun
Until I'm sin free
Like when we were young.

Simon McAlear (London)

Omega Point

In mist and rain, see Life begin
in hilly terrains, where fountains spring.

Two streams of Life unite and onwards flow
Their course and destination no human soul may know -
Save in this single affirmation
Convergence the destination.
Through pastures green where sun-blessed breezes blow
or forests dark, where tangled thorn-clad creepers
Strangle the listless hearts of heart-awakened sleepers.

Awake, my soul; in unity of Thee and me
My soul is master of the sea -
My soul, awake, in unity of Thou and I
My soul is mistress of the sky.

Come on, come on; come on with me
till our river is one with the endless sea.

Till the endless sea in mist and rain
begins the cycle all over again.

Sidney Fisher (Langport)

Two Worlds

Transported to a magic scene
A place so sacred where
A part of me
Has always been

A dream, a dream.

Where ancient woods
Their stories tell
Where insects thrive
Where water flows
With everything alive.

Yet, there is
The other part of me
Away from woods, just memory
Struggling in London's Underground
With many others outward-bound
To noisy traffic,
An ugly street.

Can the two worlds ever meet?

Perhaps it is my never-ending task
To ask and ask and ask.

Lily Seibold (London)

Winchester

Have you been to our historic city?
If you have not that's a pity.
King Alfred statue in the Broadway there
Bringing memories to share.
Abbey grounds with lovely flowers
Where children play for many hours.
Stop at the Guildhall to look around
Things of history to be found.
Take a look at the cathedral
So many visitors they form a queue.
Stained glass windows of long ago
Ask a question for, if you want to know.
It's so lovely being there
When beautiful voices fill the air.
The Butter Cross and the West Gate too
Many things to see and do.
Goodbye Winchester you will say
We will return another day.

Monica Ebbs (Winchester)

Not Far . . .

When I must go - I will leave the door ajar
then you will know that I have not gone far,

. . . only as distant as a loving thought
or a moment in time that you have caught

of love exchanged in boundless measure
and fond memories - ever there to treasure.

. . . Maybe you will recall, or sense, a gentle touch
that, given in love can mean so much.

Though now no longer meeting face-to-face
distance cannot dim the memory of a fond embrace.

Love and kindness never die - they forever live
in every heart that, openly, can receive - and give.

Remember, when I am no longer there,
a thought in silence and in a gentle prayer
will eternally span all space and time . . .
then in your heart - know - my love is forever thine . . .

I will, into eternity, leave the door ajar-
I have not gone far - I shall always be with you.
. . . just as near or far as your own heart desires.

Colin R Paine (Banbury)

Song Of True Devotion

Miss Jennifer Jean
Is oft to be seen
Astride a white horse on the beach,
So I donned my old spurs
They are rather like hers
Though the quality's out of her reach.

So we galloped away
'Til the end of the day
When twilight emblazoned the sky
Then I looked for my watch
And my bottle of Scotch
And kissed her sad eyes with a sigh.

Miss Jennifer Jean
Is ever so clean
And joyfully sprays every room,
But admirers beware
She has polished the stair
Objection will lead to your doom.

A P Dixon (Basingstoke)

Summer Rain

Grey days.
Rain
Like eels
Slithers down from
Slippery skies,
Sliding furtively
Along ditches
And down drains.
Children
Huddle at windows.
Tears fall,
Matching the drops
Crying down
Transparent panes
For empty swings
And rusting slide.
Yet flowers bloom,
Colours bright-washed
Under the dripping
Umbrella of the trees.
We sigh -
And wait for the sun.

Diana H Adams (Winkleigh)

My West Country Home

It's a Cotswold stone house this place I call home
With mullion windows and a line for the phone
At the front there's a porch with stained glass in the door
And creamy stone flags are laid on the floor
It stands in a garden all on its own
With wrought iron gates, 'twix pillars of stone.

And round at the back there's an acre at least
Of paddock and orchard; for chickens and geese:
There's walnuts and pears, a big swing of course!
A hayrick, a pigsty and a shed for the horse,
But the pride of the orchard is the apples we grow
That go in the cider to give us that glow.

We make it ourselves in the old cider press,
It squeezes the apples, the old ways are best;
In the pit the juice froths for many a day,
Then golden and still it is taken away
To mature in wood barrels
For next year's harvest day.

Ray Davis (Stonehouse)

675

The Session

My legs took me to Boots
To the make-up counter, to be precise.
'Can you help me with my face?'
I tentatively asked.
The make-up girl eyed me up and down
And her welcoming smile became a frown.
Her questions hit me like unwelcome arrows.
'Do you usually like the natural look?'
(She could read me like a book.)
Out came the pinks, browns, greens and the blues,
And that was just the lipstick.
Every item cost the earth
And I only had £5.50 in my purse.
'What do you think?'
She held the mirror in front of my face
And gave me a theatrical wink.
'Very nice,' I fibbed and
Sheepishly left without buying a thing.
What a glamorous mess, I thought
And gave myself a cleanse and a wash.
'Oh for the natural look.
In future I'll stick to my lipgloss!'

Sarah Diskin (Worthing)

The Homecoming

Was that the light that burn'd in the stillness of night?
Or was it, bereft eyes that glowed in the dark?
Was that a fire that burn'd the ambitious moth alight?
Or could it have been love? That relentless spark
Those countless desires that were waiting to cinder
And wild tempest anxious to scatter ashes whom linger.

Those flowers that were gathered for his festoon
Were they not laid beside the beloved's tombstone
Of that brave, young lad separated amid his platoon
With a picture of his love in his hands killed alone?
And was that not the lady in that picture who stood
Near the soldier's epitaph mistaken for dried wood?

And did you not see that saintly soul gazing down
With the crying white clouds, showering tears a few
And the sprites with saffron and frankincense had flown
Amidst the funeral gathering, oh! Only if you knew!
The seraphic atmosphere filled with joy and praise
O - only if you heard! The divine songs of his grace.

Hamza Ismail (Luton)

Profile

We are sexual, telepathic, word-orientated goofs,
We are nebulous, necromantic, prehensile,
We are roaming, reared and romantic,
We are benign, bovine and bizarre,
Our residencies are eclectic,
Places, like time, happen anywhere.
We have free will yet constantly fight our own destiny,
And cannot subjugate matter over fidelity,
We are born to remember ourselves,
Holding stature in the face of volition,
The road is fraught with danger,
We are supernumeraries on the stage of the world theatre,
Human life is both precious and dispensable,
The societies that have occurred are meretricious,
Tribal chaos veneered by bouncing colour,
Adult schizomania rages, civilisation's final stages,
We are lumpen, incarnate, mind-altered,
The world is a representation of our complexities,
By computer programmed serendipity,
And we are myriad, scattered, running,
Peopled in a thousand continents,
Jolly on the hop, a multifaceted being.

Fergus Hilton (Dawlish)

Whispering Rain

Whispering rain filtering
Through my mind
Like yesterday, when in a
Dark moment, I thought of you
And suddenly the rain turned
To sunshine.

It was just a dream of long
Ago, when we were young.
To think of the times we
Roamed hand-in-hand
Where our hearts and
Souls entwine.

With a smile to breathe
And know you are close by
Though far away, dear memory
Now to walk at journey's end
And to reach destiny, knowing
You are mine.

Joyce Gale (Bristol)

Summer Steps

Summer afternoons
go up-river
under green low leaves
cathedral cool
light slow wheel of gold
windows high above
spinning in a huge sky.
Her, up flutes
of falls, river rocks down
through gullies
water fleece, curls, eddies,
long day bleeds
into sunset behind trees;
wind whispers
her secrets to river
tumbling towards sea,
indigo blue sky, she folds
her cloak of stars
about her shoulders and soft
stepping down into summer
water, she kisses moon
into melting river.

Teresa Webster (Falmouth)

One In A Million

Many congratulations Forward Press,
On your forthcoming anniversary,
With over a million poets in print,
With our works shelved at the British Library,
Recorded for the future, forever, for infinity,
Success is your watchword I guess.

Knowing just how fair and generous you are,
I've estimated that one of my poems,
Was exactly the millionth poem to be selected and printed,
I was wondering if that meant you would be writing out for me,
A cheque for a million pounds,
And on the big day, send for me a chauffeur driven limousine or car.

Perhaps not, merely a passing whim,
Another pipe dream goes up in a cloud of smoke,
Another ambition slips from the jaws of hope,
So I wrote these few short words instead,
But I really don't mind, it's been a pleasure down the years,
To your table, some of my written words to bring.

Peter John Littlefield (Bournemouth)

To George - The Newly Diagnosed Diabetic

So, you are a diabetic then
And can only think of when
Anything you could eat or drink,
Now you have to stop and think.
Don't worry, there are lots of ways
To brighten up those difficult days.
You will welcome the loss of weight
As you step out with lighter gait.
Slim and handsome you will become,
You could well have much more fun,
It might be worth it in the end
If the rules you do not bend.
From those sugars run a mile
Do not let it cramp your style.
Just you fight it all the way,
I know that you will win the day.
Life does not have to be too bad
Don't let it catch you looking sad.
So you are a diabetic then
In that case I will see you when
Fortitude has blown the blues away
And your winning smile is back to stay.

S Rosemary Ward (Aylesbury)

A Dream

Last night she came with a bright
Smile spread from her white
Teeth. Her lips were lightly fold.
She was silent, but her eyes told
Me all, Greek to common ear.
My passionate heart made me hear.

Slowly she swaggered and came
To me like a charming dame.
The rhythm of footsteps filled my
Mind like a singing lark soaring high.
She looked and looked at me,
But still silent with a mysterious glee.

I spread my hand to touch her hair.
At once she vanished, came she never.
I cried, I awoke and opened my eye,
But saw none and heaved a sigh.
I awoke, alas! Only to spoil her spree.
It was all dream, but a sweet memory.

Asaduzzaman Malik (London)

A Magical Place By The Sea

It is a magical place by the sea,
Quaint granite buildings beside clear blue waters,
There is an outcrop known as 'the island',
It was once, but no more to be,
A bay named after the town,
A harbour and beaches with true golden sand,
A castle that sits upon a lush green hill,
Shops and curios aplenty to browse around,
It was once a fishing port with a mighty fleet,
Not aware what fate the future held,
Now it has become the destination of thousands,
They come for a unique holiday treat,
Narrow cobbled streets built for horse and cart,
Where I used to run and play as a child,
Such good times never to be forgotten,
So lucky was I with all this as a start,
They say the air and light here is so clear,
Like no other place on Earth,
Attracting many famous artists throughout the years,
Little wonder I hold this place so dear,
This magical oasis is my town,
This is St Ives!

Terry Plummer (Hayle)

The Valuers

Just one hair.
The comb a slender thread of Art Deco:
A mirror, elegant and long, its shaft a twisted fish -
The brush - an urchin, spiked with silver.
Before the gilded glass they lay,
Serene within their own complicity.

'Nothing here - that I can see. Let it go.'
'Wait.' The dust upon the polished wood was recent.
Everything neat - but old. So old.
Silence ticked around the shadowed room.
I picked the hairbrush from its matched companions,
Pressing the soft pale bristles with my thumb.

Just one hair.
I took the brush and went into the light.
Silver. Pure, pure silver.
A fond remembered thread.
I know I spoke quite softly as:
'These have value,' I said.

R Allen (Harrow)

Rock Cottage On The River Wye

Hugging the crumbling riverbank, it stands alone,
Revelling in its solitude.
Hidden in its shroud of greenery, it is protected,
Time has passed by unnoticed.
Its watery companion curls past its door,
Carrying majestic swans.
Streaks of electric-blue at dusk flash by,
Betraying the shy kingfisher.
The air is still, the quiet broken by the lazy hum of bees,
And the cry of little owls.
At night the black satin sky is pierced by stars,
Watching over the cottage.
There is no alarm to wake you here, only the dawn chorus,
Gently nudging you to stir.
The scent of flowers and riverbank shrubs pervade the air,
Carried on a wispy breeze.
Inside the leaping flames of the open fire warm you,
Reminding you of your childhood.
You can watch the dancing shadows on the walls,
And paint your pictures.
There is no guilt if you do nothing, only look and listen,
This is where you find yourself.

M Lawrance (Englefield Green)

Healing

The patient awaits their healing
Secure in the knowledge
That a blessing
Will come their way
Faith or no it matters not
Universal power comes into play

Healing energy from the spirit plane
Transcends the link between
The two worlds
Harmony is present and
Time matters not
Universal power now unfurls

The healer is an instrument
An ambassador willingly used
In this mediumship
Transmitting, receiving, it matters not
When universal power
Completes its trip.

David Thompson (London)

We Walked

In the period between the rain of last night
And the storm of this evening, we walked.
As though the clouds waited for our moment together
So that we could capture our peaceful mood
Of care and endearment, touch and contentment,
Like new lovers revelling in and praising their self-involvement.
Our words and ideas of future belonging,
Dreams and happiness
Make our time seem youthful and vibrant
Like the budding spring flowers that surround us.
Yet, despite the scene not being a beach
That we so longingly crave,
We still remained captivated by its personality.
As the scenery complemented our walk,
You were the centre of my world.
I did not count every step,
Nor become distracted by passers-by.
For you occupied my mind and complemented my view
And with that sentiment I breathed out.
The cool breeze caught it and stored it.
Waiting for our moment
To be remembered.

Michelle Dixon (Poole)

Studland Ferry

Sombre purple clothes the hills
Where darkling heather grows
By twisted track on hillsides steep.
The wind of winter blows
Down to the shore to meet the sea
And drives across the bay.

Cormorants in arrowed flight
Speed noiseless overhead
From sandpits in the harbour mouth
To fish the ocean bed.
Seagulls mew and wheel about
And sweep across the bay.

Grey-green seas run;
A sudden shower of rain
Splinters on the heaving deck
And washes clear again.
On massive chains the ferry strains
To reach the further shore.

K Merle Chacksfield (Swanage)

Blessed Are They That Mourn

When all the pomp and glory dies,
Or a little life snuffs out,
Or a young life is killed by a crazy bomb
Or a young bomber dies for glory
What then? Do souls just ride in middle mist?
And wander lost between Heaven and Earth.
The bells ring out, the mourners come,
Crying loudly for their loss;
Mounds of flowers rise lovingly
If only . . . they had slept late
And missed the fateful train -
If only . . . we had kissed a fond farewell
If only . . . we had parted friends.
If only this, if only that . . .
Rejoice in their lives, their happiness.
Which leave a glow on Earth behind
Where they find a rest, a blessedness
In Christ, a peace we cannot know.
Taken in youth and unprepared,
Age shall not weary them, they go
Rejoicing, into Heaven's arms -
Alive in our memory.

Betty Shipway (Basingstoke)

How Can I Make Ends Meet?

Each Monday I draw my old-age pension,
Which is not a lot I hasten to mention,
But no matter how frugal I try to be,
I'm unable to make ends meet, you see,
For it's not fair and it's not funny,
When there's too much week left at the end of my money.

From charity shops my clothes I buy,
I make my own cakes and bake my own pies,
From jumble sales I get bargains galore,
Sheets for my bed, a rug for my floor,
I save on fuel when days are sunny,
But there's still too much week left at the end of my money.

Although the number of bills are many,
I can honestly say I owe not one penny,
I do not smoke, I do not drink,
What more I can save I cannot think,
Oh! Show me a land of milk and honey,
Where there's no week left at the end of my money.

Freda Pilton (Tiverton)

Aldworth Giants

Of Aldworth giants there are just nine,
And all in solid stone recline,
Here they pass their endless days,
In prayerful hope and silent praise.
Of Aldworth castle not a trace,
The mound is there but not the place.
It seems ironic that they lie,
In castle keep of church nearby.
These Norman knights with William came,
To serve their king was all their aim,
But what with wars, crusades and routes,
The male line quickly fizzled out.
Now they're only left in stone,
They've made the church their final home.
In fact it could be said they're caught,
With feet in chancel, head in porch.
So much room they take within,
They could not pack the village in.
They built another aisle to take,
Three more tombs for pity's sake!
Did they achieve the heaven they sought,
Or was this pomp and show for nought?

Graham K A Walker (Reading)

Thank You!

Thank you for loving me
With a love so tender,
For the most passionate love letter I ever received
You were the sender
And of all the pieces of my broken heart
You are the mender.

Thank you for protecting me
When in battle I must not give up the fight,
And though weary and disheartened
I must still do what is right
To prevent darkness
Conquering the light.

Thank you for providing for me
When debts are piling high,
When money's short and things look bad
And nothing seems to work, no matter how hard I try,
When poverty and hardship
Make me just want to curl up and die!

Natasha Yogaratnam (Uxbridge)

My Childhood Days

Oh how I loved my childhood days
So innocent and pure.
When children laughed and skipped and played
From dawn till set of sun.
And Christmas time brought great delight
To anxious little ones
While parents made the festive time
As happy as could be
With presents for each child, young and old
And traditional foods, drinks and cakes.
Those days of fun have long since gone
And schooldays came for us to learn
To read and spell and count and write
So that when we leave the schools behind
We'd take our place in the adult world.
To choose a career and work and earn
To build a future for ourselves
But now that age is creeping on
And life is not the same;
How I long for childhood days that will never be again.
So I thank the dear Lord for life and hope
And His great love for me, and my faith in Him.

Josephine Welch (London)

Winter

Across the Downs the winds do blow
And scatter all the leaves below.
At home, the fires glow in the grate
And cards from friends all prove the date
Is getting near the festive day
To celebrate with carols gay.

The trees dance in the breeze and show
Their leaves, which gained a fiery glow,
Then floated dancing to the ground,
Where bluebells in the spring abound
But now they sleep the winter through
Until in spring they'll rise anew.

So let us dance the year away
And fill our lives with joy each day.
We'll celebrate the Christmas season
And show our winter has a reason
To join with family and friends,
And show that true love never ends.

Annie Mouse (Brighton)

Ode To 9/11

The world changed on that fatal day
Five thousand souls were blown away
The western world was up in arms
Eastern world got quite alarmed
Out of the evil that arose
Armies gathered to be opposed
You could not help but cry a tear
For the nations who lived among the fear
Try to imagine what it was like
Last moments away from the end of a life
A lot of brave people died in vain
As they fought the horror brought by those insane
Families who lost loved ones will never forget
Sight of airplanes turning to flaming jets
No solution as yet to be found
Invading the enemy by air and by ground
Peace seems the last thing on world leaders' minds
But peace is the only way for countries to be combined
'Live and let live,' I heard someone say
All we've got left now is to hope and to pray
May your God go with you,
                          Amen.

Robert Henry (Letchworth)

Close To Heaven

When you've been kissed by the falling rain,
Or slept awhile in a field of grain.
Been gently tanned by a summer breeze,
Surveyed God's clouds through the shady trees.

Picnicked beside a babbling brook,
Canoodled in a shady nook.
Walked hand in hand through a leafy glen,
Or followed a deer through a marshy fen.
Living with God's creatures, day by day,
Can Heaven be so far away?

When you've been touched by a gypsy hand
Or been a part of a travelling clan.
Slept in a wagon beneath the stars,
Breathing contempt at trains and cars.
Laughed as the snow fell from the skies,
Sorrowed as tears fell from your eyes.
Living and breathing the Romany way,
Can Heaven be so far away?

Michael Pidgley (Totton)

Humbug!

What
Really bored her
When Christmas was near was
'Turkey talk' and Christmas cheer.
The Christmas build-up came too soon,
With consumers dancing to the retailer's tune.
'Commercialised consumerism' gets worse every year,
This ain't about Jesus, it's a moneymaking affair.
Mark up the prices they're sure to go,
The consumer will pay it, it's Christmas you know!
Two days later
Put the prices down again
Disguise it as the winter sales
And make them keep on paying.
It's hard to believe that we eat all year
'Cause that turkey dinner's such a grand affair.
Who had what veg, was it peas, sprouts or carrots?
What did Santa bring, did you get that coat from Harrods?
It bored her and bored her and got too much to bear,
Then like programmed computers
They chanted
Happy New Year!

Judith Desbonne (Bridgwater)

Spring At Last

Listen to the birds
Singing oh so dear
I haven't heard them sing like that
Since earlier last year.

The flowers wait to open up,
What colours they will bring,
Though it takes us by surprise each year,
I do believe it's spring.

I forget how green the leaves can be,
They cover healthy trees,
I missed all those lovely creatures,
The butterflies, the bees.

So I fold away my winter clothes,
Let out a great big cheer,
Then step into God's garden,
For my favourite time of year.

Louise Bradley (Brixham)

I Promise

Come, let me keep you warm,
Throughout the savage bite of winter,
Be your cooling breeze
When heat rises with the sun.
I will be your feast
In knawing pangs of famine,
At the break of day,
Until our time is done.
Let me make you smile
And hold your hand in pleasure,
But soothe you,
When sorrow creeps inside your soul.
Let me share our days
Of triumph and disaster,
Let me show my pride
In all your goals.
Come, let me love you always,
Through our life together,
Supporting, sharing, living, every day,
Knowing we will grow old forever,
Thankful, for our lives,
In every way.

Debbie Ingram (London)

Perfection

Perfection is nothing but a myth
Find it, and you have nothing to measure it with
Perhaps I am looking in the wrong place
Is it inside me, or on another's face?

Is it in love when the blood runs fast
But when all passion is spent, it doesn't last
Then love just becomes a game of chance
Blowing in the wind, perfection's dance.

I seek again in another sphere
Perhaps the missing link is here
Perfection must be coming my way
But it is gone, and here is another day.

I am getting tired, life is not so kind,
Perhaps after all it's only in the mind
But now spring is here, the world looks good,
I am living again because I think I should.

Gordon Watts (Clevedon)

Research

The spies were aching travesties; discerning, flinching
through the backward lens atop the secret smiles; the broken
trust; the sighing mental intrepid scans of the magnified
selves of the photograph pocket. Who is to know when
knowledge is the one possessor of them all: who scours
without archetypal betrayal of the systematic punchline
of humanity, draped in solid liquid dust and shod
beneath thousands of acres of text? It's a man, woman,
child, taking journeys into themselves, as they
hunt for chemical bloodshed unheard of to silent
minds apart from blush-spoken whispers of sapphires
in trees. The knees of politicians shape the moulds of
weariness in far-off shelters to discourse, with unearthed
chasms of remorse dug broken from guilty emptiness of
mines pumped out with anti-structural tools to
catalyse our fate. Our infrastructural is crumbled
away by the ruins of thought from thought decay. So
stand and watch at the gloomy canyon, free of
shifty concords, free of open-ended circled bushes
beaten round, discovered all that one might find.
For curiosity is in our nature, right? And
civilization is clearly not.

Sumil Thakrar (Norbury)

Mystery Of Life

Some hurry through life without wondering why
Or who made this Earth, the sea and the sky
What purpose is there for us to be born?
T'wist good and the bad, sometimes we are torn.

It's hard to explain why some folk grow old
While others die young, God's wish we are told
Some people thru life will suffer great pain
It sometimes is hard to always stay sane.

On this road of life, it's often quite rough
Sometimes to survive, one needs to be tough
The weak may succumb . . . some stumble and fall
Along rocky paths, for help they may call.

If only we knew this mystery of life
Birth, life, death . . . disbelief can be rife
All will be revealed when God calls to us
And life after death could be a big plus.

Kevin Erickson (St Albans)

689

A Busy Day

I went to the office this morning
To work out the wages and tax,
But the phones were ringing
And doors were banging,
Messages coming in on fax.
I decided to down pen and paper,
Make coffee to soothe my nerves,
But the boss came in,
With a cough and a grin,
'I've a new job for you tonight.'
You see, my boss owned many fish shops,
I helped in them now and again,
It was a change from the books and the typing,
I enjoyed the challenge and fame.
The shops were busy on Fridays,
And often on Saturdays too,
We laughed and joked while serving the fish
Till someone called out, 'She's a tasty dish.'
But the boss replied, 'She is not for sale.
Do you want this one's head, or this one's tail?'
So that was the end of a busy day.
We will close the shop and give staff their pay.

Elsie Keen (Uxbridge)

Country Childhood

The smiling hills of my childhood speak great strength to the heart of me,
The bright river's waywardness murmuring is very much part of me,
The song of the birds and cattle soft lowing, touches the deep in me,
The moon on the trees and the light of the stars makes something to weep in me.

I loved the sight of the heather, as the distant moorland I trace,
The feel of the dew on my hand, and the rain on my upheld face,
I loved the pools in the forest, the wind in the highest trees,
The butterflies summer outpouring, the haunting of laden bees.

And the cloudy skies a-gleaming is part of my halcyon day,
The green of the meadows a-ripening, holds promises of gold of hay,
The hedgerows bejewelled glory of joy, of summer and spring,
The mist of the morn arising, and the rush of the bird's first wing.

Bright were the days of my childhood, with skipping days in the sun,
Soft were the nights of its passing, as slowly each day was done -
Now as the years pass quickly, and sunset glows o'er the world -
The sweetest dreams are realised, as the rainbow is brightly unfurled.

Elizabeth Killick (High Barnet)

The Photo Album

Found in a shop in Camden Passage,
a short stop from Sadler's Wells,
among the magic lanterns
the owner buys and sells,
on a ledge, a photo album, gathering dust,
lying abandoned, just an idle curiosity,
moments of lives caught within a frame,
snapshots of people who have no name.
What can we tell by such a fleeting glance,
from the backgrounds, their clothes, their stance,
cashmere, tweeds, leather shoes and pearls?
Perhaps adventurers, daughters of earls,
colonialists, planters of rubber or tea,
or civil servants with files to oversee,
administrators in the Diplomatic Corps
with home leave taken via Singapore.
The album travelling across oceans and on trains,
protected from humidity, mildew and the rains,
carried overland through the mud and the briar,
and brought back when they were ready to retire
to Cheltenham, the Cotswolds or the Yorkshire Fells.
Then, how did their photos end up near Sadler's Wells?

Heather Grange (Plymouth)

Our Tommy

Wear no band of black
For Tommy in Iraq
Don no funeral shroud
For one so young and proud

Weep not by the grave
Of a son we gladly gave
But tell us if you can
How this cruel war began

You told us it was just
To kill for yards of dust
And now I can't recall
Why we are there at all

I have no hate nor spite
For those we chose to fight
Just piteous despair
For *you* who sent them there.

Les Porter (London)

Heartache

(In memory of Alisha Marie Grebby)

Ten tiny fingers upon your little hand,
Ten dainty toes on your feet to help you stand,
I look into your sleeping face and my heart is filled with love,
How can something so beautiful now be an angel above?
Your eyelashes so long upon your sweet face,
No one will ever take your place,
The joy we all waited for is now replaced by tears,
The numbness, the heartache, along with all our fears,
I want to hold you in my arms and never let you go,
My darling child, how I love you so,
A part of me went with you the day you were called home,
I feel that my world has stopped and I feel so much alone,
I gently place you down for one last time,
Tears are on my face as I whisper, 'Peace be thine,'
Without you I am nothing, and never will be again,
All I feel is heartache and a huge, huge pain.
My darling child you will be loved and missed every single day,
Goodbye is too final a word for me to ever say,
God only gave you to us to borrow,
Loved today, yesterday and for all the tomorrows.

Sandy Ward (Abbots Langley)

Gosport Waterfront

Small anchored boats
Bobbing gently
As a ferry passes,
Under a streaked blue sky.
At the marina,
Anglers leaning on a rail
Await their fish's response;
Yachts edge into narrow spaces,
Fenders banging the wooden pier.
Sunbathers sprawled on seats
Oblivious behind their paperbacks
As school children march by,
Voices babbling together.
But old men in wheelchairs
Look across that stretch of water,
Remembering when it teemed
With wartime vessels;
The troops are still departing
In their minds.

Julia Perren (Ryde)

Equinox

Cold pinpricks against the ink-black night,
Through rents in ragged clouds,
The rising constellations glisten.
The winter sky is taking shape,
Marking the turning of the year.
Harvest Moon to Hunter's Moon,
New Moon to Old Moon; waxing, waning.

Distant - so infinitesimally distant -
Across the void of time and space,
Those sisters, the Pleiades, ride the night,
Scudding the racing clouds,
Heralding the ascendance of Bull and Hunter,
Borne upon a westering wind, they scout the skies
And usher in the Season of Storms.

Beneath the changing heavens,
Amid a darkened landscape, moist with chilly dew,
Autumn's mellow harvest sinks slowly into sere.
Summer's gentle pulse has long subsided.
It is the time of decay and lengthening shadows.
Nature's ebbing rhythms contract and coalesce.
The ageing year lies poised upon the cusp of winter.

Rob Atkins (Sandown)

Today . . .

Hey!
Today -
Turn around
For new things are to be found.
Quick!
No - it's no trick
That the past
Is vanishing fast
Deep into your memory.
But wait - there's more to see,
In this direction look!
Unfolding as a book,
The way ahead
Is waiting to be read.
Excitingly new,
It's all in store for you -
Hey!
From today -
Your special birthday.

Judy Marshall (Winchester)

Dartmoor April 2008

The sky is a pale grey dome
Over the moor today;
The savage wind,
Aware of its merciless power,
Howls in a bluster of venom;
Raindrops sting the skin.

Up on the moors,
Exposed to the raging storm,
No hint of life reveals
The chosen shelter
Where the sheep and ponies hide,
No birds sing
As they did
In the brightness of yesterday;

Instead, the sodden turf,
The creaking gorse,
Suffer the battering unseen,
Waiting for those skies to blue again,
The warming sun to glint again
And life to stir,
And show itself once more.

Jacqui Fogwill (Tavistock)

Silent River

At Blackfriars Bridge, you stand on the stair
slowly descend to the walkway
feel cut by the icy-cold air.
(London is bleak and lonely
when no one else is there).
Look down to the river
pulled by the tide, look at it,
so black no colour escapes,
so oily, fluid, silent, unstoppable,
powerful swallower of feeling,
everything, that is, but the cold
that cuts through and strips you bare,
the hard steel blade of the icy-cold air.
As you walk the embankment, take care!
Be sure not to stop, or stand on the wall -
One slip, you fall and get swallowed up
By the oil black river that silently flows,
leans round the bends and slithers and slides,
joins with the sea, mixes and hides, and never returns.

Raymond Lancer (Harrow)

You Woke Me Up

I heard you come in
You woke me up
I was having a dream
But you woke me up

The mind was dark
My dream was too
I was having a dream
But you woke me up

There were demons and monsters
And blood on my hands
I was having a nightmare
I couldn't wake up

The angels were crying
Their swords had fallen
I was having a nightmare
I want to wake up

I hear your voice
I feel you near me
I was having a nightmare
Now it's gone and you're here.

Caroline Jacobi (Dunstable)

Mike's Hairdressers

(With apologies to Mike)

If you're in need of a haircut,
Then go along and see Mike,
Where he will do this for you,
Just any way that you like.

You'll get a nice warm welcome,
As you open the door and go in,
Good morning Sir, nice to see you,
I take it you would like a neat trim.

So with a little snip here,
And a little snip there,
Oops I'm so sorry Sir,
There goes your right ear.

Not to worry Sir,
About a thing like that,
Just on your way out,
Keep it under your hat.

Peter Byron (Southampton)

Computers Don't Bite

'Computers don't bite' a course in IT,
I wonder if this is the thing for me,
The only way that I will know,
Is to join a class and give it a go.

We were shown how to 'boot up',
That meant switch on,
Our screens came to life before very long.
Asked for the 'password', we all typed it in,
Now our IT course was about to begin.

The mouse was the gadget which we clicked to move on,
The tutor was there if you got it all wrong.
We learnt how to drop, drag and write our names,
We drew some balloons and coloured in frames.

First Word and Excel, then searched with Webwise,
Learnt how to email - quite a surprise.
As we sent to each other it felt really grand,
It was good to see we had it in hand.

We didn't get bitten, it was really quite fun,
Sign up for a course,
IT life's begun!

Enid Thomas (Bracknell)

A Lancashire Carnival

I heard the sound of the clogs on the road
And the tap of the knocker-up's cane
The hooter sounds calling all to work
And the wheels of the winding gear start to turn
As I watch from the upstairs room
I was just a girl waking up
In a Lancashire mining town
Each year we had a carnival
With floats (no longer allowed)
We had carnival queens
With three attendants
All dressed in home made gowns
Church representatives paraded as well
With many carrying banners
There were Guides and Brownies
Cubs and Scouts and Sunday school
Members all dressed in their best
Dancing troops put on displays
And the town band played for all.

Christine Youd (Newton Abbot)

What Has Happened?

Where has our love for each other gone?
What has also happened to our passionate years?
Where's the days we had romantic walks?
What has happened to our laughter and shed tears?

Where's those moonlit walks we used to have
Or the times we spent in hot passionate nights?
What about our dances and candlelit meals,
What about me driving you to the sights?

Where are the times we spent on beaches?
What's happened to the times we hugged by coal fires
Or times we sailed on the open sea,
And times we kissed and were full of desires?

Now your love for me has almost gone
Though sad inside, I show a fake mask,
Romantic walks have become a drag
Making you laugh, has become such a hard task.

Nice drives now seem dull and unending
Your love's gone cold, like logs fires now rarely made,
Sexy nights now seem dark and gloomy
Like a candle's flame our love's about to fade.

Donato Genchi (Luton)

My Friend At The Window

I'll never forget how I felt that morning when I was abruptly awoken
by the chilling sound of chainsaws gnawing into innocent bark,
men talking and laughing, just going about their job,
not a second thought for the murderously callous act they were about
to commit,
a beautiful majestic horse chestnut tree standing tall,
conversing with the breeze, a tree among trees,
branches dancing and weaving through shafts of light,
greeted their last dawn and bid a sad farewell to their last night,
it had stood a hundred years or more,
it was my friend at the window, a stone's throw from the door,
and now because of a bureaucratic council of this nanny state,
we just sit back and watch helplessly
as another nature made skyscraper will meekly suffer its fate.
The next day I took down the rubbish and walked over and through
what would have been the trunk of that glorious tree,
to my saddened surprise as I knelt on the paved area amongst the freshly laid gravel I found
two lonely horse chestnut pods decaying,
housing infant conkers that will forever cease to be.

Steve Sayers (Woking)

697

Let The Wind Blow

Whichever way the wind blows
Carry my message loud and clear
Across the lands far and wide
Forever in my image.

Let the flowers grow
Bright and sweet
Let the rays of the sun
Shine clear.

Let no darkness
Fall on thee
For I am ever near
Let your heart beat to my song.

Let your love be true
So that with each shower of rain,
The freshness is for you,
Let your life be cleansed.

Sing your love with every breath,
Let laugher fill the air,
Join the chorus of the birds,
They will know, you to me, are dear.

Jeanette Jackson (Paignton)

The Venue For Your Menu

The sort of food we used to favour
Had a clear distinctive English flavour.
Roast beef, fish and chips, spotted dick or jelly and cream
Was enough to satisfy a food lover's dream.
Search today and you'll find it rare
To savour the delights of homely national fare.
Down most high streets you'll find a varied selection
Of international cuisine promising culinary perfection.
Whichever you choose is a question of taste
And your choice should not be one made in haste.
Chow mein, korma and madras, pizza, pasta and Satay sauce
May not suit your palate as a matter of course,
But if you dine out on a regular basis
You'll eventually choose a favourite food oasis.
The fare will not be the only criteria,
Ambience and service not found in the local cafeteria,
Together with a pleasant location, will each hold
their persuasions,
To ensure you have your place for those celebratory occasions.

Allen Jessop (London)

Résumé

'Tis twenty years you be today
As you stand fore the mirror
Success has come tenacious way
Now bright light not a glimmer

Your invites sent all scribes aware
Their quills are poised and ready
Words will explode, rhyme will appear
A million poets stand steady

What you've achieved is quite unique
Allowed us poets to write and speak
From this a few have carved careers
For most of us it's sweat and tears

We persevere and forward press
Each one of us must face the test
Of editors who check our script
We do our best to make lines fit

Sincere congrats are call of day
We doff our hats with quills and say
'You have done well and now move on
Your twenty-first it must be fun'.

Trevor Perrin (High Wycombe)

Leaving Work In Winter

Now, when we leave work it is night.
We plunge into a hard land,
Where the paving stones throw back our sounds.
The chill air drips,
And where the office building gleams with its own grey light,
The wind whips round.
I search for the muted lights
At the edges of shops,
In the moving bus,
Like a strange reflection of the sun
Holding out warmth for us.
I am in no-man's-land, where no one claims me.
It is the time of the universe
Standing still around me.
At last, on the open platform,
I see the train winding its way along the track,
Like the day I've just had,
That comes to a standstill in my mind
And then unravels back.

Deborah Binstock (Hendon)

The Moonlight Goose

On a late summer evening,
A gloomy sunset filled the sky,
I watched in amazement
At the golden fleeces sailing by.

One fleece fell on a burnt-out tree
And changed into a silken goose,
It ran about the field in glee,
Shaking its feathers loose.

It honked just like the geese of Rome
And flapped above in splendor,
Singing a lovelorn song of joy,
So pretty and so tender.

Then night came down, grey inky black,
The gosling flew away
But first it took a sideways glance
Through a field of hay.

There it laid a lovely silver egg,
Which turned into a moon,
This did not hatch, but coldly shone
Amid the starlight swoon.

David Hazlett (Reading)

To My Husband

Have I met you?
Have our paths crossed?
Is it too late or are you far in the midst?
My adored one being on this Earth
At this time without you, to be on my own,
But whole until you become me
And I become you, unite, as one.
The journey has been long,
Wrong choices I made in the past,
Didn't know then,
This means I need to complete you,
But how do we get to the finish line?
If you've never seen me and I've never seen you,
I do not date, I yearn for everlasting love,
Obedience is better than sacrifice.
We were born for one another,
God willing we will be together.
We will marry, live happy ever after,
Before you and I die.

Elisabeth Senghor (London)

My Friend

One day I sat gazing,
Just sitting on the floor,
As I looked out of the window,
My emotions feeling raw.

The moon staring back at me,
Shining on my tear-stained eyes,
Just glistening in wonder,
Amongst the star-filled skies.

I waited for a long time,
For someone who would be,
The light to brighten up my life,
Like that moon on the sea.

Then suddenly I'd remember,
A friend who is so dear,
And yet they feel so far away,
Even though they are quite near.

Then I eventually realise,
You were there, up to the end,
And gave me hope to carry on,
Thank you for being my friend.

Ruth Bray (Plymouth)

Rebellion

Kissed my father in the street
Screamed I love you! to the world
And meant it with a will that drove me deep
Beneath the Earth
Crossed the brow of bitter city
Steamy with its sticky hate
Just to hear the broken record of my
Baby's garbled words
Ducked inside a park and rode the only swing
Left on its chains
Whistled at a group of angry women dressed to
Slay
Called my mother, took her shopping
Held her hand across the road
Quit my job without a word
Live to fight another day
Rebellion, ah rebellion!
Ain't nothing like it anywhere, or anymore or anyhow, or anyone . . .
Rebellion, sweet rebellion, sweet rebellion.

Laudis Noel (London)

War Cry

I raise my hands
Head flung back
Hailing in strength
Countering the next attack

I roar
Towards the sky
I roar
A lioness's cry

Lift me up
So I can be
Your true creation
Lay your hands on me

Lift me up
I need to see
I'm not forgotten
There's a place for me

Lift me up
Don't pass me by
I roar, I roar, I roar
My latest war cry

Angelia Burke (Edmonton)

Out Of Emptiness

Suddenly there's silence,
Nothing to be done,
A dull day, no sun,
But it's Sunday morning, Sun day,
The wind comes, the branches rise and fall,
Still no sun,
Silence, not even traffic,
The world may have stopped going round,
Whatever next?
But -
There is wind, there is breath and breathing,
Something wants to move,
There is always want,
The pulsing blood needs to connect,
A bird sings, bravely, it seems,
And there are, in fact, things to be done,
'The claim of the object' as Jung and Churchill knew it,
Something within to be touched,
If we haven't lost touch.

Elizabeth Rainsford (Shaftesbury)

Strap-Hanging

Freeland Crabtree is no longer well and alive;
A sworn statement on oath I cannot give.
But I feel he's expended his allotted years
And joined the resting place with his academic peers.

But last week, I thought I glimpsed him in the city rush
On the tube between Marble Arch and Shepherd's Bush.
Strap-hanging he was - or else his spitting image
With greying temple hair and his designer visage.

I looked up again from the book I was reading
But he had unhooked, flown, just a shadow receding.
Perhaps my mind had indulged in its usual skittish games
Playfully fitting faces to erstwhile well-known names.

I knew him as a schoolmaster, many years ago:
A fair and respected figure, alike to friend and foe.
A constructive critic with incisive thoughts and brain
Evoking memories and ideals which returned to me again.

That evening, I glanced through my jumbled bookcase
And a leather backed volume seemed to jump out of its place.
For there on the front page, copper plate, he had signed it for me,
'Walk upright, see everything, absorb all', Freeland Crabtree.

Robert Main (Bedford)

Sign Of The Times

What is wrong with today?
The sun shines, the flowers are gay,
But this heavy feeling falls on my head,
It's not all it seems, there's a vast flowing stream of depression and slump.
The news gives us worry, those awful knife killings increase.
People hating each other, another life spent.
Folk doing their duty are jeered at and scorned.
Has decency gone forever?
Oh how it should be mourned.
Come back values of yesteryear.
All those electrical gadgets and fancy mod-cons.
Can't we live with true values, Mum, Dad and kids,
Has TV addled our brains with soaps all the rage.
What happened to reading? It's all on the Net,
No need to learn is all that is said.
So why is knife culture so strongly pursued?
Is it taken with drugs the mind cloudy, mis-used?
What has damaged our youngsters, please answer me this,
Is it just wanton and Godless, the Devil's last hiss?

Rosemary C Whatling (Leighton Buzzard)

Time's Arrow

Time rushes forward, we ride the arrow's shaft
The dye is cast, no turning for this craft
Out from the past, from cot to grave
Unknown future beckons meek and brave

And yet time's features constantly recur
Night follows day, the seasons four,
Moon phases too, and even rocks do tell
Of ice age cycles on some huge Mayan carousel

Or is it merely semblance, this inexorable flow?
Do we spiral to the future or does God know
That all that was and will be, simply is,
Everything present to the glory that is His?

It may be so, yet Einstein clearly shows
That space-time stretches, bends and warps, but forward flows
Yet in some later models of his universe
Theory permits time's arrow to reverse

So if through some 'wormhole' we could time retrace
Prevent our own conception taking place
Priests and moralists must then decide
Whether such meddling would be suicide.

Aidan Power (South Croydon)

Only A Mum

I am saddened greatly by his eyes,
They reveal such truth and hurt, no lies.
He flits from pillar to post each day,
Like a manic pinball on fast play.
Now his engine it runs but his petrol is low,
Need to fill him up so he can go.
But when will he stop and understand
That sometimes he needs to hold my hand?
I've never before cried such tears of despair,
I didn't know caring was so unfair.
But he pushes and pushes till the walls come tumbling,
My walls were my strength, I'm stumbling, I'm stumbling.
I've got him but who's got me?
Is there anyone there? I just can't see.
The noise is increased and the pressure will soar,
So bad is my rage I will scream, I will *roar!*
And he sees this great beast who stopped all the fun,
I'm sorry, I'm sorry . . .
I'm only your mum.

Hayley Smart (Potters Bar)

Resurrection

Come take this crippled body
And cleanse it to the core;
Empty it of worthlessness
Forever, I implore!

Vanquish all the vanity
Grandiloquence besides.
Prick the gross pomposity
Wherever it resides.

Stop-up the shadow chasing;
Alert the ego too.
That what it thinks will aid it,
Is twice removed from true.

Please hasten with the kindling
For time is getting thin.
To smoke out foolish phantoms
That lead a man to sin.

Then come the resurrection,
With mind and body twinned.
Tomorrow can reclaim him
From yesterday's waste-bin.

Bernard Doogan (London)

Why Am I Here?

I just got old, so where did I go?
Why am I here, does anyone know?
My family told me they knew best
And put me in a home for a well earned rest.
Through the big doors I'm shaking with fright,
I do hope I settle on this my first night.
Would you understand if you were me?
I had a home with my own front door key.
Sat in this room I feel so alone,
Feeling so sad, is this my new home?
Will I like them - or will they like me?
Should I come out, or watch my TV?
Don't want to be a trouble, I feel so unwell,
I've been told, 'just ring your bell'.
Can't drag myself down for dinner tonight,
Hope they don't mind if I ask for a tray.
Do you understand, I hope you'll agree,
The reason I'm here
Is to be cared for you see.

Marie Harvey (Paignton)

The Scots Were Bold

Memories come to me as sweet and dry as a true Scotch
For what is life without the tales to tell?
I be this drifting mouse
Held to the sway of fate

No mystery is there in my glass
For life has made me still
Not rushing for a morsel
Nor a cracker

Aye I used to pull
Well we all did
Rushing to fill the Friday night
With a flirt

If I could live again
To Bruce's door I would stand
The time was great
The Scots were bold

I be a quiet mouse
Sitting and thinking
By his immortal side
Dunfermline Abbey.

Ajarn Anton Nicholas (London)

Afterglow

After spending a little time with you,
The best time spent in the world,
For three days Heaven is brought down to earth,
Three days of heaven, and it feels like the birth
Of the luckiest person ever to live
Who basks in the afterglow you give;
And while you give I return your love,
So we share the experience of life,
With no conditions to which we abide
The once-closed doors are now open wide,
To let your voice ring clear as a bell,
Saying, 'Come on love, come on inside,'
For now I'm within, no longer without,
To remove the slightest trace of a doubt;
But no one said this was easy to do,
To get love to grow, to start life anew,
For everything I do, I do it for you,
As my world is coloured a devotional blue,
How could I do anything but love you?

Andy Gresty (Oxford)

Time Is Master

Never still the hands
Of time, as he winds his
Way forward
No going back

As the river winds so
Doth the clock, as the
Water flows, so doth
The time, river and time

Are as one, the hands
Are restless and the
River knows time waits
For none.

Not a ripple will
She echo, time is on
Her side, should he
Forget, then she
Will wait

For, time is the master
And she
His mistress.

Jeanne E Quinn (London)

Back to the Engine

Houses, scrubby trees, the
rails and landmarks
fly back from sight
into the misty past.

Out of eye's corner, through
the murky glass,
present erupts,
catches sun's shine through clouds.

The rails, the scrubby trees,
forsythia gold
at Preston Road,
green sward and hospital

Bring Harrow Hill where spire
of Mary's church,
millennium nigh,
mind out of time up-points.

Enid Ellis (Harrow)

A Moment Away From It All

Here is where I find you
In a forgotten, unvisited piece of Bletchley town
Remembered only by me
When my adult world gets me down.

I still see our initials are carved into the tree
They are a little worn
And a little weathered
But all that remains of what was you and me.

I walked down the path
That we always walked home from school
Sweating in the summer sun
Or ploughing our way through the leafy autumn fall.

I see a person in the distance
Each time it happens I wonder if it is you
Taking a trip down memory land
Coming here as I do.

I can't remember your last words
Or where it all went from here
Maybe the answer or maybe you will find me
As I come here year after year.

Steve Prout (Milton Keynes)

The Glorious South

What a glorious place is England's south
With historic ships in old Portsmouth
When Pompey won the FA Cup
All night we did sing and dance and sup.

The weather here is always better
The north it seems is so much wetter
The beaches here are fine and dandy
A shame we can't have more that's sandy.

And down the road we've a forest new
With lots of deer and ponies too
And trees and streams and lots of space
I doubt you'll find a more relaxing place.

Although I've travelled most of the land
It's the south of England I find most grand
If when I die I go to Heaven
I'll give it ten but the south gets eleven.

Dick Hardy (Havant)

God Calling

God's peace is all around us
Each and every day,
But do we always stop and think
To give our thanks and pray.

Our Heavenly Father does know best,
Then Jesus He will do the rest,
So give to Him a listening ear
And carry out His plans without a fear.

Jesus is with us every day,
All we have to do is pray,
Then His guidance will see us through
And show us what we have to do.

Those who serve Him know this is right,
So keep Jesus in their sight,
This they feel they must do,
It also can apply to you.

So just get busy from today,
Do the best for him you can,
Remember even the smallest task
Could be part of His plan.

Will A Tilyard (Yarmouth)

Perhaps

The river shivers in the early dawn
The shadow of the tree lies stark
The wind is gentle but very cold
As the world emerges from the dark

The black sky slowly turns to grey
And the flowers blink and wake
The dew lies heavy on blades of grass
In the distance, on the river, a drake

The sun has now risen high in the sky
Off the river, a shimmering haze
A kingfisher dives, just a glimpse of blue
Reflections glow, the world is ablaze

Late afternoon is a tranquil scene
Gently now, the river laps
Heard on the wing, a nightingale's song
Tomorrow, tomorrow, perhaps.

Barry L J Winters (Newton Abbot)

Somerset My Home

The beauty of the countryside,
Rolling hills, woodland and moors,
The coastline with its rugged cliffs,
And Exmoor with its tors.

Georgian Bath in all its glory,
Cheddar caves and Wookey Hole,
Somerset has so many treasures,
Which are something to behold.

Castles, parks and stately homes,
Where visitors look around,
A precious heritage for me,
Somerset knows no bounds.

The levels amass with wildfowl,
When in winter they arrive,
Starlings with their aerobatic swarms,
Spectacular when at dusk they dive.

Pathways to secret places,
Where on horseback you can ride,
But Somerset is home to me,
Where evermore I'll bide.

Caroline Russell (Crewkerne)

A Gift

My love, woo me not with words as so many others have done,
instead, show me your heart through your eyes.
For words can be cheap, when said just for fun,
and are too often a cover for lies.

Too many before you have made promises and spoken of love,
whispering words, oh so tender and sweet.
But they were not my true soul mate, my gift from God above,
yet still, they made my fragile heart weep.

You too have been broken, by a love that was not true,
so for you, trust was a thing of the past.
But your natural reserve and suspicion may overcome you,
spoiling the chance of a true love that can last.

So my love, all I will ask of you; forever and today,
will not be demanding or for gestures oh so grand.
I only ask of you, never to hurt or casually throw away,
my heart, which I hold out to you in my hands.

Deborah Wainman (Essex)

A Moment In Time

A moment in time fast or slow,
A magic, a picture at once will grow,
A feeling, a rapture, a look in two eyes,
An instant flow in bondage lies.

A moment, a fraction of love or sadness,
A touch, a feeling, a joy, a gladness,
A wedding, a couple in love,
A newborn baby, a cooing dove.

A happiness, a joy with nature blends,
Majestic beauty before you stands,
A whispering, a singing lark,
In broad daylight or shadows of dark.

In the silence a hushful echo, a gentle sigh,
And endless beauty surrounds your eye,
A silence, a stillness, a throbbing heart,
Pervades your being, living each part.

This moment in time will linger on
Till end of life when all is gone,
A heritage, an heirloom,
Will blossom on into full bloom.

Shula Bailey (East Grinstead)

Snowflakes

When I see flakes fall through trees
All seem alike, as they brush my knees,
And as each falls upon the ground
To snugly fit one glittering mound.

Why is it I prefer them to be
High and free, like birds in a tree?
Would they be forever free
If they travelled on with no ground to see?

And if they did, what colours warm
Would sunbeams dance along their form?
Transfer them into their own true selves,
Their patterns diverse, as they drift and change.

The image of such amazing displays
Should stay in our minds' eye always;
Should not our lives be like this too?
But I don't expect they will, do you?

Christine A Dunn (Ashford)

Button Your Hip

Molly was a draper
She used to own a shop
Sewed on many buttons
Zippers made it a flop

Those new fangled zip things
Took so much sewing on
Adhering to straight lines
Start to finish belong

We all know how they stick
Inauspicious moment
When that damned slider jams
Raging temper foment

We twist and tug the things
And tactfully seek help
When freed it ensnares you
Followed by some loud yelp

Molly's back in business
Replacing broken zips
With nice fashion buttons
So trousers hang off hips.

David Youlden (Newquay)

Sand That Stretches

Sand that stretches to the sea
Footprints, those of you and me
Glistening on the water's face
Lasting memories to embrace

If there was to be a cloud
Our hearts combined would shout out loud
As soul mates we would then destroy
The storms that try to spoil our joy

Life could never be as fine
As basking in the warm sunshine
I am yours and you are mine
Together till the end of time

Footprints that will ever last
Steps to reflect upon our past
Together we are meant to be
Like sand that stretches to the sea

Stephen Morrison Hay (Littlehampton)

Michelle's Security Dream

Michelle was a little girl
But a lady she wanted to be,
So she dressed up in her mummy's clothes
And looked into the mirror to see. . .

She glanced sideways at herself . . .
And her magic wand she waved
And there she was in Dream Land,
With all her pennies saved.

She bought a clown and lots of dolls,
And a puppy of her own,
She spent lots of pennies to have some fun
In a dream land of her own.

And now a lonesome Michelle . . .
A lady she no longer wanted to be . . .
It's far better to be a little girl,
Where everything comes free.

So she waved her magic wand once more
And prayed that she could be
A little girl at her own back door . . .
Where Mum and Dad might be!

Lynn Smith (Stotfold)

The Magic Garden Of Aphrodite

From an ancient laurel coppice,
Through a twirled black wrought iron gate,
Sunlight dances round blue iris,
Falling golden on blue black slate.

Peeping through ivy, Virgin Mary,
Reigns over jostling profusion;
Sweet violets of Aphrodite
Vie among tansy infusion.

A horse rug draped over a gate;
Bridles hung from a bough of yew.
Groundsel, comfrey, thistle and rue;
Robin waits pertly for his cue.

In soil like dark roasted coffee
By summer house, forget-me-nots
Share with annual meadow grass,
The *parfait amour* of this spot.

Joan Woolley (Arundel)

The Story Of My Life

Forty years I have spent on this Earth
So much has changed since the day of my birth
Tears and sorrow, pleasure and mirth
What does it mean? What is my worth?

Family members that were here but now gone
Aunties and uncles and grandparents pass on
Some lived through decades, others not as long
They are close to my heart and my memories stay strong

I have lived in London all my life
I am a daughter, a sister, a mother and a wife
Spent my teens living on the blade of a knife
Missed most of school and caused nothing but strife

Weighed 24 stone after my four girls were born
Living in poverty and feeling forlorn
Agoraphobia, depression and sleep apnoea were my thorns
Then reached 35 and my new life had dawned

I started working in my local school,
Took a course in college which proved I'm not a fool
9 stone lighter and I'm having a ball
My life has new meaning, and that is not all.

Karen Barry (London)

Ego

Perverse with darkness,
Darkness is a pitch-black cloth.
It wraps itself around the soul.
The soul is consumed by it.

The soul becomes lost
And the shadow is mangled
Across the silver moon,
With an hallucinating grin.

And the illusions bombard,
Possessed by a delusion
And the drab bells ring loud,
And the hellish sounds heard

Again, among the rigid flesh
And the dark selfishly instilled.
Inner lust looms, unleashed.
The ego breeds by mindless will.

Dharminder Gill (Hounslow)

Why Is It?

Why is it some days we are worried and blue,
and some days happy and gay?
Is it because of the rights and the wrongs,
that each of us do every day?

Why is it sometimes we help one another,
and sometimes just harden our hearts?
Is it because we think 'life' is a play,
and that we are just acting our parts?

Why is it somehow when we cannot see straight
and somehow we cannot think clear?
Is it because of tears in our eyes,
or thoughts of someone that's dear?

Why is it somewhere we've seen things before,
that somewhere we just cannot place?
Is it because our memory's at fault,
that our hearts soon forget a friend's face?

Why is it someone we love most of all,
that someone who cares for our love,
Is the one we most hurt if we don't ask them for
the answers above?

G F Davison (Bedford)

Silly Stupid Man

Now we're in a state of war,
That 'dark abyss' again,
Is there no one out there
Who's just a little sane?

Is it fight for freedom
Or just the thick black oil?
Think of all the countries,
War is going to soil.

Doesn't Man do quite enough?
His life a constant toil.
Must we really start again?
Everything to spoil.

He should have learnt with Vietnam,
The trenches and the Somme,
The bomb delivered on Japan,
Silly stupid Man.

Barbara Shaw (Cowes)

Criticism

Criticism - I don't need it,
Yes, my views are very strong,
It's not as though I'm always right,
Simply that I'm never wrong.

Criticism - I can't stand it,
Just who do you think you are?
Adamant that your opinion
Is superior by far.

Criticism - how I hate it!
I can't take it that's for sure.
I've listened to your words of wisdom,
Don't expect me back for more.

Criticism - I protest loudly,
But in my heart I fear it's true,
I'll pretend that I've not heard it,
Then start criticising you!

Criticism - just once perhaps,
I'll ponder on it overnight,
It's true I'm hardly ever wrong,
But maybe I'm not always right!

P Parr (Lauceston)

Captivity

If I were a fly in a spider's web
Or a caged bird never to fly
Or a fish in a bowl so small it is cruel,
Or a wild bear chained up till he dies.

If I were a child in the hands of a pimp
Or a dog kicked daily for fun
Or spent my whole life encapsulated in pain
Or too crippled to walk or to run.

If I were a soldier tormented by thoughts
Of friends killed - or disfigured for life
Or I lived in a country so short of food
Just to live is endurance and strife.

Then maybe I would have cause to complain
On reflection, I haven't and I don't
So I'll just keep up my struggle and smile when I can
But moan and complain I won't.

Jacqueline Rowlands (Newquay)

Springtime Song

Intensity of nature to breed and illume,
In principle spring shows its bright significance,
Earthly mind salutes whole-heartedly earthly perfume,
Earth and nature show fine appearance.

Each spring presents to us its wonderful nature,
Brings the beautiful nature to our loved Earth,
Injects bliss much better than our literature,
Nature salutes and gives beautiful birth.

Sun and daybreak salute beautiful flowers each day,
Giving us joyful life throughout all of sunny May,
Earthly star in merciful day, the brightness sways,
We adore earthly nature that clouds may sway.

Oh, each spring's beauty reflects those revolving,
And the glistering spring does feed our earthly life,
The daylight holds beauty that's daily floating,
The pleasing spirit does observe daily strife.

Loving joy starts in early flowery blossom,
We do live the glistering spirit in morning,
That reveals Heaven's beauty, that shows its wisdom,
Each spring's light warming Earth and us entertaining.

Milan Trubarac (Slough)

When The Fat Lady Sings

And when the dark cloud hovers low
I'll know that it's my time to go
And seek a place among the stars
This ragged journey ends.

I'll climb the hillside full of bloom
And with my thoughts await the moon
A beacon sent from afar
A guiding hand, a friend.

A last look at the maiden fair
A last kiss form July's sweet air
But save the willow no tears at all
No mooning hearts shall bleed.

My memory scrapes but one last time
My feet upon the beacon climb
My senses on a spiral fall
One less this happy breed.

Rick Charles (Dursley)

Appledore In Devon

A little jewel, set where two rivers meet
and flow in quiet fulfilment out to sea.
White-painted houses climbing up the hill
or plunging sharply to the ancient quay.

Old shipyard, once the scene of active skill
lies quiet now, with little to be done,
(though men with household names once laboured here)
the dry dock empty, drowsing in the sun.

Across the water lie the golden sands
of Instow, framed by woods of fragrant pine,
and fishing boats slip quietly home at night
to background music of the church clock's chime.

Now on the quay a modest building waits,
a Mission Hall, once filled with love and song,
the fisher's refuge from the storms of life.
But times have changed. Those eager crowds have gone.

Yet still the local children fill the hall
and sing again the songs of yesterday.
They wonder at the Christmas story told
and celebrate the joy of Easter Day

Hazel Bradshaw (Cheltenham)

The Scaffolders

He carried in his hand a rod -
(It seemed too long to hold)
He wielded it with great aplomb,
Just like a warrior bold.

He stood with grace before the house
His eyes were raised on high,
He took a step towards the wall -
Then let the scaffold fly.

It sailed right up into the sky -
(And seemed to hover there).
But then another hand appeared
Which caught it fair and square.

And so, before the painters came,
The stage was set to start -
A crew of brilliant scaffolders
Had already played their part.

Mary Baird Hammond (Chelsea)

Snowdrops In Winter

'Mrs Pearson.'
Ice-cold fingers of fear grip my heart
as the cheery nurse puts her head around the door
and calls my name.

For a second I do not respond.
Too many emotions block my ability to hear.
I am being called - why?
Will she say the words I dread to hear?

I think no more of the solace of hot coffee
and rush to the door.
Six pairs of eyes bore holes into my back
as she closes it behind us.

I search her kind, tired eyes
as deeply as I have searched those of my husband.
We are partners now: she knows his body better than I
but the intimacy of his soul is mine alone.

'Mrs Pearson,' she repeats. 'Good news!'
The ice-cold fingers begrudgingly loosen their grip
as hope bursts forth as surely as
snowdrops through the cold, hard earth of winter.

Suzie Hunt (Ascot)

The Jewel House

I will build a starry house
With gold and silver walls
The floors will be of amethyst,
And diamonds - the walls

The roof will be of turquoise
With opal and ruby slates
The windows made of topaz,
And emeralds - the gates

The sapphire doors will open
To lustrous pearl and jade
The stairway rosy garnets
With onyx steps inlaid

My house will last forever
I'll live there, long apart,
No people will its door invade
The house is in my heart.

Barbara J Settle (Portsmouth)

So Close

You're the star in the sky
Along with the moon
You're the sun in the day
Along with the sea

You're so far away
I wish you were here
To come and save me
From my darkest fear

Thinking about you
Most of the time
Wasting my life away
Wishing you were mine

In my dreams I'm with you
But in reality it's nowhere near true
There's only one more thing
That can explain how I feel

If all the stars were people
It wouldn't matter where you'd be
'Cause you'd be the biggest
And brightest one to me.

Chloe Catlin (Worthing)

Obtuse

'What do you do with yourself all day?'
Comes the heat of hostility,
Across the room.
Or is it implied inferiority?

What would you like me to say?
That I am of no significance?
The cipher.
And now I am bathed in omniscience.

Those words define me anyway,
Although I know what I mean.
For I am stoic,
And fight my battles unseen.

'What do you do with yourself all day?'
Comes the false superiority.
And he waits:
To judge my validity.

Janine Parry (Bracknell)

Faithful Friend

The old dog lies before the fire
He seems so very sad
He knows his life is nearly over
And in some ways he is glad.

He can no longer run and play
In the green fields beyond
His master has to wait for him
There is no magic wand.

It is not easy to say goodbye
But we will meet again
I will once more catch the ball
When you throw it down the lane.

My time is over and I must go
Farewell my friend, adieu
Look out for me, you will hear my bark
When you are feeling blue.

I lick your hand and breathe my last
The tears roll down your face
I am still here my young master
In your dreams, we will still race.

Sue Godsell (Bristol)

Why Lies?

Wonder why, we have so many lies,
Because they're so easy to tell?
For when you are found out,
Your ego is gone. So rebel!

As for those that are honest,
They don't have to seek revenge.
But really can only laugh,
For now you've lost a friend!

So are you ever to be trusted,
In anything you say or do?
For you've only cheated yourself,
Others will always see through!

People only want the real you,
That may sound a bit of a bore.
But we are all individuals,
The beauty of life to score!

Ann Beard (Bridgwater)

Eccentric Endorsement

Concerts sponsored
by a shop
clubcard points
for a culture shock

Violas play
so tenderly
Artichokes, buy one
get one free

Piano notes
envelop, caress
Car insurance
10% less

The music's played
relieves all stress
more quickly than paying
at ten items or less

Music from ages
presented for you
As you say, 'Thank God
there isn't a queue!'

Andrew Blundell (Honiton)

Destroyed Promises

Dreams are shattered, promises broken,
A thousand words are left unspoken,
Mixed up feelings are strewn everywhere,
How could you leave me standing there?

My eyes were afraid, my whole body shook,
You walked away without a second look,
After so long you still tried to lie,
But I could see what was going on inside.

Happy memories are all that filled my mind,
You were always so loving, gentle and kind,
What changed to make you cruel and cold?
I hurt at all the failed promises you told.

Everything I wanted was all that you were,
My falling tears make this whole scene a blur,
Our beautiful commitment, completely gone,
Please give back my heart and let me move on.

Jennifer Smith (Saltash)

Two Loves

The first is the burning bright, high in the sky, mountain colour
changing daily of it; then for my eyes only not seen
by any other of it.
The highly charged, put on a pedestal, purely wonderful individual.

A love like that can only fly, bearing lofty thoughts.
A love like that cannot survive the normal life so fraught.
So came the choice to leave it there exquisite by itself
Just as a perfect piece of glass may be left upon a shelf.

Onto the next - a different love, though in a way as strong -
This love runs on a lower track and sings a different song.
She's a transformed person now, though very much the same,
The new love is another one who bears a different name.
This love is constant and lasts the many years they share,
What makes it last is hard to tell - it's not without its care.

To look too close at either love would not offer clarity
As to why she had to make the move with such alacrity.

Perhaps she thought her leaving would not cut the bond between them;
as if in taking legal steps the thread of love would break.
In fact she found as time went by the attachment still remained.
And stayed with her forever, a constant burning flame.

A Carrey (Bideford)

Toast To My Wife

May your dreams at night be carefree, may your hopes for life come true.
May your wishes all be granted, may your loved ones cherish you!
May your life just be so happy, that you wish it never ends.
May the joyful hours each evening be shared with all your friends!

May the black clouds that can gather, be swiftly blown away.
May the dark clouds turn to sunshine, at the start of each new day.
May you grow to love me also, in the way that I love you.
May my faults all be forgiven, may my stories all be true!

May our children not forget the good things we have said.
May their lives all be as happy as the life that we have shared.
May they sail through troubled waters to reach the calming coast.
May their quarrels be forgotten, may they reach life's winning post!

May we walk together daily, a journey with no end.
May the happiness await us, around each unknown bend.
May we both grow old together, as time goes slipping by.
May calm and peace surround us, until death brings a goodbye!

Robin Neill (Rickmansworth)

Trenow Cove

Across the bay a soft light streams
Free as a leaf on fickle winds,
Wave upon wave my thoughts are borne
Onto the shore where the land ends.

As in the time of Genesis
Came the first light, the heavens, the deep,
Here the storm petrels made their home,
Mingling in foam now shy terns sleep.

Hypnotically the ocean shifts,
Dissolves, reflects, transports, suspends,
Boundaries are found and disappear,
Energy spent where the land ends.

Relentless tides, unstoppable,
Tumbling, receding all alone,
Matrix of life, a hostile place
Accommodating all or none.

Rock pools and boulders, overhangs
Shelter to secret sealife lends,
Stardust we are, stardust reflects,
Onto the surf where the land ends.

Frances M Searle (Helston)

The Real Me

It took just over half my life
To find out who I am
Whilst it meant a lot to me
The rest couldn't give a damn!

Born a male and stuck with it
For many, many years
I now have a chance to be myself
-it brings me near to tears.

It's like going back to school again
To learn the female ways
But when I get to where I want
The past will be a haze.

I told the doctors and the like
I want to die so happy
They said that they would grant my wish,
'To be a lass - not a chappy!'

Krystina Baker (Guildford)

This Golden Pen

My golden pen hasn't broken
The one that writes these words
And from this heart, the one I've spoken
I hope and pray someone's heard

Please hold the flickering candle
It again blew out last night
This life is so hard to handle
When darkness blinds my sight

The flames a warmth to be with
The light's an ever glow
Such comfort inside it does give
That I'd like for you to know

The stable door has stopped banging
No horse lies on the straw
My picture of life is still hanging
How long for? Well I'm not sure

So shield the wind from the candle
As the hot drips cover the floor
Try as I might I can't stand all
The burns from the wax anymore

D A Garment (London)

Somerset

Oh, I am very fortunate
To live just where I do,
For Somerset's a lovely place
With many a gorgeous view.

There's Cheddar Gorge and Cheddar Caves
And Glastonbury Tor,
And Glastonbury Abbey too,
And Wookey Hole, and more.

Now Wells Cathedral, there's a sight;
And Butleigh Monument.
Montacute House is open now;
Is it not time you went?

But best of all is Somerton.
Right in the Market Square,
Are the Buttercross and Parish Church,
I hope to see you there.

Jillian Mounter (Somerton)

Wings Of Learning

Wings of Learning gently turning,
Frogs to princes overnight,
Leading us from inner darkness
By the hand into the light.

Balmy summer, country fragrance,
Parakeets and hummingbirds,
Harmony in every detail,
Lost in awe and lost for words.

Starry nights and walks in parkland,
Arm in arm in silent thrall,
Night-time dancing, songs and talking:
Special memories for all.

International presentations
Passions, minds and souls inspire:
Charismatic organisers,
Setting every heart on fire.

Wings of Learning, we are yearning
For the time when, yet again,
You and they who so inspired us
Feel once more that joy shall reign.

Robert Gillan (Bath)

Ideals

In America a man used to wait by a 'phone.
In Russia, it happened too.
Just one ring, and the switch would be thrown;
The end of me and you.

In Germany, a wall kept families apart,
And in South Africa, intolerance was rife.
Imagine the feelings people had in their heart
When oppression gave way to new life.

All over the world, we're beginning to see,
Leaders known for their hard-line stance,
Coming together with an old enemy,
To give peaceful methods a chance.

Many have paid the ultimate price,
For someone to hear their voice,
We must not forget the sacrifice,
To achieve freedom, equality and choice.

Sally Millett (Christchurch)

Cornwall

There's sea and sand, walks galore,
Forest, coast and so much more,
Cornish pasties, clotted cream,
Miles of sand, a childhood dream.

Shows and sights beyond compare,
Bars and cafes everywhere,
Fun parks, peace, tranquillity,
All await for you and me.

Surfing, sailing, swimming too,
Lots and lots of things to do,
Or just relax, enjoy the view,
It really all depends on you.

A welcome waits at each event,
Hotel, caravan or tent,
Tin mines, gold mines, to explore,
Films, theatre and much, much more.

Cycle rides on the Camel Trail,
Come by car, fly or rail,
Don't miss out there's fun for all,
In beautiful Kernow (Cornwall).

Kathleen Townsley (Liskeard)

Soulmates

Along the water's edge we walked,
In silence, there was no need to talk,
The sand and stones beneath our feet,
Was it by chance our souls did meet.

We had a place we used to go,
A place that only you and I did know,
To swim, then lie beneath the sun,
And stay hand in hand till day was done.

I'd love to be there with you now,
Alas your soul has passed on,
The sea's still there, all clear and blue,
All that's missing my dear is you.

My heart will always hold you so dear,
And I know your presence is ever near,
Life must go on, or so they say,
It doesn't stop me missing your smile every day.

Wendy Walker (Bournemouth)

The Rain

Falling and splashing
On pavements and tiles
Reflections of people
But wearing no smiles

Wet leather shoes
Squelching and squeaking
Hurrying with heads down
But no one is speaking

Grey lowering skies
Cast over with gloom
Rain dancing and stinging
And warm lighted rooms

Cold crystal droplets
Shivering on trees
And full gushing gullies
Like miniature seas

That is the rain
On a cold March day
Then suddenly the wind gusts
And blows it away.

Alison Miller (Seaton)

Spring

April showers under sunlit rainbows bring,
A garden teeming with life, welcoming spring.
Every drop replenishing the plants to grow,
New roots break through, up they go.

Frogs croak and jump in pond's delight,
Fish chase marble-shaped bubbles of light.
The raindrops sometimes turn to hail,
Clattering on shed roofs to no avail.

It's as if nature's burst into life,
Shrugging off winter's dormant strife.
The overladen drenched shrub leaves,
Sparkle in sunbeams of yellow and cream.

The birds nest and cheerfully sing,
Adding to the vibrancy of spring.
In my garden this season to me,
Is by far the best place to be.

Andrew Haylock (Yeovil)

Too Old For Mathematics

Mathematics gets much harder as the years go rolling by,
In our eighties syllogisms might still put us on a high,
In our nineties our poor brain is just refusing to abstract,
So, instead of mathematics, we must find another act!

Writing poems is one option, there for rhythm we must care,
Pentametric iambic verses with Bill Shakespeare could compare!
Dizzy heights of ancient sonnets our poor efforts will not reach,
Putting images together in our schools they do not teach!

Poems must be put together out of images that fit,
Clothed in rhymes and rhythmic structure to excite the reader's wit!
So the beauty of the pictures that are painted in each line,
Is enhanced by careful timing, which with rhyming we combine.

Ere you start to write your poem, sing a song that has no words,
To your mind will leap the pictures of green trees and singing birds,
Thus your song provides the meter for the poem that you write,
But your soul provides the pictures which convey that all is bright!

Putting thoughts in rhythmic verses makes your mathematics sing,
So perhaps it is not true that mathematics is no king!
It comes in through your back door when you're writing out your verse,
Mathematics is an art form every time the text is terse.

Zoltan Dienes (Totnes)

With Apologies To Elizabeth Browning

'How do I love thee, let me count the ways'
Can I then steal from Elizabeth B?
She said it all, far better than I may,
But I sing praises just as much as she.

Your smile, your squeeze of flesh-warmed hand
Shared summer country lanes.
Snow glistened on bleak silhouette of land
And falling rain on misted windowpanes.

A bonfire, sparks flying in a stream,
Fireworks exploding on a winter's night,
Children's laughter held upon a dream
Of hand clasped sparklers of light.

Memories of life from these are sown
So cherish in an ever-changing world
'Those Brownings' never could have known
Of our own place where dreams are curled.

Peggy Day (Ashford)

Break In, Break Out, Break Through

You have to digitally break the code
To crack the vault inside
And have to physically break the bank
Cos your money can be awfully tight

You're breaking even in a business year
Even though you've had a bumpy ride
And breaking records can be sweeter still
When the eyes of luck are by your side

You break the mould to make yourself shine through
When all around can only criticise
And break the rules in everything you do
To follow blindly would be most unwise

They break the law because they won't conform
Like an animal encaged inside
We break the habit when addiction storms
And break cover for a place to hide

We try to break off more than we can chew
And take on more than we can stand
They will not break us 'til we've fallen through
But we will break out because we can.

Martyn Leroy (Swindon)

Flood

Downwards I spiral as thoughts hurl their worst at me
Tearing like razors at what they call mind,
Once a calm lake with an air of tranquillity
Now raging torrents, no flood plain defined.

Though I crave silence the noise is unbearable
Rhythm of horses' hooves close by my ear,
Thousands of voices resound in my cranium
Dark thoughts flash brilliantly, quickened by fear.

High is the tide of encompassing helplessness
Urgent the need to escape from the now,
Memories of failings pursue me relentlessly
Time to start running, it's all I know how.

Reason exchanged for resolve to spark impetus
Blood powers the body and heart fires the brain,
Senseless my mind with the ache for oblivion
Give me obscurity; softened by rain.

Claudia White (Lancing)

If I Was A River

If I was a river,
I would flow on forever.
My destination is to cascade into the sea,
My fruitful journey and destination as only can be.

Soothing symphony as I dance over stones,
Happy to not yield fishes to the fisherman who moans,
Caressing and cool is my watery way;
To the teenagers swimming happily today.

As I twist and turn, meandering along,
I pass yet more picnic crowds - what a partying throng.
Sharing my life with flowers, trees, birds and fish,
For a more pleasant journey I could not wish.

When the humans go home as the darkness falls,
The moon sides from behind a cloud, flirtingly to me she calls.
There she will tease me with her moon beams silver,
Ever sparkling on my surface, I could have this affair forever.

You could never say a river's life was a bore,
Or even to flow for miles was such a chore.
Please remember my children will flow and live on,
Even when I join the sea and am gone.

Sue White (Portland)

Moonbeams

Cover me in sunshine
A golden cloak to wear
A fairy dell, a wishing well
And flowers in my hair.

Cover me in moonbeams
A canopy of love
And in my hand a wedding band
That lights the sky above.

Cover me in raindrops
To wash my cares away
A soothing shower on eager flower -
I wish that I could stay!

Cover me in stardust
A galaxy to roam
A journey bright, on starlit night
And then, please - take me home.

Phillippa Benson (Bideford)

Betwixt Land And Sea

Diamonds glinting on the sea
Gentle waves beckoning me,
Leave your carriage, stay awhile,
They call, full of summer's smile.

Reluctantly I speed by
Towards land I turn my eye,
Deer roam on rolling meadows,
Seeking shade in trees' shadows.

Devils racing on the sea,
Surging waves threatening me,
Go away, we'll swamp your train,
They roar, full of winter's rain.

Crawling along, I'm spellbound,
Tidal waves flood low ground,
Deer huddle 'neath bare branches,
View scene from higher vantage.

No matter what time of year,
It's a joy to travel here,
A magical rail journey,
On tracks betwixt land and sea.

Sue Rowe (Tavistock)

Heroes (Carers Support Group 3)

I met heroes today.
No super powers
Or feats of derring-do
Were on display.

Just courage shining,
Diamond bright and soft.
As people held
Their open hearts aloft.

And told sad tales
Of love's responsibility.
Wrapped in gentle
Stoic dignity.

Then quietly left
To carry on their day.
To shoulder soul taking burdens
Till death takes them away.

Miki Byrne (Tewkesbury)

I Still Crave The Love Of My Dad

I know not what to call you,
Though I refer to you as Dad.
My heart urges to love you,
But my emotions for you are blank.

Reserved in my heart a special place -
Just waiting for you to claim;
There lies an empty space;
Replacing happiness with pain.

I've spent years imagining your face,
Still more years running without a cheer.
Now it pours, leaving traces of my face,
You're still not here to dry my tears.

My child's given me a new lease of life,
My true friends God has revealed;
I dance with the love of my life,
But the love of my dad is still concealed.

Now slowly my yearning fades -
As I learn to trust in God's perfect plan;
Realising His love never fades,
But I still crave the love of my dad.

Janice S Ramkissoon (Luton)

The Mirror Of Time

The mirror or time does not lie,
But reflects what it sees at a glance;
The image it gives is the truth,
No appeal, no deceit, no fresh chance.

It may catch us when quite unaware,
The identity real and exposed;
In a flash we may hide from the truth
With a smile that remains quite composed.

The impersonal mirror of time
Will not show compassion or hope,
But only the rush of the years
And a future that's vague and remote.

Then hasten away when we can
From the stories we read from each line;
For the mirror reflects what has been
And the future's not ours to define.

Vanda Gilbert (Lymington)

In Praise Of Monday

It's heigh-ho for Monday - the day after Sunday
The very best day of the week . . .
Hubby's gone off to earn - children gone off to learn . . .
(I must ring the plumber re: leak!)

The house is untidy - been like that since Friday
But now there is plenty of leisure . . .
First, two cups of coffee - then one secret toffee -
I'll tackle the housework with pleasure.

No people to cook for - but washing to look for
Some pieces of cheese I can munch.
Yes, Monday's much better (I must write a letter)
I'll just have a sandwich for lunch.

For 2 until 4 I'll not do much more
But happily catch up with knitting . . .
Who's that at the door? It's my sister-in-law
Oh bang goes the chance for some sitting.

Oh how I love Monday - the day after Sunday
Why do people call it their blues day?
A day for unwinding - with no one fault finding . . .
It's a shame that tomorrow is Tuesday!

J Baum (Edgware)

My Birthday Wish

'It's my birthday soon and I've thought of a present
I would enjoy more than anything from you.
It won't cost you Honey! Or your bank account dent,
Even though to you my present will be brand-new.

My desired present would exceed the value of silver or gold,
And be elevated above the diamond, sapphire or the ruby.
Without a doubt this treasure I long to uphold,
Surpass the depths of wisdom and shines like a star to me.

The present I yearn - my natural gift on entry into this world.
It is part of me - my gift and I can never be separated.
It belongs to me and was chosen from a multiple field.
It is me, together I feel complete and elevated.

My natural gift long discarded - substitutes can ever take its place.
Nicks are sometimes fun, and pets reveal the same.
Without it I feel non-existent, like having no face.
What birthday present do I wish? Call me 'Lesley' my correct name.'

Lesley Hunt (Bristol)

Left Behind

I still remember the day you left me.
The hurt and sadness I felt inside.
I couldn't help but blame you,
For leaving me behind.

I now know I was grieving,
And needed someone to blame.
I'm sorry for having these feelings.
I feel alone and so ashamed.

Now I know you're with the angels.
I feel it in my heart.
I know they will watch over you,
For the time we are apart.

Please remember that I love you,
With all my heart and soul.
I will never forget our special times,
Whatever I do, and wherever I go.

One day we will be together again.
Until then be patient my love.
But for now whenever I feel alone,
I will look up at the sky above.

Michelle Anne Thorpe (Plymouth)

Compulsive Shopper

The lady lives at number four
And every day she slams her door
Says swift 'Goodbye' to husband 'Fred'
What a merry dance he's led

He works so hard to earn some cash
All spent by wife in frenzied dash
From shop to shop her eagle eye
Looks for bargains she can buy

She carries home her prize possessions
Building up her one obsession
Never satisfied is she
Every day a shopping spree

Each one bringing such a high
Poor old Fred can only sigh
Shake his head and carry on
Working while his wife is gone!

Sonia Richards (Exeter)

Would That I Could

I wish I could be present
On the day they put me down,
An inconspicuous spectator,
As I slide into the ground.

To listen to their comments,
And see individual emotions,
Judge if after all I'd made it,
To their ideal, measured notions.

To mingle unobtrusively,
Whilst my history is retold,
Was it that hilarious -
As each story does unfold.

Will comments from distant relatives
Refer to hoped for legacies,
Or will each be there on merit -
As part of eulogies?

There really is a worthy case,
To be present at your end,
And you pray the cast will not forget,
You really were a friend.

Mike Bennett (Barnstaple)

What Do I See When I Look At You?

You asked me, 'What do I see when I look at you?'
I see a love rare and true
The way you light up my life
Especially when you made me your wife.

I see a best friend
Always there with a willing ear to lend,
A warm hand always outstretched
Our dreams built together never seem too far fetched.

I see a kind and gentle man
Always ready to lend anyone a hand,
A father and a lover,
To your family - a brother.

I may not always show
How much you have helped my love to grow,
But my darling, without you,
I am only one half of a whole.

June Toms (Liskeard)

Cornwall

The country lanes so winding
The gorse upon the moor
The thatched roof on the cottage
Wild flowers by the score.

The walk along the cliff tops
The seagulls piercing cry
The blossom in the springtime
So pink against the sky.

The golden sand upon the shore
The brightness of the sun
The softness of the shadows
When day at last is done.

The place of many legends
That mystifies the mind
Of castles and cathedral
That have stood the test of time.

No greater gift could I have
Than the birthright that is mine
To be a son of Cornwall
Now and for all time.

Elaine Tamblyn (Truro)

I Am A Tree

I am a tree, tall and grand
At the edge of a forest is where I stand
I reach out my branches to lend a hand
So insects and birds can safely land

I am a tree with leaves so green
Whose blossom in springtime's the finest you've seen
My branches are long, strong and lean
Come and see me, you'll be glad you've been

I am a tree in which squirrels nest
Standing apart from all the rest
Holding myself firm, trying my best
Not to bow down to the winds from the west

I am a tree that is very old
Whom loses leaves when the weather turns cold
Yet still stands up proud and bold
Till Man cuts me down and my wood is sold.

Nicola Hopkins (Bracknell)

Modern Times

There's an internut on the Internet,
Causing havoc far and wide,
Not a dribble or a trickle,
But a storm-force tide.

He's messed up all the websites,
Big business deals have crashed,
The stock exchange is extra mad,
All stocks and shares are trashed.

No surfing to broad our outlook,
No games to stir the mind,
No Jeeves to solve our problems,
What a bloody awful bind!

He comes from a well-heeled family,
A disgruntled much spoiled pest,
He's blanked out all the emails,
And the mouse is sorely stressed.

Twenty-five hours a day our workload,
All doing our very best,
Perhaps the internut on the Internet,
Thinks we need a well-earned rest.

Germaine Lane (South Molton)

The Farmer (For Len)

Some, are born to be leaders,
Others, to do ordinary things,
If yours, is the life of a farmer,
Then you are surely born a king.

The fields and hedgerows your kingdom,
Blue sky is your castle above,
Then yours is a life full of wondrous things,
Just doing the job that you love.

As spring, gently awakens from winter,
To breathe life across the land,
The farmer will be there to greet her,
As she stretches out her comforting hand.

Long days in the fields you toil,
Beneath a golden sun,
But the time has come to rest old friend,
For all the work is done.

Gillian Longman-Hart (Wareham)

Recession

Whatever are we going to do
When the recession hits, me and you?
Everything today costs such a lot
We have to make do with what we've got.

Politicians say they know what to do,
But they don't live like me or you.
They've got much more money, not like us,
They've got big cars, we take the bus.

The last time this happened was in '92,
I remember it clearly, how about you?
That time we managed to get ourselves straight,
But this time so many have left it too late.

No pay rise for workers, they've all gone on strike,
No money for petrol, it's back to the bike.
The children go hungry, food costs so much more,
They can't sort this one out, of that I am sure.

So, come on you statesmen, start putting things right,
So people can sleep more peacefully at night,
Sort this mess out, that's what you're paid for,
So we can get back to normal once more.

Maureen Ann Baker (Portsmouth)

The Christening

A dear little girl with a beautiful face
Wearing a dress of satin and lace
Going to church for her special day
Three cheers for Antonia, hip, hip, hooray!

The flowers at the font smelt fragrant and sweet
We all stood round, the words to repeat
And then she came home for a nice little tea
Grandma and Grandads, your parents and me.

And when you are older, the stories I'll tell
Of soldiers and sailors and airmen as well
We'll have some outings just, you and me
Spend days together down by the sea.

And when you are older how happy you'll be
Knowing you're loved by your family and me
Laughter and joy and everything nice
May they all be yours in a wonderful life.

C M Garland Adams (Teignmouth)

God's Great Love

God is love, unbounded, timeless.
His great love created me.
But before me all creation
By God's loving came to be.

God's great love was cause of weeping
When the world fell into sin.
But that love remained undaunted;
God's great plan did then begin.

God's great love came down at Christmas,
Love all lovely, love divine.
Incarnation, love in action;
Words and deeds became a sign.

Jesus' Cross, the sign of God's love;
Love was crying on that tree.
This love-sign is for God's children,
Drawing all humanity.

God's great love will triumph always;
He loves all, including me.
His embrace is all-forgiving;
Love is Heaven's guarantee.

Peter J Millam (Bognor Regis)

War

The hour approaches meant for detention
A sigh from those looking for ascension
Business affairs and issues relent
Curious minds follow the bitter scent

Eager hand stretches to scratch
To open the gate and find a way to detach
The new life seems much like a game
A camera capturing life in a single frame

Desert sands seek rain for lubrication
Criminal minds seek psychology for exoneration
The Earth has detected poison in her soul
The olive trees are burnt, there will be no more oil

All has changed, we need a new map
Genetics have created flowers without sap
Soldiers in the trenches hide from the shells
Deaf to the never-ending ring of church bells.

Emily Petrolekas (Wimbledon)

For Joshua - Born 25th July 2006

The first gift your mother gave you were two soft spring days,
So gentle, the sweet smell of summer to come,
Gentle breeze, lost to her forever in her willing pain,
Given up with joy at the coming of your little form.

Little boy, so waited for and loved even before we saw you,
And then, your tiny face, now so familiar,
Bearing your father's nose and your mother's lovely mouth
With pride we all declared Joshua is born!

Your constant smiles fill our days of summer, into autumn
Your every achievement enthrals, and impresses us
Years of love stretch out before you, and although we call
You our big boy we know it is your dawn.

So familiar to us, but will we be to you?
We want so much to be held in your thoughts
In future times, and hope some scent or word will
In your brain sweet memories form.

Your future has been written, we cannot know
How far or where it takes you,
But hope, jealously, that somewhere in your far off time
Some comfort to you of our memory be drawn.

Mary Anne Clock (High Wycombe)

The Best Things

The best things in life are free, they say,
We should enjoy every single day,
The air that we breathe, the rain and sun,
Are free to each and every one.

To have our family and friends,
To have a love that never ends,
Our work and play, and our leisure,
Are all things that we should treasure.

Birds in the air, the sea and sky,
Mountains and scenery to catch our eye,
The scent of flowers and new mown hay,
Are some of the things to brighten our day.

We should be thankful for all of these things,
To enjoy what every new day brings,
The best things in life are there for us all,
So accept what we have, they will never pall.

Joan Corneby (Thatcham)

Summer Christmas Trees

Grass bright as emerald, long and lush
Waiting for sun and rain, moon and stars
Children with picnics, lovers with no need of food
Dancing in the park.

Hedges white with hawthorn and burgeoning growth
Lowly cow parsley deserving of a second glance
Lace plates as delicate as a million snowflakes
Juggle on sturdy stalks of bitter green.

Chestnuts line the avenues
Like rows of summer Christmas trees
Their stiff white candle blooms ablaze
To light the traveller's inward gaze.

Seas of barley, with no tide to keep
Compliment the unyielding wheat
Poppies stain the earth with crimson streaks
Give back fire to the setting sun.

Drab dwellings overnight become a child's delight
A fairy tale of roses round the cottage door
Full fat blooms seduce the bees to enter in their secret parts
Summer has come.

Maureen Elizabeth Goff (Salisbury)

The Beach

I love the beach, miles of clean golden sand,
I dream of this beach in our beautiful land,
The ripples so cool, they touch my feet,
They soon run away leaving marks very neat.

I sit on the beach where hours do not end,
A quiet little song to the sea I send,
Peace is bestowed just watching the blue sea,
I never get tired of its beauty you see.

The sound of the waves brings me great pleasure,
It is such a joy beyond any measure,
The white waves comb the beach, as if to say,
'We are coming back, we will not go away.'

I stroll on the beach, I love to be there,
Prints I leave disappear, with feet so bare.
When I am home I recall this tranquil scene,
I long to be there, on the beach I have been.

Kamala Dias (Hounslow)

Two of me!

I feel lonely but I am not alone
I am lost even though I am found
I am tired but cannot sleep
I shout loud but hear no sound.

I am confused but think clearly
I am sad but wear a smile
I am here but I am hiding
I'm an adult but feel like a child.

I feel wanted but ignored
I feel desire but I am restrained
I am angry but remain calm
I am free but I feel contained.

I give all and get nothing
I am passionate but act shy
I want to erupt but hold it in
I tell the truth but to myself I lie.

Is this me or someone else
Am I split when once I was whole?
Two halves of the same person
And over neither I have control . . .

J Howson (Bedford)

Forgive

Forgive and forget, can it be true?
To forget can sometimes be hard to do
the pain that is caused by someone's wrong
can stay with you forever so long.

It plays on your mind every day
I wish it would all just go away
there must be a way to give me release
I just want a life that's filled with peace.

I can't believe this happened to me
I need to find a way to be free
free from the trouble inside my head
it wakes me up at night in bed.

To forgive would be a wonderful thing
but it has to come from deep within
to understand why would be a start
then perhaps to forgive would come from your heart.

Martyn Lock (High Wycombe)

743

The Fate Of This Land

The snow falls thick upon this land,
Where silence drowns out the words
Of a peaceful song, that's long forgotten,
Of a time, so long ago.

And of that time, so long ago,
When spring was fresh in our hearts,
When the land stood tall and free and peaceful,
Did the sun defy the dark.

Yet the sun no longer could defy,
Whence the snow and silence came,
And the hope of our people, without the song,
Let the emptiness shroud them all.

But lo! In that shrouding emptiness,
Was one that could not accept,
And that one shines brighter than a hundred suns,
Reflecting the white of snow.

And in this snow, there'll be a time,
When the sun that lights this land,
Shall burn bright in thy soul, and melt thy heart,
And the snow shall cease to fall.

Nicky Hockin (16) (Bideford)

Round The Island Race - 2008

What a wonderful sight,
Off the Back of the Wight,
There are hundreds of yachts
With their spinnakers bright.

They've rounded the Needles,
And are now on the run
To St Catherine's Point -
Where the lifeboat's just gone!

There's a good south west wind
Blowing 'five', gusting 'six',
Across an ebbing neap-tide -
Quite a challenging mix!

But there's glorious sunshine,
In a cloudless blue sky -
And it's forecast to last
'Till they're all home and dry!

Leslie V Hall (Newport)

744

For You

Take the step and take the chance,
For I am here to guide,
Through each turn life appears,
I will always be by your side.

When each struggle takes a hold,
I'll be a soft place to fall,
When lost and searching for the way,
I'll answer to your call.

When happy times are here to stay,
Laughter and cuddles shared,
Memories made for times to come,
And I will always be there.

As time moves on and age appears,
My hopes you've raised above,
As pride warms through my inner self,
You, I'll forever love.

And when I touch the angels' wings,
Smile, no matter how hard,
Be not sad, for I am here,
Always over you I will guard.

K M King (Bournemouth)

Garden Tools

There's so much joy in a garden,
Away from the sheep and the goats,
The pleasure of planning and planting
Like messing about in boats.

It's digging a lot and thinking,
Big decisions have to be made.
You can't be decisive in using a fork,
But you can call a spade a spade.

The trendy gardener doesn't use tools
Like the old-fashioned shear which survives,
No, it's trimmers and strimmers all powered and smart,
A far cry from old dinner knives!

But the trowel and the dibber still have their place,
When hoeing and weeding is done.
So, forget garden tools, and sit in the shade,
Oh no! We've hardly begun!

Ian Pulford (Cheltenham)

745

Caribbean

Steel drums beating,
Masks and dragons swaying,
Calypso music pulsating, street dancing
Herald the arrival of Junkanoo.

Azure sea lapping,
Glossy green seaweed forms a band,
Coral and crushed shells
Are revealed on dazzling white sand.

Sandpipers scurry along the shore,
An eastern bluebird darts along
While yellow birds twitter a song,
Starfish and conch lay dormant.

Mangroves, oleanders line the banks,
Palm trees shade the villas,
Bougainvillaea combined with
Frangipani waft their scent.

The sea recedes and behold a reef,
While swimmers explore beneath,
The sun becomes a ball of fire,
It's party time in the Caribbean.

Diana Herke (Maidenhead)

Love

Love is not always easy - to give
But the essence of life is in how we live
The love of a parent for a child
With the innocence born, still meek and mild.

Love can be given, it doesn't cost
Sometimes it's showered, but never lost.
It colours our lives, like a brilliant gem,
You give it away, and it returns again.

The language of love, it is sometimes said
Can be fiery, and tempered, yet never ill-read.
It's not always easy, maybe hard to define,
But clear to succumb, with a free heart and mind.

People have written over the centuries of time
How love's own path - is ever sublime.
It is beauty, and seeing special things
Like a soaring bird, when your heart - *has wings*.

B M Woolnough (Pulborough)

View From The Top Deck Of A Bus

The road is long and winding
Like a ribbon through the hills,
Fields and forests aplenty
No factories, shops or mills.

Cows and sheep in meadows graze,
A sight to behold
For both young and old,
On these glorious halcyon days.

Wheat and corn and grasses
Swaying gently in the breeze,
Cool water runs in rivulets
That help you feel at ease.

Wild flowers in profusion
So many birds that sing,
Take time to look around you
You'll feel just like a king.

Now when all around are troubles
You can visit this wondrous sight,
Wherever you care to travel
On this beautiful Isle of Wight.

Joy Hanlon (Ryde)

New Love

Our dreams and wishes will come true
Of promises we make
Our love is oh! So new
Remembering our first date.

The days we spend apart
Seem longer every time
So please don't break my heart
I know you will be mine.

Those days you come to stay
Will seem just like a dream
So please don't run away
When we walk down by the stream.

Our dreams and wishes have come true
And worries far away
Our love that was so new
I know it's here to stay.

Phyllis Nichols (Bickleigh)

Baby's Smile

When Baby smiles, the sun shines through
The dullest day;
When Baby smiles, the tears dry up
And go away;

When Baby smiles, a Mother's Heart is glad
And she smiles too;
When Baby smiles, the worries fly away
And hope holds true;

When Baby smiles, perhaps a new tooth shows
Some progress in its growth;
When Baby smiles, a dimple forms
And pleases both;

When Baby smiles, after pain and tears -
All's well again;
When Baby smiles, who cares what weather,
Be it sun or rain!

When Baby smiles, the Family feels as one,
Yet set apart;
When Baby smiles, the whole world smiles as well,
So glad at heart!

Donoveen Alcock (Woodbury)

Time

Why does time always go so fast?
Soon the present becomes the past,
One moment he's here, the next he is not,
One moment remembered, the next is forgot.

From the time we are born right up till we die,
Nothing can stop Father Time passing by,
From baby to child in the blink of an eye,
Soon will be adult and life passing them by.

The long winter day and the storm in the night,
The warm summer sun with the sun shining bright,
The cool autumn wind and the cool autumn rain,
Then the soft breeze starting the seasons again.

Happy times and sad times, what will our future be?
The only thing for certain is our future we can't see,
Though upon reflection do we need to know,
The mysteries of time and space and what happened long ago.

Gillian Todd (Bridgewater)

Forward Press

Forward Press is celebrating
20 years of publishing.
Over one million poets
Old and new.

With no age limit
Everyone can do it.
Writing verse is easy,
If you take the time to try.

Old and young can write
The thoughts that are in their minds,
About the life they live,
Or what they see around.

Seaside scary rides
Or even sitting on the beach.
Those memories are in your head,
You only have to reach.

Inside your head like filing cabinets,
They sit stately in a row.
So ease each drawer open
And the poetry will flow.

John Murdoch (Reading)

Gangster Rap

Why are you so quick to judge me?
It's my life; my choice; and my decision . . .
I don't believe in much -
So I chose my own religion.

Sometimes I wonder if I need this thrill;
I definitely don't need the money . . .
I'm laughing like mad as I drive away;
But I know it's not that funny.

I don't like hurting innocent people.
I had nothing - I needed more!
Understand that I'm not deliberately violent;
But I change when I walk outside my door . . .

Believe me when I say I'm not selfish;
I really do enjoy giving . . .
I hope you're contented in your day job;
Because I rob banks for a living . . .

Lauren Masterson (Salisbury)

For James

My love passed over in the spring,
 for him no further pain.
How could fate leave me so
 with loneliness again?

As days dragged by
 how I wept and wept.
For memories of long gone years
 which now I can't accept.

In time my love became so close
 protecting me from harm.
Great love was shown, which humbled me,
 kept safe from all alarm.

I prayed for release from Earthly bonds,
 to be with my love once more.
This life holds no joy for me,
 each day becomes a chore.

I crave the joy which now he knows
 while I pray for help from above.
Angels will bear my soul away
 into the arms of my love.

Elizabeth Elcoate-Gilbert (Newbury)

The Lady With The Urn

In the Sinah Warren gardens
A lady with an urn
Stands by the charming walkway
Just upon the turn

At some stage in her being
In a moment less than calm
The savage tribes descended
And the lady lost her arm

Unfailing still she carries
Her battered Grecian urn
Her graceful style a lesson
For modern girls to learn

What a way to 'urn' a living
In her 'armless statue way
For sure she's not for turning
The lady's here to stay

Ray Ryan (Great Missenden)

Longing

Feel like I am sinking
Can't make my way to the top
Unable to breathe or see
Wish this feeling would stop.

Drowning in a sea of confusion
Can't seem to fight anymore
The rising tide of desperation
Not knowing if I'm here at all.

Want to cry all of the time
Don't know why the tears fall
Why I ache so much inside
When I never get your call.

Why do I feel so desperate?
Why do I need it so much?
When you are not near me
Why do I long for your touch?

I don't know how much longer
I can go on like this
Waiting for time to pass
Until once again I can taste your kiss.

J Webb (Hemel Hempstead)

Kingsmead

'Don't go back,' it's always said,
For nothing stays the same
But I have been invited back
To Presburg Road again.

Like a beacon Kingsmead shone
Inside my weary brain,
Illuminating all those times
When life brought grief or pain.

This is the house where I did dream
Of all that I might be,
When Kingsmead was my childhood home
And cast its spell on me.

My brother's gone, my parents too,
But now there are no tears,
For I am back where they belonged
And feel good spirits here.

Mary Rutley (Epsom)

To My Dearest Mother

Mothers like you are truly one of a kind,
what we take for granted is rare to find.

If only I could turn back time, and have another chance,
just to be able to see you when I please,
to be able to roam around freely holding your hand.

Unfortunately none of this can come true,
as it seems that I committed a terrible sin of falling in love,
for which I paid the price of being disowned by my family.

However I understand that your hands are tied, no matter how
hard to try. If only you had the courage to follow your heart
and speak your mind.

I miss you tremendously and wish that I could do more for you,
to prove and show that my love for you is true.
Despite the current terms and conditions of contract,
I still love you endlessly and will keep on doing so for eternity.

I will always be there for you, to comfort you in times of distress,
to share our moments of happiness together,
just remember I will always be there for you as your best friend.

Love always from your one and only daughter.

Sajida Hassan (Watford)

Reflecting On The Whole Of A Life

(For my dear friend Hans, 88 years old; waiting in hospital to learn his fate)

He feels he's plucking at the end now,
His pain-riddled foot like a doorway
Opening to the great Absolute of death.
He goes into the hospital on Monday
And in his heart lurks fear he may not come out.
Half a diabetic leg has already been severed
And if they claim the remaining foot
He knows further conversations with God
Will take place face-to-face.

So what is it like to see yourself
As finality, the whole continent of who you are
Soon to vanish into faceless air;
Remembering as the flicker ebbs
How vast you were inside.
Do memories turn to ash and genes transmute
To stars? He blinks and waits.
The ribbon of his life still tied to earth.

Karen Eberhardt-Shelton (Kingskerswell)

A Celebration . . .

When you wish upon a star,
Twenty years on, is where you are . . .

Three *big* cheers . . . and hip hooray,
'Forward Press', are twenty today . . .

Publishing over a million poets across the nation,
Well done, a great achievement, time for celebration . . .

Through you, new poets, have been found,
You helped them all, to get off the ground . . .

Largest publisher of new poetry in the world,
At last, us poets, can now be heard . . .

Corks popping, and glass of bubbly champagne,
To the next twenty years, go on, you can do it again . . .

So, whatever you do, on this, your special day,
Just, do it, in your very own celebration way . . .

And may all your future dreams, and plans, come true,
For a great publishers, yes, that really is *you* . . .

Many congratulations, to you all, from me . . .
I am a published Surrey poet, of Stream Valley.

Jenny Williams (Farnham)

Changes

Twenty years on - how things change!
My life and others - even yours,
Things maybe to give us pause.
Is it my age or do others find
Distasteful changes they really mind?
Buildings of towering ugly brick
Where once the trees and plants grew thick.
Small friendly local shops replaced
By vast and soulless trading space.
And my beloved seaside town
With structures that should be torn down.
Treasured theatres authorities ignored,
Despite all protests and promises abroad.

But twenty years on despite all that,
Despite all excuses and political chat,
We still fight on for the things we believe,
For the good we see and the love we receive.
So look to the future not to the past,
To important things, the things that last.

Ann Dodson (Bournemouth)

The Funeral

We're gathered at the crematorium,
stiff, ill at ease in black, not saying much.

The long black shiny car comes sliding up
and in we file to where the coffin is,

There at the front and in plain view throughout,
As the vicar speaks of her and final things.

Outside, a cold wind blows. Finding no words,
our eyes red-rimmed, we huddle close, and though

we stand upon a rosebush-bordered walk
beside a pond where fish are glinting gold,

and cars are lined up on a gravelled drive
to take us off to warmth and food and drink,

right now, we're just as others must have been
millennia before, in skins and hides,

with matted hair, out in the rain and wind,
around some final place scraped from the earth

laboriously, with tools of bone or flint,
comfortless, afraid, their numbers down by one.

Geoff Parker (London)

Poets In Parks

Sam Johnson jumps over the railings into St James' Park
to roll with a shilling whore, who has no conversation.
It's even too dark for the girl to yuk at his scrofula.
He grizzles, reforms, and of course will never tell Tetty,
while Boswell is still just a blob, unable to comment.

Green Park and Hyde Park are loud with loose-tongued linnets.
John Clare is declaring, much good in the end it will do him!
but he's dazzled by lovely ladies passing on horses.
Pope's up from Twit'nam, politic-chatting with Dryden
who has strolled from his pad in the nearby Park Lane Hilton.

On Hampstead Heath, blood not yet spotting his hanky,
Johnny Keats is frisking with Coleridge, while Percy Shelley
nearby on Primrose Hill, is bored into going
down to chuck stones at Parliament and Buckingham Palace.

Look, poor Keats has started to cough, while in Phoenix Park
over the water, Dean Swift grows gloomy. The rest are glaring,
but being so dead, know they can't do much about it
while I'm wand'ring, a little longer, on Wimbledon Common.

Ron Taylor (London)

754

Five In The Morning

Five am creeps down
   the street
    whey-faced and sickly.
Moves in the open spaces
   leaving a ghostly trail
   behind him
Shadows huddle
   under hedges.
His wispy light seeps
   through gaps
   in curtains,
    slides under doors.

At the corner
   he shakes hands
   with six o'clock,
is dazzled by
   her radiant smile.
Then slips away
   from the sound of
   door knockers
   rattling.

Alison Batcock (Bognor Regis)

Come Back St. Austell!

June 2003
There used to be a Liptons in St Austell
There used to be congested two-way street,
There used to be a building down the road from here,
Where villagers of Trethowel used to meet.

There used to be a Broad's store full of goodies,
Where the buses once an hour used to go,
We used to see policemen and we'd know them all by name.
Now nothing's left, as you and I all know!
The milk is gone with cream on top
And so have all our smaller shops,
Let's get to work and get them back,
We'll pull out all the stops!

July 2008

At last a car park's being erected,
Although delayed, as most expected -
Let's hope the vandals don't abuse it,
I wonder if *I'll* get to use it!

Jean M Tonkin (St. Austell)

A Life Well Lived

Dancing motes upon the water
Diamond gems upon the lake

A moment's joy

Sun's caress upon my cheek
Gentle breezes upon my brow

A moment's joy

Dewdrops sparkle
Wild birds' calling

A moment's joy

The sound of a brook running
A butterfly's errant flight

A moment's joy

The smile of a friend
The touch of a hand

A moment's joy

Many moments of joy
Make a life well lived.

Stuart Stoter (Reading)

The Magnolia Tree

This beautiful tree flowers just once every year
So splendid yet so vulnerable the winds blow and the flowers fall
A lot like us we break and fall as hard words and actions
beat us down
The scent so magical in the air, a bit like us when we
Use the right words,
The right touch our spirit soars into the sky.

This beautiful tree never loses its way every year
Its buds appear in a mass of splendour
Its flowers may fall as the wind blows in gusts
But it still comes back to face another year
Because it knows life is very precious.

We have to be like the magnolia
Take the knocks in life but always remember
That life is very precious and we have to pick ourselves
Up and carry on.

So when you're feeling down, think of the magnolia tree,
Picture it, smell it, and the light of life will appear.

Lynne Whitehouse (Poole)

Morning

Softly, step softly,
The morning is sighing
Whispering sunrise, the shadows are flying,
Murmuring breezes awaken the river
Now bathed in pure light of sunshine and silver.

Gently, step gently,
Disturb not the dewdrops,
Hark, now, a sweet sound is heard in the treetops;
Birds of the air singing songs of the morning,
Praising the beauty as new day is dawning.

Gathering strength now
The morning is singing,
Filled with the sounds of a million things living
A million new lives that the sunshine is forming -
Be glad that you've witnessed the birth of a morning.

Silently, silently,
Live through your senses,
Forget all your acts and the foolish pretences,
Let go of your heart, let it fly with the swallow,
Rejoice in today, let there be no more sorrow.

Dorothy Kemp (Dunstable)

Helmand

(Helmand was the Poem of the Month
on the Daisy Goodwin poetry website in November 2007)

Night on the cold plain,
invisible sands lift,
peripheral shadows stir,

space between light and dark
shrouding secrets;
old trades draped grey.

Here too poppies fall,
petals blown on broken ground,
seeds scattered on stone

and this bright bloom,
newly cropped,
leaves pale remains,

fresh lines cut;
the old sickle wind
sharp as yesterday.

John Hawkhead (Yeovil)

Welcome

The single electric light bulb
encased in a metal mask
deep in the concrete ceiling
throws its unrelenting harsh beam
onto damp grey walls,
illuminating initials and messages
gouged out to loved ones
by dying, broken men.

The all-embracing stench of sewage
emanating from the uncovered hole
in the middle of the blood-encrusted, unswept floor,
bare but for the biscuit-hard mattress
and metal washing bowl in one corner.

No window to allow sight or sound of life
to penetrate the cloak of hopelessness
that impregnates the squalid atmosphere.

Tortured voices urge me enter.
The clanging door echoes behind.
Utter despair pervades my soul
in this, my final resting place.

Peter French (Tring)

The Edge Of Love

O, one who is most unknown
Dwarves a polestar and drives love's moan
Where, endlessly sinking, death's fled groan
Delves the dead and kills
Fires and children, crafted by their thrills.

O, the eyes of love reach the edge of love
And love lies loaded with its fresh shells.

With every cry of light burning down till midnight
The flares of screaming and the silence of the speared moonlight.

O, one is most unknown
Razes a polestar and dreams against the seared son.

As an exodus from the garden, mad woman lies
Stained with the liquids of a sea-in-harness.

With every life let free from the tar-bled Thames,
Man-waging grief lights the embers of the stemmed seas.

O, man and girl die in Heaven, eternally,
Dammed by a fist, shaped with a war-waged tattoo.

James Bellamy (London)

The One And Only . . .

She flew like a bird,
Nothing could compare
To her grace and perfection
When she took to the air.

The sound of her engines
As she moved through the skies,
The Queen of all aircraft,
No other would rise
To the heights she attained
In everyone's eyes.

Never will a plane
Be so loved and adored -
But time passes on
And things 'go by the board'.

Now she's come back to Filton
The crowds will all throng
To see her once more
Where she belongs.
A flightless bird for eternity.
Concorde - in all her majesty.

D J Williams (Kingswood)

Standing Alone

Standing alone in the big house
not even a mouse can be heard
from the window the clouds skip by
she opens a drawer, finds his old tie

she glances in the full length mirror
her figure isn't what it was
but she doesn't really care
just stares at life rushing past
all too fast

once it was good and nice
even with the mice scampering
about for cheese,
'Please,' she pleads, 'why am I lonely
and getting old?'

she feels the cold now too
maybe it's flu
because of the snuffles and sneezes
that come in on the autumn breezes.

Jon B Baker (Yeovil)

759

Waiting

Amid the driftwood of her life she sits,
Her hands, once nimble, quietly resting on her knee,
No more the busy passing of the time;
The hands that knew their art with skilful powers
Now lie like empty gloves for idle hours.

The voice that once commanded and reproved
Enticed and soothed, lies silent on her tongue.
Her lips shaped for smiles and kisses are now carved
From the very stone that has her heart in thrall;
Speak her name, does she not hear the call.

To some distant shore her errant spirit fled,
Taking with it ways where minds can meet.
Her eyes without depth or spark of life
Gaze on a country beyond human sight,
Where worldly wonders have no means to excite.

Implore a miracle to wring a change,
Entreat the magic that will return
The precious essence to a graven form.
Dare to dream that salvation lies, a wonder most profound,
Coiled in a distant test tube, just waiting to be found.

Joan Hawkes (Trowbridge)

A Mystery?

People astride enormous lions,
Rainbow bubbles amid the air,
Birds escaping little people,
A scene enclosed, unusual? Rare?

Swordsmen staring at humanity,
Reflecting on their lives gone by,
Astride his horse is past nobility,
His head inclined towards the sky.

Majestic creatures spraying water,
Close to where the fountains lie,
Sunlight reflections enhance the aqua,
Before the evening clouds drift by.

This view is no mysterious scene,
Where humans come to sit and stare.
This daily sight is for all to see,
In our familiar Trafalgar Square.

Margaret Nicholl (Enfield)

Tribute At Coniston Water

A cold stillness fills the air,
Covering the glassy surface of the lake.
Trees stand like sentinels against the sky,
And gazing sadly to an unmarked place,
We stand by Coniston Water.

The 'Bird' took flight and somersaulted
Then plunged into the icy depths.
It vanished in one brief moment,
Leaving behind a startled crowd
Watching, breathless, by Coniston Water.

Not in vain this sudden break
With life, so bravely filled.
Patient climber of his own 'high mountains'
Never flinching from a certain death
Which came on Coniston Water.

We shall remember this man of speed,
And all he tried for England.
With nerves like steel and determined mind,
We followed a hero's uncharted path,
When he flew across Coniston Water.

Marlene Sarah Jones (Mill Hill)

I Remember The Days

When I remember the old time days,
things were so beautiful so amazing,
the things I remember as the years go by,
make me so amazed as I look to the sky.

Changes in the world today,
still we have to smile from day to day,
going our ways from day to day,
don't let anything stop us on the way.

We have to carry on, this is the only way,
why worry just let us go on our way,
we know we will make it just kneel and pray
when the days look grey.

We will sing and clap for joy all the way,
meeting people on our way.
Come on just walk this way today,
It is a beautiful day why worry just come the way.

Shirley Lovell (Wood Green)

The World In You

It's seeing you in the fields
That makes them green.
Your laughter stirs the larks to soar
Your voice their hearts to sing
Your whisper shuffles the corn in waltzing waves
And your eyes ripple the dancing stream.

When you're not there, it clouds the sun,
Without you, I cannot feel the wind
Flowers furl their umbrella petals
And myriad colours lose their hue.

It's autumn now
We walk through fallen leaves
Small dreams rustling while we tread
Scuffled silent as our path moves on.

The mistletoe and ivy of our hands
Entwines and binds,
The knotted oak of our hearts
Shelters us with dappled-green shade.
It's colder now
As we tread our way to winter.

Kate Hammond (Twickenham)

Changing View

The view from my window is profound
pleasant space gone, levelled to the ground.
Church patio and steps from arched door to the street
once quiet oasis, a one tree retreat.

Making room for who knows what?
Pretty garden views or an office block.
Machinery swinging buckets around
invading silence with a loud clanking sound.

Walls knocked down to rubble and dust,
mortar and bricks built and adjust.
Workmen shovel cement here and there
noise is loud, they seem not to hear.

Lorries filled to the brim,
ferrying materials out and in.
What vandal dared to change our scene,
from the pleasant one it long had been.

E Sawyer (London)

On The Move

Moving afar by bus, not car,
To a change of scene.
Mountains that soar majestically high,
Your eyes have to rise
To meet the sky.

Like a joyful child -
Running away from its mother,
Seeking the freedom of open spaces,
Beholding land stretching - far and wide,
God's peaceful countryside!

Needing to be on the move,
To experience the rhythm of life.
Never looking back!
This is the joy of living,
There is nothing that I lack!

Flowing like a river,
On its way to the sea.
Getting there in the end,
To await life's destiny.
Not knowing what's around the bend!

Linda Webster (Redruth)

Poem Written On My Eightieth Birthday

I don't feel eighty at all,
More like eight when I awake
And my two dogs follow me in
From the hall and help me
Put my socks on
By lying on my feet
Winding themselves around my legs
And rolling on the ground.
They set, and bow and stretch
And leap and bound around,
Making a complete cacophony of sound.
They look at me with great expectancy,
That's what it means to be a hound.
They know I'll take them for a walk
In whatever kind of weather,
So let us head off up to the hills
And roll about among the heather.

Stewart Gordon (Sidmouth)

It's Carnival Time

It's carnival time in Burnham-on-Sea,
There's great excitement, with plenty to see,
The women are busy with needle and thread,
Working all hours to get ahead.

The men are busy upon the floats,
The painters are choosing different coloured coats,
Weird creatures start to appear,
It's carnival time in Burnham it's clear,
From dogs and cats to snakes and rats,
Everyone's wearing fancy hats.

Nursery rhyme characters and clowns,
Skeletons and ghosts take over the town,
Elephants and tigers, lions as well,
Balloons, toffee apples and necklaces to sell.

There will soon be a fantastic night,
Burnham will be lit up from the float's light,
Music and laughter will fill the air,
It's carnival time I do declare
And when it's all over to add to the cheer,
Some will go to the pub for a good pint of beer.

Violetta J Ferguson (Burnham-on-Sea)

The Blackbird

In a tree a blackbird sat
Underneath lay pussycat
His tail was moving
From side to side
I would like to know
What's on his mind
He's like a little tiger
His eyes fixed on that bird
I said,' You leave
That bird alone
And why don't you
Just go on home
Leave the blackbird
In the tree
So that he can sit
And sing to me.'

Kathleen Poole (Gloucester)

June Past

Sea swishing, soothes my head,
Sun warms my mind
Nostalgia touches my thoughts -
Nudging memories that bind
Us invisibly.

Sand sticks between my toes
Gratingly fine.
Reminiscent of long ago -
Spurring ideas which are mine,
But with you in view.

Mountains watch over me
Looking always down.
But ever caring and secure -
Lifting a fleeting sad frown
Of a June long past.

Seagulls soar on the breeze,
Plaintively pulling
My visions back to the present,
Lying here, the sea lulling
Gentle thoughts of you.

Susan Naile (Exmouth)

Just True Love

The hair upon your little head is as soft as thistledown
Your little lips pursed as a folded rose.
To hold you in my arms, I feel like a queen in a crown.
I touch my lips in a kiss on your little nose.
Nothing can be sweeter than the swell of my heart,
So filled with joy, happiness and love.
No one shall tear us apart,
You are part of me, my own little dove.
I hope the years will be good to you.
I'll try to be here, never far away, just call and I'll be there.
Love like ours will always be true.
I'll be there at all times to show that I care.
And as the years pass on their way,
At the end, I hope remarks will say
She really did her very best
As you go to your very last rest.

Phyllis Wright (Basingstoke)

Total Darkness

*(I dedicate this poem to Ellen who became blind
9 years ago)*

If she closes her eyes
What does she see?
A big black space
That is foreign to me.

To enter your world
I've covered my face
Hands stretched in front
I walk at a snail's pace.

Am I nearing the door
I talk to myself?
Soon to find out
My head hits a shelf.

Ellen, how do you manage
To cope every day?
You're proof of mankind
Where there's a will
There's a way.

Brenda Bartlett (Sutton)

Moments Of Your Life

That first glance,
That first chance meeting
The way the world was altered on that day.

Fate played its hand
And naught withstands how it plays out,
Crossroads in sight, take left or right,
It's in your hands.

What leads you there,
Your life since birth,
Experiences gained whilst on this earth?
Decision made, you stand or fall - *your* choice withal.

That spark,
That flame,
That voice which called your name;
That gold which never loses its bright glow.

The pain, the loss,
That glory turned to dross,
Yet 'neath those ashes still the gold doth show.

Brenda Heath (Torquay)

Dreams

Dreams of you are haunting me
Although I know it's wrong,
I'll love you through eternity

But to me you won't belong.
For another occupies your time
And for her, you play love's song.

For her, your smile sublime
That smile that sets me all aglow
For her, church bells will chime.

If for me, you'd some affection show
I'd give you love in oh so many ways
No other one you'd ever want to know.

I'd never have to dream away my days,
Pretending that you always will be near,
Or live my life, in this romantic daze,

But, in my mind it's very clear,
Dreams of you are haunting me
And oh my love, my dearest dear,
I'll love you for eternity.

Joyce Walker (Borehamwood)

À Monsieur N Dahl

(Dedication of Rachmaninov's Second Piano Concerto)

*Dr Nikolay Dahl, a talented amateur musician,
successfully treated Rachmaninov for depression
after the failure of his first symphony.*

An émigré, barred from his native place,
He never lost his stoic Russian soul;
Slav melancholy, curbed by iron control,
Shaped the inscrutable haunted public face.
Early success came at too swift a pace;
A symphony was his ambitious goal.
It failed. Rejection took a savage toll:
He fled the hall to cover his disgrace.

He thought he never would survive the shock
Of the work's universal condemnation.
A three-year breakdown and composer's block
Froze his creative mind in hibernation.
Only the friendly doctor could unlock
The pent-up sources of his inspiration.

Geoffrey Riley (Marlow)

Thoughts On Trees

Does a tree have feelings? Does a tree feel pain?
Does a tree feel pride in growing, when it comes to life again?

In spring, when leaves adorn it and blossoms bloom so fair,
Does a tree admire its beauty and its strength in growing there?

In summer, when the fruit bursts forth and ripens in the sun,
Does a tree feel pride in what it bears? Its gift to everyone.

In autumn, when its leaves descend and leave its branches bare,
Does a tree feel chilly in the winds that blow about it there?

In winter, when it's snowing and everywhere is bright,
Does a tree feel warmer deep inside when it's dressed
                                                    in sparkling white?

Does a tree feel glad at Christmas, when it twinkles
                                        with small lights?
And tinsel decorates its boughs that brighten up our nights.

Does a tree feel sadness later, discarded and forlorn,
When it's no longer needed and it lies out on the lawn?

I think a tree has feelings, I believe a tree feels pain,
So think before you fell it, and please, let it remain.

Anne Dyson (Basingstoke)

Bank Of Freedom

Patiently gazing into the clear flowing river,
A heron stoops like an old man,
From the grassy bank, he spotted eels slithering around,
He waded into the shallow water carefully stalking prize,
Eagerly waiting to withdraw his catch of the day.
Swiftly he's caught a wriggling fish, firmly clamped in yellow bill.
This is truly one of nature's skilled fishermen, since time began.
Returns again to the grassy bank, now satisfied with this refill.

Soaring high above this wooded vale,
Sharp eyes focused on unsuspecting prey.
A buzzard swoops suddenly, talons ready to collect earned pay.
In meadows and hedgerows wildlife dine from nature's rich store
Plentiful reserves no need to stockpile,
But the willey fox returns for even more.
Although belly full, it's just his way, to bury his kills, for hidden treasure.

Grey squirrels dart from branch to branch,
Seeking a hollow to deposit their valuables in vaults secure,
Stopping briefly, ensuring no others follow.
Intending to steal these winter savings at leisure.

Pat Leat (Exeter)

The Big Race

Women like flowers,
gentlemen,
   and horses.
The Royal Ascot is open.
Horses are ready to run.
The show and game
     just begun.
The trophy is always
     for the best,
so you are welcome
     as a guest.
Who will be the winner
is the biggest surprise.
All the horses are splendid
     and fast.
Old-fashioned clothes,
     colourful dresses
     and interesting hats.
The Royal Ascot is now open,
     the big horse race
       has begun.

Martha Angelica (London)

Incommunicado

Your silence
is full of inner groaning,
night murmur,
crushed desire.
Confusing hope
with wisdom, you
nightly starve
beyond sustaining.

The coming day milks over
your dreams and gagged,
to work you go.
What words can rise
to meet this lumpen pleading?
The river dredged,
the Earth disgorged,
the moon coiling at the needy hour.

Once the night flowed
between us: now you stumble
as a new dirge claims your buried day.

Gloria Tessler (London)

See Me Hold This Space

My life! What life?
I'm going nowhere.
I'm a no-hoper in bloody despair.
I have no feelings, there's nothing to feel,
I'll finish up in prison,
It's a mint deal.
My mom's spaced out
And my dad's gone AWOL,
I live in the moment,
Don't care at all,
You can think what you like,
I don't give a toss!
I am who I am, I'm the boss.
On the streets it's the same to me
As the fight games I play on TV.
My gang's my life,
My brother's my knife.
Cut through the claptrap,
See what you see,
I'm a person,
You could be me.

Sue White (Buntingford)

A Poem In Haste

A poem in three weeks' time?
How could you be so unkind
To give us so very little time
To write a poem.

A click of the finger
Will not make one appear.
nor a magic wand
produce a Browning I fear
For it's a hard slog
which takes its toll
but which in turn
achieves its goal.

So please in future
give us the chance
to write a poem
which will enhance
our status as a poetic bard
and let our talent play its part
in making us top in the chart.

Doris Sherman (London)

Oceanic

The tiny waves do sing and spring in tidal waters fresh with day.
The natural beauty of the day spins on in everlasting solitude.
Bright light plays on this summer morn -
The dolphins dip and dive.
Tiny prawns glide through the aqua hue - so bright,
Oh so unimaginable to my eyes . . .
Dazzled, bewitched I stand upon the sight of,
Summer's golden mantle bright, transfixed.
Exquisite beauty, it is, of course, a gift.
As on the scene *I sit and rest* . . .
Day draws on, O blessed light - it becomes a shadow deep . . .
So nature's wealth is spread abroad, the tiny clusters
On the greenwood tree . . .
Massed Marsh marigolds nod their head to me.
Little acorns stuck in green upon the giant oak.
Candle flowered horse chestnut - the aura of the oceans swell
The season passes on.
Wood anemones in tinkerbell wood, bluebells cast the shadow - blue
Pale night appears as Plaides comes and shows her all.
Beautiful in the moonlight, an owl cries out his plaintive call,
And the wind takes it all . . .

Carol Palmer Ayres (Weston-super-Mare)

Proud Of London

London is a special place.
I am a Londoner by birth, born in the East End.
Some people say it is the world's best city.
A big part that makes London so great is its diversity.
It influences our food in the world's best city.
I am proud of London because of its diversity.

Say yes to hope and no to hate.
London is proud of its diversity.
It influences our culture in the world's best city.
I am proud of London with its unique history.
Let's be proud of London and say no to hate.
Say yes to hope and vote to defeat racism.

London is a city of immigrants, it always has been.
The city was created by the Romans and always will.
I am proud of London and its diversity.
London's diversity brought people together, it won the 2012 Olympics.
London is a world in one city.
It influences our entertainments and sport in the world's best city.
I am so proud of London due to its diversity.

Errol Baptiste (Ealing)

Padma's Secret

High in the Himalayas
Swept by sun and wind
Live a tribe of people
Who have a secret
They know how to fix the world below
When it implodes
They call it Padma's Secret
In Iraq they don't have Padma's Secret
The caretakers of capitalism
Sacrifice on oily altars
They have a new three card trick
Shuffle freedom, democracy and oil
To produce peace
If you fail you die
Baghdad death in the sun, Tenochtitlan undone
Here in white-walled Spain
The sun demands no sacrifice
Between the mountains and the sea
Small birds greet each other incessantly
And I remember the Aztecs
Sacrificed merely to guarantee the light of day.

Patrick Daly (Finchley)

Red Onion

Whoever would think
As I stand at the sink
A red onion would shout
At me madly,
'Take a picture of me
I'm tasty and free
Don't let me down!' he cried sadly.

So out came the flash
Skins in the trash
Onion all rosy and ready
He looked rather nice
Sporting his stripes
Now will the camera stay steady?

Well you see after all
The deed came out tall
Now it's time to eat onion for dinner
He does not mind
The digital is kind
And everyone turned out a winner.

Katrina Graham (Hemel Hempstead)

Much Ado About . . . ?

Now where on Earth did I put it?
It's really very strange -
Was it upstairs - or was it downstairs?
Did I put it in the range?
Of course I didn't! That's stupid!
It would be burnt to a crisp, by now -
I'll really have to think much harder -
There are beads of perspiration on my brow.
Let's recall when last I saw it -
Was it today, yesterday, or when?
And where was I when I last saw it?
Was it England or Scotland, ye ken?
Now when did the children come to visit?
Just let's have a little wee think -
I remember standing here in the kitchen
when they all asked me for a drink -
Now whether it was lemonade or orange -
I can't recall - I really have to think -
But what does it matter if I've lost it?
The trouble is . . .
I've forgotten what the *it* is!

Valma June Streatfield (Reading)

Grim Times

Like tumbling leaves they all fall down
With wounded hearts
The gallant ones

Striking swords in the back
Stabbing to the ground
The pitted ones

No tomorrow to look back
Their loved ones ever mourn
There are rows of crosses now in line
Only poppies to adorn

A thriving harvest could be there
But now we will never see
Only left with sad memories -
-Bear, the crosses where should stand a tree

Killing nature all around
Where sons and fathers tilled the ground
Harvest of love could now be there
Now we can only stand and stare.

Dorothy R G Morley (Leyton)

The Civilised Man

Shall a civilised man not embrace
What makes him a civilised man?
How does the civilised man ignore
What is civilised, and acts to endure?
For the civilised man to be extinct;
Who could endures?
Chaos looms and exacerbates, and cries
For the return of the civilised man.
Under the canopy of the heavens, Man's
inhumanity to his fellows bears no reverence,
The imperative of a civilised man
Characterises his inextinguishable will
To uphold things civilised.
Will the civilised man ceases to exist?
Must not the civilised man persists?
Arise, arise, civilised man,
This terrestrial orb would degenerate
Into barbarity without you
You civilised man, are invaluable
And Olympian who holds together
All who wish to be free.

Leslie Aarons (Luton)

1978 - 2001

This seat where I sit has a memory plaque
To a youth who knew no turning back,
Whose luck ran out at twenty-three
Surfing the waves and riding the sea.

I'd like him to know I love this place
This youth of unknown creed and race.
The gulls still circle overhead
But my thoughts lie with the one who's dead.

Do his parents uses this seat?
Watch other surfers with ambling feet,
With arrogance, without a care,
Expensive boards, long flowing hair.

And long to warn of dangerous rocks
Currents pulling at their locks.
Beware, take care - and yet their son
Would understand the sense of fun.

My thoughts confused; my feelings deep
I linger with gratitude on this seat.

Barbara Best (Slough)

Our Week In Hayle

We've always lived in Plymouth
But across the bridge and down
There's a pretty place in Cornwall
Where we stayed away from town
The beach just stretched for miles
You could even see St Ives
Well it was far in the distance
Stretching just below the sky
The caravan was cosy
Where we lived about a week
With all mod cons
Like pots and pans
To suit our every need
We sampled Cornish pasties
Scampi, chips and home-made scones
Ice cream that melted in your mouth
And all too soon had gone
You couldn't ask for better
So we've booked to go next year
I wonder what adventures we will have
Farewell, my dears.

Jeanette Gaffney (Plymouth)

20 Years Of Forward Press

Poems long, poems short,
Reflecting the colourful tapestry of life.
Humorous poems, serious poems,
A poem that is fun.
We struggle to juggle our words
And to create laughter or emotion.
Ordinary people producing extraordinary
Crafted pieces of work.
Simple poems, complex poems,
We paint with our words,
Creating pictures on subjects galore.
Readers and writers alike keen to admire
The contributions of others.
Happy 20th birthday Forward Press
And thanks for the great opportunity
Of seeing our work in print!

Margaret Cutler (London)

The Dance Of The Moth

He is drawn to the light
He touches it and glows
Dancing in circles
He spirals around and around
Wanting to enter the light
It is not yet time
The light is . . .
A long wait
Perhaps eternity
Flutter and fly
Precious moth
With your paper wings
Beware the bat
Because . . .
He may bring death
For you to touch
The light is extinguished
Silence
Stillness
Emptiness
Without the dance of the moth.

Ivana Cullup (Windsor)

A Message To A Gardener

Don't be cross with the poor old magpie
It's not his fault that he can't stay in the sky
Nature made him stay below with us.
So please dear gardener, don't make a fuss
When he visits your garden so grand.
Do you know the day is close at hand,
When those annoying birds will fly away
Remember sparrows that use to stay?
They stay no more, starling too.
Nothing is forever, that is true.
So please take heart gardener dear
Your garden will last a bit, no fear,
But only with the birds that land
And eat the grubs in the garden you planned.
Pray welcome the magpie with the rest
Don't think of him as a deadly pest.

Hilda B Mason (Harrow)

O' Glorious Devon

Land of beauty, land so bright,
Where you can see a starry night.
And in the morning of pearly dawn
You can see fields of golden corn.
On the green, green grass contented sheep graze,
The horizon a clear blue haze,
As once again on a summer morn,
Wild flowers bloom with many a birdsong.
Up high the lilting melody of the lark,
And dogs go barking in the park.
As children wend their way to school,
Alas nobody walks now, the motorcar rules.
Yet still the seasons come and go,
Spring and summer plus harvest glow.
Winter comes when least expected,
Just make sure your crops are protected.
And cows come mooing down the lane,
As fields and meadows wait for rain,
To replenish the thirsty earth,
This will always give it second birth.
O' glorious Devon.

Rosemary Peach (Torquay)

Moonlight Shadows

Shadows drift in moonlight mist
Skeletons click with every movement
Blackpools of light for those eyes
Nothing deeper inside
Movement slow
Movement dead
Breathing ceased
Tears streaming down young one's face
Shadows leap with lust alone
Coldness barks as the wind blows
Chasing sandy seas
Holding out for love ones lost
Cursed men walk, not holding back
Camera light. Shutter quick
Iris moves. Blank picture clear
The shadows drift in the moonlight mist.'

Natalie Clark (Reading)

The Museum

Beyond bustling streets,
inside rest cool marble statues
standing upon solid feet;
about the echoing halls
like grey pebbles on a lonely beach.
Their waxy, smooth features,
paler than chalk
reflections dimly reach the floor
that echoes soft footsteps in
squeaking talk.
Rich, wide gardens gleam,
through the tall windowed door
and clouds wreath a brilliant
sky's endless walk.
Battered objects hued with rough age
sit in rows; above, white lights
like burning embers rage
gleaming hard upon withered bowls.
A half broken long sword points
its hard metal blade as if it
would be by a distant soul.

Mark Paros (Edgware)

Spring's Smile

Softly and slowly the season is moving on
You know it is winter as the robin sings his song
Gently each leaf drops lightly to the ground
Seagulls, buzzards, calling, autumn colours all around
Bare trees stand majestic resting for a while
Working hard beneath the soil, ready for spring to smile,
Rain and wind and snow restore the sun's thirst
Now watching for the buds which one shall be the first
Do not despair throughout this time but rest as nature does
Soon it will be time again to put away scarf and gloves
Still see the beauty, each outline of the trees
As now they sway devoid of leaves amongst the winter's freeze
Keep watching for soon you will see once again
Blossoms start appearing, all will be the same
Without this restful time nature would not survive
So enjoy all the seasons, enjoy just being alive.

Sue Starling (Minehead)

Silent Tears

Many are we
Who weep in vain,
The silent tears,
The aching heart,
On pillow slip,
Soft falling rain,
For dreams of love,
That seem obscure,
The passing years,
The wish so pure,
Material wealth,
To some may be
For happiness,
A necessity,
He who desires,
A deeper bond,
A path of souls,
That leads beyond,
Seek longer still,
Till fate decides,
What washes in on new spring tides.

Ann Pilcher (Penzance)

A Summer's Day

As dawn breaks I see a hot summer's day.
Across the fields butterflies are at play.
The smell of fresh grass and flowers in bloom,
The roses beside me smelling sweetly of their perfume,
The rabbit stops, then travels on,
Leaping as he goes in the morning sun,
I stand on the bridge and listen to sounds below,
As the stream travels by, you can hear the gentle flow,
The skylarks just above me are adding to the sound,
To walk, stop, listen, so much pleasure to be found,
I turn for home, feeling totally at ease,
Nature always gives its all to please,
The animals graze in the lush green grass,
Hardly a glance when I walked past,
The day may be over but tomorrow I will say,
Thank you for giving me another summer's day.

Wendy Jones (Newbury)

Horses

Out of the blue of a pale morning
they crested the brow of the hill;
then I was a child, with age I remember them still.
With never a falter in their stride
they came on like a billowing tide.
And oh, the thrill and terror as they ran wildly by,
panicked and untamed were they
black and chestnut and dusty grey
wild were their galloping legs and cruel their pounding hooves
as they sprayed mud sky-high from the rutted rain-filled grooves.
Their coats were lathered with running sweat
the wind blew through their manes
and they were mad and uncontrolled for the want of bridle and reins.
There was fear in each rolling eye
as the bolting horses thundered by,
passed in a trice and fled away
and I can hear them to this day
as the tumult became a thread of sound
fading away over stony ground
where I stood alone in the quiet lane
under the still blue air.

Brenda J Smith (Gillingham)

Being Published

I had never had anything published before,
But then Forward Press published me in 2004.
They're in a book entitled 'Here In My Mind'
If you look inside you will find
Lots of poems, eighteen written by me
A photograph and a short autobiography.
My favourite's 'Mixed Blessings' about a girl of mixed race -
'I have a beautiful golden face.'
There's one about cannabis and the bad things it did to me,
One about my mum and dad's anniversary.
There's a get well poem to Frank Bruno and one to John Thaw too,
His widow Sheila Hancock wrote to me to say thank you.
There's a few about Dean who was my boyfriend,
But now that relationship has come to an end.
Thank you Forward Press for publishing me -
And may you continue to publish poems for another twenty.

Anne Voce (Plumstead)

Changes

Changes must happen on our way through life.
Some may seem wrong, but many are right.
So don't look back, ahead you must go.
Another step forward to continue to grow
in your mind, in your heart - you'll find the way.
Then at last comes that moment.
At last comes that day
when you realise
you made it through the changes.

Changes manifest themselves in many a form,
and fate holds our destiny from the moment we're born.
Each life is a story which in time will unfold.
So be brave, my friend, be strong, be bold and . . .

Don't look back, ahead you must go.
Another step forward to continue to grow
in your mind, in your heart - you'll find the way.
Then at last comes that moment.
At last comes that day
when you realise
you made it through the changes.

Susan Shaw (Yatton)

Bobby The Plough Horse

Don't need a timetable for buses and trains.
Just a means of transporting me far, far away.
There isn't a town, not a car to be seen,
But there are farms, fields and meadows and landscapes are green.
It's a crisp autumn morning and the harvest is home.
I am there by the gate with my plough horse alone.
The seagulls are wailing and the breeze through the trees
And my face feels the touch of the soft falling leaves.
He is harnessed and ready, he stands for command.
I tell him 'Walk on!' and his feet tread the ground.
The furrows are soggy, muddy and deep
And finds it a problem to lift up his feet.
Once we have started we are on our way.
We will work close together as we go through the day.
He's a big sturdy fellow yet so gentle and kind
And looks after me with his brown knowing eyes.
We will stop for a time for lunch and a rest.
He buries his muzzle and head in my chest.
I will give him some hay and an apple or two
And we start off again refreshed and renewed.

Eileen Kay Gingell (Milton Keynes)

Where You Belong

An invisible shroud surrounds me
With wings upon its back
This gift of freedom given me
Life is back on track
Like a butterfly emerging
From its chrysalis trap
Taking to the skies
The world a living map.

Sitting by the shore
As the waves crash all around
Ringlets of seaweed abound
Above the angry sound
One knows that it will return
With greater power and strength
A visual gift Heaven sent.

As the darkened sky displays its wares
Twinkling and sparkling like fluorescent flares
What message does it hold for me?
'Life goes on when you are strong
You are where you belong'.

Gloria Hargreaves (Weybridge)

Wild Thoughts

I thought I saw an elephant go flying into space
I thought I saw a snail win a hundred yard race,
A giraffe and a chimpanzee were trying to do the twist
When they were both knocked out by a monkey's fist.
The flowers in the garden were laughing off their heads
The cabbages were lying in the strawberry beds
Whilst the ladybird and earwig were singing a duet,
A frog was trying to have a bath, without getting wet.
I thought I saw a dog with glasses on his nose
I also heard a horse say hello to a rose,
It's really quite ridiculous these wild thoughts of mine
Whoever heard of field mice drinking cups of wine.
I thought I saw the moon spinning on the ground;
Then I picked up a shilling and thought it was a pound
I thought I saw a flea churning butter in the park;
He said he was doing it just for a lark.
A squirrel hiding nuts, said he'd hid one in a cloud
A sleeping weasel watching just laughed out loud.
Then a lady with a suitcase stood upon her head,
And said, 'I've had enough of this, I'm going back to bed!'

Gwendoline Dillon (Bristol)

Voyages

As listless sun lays on
December burning fog
Planes fall from the sky
Rolling comets and shadows
Break the London silence
My mind trapped between
Palm trailed shores and
Scarlet tropic smoke.

Labyrinths of broad
Boulevards in grey Paris
Melt in windless rain
Unravelling eucalyptus
Melbourne burns in green.

I watch Ceylon seas screened
By haunting darkness, by ripples of
The sea, my childhood's horizon
The broken promises of absence
Cold, clammy, sand beneath my feet
As I turned away far from the night
Stars despondently shone.

Daisy Abey (Sutton)

My Dorset

The delight of nature's artistic hand
Has fashioned the coastline, rocks and sand.
From chalky cliffs to craggy rocks,
Even yachting and boating docks.
Varied hues and many moods,
Beaches for everyone, even nudes.
Slipping rocks, striated, Jurassic
Lead to views amazing, fantastic.
Sandy coves with sparkling waves,
And in the cliffs, some hidden caves.
Inland, heaths hold habitats
Of rarer breeds, including bats.
Lizards lurk and birds abound,
As if they're born on hallowed ground.
Sometimes, driving, deer leap out,
Scaring motorists without a doubt
They live throughout the heaths and trees.
(If you want some honey, there are also bees.)
You can keep the manmade expensive attractions,
Nature's beauty has no subtractions.

Christine Bridson-Jones (Wareham)

783

Where The Sweet Roses Grow

'Will you walk with me my lady through the garden smelling sweet
Of roses and lavender with soft grass at your feet
And sit with me my lady on the seat beneath the bower
Where we may talk of many things to pass away the hour
Then perchance my lady, I may take your hand
And lead you down the secret path to where the small boats land
We may stroll along the riverbanks, share our hopes and dreams
Knowing my lady, all is not quite as it seems.'

'Oh Sir, it sounds delightful I really cannot wait
I'll pack a picnic basket our hunger for to sate
And Sir I will walk barefoot if I may be so bold
The day is warm and sunny so I will not feel the cold
And Sir may I touch your cheek with finger tips?'
'Only if, my lady, I may kiss your soft red lips.'

'Sir, when our lovely day comes to an end
Back up the pathway we'll slowly ascend
Up to the big house where we came from
To work in the kitchen, Rosie and Tom
But on our days off where no one will know
We'll be Lady and Sir where the sweet roses grow.

Joyce Lodge (Looe)

Moving On

No reason now why people should
Remember where the farmhouse stood.
Still, sad though that they never knew
The peaceful place where elm trees grew.
Where cows were milked and calves were born,
Where fields were filled with waving corn,
Where meadowland gave way to fen,
Where time stood still since way back when,
Where orchards grew greengage and cherries,
Where hedgerows heaved with elderberries,
Where swan and heron glided by,
Where skylarks swooped from way up high,
Where plough and scythe had worked the land,
Where skills were shared and futures planned,
Where none foresaw the unexpected,
Where dreams were dashed and hope rejected,
Where nothing really stayed the same,
Where no one person took the blame.
A lifestyle left without a trace,
Another time, another place.

Sandra Clarke (Dursley)

A Bristol Love Affair

(Homage to Betjemen)

White pleated skirts sway in the breeze;
Intense lady-bowlers dip at the knees;
Following through with eagle-eyed stance,
Toing and froing, in stately-trod dance.
'Good shot': 'Well bowled': a few dignified claps;
Quiet contentment, and tea with the chaps.

Joan Hunter-Dunn is now Joan Fortescue -
The Green, here, on Saturdays; Sundays, the pew.
Freckles remain on the cheeks and the nose -
Tanned and resplendent, our Bristol-born rose.
Grand slams forgotten, she glories in grace,
As she basks in attention; with radiant face.

The Major is waiting to whisk her away,
Past Bristol landmarks, to finish the day
With drinks at an hotel, or new, trendy bar;
Then home, changed for dinner, and out in the car
To some Bristol night spot that's classy and bright:
And home, past the bridge, with the world put to right.

J Myrtle Goulden (Bristol)

December / January

December

Santa and reindeer
Ice and snow
Tinsel and turkey
Holly and mistletoe

Excited children hang up their stocking
Gifts lie under the tree
The hyacinth and the amaryllis
Their colours for all to see

January

The weather is cold
It may even snow
The rain will fall
And the winds will blow

People make resolutions
And break them too
The year is just starting
So everything is new

Patricia G Stone (Totnes)

Lady, My Dog

(Lived to 16½ years)

In my darkest despair
You were always there
To lift my spirits
And kiss my hair.

Eyes that could see
What nobody knew.
This terrible pain
That I've been through.
I will never forget you
Or ever could.

Now life's moved on
And both of us too.
I'm getting older
And so are you.
Sixteen years we have
Been together.
I wish it could be
Forever and ever.

S Bannister (Plymouth)

The Milestone

Here I stand, a figure of stone,
The silent witness of all who pass.
An unchanged message, seldom read.

Half-buried in soil, with ivy collar.
Layers of paint announce my age.
A roadside sentry no longer to attention.

If I could speak, what I have seen.
Galloping mail coach, horn a-blowing.
The prize of riders in hot pursuit.

Chasing cars, headlights roving.
Criminals and victims changing places.
Law and order interlaced.

Around the clock, I keep my vigil.
Darkness brings my wildlife friends.
With humans sleeping, nature thrives.

Oblivious to the changing weather,
I stand here, with no opinions.
The constant reminder of a bygone age.

Susan Dean (Dorchester)

The Linnet

I thought my garden quite complete,
With lawn set down midst trees and shrubs,
A rockery with heathers strewn,
And beds packed tight with scented blossoms.

An aviary of birds whose song and beauty brightens every day,
Telling sparrows, blackbirds, tits,
They too are welcome here to stay.

And then, one dull October morn,
A new song fell upon my ear,
I turned, and there upon a tree,
A grey-brown linnet sat alone.

She sang, and in the aviary,
The other birds joined in with zest,
As if they knew this tiny guest,
Could teach them songs they'd never heard.

Now every time I hear her song,
I feel so grateful that she came,
And hope that she for many years,
Here in my garden, will remain.

Doreen Clayton Fergusson (Cullompton)

The Statue

There is a statue waits outside my door,
Through balmy days and nights of winter hoar -
I wish it wasn't there anymore.

Its stony skin is cracked and green with moss,
Its heart is cold and feelingless with loss
Of more than just its arms and surface gloss.

It watches me with sightless eyes that know
The image I portray is but a show;
And saying nothing tells me so.

Its ears are tuned to everything I do,
From fixing lunch to visits to the loo -
There must be something I can do.

But no . . . unless I speak aloud its name,
And by so doing give away the game,
My life must always be the same . . .

And yet . . . perhaps it's just that I should suffer so,
Forever looking backwards as I go
Towards the child I didn't grow.

Joseph Clift (London)

Drinker's Lament

Pig's ear, apple fritter
Fill my glass with a pint of bitter,
Think of a world full of sorrow,
It's a long night till tomorrow,
Sadness lessens with each swallow.

Another pint in which to think,
The answer coming at the end of each drink.

Sad things happen on this Earth,
Not much room for joy and mirth,
Each day cries for a universal answer,
For me another pint will find it brighter
In someone else it'll find a fighter.

The cold light of day looms foreboding,
Hangover and depression fill the daylight hours,
Whatever happened to a world filled with flowers.

Pig's ear, apple fritter
Fill my glass with a pint of bitter,
Farewell my loved ones and as time passes,
Think of me and raise your glasses.

M D Martin (Rickmansworth)

Time Cannot Heal

Time cannot heal heartache,
Stop a silent tear
Nor can it take away the memories of someone we loved so dear.

If tears could build a staircase and memories a lane,
I'd walk right up to Heaven and bring you home again.

In our memories you'll live, with beauty and grace,
In time remembering you will bring a smile to our face.
When speaking of your life, we are filled with honour and pride,
You're not here anymore, yet we know you stand by our side.

Now your home's in Heaven,
And there you'll always be.
You're in my heart and my soul,
You mean the world to me.

Goodbye, God bless and a final kiss I send
On a train to Heaven and at peace you are.
Shining right above, our guiding star.

We are so sorry to have lost you and will think of you always.
Love you forever, Laura.

Laura Perkins (Wantage)

Cats

Cats are wise;
They view the world through contemplative eyes
Of emerald hue
Or cerulean blue.

Cats are restful;
They calm the troubled soul as they sit
Immobile,
Considering the infinite.

Cats are quicksilver;
Alert to the flick of a shadow of leaf or cloud
Upon the grass.

Cats are cruel;
Tormenting the defenceless bird or mouse
With tooth and claw -
Nature in the raw.

God created cats;
His infinite wisdom shines from their eyes,
Calmly, inscrutably
Eternal.

Irene Grant (Reigate)

Flower Bud

A bud is a flower,
Just waiting to bloom,
Waiting for sunshine to warm up its room.

Wrapped up with its petals, keeping warm,
Waiting for sunlight,
To power over the storms.

Beautiful colours lay waiting inside,
All the good gardeners,
Waiting for their pride.

Up pop the daffodils, yellow and strong,
Along with the crocuses,
In the fields they belong.

Waiting all year to see the sunlight,
Along come the pickers,
To share the delight.

From store to shop, they get sold,
Bringing colour and love,
With their buds, unfold.

E P Dunn (Plymouth)

Please Don't Betray Our Love, My Dear Wife Smreeti

At this moment in time, my dear wife Smreeti,
my thoughts are on our marriage, now in its fifth year.
I sit alone in solitude and think about you; about us,
and am still stunned in the cold manner
in which you just walked out on me.
after an unexpected phone call that you had arrived
back in London from India.
it felt so strange when you reappeared back home as a 'guest'.
and when I hugged you, your body grew stiff
and your lips were pursed so tightly.
the manner in which you opened our bedroom window so wide
when I sat and watched helplessly as you collected your belongings
and then left in someone's car whom I never knew,
without any introduction, telephone number or home address.
And now, my mind is blank; I just feel emptiness inside.
I think of all those precious moments we spent
alone outdoors; just the two of us.
I gave you my heart and in return, it seems you left me.

Rajeev Bhargava (Harrow)

The Wanderer

As I ramble through the pass
Between the mountains high
I sometimes sit upon the grass
And gaze up in the sky.
I look for the golden eagle
A very splendid bird
And if it's quiet, I will hear its call
Like no other I have heard.
Soon it's time to be on my way once more
Passing primroses, bluebells, by the score.
Slowly walking down the hill
Beside a stream that's never still
Passing falls and a little bridge
Raggy sheep upon the ridge.
A deer or two, maybe a hare
Mischievous squirrels playing there
Now I've reached the road below
Left the mountains their peaks in snow
The countryside is rough and crude
This lovely Cumbria in solitude.

P B Sewell (Godalming)

To My Ysha - My Beloved Yorkshire Terrier

The most wonderful sight
I could ever behold
Was his bright, loving eyes
And a nose so cold.
We played together he and me
I knew the joy in my heart
He could see.
His little legs could outrun me
As we played *his* game -
Run around tree.
But, alas, the years must have their way
And I lived in dread of that fateful day
The love of my life he'll always be
I'm glad my tears he cannot see.
His cuddles and licks are all now gone
But his memory will always linger on
I know he looks down from above
And each star I see is his eternal love.

Wendy Tirebuck Souter (Plymouth)

More Houses

A derelict bit of land where once a factory stood,
Graffiti on the crumbling walls, artistically quite good.
Concrete roads with cracks from which young saplings grow,
Spiked rusty railings, stand like soldiers in a row.
Pulley wheels and narrow gauge, railways line
Windows with broken glass, a fading *Keep Left* sign.
But now men with giant tractors have come
And cleared the brambles, which make the rabbits run.
Suntanned men with yellow hat and yellow vest
Clear the undergrowth, and last year's blackbird's nest.
Bulldozers push earth into piles and heaps,
And gouge ditches which are wide and deep.
Tarmac is spread on a newly made road,
Bricks arrive by the lorry load.
Scaffolding and drainage pipes,
Sweating brow, backhand wipes.
A new housing estate is being built here,
People will be living here within this year.
Walls go up and roofs go on,
But the rabbits and blackbirds have gone.

Keith Coleman (Newport Pagnell)

Tea Time

Look at me, how badly dressed.
I walk too tall for one so cross,
For one so small,
For one so out of place
In this fine room.
The girls, with golden beads,
Cold pearls,
Line up like bells
And nod their heads,
Ding dong.

Better where the walls are grey.
The food, too hot (quite over keen),
Discarded now.
A whiff of smoke,
Hysteria prevails out there.
It makes me laugh
To sip my tea.
Remaining unconvinced
I hold their gaze
Too long.

N Stringer (Croyden)

London

Londidnum was a silly name,
Now we're holding the Olympic games
Find a nice place to eat
Walk to Two-Two-B Baker Street.
We had the seven/seven disaster
A man with a red flag don't go faster
Docklands airport, more planes in the sky
Take a ride on the London Eye
Pearly kings give you a smile
Do the Lambeth Walk over the square mile.

We put the beer into the fridge
Shops once stood on London Bridge
Jump on a London red bus
Be a real Cockney like us
You hear the sounds, get the smells
Get a wake up from Bow Bells
Walk across some finest green
Have a visit to our great Queen
We've got joy, our share of crime
Come to visit London anytime.

Colin Allsop (Leyton)

Sun, Sea And Sandwiches

Early morning, let's go to the coast.
The sun is out ideal for most,
Pack a lunch,
Bucket and spade.
Lilo, lotion and a sunshade.
Into the car and join the queue,
Held up now 'enjoy the view'
Arrive at ten, park and then?
Head for the beach,
It's out of reach.
The grass will do,
With kites and ice cream,
Souvenir shops with postcards too,
Found a spot just on the sand
Let's make a sandcastle
And have a small parcel
Of something to eat.
The wind starts to blow
And now, we know.

We're having *sand*wiches . . .

Gerry Dymock (Harmondsworth)

A Cornish Gem

The tour coach stops, this summer's day
Where the plateau ends,
What a view!
Below a bay with waters greeny-blue
On the far side, four miles away
A church spire between small harbour
And that Cornish town
Of opera renown
(No pirates there today.)

From the hill tops to the plain below
Marazion goes down
When water is all about
From where town and harbour meet
Ferries go to a tiny mount
With church and castle crowned.
Once a monastery, now a baron's seat.
At the Mount's foot by the tiny harbour
Are the houses of the islanders,
This is St Michael's Mount,
The jewel in Mount's Bay.

Frances Joan Tucker (Exmouth)

The Hair Display

A few days ago I was selecting some very nice fruit from the local market when I unwittingly heard the conversation of a young stall holder to his mate. It went something like this:

The old 'Barnet Fair' was feeling quite long
so thought I'd hop down to 'Anton's Salon'.
The advert said 'the complete male coiffeur'.
Anton enquired, 'The full treatment, Monsieur?'
Now I knew that it looked a bit of a hash,
thought it's not before time, better have a bash.
He clipped it, he trimmed it, brushed it with care,
twisted me around in his revolving chair.
He singed it, shampooed it, soaked my head with a tonic,
said it would attract the girls, made me feel bionic.
He massaged it, blow dried it, set it in modern style,
told me to relax, to cool it for a while.
Covered it in jelly called 'Essence of Squid',
blew it into shape again, saying, 'I hope there's no rain, that's forty-five quid
I wandered home feeling tired and worn,
slept in the chair, awoke with the dawn.
Looked in the mirror, felt quite sick.
I paid forty-five quid for strawberry-coloured hair that looks twice as thick.

Robert Dives (Haywards Heath)

The Rainbow - Benedict XVI At Auschwitz

Herded by murderers, they went this way.
Line after line they passed; day after day.

A man walks through the rain. He's come to pray.

It's lonely in the cold grey shadows there.
Evil seems lingering in the lifeless air
And the great world sunk deep into despair.

Man born for love is turning from Love's Light
Blind to the beauty fairer than the height
Where the stars are, blaze, flaming silver-white.

The wall of death towers desolate and bare.
Is God Himself no longer anywhere?

Yet still the man is standing there in prayer.

And now when noon of day seems dark as night
A rainbow shines with colours made so bright
Only God who is Love could bring this Light.

Diana Momber (Falmouth)

Our Place

Wait for me where leafy glade bows low on mossy bank,
Where waters gently lap the pebbled shore,
And breezes more softly rise to kiss
Your cheek and whisper sweet promises,
And wait for me my love.

Wait for me where gold brown leaves reflect,
The sun on shrinking bough where misty shafts of
Silvered light reach down to touch the withering stems
Of rush and reed that dip a last farewell
And wait for me my love.

Wait for me where icy winds blow fierce on hoary bough,
Where silent snowflakes fall on stunted larch,
To hide the greying coldness of the earth,
Where cloaked against the winter's blast small creatures sleep
And wait for me my love.

Wait for me in sun and song and laughing breeze,
Stirring the ripples o'er the bay to whirl and dance,
With wakening buds that burst in wondrous harmony
And there shall I be my love.

S Cameron (Taynuilt)

Prisoner Of The Gutter

I'm a prisoner of the gutter I have no self-esteem
I live upon the cobbles and all I do is dream
With nitty hair and dressed in rags, I beg for money to buy fags
Surrounded by the debris with rats and mice and whores
My only friends are beggars and those who flout the laws.

A penny for your thoughts Sir, a penny in my hand
A sixpence in my pocket that would make life grand
But only shadows pass me on streets once paved with gold
But that's another story; I'll tell when I grow old.

Gaslights flicker as the night draws in
Loose women on corners drinking gin
A penny for your time Sir, a penny in my hand
A sixpence in my pocket Sir, I know you understand.

I rest my head upon the boxes and watch stars dance in the sky
I close my eyes and go to sleep and let the world just drift on by
Dawn breaks, birds sing, freshness in the air
Children crying, people sighing, life seems so unfair
I have one hand on God's ladder, one foot on the Devil's hole
Will my God lift me up another rung, or will the Devil take my soul?

Michael Bowden (Dunmow)

Waiting For Something

The clear thought was enough
like some possession in a room
only detached from the main building,
labour was my lot, not some
slip of paper or empty image.

Soil full of brambles and briar
and the graven image is our chariot,
given to us by the brutish
knowledge of Man.

At twilight, creatures in feathers
feast on a banquet of song,
wings like angels whose tongue
call through ancient woods
and mock the graven image.

Yes Mock Dagon and Mock Baal
and the molten image is falsehood,
who for apparition is ingenious
in the way of iniquity,
at twilight creatures in feathers do sing.

Jeremy Jones (Reading)

Paper Jack

Never had there been a more eccentric fellow,
Carrying all his worldly goods about his neck.
With a demeanour nothing short of mellow,
Neither hot sun nor winter snow stopped his morning trek.

His body wrapped in clean but crinkled newspapers,
He trampled through Beddington along the village streets.
It's a wonder village ladies never suffered vapours
But they often made him cakes and pies as welcome treats.

He bathed in the River Wandle, even slept in a shed I'm told,
Always eating outside like a gypsy, never snuggled in the warm.
Tough as old boots, his arms were always bare despite the cold,
All loved this kind and gentle man with the innocence of a faun.

Wreathed in mystery, this ex-surveyor, once shone
                    with quiet dignity,
Crossed in love some thought but many theories were proposed.
Still, he'll be fondly remembered, with warmth
                    or sometimes pity,
Now the unread pages of his odd life have finally,
                    quietly closed.

Teresa Tipping (Croydon)

The Somerset Levels

Flat, soggy, yet startlingly beautiful
In its bare bleakness
White ethereal mists, rise at dusk,
From primeval rhynes,
Which cross-cross the ancient landscape
Teeming with life
From tiny thought, to be extinct snails
To playful otter,
On their banks, the yellow iris grows
In bright profusion
Eclipsed by brown-headed bulrushes
Standing straight and tall
While underfoot lies the black-gold peat
Formed aeons ago
By long-dead trees and foliage
Once under the sea
Starlings in their thousands come at dusk
To rest in the sedge
While the ancient Tor of Druid fame
Stands guard over all.

Dora Watkins (Bridgwater)

Sweet Peas

Pale pink and delicate lilac
white and almost cerise,
overwhelming perfume
beautiful sweet peas.
Various hues of lemon
some of violet shade,
soft velvety petals
elegantly displayed.
Blooms like fine tissue paper
carefully fashioned and groomed,
unique in design by nature
fascinating blooms.
Their fragrance fills the sultry air
attracting butterflies and bees,
Nature almost perfected
wonderful sweet peas.
Exquisite in formation
their aroma floats on the breeze,
purity unblemished
beautiful sweet peas.

Patricia Frampton (Newport)

Call Me

My number scrawled on her bare arm,
My words whispered with hypnotic charm,
Call me, call me, call me!
My mantra for Saturday night,
Go home - she tells me, problem is
Home is her heart, should I obey the urge
To wrap myself in her warmth?
No, better wait two or three days,
Prayer will draw us closer to erase fear
And conquer the physical divide,
She works office hours
I dwell in the poetic doldrums of the mind,
We disguise our desire with the silence
Of indifference, she calls, I answer,
We confer on the phone in the hope of . . .
Our date ends in my living room divan,
We smoke fag ends, blabber, and when
The talking is done - we are reborn like
Children determined to brand each other
Before we breathlessly cross the finish line.

Carlos Nogueiras (London)

For You

I am the gentle breeze,
The grass beneath your feet.
I am there above you
Where Earth and Heaven meet.
I am there at break of day
And there at Eventide
To comfort you in sadness
Be there at your side.
In your dreams reach out for me
I am always there
To lighten all your darkest hours
To show you that I care.
I am the summer rain that falls
From darkened skies above
To wash away your grief
And shower you with love.
I will kiss away your tears
Do not cry for me
I am always there for you
For all eternity.

Jane King (Chesham)

A Winter's Night

Silently, softly, the flakes flutter down,
Onto roads, gardens and roofs in the town.
Twirling, whirling, dancing around
Till finally landing to carpet the ground.
Birds and animals leave their track,
Whilst going off hunting, or coming back,
After the shower moon and stars shine,
Jack Frost flies overhead sprinkling his rime,
Next morning we awaken to an eerie light,
Everywhere outside lies pristine white.
Children peer out, their faces aglow,
Eager to go out and play in the snow.
But alas, everyday life cannot be halted,
The gritters arrive, the roads are salted,
People on foot soon appear,
Cars, carefully driven, in first gear,
Soon all to be seen is dirty brown slush,
Gone is the quiet, gone is the hush,
Did it really happen, this winter scene,
Or, was it only - just a dream!

Dawn Furse (Launceston)

Cressbrook Dreaming

This land is but a dream
With silent valleys and running streams
With Spirit in the earth around
Heartfelt moments can be found
In weir and brook and hill and peak
Your solitude is what I seek
To give my mind, my heart, my soul
Your wondrous secrets to behold
Who knew I would find such a treasure?
That gives me real earthly pleasure
No other wealth holds such a key
To find joy in eternity
Of nature's gifts of land and sky
And hills and peaks to look up high
I walk, I climb, I run and dance
My life you definitely enhance
Thank you Cressbrook, thank you land
You hold my heart in your mighty hand
Of hill and tree and brook and stream
I will always dream . . .

Karen Harvey-Zahra (Fareham)

Have I Told You Mother (Our Mother)

Have I told you lately of how much I love you,
Dear sweet Mother of mine.
Have I told you in my dreams each night,
With tender love divine,
When you look upon me with your smile,
Have I told you what it means to me.
Gold and silver could never buy,
The smile that my eyes can see,
Hands that worked and toiled for us,
When 'ere we could understand.
Have I told you lately, the marks I see,
Of love within those hands.
Dear brown eyes, precious jewels
That's seen sunshine, cloud and rain,
While through the years the warmth shines through,
Reflecting love the same,
Love's sweet foundation I have learnt,
From your dear heart so true,
Golden are each moments' spent -
Dear Mother, when it's shared with you.

Selma Brown (Penzance)

Catherington Lith- Hampshire

The cold chill wind in wintertime
Howls round the church and yard.
The hilltop so exposed and bare
Is iced with frost so hard.
The pond is frozen next the school,
The pub's warm welcome light,
The winding lane with cottages
Their thatches thick with white.
Returning through the churchyard
Descending o'er the hill
We greet snug-coated horses,
They stand so very still.
Their breath hangs round their nostrils
So warm it steams, then here
We leave them to descend again
Through woodland, sheltering deer.
Then on mud track we trudge for home
And gather wood, the way.
We light our fire and thaw our toes
And nod and dream away.

Jean-Margaret-Paul (Waterlooville)

Please Beware, I'm Dangerous

I'll cut your heart into tiny fragments
And make each one my own,
I'll drain you of every emotion
You'll never be alone.
I'll make you so frustrated,
And smother you to death,
Until I hear my name
On your each and every breath.
I'll break down all your defences
And silently sneak through,
And now you can't be sure
If I am me or you.
The pieces of your heart and
My name upon your breath
It's clear that I'm part of you,
There's nothing of you left.
So please beware I'm dangerous
Never let me roam,
Because I'm so in love with you,
I'll make your soul my home.

Lyndy Phillips (Weston-super-Mare)

My Fake Cat

I have a cat that is not real, but real she is to me.
She nods her head and miaows out loud when sat upon my knee.
She is so white and fluffy with sparkling two green eyes,
But pull her tail and she will give a nasty big surprise.
She is so sweet and lovely and gives me hours of joy,
So very, very wonderful though she is just a toy.
She sits upon her chair of blue and waits for me to cuddle
And best of all she never makes a big and nasty puddle.
She is the best of all the cats that are about the town,
She always looks so happy and never wears a frown.
I treat her very gently because I love her so,
To me she is a real cat, I call her Mitzy-Mo.
I'm glad the day I bought her, she means the world to me,
I'll always take great care of her so wonderful is she.
She also shuts her lovely eyes and sometimes goes to sleep,
I always say a prayer for her and a kiss for her to keep.
And when I stroke her soft white fur she nods her little head,
As if she knows the day has gone and time to go to bed.
And now I'll end this little tale of my pussy cat so true,
She will always make me happy and never make be blue.

Josephine Blackford (Andover)

Upwardly Mobile

Open plan
Modern man
Mainline computer
Trouble shooter
Swivel chair
Spiky hair
Lapel rose
Designer clothes
Golden earring
Power steering
E-Type Jag
King-size fag
Double scotch
Cartier watch
Yuppie flat
Persian cat
Mobile phone
Credit loan
Solvent still
Treadmill.

Carolyne Calder (Newbury)

Remorse

Long ago with sadness in my heart
To live in the city I did depart
But I realise it's not my life
With all its strident noise and strife
Always yearning in my heart
For the home I did depart
Long to see again my valley home
Where the deer and ponies roam
Its tranquil glory, so serene
Makes a peaceful scene
To see again the seasons unfold
From winter snow to summer gold
I long to walk again
By its rivers and many a leafy lane
To hear the wild birds' song
And know it's here I belong
I shall return one day I know
And make the journey somehow
To ease the longing in my heart
And never ever more depart.

A Mitchell (Bournemouth)

Cathedrals Of My Days

In the chapels of my heart
and the churches of my life,
are the meanings of my thoughts
and the reasons for my ways.
So come inside this abbey -
the cathedral of my days,
skilful art, my mind so sharp -
of knowledge found, kept and taut.
So welcome to my minster,
the priory of my being,
where spirits sleep and angels weep
and many fools have tried to creep.
So deep inside my soul,
are the vaults of new beginnings
and the crypts that do so whisper
when the bells of time do toll.
So enter these my houses,
there's wisdom here to find,
among the many choices
in the temples of my mind.

David J S Golding (Exeter)

Rural Rhapsody

Passing through East Sussex
On the road to Tunbridge Wells;
I behold a rural paradise
And my heart, with loving, swells.
Love for the English countryside,
An inspiring awesome scene.
I hear music deep within me
Of a rhapsody in green.
If I were a skilled musician
With this view of inspiration,
I'd compose a glorious symphony
For performance to the nation.
Or as a landscape artist
I would paint a picture there;
To hang in a public gallery
For everyone to share.
But sadly, I am neither;
So how can I express
This beauty that surrounds me,
In all my humbleness.

Doris Ainsworth (Crawley)

Childhood Days

I remember those days so clearly
They might have been yesterday
Long, hot, sunny days
Tea on the lawn, the chink of cups from the kitchen,
The smell of cut grass,
Bike rides through the long country lanes
Birthday parties with pretty frocks
Presents and a birthday cake with candles
Days in school with friends
Long summer evenings sitting in fields of corn,
The smell of apples in an old barn,
Warm rays of sun with dust motes dancing in the air
Snowy days by the fire with big thick storybooks
Christmas morning, waking early, presents by the bed
Yes, those sweet, long, happy days of my childhood
Long, never-ending days full of love and laughter
And night-time with a loving mother to tuck me in,
With a kiss goodnight
Yes, all this I remember
But now, oh so long ago.

Hazel Webb (Hoddesdon)

Sheila's Perfume

And in my garden I planted a rose,
With no idea what colour it would be.
The label on the stem said, 'Sheila's Perfume'
That name alone meant everything to me.
The rose - your rose - turned out to be bright yellow
With scarlet trim. It had a gorgeous scent.
It's lovely, but not half as fair as you were.
I bought it out of grieving sentiment.
I plucked a bloom and put it in a vase;
For days its sweet aroma filled the air,
But, mortal too, it drooped and died, as you did;
Brought echoes of my infinite despair.
Nothing can bring you back no rose can be
More than a token of unending grief.
You were the blossom in our life together
While I was just your life-supporting leaf.
But now my leaf hangs through the sunless days.
In weariness, bereft, its flower sped.
Slowly it withers, by no one regarded,
Till winter drops it to its loamy bed.

John Goodspeed (Plymouth)

The Maltese Rose

It retains a longing fragrance
Like the island where it grew
The mystery rose of Malta
Its location known to very few
So many roam the island
Searching for this rarest rose
Very few have had the pleasure
Of finding where it grows
Within its petals hides a secret
A perfume it expels
Dew drops send its petals nodding
Like the ringing distant bells
A sweet aroma rises
Enchanting insects and the birds
Reminding all lovers who whisper
The three little words
All colours of the rainbow
To leaf and petal in full bloom
The beauty of the Maltese rose
From September through to June

Ernest Hannam (East Grinstead)

Happy Hospital Stay

Here I sit in my hospital bed,
Out of the windows the sky turns red,
Clouds passing quickly silhouettes of which you could be fond,
Aeroplanes crossing to the airports beyond,
Nurses doing their duties efficiently,
Sorting out catheters and cannulas,
Pills and potions,
For those with less motions,
Blood pressure, oxygen levels and temperatures taken,
Not all of this done when you're fully awaken,
Us poor patients in pain and discomfort,
Nurses caring and sharing in a professional way,
To make sure we have a comfortable day,
Bells are ringing for help and understanding,
Patients brought back from theatre,
Made better or bits taken away,
Fast asleep in a dream world
A wonderful place to be,
An eye opener I can tell you,
From a patient just like me.

Marian Clark (Thatcham)

Bournemouth

You said write a poem
And gave a closing date
To tell of where you're living
What you like or what you hate!
Well I live in Bournemouth
Which is pretty cool
We say the sun shines daily
And that's usually the rule
We all love the winter
The autumn and the spring
But not so much the summer
Oh the problems the grockles bring!
They fill the roads with traffic
Car parking they demand
Then out come hampers and sunshades
And they cover all the sand!
I suppose we should be grateful
At least they pay their way
Then they're gone by October
And won't be back till May!

Rowena (Bournemouth)

Carter's Town

In nineteen hundred a farm did stand,
In a green and pleasant Oxon land.
Bought by Bill Carter who divided it up
In plots for sale to sow and crop.
Men, mothers and children dug the land,
No tractors, etc, all by hand!
Wells for water, a house for all
They built and lit them with lamps of oil.
Greenhouses up, chicken runs placed,
Orchards planted, elements faced.
They named it Carterton after old Bill,
Hundred years later it's with us still.
No market gardens now, no eggs to sell,
Co-op supermarket does it all so well.
RAF Brize Norton, planes in the air,
Part of Carterton; just over there.
We are now a town, expanding fast,
Did William Carter think it would last?
In Carterton that farm still stands,
In a town seventh largest in Oxon land.

Wendy Morgan (Carleton)

Age And Beauty Doesn't Matter

Met
On the internet
She
Said thirty-three
Saw
Was nearer fifty-four
She
Said you're no Greek God
As
Claimed on your blog
We
Laughed together
Then
We dined
And
Love redefined
We're
Laughing still
Through
All our happy years.

John Anstice Brown (Hitchin)

Place Of Renown

Hills
dawn draped ethereal
shield a sun-kissed valley
as mellowed doorways
gorge invading shoppers
students
wanderers
around a city loved
by revellers
sheltered ladies
captains
kings
surveying springs
crescents
sally lunns
while scenic isles rise from the valley shroud
lap custom
passion
fashioning a cultured bath
within the hills.

Faith Dolman (Bath)

807

Village Life

The old men on the village seat,
With dimming eyes and weary of feet.
Autumn sends the red leaves flying,
Their summer memories slowly dying.
The fire has gone out the forge is cold,
Bellows and nails asleep their stories told.
The hammer and anvil is silent now,
Where have the horses gone that pulled the plough?
Moorlands of brambles, heather and yellow flowering gorse,
With farms and woodlands and a lazy river winding its course.
The abbey of ghosts and people long gone,
The saints walk along paths in silent song.
Many are the crosses of bygone days,
To the rock, to the rock, the lepers seek their way.
The past is cancelled and buried deep,
Yesterday is but a dream and it's time to sleep.

Sheila May Burden (Bodmin)

Dartmoor

Dartmoor in summer, when the fern is green,
A sight by a million visitors seen,
Rivers and streams run sparkling and clear,
A delight to every eye and ear.
But how many *feel* the place? I ask,
Who only see its summer mask.
When green fern into curled brown bracken fades
And chattering brooks become cascades,
When winter winds over all do blow
My feelings even deeper go.
Each stream, each tree, each path, each tor,
Only emphasise the more,
This is my heritage, my ancestry, my past,
The die in which my love was cast.
Not entombing fog nor icy rain upon my face
Can diminish my feeling for this place.

Sylvia Ashton (Plymouth)

Untitled

Sky Watching
Faces and monsters etched in clouds
Magic cities and oceans
    that disappear in the
        blink of an eye
Burning sun consumed by evening
        drawing on
Milky glow round a full moon
        circled with a promise
            of rain
Ebony sky stained with silver stars
Pushed over the globe with the
    dawn breaking through
        flashes of peach streak the sky
           castles are built
               birds will fly . . .

C C McCarthy (Torpoint)

Stately Home

Marbled pillars, graceful curve, a staircase of beauty, but oh - so cold.
No carpet spoils its symmetry, my toes curl in sympathy with inhabitants of old.
Glass cases full of china, how I long to hold it in my hands
Feel its age-old beauty, and glistening raised gold bands.
Smocked and bewigged ancestors - long dead - gaze benignly from the walls,
At lesser mortals such as we, who timorously walk their halls.
What sumptuous luxury the bedrooms portend - with enormous four-poster bed,
How cosy to close the curtains when resting one's weary head.
Red velvet plush on carved back chairs, a cautious prod with finger -
Reveals a yielding softness, made for folks who wish to linger.
The patina of great oaken chests, some with wide brassed bands,
Pay silent tribute to mob-capped housemaids with work worn busy hands.
Looking from the window at the curved and gravelled drive,
It's easy to picture a carriage sweeping round when guests arrive.
Or 'milady' in billowing crinoline, strolling on the grass,
P'rhaps taking tea beneath the cedars as long days of summer pass.

W Perrett (Salisbury)

The High Street

Within the Sussex countryside, nestles this historic town.
An ancient stone church can be found,
Witches and wealthy lay beneath the hallowed ground.
So many beautiful buildings remain unseen,
Behind secret gates and hidden paths they stand.
A hundred secrets hide deep within the walls,
Of which many will remain untold.
The hospital once so small and sound,
Today the name is world-renowned.
Black and white beams line the street,
Where once, only country folk did meet.
Now cars and buses rush by.
No time to see with naked eye,
No time to rest, take in its treasures.
Take time, now all is said,
Stroll round East Grinstead.

Jennifer Walsh (East Grinstead)

Pussy Cat

'Pussy cat, pussy cat, where have you been?'
'I've been down the garden you know
Watching the frogs and chasing the bees,
Then I sharpened my claws on a couple of trees,
Having done all those things, I'm now terribly tired
So I'll go up to bed for a nap
And when I come down I might fancy some lunch,
Please make sure it's ready, there's a good chap.
Then I'll probably stroll down the garden again,
You must be there to open the door,
I may want to go out, then again I may not,
It depends on the weather, it might be too hot.
I just want you to be there, you know how it is
I simply won't go through that flap.
It's got nothing to do with my waistline at all
I'm just pleasantly plump and that's that!'

Ann Fairman (Waltham Cross)

Amber

Solid sunshine; layered by dreaming summer days
Pine resin, which oozed before the step of man
In forests in deepest green and blue.
Needled fingers traced the movement of sun and moon
Saw stars which fell across the firmament
Producing a drop of time, to hold forever in your hand.
Baltic bounty which traced a channel from beneath the bark
A golden glistening teardrop to entrap the unwary insects
Which are drawn by the sad sigh of wind filled branches
Curious as the sorrow of such mighty monuments.
Foolishly to alight as gently as spore or seed
No more than a touch would hold them fast; for eternity.
This graceful globule, swept up upon a strange shore
Many miles and many millennia from its origins
Has within its heart, that which man often yearns for;
Time past.

Jackie Garth (Redruth)

Cornish Moon

Breath hanging in the air
Of a misty Cornish valley,
Bathing the trees in silver light,
Bringing the ghosts of bygone days
To life, as whispering leaves
Dance in the moonlight;
Holding one's breath inside,
Heart beating in anticipation
Of some other movement in the stillness,
The jagged blades of grass
Emerging from the mire
Under a Cornish moon
Frozen in time and isolation,
Remembering times past,
Honouring them yet welcoming tomorrow
With a fond embrace.

Sandra Holmes (Perranporth)

The Moody Barman

I'm the barman, the lads call me Terry,
They're drinking half pints, getting merry,
The girls, now and then,
Say hello to the men,
But they're down in the lounge drinking sherry.

The dry, the medium, the sweet,
The ladies, aloof and elite,
Let us raise a glass,
To the chattering class,
That eat fish and chips in the street.

That brought a smile back to my face,
Here's my helper, he's taking my place,
To the girls then for lunch,
With a bottle of punch,
I'll get there in time to say grace.

Irene Wilson (Frome)

Thank You Lord

Thank You Lord for my mixer
I can produce two big cakes
In half an hour
And that includes preparation
And clearing away.

Thank You Lord for friends
People to celebrate with
People to cry with
People to raise funds with
People to introduce to others.

Thank You Lord for work
Both paid and unpaid
The menial and the challenging
Recreation is so much better
After a day's hard graft.

Barbara Tozer (Caterham)

The Attic

Rest well, dark dust of ages,
Tell me, did you once have dreams?
Were you ever polished and brassed?
Like the old stairwell and its beams,
Now glass broken in your crusted corners,
Scattered literature strewn upon your ground,
If it wasn't for me and my footsteps,
You too could create a ghostly sound.
Though you sleep well, you awake through your beauty,
Your antics shadow you well,
They stand with you in companionship
And rest peacefully where they fell.

Ellen. Calloo (Enfield)

Forward Press - Congratulations

Press forward let us go hand in hand
Cheerfully you take command,
We stumbled but weren't prepared to stay down
You fashioned and grafted all over town,
We ploughed, worked hard, we went to press
Followed through in the wilderness'
We scaled the heights, saw the beauty appear
And followed with pride year by year,
Steep was the climb but with passion we stand
We survived clung together now with banners in our hands,
Forward Press we salute you with pride, in your 20th year
Let us all celebrate now, loud and clear!

Mary Joseph (Stockwell)

Fortune Teller

You tell of my future
You tell of my fate
You swish your tea leaves
On the edge of your plate
And tell me the wisdom
Life versus death
You look up at my face
With bated breath
You open your mouth
To talk of my doom
But before you can speak
I see my ghost in your room.

Denise Longhurst (East Grinstead)

Indispensible Man

Someday when you're feeling important
Someday when your ego's in bloom
Someday when you take it for granted
You're the best qualified *man* in the room
Take a bucket and fill it with water
Put your hands in it up to your wrists
Pull them out and the hole that remains
Is the measure of how much you'll be missed
The morale of this is quite simple
You must do the best that you can
Be proud of yourself, but remember
There is no indispensible man.

Bonnie Austin (Ventnor)

Untitled

You speak to me as if I'm dirt
The words you use, they really hurt
They make me feel, I don't want to live.
Yet still I have a lot to give.
Be kind and show some compassion
Or one day you may get your ration
Or slights, rebuffs and hurtful phrases
For like the moon, things come in phases.
So try and feel what others endure
Remember, you are not so pure
One day you may be old and sick,
For the clock is going by, *tick, tick, tick!*

Marian Ruth Turner (Bath)

An Ode To A Poem

A poem is not a poem -
'Til it becomes a song!
'Til somebody with magic
In their music comes along!
A poem is like an angel
Getting ready to be heard -
When someone puts a melody
Behind each written word . . .
And when that angel starts to sing -
You'll know I wasn't wrong . . .
A poem is not a poem -
'Til it becomes a song!

Russell Humphrey (Bushey)

For Lou On Leaving Home

When you're lost, not knowing who to turn to,
Just remember I'm always here to show you
The path to follow, I'll help you if I can,
But will you let me take your hand or will you simply ban me
From trying to shelter you and keep you safe from harm?
I want to shield you from the cold, keep you snug and warm,
I know our worlds are different in oh so many ways,
And I would never let you down in your darkest days.
So anytime you're feeling sad or feeling all alone,
Remember I am always here to welcome you back home,
I know my hair is streaked with grey, my eyes are not so bright,
But if you need me I am here to try and put things right.

Doreen Walters (Weston-super-Mare)

Thoughts From The Forest

Silver birches simmer in the gentle summer breeze,
Sparkling sunlight filters through the young leaves on the trees.
Birds sing out their happy songs, in simple joy of living,
Not knowing, and not caring for the happiness they're giving.
But, as we look and listen, do we appreciate,
These gifts that have been given us, do we ever contemplate?
That there are those who cannot see the colour of the sky,
And those who cannot hear the sound of birdsong way on high?
Such things we take for granted, the gifts of sight and sound,
Just to be able to see and hear what's happening all around.
So, should we sometimes give a thought when gazing at the sky,
Or listening to nature's sounds - but for the grace of God go I . . .

V Slater (Poole)

Ferry

Darkness grows in clouded skies
Mauve of night chasing orange glows;
Waiting to cross this river border
Strangers chatter drunken banter
Biding time till passage passed,
Blue-tinged tones of summer and white foaming tides
Grey clouds breeze by under sullen skies;
Both sun and moon hidden from view
A falling star traverses the void speeding across the sky,
Now departing, gone but not forgotten
Ferry clanking and clatters away,
People stray to the pub till the end of this day.

K M Clemo (Torpoint)

Refulgent Granite Peninsular

Mamvro, land of our mothers
Bennathow, our blessings said
Splann, our word for brightness
Bara, our Cornish bread
Haf, our word for summer
Kernow, our heart and lungs
Home of our Celtic forebears
Who spoke proudly our Cornish tongue
Refulgent granite outcrop, pounded by sparkling seas
Almost lost your language, risking beloved land
For voices once silenced cannot again resound
Cornish, in Cornwall, so wonderfully profound.

Amber Smithwhite (Paignton)

Today

I opened the curtains looking out of the window,
Wondering what today would be like,
Across the sky there came a shadow
It's going to rain, I'm sure that's right,
We all know that sun will follow
The birds tell us, they are so bright!
Then I look at flowers taking a bow
Everything's in place until night
We know that night follows daytime
That winter follows summertime too
We aren't in charge, God makes it fine
He knows just what to do.

Joyce Shipton (Stroud)

The Crossing, Tranquil Vale, Blackheath

When a child lifts up its hand to
Grasp yours the trust implicit in
The gesture bears down upon you,
Be they stranger or kith and kin.
Thus it was when I took the hand
Proffered to me at the kerbside.
Crossing to the traffic island
It held mine firm against the tide,
Releasing me with easy grace
To face the rigours of the day.
Mother and child left without trace,
But the gesture remained to stay.

Roy Richards (London)

Renaissance Angels

In robes of azure,
On flaked backgrounds of or,
A seraphic, serene angelic scene.
On panels of oak,
The celestial folk -
Awesome expressions,
Enhanced by halos,
With wings of fire.
Tranquil, on lyres
They play and strum.
Timeless and ethereal
-Our senses are numb.

Kieran F Harford (London)

My Dearest Dear

My dearest dear - save me a dream,
that in a moment it will seem -
love is drifting thro' the night
as dreams entwine-tho' not in sight.
To feel the softness of your hand,
in this enchantment we do stand -
when you gently touch my cheek
I hear those words we need not speak.
As a sigh from the sky above,
softly comes the warmth of love -
a fleeting glance that's so serene
my dearest dear - save me a dream.

Jon Arden (Gloucester)

Remember Me

Remember me from time to time
Listen can't you hear me
Beloved daughters, sons of mine
As life hastens you away
Along the path you follow
Listen you will hear me
My spirit free of earthly bounds
And as I rest in sacred grounds
I'm on the wind and in the air
In sunny days and darkest nights
If e'r you need me I am there
Listen you will hear me.

David Peter Rutherford (Mottingham)

A Baby's Eyes

There is beauty in a sunset,
There is beauty at sunrise,
There is beauty full of wonder
And it's in a baby's eyes.
There is music in its laughter
And contentment in its sighs.
There is sunshine in its lovely smile
And there is beauty in its eyes.
Beauty is intangible and is sometimes in disguise,
But it's lovely when you find it
And it's in my baby's eyes.

Alexander McIlquham (Cheltenham)

Life For Sale

Careering through love, selling metaphorical onions
braking hard downhill to evade impetuosity
I plunged into life's stingers at the bottom of the hill.

Changing direction to a life on the sea
I learned to swim with the tide, Piscean I hoped
but proved to be more crustacean than scaled, I failed.

Whoever said 'a woman needs a man
like a fish needs a bicycle'
had never felt the pangs of love or cried such onion tears
and fled downhill in tandem towards the empty years.

Patricia Brown (Barnstaple)

Celtic Praise

Combrogi warriors of our past, fought and won by brawn and stealth,
Standing proud, defeating all, accumulating nations' wealth.
Communication, dialect, skilled leaders played their part.
Forging Celtic attitudes, a nation set apart.

Millennium warriors straddle time and play a different game.
No longer shields and spears forged with care win Celtic fame.
Technology, the will to learn, new industries are waiting.
Music, culture, friendships made -all hatreds past forsaking.

Into a thousand years we stride, a nation proud and clever.
Forget the past? No, not we. It lives with us forever.

B Priday (Eastleigh)

A-Z of Authors

R J Raymond (Guernsey) 333
R Muncie (Maidenhead) 605
R Niall (London) 501
Rob Atkins (Sandown) 693
Rob Barratt (Bodmin) 251
Robert Denis Spencer (Great Missenden) 267
Robert D Hayward (London) 123
Robert Dives (Haywards Heath) 794
Robert Gillan (Bath) 726
Robert Henry (Letchworth) 686
Robert King (Southampton) 519
Robert Main (Bedford) 703
Robert Morgan (Waterlooville) 326
Robert Reddy (Taunton) 485
Robert Smith (Romsey) 431
Robert Yates (Stoke) 255
Robin Neill (Rickmansworth) 723
Rod Legge (Lymington) 97
Roger Turner (Cheltenham) 307
Roland G Clarke (Andover) 410
Ronald Baron (Plymouth) 177
Ronald Frost (London) 185
Ron Isaacs (London) 493
Ron Taylor (London) 754
Rosaleen Caffrey (Luton) 525
Rosamund McGarry (London) 183
Roseanne Harten (Plymouth) 107
Rose Mary Childs (Haywards Heath) 27
Rosemary C Whatling (Leighton Buzzard) 703
Rosemary Hull (Newbury) 423
Rosemary Peach (Torquay) 777
Rose Mills (London) 635
Rosie Crocus Smith (Millbrook) 52
Rosie Powlesland (Chalfont St Giles) 272
Rosina Winiarski (Dulverton) 500
Ros Kane (London) 634
Rowena (Bournemouth) 806
Rowland Patrick Scannell (Epsom) 304
Roy Court (Teignmouth) 264
Roy Glanville (Andover) 514
Roy Gunter (Anerley) 315
Roy Hobbs (Christchurch) 29
Roy Merrett (Bristol) 173
Roy Richards (London) 818
Roy Williams (Plymouth) 467
Russell Humphrey (Bushey) 815
Russ Parker (Bordon) 543
Ruth Bray (Plymouth) 701
Ruth Clarke (Shoreham-by-Sea) 517
Ryszard Lipinski (Weston-super-Mare) 354
Rywa Weinberg (London) 490
Sajida Hassan (Watford) 752
Sally Busby (Shipham) 103
Sally Flood (London) 595
Sally Millett (Christchurch) 726
Sally Wyatt (Wallingford) 616
Sam D Kingdon (Southampton) 391
Sammy Michael Davis (Bournemouth) 669
Sandra Clarke (Dursley) 784
Sandra Curtis (Ilminster) 314
Sandra Eros (London) 306

Sandra Holmes (Perranporth) 811
Sandra Una Brisck (London) 331
Sandylea (Milton Keynes) 577
Sandy Ward (Abbots Langley) 692
Sara Glass (Bristol) 571
Sarah Anne Day (Bristol) 442
Sarah Diskin (Worthing) 676
Sarah Dodds (Weybridge) 213
Sarah E Fernandes (Bristol) 665
Sarah Lindsay (Bournemouth) 434
Sarah Wright (Brighton) 473
Sara Jane Berry (Witney) 660
Sarathin (Joseph Noel Thomas Nice)
(London) 470
S Bannister (Plymouth) 786
S Cameron (Taynuilt) 795
Sean Donaghey (Charlton) 617
Selma Brown (Penzance) 800
S G A Bennin-Sam (London) 99
Sharon (Blossom) Brown (Oxford) 476
Sharon Elizabeth Benjamin (Stratford) 303
Shaun Smith (Plymouth) 171
Shaun Usher (Epsom) 244
Shazia Afzal (Luton) 253
Shazia Kausar (Reading) 444
Sheila Booth (Ruislip) 243
Sheila Brown (Hayle) 433
Sheila Dodwell (Taunton) 520
Sheila Evans (Torquay) 462
Sheila Fermor Clarkson (St Austell) 239
Sheila May Burden (Bodmin) 808
Sheila Scorse (Helston) 356
Sheila Seecharan (London) 516
Sheila Wilmot (Bristol) 235
Shelia Page (Newbury) 152
Shirley Davies (Barnet) 502
Shirley Davis (Cinderford) 587
Shirley E Parker (Plymouth) 600
Shirley Lovell (Wood Green) 761
Shirley Mungapen (Southampton) 498
Shirley Nicolaou (London) 419
Shona Chester (Eastbourne) 382
Shula Bailey (East Grinstead) 711
Sidney Fisher (Langport) 672
Sid Stovold (Farnborough) 440
Simone Brightstein (Bradford on Avon) 171
Simon Genchi (St Albans) 321
Simon Marshall (Eastleigh) 131
Simon McAlear (London) 672
Simon Plant (Bristol) 71
S M Tajul Islam (East Ham) 197
S M Thompson (Southampton) 383
Sneh Brahmbhatt (16) (London) 199
Sonia Richards (Exeter) 735
S Papier (Stepney) 381
S Rosemary Ward (Aylesbury) 679
Stella-Rose Benson (Penzance) 117
Stella Goorney (Bath) 568
Stella Robinson (London) 25
Stephanie Harvey (Bristol) 651
Stephanie Jean Hope Bridewell (Andover) 386

Forward Press Information

We hope you have enjoyed reading this book - and that you
will continue to enjoy it in the coming years.

If you like reading and writing poetry drop us a line, or give
us a call, and we'll send you a free information pack.

Alternatively if you would like to order further copies of this
book or any of our other titles, then please give us a call or
log onto our website at www.forwardpress.co.uk

Forward Press Ltd. Information
Remus House
Coltsfoot Drive
Woodston
Peterborough
PE2 9JX
(01733) 890099